L(n)

ACPL ITEM
DISCARDED

Y0-BSM-658

SEP 11 '78

FILM REVIEW DIGEST ANNUAL 1977

Edited by David M. Brownstone and Irene M. Franck

A Hudson Group Book
Published by kto press
A U.S. Division of Kraus-Thomson Organization Limited
Millwood, New York 10546

International Standard Book Number:
    0-527-29321-0
Library of Congress Catalog Card Number:
    76-640962
KTO Press, Millwood, New York 10546
A U.S. Division of Kraus-Thomson
    Organization Limited
© 1978 by KTO PRESS.
Extracts of film reviews
    published with permission.

Film Review Digest, its editors and publisher
disclaim responsibility and liability for statements, either of fact or of opinion, made by
reviewers.

Printed in the United States of America
Designed by Kristine R. Knapp

table of contents

Film Rating Classifications

G-General Audiences
PG-Parental Guidance Suggested
R-Restricted
X-No One under 17 Admitted

preface

The **1977 FILM REVIEW DIGEST ANNUAL** incorporates more than 1,500 reviews that appeared this year in two dozen American, British, and Canadian publications. Reviews of approximately three-hundred feature films that opened in the United States this year, some of which are not yet in general release, are included.

In this second **FILM REVIEW DIGEST ANNUAL** all reviews that appeared in the Fall 1976, Winter 1976, Spring 1977, and Summer 1977 issues (Volume 2) have been cumulated alphabetically by film title. The volume contains a complete, cumulated **General Index**, including people and film titles (both foreign and U.S.) mentioned in the **1977 FILM REVIEW DIGEST ANNUAL**. A separate **Index of Reviewers** follows the **General Index**, thus providing a complete index to all critics whose reviews appear in the volume. An award section is also included, containing the important film awards of the year.

Appearing with the reviews of each film included is important production information, cast and crew listings, country and year of origin, as well as the original name of the film (as available) for foreign films. Motion Picture Association of America ratings are provided when appropriate. The reader should note that United States running times are used throughout the publication.

In some cases, new films reviewed may have a small number of reviews; this reflects the arrival of many reviews after the Summer 1977 issue had gone to press.

The **1977 FILM REVIEW DIGEST ANNUAL** is intended to provide a much needed reference source for scholars, film buffs, and those simply interested in how current films are critically received.

A list of periodicals from which reviews are excerpted in the **1977 FILM REVIEW DIGEST ANNUAL** follows.

The Editors

list of periodicals

The Christian Science Monitor
One Norway Street
Boston, Mass. 02115

Cineaste
333 Sixth Avenue
New York, N.Y. 10014

Commentary
165 East 56th Street
New York, N.Y. 10022

Commonweal
232 Madison Avenue
New York, N.Y. 10016

Esquire
488 Madison Avenue
New York, N.Y. 10022

Film
British Federation of Film Societies
81 Dean Street
London W1V 6AA
England

Film Information
Broadcasting and Film Commission
National Council of the Churches of Christ
475 Riverside Drive
New York, N.Y. 10027

Film Quarterly
University of California Press
Berkeley, Calif. 94720

Films and Filming
Hansom Books
Artillery Mansions
75 Victoria Street
London SW1H OHZ
England

Films in Review
National Board of Review of Motion Pictures Inc.
210 East 68th Street
New York, N.Y. 10021

Jump Cut
P.O. Box 865
Berkeley, Calif. 94701

Los Angeles Times
Times Mirror Square
Los Angeles, Calif. 90053

Monthly Film Bulletin
The British Film Institute
81 Dean Street
London W1V 6AA
England

Ms.
370 Lexington Avenue
New York, N.Y. 10017

The Nation
333 Sixth Avenue
New York, N.Y. 10014

The New Leader
212 Fifth Avenue
New York, N.Y. 10010

New York Magazine
755 Second Avenue
New York, N.Y. 10017

New York Post
210 South Street
New York, N.Y. 10002

The New York Times
229 West 43rd Street
New York, N.Y. 10036

Newsweek
444 Madison Avenue
New York, N.Y. 10022

Rolling Stone
78 East 56th Street
New York, N.Y. 10022

Saturday Review
488 Madison Avenue
New York, N.Y. 10022

Sight and Sound
British Film Institute
81 Dean Street
London W1V 6AA
England

Take One
Box 1778
Station B
Montreal 110
Quebec, Canada

Time
Time & Life Building
Rockefeller Center
New York, N.Y. 10020

The Times (London)
200 Gray's Inn Road
London WC1, England

The Village Voice
80 University Place
New York, N.Y. 10003

Women's Wear Daily
Fairchild Publications, Inc.
7 East 12th Street
New York, N.Y. 10003

FILM REVIEWS

Film Review Digest

ABDUCTION

Director: *Joseph Zito.* Screenplay: *Kent E. Carroll.* Based on the novel *Black Abductor* by James Rusk, Jr. Producer: *Mr. Carroll.* Photography: *Joao Fernandez.* Editor: *James Macreading.* Distributor: *Venture Distribution, Inc.* Running time 100 minutes. Los Angeles opening November, 1975, at several theatres. Classification: R.

Players: *Judith-Marie Bergan, David Pendleton, Gregory Rozakis, Leif Erickson, Dorothy Malone, Lawrence Tierney, Presley Caton, Catherine Lacy.*

See Volume 1 for additional reviews

Monthly Film Bulletin, 7/76 (p. 143)
Jill Forbes

"Disclaimers notwithstanding, *Abduction* is clearly based on the Patricia Hearst affair. It is a strange form of narcissism which leads Americans to transform yesterday's news headlines into today's feature films . . . *Abduction* . . . falls well short of making a contribution to popular mythology, despite the extravagant statements of the capitalist villain Prescott, to the effect that his whole way of life is threatened. Instead, it falls back on a crude psychological ploy which suggests that Patricia Prescott was bored by all the good things privilege can buy and secretly yearned for the clutches of a black revolutionary rapist when in the arms of her sedate and studious boyfriend. Furthermore, there is some confusion as to exactly which revolution is being sought . . . But the film is successful at showing Patricia growing in self-

awareness and political understanding, despite the flimsiness of the theoretical basis. Joseph Zito is especially good at combining long takes with voices and sounds off to capture Patricia's bewilderment subjectively, and in presenting the clash between Prescott and the revolutionaries as a conflict of perception . . ."

©Monthly Film Bulletin, 1976.

ACROSS THE GREAT DIVIDE

Director, Screenplay: *Stewart Raffill.* Producer: *Arthur R. Dubbs,* Music: *Gene Kaver, Douglas Lackey.* Distributor: *Pacific International Enterprises.* Running time 95 minutes. New York opening December 20, 1976, at the Guild 50th and Embassy Theatres. Classification: G.

Zachariah Coop: *Robert Logan.* Holly Smith: *Heather Rattray.* Jason Smith: *Mark Hall.* Indian Chief: *George (Buck) Flower.*

New York Post, 12/21/76 (p. 20)
Archer Winsten

"... a carefully composed animal-and-travel picture using the Disney formula for innocent children and animals that threaten but don't eat you up ...
continued on next page

1

continued from previous page

... adventures with a huge bear, a couple of mountain lions, a pack of howling wolves, buffalo, friendly Indians, raging rivers and naughty mountain men. It is very probable that they would have never reached their destination, Oregon, without the help of Coop, who insists on helping them though Holly questions his intentions regularly and shoots her rifle in his vicinity several times.

Everything turns out for the best in the end, as you knew it would. The animals behave themselves in performances that are a tribute to their handlers, especially the bear who is huge, muscular and King Kong-like when he stands up ..."

Reprinted by Permission of New York Post.
©1976, New York Post Corporation.

ACT OF AGGRESSION (L'AGRESSION)

Director: *Gerard Pires*. Screenplay (French with English subtitles): *Jean-Patric Manchette, Mr. Pires*. Based on the novel *The Shrewsdale Exit* by John Buell. Producers: *Alain Poire, Pierre Braunsberger*. Photography: *Silvano Ippoliti*. Music: *Robert Charlebois*. Producer: *S.N.E. Gaumont; Les Films du Jeudi; Les Films de la Seine; Primex Italiana*. Distributor: *Joseph Green Pictures*. Running time 94 minutes. New York opening December 3, 1975, at Trans-Lux 85th and 8th Street Playhouse Theatres. Classification: None. Origin: France.

Paul Varlin: *Jean-Louis Trintignant*. Sarah: *Catherine Deneuve*. Andre Ducatel: *Claude Brasseur*. Escudero: *Phillipe Brigaud*. Helene: *Michelle Grellier*. Patty: *Delphine Boffy*.

See Volume 1 for additional reviews

Los Angeles Times, 11/10/76 (Pt. IV, p. 13)
Kevin Thomas

"With *Act of Aggression* . . . the *Death Wish* syndrome that emerged in the French cinema with *The Old Gun* continues to spread—like a disease.

Jean-Louis Trintignant and his wife (Michelle Grellier) and little daughter (Delphine Boffy) are on their way to a Riviera vacation when they are suddenly hounded by a trio of black-leathered motor-

cyclists. Trintignant gives chase, the bikers retaliate by splashing oil over his windshield, causing his car to go off the road. They beat up Trintignant, who regains consciousness to find his wife and daughter raped and murdered.

Naturally, Trintignant is consumed with revenge, but the way he goes about it is highly improbable in this most contrived and discursive film . . ."

©Los Angeles Times, 1976.

ADVENTURES OF THE WILDERNESS FAMILY, THE

Director: *Stewart Raffill*. Screenplay: *Mr. Raffill*. Producer: *Arthur R. Dubbs*. Music: *Gene Kauer, Douglas Lackey*. Distributor: *Pacific International Enterprises Inc.* Running time 101 minutes. New York opening December 19, 1975, at the Embassy and Guild Theatres. Classification: G.

Skip: *Robert Logan*. Pat: *Susan Damante Shaw*. Jenny: *Hollye Holmes*. Toby: *Ham Larsen*.

See Volume 1 for additional reviews

Los Angeles Times, 12/23/76 (Pt. IV, p. 10)
Linda Gross

"The reason that *The Adventures of the Wilderness Family* . . . is such a super movie is that it touches the heart of children's fantasies about family togetherness.

The low-budget feature, filmed on location in the Utah mountains and Canadian Rockies, has technical flaws and a predictably hazardous plot. But nothing mars the beautiful scenery, exceptional wildlife footage or sunny depiction of a family having fun together . . .

Stewart Raffill's script is an intelligent blend of domestic harmony, resourcefulness and adventure.

Logan is warm and sturdy as the father. Miss Shaw is pretty though slightly self-conscious as the mother. Miss Holmes is wise and sweet without being cloying as the girl and Larsen, with a devilish grin, is truly endearing as the boy. The golden retriever, bears, raccoons, wolves and wild geese all figure prominently and perform commendably."

©Los Angeles Times, 1976.

AGAINST A CROOKED SKY

Director: *Earl Bellamy.* Screenplay: *Douglas Stewart, Eleanor Lamb.* Producer: *Lyman D. Dayton.* Photography: *Joe Jackman.* Editor: *Marsh Hendry.* Music: *Lex de Azevedo.* Distributor: *Doty-Dayton film in association with Film Associates.* Running time 85 minutes. Los Angeles opening December 16, 1976, at several theatres. Classification: G.

Players: *Jewel Blanch, Richard Boone, Shannon Farnon, Gordon Hanson, Geoffrey Land, Stewart Petersen, Clint Ritchie, Vincent St. Cyr, Brenda Venus, Rich Wheeler, Henry Wilcoxon, Margaret Willey.*

Los Angeles Times, 12/17/76 (Pt. IV, p. 26)
Linda Gross

". . . The film works as an adventure story but falls short in its portrayal of human beings. The tone of the condescending screenplay by Douglas C. Stewart and Eleanor Lamb is set when the sister says to her brother, 'You can't have any greater love than to give your life to a friend.' The film is understandably more effective when it departs from this greeting card sensibility and dwells on the more sturdy friendship between the selfish trapper (Boone) and the boy, in the process of becoming a man (Petersen).

Earl Bellamy's direction is generally lethargic but the sequences involving the boy pitted against the wilderness have a natural grace . . .

The Utah locales, photographed by Joe Jackman, are starkly beautiful."

©Los Angeles Times, 1976.

AGUIRRE, THE WRATH OF GOD

Director, Producer: *Werner Herzog.* Screenplay (German with English subtitles): *Mr. Herzog.* Photography: *Thomas Mauch.* Music: *Popol Vuh.* Distributor: *New Yorker Films.* Running time 90 minutes. New York opening April 3, 1977, at the D. W. Griffith Theatre. Classification: None. Origin: West Germany, 1972.

Aguirre: *Klaus Kinski.* Don Pedro de Ursua: *Ruy Guerra.* Inez: *Helena Rojo.* Flores: *Cecilia Rivera.* Emperor: *Peter Heiling.* Slave: *De Negro.*

New York Times, 4/4/77 (p. 43)
Vincent Canby

". . . Werner Herzog's absolutely stunning 1972 German film . . . was shot by Mr. Herzog . . . on locations of breathtaking beauty (and, I must assume, of horrendous difficulty) in South America, but it's no ordinary, run-of-the-rapids adventure . . .

Aguirre, the Wrath of God is simultaneously a historical film (to the extent that it follows events as they are known) and a meditation upon history. Aguirre is truly mad, but as played by Klaus Kinski, whose crooked walk and undiluted evil recall Laurence Olivier's Richard III, he is the essential civilized man, a fellow who, in Mr. Herzog's vision of things, must be lunatic . . .

The film is incredibly rich and lush looking. It is tactile. One can feel the colors of the jungle and see the heat. The conquistadores endure terrible trials—whirlpools, Indian attacks, rebellion within their own ranks—yet the mood of the film is almost languid . . .

Contrasting with this peculiar languor is the radiant madness of Aguirre, who hypnotizes his soldiers into following his wildest instructions, who sneers at men who seek riches when power and fame are all that matter, who aspires to be nothing less than the wrath of God, and who, at the end, is planning to create a new dynasty by marrying his dead daughter. He's mad but he's a survivor.

This is a splendid and haunting work."

© 1977 by the New York Times Company.
Reprinted by permission.

Christian Science Monitor, 4/4/77 (p. 23)
David Sterritt

". . . the astonishing *Aguirre, the Wrath of God*, first shown in 1973, but just released commercially in the United States. Its story is exciting and its setting is exotic. And it ingeniously combines Herzog's gift for deep irony, his strong social awareness, and his worthy ambition to fashion a whole new visual perspective on the world around us via mystical, evocative, yet oddly direct imagery. It is a brilliant cinematic achievement.

The year is 1560. Spanish conquistadores cross the Sierras of Peru in search of the golden Inca city, El Dorado. The jungle becomes impassable, and the commander, Gonzalez Pizarro, sends a crew down-river to find out what is in store. Included in the party are a leader and his wife, a self-indulgent nobleman, and the talented but loutish Aguirre with his young daughter.

Aguirre stages a mutiny and presses on in the name of his own power—a proto-Hitler with a gospel of force and a lust for conquest . . .

Clearly this is Herzog's *Heart of Darkness.* It is also a subtle comment on the Fascistic urge that he and other young West German filmmakers occa-

continued on next page

continued from previous page

sionally find necessary to concern themselves with, often on a detached and quizzical level.

Yet *Aguirre* operates as grippingly as most thrillers even as it spins its allegories . . ."

Reprinted by permission from The Christian
Science Monitor © 1977.
The Christian Science Publishing Society.
All rights reserved.

AIRPORT '77

Director: *Jerry Jameson.* Screenplay: *Michael Scheff, David Spector.* Producer: *William Frye.* Photography: *Phili Lathrop.* Editors: *J. Terry Williams, Robert Watts.* Music: *John Cacavas.* Distributor: *Universal Pictures.* Running time 117 minutes. New York opening March 25, 1977, at several theatres. Classification: PG.

Don Gallagher: *Jack Lemmon.* Karen Wallace: *Lee Grant.* Eve Clayton: *Brenda Vaccaro.* Joe Patroni: *George Kennedy.* Philip Stevens: *James Stewart.* Nicholas St. Downs 3rd: *Joseph Cotten.* Emily Livingston: *Olivia De Havilland.* Stan Buchek: *Darren McGavin.* Martin Wallace: *Christopher Lee.* Chambers: *Robert Foxworth.* Eddie: *Robert Hooks.* Banker: *Monte Markham.* Julie: *Kathleen Quinlan.* Frank Powers: *Gil Gerard.* Ralph Crawford: *James Booth.* Anne: *Monica Lewis.* Dorothy: *Maidie Norman.* Lisa: *Pamela Bellwood.*

New York Post, 3/26/77 (p. 35)
Archer Winsten

"*Airport '77* . . . has consolidated the thrills and chills of hijacking, air disaster, Grand Hotel assembly of varied characters, and underwater rescue. If the whole bunch had fallen into a live volcano, they, and their participant audience, could hardly have been in greater peril . . .

If you buy this kind of melodrama, *Airport '77* can be a very suspenseful exciting cup of strong tea. If not, it is equally possible to sneer at it as another one of those disaster compilations, each one bigger and better and worse than the last. If you really want to, you can spend the whole picture wondering how they made that 747 do all those things without disintegrating. Technically, it's a dilly."

Reprinted by Permission of New York Post.
© 1977, New York Post Corporation.

Los Angeles Times, 3/25/77 (Pt. IV, p. 1)
Charles Champlin

". . . It is possible to wish that *Airport '77*, the second sequel to the very successful original, were some other picture altogether. But, accepting what it intends to be and to do for its audience, you are bound to say that *Airport '77* is a shiny, corny, crafty triumph of commercial filmmaking, certain to bring a fortune at the box office (and to be forgotten as quickly as the message in a fortune cookie).

The flight of fancy is actually this time quite a bit further fetched, embracing the charms of *Poseidon* as well as *Airport.* Jack Lemmon is the pilot of a 747 lavishly customized for billionaire James Stewart. Hijacked on its maiden trip to Florida, the plane does not simply crash, it sinks intact to the ocean floor, leaving passengers and crew in a pretty pressurized pickle under what looks like 50 feet of water . . ."

©Los Angeles Times, 1977.

ALEX AND THE GYPSY

Director: *John Korty.* Screenplay: *Lawrence B. Marcus.* Based on the novella THE BAILBONDSMAN by Stanley Elkin. Producer: *Richard Shepherd.* Photography: *Bill Butler.* Editor: *Donn Cambern.* Music: *Henry Mancini.* Distributor: *Twentieth Century-Fox.* Running time 98 minutes. New York opening October 3, 1976, at the Sutton Theatre. Classification: R.

Alexander Main: *Jack Lemmon.* Maritza: *Genevieve Bujold.* Crainpool: *James Woods.* The Golfer: *Gino Ardito.* Judge Ehrlinger: *Robert Emhardt.* Treska: *Tito Vandis.* Public Defender: *Bill Cort.* Roy Blake: *Todd Martin.*

New York Post, 10/4/76 (p. 9)
Frank Rich

"I really think we could live without another movie about a tired, emotionally hardened middle-aged man who falls in love with a free-spirited young woman who leads him to rediscover the joys of life. *Alex and the Gypsy* . . . is the latest example of the genre, and even if it were well done (which it is not), it would be emotionally banal, predictable and cloying. *Alex and the Gypsy* is all these things and rather spectacularly numbing besides.

In this variation on the familiar theme, we learn all about the torturous relationship of Alex (Jack Lemmon), who is a smalltown-bailbondsman, and

Maritza (Genevieve Bujold), who is, yes, an honest-to-God gypsy . . .

Lemmon . . . plays Alex at an abrasive pitch . . . As for Miss Bujold, she's an actress who can do no wrong, and she does no wrong here. She just does nothing, which is, I'm sorry to say, precisely what her role and the film that contains it are worth."

Reprinted by Permission of New York Post.
©1976, New York Post Corporation.

Film Information, November 1976 (p. 5)
Dave Pomeroy

". . . *Alex* is not easily classifiable: at one level a straightforward story of a love-hate relationship but with the subthemes of loneliness and freedom; at another level a hymn to that ebullient spirit, in the face of life-denying modern preoccupations, symbolized by the life of the gypsy . . .

The bulk of the film . . . depicts Alex's almost comically manic efforts to keep Maritza (sometimes literally) chained to him, ostensibly so that he will not lose his bond money, but at a deeper level as they explore the paradoxes of bondage and freedom in a context of mutual loneliness and need . . .

Some nudity in the bedroom scenes and a fair amount of raunchy language lead into the R rating."

©Film Information, 1976.

New York Magazine, 10/18/76 (p. 81)
John Simon

". . . *Alex and the Gypsy* has an appalling screenplay by Lawrence B. Marcus that bears almost no relation to Stanley Elkin's novella, *The Bailbondsman*, on which it purports to be based. And, over and above its general banality and unbelievability, this is a weirdly midriffless script . . .

. . . Korty's direction is, as usual, well-meaning but pedestrian, as is Bill Butler's cinematography. As Alex, Jack Lemmon hauls out his standard bag of tricks that, for all their deftness, never struck me as much more interesting than card tricks. Genevieve Bujold's copious talent and charm can do little for the synthetic phantasm of a Maritza, and her 'gypsy' accent is easily the noblest (and least credible) Romany of them all. James Woods is likewise defeated by the cockamamy role of Crainpool, and there is a dependably dreadful score by Henry Mancini . . ."

©1976 by the NYM Corp. Reprinted with
the permission of NEW YORK Magazine.

Los Angeles Times, 10/8/76 (Pt. IV, p. 1)
Kevin Thomas

"*Alex and the Gypsy* . . . is a terribly romantic

and at times wildly farfetched film that clearly not everyone is going to be able to accept. Yet it is exactly the sort of 'little' picture that after a blitz opening sometimes returns to acquire cult status.

Originally titled *Skipping*, and based on a Stanley Elkin novella, *Alex and the Gypsy* is not without flaws, but they are more than compensated for by the perceptiveness and life-loving sensibility of director John Korty and writer Lawrence B. Marcus. In short, *Alex and the Gypsy* as a love story with some comedy and more pathos is welcome relief from the bloodbaths that so many movies are these days.

Above all, *Alex and the Gypsy* offers Jack Lemon a part with the size and range of *The Entertainer*, his recent TV movie . . ."

©Los Angeles Times, 1976.

Village Voice, 12/20/76 (p. 57)
Andrew Sarris

". . . *Alex and the Gypsy* is much better than its weak grosses and bad notices would indicate. It is not the most endearing movie in the world: both Lemmon as a professionally suspicious bailbondsman, and Genevieve Bujold as an old gypsy flame in need of his services, give rasping, often indecorous performances. Director John Korty lets the plot (from Lawrence B. Marcus' screenplay based upon Stanley Elkin's novella) sneak up on the audience . . . *Alex and the Gypsy* . . . displays a gutsy modernity which was once considered the trademark of the New Hollywood. The movie even dares to be subtle in its evocation of the rattier side of a small California town . . ."

Reprinted by permission of The Village Voice.
Copyright ©The Village Voice, Inc., 1976.

Films in Review, November 1976 (p. 567)
Rob Edelman

". . . *Alex and the Gypsy* is a mess.

Lemmon appears as an obnoxiously cynical bailbondsman, and Bujold is his ex-girlfriend, a short-tempered gypsy in his charge who is on the verge of a long jail term for having stabbed her husband. Lemmon has a Save the Tiger-ish role, yet his part—and ultimately his performance—is hardly more than a caricature, and Bujold just goes through the motions as a one-dimensional bitch. While the character's loneliness, isolation, and inability to communicate should evoke sympathy,

continued on next page

continued from previous page

both are so crass and unattractive that it is impossible to feel anything for them but contempt.

Alex and the Gypsy is so haphazardly pieced together it takes half the film to realize that several sequences are flashbacks, and Lawrence B. Marcus' screenplay is unworkable."

©Films in Review, 1976.

ALI: FEAR EATS THE SOUL (ANGST ESSEN SELLE AUF)

Director, Screenplay, Producer: *Rainer Werner Fassbinder*. Photography: *Jurgen Jurges*. Editor: *Thea Eymesz.*Production: *Tango Films*. Distributor: *New Yorker Films*. Running time 94 minutes. Los Angeles opening November 1976 at the Monica II. Classification: None. Origin: West Germany.

Players: *Rainer Werner Fassbinder, Peter Gauhe, Irm Hermann, Brigitte Mira, El Hedi Ben Salem, Karl Scheydt, Barbara Valentin.*

Los Angeles Times, 11/3/76 (Pt. IV, p. 1)
Kevin Thomas

". . . the course of Emmi and Ali's relationship reminds us, of all things, of the dangers of complacency. Fassbinder, however, culminates with a testament to the power of love and also of hate as he drives home the price of bigotry exacted of its victims.

The way in which Fassbinder maneuvers the twists and turns in his story is nothing short of dazzling. His empathy with Emmi and Ali is expressed with the utmost tact and eloquence. Brigette Mira shows us the heroic in a seemingly ordinary woman, and El Hedi Ben Salem invites us to see ourselves in his seemingly exotic person.

Like all remarkable films, *Ali: Fear Eats the Soul* is studded with unique and striking moments. Perhaps most stunning, in the context of the film's specific protest, occurs when Emmi, just married, joyously hustles Ali off to what is obviously the first expensive restaurant she has ever been in. Extolling its reputation she informs him that it had been Hitler's favorite."

©Los Angeles Times, 1976.

ALICE IN WONDERLAND

Director: *Bud Townsend*. Screenplay: *B. Anthony Fredricks*. Based on the novel by Lewis Carroll. Producer: *William Osco.*Photography: *Joseph Bardo*. Editor: *Shaun Walsh*. Music: *Bucky Searles*. Distributor: *General National*. Running time 75 minutes. Los Angeles opening June 1976 at several theatres. Classification: X.

Players: *Kristine De Bell, Larry Gelman, Allan Novak, Tony Tsengoles, Sue Tsengoles, J. P. Parradine, Bradford Armdexter, Ron Nelson, Kristen Steen, Nancy Dore, Terry Hall, John Laurence, Juliet Graham.*

Los Angeles Times, 6/24/76 (Pt. IV, p. 15)
Kevin Thomas

"Two years ago Bill Osco, young producer of X-rated pictures, scored a success with *Flesh Gordon*, a mildly racy and very funny spoof of the '30s serial and comic book hero that was also a loving, painstaking homage to the original.

Now Osco's back with an X-rated version of *Alice in Wonderland* . . . that isn't nearly so inspired. Indeed, it's hard to tell whether its aura of insipidity is by accident or design. At best it's only intermittently funny and, although not for prudes, it could surely receive an R-rating with only the slightest of cuts.

Alice (Kristine De Bell) is a beautiful but repressed librarian who becomes liberated when she accepts the invitation of the strange-looking Mr. Rabbit (Larry Gelman) to step through a looking glass. Scantily clad, Alice undergoes sexual awakening in her adventures with various Lewis Carroll characters.

Along the way there are some fairly syrupy and highly forgettable songs. Indeed, if it weren't for a certain amount of nudity, simulated sex and blunt talk, *Alice in Wonderland* would seem like just another innocuous kiddie show . . ."

© Los Angeles Times, 1976.

ALL SCREWED UP (TUTTO A POSTO E NIENTE IN ORDINE)

Director: *Lina Wertmuller*. Screenplay (Italian with English subtitles): *Ms. Wertmuller*. Producer: *Romano Cardarelli*. Photography: *Giuseppe Rotunno*. Editor: *Franco Fraticelli*.

Music: *Piero Piccioni*. Production: *Euro International*. Distributor: *New Line Cinema*. Running time 105 minutes. New York opening January 14, 1976, at the Eastside Cinema. Classification: PG. Origin: Italy, 1973.

Gigi: *Luigi Diberti*. Marluccia: *Lina Polito*. Carletto: *Nini Bignamini*. Adrelina: *Sara Rapisard*. Biki: *Giuliana Calandra*. Isotta: *Isa Danieli*. Bagonghi: *Eros Pagni*.

See Volume 1 for additional reviews

Los Angeles Times, 4/23/76 (Pt. IV, p. 1)
Charles Champlin

" . . . Wertmuller may not have been making films long, but long enough to acquire old tricks to get up to. Once again, country innocence visits the wicked and destroying city and comes away much the worse for the experience . . .

Wertmuller's women in *All Screwed Up* are no longer the grotesques of the other films; they are victimized equally with the men in the hostile city and they respond as they can. One (Giuliana Calandra) organizes the commune and charges extra for everything, vacuuming up the loose lira with ruthless acquisitive efficiency. Another sacrifices warmth for the cold comfort of saving. Another sells herself on the far side of the city so her friends won't know.

As in *Seven Beauties*, Wertmuller generates scenes of bizarre power, here notably in some grand operatic processions in the hellish kitchen, with the waitresses and the cooks like contending armies, attacking with shrill invectives. It is a madhouse and, indeed, madness seems very near by . . .

. . . Yet . . . as in *Seven Beauties*, the calculated efforts to generate emotional responses seem unsuccessful because the calculations are so evident. And although it is no problem to seize the point intellectually, the indictment itself reads rather old-fashioned and for the most part impersonally . . ."

© Los Angeles Times, 1976.

ALL THE PRESIDENT'S MEN

Director: *Alan J. Pakula*. Screenplay: *William Goldman*. Based on the book by *Carl Bernstein* and *Bob Woodward*. Producer: *Walter Coblenz*. Photography: *Gordon Willis*. Editor: *Robert L. Wolfe*. Music: *David Shire*.

Production: *Wildwood*. Distributor: *Warner Brothers*. Running time 136 minutes. New York opening April 7, 1976, at the Loews Astor Plaza and Tower East Theatres. Classification: PG.

Carl Bernstein: *Dustin Hoffman*. Bob Woodward: *Robert Redford*. Harry Rosenfeld: *Jack Warden*. Howard Simons: *Martin Balsam*. Deep Throat: *Hal Holbrook*. Ben Bradlee: *Jason Robards*. Bookkeeper: *Jane Alexander*. Debbie Sloan: *Meredith Baxter*. Dardis: *Ned Beatty*. Hugh Sloan, Jr.: *Stephen Collins*. Sally Aiken: *Penny Fuller*. Foreign Editor: *John McMartin*. Donald Segretti: *Robert Walden*. Frank Wills: *Himself*. Bachinski: *David Arkin*. Barker: *Henry Calvert*. Martinez: *Dominic Chianese*. Kay Eddy: *Lindsay Ann Crouse*. Miss Milland: *Valerie Curtin*. McCord: *Richard Herd*. Carolyn Abbot: *Allyn Ann McLerie*. Angry CRP woman: *Neva Patterson*. Al Lewis: *Joshua Shelley*.

See Volume 1 for additional reviews

Sight and Sound, Summer 1976 (p. 189)
Richard Combs

". . . the film seems to have emerged as a remarkably pure distillation of the original. It touches on all the essential moves and revelations of the investigation, while allowing hardly any of the usual embellishments—a bit of comedy with an obstructive secretary is the most obvious.

But in dealing with so complex (and recent) a political phenomenon as Watergate, the film perhaps best shows its mettle by compiling its evidence with all the clipped allusiveness and atmospheric tension of classic mystery fiction. Having broken down *Klute* and *The Parallax View* into a succession of almost self-contained episodes, each striking with some unexpected shock against what had gone before, Alan Pakula seems to have found the documentary equivalent for *All The President's Men*. Such crisp dramatic counterpoint is part and parcel of the way he persistently restricts his canvas . . ."

©Sight and Sound, 1976.

Commentary, 7/76 (p. 60)
William S. Pechter

". . . here we have a depiction of the unmasking of a true conspiracy, done by film-makers sympathetic to conspiracy theory, that is nevertheless oddly deficient in conveying a sense of conspirator-

continued on next page

continued from previous page

ial menace. That we know how the story ends doesn't seem explanation enough. Rather, despite its thriller trappings, the film seems unable to get around the fact that our common perception (via our common experience) of this conspiracy story is unalterably not one of detective-reporters on the trail of CIA-caused massacres or mysterious as-sassination networks, but—through such public spectacles as the televised hearings and the White House transcripts—one of the conspirators' own desperate ineffectiveness, and of the high and the mighty brought low. Here, exposed, is an actual conspiracy, and one leading directly to the Oval Of-fice, and yet the President himself, with all the agencies of government supposedly at his dis-posal, was unable to prevent its disclosure to the public . . ."

© Commentary, 1976.

Saturday Review, 5/1/76 (p. 44)
Judith Crist

"*All The President's Men*, based on the 1974 Carl Bernstein-Bob Woodward book reporting their investigation of the June 17, 1972, Watergate bur-glary and its ramifications, is just that—and therein lies its excellence and the integrity of its makers. What might have been an exploitation flick, a two-star vehicle, a romanticization of actuality, or the fantasy that so many fact-based works become on screen is, instead, not only the most authentic film about journalism in my experience but also a sus-penseful, engrossing account of the prologue to the major moral and political horror of recent years . . .

Hoffman and Redford, both at their best, are submerged in their roles with an authenticity to match that of the somehow ominous Washington scenes, filmed on location, and the cold reality of the exacting replica of the Post's newsroom and offices, constructed in Burbank, Calif. Pakula has so skillfully disciplined his performers that one is startled in retrospect to discover familiar names in the supporting cast . . . What emerges through Gordon Willis' lens, then, is a film of brilliant con-trast, one depicting the day-in, day-out plodding, painstaking work of investigative reporters against a familiar background suddenly filled with forebod-ing, turned sinister as the surface of corruption is touched upon . . . "

© Judith Crist, 1976.

Film Information, 4/76 (p. 1)
William F. Fore

"*All The President's Men*, the long awaited film version of the best seller by Woodward and Bern-stein, doesn't disappoint the viewer. How two fledg-ling reporters wheedled permission to investigate the Watergate break-in and how, step by inexora-ble step, they uncovered the corruption and collu-sion which led to the highest centers of power, cer-tainly ranks among the most exciting, fascinating and awesomely important stories of our time . . .

Fortunately, Redford's handling of the material matches its importance. For this is no long-ago Zola protesting the Dreyfus case, nor is it *Z* revealing corruption in a far-away country, nor is it may-have-been events in *Seven Days in May*. *All The President's Men* is current, true—and it happened to *us*. For this reason, verisimilitude is of the es-

Robert Redford (left) and Dustin Hoffman (right) talk with their editors about Watergate in **All the President's Men**.

sence. Even at the expense of occasional plodding (after all, no one took a shot at Woodward or Bernstein, no cars tried to run them over) the film is accurate both to the facts and to the truth of Watergate . . ."

© Film Information, 1976.

New Leader, 5/10/76 (p. 23)
Robert Asahina

" . . . one explanation of the striking differences between the book and William Goldman's screenplay is that Goldman and director Alan Pakula took the promotion seriously and gave us a real 'detective story,' a romantic thriller with only the most tenuous connection to the facts. The movie makers were undoubtedly subject to constraints of time (the film concludes in January, 1973, more than a year before the book does) and dramatic structure as well. But the account of Watergate in the cinematic *All The President's Men*, the uses and misuses of the truth, seem most of all to reflect a peculiarly skewed political vision . . .

We go into the movie aware that the fears of the protagonists are not fantasies, that a conspiracy is waiting to be exposed. Although our knowledge might seem to undercut the suspense, it actually renders us that much more ready for Pakula and Goldman's distortions. *All The President's Men* is really a new version of *The Parallax View*, with the spurious legitimation that the paranoia is factually justified. No matter that the 'facts' have been badly twisted . . . "

Reprinted with permission from
The New Leader, 1976.
© The American Labor Conference
on International Affairs, Inc.

Village Voice, 4/12/76 (p. 131)
Molly Haskell

" . . . So studiously does the film avoid the easy payoffs of grand moments and cheap ironies . . . that it would be anticlimactic were it not for the inherent drama of the material, and the consistent, subtle intelligence with which it is handled . . .

From top to bottom, the casting is impeccable. More than impeccable, it is the heart of the movie: Martin Balsam as Simons, the Managing Editor; Jack Warden as Harry Rosenfeld, The Metropolitan Editor; and more vivid than if he had stepped out of obscurity to identify himself, Hal Holbrook as the mysterious Deep Throat. Stephen Collins as the anguished defector from CREEP who provided the reporters with most of their information, and suffered the most, leaves us feeling just the way he left them feeling—a little dirty . . .

By taking the path it does, and by stopping short of catharsis, the film avoids the obvious and earns our respect. But there is something missing, too, some ultimate confrontation not only with the factual truths, but with the inner ones. It is a film

characterized less by genius or inspiration than by intelligence, but intelligence carried to the nth degree . . . "

Reprinted by permission of The Village Voice.
Copyright © The Village Voice, Inc., 1976.

The Sunday Times (London), 5/2/76 (p. 35)
Dilys Powell

" . . . The investigations, the interviews are conducted, most of them, in darkened rooms; even the exteriors are often shadowed; it is a violent contrast with the newsroom, huge, bleak, not a corner escaping the brutal white light. It is to the newsroom that the two reporters belong. They are the servants of its demand for the pitiless truth. And that, I suppose, is where the justification for the making of *All The President's Men* lies. The film is not about the fall of Nixon, or the disgrace of political aides, or the complicity of great departments. It is a stunningly well-made reconstruction of a hunt for facts. One may have qualms, as I have, and still admire the brilliance of the job done. I don't think anything as close to life—close in time, close in personalities —has been done in the cinema before."

© The Sunday Times, 1976.

Commonweal, 4/23/76 (p. 276)
Colin L. Westerbeck, Jr.

" . . . Despite its title, the men whom *All The President's Men* is about are Woodward and Bernstein themselves. This is disappointing . . . It's as if the porno movie were focused on the man all the time instead of the woman. We begin to feel cheated, as we would in a grind house, when we figure out that the plot here isn't just a pretext for showing us what we really came to see. In a sense, Woodward and Bernstein, and filmmaker Alan J. Pakula, are defeated by their own material. Its very strength is their failure, for Watergate is of such interest to us that it overwhelms any interest we might have taken in Woodward and Bernstein.

It is essentially the background of their story that we are focused on. We find ourselves trying to peer around them, wishing that they would get out of the way and being irritated that they don't. The production values of the film seem almost to anticipate and acknowledge our impatience . . . the filmmakers must hope that if the background we see is absolutely authentic, it will make up for not giving us the background we want.

So we are stuck with Woodward and Bernstein, and a movie that, to be honest, doesn't do much to compensate us for our loss . . . "

© Commonweal, 1976.

continued on next page

continued from previous page

Monthly Film Bulletin, 5/76 (p. 95)
Louise Sweet

"The unrelenting sound of Bernstein and Woodward's typewriters, and the loud affirmation of 'Hail to the Chief' as Nixon takes his oath of office, mingle at the end of *All The President's Men*; symbols of the watchdogs and the wielders of power who throughout this powerful film compete for a hearing. Meticulously faithful to Bernstein and Woodward's published account of their investigation, the film is an understated treatment of a terrifying series of disclosures, as the reporters' researches gradually uncover a trail of corruption leading through the offices of high-ranking aides and representatives, the Department of Justice and the FBI, just stopping short of the final door, behind which—in the opening and closing images—an unperturbed, smiling Nixon continues to perform . . . Nowhere does the style overwhelm events, as the film (like the book) reveals both the workaday dimension of evil and the closed quality of America's open system—and the effort required to separate men from the institutions that protect them. For the mood of the film—despite its scrupulous attention to the groundwork of investigation—is still largely buttressed by its sense of power being mythologized and rendered invincible; and by the way the pursuit of truth is complicated by the fallibility of the pursuers themselves, who are motivated by some of the same need for acclaim . . ."

ⓒ Monthly Film Bulletin, 1976.

Nation, 4/24/76 (p. 505)
Robert Hatch

" . . . The effect of *All The President's Men* is not to make Watergate more real but to make it more remote. It moves CREEP out of political history and into the land of SMERSH. It elevates John Mitchell from a disreputable steward of political arrogance to a disembodied ogre of corruption. It glorifies journalism (and I agree that the *Post* and its news staff deserve some glory) with an updated version of *Front Page* razzle-dazzle. I kept expecting someone to yell 'scoop.' The only people in the film who project feelings you can assimilate are the supernumeraries, from whom Bernstein and Woodward sweated their drops of information . . .

But the distancing effect of the picture may be the secret of its enormous success. People go to it, I'm reasonably sure, hoping somewhat morbidly that a screen re-enactment of the miserably inconclusive story, which began with a bungled burglary and ended with an opportunistic pardon, will somehow confirm their worst suspicions. It doesn't do that, and they should feel a bit cheated. But it does something else instead: it takes Watergate out of their remembered past and puts it in the pastime category of *The Ipcress File*, *Blow Up*, and *The Manchurian Candidate* . . ."

ⓒ The Nation, 1976.

The Times (London), 4/30/76 (p. 11)
David Robinson

" . . . The script apparently gave problems. It was basically written by William Goldman (writer of *Butch Cassidy and the Sundance Kid*) who gets screen credit, but was then argued over (often bitterly) and reworked by Redford, Bernstein and the director, Alan Pakula, with advice from the people at the *Post*. The result justifies the effort. Staying all the way with the original Woodstein book, ingeniously interpolating fragments of actuality into the re-creation of events (pudgy Ron Ziegler ferociously denying; Spiro Agnew ranting incoherently; Nixon beaming through the ceremonies of office apparently unperturbed by awareness of the gathering storm), every instant of the mosaic-built story is gripping . . .

Given this degree of dramatization, the method of documentary reconstruction is a triumphantly correct choice. It is handicapped inevitably by the presence of Redford and Dustin Hoffman in the main roles . . . In the event, then, the failure of the film really to characterize the two reporters or their relationship to any extent is a positive advantage . . ."

ⓒ The Times, 1976.

New York Post, 4/8/76 (p. 22)
Frank Rich

" . . . this film is a rare and classic example of what Hollywood can do when it's willing to bank on good taste, shrewd intelligence and deep personal conviction. Though not perfect, *All The President's Men* is an absolutely breathless entertainment, and it successfully carries the weight of history on its shoulders . . .

It works as a detective thriller (even though everyone knows the ending), as a credible (if occasionally romanticized) primer on the prosaic fundamentals of big-league investigative journalism, and, best of all, as a chilling tone poem that conveys the texture of the terror in our nation's capital during that long night when an aspiring fascist regime held our democracy under siege . . .

. . . it's hard to recall an occasion when stars of this magnitude have given less egocentric performances—so careful are Redford and Hoffman to avoid overshadowing the story they wanted to put out. They got what they wanted—*All The President's Men* is a powerful tribute to our free press—and in the process they have, for the moment anyway, valiantly given Hollywood back its good name."

Reprinted by Permission of New York Post.
ⓒ 1976, New York Post Corporation.

Films in Review, 5/76 (p. 311)
Charles Phillips Reilly

" . . . Most of us had become over-saturated with

the Watergate story. The saturation and awareness of the outcome created the film's major problems: how to sustain suspense; how to 'flesh out' a very tangled web of familiar and unfamiliar conspirators; how to dramatize events, often banal. Pakula has overcome these difficulties by using this extraordinary script intelligently, building up detail upon detail to unfold the plot as well as to let us 'see' these characters. Gordon Willis' camera gets the feel of Washington as well as the *Post*. Hoffman and Redford are made for their parts, along with Jason Robards (Ben Bradlee) who almost steals the picture; Jack Warden (Harry Rosenfeld), and Jane Alexander, who is exceptional as the Bookkeeper.

The editing by Robert Wolfe paces the picture beautifully, allowing the audience to identify with the two reporters struggling to do what begins as an ordinary reportorial task, but which ends as an involvement in the salvation of a nation . . .''

© Films in Review, 1976.

ALL THIS AND WORLD WAR II

Director: *Susan Winslow*. Producers: *Sandy Lieberson, Martin J. Machat*. Musical Director: *Lou Reizner*. Words and Music: *John Lennon, Paul McCartney*. Editor: *Colin J. Berwick*. Production: *Martin J. Machat/Eric Kronfeld Presentation—Lou Reizner Production*. Distributor: *Twentieth Century-Fox*. Running time 87 minutes. Los Angeles opening November 11, 1976, at Pacific's Cinerama Dome. Classification: PG.

New York Post, 12/27/76 (p. 41)
Archer Winsten

"*All This and World War II* . . . describes itself as unique. What makes it so is the startling notion of combining documentary footage with appropriate scenes and sentiments from fiction movies concerning the period and then accompanying 'all this' with words and music from those famous Beatles, John Lennon and Paul McCartney, as performed by no fewer than 24 groups . . .

With people of a certain age, and plentiful movie experience, like myself, the picture is a long and well-packed collection of highlights of the period. You might consider it a trip down that particular Memory Lane, the most obvious events revisited.

For younger people, still able to identify well-known movie stars of the past and present and cognizant of historical figures as well, it could be highlighted history against a backdrop of the latter-day popular music that is their preference. It's

probable they could enjoy it more than I did, as an offended antiquarian.''

Reprinted by Permission of New York Post.
© 1976, New York Post Corporation.

Los Angeles Times, 11/12/76 (Pt. IV, p. 31)
Kevin Thomas

"*All This and World War II* . . . is a tasteless, even offensive attempt to get some more mileage out of some Beatles standards and some wartime Fox MovieTone News footage by combining the two—and then, of course, topping the whole thing off by producing a soundtrack album featuring an array of top recording artists rendering the words and music of John Lennon and Paul McCartney.

The facile tone of this glib, shallow enterprise is set early on when we hear Helen Reddy singing 'Fool on a Hill' as we watch Hitler at ease in Berchtesgaden—as if the most evil man of the 20th century could be dismissed so easily! . . .''

© Los Angeles Times, 1976.

Film Information, January 1977 (p. 4)
Suzanne Bowers

"The music of John Lennon and Paul McCartney enhances this compilation of film footage of the World War II years. There is a little bit of everything: newsreel footage of Clark Gable and Charlie McCarthy being sworn into the service, the London Blitz, and Japanese-Americans being shipped to internment camps; some scenes from *Tora! Tora! Tora!* showing the attack on Pearl Harbor, and clips from other Hollywood movies.

The music is performed by twenty different singers or groups, including the Bee Gees, Elton John, Helen Reddy, Rod Stewart, The Four Seasons, Keith Moon, Tina Turner, and Frankie Laine. The attempt to mesh the contemporary songs with the appropriate footage is not always smooth, and several songs are totally unsuitable for the visuals they accompany. Often the tone is too knowingly ironic, as when Hitler struts around his mountain retreat as Helen Reddy sings 'The Fool on the Hill,' or tons of bombs are dropped to the tune of 'All We Need Is Love.' . . .''

© Film Information, 1977.

ALPHA BETA

Director: *Anthony Page*. Screenplay: *E.A. Whitehead*. Based on the play by Mr. Whitehead. Producer: *Timothy Burrill*.

continued on next page

continued from previous page

Photography: *Charles Stewart*. Editor: *Tom Priestley*. Distributor: *Cine III*. Running time 70 minutes. New York opening August 4, 1976, at the Quad Cinema 2 and Thalia Theatres. Classification: None. Origin: England.

Frank Elliot: *Albert Finney*. Nora Elliot: *Rachel Roberts*.

Women's Wear Daily, 8/2/76 (p. 9)
Christopher Sharp

"Not even the expert performances of Albert Finney and Rachel Roberts can cover the weaknesses of *Alpha Beta* . . . Since the film is neither crass nor flimsy, there is no fun in pointing out its weaknesses. It is a seriously conceived, honest film about a disastrous marriage, using only Finney and Roberts for a short 70 minutes . . .

. . . At best the film succeeds at sustaining a high-pitched intensity. The intensity dominates the film so totally that the changes in the lives of the couple are blurred . . .

Students of the art of acting should not miss this film. In spite of the one-dimensional outlook of the film, both Finney and Roberts achieve a searing energy that neither wavers or breaks. The director has been careful to isolate the two performers from distractions—he has succeeded in that, but they are even isolated from a developed plot . . ."

©Women's Wear Daily, 1976.

New York Magazine, 7/26/76 (p. 56)
John Simon

". . . The direction is incisive, but there remains the incontrovertible fact that this is a filmed play that one should have seen on the stage. Failing that, however, it is still a magnificent experience to watch Rachel Roberts and Albert Finney reenact on film the union, in George Meredith's words, of this ever diverse pair. It is acting at its very highest: Anyone who cares a rap about performance penetrating to the essence of humanity owes himself this experience. Watch Finney change from act to act (the movie preserves the act division): He goes from a baffled but still belligerent young husband to a cocky, irresponsible lecher, and thence to a man prematurely old and exhausted but clinging to some illusion of independence. It is not one but three glorious performances rolled together . . . Rachel Roberts is no less superb, but her part has fewer dimensions. Yet how piteously she ages, becomes more thrall to despair, and still preserves a spark of pugnacity, however dulled and enfeebled . . ."

©1976 by the NYM Corp. Reprinted with the permission of NEW YORK Magazine.

New York Post, 8/5/76 (p. 16)
Frank Rich

". . . *Alpha Beta* is almost a completely derivative and predictable piece of theater, and despite director Page's use of a hand-held camera to create a documentary-style visual tone, the movie never stops looking like a filmed play.

But then there are the performances. Miss Roberts has rarely been better than she is here as Nora, and, if she's overshadowed by Finney, that's due to circumstances beyond her control . . . What hurts the actress most, though, is Whitehead's apparent lack of understanding of her character . . .

Finney's role, too, is slightly hampered by Whitehead's clumsiness . . . but the actor rides over such moments and gives a beautifully conceived performance.

Just watching Frank age from act to act is a treat . . ."

Reprinted by Permission of New York Post.
©1976, New York Post Corporation.

Film Information, 9/76 (p. 3)
Frederic A. Brussat

". . . *Alpha Beta* may not be an illuminating film experience for everyone. Yet it is acted with a forcefulness that requires praise. Albert Finney captures all the vanity, anger, guilt and sizzle of Frank, and Rachel Roberts effectively conveys the forsakenness, jealousy, and exhaustion of Nora.

Alpha Beta makes a good case against perpetrating a destructive marriage—'One of the few surviving forms of ritual slaughter.' To those who have the will to endure it, *Alpha Beta* is instructive. But it is not for those who want their entertainments to be magic carpet rides away from the strains of everyday life."

©Film Information, 1976.

Films in Review, November 1976 (p. 570)
DeWitt Bodeen

". . . The entire movie, like the play, takes place in their living-room and tiny kitchen; the camera never leaves the two characters, marvelously played, as they were on the stage, by Albert Finney and Rachel Roberts. Everything on the screen is close-ups or two-shots, yet the camera has more movement in its confined quarters than is permitted the two actors.

E.A. Whitehead, who wrote the play, has adapted it to the screen. Anthony Page has directed its 70 minutes with a mounting, agonizing intensity. Released by Cine III, *Alpha Beta* did not get a first class premiere in Manhattan. But every first-line critic has praised it to the skies, and after two months it's still running downtown. *Alpha Beta* is indisputably one of the best films of the year, and Albert Finney and Rachel Roberts deserve recognition for their realistic, flawless performances."

©Films in Review, 1976.

Los Angeles Times, 10/26/76 (Pt. IV, p. 1)
Kevin Thomas

". . . *Alpha Beta*—its odd title comes from Finney's remark that if he'd say alpha, Miss Roberts would say beta, he gamma, she delta, and so on— is distinguished by the remarkably high quality of writing and acting that is so characteristic of British drama. Its two people are extraordinarily articulate for their station in life, but this theatrical convention is effectively absorbed into the level of heightened reality that the film sustains so well. Director Anthony Page, furthermore, succeeds in keeping the curse of the 'filmed play' off *Alpha Beta* by restricting the camera to extremely tight setups that become expressive of the couple's claustrophobic lives.

Although marriage remains steadfastly the target of Whitehead's wrath, this does not prevent him from creating individuals responsible for their fates . . .

Finney and Miss Roberts are both superb, completely realizing their characters right down to the tiniest details and aging subtly and convincingly. The brilliance of its stars is so exhilarating that *Alpha Beta*, although it sounds depressing, is actually a pleasure to watch."

©Los Angeles Times, 1976.

AMAZING DOBERMANS, THE

Director: *Byron Chudnow*. Screenplay: *Richard Chapman*. Based on a story by Michael Kraike and William Goldstein. Producer: *David Chudnow*. Photography: *Jack Adams*. Editor: *James Potter*. Music: *Alan Silvestri*. Dogs supplied by Frank Inn. Production: *Doberman Associates, Ltd*. Distributor: *Golden Films*. Running time 99 minutes. Los Angeles opening November 23, 1976, at the Beverly Theatre. Classification: G.

Players: *James Almanzar, Fred Astaire, Parley Baer, Billy Barty, Charlie Brill, Jack Carter, Barbara Eden, James Franciscus.*

Los Angeles Times, 11/25/76 (Pt. IV, p. 36)
Kevin Thomas

". . . This time out, the Dobermans are owned

by Fred Astaire, a Bible-quoting ex-con who hires them out for special guard jobs as he travels over the country in his large camper . . .

Most important, *The Amazing Dobermans* has provided the ever-nimble Astaire with an affable, dignified character part in which he can be both poised and charming. Franciscus is likewise appealing, and Miss Eden, her *I Dream of Jeannie* figure admirably intact, has been given the chance to be more relaxed and natural than in various arch and artificial TV movie comedies. (Her would-be romance with Franciscus seems a bit coy, but then this film is carefully aimed at the Disney trade.)

The Dobermans themselves are terrific, as usual, and Billy Barty has a good part as a circus clown . . ."

©Los Angeles Times, 1976.

AMERICA AT THE MOVIES

Producer: *George Stevens, Jr.* Editor: *David Saxon.* Associate Editors: *Joseph Parker, Ana Luisa Corley Perez.* Designer: *James R. Silke.* Narration written by Theodore Strauss. Narrator: *Charlton Heston.* Production: *American Film Institute.* Distributor: *Cinema 5 Limited.* Running time 116 minutes. New York opening September 22, 1976, at several theatres. Classification: PG.

New York Magazine, 10/4/76 (p. 86)
John Simon

". . . *America at the Movies*, the sleazily grandiloquent olio the American Film Institute has just foisted on us . . .

. . . George Stevens Jr. and his cohorts have concocted *America at the Movies* out of, we are proudly told, 83 films, 83, all mutilated and pillaged to provide us with 92 scenes of anywhere from 30 seconds' to two minutes' duration. Would you buy a poetry anthology that consists of 92 incomplete poems? Would you buy the Brooklyn Bridge? . . .

. . . Some omissions are unavoidable, but how do you explain the absence of the likes of Cary Grant and William Holden, Fred Astaire and Kirk Douglas, Loretta Young and Constance Bennett, Marilyn Monroe and Pat Neal—to name just a few off the top of my head? A curious xenophobia operates here: None of the great 'foreigners' is included, thus no Garbo or Dietrich, no Boyer or Colman. Nor,

continued on next page

continued from previous page

among directors, do we get Renoir, Lubitsch, Lang. But there is no consistency even in the chauvinism . . ."

©1976 by the NYM Corp. Reprinted with the permission of NEW YORK Magazine.

New York Post, 9/23/76 (p. 23)
Frank Rich

"*America at the Movies*, a two-hour anthology of Hollywood movie snippets slapped together by the American Film Institute, is either the longest film trailer you've ever seen or a bloated Bicentennial minute—but, in either case, it's a poor excuse for a feature attraction at respectable movie theaters . . .

. . . Early on it devolves into a mindless mish-mash of great and less-than-great cinematic moments—and those moments, even more than the musical MGM anthologies, lose their drive and meaning once they've been yanked out of the films that originally contained them . . .

What I'd like to know about *America at the Movies* is why the American Film Institute . . . decided to make it in the first place . . . the only real use for *America at the Movies* is as filler on the next Oscar telecast."

Reprinted by Permission of New York Post.
©1976, New York Post Corporation.

Village Voice, 10/4/76 (p. 123)
Molly Haskell

". . . As a project that is more institutional than commercial, *America at the Movies* doesn't really require, or call for, reviews. It's not a movie for us, but for . . . whom? Rotarians in Missouri, perhaps, or Legionnaires wherever they are. It is of interest to critics and film buffs to the extent that it shows what the AFI is up to and where its collective head is at with regard to the American cinema, of which it is now the official custodian. In this capacity, the film . . . is more encouraging than one might have expected. Except for one cataclysmic omission, which I'll deal with shortly, the clips suggest a film consciousness that is more informed, discerning, and affectionate than might have prevailed had the film been made 10 years ago . . .

. . . the omission is this: There are virtually no women in the film. The acting credits list 25 women to 85 men (that's counting the Marx Brothers and Laurel and Hardy as one each!). There's no Garbo, no Dietrich. No Bette Davis, no Joan Crawford. No Barbara Stanwyck, no Mae West. No Rosalind Russell, no Rita Hayworth. No Grace Kelly, no Marilyn Monroe, no Doris Day, no Audrey Hepburn. No Jane Fonda, no Ellen Burstyn, no Barbra Streisand . . ."

Reprinted by permission of The Village Voice.
Copyright © The Village Voice, Inc., 1976.

Commonweal, 10/22/76 (p. 695)
Colin L. Westerbeck

". . . takes the BIG moments from some of our best movies and makes them fall out of their original contexts to line up here for a parade, a Fourth-of-July parade with nineteen hundred and seventy-six trombones. The only trouble is that the parade is in truth a forced march and the homage it would pay is fake. *America at the Movies* takes the most popular American art form of this century, and reduces it to a couple of hours' worth of propaganda . . .

In each of the sections, the manifest destiny being demonstrated is made to seem a kind of cycle, a film loop in which the country's history keeps going merrily round and round. This is how all conflict is avoided in the film and anything that might be disagreeable is effaced . . ."

©Commonweal, 1976.

Christian Science Monitor, 10/14/76 (p. 26)
David Sterritt

"*America at the Movies* is a guided tour of a dream.

Anthology films have become a minor rage in recent years, with the deserved success of such efforts as the *That's Entertainment* extravaganzas and some similar reminiscences assembled for TV. *America at the Movies* is more hifalutin than most, seeking to outline the American consciousness as it has influenced—and been influenced by—the Hollywood cinema. The result is usually entertaining and sometimes thought-provoking . . .

Though Theodore Strauss' narration—spoken by Charlton Heston—oversimplifies almost everything, there are many magic moments in *America at the Movies*. And it all ends on the appropriately comic-nostalgic image of Charlie Chaplin's tramp wandering towards the horizon with his lady by his side . . ."

Reprinted by permission from The Christian
Science Monitor ©1976.
The Christian Science Publishing Society.
All rights reserved.

AT THE EARTH'S CORE

Director: *Kevin Connor*. Screenplay: *Milton Subotsky*. Based on the novel by Edgar Rice Burroughs. Producer: *John Dark*. Distributor: *American International Pictures*. Running time 90 minutes. New York opening August 1976 at several theatres. Classification: PG.

Players: *Doug McClure, Peter Cushing, Caroline Munro, Cy Grant, Godfrey James, Sean Lynch.*

Christian Science Monitor, 9/8/76 (p. 56)
David Sterritt

". . . self-satire is fun, but it can't rescue the movie from the disasters of papier-mache-type people eaters, idiotic situations, and a frequent sense of confusion as to what's going on.

Snazzy editing enlivens some sequences, but most of Kevin Connor's directing seems the visual equivalent of Burroughs' awful prose . . .

Peter Cushing is one of the most distinguished fantasy-film specialists in movies today, so I was disturbed by his campy overacting throughout. Doug McClure is his usual athletic self. Caroline Munro looks great as Diane the Beautiful. The rest of the cast does as well as might be expected with such characters as Hooja the Sly One, Ghak the Hairy One, Joobal the Ugly One (and is he ever), plus various monsters, including the Sagoths, whose voices sound like CB radios gone mad underwater . . ."

Reprinted by permission from the Christian
Science Monitor © 1976.
The Christian Science Publishing Society.
All rights reserved.

Los Angeles Times, 9/1/76 (Pt. IV, p. 10)
Kevin Thomas

". . . A kind of cross between *Planet of the Apes* and *One Million B.C.*, *At the Earth's Core*, based on a novel by Tarzan's creator, Edgar Rice Burroughs, is as silly as it sounds—but deliciously so. It has been done with considerable flair (and clearly at considerable expense), boasting elaborate sets and special effects whose obvious artificiality has been stylized enough—as the film itself has been—to seem endearingly whimsical. Children should love this AIP release, and, as camp, it's fun for adults, too . . .

Epitomizing the eccentric and unflappable Britisher and the ever-inquisitive man of science, the always reliable Cushing, in a pleasant departure from his familiar horror roles, is a delight in one of the best roles he's ever had . . ."

©Los Angeles Times, 1976.

New York Post, 8/28/76 (p. 15)
Archer Winsten

"*At the Earth's Core* . . . pursues the imagination of Edgar Rice Burroughs, the creator of Tarzan, into the bowels of the earth in what amounts to a Jules Verne-H.G. Wells Antique Sci-Fi.

Old scientist Dr. Abner Perry (Peter Cushing), backed by the rich, burly young American, David Innes (Doug McClure), has built the 'Iron Mole' which can bore its way through solid rock taking with it a chassis the size of a large missile to the moon.

So, after ceremonies reminiscent of the take-offs described by Jules Verne, they're into the bowels . . .

Although the picture and its plot rush into realms of total impossibility, the film's productive elements are rather better than average. The monsters walk, bite, fly, emit flames and generally behave like the scariest of their ilk. Dr. Cushing spouts a Victorian lingo, while the others sound contemporary . . ."

Reprinted by Permission of New York Post.
©1976, New York Post Corporation.

AUTOBIOGRAPHY OF A PRINCESS

Director: *James Ivory.* Screenplay: *Ruth Prawer Jhabvala.* Producer: *Ismail Merchant.* Photography: *Walter Lassally.* Editor: *Humphrey Dixon.* Music: *Vic Flick.* Production: *Merchant-Ivory.* Distributor: *Cinema 5.* Running time 60 minutes. New York opening October 5, 1975, at the New York Film Festival, Lincoln Center. Classification: None. Origin: Great Britain.

Cyril Smith: *James Mason.* The Princess: *Madhur Jaffrey.* Delivery Man: *Keith Varnier.* Papa: *Nazruh Rahman.* Blackmailers: *Diane Fletcher, Timothy Bateson, Johnny Stuart.*

Film, 5/76 (p. 4)
Lesley Robinson

"In an elegant flat in a fashionable part of London, an exiled Indian Princess and her father's old tutor, Cyril Sahib, are watching some home movies. This is how, every year, they commemorate the dead Prince's birthday. The movies—processions, tiger hunts, family celebrations, magnificent buildings—remind them of the splendours of royal India, ended by Indira Gandhi's egalitarian policy . . .

If British cinema is moribund, this is at least one sign of life. It's a finely wrought film, as compressed as a Somerset Maugham short story, and as compelling. James Mason and the Indian actress Madhur Jaffrey are superb. For a perceptive insight into the spirit of India, and an aesthetic experience of the highest quality, see this movie . . ."

©Film 1976.

BABY BLUE MARINE

Director: *John Hancock.* Screenplay: *Stanford Whitmore.* Producers: *Aaron Spelling, Leonard Goldberg.* Photography: *Laszlo Kovacs.* Music: *Fred Karlin.* Distributor: *Columbia Pictures.* Running time 89 minutes. New York opening May 5, 1976, at several theatres. Classification: PG.

Marion: *Jan-Michael Vincent.* Rose: *Glynnis O'Connor.* Mrs. Hudkins: *Katherine Helmond.*

continued on next page

continued from previous page

Sheriff Wenzel: *Dana Elcar*. Mr. Hudkins: *Bert Remsen*. 'Pop' Mosley: *B. Kirby, Jr.* Marine Raider: *Richard Gere*. Mr. Elmore: *Art Lund*. Drill Instructor: *Michael Conrad*. Barney Hudkins: *Michael Le Clair*. Capt. Bittman: *Allan Miller*.

Women's Wear Daily, 4/28/76 (p. 35)
Howard Kissel

" . . . In some ways material like this is easier to do in 'stills' than as a story because we are only willing to suspend disbelief for so long—we can't really accept the notion that even in a past we didn't know everything could have been so basically sunny.

Baby Blue is about a young man who fails basic training as a Marine and is sent home in an embarrassing 'baby blue' uniform. En route he meets a highly decorated Marine who wants to desert, who knocks him out, steals his light-blue uniform and leaves him his bemedaled one in exchange, which the youngster has to wear on his trip home. Needless to say, he is given opportunities to show that even if the Marines didn't consider him suitable material he is nevertheless heroic stuff. This is the sort of material Preston Sturges has explored with greater success but Hancock's aims are limited and his story is without pretensions; because he gets solid character performances out of his beautifully chosen cast, the film works within its modest intentions . . ."

© Women's Wear Daily, 1976.

New York Magazine, 5/10/76 (p. 65)
John Simon

" . . . Despite his name, John Hancock has precious little signature as a director, though the film is, on the whole, well cast and acted even in the tiniest parts, for which Hancock must receive some credit. The small-town atmosphere is, at times, all but caught just when a cliche or bit of posturing undercuts it . . . Indeed, the very climax, meant to invest our antihero with true heroism, is contrived and insignificant, and lacking in resonance. Jan-Michael Vincent and Glynnis O'Connor are believable enough young lovers, but their young-love story holds little interest.

Laszlo Kovacs, one of our trickiest cinematographers, starts out with some persuasively atmospheric boot-camp shots that are not excessively mannered. Soon, though, while avoiding artifice, he falls into mere ordinariness . . ."

© 1976 by the NYM Corp. Reprinted with the permission of NEW YORK Magazine.

Film Information, 6/76 (p. 2)
David Bartholemew

"A World War II term 'baby blue marine' refers to those unfortunates (or lucky ones, depending on your point of view) who wash out of marine boot camp training. The light blues they are sent home in become a sissy-ish badge of their failure. If you can accept muscular Jan-Michael Vincent as such a flunkie, you're half-way there to enjoying the pleasantly old-fashioned movie . . .

. . . Hancock has always exhibited a fondness for losers and innocents, and he keeps this lightweight concoction afloat, mainly by drawing strong performances from his cast. O'Connor and Vincent make attractive lovers, and Vincent has shucked his usual action image of revenge-aroused, violent but moral force. Considering his wholesome, lean, blond appearance, there's just no one around who can play a 'good boy' better than he . . ."

© Film Information, 1976.

New York Post, 5/16/76 (p. 23)
Archer Winsten

"*Baby Blue Marine* . . . offers the improbable spectacle of Jan-Michael Vincent portraying a boot-camp Marine relegated to the idiot group because he can't do anything . . .

Romance and melodrama out of the Japanese internment national error keep this odd recollection of things past movingly unexpected. The ending is wrapped up very much as if we had been listening to a personal memoir which is, after all, what it is in good part. Author Stanford Whitmore did graduate from high school in 1943, joined the Marines, and did see 'baby blues' leaving on the bus. And yet, he himself didn't go through it, and in some strange way, this picture doesn't either despite all the genuine people, places, and behavior.

Instead it's a rickety structure of strange events that make you think they're contrived rather than inevitable results of what had happened earlier . . ."

Reprinted by Permission of New York Post.
© 1976, New York Post Corporation.

Monthly Film Bulletin, 9/76 (p. 188)
Verina Glaessner

" . . . Although its nominal concerns are with American involvement in World War II, Hancock and scriptwriter Stanford Whitmore deliberately play it as a kind of exorcism of the Vietnam trauma. This aspect becomes most fascinating in the hero's rather ghostly encounter with the white-haired marine raider . . . He leaves Hedge to don the cloak of heroism (minus the pain), to which, the film suggests, he has every right, making him a clean hero returning to a clean country. Coming straight from a similar role in *White Line Fever*, Jan-Michael Vincent is an obvious choice for Hedge, making him a character so evidently without guile that he virtually rekindles the conviction that 'all the old ways won't die.' Unfortunately, Hancock tends to linger all too lovingly over his material, squeezing out the last drop of poignancy . . .''

©Monthly Film Bulletin, 1976.

in *The Odd Couple* to make an uncouth and very human slob out of his coach Morris Buttermaker, is at his best as he lets intimations of decency creep into his shrewd boozer's squint and a touch of sentiment to leaven his scowl. The kids are first rate, with scrappy Chris Barnes, near-catatonic Quinn Smith, and every other Bear outstanding. Joyce Van Patten is fine as a tough league lady, and Vic Morrow is very good as a coach who has all the proper patter down too pat . . .''

© Judith Crist, 1976.

BAD NEWS BEARS, THE

Director: *Michael Ritchie*. Screenplay: *Bill Lancaster*. Producer: *Stanley R. Jaffe*. Photography: *John A. Alonzo*. Editor: *Richard A. Harris*. Music: *Jerry Fielding*. Distributor: *Paramount Pictures*. Running time 102 minutes. New York opening April 6, 1976, at the Paramount and Sutton Theatres. Classification: PG.

Coach Morris Buttermaker: *Walter Matthau*. Amanda Whurlizer: *Tatum O'Neal*. Roy Turner: *Vic Morrow*. Cleveland: *Joyce Van Patten*. Bob Whitewood: *Ben Paizza*. Kelly Leak: *Jackie Earle Haley*. Ogilvie: *Alfred W. Lutter*. Joey Turner: *Brandon Cruz*. Tanner Boyle: *Chris Barnes*. Ahmad Abdul Rahim: *Erin Blunt*. Engelberg: *Gary Lee Cavagnaro*. Joe Agilar: *Jaime Escobedo*. Regi Tower: *Scott Firestone*. Miguel Agilar: *George Gonzales*. Jimmy Feldman: *Brett Marx*. Rudi Stein: *David Pollock*. Timmy Lupus: *Quinn Smith*. Toby Whitewood: *David Stambaugh*.

See Volume 1 for additional reviews

New York Magazine, 4/29/76 (p. 85)
John Simon

'' . . . *The Bad News Bears* deals not only with baseball, America's favorite pastime, but also, being Little League baseball, with America's favorite people—kids. And not just any old kids, but a wonderful gallery of angelic kids, precocious kids, hilariously oddball kids, lovably ethnic kids, sweetly pathetic kids—in fact, everything but ordinary kids . . .

. . . the film has genuine virtues . . . Ritchie has directed the kids most persuasively, even when the script gives them deeds and dialogue that are not really credible. (At other times, though, they are.) From Matthau he gets one of his crustiest and unforcedly funniest performances, which does not even let such dazzling youngsters as Tatum O'Neal, Alfred W. Lutter, and Jackie Earle Haley steal the show. And Ritchie is marvelous at shooting action on the diamond, whether comic or tense. But he is most brilliant in moments of waiting, between plays or ploys, when people are nervously twitching or fidgeting, blinking or scratching themselves—when expectant emptiness begins to burst at the seams. Add to this fine cinematography by John A. Alonzo and jolly background-musical fiddling with the score of *Carmen* by Jerry Fielding, and you've got yourself a ball, if not a hit.''

© 1976 by the NYM Corp. Reprinted with the permission of NEW YORK Magazine.

Saturday Review, 4/17/76 (p. 47)
Judith Crist

"*The Bad News Bears* is unbeatable as all-around satisfying entertainment, replete with the 'something more' that gives light comedy its tang. Written by Bill Lancaster, son of Burt, in his writing debut, this Michael Ritchie film goes to the heart of the matter of children's competitive play . . .

. . . We stick to the ball field and the grandstands for the most part, and we see, with a remarkable subtlety that builds amid laughter and slapstick, adults and children arriving at some unsavory and some very rewarding truths about themselves.

Matthau, going even beyond his Oscar Madison

Los Angeles Times, 4/7/76 (Pt. IV, p. 1)
Kevin Thomas

"*The Bad News Bears* . . . is nothing but good news.

Starring Walter Matthau as the boozy, broken down coach of a Little League baseball team and Tatum O'Neal as his tough little star pitcher, it's the best American screen comedy of the year to date . . .

Bright, pugnacious and utterly realistic as most children seem to be today, these kids are drawn with much accuracy and are played beautifully. Especially resilient and self-sufficient is Miss

continued on next page

continued from previous page

O'Neal's pitcher, and she is again the charmer she was in *Paper Moon*. (An occasional strong word stood out uncomfortably in that period piece; here the frequent foul-mouthing among the kids must be admitted as typical of today.)

Indicative of the film's apt casting right down the line is Vic Morrow's hard-driving coach of the Bears' potent rivals, the Yankees, and Joyce Van Patten's hearty, no-nonsense league official. Another key Bears teammate, besides Jackie Earle Haley, is Alfred W. Lutter, again the precocious kid he was in *Alice Doesn't Live Here Anymore*.

Smartly produced (by Stanley R. Jaffe) and designed (by Polly Platt), *The Bad News Bears* has an especially witty score by Jerry Fielding, who has incorporated familiar themes from Bizet's *Carmen*, which at once conveys the deadly seriousness of sandlot baseball to its players—and a gentle sense of absurdity that this should be the case."

© Los Angeles Times, 1976.

Village Voice, 5/3/76 (p. 123)
Andrew Sarris

"*The Bad News Bears* is a pleasant enough piece of entertainment about a Little League team of lovable misfits rising from the bog of defeat to the brink of victory. Walter Matthau growls his way through the role of the team's drunken manager with rumpled expertise. The kid ensemble —headed by Tatum O'Neal, Jackie Earle Haley, and Alfred W. Lutter—reaches new peaks of precociousness both on the field and in the dugout. This concoction should have been packaged for the Radio City Music Hall. It is sleek '70s sentimentality at its best. Indeed, by the time the picture is over you want to reach out and hug every one of the children and then give Matthau an appreciatively firm handshake for a job well done. Of course, it is all too good to be true and too neat to be convincing. But who cares? . . ."

Reprinted by permission of The Village Voice.
Copyright © The Village Voice, Inc., 1976.

Film Information, 5/76 (p. 2)
David A. Tillyer

" . . . *The Bears* is a movie for those adults who, insecure with their own abilities, attempt to win life's accolades through their progeny. In this film, tension builds to a feverish pitch as the team approaches the inevitable championship and Matthau and Vic Morrow, playing an opposing coach, square off for a no-holds-barred brawl. This section

offers classic scenes of children resisting parental pressure. Director Michael Ritchie (*Downhill Racer*, *The Candidate*, *Smile*) deserves high praise for his work with his crew of moppets, many of whom had never acted before. Together they come off as a team; individually they sparkle freshly with clean cues and priceless lines.

In *The Bears* we see only one facet of the lives of nine kids and the adults in the league. With so many characters, none is fully developed. It's a long film and yet it doesn't tell a full story . . . one wonders about Matthau's character and his relationship with Tatum and her mother, barely mentioned in the film.

Still, the action is lively and incisive statements are made about the nature of American competitiveness . . ."

© Film Information, 1976.

Sight and Sound, Winter 1976/1977 (p. 58)
John Pym

"Sustained by an individual and highly polished standard of comic invention, *The Bad News Bears* . . . remains easily the most accessible and tidily complete of the four feature films (the others being *Downhill Racer*, *The Candidate* and *Smile*) in which Michael Ritchie has developed and extended his ruminations on the peculiarly American requirements for winning at sports, politics and pageant. Unlike its more quizzical and open-ended predecessors, *The Bad News Bears* is an unmistakable commercial picture (the kind, Ritchie intended, to make an audience feel good); it has the straightforward attraction of a sentimental yet witty script, an oddball cast of unaffected and genuinely engaging boys, and two old-fashioned stars, Tatum O'Neal and Walter Matthau, skillfully rehearsing their respective images of tough precocity and lovable misanthropy . . ."

© Sight and Sound. 1977

Film, February 1977 (p. 12)
Peter Cargin

". . . *The Bad News Bears* is about a kids' baseball team and their reluctant new coach, who attempts to knock some shape into them for a fee. Behind this simple story line Ritchie continues to bring us more facets of the two themes which have been common to nearly all his films. These themes are, I believe, the depiction of small-town America and the American concern with winning . . .

. . . *Bears* is about another small town; moreover it concerns itself with a team about to start another season of contests, but in the course of the film the whole idea of winning being the most important thing is questioned . . .

Like all good films this has considerable depth

beneath the seemingly bland surface and simple story line, and it will last unlike many more portentious efforts on the same theme."

©Film 1977

Films in Review, 5/76 (p. 312)
Michael Buckley

" . . . An amusing comedy that doesn't score a home run, due to the lack of character development in the screenplay by Bill (son of Burt) Lancaster, this film should still be a popular three-base hit.

As the coach, Walter Matthau repeats his *Odd Couple* character, and is herein named Morris Buttermaker. Tatum O'Neal, youngest possessor of an Oscar, skillfully handles her second screen assignment . . .

One of the film's best performances is given by Jackie Earle Haley . . .

All members of the team acquit themselves admirably, with particular standouts being Alfred Lutter (Ellen Burstyn's precocious son in *Alice Doesn't Live Here Anymore*) as a boy who knows everything about the game except how to play; Chris Barnes, whose temper is shorter than he is; Gary Lee Cavagnaro, the overweight catcher who also has a big mouth; Erin Blunt, who aspires to be the new Hank Aaron; Quinn Smith, the smallest player, whose runny nose is a constant problem . . .

Michael Ritchie, whose last achievement was the underrated *Smile*, directs in expert fashion. *The Bad News Bears* just misses being a big league success."

© Films in Review, 1976.

The Times (London), 11/12/76 (p. 9)
David Robinson

" . . . For all its sweet-sour undertones, it is a very funny film indeed, as the strained melodies of Bizet's *Carmen* underscore Buttermaker's efforts to woo his dangerous charges like a matador playing his bulls.

Matthau, who is sometimes inclined to coast when a part does not fully engage him, is at his funniest here. His beady eyes peer cautiously out of the leathery folds of his face, his mouth always crumpled somewhat towards one side as if in readiness to snarl an imprecation at someone coming up unexpectedly from behind.

The team is a match for him in comedy and cranky eccentricity . . ."

©The Times, 1976.

Monthly Film Bulletin, November 1976 (p. 228)
Tom Milne

" . . . *The Bad News Bears* is miraculously funny and entirely delightful. Walter Matthau, of course, has (and makes the most of) a tailor-made part as the beer-swilling slob trading insults with his charges and generally getting the worst of it . . . In scene after scene, one has to be quick to catch the drift of Ritchie's wit: the casual camera angle revealing that Buttermaker has resorted to a bail bond firm as sponsors for his team of moppets; the smart oneupmanship of Amanda's lightning patter to tourists explaining why the maps to film star homes she is touting are marked 25 cents but cost $2.00 . . . All these are featured comic set-pieces, as it were, but the real triumph of the film lies in the incredibly funny background panorama of baseball scenes where, with a helpless bafflement and perfectly timed dexterity that Buster Keaton would have been proud to own, the Bears fumble, drop or entirely miss every ball that comes along in an amazing variety of ways . . ."

©Monthly Film Bulletin, 1976.

The Sunday Times (London), 11/14/76 (p. 39)
Alan Brien

" . . . The groggy maypole on which all the juvenile strands depend is the beer-logged, failed pro, Walter Matthau, face like an old baseball glove with the eyelets torn, who is that least forgivable of American dropouts, not so much a has-been as a hasn't-been. Reluctantly rescued from his sinecure of cleaning out swimming pools, uncomfortably sobered by the baleful stare of the Bears, bested even in his exchanges of barroom insults, he winches up his grin, adjusts his nose to a jaunty angle like an unlit cigar, and almost falls flat on his face. The tensions of winning are worse than the trauma of losing and he throws the key match to save their childhood. No one can embody this role, somewhere between Spencer Tracy and W.C. Fields, more capably than Matthau, dominating a screen full of relaxed, unself-conscious youngsters as though he did not know the camera had been invented . . ."

©The Sunday Times, 1976.

BAMBINA

Director: *Alberto Lattuada*. Screenplay: *Ottavio Jemma, Bruno Di Geronimo, Mr. Lattuada*. Producer: *Silvio Clementelli*. Distributor: *Buckley Bros. Films*. Running time 97 minutes. New York opening April 1976 at the Paris Theatre. Classification: R. Origin: Italy.

Players: *Luigi Proietti, Irene Papas, Teresa Ann Savoy, Bruno Cirino, Mario Scaccia, Lina Polito, Isa Miranda*.

continued on next page

continued from previous page

New York Magazine, 5/10/76 (p. 65)
John Simon

" . . . Clotilde is a wealthy sixteen-year-old retardate, who urinates equally in her bed, in her panties under the gaze of her mother's guests at an elegant soiree, and on her lover's best suit when she rides him as they play horsey. *Bambina* is a semipornographic *Lolita*, with lots of southern Italian gusto and a curious happy ending. Saverio, the mature, materialistic land developer has given up everything for his sexy Kewpie doll with the underdeveloped brain . . .

This is, you may have gathered, a fairly demented little film. But it believes in itself with remarkable singlemindedness . . . there is something to be said for the notion that a shared private obsession is preferable to endless public exploitation. Unlike, say, *Malizia*, *Bambina* is not evil.

It is not, however, a good film, and deserves only the kind of sympathy we grant madmen from whose mouths drop flashes of insight. There are some good performances. Luigi Proietti is an amusing Saverio . . . Irene Pappas is a compelling presence as Clotilde's rich, mercilessly mercenary yet not unmotherly mother. As Clotilde, Teresa Ann Savoy is amazing . . ."

© 1976 by the NYM Corp. Reprinted with the permission of NEW YORK Magazine.

New York Post, 4/26/76 (p. 23)
Archer Winsten

"*Bambina* . . . is an Italian item so fundamentally different from almost any film you can call to mind that it's hard to characterize. Set in southern Italy where male 'macho' is the source of much cinematic jest, it takes off in another direction. Free to utilize sex, it brings up an aspect no one has thought to handle until now. Call it total reversal or black humor, what happens is going to strain your credulity, at the same time providing elements that give you pause . . .

. . . Irene Pappas is a handsome mother of great personal distinction, and Proietti is able to make mental transitions with admirable facial subtlety that carry across to an audience. Teresa Ann Savoy is unquestionably the most attractive halfwit in the movies, and Alberto Lattuada has succeeded in walking a tightrope of film-making and story telling without falling on his head . . ."

Reprinted by Permission of New York Post.
© 1976, New York Post Corporation.

BAWDY ADVENTURES OF TOM JONES, THE

Director: *Cliff Owen.* Screenplay: *Jeremy Lloyd.* Based on the musical by Don Mac-Pherson and Paul Holden. Producer: *Robert Sadoff.* Photography: *Douglas Slocombe.* Editor: *Bill Blunden.* Distributor: *Universal Pictures.* Running time 94 minutes. New York opening September 1, 1976, at several theatres. Classification: R.

Tom Jones: *Nicky Henson.* Squire Western: *Trevor Howard.* Mr. Square: *Terry-Thomas.* Dr. Thwackum: *Arthur Lowe.* Jenny Jones (Mrs. Waters): *Georgia Brown.* Black Bess: *Joan Collins.* Squire Alworthy: *William Mervyn.* Blifil: *Murray Melvin.* Sophia. *Madeline Smith.*

Los Angeles Times, 9/29/76 (Pt. IV, p. 12)
Kevin Thomas

" . . . Sadoff's stage production was fast, funny and mildly risque, one-dimensional and . . . apt in a nightclub or dinner theater context. However, *The Bawdy Adventures of Tom Jones* falls far short of any of its predecessors. It's a cheap, crude, sexed-up rehash with only three actual musical numbers, all of which are forgettable . . .

Actually, *The Bawdy Adventures* consists mainly of Trevor Howard, cast as Squire Western, father of Tom's true love Sophia (Madeline Smith), mauling every servant girl in sight, and of Tom forever being caught with his pants down. Alas, the way Howard roughly exercises his droit de seigneur causes the film to take on a crass, unappetizing male chauvinist fantasy role . . .

. . . this new edition of *Tom Jones* is more boring than bawdy."

©Los Angeles Times, 1976.

New York Post, 9/2/76 (p. 23)
Archer Winsten

" . . . They've collected some pretty good British name actors. Trevor Howard to play the hard-drinking Squire Western, Terry-Thomas to be Mr. Square, Arthur Lowe for the Dr. Thwackum role, Georgia Brown as Jenny Jones, Joan Collins to show up as Black Bess, a masked robber, William Mervyn as Squire Alworthy and Murray Melvin to be Blifil. Net result is that you have a strong feeling of theatrical revival, with costumes and settings done in A-1 Pinewood Studios, London style.

But that's the end of it. Nicky Henson is a Tom Jones of no distinction at all, and director Cliff Owen moves his huge cast from garden to horse without any embellishments designed to grab attention.

Gradually the picture sinks beneath its impedimenta of musical, classic and new material that adds up to fuss-and-feathers cluttering up the landscape . . ."

Reprinted by Permission of New York Post.
©1976, New York Post Corporation.

BEAUTIFUL BORDERS (CHULAS FRONTERAS)

Documentary. Director: *Les Blank*. Producer: *Chris Strachwitz*. Distributor: *Brazos Films*. Running time 58 minutes. New York opening December 31, 1976, at the Film Forum. Classification: None.

Note: There is no cast in this film.

Village Voice, 1/3/77 (p. 39)
Michael Goodwin

"When filmmaker/folklorist Les Blank gets interested in some new kind of music, I get interested too. And this time it's Norteno—the music and people of the Texas-Mexico border. Blank's new film, *Chulas Fronteras* . . . calls for dancing in the street with a bottle of Pearl beer in one hand and a chili reileno in the other . . .

Chulas Fronteras . . . was completed in mid-1976. It's a perfect introduction to Norteno—with performance footage of the top musicians, interviews with disc jockeys and *campesinos*, guided tours of back-room recording studios, and subtitled translations of no fewer than 16 musical numbers. It's the first road map through a virtually unknown (at least to Anglos) musical landscape; it's also a joyous, angry, complicated film . . ."

Reprinted by permission of The Village Voice
Copyright © The Village Voice, Inc., 1977

BEWARE OF A HOLY WHORE

Director, Producer: *Rainer Werner Fassbinder*. Screenplay (German with English subtitles):

Mr. Fassbinder. Photography: *Michael Ballhaus*. Distributor: *New Yorker Films*. Running time 103 minutes. New York opening November 11, 1976, at the Film Forum. Classification: None. Origin: West Germany.

Players: *Marquard Bohm, Lou Castel, Eddie Constantine, Rainer Werner Fassbinder, Hannes Fuchs, Ulli Lommel, Werner Schroeter, Hanna Schygulla, Margarethe von Trotta.*

Los Angeles Times, 10/29/76 (Pt. IV, p. 20)
Kevin Thomas

". . . Like Fellini's *8½*, Truffaut's *Day for Night* and most especially Godard's *Contempt*, Fassbinder's *Beware of a Holy Whore* uses the film-within-a-film device to contemplate the nature of film itself. Essentially, what Fassbinder discovers is that he and everyone else involved need to make films in order to give their lives meaning, no matter how treacherous the process. In showing this is so in such a manner so unsparing of himself and his colleagues, he invites us, the viewers, to recognize how intense is our own need for the cinema . . .

. . . except for Constantine, everyone else is enormously and excruciatingly self-indulgent, yet Fassbinder views one and all with such insight and compassion that this most demanding (yet resonant) of films never becomes a bore in its portrayal of the bored. In fact *Beware of a Holy Whore*, a piercingly beautiful film, confers upon its people the very sense of grace they hunger for so deeply."

©Los Angeles Times, 1976.

BIG BUS, THE

Director: *James Frawley*. Screenplay, Producers: *Fred Freeman, Lawrence J. Cohen*. Photography: *Harry Stradling, Jr.* Editor: *Edward Warschilka*. Music: *David Shire*. Distributor: *Paramount Pictures*. Running time 88 minutes. New York opening June, 1976, at several theatres. Classification: PG.

Dan Torrance: *Joseph Bologna*. Kitty Baxter: *Stockard Channing*. Shoulders: *John Beck*. Father Kudos: *Rene Auberjonois*. Shorty Scotty: *Ned Beatty*. Dr. Kurtz: *Bob Dishy*. Ironman: *Jose Ferrer*. Old Lady: *Ruth Gordon*. Professor Baxter: *Harold Gould*. Parking Lot Doctor: *Larry Hagman*. Sybil Crane: *Sally Kellerman*. Claude Crane: *Richard Mulligan*. Camille Levy: *Lynn Redgrave*.

continued on next page

continued from previous page

Los Angeles Times, 6/24/76 (Pt. IV, p. 1)
Kevin Thomas

" . . . An appealing silly spoof of disaster epics written by the authors of that inspired send-up of swashbucklers, *Start the Revolution Without Me*, *The Big Bus* is a satisfying summer refresher, not great maybe, but the kind of picture that's relaxing and a lift to the spirits. In short, it's entertaining . . .

Directed by James Frawley with an unflagging sense of fun, the prime asset of *The Big Bus* is unquestionably its zany, cliche-skewering script, written by Fred Freeman and Lawrence J. Cohen. Bologna and Miss Channing, who is in her third film and looks like a cross between Elizabeth Taylor and Maureen Stapleton, are nicely teamed, as are Miss Kellerman and the all-too-seldom-seen Mulligan."

© Los Angeles Times, 1976.

The Sunday Times (London), 11/7/76 (p. 38)
Alan Brien

" . . . a free-wheeling, accident-prone vehicle programmed to send up and run down all disaster movies . . .

Director Frawley, still affectionately remembered here as one of the American satirical stage company, *The Premise*, joins with writer-producers Fred Freeman and Lawrence J. Cohen to keep as many gags going as he has mouths to fill. And he doesn't just stick to disaster-jokes but lobs in a few sour anti-romantic cracks as well. It's all fast, bright, surface stuff, almost obsessively intent on never letting a laugh get away, misfiring, back-firing, skidding and crashing gears gaily all the way, often quite as thrilling, if not always as ludicrous, as some of the films it mocks."

© The Sunday Times, 1976.

Monthly Film Bulletin, November 1976 (p. 229)
Richard Combs

"*The Big Bus* is a spirited collection of gags on the disaster movie syndrome, which, disappointingly from the director of *Kid Blue*, never quite coheres into something all its own . . . Disaster movies are so limited as a genre that even a parody winds up looking very simple-minded, unless it also aims its barbs at the climate—historical, emotional and commercial—that makes all the stunts and super-destructive thrills possible. But *The Big Bus* effortlessly glides on the surface—its comic routines made all the more seductive and rather benumbing by the fact that they are as expensively and elaborately produced as anything in the disaster cycle . . ."

© Monthly Film Bulletin, 1976.

The Times (London), 11/25/76 (p. 9)
David Robinson

"It is a good week for comedy. *The Big Bus*, directed by James Frawley who made *Kid Blue*, is that rarity among films, a successfully sustained parody. It sends up the disaster movie of the *Airport* school, with the story of the first nuclear powered bus, Cyclops, on its nonstop maiden trip from New York to Denver. The writers, Fred Freeman and Lawrence J. Cohen, haven't missed a trick. The driver, who is in love with the designer's daughter, has a past: he is suspected of eating 110 passengers when his bus broke down on Mount Diablo. In the operations room, the controller is having trouble with his boyfriend. The passengers are the usual ship of fools who take tickets for disaster movies, or at least almost so . . ."

© The Times, 1976.

New York Post, 6/24/76 (p. 21)
Frank Rich

"What, you may ask, is a movie called *The Big Bus*? Well, I'm not absolutely sure—but I think *The Big Bus* is a movie about a big bus. Not just any big bus, of course—but a really big bus. A really, really big bus that goes very, very fast . . .

And what, you may also ask, is happening on the big bus in *The Big Bus*? Well, what happens is that a lot of people stand around and act silly. Some of these people . . . are highly regarded actors who are, apparently, on a busman's holiday. Others . . . are comic types who have been encouraged by *The Big Bus*'s director . . . to bulge their eyes whenever they feel a joke coming on . . .

A prologue to *The Big Bus* says that it's a satire of disaster movies—only with a big bus instead of a big plane or a big ship. And maybe it is. But I'd bet you a one-way ticket on the Concorde that *The Big Bus* is, instead, a conspiracy to drive the moviegoers of America completely out of their minds."

Reprinted by Permission of New York Post.
© 1976,New York Post Corporation.

Saturday Review, 8/7/76 (p. 45)
Judith Crist

"*The Big Bus*, a happy takeoff on all those *Airport* adventure spectaculars, is so full of talents and ideas that I, for one, am not going to quibble about whether it works all the way or not. Written and produced by Fred Freeman and Lawrence J. Cohen, and directed by James Frawley, it crams the first nuclear-powered bus chock-full of fine comedic performers and takes them on a disaster-ridden nonstop ride from New York to Denver. The hero is Joe Bologna, a driver accused of cannibalism after a bus wreck, trying for a comeback under the aegis of Stockard Channing, daughter of the inventor and interior designer of the lunatic vehicle. The passengers include Rene Auberjonois as a falling-away priest, Sally Kellerman and Richard Mulligan as a love-hate couple, Lynn Redgrave as a lubricious couturiere, Bob Dishy as a veterinarian delicensed for putting an IUD in a rabbit, and lots more . . .''

©Judith Crist, 1976.

Newsweek, 7/12/76 (p. 69)
Jack Kroll

". . . *The Big Bus* makes fun of disaster movies, but ironically there's almost as much laughter—nervous laughter—at a film like *The Towering Inferno*, and the nervous laughter is more fun because it involves our primal fears as well as our funny bone.

The central joke in the script by Fred Freeman and Lawrence J. Cohen is to take the most plebeian method of public transportation—the bus—and upgrade it to Titanic or Hindenburg status by turning it into the world's first nuclear-powered bus, a multisectioned monster that includes cocktail lounge, swimming pool and bowling alley. The movie rumbles a long way on this TV-sketch kind of idea, thanks to reasonably clever special effects, reasonably sly direction by James Frawley, and a passenger list of deft performers on this bus of fools. Funniest is Joseph Bologna . . .''

©Newsweek, Inc. 1976
reprinted by permission.

New York Magazine, 7/12/76 (p. 74)
John Simon

". . . These characters are denied a single witty line, and are merely pushed into outrageous exaggeration, as if grade-school notions of jadedness or hysteria were the soul of wit. Alas, these poses and paroxysms are stupid and offensive, and it is small wonder that Lynn Redgrave, Richard Mulligan, and Sally Kellerman are made to look ridiculous, as is virtually everyone associated with this venture . . .

It is just barely possible that all this could have been mildly amusing if it had been written, directed, and acted with the straightest of faces, the satirical intent dribbling out only gradually and, as it were, by accident. But that would have been well beyond the means of the writers and James Frawley . . .''

©1976 by the NYM Corp. Reprinted with
the permission of NEW YORK Magazine.

Village Voice, 7/19/76 (p. 103)
Molly Haskell

". . . The nonsensical nuclear bus, rigged out in all the 'marvels' modern technology and the leisure industry can produce, is on its virgin nonstop run from New York to Denver, but the movie is as laden down with gimmicks as it's hell-on-wheels. When the usual assortment of misfits arrive *Airport* style at Port Authority it's not as funny as the original. Is Ruth Gordon, for example, really a parody of Helen Hayes, or isn't she rather the Helen Hayes of comedy!

Joseph Bologna is enchanting as the driver with a black mark on his professional escutcheon (he is accused of having devoured 104 missing passengers when his bus got stranded in a mountain pass, and the scene in which he is accosted by his lynch-minded colleagues in a busman's bar is very funny). But like so many interludes in the film, it tries too hard . . .''

Reprinted by permission of The Village Voice.
Copyright © The Village Voice, Inc., 1976.

Christian Science Monitor, 7/7/76 (p. 22)
David Sterritt

". . . Even when *The Big Bus* pokes fun at sacred cows, the mockery is aimed not at real people or institutions, but at stereotypes and cliches that have dominated the movies ever since Edison. If you like the grand old absurdity of grand old Hollywood, you'll be extra charmed by the 'inside' humor that is no more 'inside' than a box office hit or a cast of thousands. If you're not a buff, don't worry—there is nothing here more subtle than a good guy frightening off a menacing mob with a broken milk carton. And by the way, these jokes look funnier than they sound. That's the mark of a good movie, and not merely a promising screenplay.

A host of good actors brings off the comedy under the direction of James Frawley, who achieves Mel Brooks' mania without too much of Mel Brooks' shouted repetition . . .''

Reprinted by permission from The Christian
Science Monitor © 1976.
The Christian Science Publishing Society.
All rights reserved.

Film Information, 9/76 (p. 4)
Dave Pomeroy

". . . *The Big Bus* has been produced with such consummate bad taste, schlock acting and feeble attempts at verbal and visual humor that whatever laughs are engendered are *at* it rather than *with* it. (Here is the one halfway decent line: a cashiered veterinarian says he was thrown out of his profession because 'I was the only one with the courage to put an IUD in a rabbit'—that, mind you, is the *best* line in the film.) . . .

continued on next page

continued from previous page

It's all much too broad and obvious. Stockard Channing, made up to look like a cross between Elizabeth Taylor and Shelley Winters, fulfills none of the promise as a farceuse she offered in *The Fortune*. Of the all-star cast only Ruth Gordon brings some wry humor to her throw-away lines . . ."

©Film Information, 1976.

BIG DIG, THE
(TAALAT BLAUMILCH)

Director, Screenplay: *Ephraim Kishon*. Producers: *Rony Yacov, Mr. Kishon*. Photography: *Manny Wynn*. Music: *Noam Schariff*. Distributor: *Canal Films*. Running time 83 minutes. Los Angeles opening November 1976 at the Royal Theatre. Classification: None. Origin: Israel.

Players: *Nissim Azriki, Shraga Friedmann, Rina Ganor, Miriam Gabrielli, Zahrira Harifai, Avner Hizkaiyahu, Shai K. Ophir, Aviva Paz, Avraham Ronai, Oded Teomi, Natan Wolpowitch, Bomba Zur*.

Los Angeles Times, 11/24/76 (Pt. IV, p. 6)
Linda Gross

"*The Big Dig* . . . is one of those rare, ironic charmers like *The King of Hearts* which suggests that sanity is as illusive as lunacy.

The film concerns a city's reaction to a madman (Bomba Zoor) who escapes from the local asylum in a milk van that drops him in the middle of Tel Aviv, whereupon he steals a compressor and starts to dig a canal to transform Tel Aviv 'into the Venice of the Middle East.' . . .

The Big Dig has been produced, directed and written by noted Israeli humorist Ephraim Kishon. As a parable of power, the film is ingenious and satisfying. His script has a healthy irreverence for rules and authority, as well as warm and funny characters in hilarious situations.

Zoor, a Peter Ustinov look-alike, plays the enterprising madman with silence and true sweetness . . ."

©Los Angeles Times, 1976.

BINGO LONG TRAVELING ALL-STARS & MOTOR KINGS, THE

Director: *John Badham*. Screenplay: *Hal Barwood, Matthew Robbins*. Based on the novel by William Brashler. Producer: *Rob Cohen*. Photography: *Bill Butler*. Editor: *David Rawlins*. Music: *William Goldstein*. Production: *Motown*, in association with *Pan Arts Enterprises*. Distributor: *Universal Pictures*. Running time 111 minutes. New York opening July 16, 1976, at several theatres. Classification: PG.

Bingo: *Billy Dee Williams*. Leon: *James Earl Jones*. Charlie Snow: *Richard Pryor*. Willie Lee: *Rico Dawson*. Esquire Joe Callaway: *Stan Shaw*. Rainbow: *DeWayne Jessie*. Isaac: *Tony Burton*. Sallie Potter: *Ted Ross*. Bertha: *Mabel King*. The Prostitute: *Anna Capri*. Mr. Holland: *Joel Fluellen*. Pearline: *Sarina C. Grant*.

Film Information, July/August 1976 (p. 2)
Annette Samuels

". . . filmed mainly in Macon, Georgia, is funny and it's serious. It gets down to the nitty gritty of life as it was for Negro players during the late '30s in the Negro National League.

'Bingo' Long, veteran pitcher for the Negro National League and star player for the St. Louis Ebony Aces, is played by Billy Dee Williams, who, no matter what you do to him, is always going to be the pretty man on the screen.

Leon Carter, genial catcher for the Cincinnati Elite Giants, is played by James Earl Jones. And a better actor could not have been found for the role. He is big, hulking even. And he is, indeed, the binding, calming factor that keeps The Bingo Long Traveling All-Stars & Motor Kings together.

Richard Pryor, as Charlie Snow, the third baseman who dreams of passing himself off as a Cuban in order to get into the white major leagues, is comedian personified throughout the film.

But it's the co-stars that pull it all together. It's not likely that you will forget 'Sallie Potter,' the villain played by Ted Ross, the Cowardly Lion from *The Wiz*, the Broadway musical. Nor will you forget Mabel King who plays 'Bertha DeWitt,' the one female owner of a Negro team who is as tough as nails. She played the wicked witch in *The Wiz* . . ."

©Film Information, 1976.

Los Angeles Times, 7/16/76 (Pt. IV, p. 1)
Charles Champlin

"The same instinct, translated from music to

movies, made box-office successes of *Lady Sings the Blues* and *Mahogany* and there is now the same sweet smell of success about *The Bingo Long Traveling All-Stars & Motor Kings* . . .

The ingredients of *Bingo Long* are neither new nor secret. Like *Mahogany*, the movie remembers everything Hollywood knew how to do and did with such confident skill in the days of its glory. *Mahogany* was the popular three-handkerchief romance; *Bingo Long* is the two-boxes-of-popcorn action thriller laced with comedy.

It has sustained high energy, a lot of warmth, basic emotions (fear, greed, anger, sorrow, triumph) and a trio of engaging and sympathetic stars nicely supported all down the line.

Richard Pryor has the principal comic role, as the ballplayer hoping to make it into the majors by passing either as a Cuban or an Indian. Pryor becomes the clubhouse card rather than a visiting comedian, and the performance melds perfectly with the others.

James Earl Jones is the slugging catcher, and somehow he exudes that calming solidity you associate with the savviest of players . . .

Williams, the leading male star of the Motown films, gives a straight and intense performance . . ."

©Los Angeles Times, 1976.

Village Voice, 8/2/76 (p. 93)
Andrew Sarris

". . . the acting in *Bingo Long* attains the highest level of charm and subtlety. Billy Dee Williams is particularly skillful as Bingo Long, a part that could have easily fizzled in flamboyance. Williams, who has hitherto displayed admirable restraint in such emotional exercises as *Brian's Song* and *Lady Sings the Blues*, shows an interesting range for a leading man. He could have easily been overwhelmed by the artful bellowing of James Earl Jones as the antirhythm disciple of W.E.B. Du Bois. Instead, the two actors shared a marvelous rapport between the lines of their shared jokes of survival. If they as characters are prepared to do almost anything to make a decent living, Richard Pryor's flaky Charlie Snow is prepared to do absolutely anything, down to passing, in turn, as a Puerto Rican and an Indian. Pryor's eccentric rhythms supply a pleasant counterpoint to the stabilizing duet of Williams and Jones as the pitch-catch battery of Bingo Long and Leon Carter . . ."

Reprinted by permission of The Village Voice.
Copyright © The Village Voice, Inc., 1976.

New York Magazine, 7/26/76 (p. 54)
John Simon

". . . John Badham, a director fresh out of television, has some dizzy old cinematic devices up his tricky mitt; it may well be that television is where

traditional cinematic knowhow has been nurtured by aspiring cineastes. Badham gives us, for instance, that old-time fascination with the eccentric ingredients that make up a crowd, or the zany opticals, such as a pitched ball exploding into the image to start a new scene. It is not just baseball, it is even more cornball, but some of it works, especially as helped along by a perfervid, ebullient cast . . .

More than the writing and directing, more than Bill Butler's proficient but unspectacular cinematography, more than the comedy on the road or the comedy-drama on the diamond, what captivates us is the acting. As Bingo, Billy Dee Williams happily blends the virtues of the dedicated actor and the matinee idol. As Leon Carter, James Earl Jones demonstrates that he is at his best in down-to-earth comedy laced with a touch of seriousness; for farce, there are Richard Pryor and, some menace notwithstanding, Ted Ross. In fact, there's no loser in the entire large cast . . ."

©1976 by the NYM Corp. Reprinted with the permission of NEW YORK Magazine.

Saturday Review, 8/7/76 (p. 45)
Judith Crist

". . . a pleasant summertime bit of foolery about a black baseball team in the thirties during the Depression, when the color ban in big-league baseball was intact and the Negro National League was enjoying its heyday. Like *The Bad News Bears*, this is more than a baseball comedy, focusing on personality and friendship while revealing the fascinating past of a national pastime. Above all, it is good-humored and kindly—so much so that a couple of brief 'everyday' cruelties jolt one back to an unpleasant reality . . .

. . . one should indeed heap praise on the cast: Billy Dee Williams and James Earl Jones, as the dedicated Bingo and the good-hearted Carter; Richard Pryor, a player determined to crack the majors as a Cuban or an American Indian; Stan Shaw, the rookie who finally breaks the color barrier via the Dodgers; Ted Ross, a villainous undertaker; Mabel King, a canny widow; and many more . . ."

©Judith Crist, 1976.

Newsweek, 7/19/76 (p. 77)
Janet Maslin

". . . *Bingo Long* wants us both to admire Bingo's principles and chuckle at the sight of him pitching in a gorilla suit. It also hopes that we'll both respect its documentary underpinnings and choke back a lump in the throat when one player, who has been struck dumb at the beginning of the film, miraculously regains his power of speech at the finale. It

continued on next page

continued from previous page

intends to be discerning about black culture, while showing that an enthusiastic black baseball audience has a highly choreographed sense of natural rhythm. It would like, in short, to have its chitlins and eat them too.

Throughout, *Bingo Long* also affects an insistent cheerfulness. . .

Still, this is nothing if not a crowd-pleaser, thanks to a witty if scrambled screenplay . . . and to extremely deft performances. Williams, as usual, is very much the handsome matinee idol . . . but he moves gracefully through the inconsistencies of his role. Jones' unflagging intelligence and good humor likewise transcend the script's most precarious moments. Richard Pryor is likely to make the biggest hit with audiences, since his is the simplest and funniest character . . ."

©Newsweek, Inc. 1976
reprinted by permission.

New York Post, 7/17/76 (p. 15)
Frank Rich

". . . In recent years, no Hollywood film about black Americans has attempted, as this movie does, to combine ambitious thematic intentions with high-spirited comedy, top-notch production . . . you admire it more for what it attempts than for what it actually delivers; out of extraordinary materials, this film's creators have fashioned a singularly ordinary movie.

. . . *Bingo Long* is . . . a perfectly inoffensive little farce, in which modest pleasures and dull stretches co-exist in equal abundance and that seems, under the circumstances, a terrible waste . . .

Properly executed, this film could have been both an entertaining baseball picture and a fascinating portrait of the precarious lives led by talented blacks during the years when they were officially excluded from this country's social mainstream. But though *Bingo Long* does at least touch these bases, it never becomes a truly top-flight comedy, it never really gets inside its characters, and it doesn't even offer too much in the way of exciting baseball . . ."

Reprinted by Permission of New York Post.
©1976, New York Post Corporation.

Christian Science Monitor, 7/30/76 (p. 22)
David Sterritt

". . . In sum, *Bingo Long* moves from the sad to the preposterous, keeping up a roistering batting average in both categories despite some seventh-inning stretches of dullness and enough ball-park language to merit a PG rating.

Credit goes to director John Badham for coaching such a winning series of jokes and mini-dramas, and to all the cast—Billy Dee Williams as Bingo, the organizer; James Earl Jones as his mentor,

sidekick and catcher; Richard Pryor as the aspiring Cuban who meets a tragic snag in his career; and the whole mad crew of beautiful blacks who make *Bingo Long* one of the most meaningful comic curveballs in quite a while."

Reprinted by permission from The Christian
Science Monitor © 1976.
The Christian Science Publishing Society.
All rights reserved.

The Times (London), 11/5/76 (p. 9)
David Robinson

". . . a freewheeling comedy that wears its sophistication lightly . . .

The laughter has a sharp edge: the team finds that the only way to acceptance by the white audience is to clown it up Uncle Tom style (shades of the Harlem Globetrotters).

Sometimes the comedy seems to be having a bit of a fight to make its way through the showiness with which director John Badham compensates for his uncertainty over timing and emphasis; but in the outcome, the performances carry the film triumphantly—the well-matched charm of Billy Dee Williams and James Earl Jones; the fruity villainy of Ted Ross; and Richard Pryor as a player forever trying to pass himself off in a more acceptable racial guise, like Cuban or Redskin."

©The Times, 1976.

Films in Review, October 1976 (p. 505)
Frank Jackson

". . . Within this film the black baseball leagues and the black way of life are essentially outside the mainstream of American life, but aside from a few snide comments, the film never really condemns white society. Segregation is just a fact of life. The real villain of the film is baseball management, in the person of a black capitalist (Ted Ross) who capitalizes on the misfortunes of his black players . . .

The scene-stealer, however, is Richard Pryor, who plans to crash white baseball by masquerading as a Cuban ballplayer . . .

Though the player-management conflict is an integral element of the film, the emphasis is on nostalgia and humor. In '39 baseball was a game first and business second. The grand old game, as depicted in this film, might even be enough to make Bowie Kuhn laugh."

©Films in Review, 1976.

The Sunday Times (London), 10/31/76 (p. 35)
Alan Brien

"On celluloid, American blacks suffer a fate worse than the Indians. Until recently, in Westerns, they were edited out altogether though a quarter to a third of all cowboys in frontier days were black. And an all-black film, like *The Bingo Long Traveling All-Stars & Motor Kings* . . . is still a refreshing rarity . . .

There's some quite chilling violence, a lively touch of sex, but it is all deflected with a joke and some of the comic knock-about as if director John Badham, like his ball-players, was determined to keep it cool. The baseball sequences are easy to follow, for it is the people who hold our attention, especially James Earl Jones' radical rake, Leon, and Richard Pryor as a crafty climber determined to pass if he has to learn Spanish to pose as a Cuban. As Bingo Long, Billy Dee Williams shows himself a handsome, relaxed, funny, smart actor who'd be pinned up above Robert Redford if he were white."

©The Sunday Times, 1976.

Monthly Film Bulletin, November 1976 (p. 229)
Tom Milne

"In his frenzied assault on the cinema, Motown's Berry Gordy has hitherto (*Lady Sings the Blues*, *Mahogany*) been dogged by disastrous scripts, bad direction, and a schizophrenic attempt to sell the new black consciousness in time-honoured dream factory wrappings. With a sharpish and skeptically witty script by Barwood and Robbins (who wrote *The Sugarland Express*) from a factually based novel, apparently sidestepping racial issues but in fact quietly probing away at old sores in the unforced irony with which it observes how easily the Negro could be conned into making his way in a white world simply by shedding his dignity and becoming a clown, *Bingo Long* . . . boasts some marvelous locations in the backwoods of Georgia, a whole flurry of fine performances (notably from Richard Pryor as an All-Star obsessed by the possibility of infiltrating the white teams as a Red Indian or a Cuban), and several very funny scenes . . ."

©Monthly Film Bulletin, 1976.

BIRCH INTERVAL

Director: *Delbert Mann*. Screenplay: *Joanna Crawford*. Based on the novel by Ms. Crawford. Producer: *Robert B. Radnitz*. Photography: *Urs B. Furrer*. Music: *Leonard Rosenman*. Distributor: *Gamma Three*. Running time 105 minutes. New York opening May 2, 1976, at 68th Street Playhouse. Classification: PG.

Pa: *Eddie Albert*. Thomas: *Rip Torn*. Marie: *Ann Wedgeworth*. Jesse: *Susan McClung*. Samuel: *Brian Part*. Esther: *Jann Stanley*. Charlie: *Bill Lucking*. Hattie: *Margaret Leary*. Mrs. Tanner: *Anne Revere*.

Film Information, 4/76 (p. 2)
Robert E. A. Lee

" . . . As with all his films, Radnitz used actual locations. In *Birch Interval*, he took his film crew to the Amish country of Pennsylvania. The resultant sense of authenticity is one of the film's outstanding qualities. Directed by award winner Delbert Mann (*Marty*), adapted by Pennsylvania-born Joanna Crawford from her own novel, *Birch Interval* takes place immediately after World War II.

As is his wont, Radnitz introduces child actors of minimum experience and realizes from them some fine performances of unusual believability. Susan McClung plays the role of an 11-year-old girl who struggles with adult problems and grows through her ordeal. During her mother's temporary 'desertion,' she spends the summer in Pennsylvania with her uncle and aunt and cousins and grandfather. Eddie Albert is the strong-willed grandfather and Rip Torn is the uncle, Tom, an eccentric loner, a free spirit to whom the children genuinely relate.

A very interesting dimension of *Birch Interval* is the insight it gives into the life of the Amish people among those known as Pennsylvania Dutch . . ."

© Film Information, 1976.

New York Magazine, 5/10/76 (p. 64)
John Simon

" . . . the cinematic rhetoric, under Delbert Mann's direction, outdoes the verbal. There are lap dissolves as slow as a spring thaw; repeated superimpositions of Jesse's wide-eyed face over the goings-on; a hoary montage of a dead hand clasped in living ones such as hasn't been seen since the heyday of Lewis Milestone or Clarence Brown. Camera positions are static and predictable, but worse yet is the photography . . .

Eddie Albert valiantly brings Pa to the verge of believability; Rip Torn uncharacteristically underplays Thomas, but manages to make even his underacting hammy; and the only thing one can say for Susan McClung as Jesse is that she isn't cute. The others do what they can; what is sad though, is the waste of the admirable Anne Revere, seen all too rarely for political reasons, in the poor and poorly directed part of Mrs. Tanner . . ."

© 1976 by the NYM Corp. Reprinted with
the permission of NEW YORK Magazine.

Saturday Review, 5/15/76 (p. 51)
Judith Crist

" . . . *Birch Interval* is concerned with a turning point in childhood, one reached with an awakening appreciation of human relationships, and with an acceptance, rather than a judgment, of loved ones. The story, set in 1947, is of 11-year-old Jesse

continued on next page

continued from previous page

O'Casey, a New York City child sent to live with her mother's family in the Amish farm country of Pennsylvania . . .

. . . through Jesse's eyes, we see with all the ellipses, mystery, and matter-of-factness that form a child's view of an adult world, and with all the cruelties and righteousness and rigidities that are part of a child's world. Like her, we are saturated in the seasons, share the exotica of the Amish community and the adventures of children's games, and probe the partial conversations overheard, the inexplicable actions of adults, the seeming harshness of a loving heart, the unexpected kindness of strangers. All this is by the indirection of Delbert Mann's direction, which keeps us in empathetic thrall to the child's viewpoint; her quest and her discoveries become ours. This identification is made easier because, as in the past, Radnitz has chosen an unknown as his protagonist—Susan McClung, a gifted 11-year-old San Franciscan, whose Jesse is a lovely, solemn, sensitive child. And, as before, Radnitz has chosen first-rank professionals to portray the adults . . ."

© Judith Crist, 1976.

New York Post, 5/3/76 (p. 22)
Frank Rich

" . . .*Birch Interval* has been directed by Delbert Mann, a long-time hack who isn't fit to direct an episode of *Little House on the Prairie*. Mann's technique for showing us the adult characters' behavior from Jesse's point-of-view is to superimpose the girl's face over a montage of portentous tableaus; his idea of creating tension is to have extras stand and gape like living statues as the protagonists suffer through their emotional outbursts . . .

Though it may be a blessing in disguise, Mann also appears to have left about half of *Birch Interval* off the screen . . .

Except for Torn, who shows surprising restraint as the bonkers, mock-Sherwood Anderson uncle, the cast is as miserable as the material. Albert seems particularly embarrassed as the family patriarch, but then, I can't remember when an actor has had so many gruesome lines in a single movie . . ."

Reprinted by Permission of New York Post.
© 1976, New York Post Corporation.

Christian Science Monitor, 5/14/76 (p. 23)
David Sterritt

" . . . At its best moments *Birch Interval* breathes childlike innocence and mystery, as adults play out their disturbing games while children stand in the foreground, waiting, watching, wondering, and learning. It is a slow and sometimes sad film experience, a straightforward drama with a share of barely hidden complexities . . .

It is unfortunate director Delbert Mann has not generated more visual vitality to match both the sincerity of producer Radnitz's conception and the folksy detail of Joanna Crawford's screenplay (based on her novel). The deliberate pace of *Birch Interval* seems appropriate to its story and characters, but the listlessness of many of its images drains the film of energy. Moreover, when the film tries hardest to burst alive—in a climactic scene involving an ambulance, a toubled boy, and a father's self-respect—the filmmakers pay insufficient attention to motivation and thus strain credibility. It is a regrettable lapse in a potentially powerful scene . . ."

Reprinted by permission from The Christian
Science Monitor © 1976.
The Christian Science Publishing Society.
All rights reserved.

BITTER TEARS OF PETRA VON KANT, THE

Director, Screenplay, Producer: *Rainer Werner Fassbinder*. Running time 124 minutes. New York opening June 1976 at the Waverly Theatre. Classification: None. Origin: Germany.

Players: *Margit Carstensen, Irm Hermann, Hanna Schygull, Eva Mattes, Katrin Schaake, Gisela Fachelday*.

New York Post, 6/12/76 (p. E-12)
Archer Winsten

"*The Bitter Tears of Petra von Kant* . . . a good look at German bisexuality among women.

As directed and written by Rainer Werner Fassbinder, it shows a successful fashion designer, Petra von Kant (Margit Carstensen) as she browbeats her secretary Marlene (Irma Hermann) unmercifully and then falls in love with Karin (Hanna Schygull), a beautiful slut of little culture and less ambition . . .

As a study of the games women play with each other, *The Bitter Tears of Petra von Kant* is a chilling reminder that reason has little to do with it . . .

It is a gloomy little picture, well staged in the claustrophobic room, impressively acted, and talked out at great length . . . The penalties of success and emotional commitment have seldom been given a grimmer presentation."

Reprinted by Permission of New York Post.
© 1976, New York Post Corporation.

The Sunday Times (London), 5/11/75
Dilys Powell

" . . . At first one is inclined to think that the deliberate postures, the calculated compositions in the
enclosed set have little to do with what one used to
call cinema: why not give one's time and space
instead to the familiar excitements . . . But the
screen changes and rejects the old rules; it must be
allowed to choose its own way; helplessly one is
trapped in the stifling room where Petra von Kant
(Margit Carstensen) lives insulated against all
worlds except her own. A fashionable dress
designer, she is slavishly attended by the silent
Marlene (Irma Hermann) who in fact does the de-
signing, runs errands, suffers abuse and watches
from behind a screen of distance and darkness the
passionate love from which she is now
excluded . . .
    . . . Fassbinder's film has an extraordinary com-
mand. But after more than two hours, I am glad to
escape from the Poussin, from the dressmaker's
dummies, from all the airless hothouse fantasies;
for essentially this strange, prehensile piece is not a
human study but an exercise, a means of confronting the abstract ideas of emotional tyranny and
emotional abasement."

© The Sunday Times, 1975.

The Times (London), 5/9/75
David Robinson

The Bitter Tears of Petra von Kant is dazzling in
the brittle brilliance of its execution, the precision of
its structure and movement, the total, hermetic
self-containment of the tiny world it creates. This
result was possible, within the very slender means
available, because the director, Rainer Werner
Fassbinder, was working with his own text, written
for his own theatre, and with his own company . . .
    What is remarkable in the work is that with all the
confinement, with the extreme—theatrical— formalism of the action and structure, it is still transmuted completely into film, without any sense of
having belonged to any other idiom . . .
    It is high camp: the dialogue as formalized as
Racine . . .
    The geometrical composition of the images and
the groupings of the people always express in precise terms the current emotional composition of the
group; the tableau with which Fassbinder ends
each sequence crystallizes exactly each successive and progressive crisis. The novel pleasure of
this exercise in chamber cinema lies in the brittle
perfection and the lucidity with which the idiom is
equated with the content."

© The Times, 1975.

Monthly Film Bulletin, 5/75 (p. 99)
Richard Combs

" . . . In this etiolated atmosphere, props and

lighting assume a rich and perverse significance:
the mannequins dotted about the apartment later
wind up in Petra's bed in a parody of love-making
after Karin's desertion: the lush textures of light and
shadow emphasize both the opulence of the setting
and the emotional deviousness which relegates
Marlene to the dark corners of the room, typing or
sketching; and Petra's records (*Smoke Gets in Your
Eyes*, *In My Room*) add incongruous but suitably
plangent notes, with *The Great Pretender* rising
over the very last shot of the abandoned heroine,
suggesting her failure to make this particular imitation of life stick . . . like the paintings scattered
through *Fear Eats the Soul*, both identifying and
satirizing their milieux, a principal icon here is the
enormous mural covering one wall, with its classical
nudes in easy, bacchanalian love-play mockingly
overlooking the attenuated games of Petra's me-
nage, but also collaborating with the androgynous
(not to say drag) appearance of some of the
players to soften the strictly lesbian outlines of the
relationships and intimate some universal experiences of passion unrequited or simply too idiosyncratic to be long sustained."

© Monthly Film Bulletin, 1975.

Los Angeles Times, 10/20/76 (Pt. IV, p. 1)
Kevin Thomas

"The most truly daring movies are those that
attempt to deal directly with human emotions without relying on any plot devices whatsoever or any
sort of sensationalism.
    Such a film is young German writer-director
Rainer Werner Fassbinder's *The Bitter Tears of
Petra von Kant* . . . a demanding, harrowing drama
of agonized love laced with sardonic humor that
ranks with the best of Ingmar Bergman . . .
    To pull off a picture that's virtually all talk and
no action, its maker has to have a genuine and
compassionate insight into human nature matched
by complete honesty . . .
    Although *The Bitter Tears of Petra von Kant*
is intensely theatrical and would make a dazzling
stage piece, it is no filmed play. If anything, Fassbinder's innate sense of the cinematic shows up all
the more vividly for having been confined to a
single set. There is a sense of rightness in all his
camera setups, and his imagery is acutely, often
painfully expressive . . ."

©Los Angeles Times, 1976.

BITTERSWEET LOVE

Director: *David Miller*. Screenplay: *Adrian
Morrall, D. A. Kellogg*. Producers: *Joseph
Zappala, Gene Slott, Joel B. Michaels*. Pho-
tography: *Stephen M. Katz*. Editor: *Bill Butler*

continued on next page

continued from previous page

Music: *Ken Wannberg.* Production: *Zappala-Slott.* Distributor: *Avco Embassy Pictures.* Running time 92 minutes. Los Angeles opening October 27, 1976, at several theatres. Classification: PG.

Players: *Robert Alda; Meredith Baxter; Denise DeMirjian; John Friedrich; Amanda Gavin; Jerome Guardino; Celeste Holm; Scott Hylands; Jac Jozafson, Jr.; Robert Lansing; Richard Masur; Vince Miliana; Erik Nelson; Gail Strickland; Lana Turner.*

Performances and settings are very high class. I mean when you have all that money and those great surroundings (houses, trees, station wagons, world cruises) you can still suffer, but you do have multiple choices. Most of the time they're all polite, and that's something when it's incest you're facing . . ."

Reprinted by Permission of New York Post.
© 1977, New York Post Corporation.

Los Angeles Times, 10/28/76 (Pt. IV, p. 20)
Kevin Thomas

". . . *Bittersweet Love* has the stuff of Greek tragedy but, alas, unfolds like an old-fashioned tearjerker, directed most earnestly if rather slowly by the veteran David Miller . . .

Writers Adrian Morrall and D. A. Kellogg have treated Miss Turner's terrible discovery with unstinting sensitivity, candor and compassion. They have created real people in an awful dilemma, and in their well-drawn parts the entire cast excels under Miller's painstaking direction. Especially vivid are Ms. Birney, an accomplished actress of ingratiating naturalness, and Miss Turner, durably glamorous and commanding in the best role she's had in too long a time. It's when Miss Turner at last reveals a secret from her past that we're best able to connect with the story.

Yet to consider how much care has obviously been expended on *Bittersweet Love* is to lament its writers did not come up with a less bizarre twist for its plot to turn upon. You can't help wishing its quality cast were caught up in a more viable drama . . ."

©Los Angeles Times, 1976.

New York Post, 3/24/77 (p. 23)
Archer Winsten

"*Bittersweet Love* . . . barges boldly but secretively into accidental incest. Brother and sister, if you want to know . . .

In the end, there's the baby, a perfectly healthy, normal specimen, and there are the two parents, victims of convention, unable to live together happily or be apart happily either.

The authors . . . and the director . . . and the three producers . . . haven't been able to come up with a better answer. You have to credit them with asking a hard question and avoiding any easy answer.

BLACK BIRD, THE

Director, Screenplay: *David Giler.* Based on a story by *Don Mankiewicz, Gordon Cotler.* Executive Producer: *George Segal.* Photography: *Phillip Lathrop.* Editor: Walter *Thompson.* Music: *Jerry Fielding.* Distributor: *Columbia Pictures.* Running time 98 minutes. New York opening December 1975 at several theatres. Classification: PG.

Sam Spade, Jr.: *George Segal.* Anna Kemidon: *Stephane Audran.* Andrew Jackson Immelman: *Lionel Stander.* Effie: *Lee Patrick.* Wilmer: *Elisha Cook Jr.* Litvak: *Felix Silla.*

See Volume 1 for additional reviews

The Sunday Times (London), 4/18/76 (p. 37)
Dilys Powell

"*The Black Bird* . . . is a jokey sequel to the unforgettable Dashiell Hammett-John Huston *The Maltese Falcon*, a sequel thirty-five years inferior. There is still a Sam Spade (the name encourages racial jokes which were not yet fashionable in 1941); but this is the Son of Spade, a reluctant private eye who can't keep his sense about him even for a partner in bed. The successor to Mary Astor is Stéphane Audran. And the old names—Archer, Gutman—recur, though not always in the same places.

. . . one or two of the original players have been brought back. The Wilmer is still Elisha Cook, though he is no longer the sliver of insolence one remembers. Lee Patrick still sits in the Spade office . . ."

© The Sunday Times, 1976.

BLACK MOON

Director: *Louis Malle.* Screenplay: *Mr. Malle, Ghislain Uhry and Joyce Bunuel.* Executive Producer: *Claude Nedier.* Photography: *Sven Nykvist.* Editor: *Suzanne Baron.* Music: *Diego Masson.* Production: *NEF/Bioscop.* Running time 92 minutes. New York opening September 30, 1975, at the New York Film Festival, Lincoln Center. Classification: None. Origin: France.

Lily: *Cathryn Harrison.* Old Woman: *Therese Giehse.* Sister: *Alexandra Stewart.* Brother: *Joe Dallesandro.*

See Volume 1 for additional reviews

Los Angeles Times, 3/2/77 (Pt. IV, p. 1)
Kevin Thomas

"... *Black Moon* is so intensely personal and so very beautiful in its rich, autumn-hued imagery—photographed by Ingmar Bergman regular Sven Nykvist—and dynamic structuring that it avoids pretentiousness. For all its bold surrealism it retains a quaint, earthy charm and much humor. 'What's going on here anyway?' asks Miss Harrison in understandable exasperation with Miss Giehse, who starts to explain—only to break up as Miss Harrison's panties suddenly descend to her ankles.

A Franco-German coproduction, *Black Moon* is being presented in an English version . . . Miss Harrison, the granddaughter of Rex Harrison, is highly appealing as a spunky girl who refuses to lose her sanity in the face of seeming madness, and Miss Giehse, who was the proud Jewish grandmother in Malle's *Lacombe, Lucien*, clearly relished the outrageous role that was to be her last . . ."

© Los Angeles Times, 1977.

BLACK SHAMPOO

Director: *Greydon Clark.* Screenplay: *Alvin L. Fast, Mr. Clark.* Producer: *Mr. Fast.* Editor: *Earl Watson, Jr.* Music: *Gerald Lee.* Distributor: *Dimension Pictures.* Running time 82 minutes. Los Angeles opening June, 1976, at several theatres. Classification: R.

Players: *John Daniels, Tanya Boyd, Joe Ortiz, Skip Lowe, Gary Allen, Anne Gaybis.*

Los Angeles Times, 6/25/76 (Pt. IV, p. 19)
Linda Gross

"*Black Shampoo* . . . is a sleazy, stupid and sluggish blaxploitation movie that won't wash.

The hero is a successful super-stud, a safari-suit-wearing, Mercedes-driving hairdresser (John Daniels) who wields a mean blow-dryer and services his rich, blonde, obnoxious clients at his Sunset Strip salon or at their palatial homes.

But whatever delusions the film has of ripping off *Shampoo* are polished off with the premise and the first five minutes of film. From then on, it's substandard macho racism that is particularly offensive in its sadistic, snide treatment of gay men . . .

Daniels, a virile and promising actor who was so fine and fiery in *Candy Tangerine Man*, has nothing to work with here.

Greydon Clark directs at a soporific pace, allowing stilted love scenes, aimless driving and boring stock shots."

© Los Angeles Times, 1976.

BLACK SUNDAY

Director: *John Frankenheimer.* Screenplay: *Ernest Lehman, Kenneth Ross, Ivan Moffat.* Based on the novel by Thomas Harris. Producer: *Robert Evans.* Photography: *John A. Alonzo.* Editor: *Tom Rolf.* Music: *John Williams.* Distributor: *Paramount Pictures.* Running time 143 minutes. New York opening March 31, 1977, at the Loews State 1 and Loews Tower East Theatres. Classification: R.

Kabakov: *Robert Shaw.* Lander: *Bruce Dern.* Dahlia: *Marthe Keller.* Corley: *Fritz Weaver.* Moshevsky: *Steven Keats.* Fasil: *Bekim Fehmiu.* Muzi: *Michael V. Gazzo.* Pugh: *William Daniels.* Colonel Riaf: *Walter Gotell.*

Women's Wear Daily, 3/28/77 (p. 10)
Howard Kissel

"... There are enough threads of plot running through *Black Sunday* so that, in the last half-hour, when they all come together, the excitement and tension are tremendous. Moreover, director John Frankenheimer achieves a marvelous counterpoint by juxtaposing images of the Super Bowl fanatics,

continued on next page

continued from previous page

whose goony behavior almost justifies Dern's pathological hatred, with the frantic movements of Robert Shaw and Fritz Weaver trying to thwart the equally frantic movements of Dern and Keller, all overshadowed by the ominous vision of the Goodyear blimp, the instrument of destruction, hovering over the game . . .

In addition to the sound way *Black Sunday* has been put together, Frankenheimer gets an exceptional performance from Bruce Dern . . .

The film is well photographed and expertly edited. John Williams' background score is perfect."

© Women's Wear Daily, 1977.

New York Post, 4/1/77 (p. 35)
Frank Rich

". . . *Black Sunday* . . . is not a thriller for the ages, but it's effective, slick entertainment . . .

The movie's premise is basically a retread of *The Manchurian Candidate* . . .

Unfortunately, *Black Sunday* isn't nearly as exciting as its classic predecessor—and not just because Frankenheimer is no longer the creative firebrand he was 15 years ago. The main problem is that the new film's script . . . lacks the density of narrative design, not to mention the wit, of the screenplay that George Axelrod wrote for the earlier film . . .

. . . There's only one real motivation for this movie—and that's the desire to make money: Why else would anyone make an ostensibly anti-terrorist film that in actuality could end up promoting terrorism? But if you see *Black Sunday* with the right expectations, you won't be disappointed: This movie may be empty and even irresponsible fun—but fun it most certainly is."

Reprinted by Permission of New York Post.
© 1977, New York Post Corporation.

Newsweek, 4/4/77 (p. 73)
Jack Kroll

"Terrorism is the shock issue of the moment, and *Black Sunday* gets that shock on screen with decisive impact and all the baroque elegance of a well-made thriller . . .

. . . In *Black Sunday*, the antagonists are Palestinian terrorists and Israelis, but the intended victims are 80,000 Americans who have come to the Orange Bowl in Miami for the annual Dionysiac frenzy of the Super Bowl.

So the complicated political issues of the Israeli-Palestine conflict are transmuted into a gigantic anti-terrorist thriller that makes no attempt to go into the issues themselves. It would be foolish, however, to expect *Black Sunday* would have the kind of political commitment that Pontecorvo gave *The Battle of Algiers* or that Costa-Gavras gave to *Z*. *Black Sunday* is American through and through in the hard, burnished brilliance of its abstract form and energy . . .

This sort of thing depends on technique and panache, and *Black Sunday* has enough to override some wild improbabilities of its narrative line . . ."

© Newsweek, Inc. 1977
reprinted by permission.

New York Magazine, 4/4/77 (p. 92)
John Simon

"*Black Sunday* is one of those films which it is perfectly enjoyable to watch but about which there is not all that much to say. One could call it (and many, undoubtedly, will) a somewhat-less-dazzling *Manchurian Candidate*, or one could fall back on that old reviewers' phrase, 'good of kind,' and leave it at that, except that columns don't get filled that way . . .

There is one structural error—the cutting out of a bit of throat-cutting by Fasil, needed to establish his fierceness and importance; but this was done to earn a PG rating, which, in the event, the MPAA foolishly withheld after all—so much for trying to play ball with that organization. Otherwise, John Frankenheimer's direction is consistently workmanlike, maintaining a sound pace, sufficient variety, and a decent measure of suspense . . .

. . . All in all, a sound commercial film, the basic stuff of cinema, and an oasis in the current American movie output. And for those who like puzzles: Can you find the line of dialogue that is verbatim a line from a poem by T. S. Eliot?"

© 1977 by the NYM Corp. Reprinted with the permission of NEW YORK Magazine.

BLUE BIRD, THE

Director: *George Cukor*. Screenplay: *Hugh Whitemore, Alfred Hayes*. Based on the play by Maurice Maeterlinck. Producer: *Paul Maslansky*. Photography: *Freddie Young, Ionas Gritzus*. Editors: *Tatyana Shapiro, Stanford C. Allen*. Music: *Irwin Kostal, Andrei Petrov*. Lyrics: *Tony Harrison*. Choreography: *Igor Belsky, Leonid Jakobson*. Costumes: *Edith Head*. Production: *Edward Lewis Production in association with Lenfilm Studios, and in cooperation with Tower International*. Distributor: *Twentieth Century-Fox*. Running time 99 minutes. New York opening May 13, 1976, at Radio City Music Hall. Classification: G. Origin: U.S.S.R./U.S.A.

Players: *Elizabeth Taylor, Jane Fonda, Ava Gardner, Cicely Tyson, Robert Morley, Harry Andrews, Todd Lookinland, Patsy Kensit, Will Geer, Mona Washbourne, George Cole, Pheona McLellan, Nadejda Pavlova, George Vitzin, Margareta Terechova, Oleg Popov, Leonid Nevedomsky, Valentina Ganilaee Ganibalova, Yevgeny Scherbakov.*

It must have sounded great around the conference table. It must have looked great on the drawing board. But, like many another movie assembled from piecemeal suggestions instead of unifying ideas, the result is less than the sum of its parts . . .

Cukor's direction has nothing to do with his celebrated Tracy-Hepburn era, or with the funny-sad comedy-drama that he helped to perfect in Hollywood's better days. Some of his fantasy scenes look like rip-offs from a junior-high pageant. But the veteran filmmaker deserves credit for making even a matinee crazy quilt from the uneven conception and silly songs he had to work with."

Reprinted by permission from The Christian Science Monitor © 1976. The Christian Science Publishing Society. All right reserved.

Newsweek, 5/17/76 (p. 111)
Katrine Ames

" . . . Filmed in Leningrad as the first major Soviet-American joint movie venture, the project was plagued from the beginning by financial, artistic and emotional troubles. But the real problem may be that the material itself is simply not Cukor's bowl of borscht . . .

Cukor is hampered further by Hugh Whitemore's and Alfred Hayes' sugary script, insipid music by Irwin Kostal and Andrei Petrov, dopey lyrics by Tony Harrison, and uninspired choreography by Igor Belsky and Leonid Jakobson. And, except for Taylor, his powerful ladies make little more than cameo appearances. Fonda is a brilliant Night —cold, black, but not entirely evil. In the equally brief role of Luxury, Gardner perfectly embodies vulgar opulence. Tyson has a bigger part but is disappointingly one-dimensional as the children's catty Cat. Taylor, who also plays Mother, Maternal Love and Light, is best as a humpbacked, beak-nosed witch, a role in which it is impossible for her to rely on her face and cleavage . . . "

© Newsweek, Inc. 1976 reprinted by permission.

Christian Science Monitor, 6/4/76 (p. 19)
David Sterritt

"The Blue Bird works so hard at making history that it forgets to make sense.

With the great American director George Cukor at the helm, *The Blue Bird* marks the first Soviet-American movie co-production ever. In a sincere attempt to do the project up right, both countries have contributed impressive amounts and physical resources.

What could be more American than Elizabeth Taylor playing four roles? What could be more Russian than dancers from the Kirov Ballet Company? What could be more international than a fantasy fable by Maurice Maeterlinck about a quest for the bluebird of happiness, focusing on children but intended as an allegory for thinking adults?

New York Magazine, 5/24/76 (p. 75)
John Simon

" . . . the filming, we learn, has provided some of the most unsmooth sailing since that famous time the battleship Potemkin put to sea. But that is no artistic excuse, any more than the casting of Elizabeth Taylor in four parts is artistically excusable. It should have been obvious even to a producer that whoever plays the Mother and Maternal Love cannot, even if she has versatility, play also the Witch and Light, for it totally destroys the symbolism. And pictures of previous productions or common sense (at least one of which should be available even to producers) could have demonstrated that Light must be played by (a) a golden blonde, and (b) an actress, since this is the pivotal role. Miss Taylor is about as much one as the other . . .

Scene after lovely scene, line after telling line, are omitted, toned down, misdirected or misacted . . . None of the supporting players does well; shatteringly, even such excellent actresses as Jane Fonda and Cicely Tyson emerge inane . . ."

© 1976 by the NYM Corp. Reprinted with the permission of NEW YORK Magazine.

Los Angeles Times, 5/19/76 (Pt. IV, p. 1)
Kevin Thomas

" . . . *The Blue Bird* has an apt ethereal look . . . Tony Harrison's lyrics and Irwin Kostal's music are pleasant and functional, Edith Head's costumes for the principals dazzling and Freddie Young's principal photography radiant. (Miss Taylor and Miss Gardner look particularly ravishing.) Hugh Whitemore and Alfred Hayes are responsible for the deft adaptation of the Maeterlinck classic.

Cukor's celebrated directing of actors and actresses still holds true. Miss Taylor does full justice to all her roles, and Miss Gardner . . . hasn't looked

continued on next page

continued from previous page

so glamorous or performed with such zest in years. But as good and helpful as all the veterans are it's Lookinland and little Miss Kensit, as able and irresistible a pair of kids imaginable, who really must carry the picture, and they do so with aplomb . . ."

© Los Angeles Times, 1976.

Film Information, 6/76 (p. 3)
Dave Pomeroy

" . . . this latest version of *The Blue Bird*, ballyhooed as an innovative example of U.S./U.S.S.R. co-operation, is such a mish-mash of styles, poor dubbing, bad continuity, and a listless approach on the part of the adult actors, that the fragile suspension of disbelief necessary to sustain allegorical fantasy flies away long before the blue bird . . .

To be fair, there are some nice moments in the film: a too short ballet by Nadejda Pavlova as the Blue Bird; using Shakespearean figures for the ghosts; Paul Klee-style art images used for dissolves. But these moments hardly make up for the sensibility lost in the conception and actualization of this extravaganza. Veteran director George Cukor leaves this project with a somewhat tarnished reputation."

© Film Information, 1976.

New York Post, 5/14/76 (p. 21)
Archer Winsten

" . . . Elizabeth Taylor appears in four of the larger roles. First she's a peasant mother of the two children, then a hideous witch briefly, then the gorgeous Light, and also Maternal Love. To tell the truth, she seems slightly uncomfortable in all of them.

A few of the other big names fare better. Jane Fonda plays her menacing Night straight and is effective. Tyson is rather convincing as a cat. Robert Morley still sounds like himself and utterly at home as Father Time. Will Geer could be anybody's grandfather, and George Cole is a good dog . . .

In short, the picture turns out to be another classic example of what international cooperation can do in the making of motion pictures. Using least common denominator compromises, throwing in big names for ballast, they always produce a dreadful amalgam of the worst of both worlds . . ."

Reprinted by Permission of New York Post. © 1976, New York Post Corporation.

Women's Wear Daily, 5/14/76 (p. 48)
Howard Kissel

" . . . The compositions throughout the film are lifeless—the actors frequently seem bunched together in the sort of groupings theater directors have to use on a shallow stage. The effect is unnatural, static and clumsy, like a filmed play.

As a result, all the high-priced talent from both East and West—stars like Elizabeth Taylor, Jane Fonda, Cicely Tyson, Ava Gardner and the Soviet clown Popov—is wasted. There is no way they can breathe life into the stilted, leaden dialog; and the dreary visual style does nothing to enhance their natural screen presence . . .

Even the design of the film is surprisingly spiritless—the sets seem to have been created by designers who were not allowed to read fairy tales as children and hence thought of the project as a historical picture . . ."

© Women's Wear Daily, 1976.

Films in Review, June/July 1976 (p. 377)
DeWitt Bodeen

" . . . A long time in production, the picture is the first American-Soviet co-production of a world classic limning Cukor's good faith as well as intelligence in his belief that there are no barriers in creative art. He has set this fairy tale in a Russia that, as photographed by Freddie Young, becomes a natural wonderland . . .

Miraculously, after 45 years of prizewinning film credits, George Cukor's work continues to amaze in its ingenuity and spontaneity . . .

Elizabeth Taylor (Mother, Maternal Love, Witch, and Light) radiates beauty and warmth, particularly in her scenes with the children. Ava Gardner is gorgeously seductive. As Luxury, caparisoned in crimson velvet, she is a sorceress for the ages. Jane Fonda bewitches as Night. Cicely Tyson (Cat), George Cole (Dog), Robert Morley (Father Time), Will Geer (Grandfather), and Mona Washbourne (Grandmother) illumine the splendid cast.

The Blue Bird will perch in your memory as a happy treasure."

©Films in Review, 1976.

BOBBI JO AND THE OUTLAW

Director, Producer: *Mark L. Lester.*
Screenplay: *Vernon Zimmerman.*
Photography: *Stanley Wright.* Editor: *Michael Luciano.* Music: *Barry DeVorzon.* Production:

Caldwell Properties. Distributor: *American International*. Running time 89 minutes. Los Angeles opening April 27, 1976, at several theatres. Classification: R.

Players: *Marjoe Gortner, Lynda Carter, Jesse Vint, Merrie Lynn Ross, Belinda Balaski, Gene Drew, Peggie Stewart, Gerrit Graham, John Durren, Virgil Frye*.

Los Angeles Times, 4/28/76 (Pt. IV, p. 13)
Kevin Thomas

" . . . *Bobbi Jo and the Outlaw* is one of those rare films that actually manages to comment upon rather than merely exploit the violence that is a staple of films of this type. Lester and Zimmerman explore the power myth and the intoxicating effect of violence . . .

If Zimmerman is strong on characterization, Lester is a terrific stylist, unpretentiously capturing a thick slice of sleazy Americana and eliciting the most natural and spontaneous of performances from his cast. Lester's illusion-puncturing films always have to them a tremendous vitality and an unfailing sense of richly nuanced rightness.

Not quite handsome but lean and virile, Gortner has a charisma and authority developed over a lifetime as an evangelist and has developed into a most effective screen actor . . .

Lynda Carter is that rarity, a former beauty queen—Miss America of 1972—who can actually act. Vint and Miss Ross are also persuasive, as is Belinda Balaski . . ."

© Los Angeles Times, 1976.

BOESMAN AND LENA

Director: *Ross Davenish*. Screenplay: *Athol Fugard*. From the play by Mr. Fugard. Producer: *Johan Wight*. Photography: *David Muir*. Distributor: *New Yorker Films*. Running time 102 minutes. New York opening April 22, 1976, at Film Forum. Classification: None.

Lena: *Yvonne Bryceland*. Boesman: *Athol Fugard*. Outa: *Sandy Tube*. Bait-shop owner: *Val David*.

New York Post, 4/23/76 (p. 22)
Frank Rich

" . . . The film version of *Boesman* was made in South Africa by a nonentity of a director named Ross Davenish. Fugard wrote his own screenplay for the film and also plays one of the two starring roles, but he would have been smarter to forget the whole idea. This play never could have worked as a movie, no matter who directed it . . .

Boesman and Lena is a novel, but hopelessly stage-bound, work in which the travails of a feuding, impoverished 'coloured' couple are refracted through an absurdist, Beckett-like nihilism. The story opens with Boesman (Fugard) and Lena (Yvonne Bryceland) being evicted from their shanty home by South Africa's ruling whites, and what follows is a narrative of their endless trek through a country in which their social status is literally that of dirt . . .

When removed from a stage and placed on a South African landscape, however, *Boesman and Lena* becomes an overwrought and trying affair . . ."

Reprinted by Permission of New York Post.
© 1976, New York Post Corporation.

2015727

BOUND FOR GLORY

Director: *Hal Ashby*. Screenplay: *Robert Getchell*. Based on the autobiography of Woody Guthrie. Producers: *Robert F. Blumofe, Harold Leventhal*. Photography: *Haskell Wexler*. Editors: *Robert Jones, Pembroke J. Herring*. Music adapted and conducted by Leonard Rosenman. Distributor: *United Artists*. Running time 148 minutes. New York opening December 5, 1976, at the Coronet Theatre. Classification: PG.

Woody Guthrie: *David Carradine*. Ozark Bule: *Ronny Cox*. Mary Guthrie: *Melinda Dillon*. Pauline: *Gail Strickland*. Locke: *John Lehne*. Slim Snedeger: *Ji-Tu Cumbuka*. Luther Johnson: *Randy Quaid*. Liz: *Elizabeth Macey*. Memphis Sue: *Melinda Dillon*.

New York Times, 12/6/76 (p. 47)
Vincent Canby

". . . The film . . . has a number of very good things going for it, in particular David Carradine's dry, haunted performance as the young Woody Guthrie who passes through the film more or less as if he were a camera, storing away impressions and emotions that only occasionally are allowed

continued on next page

continued from previous page

to erupt with dramatic force. Mr. Carradine may be taller and huskier than the real Woody, but he has the right look and manner—the reserve, skeptical squint, the texture of the countryman's skin.

Mr. Ashby and Haskell Wexler, his cameraman, have also been immensely successful in recreating the look of place and period from the drought-ridden Texas Panhandle of the 1930s, when rural America appeared to be returning to dust even before it had actually died, to the California fruit ranches and the 'Hoovervilles' where Woody sang and attempted to organize the migrant workers.

What the film doesn't have much of is a screenplay. At least, it doesn't have a screenplay that matches with dramatic conviction the intensity and drive of its largely mysterious central character . . .''

©1976 by the New York Times Company.
Reprinted by permission.

Newsweek, 12/13/76 (p. 104)
Janet Maslin

''. . . The movie spends two and a half hours and $7 million gazing wistfully at a little man and a big country, and it winds up prettily embalming them both . . .

What assets the film has are tangential to its main subject: director Hal Ashby and cinematographer Haskell Wexler elicit a bravura performance from the California landscape, and the supporting players—Melinda Dillon, Ronny Cox, Gail Strickland and especially Randy Quaid—are uniformly excellent. David Carradine brings a slow, subtle intelligence to the leading role, but he has none of the vitality the movie so sorely needs. And he is too tall, too old, too somber and too inept a singer to create any sense of what the slight, scrappy, boisterous Woody Guthrie of the '30s must have been like—or why his legend will easily survive this expensive but ineffectual 'tribute.' ''

©Newsweek, Inc. 1976
reprinted by permission.

Saturday Review, 12/11/76 (p. 78)
Judith Crist

"Producers Robert F. Blumofe and Harold Leventhal, director Hal Ashby, and screenwriter Robert Getchell have taken a huge gamble and won gloriously with *Bound for Glory*, an exquisite film about the early career of Woody Guthrie . . .

The gamble is in the leisurely pace and probing minutiae of persons and places in this two-hour-and-twenty-eight-minute film—and it is a risk that pays off in providing not only an overwhelming encounter with a human being of extraordinary quality but also a touching re-creation of a time in our history that has touched us all. Most important, we are given the gifts of talented people, who,

for once, have time and space in which to fulfill, rather than indulge, themselves. And the talents are remarkable . . .''

©Judith Crist, 1976.

Film Information, December 1976 (p. 1)
Frederic A. Brussat

''. . . *Bound for Glory*, adapted from Guthrie's autobiography, has been scripted for the screen by Robert Getchell (*Alice Doesn't Live Here Anymore*). The film pays homage to this folksinger's social conscience but does not cover up his flaws: he was an irresponsible husband and a poor father. Director Hal Ashby (*Shampoo, The Last Detail, Harold and Maude*) translates this story of Guthrie's early years with a sharp eye for detail and a vibrant aestheticism that bypasses the Scylla of sudsy biography and the Charybdis of tedious political platforming.

The film scores high marks in every department . . . David Carradine convincingly conveys Guthrie's bohemian spirit and his love for the underdog.

This is a remarkably touching and humane film with special rewards for families and youth groups in the church . . .''

©Film Information, 1976.

New York Post, 12/6/76 (p. 51)
Frank Rich

''. . . it's a decent, serious film, with aspirations to greatness.

Bound for Glory really means to be faithful to the man who fathered modern American social protest music—and even though it doesn't keep that faith, you have to admire the honor with which it goes down to defeat . . .

. . . David Carradine, who stars as Guthrie, proves to be a simply magical actor, and, happily, he's almost always on screen. When you're not watching him—and it's hard not to watch him—you can also focus on Haskell Wexler's color cinematography, which is the best to be seen in an American film this year.

Wexler brilliantly has captured the texture of Depression America . . .

. . . Getchell's writing is anecdotal to the point of structurelessness, glib, and extremely sketchy in its treatment of the many supporting characters whom Guthrie meets during his journey . . .''

Reprinted by Permission of New York Post.
©1976, New York Post Corporation.

New York Magazine, 12/6/76 (p. 123)
John Simon

''. . . I wish this were the place for a close study of Wexler's camera work in the film—it is the one

David Carradine (right) is Woody Guthrie in **Bound for Glory**, based on Guthrie's autobiography of the Depression years.

thing that sustains our continued attention to this serious and well-intentioned but rambling and superficial movie for which neither Robert Getchell's script nor Hal Ashby's direction—nor even Woody Guthrie's songs that David Carradine renders decently along with some of his own—can do much that is sufficiently antisoporific. In fact, this long and uninflected movie could easily be dismissed as a much lesser *Grapes of Wrath* with music if it weren't for the bitter lyricism of Wexler's camera. True, the many, often very brief, performances are mostly very good . . ."

© 1976 by the NYM Corp. Reprinted with
the permission of NEW YORK Magazine.

Christian Science Monitor, 12/30/76 (p. 18)
David Sterritt

"Woody Guthrie composed his autobiography, *Bound for Glory*, with the usual materials—pencil, paper, and a wealth of experiences well worth writing about. Now *Bound for Glory* has come to the screen, decked out in multi-million-dollar splendor. That the movie retains much of the book's wit, bite, and feel for the years of the great depression is a tribute to filmmaker Hal Ashby and the rising young star named David Carradine who plays the central character . . .

Bound for Glory is scarcely the scratchy, folksy little film Guthrie might have made, given a camera and a film crew, as he rode the rods and struck up his songs. But it cares so much about its places and faces that a Guthrie sort of warmth and authenticity springs to life despite the Hollywood dollars that have so laboriously and visibly been poured into every scene . . .

Paradoxically, the film's most striking asset is also its most dangerous liability. Haskell Wexler's cinematography has never been famous for restraint, and in *Bound for Glory* its fabulous images overshadow every other consideration . . .

. . . Director Hal Ashby deserves much credit for striking a delicate balance between Wexler's virtuosic pictures and Carradine's dusty portrayal. The resulting blend is one of this year's more pleasurable and meaningful movies."

Reprinted by permission from The Christian
Science Monitor © 1976.
The Christian Science Publishing Society.
All rights reserved.

New Leader, 11/22/76 (p. 28)
Robert Asahina

". . . The anguish of dustbowl life has probably

continued on next page

continued from previous page

never been so vividly pictured in the movies—a tribute to the skill of cinematographer Haskell Wexler. As Pampa is about to be struck by a dust storm, one terrifyingly brief shot of the black cloud just before it sweeps through the town eloquently captures the insignificance of civilization against the menace of nature. The soft, fine dust that permeates the air gives the early scenes a beautiful and oppressive golden haze. Indeed, Wexler's craft is emphasized by the decision to use color, rather than exploit the black-and-white images we carry in our minds from the Depression-era photographs of Walker Evans or Dorothea Lange.

The movie hits its stride as it follows Guthrie to the Coast. From hitchhiking to hopping freight cars, from brawls to one night stands, it evokes one of the most potent myths of American culture—the freedom of the traveling vagabond . . ."

Reprinted with permission from
The New Leader, 1976.
© The American Labor Conference
on International Affairs, Inc.

Films in Review, February 1977 (p. 118)
Marsha McCreadie

"*Bound for Glory*, director Hal Ashby's paean to Woody Guthrie, is an interesting odd duck of a film. The beautiful lush cinematography by Haskell Wexler invites us to contemplate leisurely the atmosphere and tableaux of the Depression Southwest, while the script and music hope to hard-drive some sociological points. We don't know whether to be lulled or stirred.

David Carradine as Guthrie (the film is based on his autobiography) nearly catalyzes these opposing pulls . . . We're just as charmed and exasperated by him as his women are . . .

Even when Guthrie becomes a successful musician and folk hero, Ashby, who directed *Shampoo*, seems uncertain about where to take the material. There's a trumped-up conscience struggle, but if Woody is all that idealistic would he be tempted to deradicalize the songs he sings on his radio program? Carradine does a good job with the music, though, and *Bound for Glory* evokes, if not probes, the man and his era."

Films in Review, 1977.

BOY AND HIS DOG, A

Director, Screenplay: *L. Q. Jones*. Based on a novella by Harlan Ellison. Producer: *Alvy Moore*. Photography: *John Arthur Morrill*. Music: *Tim McIntire, Jaime Mendoza-Nava*. Distributor: *Marvin Films*. Running time 90 minutes. New York opening June 16, 1976, at several theatres. Classification: R.

Vic: *Don Johnson*. Quilla June: *Susanne Benton*. Lew: *Jason Robards*. Fellini: *Ron Feinberg*. Voice of Blood: *Tim McIntire*.

New York Magazine, 6/21/76 (p. 74)
John Simon

"*A Boy and His Dog* is a piece of science fiction of the dog-eat-dog, world-after-the-holocaust variety; it manages to be derivative, preposterous, and mildly revolting until the very end, at which point it becomes original, preposterous, and rather more revolting. I am sorry to have to say this for three reasons: (1) because the movie is based on a story by Harlan Ellison, who once paid me a very handsome compliment in writing; (2) because featured in it is my friend Ron Feinberg, who manages to be as sordid as the rest of the picture; and (3) because the star is Tiger, a marvelous Briard or near-Briard, which is just about the nicest kind of dog there is. Yet even the voice Tim McIntire bestows on the dog—who not only speaks, but indeed is the raisonneur of the story—seems wrong to me . . ."

© 1976 by the NYM Corp. Reprinted with
the permission of NEW YORK Magazine.

Take One, 12/2/75 (p. 36)
Peter Nellhaus

"One of the best science fiction films of recent years has quietly appeared. Adapted from Harlan Ellison's award-winning novella, *A Boy and His Dog* comes virtually from left field . . .

It is the modesty of L. Q. Jones that makes this film succeed. Indeed, the lack of pretension is welcome . . .

Although the novella and film take place in the future, this is clearly an allegory of contemporary society. Much better it is to be free, if hungry, in an anarchic society, than to submit to slavery in the name of security. Vic may be sexist and crude, but he is no hypocrite.

Where the film improves on Ellison is in the character of Blood. Not only is his part expanded, but he has the best lines . . .

A Boy and His Dog deserves to be more than a cult item. And if you hate most movie animals, you will probably love Blood. Sentimental he's not.

Take that, Benji!"

© Take One, 1975.

Christian Science Monitor, 6/28/76 (p. 23)
David Sterritt

"*A Boy and His Dog* is a nasty science-fiction adventure by L. Q. Jones.

Based on an 'award-winning novella' by Harlan Ellison, the story takes place in the not-so-distant future. The earth has been ravaged by nuclear war.

Our heroes roam what used to be Arizona, warring over food and women. The boy and the dog converse telepathically—pooches have learned language, it seems, though they have lost their ability to hunt.

It is a bleak vision, riddled with violence, sex, and sexism (all explicitly depicted and discussed). It becomes no brighter when the boy invades 'down under,' where solid citizens carry on a parody of civilization in a subterranean community. Jason Robards has a small role here. All told, this is the biggest movie disaster in ages . . . "

Reprinted by permission from The Christian Science Monitor © 1976. The Christian Science Publishing Society. All rights reserved.

New York Post, 6/17/76 (p. 27)
Archer Winsten

"*A Boy and His Dog* . . . takes a harsh look at the world of the 21st century, some time after that fourth World War of five days that took place in 2007.

The surface is a desert over which Vic (Don Johnson) prowls with his talking dog, Blood, looking for old buried cans of food and an occasional female. Blood is useful in tracking down females because he can smell them at a distance.

When they find Quilla June (Susanne Benton), as it happens in a state of undress, Vic is happy. He prepares to rape her, but it turns out that that is wholly unnecessary.

After mutual pleasures they survive a fire-fight with a marauding band of ruffians . . . "

Reprinted by Permission of New York Post. © 1976, New York Post Corporation.

Village Voice, 7/12/76 (p. 115)
Andrew Sarris

". . . this is the most faithful screen adaptation of a sci-fi text that I have encountered yet in the genre. *A Boy and His Dog* is also one of the most misogynistic movies I have ever seen. Set in the 21st century after the fourth World War of five days in 2007, this movie asks us to believe in a talking dog, and the arms-length coexistence of two societies—one desert, intensive-individualistic, nomadic-hunting-for-buried-canned-goods, porn-consuming, young-hustling-inner-cityish, mostly-male-but-not-noticeably-homosexual, and the other a subterranean suburbia of mechanized, sanitized, and now sterilized Middle Americans locked into a culture conditioned by John Philip Sousa and Norman Rockwell. The plot, then, is concerned not so much with a boy and his dog as with a stud and his dog . . . Jason Robards and Alvy Moore (also the producer) deserve special mention for the malignant sangfroid of their incarnations of small town Americana death-dealing tyrants. L.Q. Jones has come up with some interesting visual gimmicks . . . "

Reprinted by permission of The Village Voice. Copyright © The Village Voice, Inc., 1976.

BREAKHEART PASS

Director: *Tom Gries*. Screenplay: *Alistair MacLean*. Executive Producer: *Elliott Kastner*. Producer: *Jerry Gershwin*. Photography: *Lucien Ballard*. Editor: *Buzz Brandt*. Music: *Jerry Goldsmith*. Distributor: *United Artists*. Running time 95 minutes. Los Angeles opening March 1976 at several theatres. Classification: PG.

Players: *Charles Bronson, Ben Johnson, Richard Crenna, Jill Ireland, Charles Durning, Ed Lauter, David Huddleston, Roy Jenson, Casey Tibbs, Archie Moore.*

See Volume 1 for additional reviews

New York Post, 5/6/76 (p. 23)
Archer Winsten

"*Breakheart Pass* . . . is a vehicle for that most popular cinema commodity, Charles Bronson of the hard face.

You will, of course, be shocked to have him introduced as a fugitive murderer. Not Bronson, our hero!

The situation is extremely complicated, though ostensibly this is a Western . . .

To put it mildly, the train is crawling with villains, many of them in cloaks of the utmost respectability . . .

Needless to say, Charles Bronson is not what he seems. He is something quite different, and it is up to him to correct the villainies of all these rascals as well as save the life of Marcia . . .

This takes a lot of tussling, on top of the train and in the snow, but Bronson, aided by Alistair MacLean on script, and Tom Gries directing, and Yakima Canutt for the spectacular sequences, is able to do it all without even wearing mittens in the snow. The man is made of iron, or something . . . "

Reprinted by Permission of New York Post. © 1976, New York Post Corporation.

Christian Science Monitor, 5/26/76 (p. 26)
David Sterritt

"Alistair MacLean is phenomenally successful at grinding out novels which become hit action films . . .

This doesn't stop his latest novel, *Breakheart Pass*, from being junk, however. There's nothing in the book but plot, and even this is ill-written and

continued on next page

continued from previous page

contrived. The enduring bestsellerhood of stuff like this never ceases to amaze me.

Nor is the movie, starring the inordinately popular Charles Bronson, much better. The grim-faced characters give us little cause to care for them, and the plot still seems too far-fetched for comfort. On the plus side, MacLean's sour prose (he wrote the screenplay, too) sounds better as dialogue in Bronson's mouth than it looks on the printed page. And the action (directed by Tom Gries) is photogenic––how can you miss a few galloping images, with a story about a train on a mysterious mission in the Old West beset with murders, intrigues, and a whole army of Indians?''

Reprinted by permission from The Christian
Science Monitor © 1976.
The Christian Science Publishing Society.
All rights reserved.

Village Voice, 6/28/76 (p. 136)
Michael McKegney

''Credited as Alistair MacLean's *Breakheart Pass*, this latest Charles Bronson flick is one of the few in recent years to explicitly attribute creative priority to its director (Tom Gries) and, no doubt numbed into complacency by a decade supersaturated with auteurism, I must confess to a somewhat shocked reaction. Not that Gries has ever seemed to me more than a technically competent metteur en scene. And with the undebatable contributions of Lucien Ballard's photography, Jerry Goldsmith's music, and Yakima Canutt's ostentatious spectaculars on second-unit action, *Breakheart Pass* shows that the tradition of film as collaborative craft is alive in the New Hollywood. Hooray for teamwork!

Now for the bad news. Vincent Canby has already noted the remarkable resemblance of the plot to the contrivances of an Agatha Christie novel, and indeed, considering this alleged western's largely train-bound setting for a series of surprising and grotesque murders, I entertained the thought of retitling it *Murder on the Occident Express*. I had plenty of time to entertain this thought, and many others. Riddled with psychological as well as narrative obscurities, the unintentional mysteries in *Breakheart Pass* outnumber the intentional ones, and thus the viewer's curiosity is continually goaded, but, in the absence of dramatic interest, just as continually dissipated . . . ''

Reprinted by permission of The Village Voice.
Copyright © The Village Voice, Inc., 1976.

New Leader, 6/7/76 (p. 23)
Robert Asahina

''*Breakheart Pass*, a new Charles Bronson film directed by Tom Gries, is a . . . satisfying example of the kind of generic swapping that might revive the Western. Gries once made a revisionist Western called *Will Penny*, an interesting failure guilty most

of all of being a rather drab film about rather drab people, but here he seems to have clicked. I can only hint at the character of *Breakheart Pass* by suggesting that it is a reworking of *Murder on the Orient Express*––sans the sterility and stifling 'quality' of that 'thriller.'

The stunt sequences in *Breakheart Pass*, staged by Yakima Canutt, are exhilarating without lapsing into camp, and the cast, including such familiars as Richard Crenna and Ben Johnson, is strong. Perhaps most important, *Breakheart Pass* succeeds in providing no-nonsense entertainment . . .''

Reprinted with permission from
The New Leader, 1976.
© The American Labor Conference
on International Affairs, Inc.

BREAKING POINT

Director: *Bob Clark*. Screenplay: *Roger E. Swaybill, Stanley Mann*. Based on a story by Mr. Swaybill. Producers: *Claude Heroux, Mr. Clark*. Photography: *Marc Champion*. Editor: *Stan Cole*. Music: *David McLey*. Production: *Astral Bellevue Pathe*; *Twentieth Century-Fox*. Distributor: *Twentieth Century-Fox*. Running time 86 minutes. Los Angeles opening July 1976 at several theatres. Classification: R.

Players: *Bo Svenson, Robert Culp, John Colicos, Belinda J. Montgomery, Stephen Young, Linda Sorenson, Jeffrey Lynas, Gerry Salzburg*.

Monthly Film Bulletin, 8/76 (p. 163)
Jill Forbes

''. . . Whether in order to overcome the difficulty of finding suitable civilian roles for the muscular Svenson, or out of some obscure conviction that 'decent' values, such as Christmas, the family and successful business are beleaguered in a 'sick' society, this film has resuscitated the pioneer . . . In *Breaking Point* violence is intelligence (McBain does not simply think on his feet, he thinks with his feet and his fists, and his gun) and once McBain stands alone it becomes clear that Bob Clark is first and foremost an action director, and there is a distinct qualitative change in the film as he moves into the climactic shoot-out. The fairly complex narrative build-up to the final action sequence is well-paced and lucidly handled, even if the ending is sheer bathos . . .''

©Monthly Film Bulletin, 1976.

Los Angeles Times, 7/7/76 (Pt. IV, p. 13)
Kevin Thomas

"*Breaking Point* . . . is something that occurs very early on in this numbskull movie, which has to be one of the most inept ever released by a major studio . . .

There is undoubtedly a film to be made about the growing phenomenon of government witnesses having to go underground and start new lives, but in *Breaking Point* the phenomenon is only a pretext for permitting its hero to take the law into his own hands and wreak a decidedly improbable—and naturally quite violent—vengeance upon the underworld.

The boners in Roger E. Swaybill and Stanley Mann's script (which are underlined by Bob Clark's ponderous, unimaginative direction) are too multiple to mention . . ."

©Los Angeles Times, 1976.

BROTHERS

Director: *Arthur Barron.* Screenplay, Producers: *Edward Lewis, Mildred Lewis.* Photography: *John Morrill.* Editor: *William Dornisch.* Music: *Taj Mahal.* Production: *SoHo Associates.* Distributor: *Warner Bros.* Running time 104 minutes. New York opening March 31, 1977, at the Fine Arts and National Theatres. Classification: R.

David Thomas: *Bernie Casey.* Paula Jones: *Vonetta McGee.* Walter Nance: *Ron O'Neal.* Lewis: *Renny Roker.* Robinson: *Stu Gilliam.* Chief Guard McGee: *John Lehne.* Joshua Thomas: *Owen Pace.* Warden Leon: *Joseph Havener.*

New York Times, 4/1/77 (p. C10)
A. H. Weiler

"Anger is the strident keynote in *Brothers*, the thinly disguised dramatization of some bloody, black militancy of fairly recent history in California. Hatred, like love, cries for balanced treatment, but *Brothers* . . . is dedicated to venting its outrage unalloyed and largely without benefit of doubt.

Although its principals are named Thomas and Jones, viewers may see close parallels between *Brothers* and the actual cases of George Jackson, the black San Quentin prisoner who was killed a few years back; his younger brother and a judge who were slain in a shootout at a courthouse, and

Angela Davis, the brilliant political, teacher-activist, who was arrested and then acquitted of charges of helping to stage a prison escape . . .

In filming lengthy sequences in North Dakota State Penitentiary, the director, Arthur Barron, has caught the raw reality of both the jail and its actual inmates. Bernie Casey, the ill-fated, driven hero, contributes a taut, thoughtful characterization of a man educated into organizing his fellow black inmates toward a seeming, ultimate victory. Vonetta McGee is decorative as the political activist the hero comes to love in a tender, underplayed affair. And Ron O'Neal is quietly forceful as the brainy inmate who introduces him to the practical values of education . . ."

© 1977 by the New York Times Company. Reprinted by permission.

New York Post, 4/1/77 (p. 42)
Archer Winsten

"*Brothers* . . . is based on the famed story of Angela Davis, the black activist and teacher, and her involvement with the imprisoned Soledad Brothers, notably the literary one, George Jackson. It's a love story, a prison melodrama, in and out of prison . . .

The main point is that a black youth, arrested and tried for a gas station robbery he didn't commit, though he was present, was persuaded to plead guilty by a lawyer promising a light sentence. Instead he was sent to the penitentiary with a sentence of one year to life.

He never did get out, dying there in the prison yard during an escape attempt.

As usual in such stories, the plot cards and sympathies are heavily stacked. The blacks are consistently high minded and noble, the whites mean-spirited when they aren't worse . . .

Given the nature of the story and its factual background, it is probable that no previously set opinions will be changed. However, as part of the record and for future opinion-making, it is a powerful statement, a tragedy with no happy movie ending tacked on for final comfort."

Reprinted by Permission of New York Post.
© 1977, New York Post Corporation.

Newsweek, 4/4/77 (p. 76)
Janet Maslin

"*Brothers* is so intent on turning George Jackson into a saint that it loses track of him as a human being. The film, a thinly fictionalized account of Jackson's life in prison and his long-distance friendship with Angela Davis, represents Jackson—here called David Thomas—as a blameless victim of circumstances who becomes quietly radicalized by his false arrest (as an accessory to a gas station

continued on next page

continued from previous page

holdup) and his experience with racism in a California state prison.

Jackson's real story was a good deal more complicated than that: he had a strong temper and a history of petty crime, and the circumstances surrounding both his death and the murder of a Soledad guard remain ambiguous even now. A thorough, thoughtful film biography might have raised some troubling questions about the thin line separating radical tactics from common criminality, and it might have examined the conditions that made Jackson's brand so compelling during the turbulent climate of the late '60s. In its determination to look only on the sunny side *Brothers* robs Jackson of all the idiosyncrasies that helped make him a hero . . .''

©Newsweek, Inc. 1977
reprinted by permission

BUFFALO BILL AND THE INDIANS OR SITTING BULL'S HISTORY LESSON

Director, Producer: *Robert Altman.*
Screenplay: *Alan Rudolph, Mr. Altman.* Based on the play INDIANS by Arthur Kopit. Executive Producer: *David Susskind.* Photography: *Paul Lohmann.* Editors: *Peter Appleton, Dennis Hill.* Music: *Richard Baskin.* Production: *Dino De Laurentiis Corporation/Lion's Gate Films/Talent Associates/Norton Simon.* Distributor: *United Artists.* Running time 120 minutes. New York opening June 24, 1976, at several theatres. Classification: PG.

Buffalo Bill: *Paul Newman.* Nate Salsbury: *Joel Grey.* Major John Burke: *Kevin McCarthy.* Colonel Prentiss Ingraham: *Allan Nicholls.* Ed Goodman: *Harvey Keitel.* Jules Keen: *Mike Kaplan.* Crutch: *Bert Remsen.* Ned Buntline: *Burt Lancaster.* Annie Oakley: *Geraldine Chaplin.* Frank Butler: *John Considine.* Chief Sitting Bull: *Frank Kaquitts.* Interpreter: *Will Sampson.* Indian Agent McLaughlin: *Denver Pyle.* Grover Cleveland: *Pat McCormick.* Mrs. Cleveland: *Shelly Duvall.* Nina Cavalini: *Evelyn Lear.* Margaret: *Bonnie Leaders.* Lucille DuCharmes: *Noelle Rogers.*

New York Times, 6/25/76 (p. C8)
Vincent Canby

'' . . . *Buffalo Bill and the Indians or Sitting Bull's*

History Lesson . . . is nothing if not eccentric, and I can't imagine anyone missing it who is interested in the continuing Altman explorations on the outer edges of commercially acceptable film form or in his preoccupation with Americana. It's a sometimes self-indulgent, confused, ambitious movie that is often very funny and always fascinating.

As in *Nashville*, the metaphor in *Buffalo Bill* is 'the show business,' though this time it's been extended—some will say overextended—to make a sweeping Bicentennial statement about the kind of men who made our country great, which is the way the film's President Grover Cleveland grandly identifies the film's William F. (Buffalo Bill) Cody, a carnival con man, somewhat more successful than most . . .

Paul Newman makes a fine, florid, egomaniacal Buffalo Bill, part fraud but also so much a product of time and place that he can't easily be held accountable for having seized the opportunities opened to him. He's the American way . . .

The film that Mr. Altman has made is even more about theater-as-life and about the making of legends (matinee idols, movie stars and Presidents) than it is about genocide . . .

The film is virtually formless in any usual way. In place of narrative drive it relies on the momentum created by its visuals . . . its prodigal way with ideas, its wit and its enthusiasm for the lunatic business of making movies. Mr. Altman makes movies the way other men go on binges—with an abandon that sometimes gets the better of him—and which should be preserved and protected.''

© New York Times, 1976.

Saturday Review, 7/10/76 (p. 62)
Judith Crist

''To each his Bicentennial offering and celebration. For movies, small doubt that the appropriate offering is Robert Altman's *Buffalo Bill and the Indians*—a celebration of the show business, the stardom, the ethic, and the verities that have been embodied in American history and epitomized by Hollywood.

It is fitting also that Altman, whose *Nashville* last year gave us a clear and devastating perception of the contemporary state of the nation, should cast his creative eye on history with the clarity, humor, and affectionate cynicism that have been the hallmarks of his work . . .

Paul Newman's Buffalo Bill, a cold-eyed but haunted man who skirts buffoonery by keeping a tight rein on his mirror-and-poster image, is the ultimate star, nightmare-ridden but quick to turn each accident or twist of events to his own advantage, discarding each moment as it becomes the forgettable past, completely convinced of the burden of posterity . . .

With moments of brilliant inspiration, and of pedestrian pointmaking, there is a surface simplicity in Altman's view—one that seems anticlimactic, as any post-*Nashville* work would seem. But it is the restatement of the obvious that counts here', an awareness of our false historic values, a recognition of the revisionism that marks one's maturity and growth. The final confidence in Buffalo Bill's eye is the warning: the great men die, the created legends endure, and history, according to Sitting Bull, is 'nothing more than disrespect for the dead'--something worth remembering at Bicentennial moments.''

© Judith Crist, 1976.

Newsweek, 6/28/76 (p. 77)
Jack Kroll

'' . . . at the heart of Altman's concept is the idea of the star, the modern world's pinch hitter for saints and heroes. Buffalo Bill was the creation of Ned Buntline (Burt Lancaster), a writer of dime novels who got the idea of turning the buffalo-butcher into a mythic figure. Altman's film confronts this jerry-built titan, with his Liberace buckskins, and Sitting Bull (Frank Kaquitts), the conqueror of Custer, now a beaten little brown man with one feather in his hair. Only Altman could get such heartbreaking laughter out of racism as Buffalo Bill matches his bombast against the chief's mystic silences, which are translated into grand rhetoric by his mysterious half-breed interpreter William Halsey (Will Sampson).

Since it is superstar Paul Newman who plays Buffalo Bill, the first modern superstar, the screen vibrates with cross-currents of meaning . . .

. . . This movie seethes with a civilized fullness of intelligence . . .''

© Newsweek, Inc. 1976
reprinted by permission.

New York Magazine, 7/5/76 (p. 70)
John Simon

'' . . . this film makes me think that the center of Altman is made not of ideas, insights, visions, but of attitudes. And attitudes are not quite good enough . . .

The screenplay Alan Rudolph and Altman have concocted is barely a screenplay at all; were someone to tell me that it was improvised *in situ* when shooting commenced in Alberta, Canada, I would readily believe it . . .

And it is not only the improvisational incoherences of the script that are problematical; there is also the notion that *texture* is all that matters, while *structure* can be allowed to shift for itself . . .

The problem, ultimately, extends beyond this picture to a certain monomania in Altman; it is all very well to want to knock off the American myths, one after another, but not to debunk the same one twice. The West got kicked in the pants in *McCabe and Mrs. Miller*; show business got its comeuppance in *Nashville*. The present film, which is really

a conflation of those two, thus ends up as a twofold tautology.

All this notwithstanding, there is, once again, substantial talent on display here . . .''

© 1976 by the NYM Corp. Reprinted with
the permission of NEW YORK Magazine.

Women's Wear Daily, 6/21/76 (p. 12)
Howard Kissel

'' . . . The trouble . . . is that though the technique is dazzling, the content is repetitious and often sophomoric. The density of the images seems a way of covering up their lack of depth. When we first see Buffalo Bill he has trouble getting his horse to make a heroic entrance. Subsequently we see him making dumb remarks about Indians and blacks. We see he is afraid of a canary. We see him apologizing to his mistress for not being able to 'perform' the night before. The point about the character was made at once but it is repeated ad nauseum, and the wit of juxtaposing history and show biz quickly begins to wear.

Because all the characters (except the Indians) are self-satiric, the choices offered to the actors are minimal. In Altman's pre-*Nashville* pictures, the style was more important than the content, but the style was conducive to getting vital, spontaneous characterizations out of the actors. Now the style seems largely geared to making 'statements' and the result is that the film, however many laughs it provides, is really lifeless.

Visually *Buffalo Bill* is gorgeous--many of the scenes seem bathed in the rich gold of the setting sun, an appropriate image for the twilight of the myth of the West.''

© Women's Wear Daily, 1976.

New York Post, 6/25/76 (p. 22)
Frank Rich

'' . . . *Buffalo Bill* has been made with such enormous conviction--it's a movie Altman was obviously driven to make--that you expect it to be one of his best movies. It isn't, but it's more than good enough. The film is full of rambunctious intelligence and, unexpectedly, it provokes more honest laughter than any other movie so far this year. It also features a star performance by Paul Newman that returns this actor, at long last, to glory . . .

Newman plays Cody as if he were a grandstanding politician--with equal measures of petulance, charm, movie-star magnetism and cold ambition--and that's how it should be. For as Buffalo Bill was a great superstar, he was also a great politician--the myths he created were politics and entertainment rolled into one . . .

The problems with the movie--the occasional halts to its free-flowing form, the shortchanging of

continued on next page

continued from previous page

some minor characters and relationships––often seem to be a function of the disruptions created by the character of Buffalo Bill . . ."

Reprinted by Permission of New York Post.
© 1976, New York Post Corporation.

Los Angeles Times, 6/30/76 (Pt. IV, p. 1)
Charles Champlin

" . . . *Buffalo Bill* is a parable on the condescending, exploitative, treacherous treatment of the American Indians by the whites, expressed as a demythologizing of Buffalo Bill, seen to be a posturing, ignorant, drunken never-was who sprang fullblown from the sozzled brow of pulp-writer Ned Buntline, and who is seen here to be shamed by the simple grandeur of Sitting Bull . . .

Buffalo Bill is played as one long Homeric hangover by Paul Newman in a shoulder-length curly wig (which he is caught without, self-scalped so to speak, in one farcical early morning confrontation with Sitting Bull) . . .

It is not quite shattering in 1976 to be told that the old West was not quite what some of the legends made it out to be. Nor is this the first time that we've been reminded that the Indians were used badly, to the point of genocide, by an invading culture that not only made no attempt to understand theirs but denied its own ideals in the name of progress . . .

You are left to remember Altman's more successful infatuations with losers and victims: the poignance of *Thieves Like Us*, the rage of *M*A*S*H*, the sprawling vitality of *Nashville*, the antic energies of *Brewster McCloud* . . ."

© Los Angeles Times, 1976.

Nation, 7/31/76 (p. 93)
Robert Hatch

" . . . At the center of . . . this is Paul Newman as Buffalo Bill, and that center does not hold. No criticism of Newman is implied; the fault lies in the conception of the character. It takes very little time and no great subtlety to establish that Cody was a slow-witted, vain, tyrannical, insensitive, self-indulgent stuffed buckskin shirt, and Newman does the job efficiently . . . Perhaps Altman, perhaps Newman—both men of civic righteousness—were unwilling to grant their hollow man any redeeming qualities of charm, humor, compassion or self-appreciation . . . such a character is hopelessly uninteresting and his position at the hub of a picture which has no strong narrative drive to hold one's attention is discouraging. *Buffalo Bill* is a chapter in Altman's chronicle of the American soul that doesn't work as well as it should because, this time, the director couldn't summon up the irony and tolerance to leaven his indignation. The film is visually exhilarating in patches and some of the side

shows, particularly Annie Oakley (Geraldine Chaplin) and her understandably nervous target-husband (John Considine), are entertaining. But on close acquaintance Bill Cody is a bore."

©The Nation, 1976.

Monthly Film Bulletin, 9/76 (p. 189)
Jonathan Rosenbaum

". . . That the film's theme is irrefutable surely deserves recognition: the genocide perpetrated by whites on the American Indian is a matter of historical record, and the systematic distortion of this fact by popular American media is no less evident. Considered purely as agitprop—neatly timed for a 4th of July American release at the start of this bicentennial summer—*Buffalo Bill and the Indians* might seem justifiable as an instrument for ramming this point home if it went about its business with some historical rigour. Unfortunately, Altman appears to know a lot more about show business than about the American Indian . . . with grinding regularity, everything that Cody does or says is pathetic while everything communicated by Sitting Bull is noble and dignified. This largely leads (in part, thanks to Paul Newman's touching performance) to Cody becoming the principal center of sympathy and attention, as a kind of surrogate for the liberal guilt of the white spectator . . . Given such a lugubrious context, it should be stressed that Altman's actors acquit themselves admirably within the relatively tight constrictions of their assigned roles . . ."

©Monthly Film Bulletin, 1976.

The Sunday Times (London), 7/25/76 (p. 28)
Dilys Powell

"After the *Nashville* show-biz the show-biz of the Wild West. With *Buffalo Bill and the Indians* . . . Robert Altman moves farther into spectacle—and deeper into judgment of an American mood. The screenplay, occasionally confusing but never dull, is by the director and Alan Rudolph; it is 'suggested,' we are told, by the Arthur Kopit play *Indians*. One is perhaps justified in saying that the stage could have scarcely accommodated the more acrobatic passages of the film . . .

But spectacle is not the point of the film, though it is needed to demonstrate the nature of the chief character. The point is in the film's subtitle, *Sitting Bull's History Lesson* . . . Sitting Bull not only declines to be made a clown but leaves his employer looking distinctly awkward. What is more, he arrives with an interpreter, played with immense dignity by Will Sampson (the Indian in *One Flew Over the Cuckoo's Nest*), who adds further to the discomfiture of the whiteskins. And that, I presume, is what Arthur Kopit's play suggested: the defeated Indians, corralled after that disagreeable business of Custer's Last Stand, are the moral victors . . ."

©The Sunday Times, 1976.

The Times (London), 7/23/76 (p. 9)
David Robinson

". . . Buffalo Bill was America's first synthetic hero. Altman's Buffalo Bill is a modern superstar, Paul Newman. 'You haven't changed, Bill,' Buntline (Burt Lancaster) tells him. 'I'm not supposed to,' Bill replies, 'that's why people pay me.' He is the prisoner of his own legend, and in his overupholstered quarters, the massive portraits and the mirrors constantly remind him of it . . .

. . . The dialogue has the unexpected freshness of improvisation (though the improvisation is done within a framework closely controlled by the director) and in the Altman manner and the way of real talk, is allowed to drift into inaudibility as it is overlapped or trailed out of earshot. Yet the whole thing has a good deal more determination than *Nashville*, which sometimes tended to pot-head meandering, and a more energetic, even vicious purpose to its ideas and subversion of myth than, say, *McCabe and Mrs. Miller*.

It takes its dynamic not from narrative progression, but in the succession of sketches and set pieces . . ."

©The Times, 1976.

Commonweal, 8/13/76 (p. 528)
Colin L. Westerbeck, Jr.

". . . In effect Altman's whole film is about the relationship between illusion and substance, fakery and the genuine article, and the difficulty of telling them apart. Sometimes Altman makes us aware of this difficulty by showing us an image—in a painting, a mirror or a photograph—instead of its subject. At other times, when he is at his best, he creates our awareness through a disparity between what we see and what we hear. The dashing figure Bill cuts shooting skeet with a pistol is undermined by a letter being read to him in which his wife accuses him of stinginess, drunkenness, infidelity, etc. A toast Bill is drinking to himself is paralyzed halfway to his mouth by a remark Ned Buntline (Burt Lancaster) makes that 'It was the thrill of my life to have invented you.' . . ."

©Commonweal, 1976.

Film Information, July/August 1976 (p. 1)
Thomas Bentz

"This is not an either/or, as its title suggests, but a neither. Rather than recapture the scope of the real Bill Cody as scout, pony express rider, and buffalo killer, or retell Little Big Horn and Wounded Knee with Indian teachers, Robert Altman instead encloses the West and its people in a corral . . .

This filmic reproduction, billed as 'an absolute original and heroic enterprise of inimitable lustre,' is indeed original, but it is not heroic. The Altman/Newman marriage is not made in

heaven—or on the range. Altman makes anti-heroes while Newman works to hold our attention. The hero does not get lost in the hills but is trampled in the traffic around him and the eight-track sounds over him . . .

The best thing about *Buffalo Bill* is its texture. Photographer Paul Lohmann mixes a yellow, brown and orange palette reminiscent of Frederic Remington's paintings. Curator Altman then sets it in motion, circling horses, moving characters, and undulating voices. Like a child on a carousel, I loved the movement and rhythm, even though I knew the ride was unreal."

©Film Information, 1976.

Take One, 8/76 (p. 39)
Will Aitken

". . . *Buffalo Bill*, like all of Altman's films, is well-crafted. Historical perspective maintained by lots of long and medium shots; close-ups used sparingly, for portraiture. Altman fills up his frames without making them busy: we've always a great deal to look at, and the anachronisms and malaprops on the soundtrack keep us chuckling (as does Richard Baskin's brassy score) . . .

What we take with us . . . once *Buffalo Bill*'s over, is the look of the picture and its sudden throw-away beauties. Just as we recall the watery greens of *Thieves Like Us*, the monotonous khakis of *M*A*S*H*—Altman's cinematographer Paul Lohmann gives *Buffalo Bill* an almost monochromatic golden patina . . .

For all its genial spirits, *Buffalo Bill and the Indians* remains a history lesson, and a simple-minded one at that. That American history is the creation of flamboyant lies and showmanship strikes us at first as an amusing trifle and then quickly becomes an epigram shaggy-dogging its way across two hours of eccentric Altmanship."

©Take One, 1976.

Sight and Sound, Autumn 1976 (p. 254)
Tom Milne

". . . Altman tackles the problem . . . by deliberately decentralising any question of the *reality* of the Indian. As the camera pulls back at the beginning of the film to reveal that the ferocious redskin attack on a pioneer shack is merely a rehearsal for one of the Wild West Show's acts, a wounded Indian extra trampled by a horse is hurried away. Subsequently, as the film bustles into the characteristic Altman flurry of sidelong jokes and overlapping dialogue while the Wild West Show marshals its characters and resources, an enigmatic shot of Indians silhouetted against the forest is laconically explained as the funeral of the dead extra before it is swallowed up by the kaleidoscopic action, leaving no ripple behind. A single Ford setup of a pioneer burial carries an automatic charge; but

continued on next page

continued from previous page

this, the film implies, is alien to our culture, our understanding, our emotions.

From this point on, *Buffalo Bill and the Indians* becomes a confrontation of myth with myth . . ."

©Sight and Sound, 1976.

Films in Review, October 1976 (p. 506)
Marsha McCreadie

". . . Altman at even his most static can be counted on brilliantly to show the faces and atmosphere of a particular time and place (aided here by cinematographer Paul Lohmann), and for witty lines in the famous overlapped soundtrack. The sharp incongruities of an outsider's vision are here too . . .

Buffalo Bill (and, it's beginning to seem, Altman as well) is at its best when observing the realistic deflating detail . . . But these clever spots aren't enough to bear the heavy moralizing the film insists on, so there's an imagined confrontation between Bill and Sitting Bull to force the point—the most heavy-handed Altman symbolism to date."

©Films in Review, 1976.

Commentary, October 1976 (p. 76)
William S. Pechter

". . . surprisingly benign, even, despite all its potential for hate-mongering, good-natured. Part of this affability seems attributable to the presence of Paul Newman, who may be a star, but is precisely the wrong kind of star—one indelibly associated with anti-heroic roles and liberal causes—to give the film that extra layer of irony which seems intended . . . But more important, perhaps because the film's point-making is so emphatic and pervasive, and the points themselves so blunted by familiarity, one can more or less ignore such things (rather as one may automatically filter out the sound of surface noise in listening to some poorly recorded music) and direct one's attention elsewhere: in particular to several deft comic touches, some nicely turned performances by a typically eccentric Altman cast . . ."

©Commentary, 1976.

BUGS BUNNY SUPERSTAR

Director, Producer: *Larry Jackson*. Narration: *Orson Welles*. Distributor: *Hare Raising Films*. Running time 90 minutes. New York opening

December 20, 1975, at the D.W. Griffith and Regency Theatres. Classification: None.

Players: *Bob Clampett, Tex Avery, Fritz Freleng*.

See Volume 1 for additional reviews

Take One, October 1976 (p. 41)
Lester Bangs

". . . The thing that's most irritating about *Bugs Bunny Superstar* is that it falls prey to the very sentimentality that never even occurred to the people who put the old ABC-TV series together. When Bob Clampett, who looks like he should be selling real estate on local TV except for the Bugs and Tweety patches on his jacket, starts talking about what a grand old hutch Termite Terrace—as they called the dump where they drew these things—was, you get that sinking, queasy feeling: you know that you're in for another dose of show-biz schmaltz . . . you may be tempted to bolt up the aisle and demand your boxoffice bucks back on grounds of false advertising—I came here to wallow in *cartoons*, not a shoddily assembled bunch of self-serving tripe by a few old artists . . .

The cartoons are well-chosen, with an expectably fair share of masterpieces, although I missed Yosemite Sam . . ."

©Take One, 1976.

BUGSY MALONE

Director, Screenplay: *Alan Parker*. Producer: *Alan Marshall*. Photography: *Michael Seresin, Peter Biziou*. Editor: *Gerry Hambling*. Music: *Paul Williams*. Production: *Goodtimes Enterprises*. Distributor: *Paramount Pictures*. Running time 94 minutes. New York opening September 15, 1976, at the Baronet Theatre. Classification: G.

Bugsy: *Scott Baio*. Blousey: *Florrie Dugger*. Tallulah: *Jodie Foster*. Fat Sam: *John Cassisi*. Dandy Dan: *Martin Lev*. Leroy Smith: *Paul Murphy*. Knuckles: *Sheridan Russell*. Bizzy: *'Humpty' Albin Jenkins*. Baby Face: *Dexter Fletcher*.

Women's Wear Daily, 5/28/76 (p. 8)
Howard Kissel

"Alan Parker's *Bugsy Malone* is an absolutely in-genious idea superbly done. Parodies of movie genres of yesteryear have become so common-place that they are almost irritating. Parker found a way to bring in all the familiar, heartwarming cliches without making it seem merely another attempt to cash in on nostalgia—he simply has all the roles played by a cast that seems to range in age from 7 to 14. This gives the whole project an innocence that makes it irresistible.

Set in New York in the beginning of the Depres-sion, *Bugsy Malone* brings in all the conventions—gangsters, showgirls, boxers. Parker has found a cast of youngsters who have obviously been watch-ing old movies since just after weaning and have all the mannerisms down perfectly. Scott Baio and Florrie Dugger as the down-and-out couple making their way through hard times combine just the right amounts of toughness and winsomeness. Jodie Foster, whom we last saw as the young prostitute in *Taxi Driver*, is again powerful as a floozy chan-teuse. Parker has directed his young cast so that they play earnestly, not tongue-in-cheek."

©Women's Wear Daily, 1976.

Saturday Review, 10/2/76 (p. 39)
Judith Crist

". . . Parker wrote the mish-mash of gangster-movie cliches and directed the cast of some 200 British and American youngsters whose average age is reportedly twelve. But putting subteens and young teens into adult costumes and makeup—and the period sets and styles are certainly lavish and handsome—has its problems: the girls come out looking like women while their partners are only too obviously little boys dressed in daddy's cut-down cast-offs, complete with fake mustaches and falsetto voices. To further destroy any illusions, Paul Williams has provided a completely charming score and ten clever songs that have been pre-recorded by adults. The on-screen youngsters mouth the lyrics—and the general result is not un-like a sixth-grade performance, say, of *Guys and Dolls* to the accompaniment of the original Broad-way cast recording.

Some of the youngsters are very good, with Jodie Foster, memorable as the young prostitute in *Taxi Driver*, and Florrie Dugger, a newcomer, outstand-ing as the gang leader's moll and the innocent young thing. John Cassisi, another newcomer, is fine as the gang leader . . ."

©Judith Crist, 1976.

New York Magazine, 9/27/76 (p. 86)
John Simon

". . . what the writer-director Alan Parker has

done to childhood in *Bugsy Malone* is no mere injustice . . . It is an indecency, an outrage. This man has taken children and adolescents and made them enact a gangster-cum-music-hall-cum-prizefight B movie just as if they were jaded adult actors in a cynical thirties or forties picture. No reason is given (dream, fantasy, movie within a movie); the children are simply there in a studio-made New York of 1929, killing, brutalizing, swin-dling, and tarting it up. To be sure, the submachine guns spout marshmallows for bullets, yet their vic-tims are 'eliminated'; the dance-hall girls are not seen actually copulating, but the implications are there; the soft drinks are only suggestive of booze, but the glorification of violence and crime are real enough . . ."

©1976 by the NYM Corp. Reprinted with
the permission of NEW YORK Magazine.

Monthly Film Bulletin, 7/76 (p. 145)
Geoff Brown

"*Bugsy Malone* marks Alan Parker's cinema debut as a feature director, although he has al-ready built up thematic predilections (plus a size-able reputation) in other fields . . . in his many commercials, he developed a highly polished style in which shots are angled and patterned with un-usual verve. *Bugsy Malone* shares the commer-cials' glossy surface . . . their rapidfire shooting style also occurs at odd moments, such as Bugsy and Blousey's idyllic open-air romp (where the style is used for parody). The film's subject matter is equally familiar, for *Bugsy Malone* is entirely acted by children—children engaged in a full-scale game of aping not adults themselves, but an adult movie genre. Parker's plot could almost have been pro-duced by a mischievous computer fed on the Warner Brothers gangster output of the 1930s . . . But *Bugsy Malone* presents the gangster genre minus its blood and bullets: the dreaded splurge guns release a charge of white mush, closely re-lated to the custard pie . . . For an adult, the world of Bugsy is at first difficult to enter, and the artificial-ity of the whole concept is uncomfortably stressed during the musical numbers, which are dubbed by adults. But one is soon won over by the cast's com-plete lack of self-consciousness and the manifold delights of the script ('Don't do that, Knuckles!' Fat Sam whines after the vicious sound of cracking bones emanates from his partner. 'It's how I got my name, boss!' Knuckles explains) . . ."

©Monthly Film Bulletin, 1976.

The Times (London), 7/23/76 (p. 9)
David Robinson

"If for nothing else, you would have to admire *Bugsy Malone* for the sheer doggedness of its ec-

continued on next page

continued from previous page

centricity. It is a nostalgia pastiche of all the cliches of the gangster movie and the musical of the early days of sound films, the novelty being that it is entirely played by children of an average age of 12 . . .

The writer-director was Alan Parker, who has come up through television commercials and a prizewinning television film, *The Evacuees*, and who clearly has a way with kid performers. The bright score is by the American Paul Williams. But if we're hoping for white hopes for the ailing British cinema, it would be more encouraging to find someone with bigger ambitions than novelty and nostalga."

©The Times, 1976.

New York Post, 9/16/76 (p. 23)
Frank Rich

"*Bugsy Malone* . . . is a determinedly stylish pastiche of '30s Hollywood movies—especially gangster melodramas and musicals—in which all the roles are played by children. For what it is, the movie is passably well-done—but who cares? *Bugsy Malone* is just another exercise in nostalgia for its own sake, enlivened slightly by its weird casting gimmick, and all the pizzaz in the world couldn't lift it above the level of empty camp . . .

Bugsy Malone does not qualify as a real movie—not because it's silly but because it isn't entertainingly silly and it isn't alive. The most crucial problems are in the script, for what Parker has written is a series of arbitrarily connected scenes whose sole point is to recall every famous howler and bit that ever appeared in a gangster film of the 'Little Caesar' era . . ."

Reprinted by Permission of New York Post.
©1976, New York Post Corporation.

The Sunday Times (London), 7/25/76 (p. 28)
Dilys Powell

". . . *Bugsy Malone* may be a kid's adventure, but it is an adult's joke, a reminiscent comment on all the gang-wars of the Hollywood screen.

The detail is a delight, from the gestures of the quartet of singing and dancing hoods to the furniture, to all the tiny appurtenances of life in a world of gang-battles. Everything is followed through; nothing disturbs the affectionate reconstruction of a film-fantasy which today, after the massacres and the bombs of real life, seems almost pacific. Is it followed through too devotedly? An adult's joke—the variations on it are numerous and ingenious, but it is a single joke; occasionally one feels a desire to break out of even so witty a cage. And extraordinary as the children are, their performance, rigorously held in the mould of the past, is bound to limit the possibilities of excitement.

All the same, by the end one is completely caught up in the narrative action . . ."

©The Sunday Times, 1976.

Nation, 10/9/76 (p. 350)
Robert Hatch

". . . The two dominant gags in this nostalgic exercise are machine guns that spray custard, alleged to be lethal, and undersized period cars operated by pedal power; those are whimsies that do not improve with repetition, and if their effect was intended to be satiric, its application escaped me. I can imagine, though with misgivings, that a travesty of the Nixon junta might be cast with children. There was something puerile about the jealousies and tantrums of the White House conspirators' club . . . But the Prohibition mobsters did not much resemble children, however vicious. They were self-made businessmen of a particularly hardheaded breed, in that they employed bullets instead of stock proxies to eliminate presumptuous competitors.

The strange thing is that, with nostalgia now selling briskly on the stands of popular entertainment, *Bugsy Malone* would undoubtedly have worked well enough with a cast of voting age . . ."

©The Nation, 1976.

Sight and Sound, Autumn 1976 (p. 255)
Philip Strick

". . . With no stars, no precedent, and only the NFFC to support it, *Bugsy* had to fight for its life in a production climate disinclined to take risks, scarcely able to afford certainties. It deserves to do well, both for being made at all, and for being made with British talent more accustomed to gloom than glory. It calls for praise not because it indicates any path to renaissance (given that *Bugsy*'s main asset is novelty, it's difficult to imagine any tolerable sequel), but because it was created with enthusiasm, humour and charm. So long as one stays with its bright perky surface, the film is an uncomplicated pleasure . . ."

©Sight and Sound, 1976.

Christian Science Monitor, 10/6/76 (p. 26)
David Sterritt

". . . This odd but charming idea is the brainchild of director-writer Alan Parker, who has assembled *Bugsy Malone* with great panache. The editing is super-snappy, the camera work is often rich, the screenplay is coy but frequently on target with its tongue-in-cheek recollections of bygone movie styles.

Most important, though, is the large cast consisting of talented and very witty children. The leaders of the pack—Scott Baio as Bugsy, John Cassisi as Fat Sam, Martin Lev as Dandy Dan— are keen satirists with firm sense of fun . . .

And special mention must be made of Jodie Foster, having a wonderful time in her own element after her role in the harrowing *Taxi Driver*. As Tallulah, 'the tantalizing vamp of the chorus at Fat Sam's

Grand Slam Speakeasy'—which serves soda pop, by the way—she is class personified.

Toss in some lively songs by popstar Paul Williams, and you have a quirkily entertaining package . . ."

Reprinted by permission from The Christian
Science Monitor © 1976.
The Christian Science Publishing Society.
All rights reserved.

Film Information, October 1976 (p. 2)
Ellen Clark

". . . *Bugsy Malone* quickly bores . . . and it's not just because of too many pie-in-the-face gags. Most of the children in the interracial cast, such as a shy boxer (Martin Lev) and a speakeasy cleaner ("Humpty" Albin Jenkins) possess real charm. But the humor of the movie rests upon parody, and with the notable exception of Jodie Foster (*Alice Doesn't Live Here Anymore, Taxi Driver*), the youngsters lack the sophistication and acting ability to amuse with their put-ons and put-downs of films ranging from the Keystone Cops capers to *The Godfather*.

Though the film flounders, parts of it entertain. As a musical, *Bugsy Malone* has luster. Most of its ten songs, written and composed by Paul Williams, boast memorable melodies and zest. And the song-and-dance routines, reminiscent of Busby Berkeley, sparkle. The sets and costumes are dazzlingly effective, the period details authentic, and the production very polished in its execution . . ."

© Film Information, 1976.

New Leader, 10/11/76 (p. 24)
Robert Asahina

". . . The story itself is a reasonably inoffensive satire of the prototypical gangster film . . .

Parker has taken his story, however, and turned it into a movie that is about as offensive as any I have lately seen. *Village Voice* columnist Arthur Bell has called it the 'first film for gay children.' My own feeling is that it will probably be less attractive to gay children than to pederasts. But both reactions reflect the bizarre nature of *Bugsy Malone*, in which all the roles—written as adult parts—are played by child actors and actresses . . .

In *Bugsy Malone*—as in recent revisionist Westerns like *The Missouri Breaks*—mannerism supplants craftsmanship; distance and detachment replace audience involvement. Both films intend and invite us to be patronizing toward what we are supposedly too sophisticated to respond to honestly . . ."

Reprinted with permission from
The New Leader, 1976.
© The American Labor Conference
on International Affairs, Inc.

Los Angeles Times, 10/13/76 (Pt. IV, p. 1)
Charles Champlin

"The risk of living in a world in which innocence has admittedly grown scarce is that you may not recognize it when you see it.

Bugsy Malone . . . is a rare, original, tuneful, lighthearted, uplifting, charming and preposterously innocent family film. It acknowledges the quite universal desire in children to dress up and play grown up. It is also a warm and affectionate tribute to the American gangster movies which, seen in retrospect, had their own repeating cast of characters and their own kind of innocence.

Written and directed by Alan Parker, who makes documentaries and commercials in London, *Bugsy* began as a story recited to his four children, and it is in a real sense a father's handmade gift, in lieu of the kind of enchantment you can't find in the marketplace anymore.

But here and there *Bugsy* has been listened to for ominous bomby tickings or held to the light as if to disclose hidden naughtiness. This seems skepticism run awry and just as likely to find evil in Evensong. There are quibbles to pick at in *Bugsy*, if only to preserve the critical franchise, but as an inspired invention, it is hard to see the movie for anything but what it is: an ably done musical romp . . ."

© Los Angeles Times, 1976.

Films in Review, November 1976 (p. 565)
Charles Phillips Reilly

"A parody of the gangland pictures of the '30s, *Bugsy Malone* employs a group of semi-talented kids to act roles more familiar to Joan Blondell, Edward G. Robinson et al. The film almost makes it with the help of some Paul Williams sentimental ballads true to the time depicted, but director-writer Alan Parker kills its chances by producing an episodic film, lacking meaningful continuity.

Jodie Foster shows professionalism as Tallulah, dancehall girl friend of Fat Sam (John Cassisi), whose gangster empire is threatened by Dandy Dan (Martin Lev), a hood whose gang has the splurge gun, a lethal weapon which annihilates foes with whipped cream . . ."

© Films in Review, 1976.

BURNT OFFERINGS

Director, Producer: *Dan Curtis*. Screenplay: *William F. Nolan, Mr. Curtis*. Based on the novel by Robert Marasco. Photography: *Jacques Marquette*. Editor: *Dennis Virkler*. Distributor: *United Artists*. New York opening September 29, 1976, at several theatres. Classification: PG.

continued on next page

continued from previous page

Marian: *Karen Black*. Ben: *Oliver Reed*. Brother: *Burgess Meredith*. Roz: *Eileen Heckart*. David: *Lee Montgomery*. Walker: *Dub Taylor*. Aunt Elizabeth: *Bette Davis*.

New York Post, 9/30/76 (p. 26)
Archer Winsten

"... the story of a beautiful old house with a bad, dangerous character ...

There's not much point in going deep into the plot. Either you believe a house can have that kind of effect, I mean lethal, or you don't.

If you do, the picture can pump up your blood pressure to new highs.

If you don't you'll be thinking you've wasted your money on some very far-fetched disasters.

Since this reviewer belongs to the latter group, it was fortunate that he didn't have to pay. The best he could say was that Bette Davis died horribly in paroxysms worthy of that great actress, that Oliver Reed achieved an athletic and bloody death . photographically most spectacular, and that Karen Black can look awfully mean when she wants to, and the make-up people are helping her ..."

Reprinted by Permission of New York Post.
©1976, New York Post Corporation.

Films in Review, November 1976 (p. 568)
Steve Swires

"*Burnt Offerings* is a superior supernatural possession thriller, haunted house variety. This story of a family (Karen Black, Bette Davis, Oliver Reed, Lee Montgomery) menaced by psychic forces which plague their summer estate succeeds because producer-director Dan Curtis has enough confidence in his material to pitch the level of suspense at a low key. While he has certain weaknesses—reverting to his TV-bred reliance on the zoom lens when a more formal visual approach would be more appropriate—he is most secure with his actors, in particular harnessing Reed's visceral screen presence.

Curtis also had the good sense to hire William F. Nolan to write the screenplay. Nolan has so structured the narrative as to accelerate gradually the accumulation of plot incident ..."

©Films in Review, 1976.

Newsweek, 11/8/76 (p. 108)
Janet Maslin

"Karen Black and Oliver Reed, amusingly miscast as an ordinary, middle-class couple in *Burnt*
Offerings, should have known better when they rented the ramshackle mansion in the woods for an amazingly low price from smirking Eileen Heckart and Burgess Meredith, her brother with the malevolent giggle. But they just don't realize that anything's odd—not when the swimming pool develops waves, or when the dead flowers in the greenhouse begin to bloom or even on a stormy night when the house begins to molt its shingles. Nor do they become suspicious when Bette Davis, as their visiting, perfectly healthy old aunt, dies in mysterious, sweaty convulsions. Black and Reed don't wise up until the ludicrous denouement. Before that, the movie merely piles on one special effect after another—none of them too special— and stalls for time ..."

©Newsweek, Inc. 1976
reprinted by permission.

Film Information, October 1976 (p. 2)
Bea Rothenbeuchner

"Fans of the supernatural/horror genre are surely among those viewers least critical of and most open to filmic manipulation. Given certain basic story elements and reasonably good acting, direction and cinematography, they will respond to material more discriminating audiences would reject. So, when a fan of the genre (like this reviewer) feels let down, a movie has to be pretty disappointing. This is true of *Burnt Offerings* ...

Producer/director Dan Curtis (whose daytime television series, 'Dark Shadows,' ran for five years) manages several scenes of appropriate terror, but on the whole does not break through the barrier separating ordinary reality and illusion. By failing to generate the tension needed to grab our attention at the film's beginning, he cannot hold it during long stretches of talk without action ..."

©Film Information, 1976.

Christian Science Monitor, 10/13/76 (p. 31)
David Sterritt

"Visited a haunted house lately? If that sort of adventure appeals to you, drop in on *Burnt Offerings*. It's as spooky as they come—and comparatively subtle, too, at least until mayhem breaks out in the final seconds of the final climax ...

These shenanigans wouldn't work for a moment if they weren't expertly filmed and deftly acted. Oliver Reed gives one of his most vigorous and varied performances as the troubled father, with Karen Black menacing as Mother. Bette Davis is restrained and sympathetic as an elderly aunt, and a gifted boy named Lee H. Montgomery makes the set-upon son thoroughly amiable. Burgess Meredith and Eileen Heckart are precisely right as the odd couple who own the place ...

Director Dan Curtis is best known for his 'Dark Shadows' hijinks on TV. He builds *Burnt Offerings* carefully, keeping the mood dark and the key low until just the right moment for a fright . . ."

Reprinted by permission from The Christian Science Monitor © 1976. The Christian Science Publishing Society. All rights reserved.

BUT WHERE IS DANIEL VAX?

Director, Screenplay: *Avram Heffner*. Producer: *William L. Gross*. Photography: *Amnon Salomon*. Editor: *Jacques Ehrlich*. Music: *Ariel Zilber*. Lyrics: *Ehud Manor*. Running time 103 minutes. Los Angeles opening December 8, 1976, at the Royal Theatre. Classification: None. Origin: Israel.

Players: *Zivit Abramson, Miriam Gabrielli, Yael Heffner, Yosef Karmon, Michael Lipkin, Amnon Meskin, Aliza Rosen, Yeshayahu Shaher, Lior Yaeni, Esther Zebko.*

Los Angeles Times, 12/8/76 (Pt. IV, p. 26)
Linda Gross

"There are certain people who feel they are old when they reach 25 and spend the rest of their days reminiscing about the good old days.
But Where Is Daniel Vax? . . . is a movie about such people. It is also an Israeli-style *Carnal Knowledge*—without the carnality—about the malaise of middle-aged misogynistic men heightened by their own mediocrity . . .
It is hard to pinpoint what Heffner is mocking the most in *Vax*—the folksinger's Americanization, disillusionment with Israel or middle-aged blues. The main character's arrogant chauvinism is as annoying as his wife's complacency. The dialogue is sardonic but also stilted. Performers seem self-conscious with each other and in their roles . . ."

©Los Angeles Times, 1976.

BYELORUSSIAN STATION

Director: *Andrei Smirnov*. Screenplay: *Vadim Trunin*. Photography: *Pavel Lebichev*. Music: *Bulat Okudijava*. Distributor: *Mosfilm*. Running time 105 minutes. Los Angeles opening December 4, 1976, at the Encore Theatre. Classification: None. Origin: U.S.S.R.

Players: *Alexei Glasirin, Eugeni Leonev, Anatoli Papanov, Vsevolde Safonov, Lyubov Sokolova, Nina Urgant.*

Los Angeles Times, 12/4/76 (Pt. II, p. 8)
Linda Gross

"*Byelorussian Station* is a fine Russian movie . . . about four middle-aged men who are trying to come to terms with growing older in a world where they no longer matter.
With absorbing scrutiny, the film chronicles the day four Soviet war veterans meet for the first time in 25 years at the funeral of a fifth army buddy whom they all 'loved best of all.' . . .
Vadim Trunin's script unfolds with the layered complexity of a novel, the characters showing a depth that extends beyond the film. Trunin eloquently depicts everyday life with humor, warmth and pathos . . .
With compassion, director Andrei Smirnov delivers the pedestrian and poetic while conveying nostalgia and a mood of regret . . ."

©Los Angeles Times, 1976.

CALIFORNIA REICH, THE

Documentary. Directors, Producers, Photographers, Editors: *Walter F. Parkes, Keith F. Critchlow*. Executive Producers: *Marshall C. Whitfield, Karen J. Whitfield*. Running time 58 minutes. Los Angeles opening March 12, 1976, at the Fox Village Theatre. Classification: None.

See Volume 1 for additional reviews

Saturday Review, 10/16/76 (p. 43)
Judith Crist

". . . two young filmmakers—Walter Parkes, twenty-four, and Keith Critchlow, thirty—have come up with a stunning hour-long documentary about the neo-Nazi movement in this country. *The California Reich* is a cool, intense, unsensational, and ultimately terrifying study of the National Socialist White People's Party in three of the four California communities where it is established. It claims 2,000 members in twenty-five cities, and neither Parkes

continued on next page

continued from previous page

nor Critchlow anticipates a takeover tomorrow. But what their film does show is the blue-collar malaise, the economic frustrations, and the psychological confusions that lead ordinary men and women into bigotries and communal hate fests. Quotations at the end of the film from 1923 editorials in *The New York Times* dismissing Hitler and his Nazis as 'comic opera' characters and 'boyscouts on an outing' provide the ultimate terror . . ."

©Judith Crist, 1976.

CANNONBALL!

Director: *Paul Bartel*. Screenplay: *Donald C. Simpson, Mr. Bartel*. Producer: *Samuel W. Gelfman*. Photography: *Bob Collins*. Action Photography: *Henning Schellerup*. Editor: *Morton Tubor*. Music: *David A. Axelrod*. Production: *Cross-Country*. Distributor: *New World Pictures*. Running time 93 minutes. Los Angeles opening September 7, 1976, at several theatres. Classification: PG.

Players: *David Carradine, Bill McKinney, Veronica Hammel, Gerrit Graham, Robert Carradine, Belinda Balaski, Judy Canova, Carl Gottlieb, Archie Hahn, David Arkin, John Herzfield, James Keach, Dick Miller, Mary Woronov, Stanley Clay, John Alderman, Paul Bartel, Roger Corman, Martin Scorsese, Sylvester Stallone.*

Los Angeles Times, 9/8/76 (Pt. IV, p. 13)
Kevin Thomas

". . . Unfortunately, it's simply *Death Race 2000* all over again but devoid of ideas . . .

Set in the present, *Cannonball!* likewise features a transcontinental car race that's just as bloody, even if the contestants confine their mayhem largely to each other. Sponsored illegally, it offers a $100,000 prize for the driver making it first from the Santa Monica Pier to a designated spot in Lower Manhattan . . .

Resourcefully made and boasting competent performances, *Cannonball!* is nonetheless just another of New World's spate of mindless destruction derbies that feature mammoth car wrecks above all else. As a result, it can only represent a

step backward for both Bartel and Carradine. Even so, *Cannonball!* will most likely be a hit at the drive-ins."

©Los Angeles Times, 1976.

New York Post, 9/16/76 (p. 24)
Archer Winsten

". . . The plot, created by director Paul Bartel with the assistance of Donald C. Simpson, is accurately described in the picture's own publicity as a 'free-wheeling, stunt-studded, dented and demented story of a road racer without rules.'

Director Bartel, already known for his specialty of 'mounting motorized mayhem' (*Death Race 2000*), has managed here to do it again in spades.

One hesitates to imagine what this picture can do to inspire teenage wheel-men to leave rubber on the road and bodies in hospitals, but some tribute must be paid to Bartel's ability to pile action on top of action to the ultimate hysteria . . ."

Reprinted by Permission of New York Post.
©1976, New York Post Corporation.

CARRIE

Director: *Brian De Palma*. Screenplay: *Lawrence D. Cohen*. Based on a novel by Stephen King. Producer: *Paul Monash*. Editor: *Paul Hirsch*. Music: *Pino Donaggio*. Distributor: *United Artists*. Running time 98 minutes. New York opening November 16, 1976, at several theatres. Classification: R.

Carrie: *Sissy Spacek*. Margaret White: *Piper Laurie*. Tommy Ross: *William Katt*. Billy Nolan: *John Travolta*. Sue Snell: *Amy Irving*. Chris Hargenson: *Nancy Allen*. Miss Collins: *Betty Buckley*.

Newsweek, 11/22/76 (p. 113)
Janet Maslin

"Brian De Palma's *Carrie* is the horror story of a teen-age girl for whom menstruation turns out to be a curse in more ways than one. The title character, played by Sissy Spacek with luminous grace and minimal hysteria, is a misfit whose fanatically religious mother (Piper Laurie) has neglected to brief her about the basics. When Carrie begins to bleed for the first time in a high-school shower after gym class, the other girls express their sympathy by jeering, cackling and pelting her with sanitary napkins. Carrie is so deeply traumatized that she begins to display telekinetic powers . . . and ultimately avenges herself upon the classmates who are planning to make her the butt of a practical joke at the senior prom . . .

Combining Gothic horror, offhand misogyny and an air of studied triviality, *Carrie* is De Palma's most enjoyable movie in a long while, and also his silliest. De Palma's direction alternates unpredictably between the elegant and the asinine, injecting an absurd lyricism into wonderfully unlikely situations . . .

. . . But De Palma doesn't invest his fancy footwork with enough authority to make it an adequate substitute for more commonplace techniques . . ."

©Newsweek, Inc. 1976 reprinted by permission.

New York Magazine, 12/6/76 (p. 125)
John Simon

". . . *Carrie*, a horror movie with grandiose aspirations to social satire. The horror is effective only once, and the attempts at humor are never very successful and come almost when one is inclined to be moved by somebody's plight, so that the nonjokes yield authentic bad taste. The plot crawls with self-contradictions and improbabilities (even if one grants, as one willingly does, the central notion of telekinesis, the heroine's ability to move distant objects by thought control), and the bad characters are ludicrous while the good ones are saccharine.

Worst of all are the big effects, drawn out to impossible lengths and shot with trashy blatancy . . . The performances are mostly humdrum or worse, except for that of Sissy Spacek in the lead: a touchingly unspoiled, intense, and various creation . . ."

©1976 by the NYM Corp. Reprinted with the permission of NEW YORK Magazine.

Film Information, December 1976 (p. 3)
Suzanne Bowers

". . . Sissy Spacek, so memorable as the young girl in *Badlands*, is physically perfect as Carrie. Her pale, vulnerable, wide-eyed face expresses all the bewilderment and awkwardness of an ostracized teenager trying to fit in with the people around her. But the big surprise is the appearance of Piper Laurie, in her first screen role since *The Hustler* in 1961, as Carrie's mother. Her deep voice, beautiful red hair and odd beauty have been enhanced by the intervening years. She renders as very believable a role that could be ridiculous . . .

The main flaw in *Carrie* is De Palma's exaggeration of details and situations to make a point and sway the viewer's sympathies. But with its excellent acting and tight script, *Carrie* is a well-crafted film that is less slick, more satisfying, *and* more frightening because of its subtle psychological buildup than other recent films of this type . . ."

©Film Information, 1976.

New York Post, 11/17/76 (p. 55)
Frank Rich

". . . *Carrie* is, pure and simply, a screamer of a horror movie, and by all rights it will be De Palma's first huge popular success, bringing him the mass audience that *Jaws* brought Steven Spielberg. And, like *Jaws*, it deserves that success: *Carrie* really delivers its punch, and it does so with style, wit and feeling rather than by slamming us in the gut with the mechanical shock effects of a disaster film or an *Exorcist* or *Marathon Man*.

De Palma reminds us that movie terror doesn't have to be cruel, but can be exhilarating—so exhilarating that you may leave this film wanting to return the next night to relive the horrifying fun . . ."

Reprinted by Permission of New York Post. ©1976, New York Post Corporation.

Village Voice, 11/29/76 (p. 53)
Andrew Sarris

". . . An innocent, ignorant girl traumatized by her first encounter with her own menstrual blood would not normally be expected to be bombarded with a barrage of Tampaxes from her peers. But if one amplifies the visual chorus of leering girls to the expressionistic level of Murnau's *The Last Laugh*, one may be suggesting that internalized guilt can be projected upon the faces of all those around us. Sissy Spacek's Carrie thus comes to represent every hellish memory of high school. And what unfolds in the film is every adolescent dream of revenge . . .

Some reviewers have complained that all this carnage is but the latest example of mindless overkill in the current crop of movies. My own reaction is much milder in that I never believed in the objective of all the people at the prom. It is all a setup, and a very funny one at that . . ."

Reprinted by permission of The Village Voice. Copyright ©The Village Voice, Inc., 1976.

Los Angeles Times, 11/17/76 (Pt. IV, p. 23)
Kevin Thomas

". . . To be sure, *Carrie* is first and foremost an all-stops-out scare show, but it makes its ancient and deadly sex-and-sin equation with breathtaking boldness so that the film becomes a dazzling metaphor for the enduring evils of ignorance and superstition—and the eternality of the supernatural. On the other hand, any of us who, for whatever reasons, were outsiders in school will identify with Carrie and recognize how accurate is De Palma's depiction of teen-age life—a depiction that allows the kids' cruelty to suggest that a primitive savagery lingering in mankind is older than time and ever

continued on next page

continued from previous page

lurking just beneath pathetically vulnerable civilized surfaces. *Carrie* appeals overwhelmingly to the atavistic—but at the same time it's outrageously witty . . ."

©Los Angeles Times, 1976.

The Times (London), 1/14/77 (p. 13)
David Robinson

". . . *Carrie* certainly seems quite deliberately packed with treats and conundrums for intending analytical critics: overdeliberate symmetries of action; little homages to the directors De Palma most admires, not excluding himself—an oddly silly and irrelevant scene of three students equipping themselves with suits for the college prom is there, it seems, only because it is an echo from an earlier De Palma film.

This in-joke fooling, and De Palma's fatal weakness for the showy angle, however daft, is the greater pity since he is in his own right a very capable manipulator of narrative. Even if he is finally defeated by one or two ineradicable inconsistencies in the plot and characters of *Carrie*, he makes a good deal out of Lawrence D. Cohen's script, based on a novel by Stephen King . . ."

©The Times, 1977.

Monthly Film Bulletin, January 1977 (p. 4)
Richard Combs

"More fancy footwork from Brian De Palma, who describes flamboyant circles around his subject while only engaging with it on the most superficial level. The content of *Carrie* is, if anything, even more highly charged emotionally than that of *Obsession*—a charge which De Palma, however, only manages to diffuse by leading his audience on with the gushy lyricism of a shampoo commercial before kicking them in the pants with the knife-wielding hysterics of the crudest Hammer horror . . . With so much artificial energy being pumped into the film, and nearly every scene being turned (stylistically, at least) into a mini-apocalypse, it is not surprising that when the real thing finally arrives—as Carrie unleashes her secret powers at the high-school prom—the effect is not so much cathartic as plainly emetic . . ."

©Monthly Film Bulletin, 1977.

Films in Review, January 1977 (p. 59)
Steve Swires

"*Carrie* is by no means just another variation on *The Exorcist*. What separates them is the difference between artistry and craftsmanship. Director Brian De Palma has so transcended his easily exploitable material as to transform it into a poignant yet in-

creasingly terrifying evocation of the tension between adolescent sexuality and religious obsession. Like the classic Hammer gothic horror films, he counterpoints supernatural forces as external symbols of sexual repression, but his concerns go further. By utilizing the device which distinguished the fantasy films of Val Lewton—that of concentrating on characterization and an accelerating narrative—he underscores the shock effects with sympathy and irony, thereby intensifying their impact . . ."

©Films in Review, 1977.

The Sunday Times (London), 1/16/77 (p. 37)
Alan Brien

". . . director Brian De Palma and cameraman Mario Tosi manage to weave around this fly-blown theme a gauzy, dazzling web of technique, a spectacular cocoon for a black fairy tale, which shamelessly calls attention to the showy brilliance of its own effects. *Carrie* itself is almost a demonstration of telekinesis at work . . .

De Palma wants you to notice his parallels and repetitions, his show-off angles and tricky crane shots, the whole Look-Ma-I'm-A-Director bit. It links him with the young Welles of *Lady From Shanghai*, and other brilliant pot-boilers, rather than the mature Hitchcock with whom he was compared after his earlier film, *Obsession*. *Carrie* is a magnificent piece of hokum for those who like bravura, baroque film-making . . ."

©The Sunday Times, 1977.

CASSANDRA CROSSING, THE

Director: *George Pan Cosmatos*. Screenplay: *Tom Mankiewicz, Robert Katz, Mr. Cosmatos*. Producer: *Carlo Ponti*. Photography: *Ennio Guarnieri*. Editors: *Francoise Bonnot, Roberto Silvi*. Music: *Jerry Goldsmith*. Production: *Sir Lew Grade, Mr. Ponti*. Distributor: *Avco Embassy Pictures*. Running time 125 minutes. New York opening February 9, 1977, at several theatres. Classification: R.

Jennifer: *Sophia Loren*. Chamberlain: *Richard Harris*. Nicole: *Ava Gardner*. Mackenzie: *Burt Lancaster*. Navarro: *Martin Sheen*. Elena: *Ingrid Thulin*. Kaplan: *Lee Strasberg*. Stack: *John Philip Law*. Susan: *Ann Turkel*. Father Haley: *O. J. Simpson*.

Women's Wear Daily, 2/7/77 (p. 16)
Howard Kissel

". . . Think of it—plague germs seeping through
the corridors of a trans-Europe express, the train itself hurtling recklessly toward a faulty bridge in
Poland, a top U.S. army man aggravating both
these problems, Sophia Loren playing a moody
best-selling novelist, Ava Gardner playing the wife
of a German munitions billionaire, the spectacle of
fine actors like Lee Strasberg and Martin Sheen
trapped in kitsch—all in one picture.

To be fair to *Cassandra* (though *Cassandra*
makes no attempt to be fair with its audience), there
are some nice surrealistic moments . . ."

©Women's Wear Daily, 1977.

Los Angeles Times, 2/9/77 (Pt. IV, p. 16)
Kevin Thomas

"'For God's sake, man, don't panic!' shouts U.S.
Army Intelligence Col. Burt Lancaster to brilliant
neurosurgeon Richard Harris soon after the beginning of the big, bad *Cassandra Crossing* . . . a disaster picture quite literally disastrous and so awful
it's unintentionally hilarious . . .

. . . The premise isn't really any better or worse
than for many other formula films, but it's done in
by its silly chatter, except for the most undemanding audiences. Even so, it's fun in a so-bad-it's-good
way, thanks to the driving energy of its Greek-born
director George Pan Cosmatos . . ."

©Los Angeles Times, 1977.

New York Magazine, 2/28/77 (p. 55)
John Simon

"*The Cassandra Crossing* could have been a
good-bad disaster movie if (a) it did not take itself
so seriously, (b) it were better acted and directed,
and (c) it made a minimum of sense. If George Pan
Cosmatos had to write the novel, couldn't he at
least have refrained from cowriting the script—or, at
the very least, foregone the direction of it? And a
basic rule would seem to be: no more than one
disaster per picture. You cannot switch disasters in
midstream and go from a plague-ridden train to the
problems of crossing a crumbling railway bridge.
There are also unforgivable performances by Burt
Lancaster, Richard Harris, John Philip Law, and
(Actors Studio members past and present please
note) Lee Strasberg. The actresses somehow
squeak by. Ennio Guarnieri's cinematography is
good in its flashy way, but Jerry Goldsmith's score
is intolerable . . ."

©1977 by the NYM Corp. Reprinted with
the permission of NEW YORK Magazine.

Christian Science Monitor, 2/11/77 (p. 18)
David Sterritt

". . . The ingredients for excitement are present,
but none are given life by director George Pan Cosmatos (who made 1973's promising *Massacre in
Rome*).

The characters seem to have stepped out of bad
'40s movies—the handsome doctor, sophisticated
wife, huffy matron, sleazy gigolo, etc.—and the film
itself cannot decide between social commentary
and trite melodrama. Matters are not helped by

Sophia Loren shields Fausta Avelli on a plague-infested
Geneva-to-Stockholm train in **The Cassandra Crossing**.

placing the pivotal bureaucrats in a World Health
Organization-type headquarters that seems to be
staffed by three people (did the budget run out before any extras were hired?).

In any event, many stars try hard to make the
silliness work . . ."

Reprinted by permission from The Christian
Science Monitor © 1977.
The Christian Science Publishing Society.
All rights reserved.

Film Information, February 1977 (p. 3)
Peter P. Shillaci

"A trans-Europe express races from Geneva to
Stockholm with a pneumonic plague carrier among
its 1,000 passengers. Fortunately, Dr. Chamberlain
(Richard Harris) is on board to comfort the victims . . .

It's hard to assign the principal blame for *Cassandra Crossing*, but a lion's share goes to director
Cosmatos who collaborated on the tissue of inconsistencies which substituted for a script. It has a
borrowed plot twist (from *Andromeda Strain*), unbelievable characters (Sophia Loren, girl novelist?),
and an ideological mugging (nailing the U.S. with a

continued on next page

continued from previous page

cavalier 'I wouldn't put it past them' type innuendo). The place for a film like *Cassandra Crossing* is on a double bill with *Silver Streak*, especially if the special effects people could stage a crash between both doomed trains."

Film Information, 1977

New York Post, 2/10/77 (p. 13)
Archer Winsten

". . . Three writers, Robert Katz, George Cosmatos and Tom Mankiewicz, with Cosmatos doubling as director, have collected just about everything you can associate with movie drama, action and suspense. Their characters are somewhat obvious in what they say and do, but this is no handicap for an audience known for its response to the familiar. Anyway, germ warfare, especially with a good, mysterious plague, has been a top news story this year after the Legionnaires sickened and died in Philadelphia.

The Cassandra Crossing is too second-hand to be a dazzler, but with all those tested elements of plot and star you can sell it short only if you're looking to be a certified faultfinder."

Reprinted by Permission of New York Post
©1977, New York Post Corporation

CLOCKMAKER, THE

Director: *Bertrand Tavernier*. Screenplay (French with English subtitles): *Jean Aurenche, Pierre Bost*. Based on a novel by Georges Simenon. Producer: *Raymond Danon*. Photography: *Pierre William Glenn*. Music: *Philippe Sarde*. Production: *Lira Films*. Distributor: *Joseph Green Pictures*. Running time 105 minutes. New York opening July 28, 1976, at the Embassy 72nd Street and Quad 4 Theatres. Classification: None. Origin: France.

Michel Descombes: *Philippe Noiret*. Commissioner Guiboud: *Jean Rochefort*. Antoine: *Jacques Denis*. Lawyer: *William Sabatier*. Madeleine: *Andree Tainsy*. Bernard Descombes: *Sylvain Rougerie*. Liliane: *Christine Pascal*. Martine: *Cecile Vassort*.

Los Angeles Times, 7/28/76 (Pt. IV, p. 1)
Kevin Thomas

". . . A watchmaker in the ancient St. Paul section of Lyons, Noiret is comfortably settling into middle age, at peace with himself and his fellow man. However, his contentment is abruptly shattered when the police arrive at his shop just as he's opening up for the day. After many mystifying preliminaries the chief of police (Jean Rochefort) tells him what's going on: His teen-age son (Sylvain Rougerie) is being sought in connection with the murder of a factory foreman.

As the shock begins to wear off, Noiret realizes that he actually doesn't know the youth at all . . .

Tavernier possesses in full strength the truly major director's special talent to absorb us so entirely in the story that we don't realize we're actually going to be asked to question some of our basic moral assumptions . . . Tavernier forcefully reminds us that society as a whole always perpetrates far greater crimes than any individual, no matter how foul his particular deeds may be . . . Noiret, in another outstanding characterization once again symbolizes for Tavernier the bourgeois complacency of an entire nation.

Yet Tavernier refuses to judge his people and instead extends to them compassion in such abundance that we cannot but recognize ourselves in both their strengths and frailties . . ."

©Los Angeles Times, 1976.

New York Magazine, 8/9/76 (p. 53)
John Simon

" . . . *The Clockmaker* cannot be consumed as a popcorn-drenched, Saturday-night movie—though even that way it cannot fail to register. Tavernier's film is more like a poem taking place in a world of details: visual and verbal details, and, above all, envenomed pinpricks of irony. There is nothing 'big' about the film: Physical violence never exceeds inexpert punches among middle-aged men; voices are raised only once or twice, and then quickly slink away; though sadness comes to displace oxygen in the air, no one ever cries. Yet the film is bursting with barely contained moral, social, and political indignation, love that cannot quite find the right words, pain too proud to strip in public . . .

From the overworked, and lately underinspired, Philippe Sarde, Tavernier has elicited a splendid score; fitful and sparing, changing idioms from jazz to baroque, but always remarkably apposite . . . . Jean Rochefort is stunningly able to make a civilized and sympathetic cop still exude an aroma of oppression and malaise; Philippe Noiret is dazzling as the protagonist who goes from stolid decency to contained heroism through intense anger and suffering . . ."

©1976 by the NYM Corp. Reprinted with
the permission of NEW YORK Magazine.

Newsweek, 8/30/76 (p. 74)
Jack Kroll

"*The Clockmaker* is an astonishing performance for a first film. The work of 35-year-old Bertrand

Tavernier, a former movie critic, is also one of the recent encouraging signs that the French film is reviving under infusions of new blood from such directors as Tavernier, Jean-Charles Tacchella (*Cousin, Cousine*), and Claudine Guilmain (*Veronique*). It's interesting that to write his film Tavernier got Jean Aurenche and Pierre Bost, who seem to have written all those absorbing French films of the postwar period before the New Wave, including *Devil in the Flesh* and *Forbidden Games*. The presence of Aurenche and Bost makes a wonderful connection between the classic tradition of French cinema and the new sensibility. Their screenplay for *The Clockmaker*, adapted from Simenon's novel, is a technical marvel that should be pondered by every young screenwriter.

Nevertheless, Tavernier's complex film bears traces of that dangerous virus, bourgeois radicalism . . .

It's too bad this moral complacency flaws an otherwise extraordinary film . . . The acting is superb, especially by Jean Rochefort as the inspector and by Philippe Noiret as Descombes . . .''

©Newsweek, Inc. 1976
reprinted by permission.

Saturday Review, 9/18/76 (p. 42)
Judith Crist

"Bertrand Tavernier, a thirty-five-year-old French critic and cineaste, makes an interesting and impressive debut as director of *The Clockmaker*, based on Georges Simenon's *The Clockmaker of Everton*. Simenon's American-set story of a middle-aged man of orderly life and habit suddenly faced by ultimate disorder has been reset in Lyons, France, and brought to remarkable realization not only by this talented filmmaker but also by Philippe Noiret, one of France's outstanding actors . . .

. . . Noiret gives a largely internal performance. Under Tavernier's hand, the human factor is kept in taut counterpoint to the tight sequences of the manhunt for an engrossing duality in the thriller aspects of the film. Noiret, for the most part, lets the upheaval of a man's roots, the revolution of his moral outlook, the resolution of his emotional ethic seep through a dogged look, a stooped shoulder, the sudden fumble of a once-secure footstep. It is a memorable accomplishment . . .''

©Judith Crist, 1976.

Women's Wear Daily, 7/16/76 (p. 24)
Christopher Sharp

"In the background of Bertrand Tavernier's *The Clockmaker* is the steady but subtle beat of an ideological message. One of the gifts that seems almost native to continental filmmakers is the facility for inserting social argument into films. Often it goes too far and becomes propagandist, but on other occasions we are reminded that the political questions of the times do settle into the lives of the most apolitical people. In the case of *The Clockmaker*, we find an ordinary, non-intellectual man thrust into circumstances that reveal the most cynical aspects of his society.

The clockmaker, Michel Descombes, is played by Philippe Noiret with a potato-faced coolness. We get the impression from Noiret's bland visage that his character will survive his difficulties in somewhat the same way Waterloo meadow had survived Napoleon and Wellington. His face is perfect for the difficult role . . .''

©Women's Wear Daily, 1976.

Film Information, July/August 1976 (p. 3)
Barbara Bauer

". . . Although certainly moving, *The Clockmaker* has been overrated. The faithful adaptation from Georges Simenon's novel of the same name is weak. This is not the fault of director Bertrand Tavernier. Rather, it is due to the fact that Simenon's novels are so short and static they cannot be accurately translated without appearing thin, and even at times boring.

The second fault is one that is common to French films. Their reasoned, distanced approach to life—often found in all forms of French art—can appear unnatural to the American temperament. Here, this characteristic is almost ludicrous . . .

Still, the acting by Philippe Noiret, Jean Rochefort, and Julien Bertheau is exceptional. Tavernier's approach to Simenon is serious and painstaking. The end product, for all its problems, remains worth seeing."

©Film Information, 1976.

New York Post, 7/29/76 (p. 17)
Archer Winsten

"*The Clockmaker*, French prize-winner of three years ago, brings its peculiar subtleties . . . as reward for those who can savor a Simenon crime story refined almost to the vanishing point . . .

The curious effect of the picture lies in its ability to hold one's attention while getting nowhere. This is largely a tribute to the Philippe Noiret performance, a masterpiece of understatement verging on no statement at all. One believes, attends, waits patiently for explanation, just as Descombes does himself, until the picture concludes with crime punished and the father maybe a little farther to the left than he was before.

It is an interesting picture, accurate in place and person, but inconclusive as a whole.''

Reprinted by Permission of New York Post.
© 1976. New York Post Corporation.

continued on next page

continued from previous page

New Leader, 9/17/76 (p. 22)
Robert Asahina

"... first is Noiret's performance itself. It would be wrong to call it brilliant, for it is quiet, subtle and restrained—the very opposite of brilliant—but it would be impossible to praise it too much ...

Sadly, however, Noiret's virtuosity is in the service of a drama that is muddled from the start ...

... the context of the film is unclear. Is it a murder mystery? A psychological drama? A family portrait? While no work of art can be easily categorized, *The Clockmaker*'s generic ambiguity makes it very difficult to locate the film's terms, much less know how to react to its characters and situations ..."

Reprinted with permission from
The New Leader, 1976
© The American Labor Conference
on International Affairs, Inc

CONDUCT UNBECOMING

Director: *Michael Anderson*. Screenplay: *Robert Enders*. From the play by *Barry England*. Producers: *Michael Deeley and Barry Spikings*. Photography: *Bob Huke*. Editor: *John Glen*. Production: *British Lion*. Distributor: *Allied Artists*. Running time 107 minutes. New York opening October 6, 1975, at the Baronet Theater. Classification: PG. Origin: Great Britain.

2nd Lieut. Arthur Drake: *Michael York*. Maj. Lionel Roach: *Richard Attenborough*. Col. Benjamin Strang: *Trevor Howard*. Capt. Rupert Harper: *Stacy Keach*. Marjorie Scarlett: *Susannah York*. Maj. Alastair Wimbourne: *Christopher Plummer*. 2nd Lieut. Edward Millington: *James Faulkner*. Regimental Doctor: *James Donald*. 2d Lieut. Richard Fothergill: *Michael Culver*. Pradah Singh: *Rafiq Anwar*. Mrs. Bandanai: *Persis Khambatta*. Mrs. Strang: *Helen Cherry*.

See Volume 1 for additional reviews

The Times (London), 5/16/76 (p. 37)
Dilys Powell

"*Conduct Unbecoming* ... a version of Barry England's play, belongs to the stage ... The plot

pivots on the unofficial court-martial of a subaltern accused of assaulting a regimental widow (Susannah York); beneath the surface of discipline and good manners some pretty bizarre things are going on. In the slow process of revelation (Michael York is admirably persevering as the defending officer) the film develops considerable tension—and so it ought, with all that talent around: Christopher Plummer, Richard Attenborough, Trevor Howard as the Colonel, a promising appearance by James Faulkner as the accused officer and a fine performance, outraged authority bending to the demands of truth, by Stacy Keach. Anyway if you can put up with an unbelievable solution to the mystery and an exaggeratedly theatrical ending, I think you might enjoy *Conduct Unbecoming*."

© The Times, 1976.

CONFRONTATION (KONFRONTATION: ASSASSINATION IN DAVOS)

Director: *Rolf Lyssy*. Screenplay (German with English subtitles): *George Janett*, *Mr. Lyssy*. Photography: *Fritz Maeder*. Editor: *Mr. Janett*. Music: *Arthur Paul Huber*. Distributor: *New Yorker Films*. Running time 115 minutes. New York opening March, 1976, at the 68th Street Playhouse. Classification: None. Origin: Switzerland.

David Frankfurter: *Peter Bollag*. Wilhelm Gustloff: *Gert Haucke*. Frau Gustloff: *Marianne Kehlau*. Doris Stelger: *Hilda Ziegler*. Zvonko: *Wolfram Berger*. Rabbi Frankfurter: *Michael Rittermann*.

See Volume 1 for additional reviews

Film Information, 4/76 (p. 2)
Dave Pomeroy

"Swiss filmmaker Rolf Lyssy's remarkable second feature film, *Confrontation*, is a study in the psychology of assassination. It is a rich, though stark, film worthy of being dealt with at several levels. Set in Europe of the 1930's Holocaust, it focuses on individual and corporate conflicts in the face of rising Nazism.

Confrontation is an example of life imitating art—a true story of one individual which illuminates passions and conflicts on a grand scale—a particularizing of the universal ...

Confrontation is filmed in black and white with interspersed newsreel footage from the '30's. The excellent editing is accomplished with quick cuts--until the one dissolve at film's end from actor Bollag leaving prison to the real 65-year-old David Frankfurter in Palestine today for a moving, concluding three-minute interview . . ."

© Film Information, 1976.

CONVERSATION PIECE (GRUPPO DI FAMIGLIA IN UN INFERNO)

Director: *Luchino Visconti.* Screenplay: *Suso Cecchi D'Amico, Enrico Medioli and Mr. Visconti.* Based on an idea by *Mr. Medioli.* Executive Producer: *Giovanni Bertolucci.* Photography: *Pasqualino de Santis.* Editor: *Ruggero Mastroianni.* Music: *Franco Mannino.* Production: *Rusconi Film/Gaumont International Sarl.* Running time 122 minutes. New York opening September 28, 1975, at the New York Film Festival, Lincoln Center. Classification: None. Origin: Italy.

Professor: *Burt Lancaster.* Blanca Brumonti: *Silvana Mangano.* Konrad: *Helmut Berger.* Lietta: *Claudian Marsani.* Stefano: *Stefano Patrizi.* Erminia: *Elvira Cortese.* Mother: *Dominique Sanda.* Wife: *Claudia Cardinale.*

See Volume 1 for additional reviews

Sight and Sound, Spring 1976 (p. 120)
James Price

" . . . *Conversation Piece* achieves its chamber music effects by the use of massive wide-screen and a majestically opulent score, and develops its introspective and auto-analytical theme with the aid of a camera style which lingers over faces and furniture and shadows as the Professor, with his magnifying glass, lingers over his paintings. Expensive technical resources which might normally be held in reserve for battles and chariot races are used here for a domestic story about the isolation of the shelf, and what happens when that self is suddenly invaded . . .

In spite of what seem to me to be major weaknesses, *Conversation Piece* is a haunting film, beautiful to look at and listen to. The centre of it all is Burt Lancaster's performance. He makes those familiar gestures with his open hands, which here seem to be attempts at policing the chaos of

events . . . His clipped style, his voice and carriage somehow expressing the control of a barely containable force, gives back to the film the solemnity and dignity which elsewhere is dissipated."

© Sight and Sound, 1976.

COOKIES, THE (LES GALETTES DE PONT-AVEN)

Director, Screenplay: *Joel Seria.* Photography: *Marcel Combes.* Music: *Philippe Sarde.* Distributor: *PRO International.* Running time 100 minutes. New York opening January 1977 at the 68th Street Playhouse. Classification: None. Origin: France.

Players: *Romain Bouteille, Bernard Fresson, Jeanne Goupil, Dolores MacDonough, Jean-Pierre Marielle, Claude Peiplu.*

New York Post, 2/7/77 (p. 16)
Archer Winsten

"*The Cookies* . . . is that rarity, a French character study that is simultaneously funny and serious, pornographic and sad.

Henri Serin (Jean-Pierre Marielle) is an umbrella salesman who covers western and southwestern France as a career but pursues an avocation of painting and an obsession with the beauty of the female behind . . .

The performance of Jean-Pierre Marielle, as organized by Joel Seria, is a compound of subtle suggestion and obsessive sexuality, excellently supported by Fresson, the painter, Pieplu, the traveling seller of religious objects, Bouteille, the priest on a bicycle, and that very pretty, young Goupil, the girl whose face is even prettier than her behind, though it is to be doubted that Henri thinks so. This is a picture to be enjoyed by the few who approach sex as neither holy rite nor routine human practice. The spice of this film is its variety."

Reprinted by Permission of New York Post.
© 1977, New York Post Corporation.

Village Voice, 3/7/77 (p. 39)
Andrew Sarris

" . . . The references to Gauguin are so pointed and frequent that it becomes clear that director-scenarist Joel Seria is attempting to say something about art, life, and society. But what? The tone fluctuates wildly between aimless merriment and unexplained bitterness.

continued on next page

continued from previous page

One of the problems is that the characters never seem to know each other well enough to engage in confidential conversation. The artist, particularly, is compelled to keep his own counsel as he adjusts from one grotesque, unfriendly situation to another. Hence we never know whether the lecher is lurking behind the artist, or the artist behind the lecher. We are never quite sure if this particular artist has any particular talent, or even if it makes any difference in the contemporary world . . ."

Reprinted by permission of The Village Voice.
Copyright © The Village Voice, Inc., 1977.

New York Magazine, 2/14/77 (p. 66)
John Simon

"*The Cookies* . . . written and directed by Joel Seria, makes every effort to be whimsical, touching, and outrageous by turns, but ends up showing mostly lots of effort. Here and there, though, a bright moment peeps through. The plot is a comic version of *The Moon and Sixpence*, even if its umbrella salesman-turned painter does not get any closer to Tahiti than Pont-Aven, and does not even begin to approach Gauguin in talent. Still, the whimsy, on the whole, is more convincing than the pathos, and even the pathos is more so than the basic hold on reality. But Jean-Pierre Marielle has a graceful comic gift, even if he is less good at moving us, and there are juicy supporting bits from several players . . ."

© 1977 by the NYM Corp. Reprinted with
the permission of NEW YORK Magazine.

COOLEY HIGH

Director: *Michael Schultz*. Screenplay: *Eric Monte*. Photography: *Paul Vorn Brack*. Editor: *Christopher Holmes*. Music: *Freddie Perren*. Production: *Steve Krantz*. Distributor: *American International Pictures*. Running time 107 minutes. New York opening June 26, 1975, at the Cinerama and 86th Street Twin II Theatres. Classification: PG.

Peach: *Glynn Turman*. Cochise: *Lawrence-Hilton Jacobs*. Mr. Mason: *Garrett Morris*. Brenda: *Cynthia Davis*. Poofer: *Corin Rogers*. Willie: *Maurice Leon Havis*. Tyrone: *Joseph Carter Wilson*.

See Volume 1 for additional reviews

Monthly Film Bulletin, February 1977 (p. 21)
Jonathan Rosenbaum

"More ambitious and less successful than his exuberant *Car Wash*, Michael Schultz's first feature can be viewed with hindsight as the promising debut of a very talented director, intermittently doing what he can with an uneven and somewhat routine script . . . And apart from such recognisably 'personal' trademarks as a taste for scatological gags and a flair for projecting the more inventive inflectives of black American speech, the mere fact that his two features have elicited such strong *communal* responses from black audiences—expressions of collective delight which are rare commodities in contemporary commercial cinema, which generally traffics in diverse forms of mutual estrangement—makes him a figure and phenomenon to be reckoned with. *Cooley High*, like *Car Wash*, begins as an irreverent, free-floating comedy and develops its more 'serious' concerns (along with its plot) rather belatedly, almost as if they were afterthoughts . . ."

© Monthly Film Bulletin, 1977.

COUNTDOWN AT KUSINI

Director: *Ossie Davis*. Screenplay: *Mr. Davis, Ladi Ladebo, Al Freeman, Jr.* Producer: *Mr. Ladebo*. Photography: *Andrew Laszlo*. Music: *Manu Dibango*. Production: *DST Telecommunications*. Distributor: *Columbia Pictures*. Running time 101 minutes. New York opening April, 1976, at several theatres. Classification: PG.

Players: *Ossie Davis, Ruby Dee, Greg Morris, Tom Aldredge*.

Los Angeles Times, 4/28/76 (p. 17)
Kevin Thomas

" . . . Ossie Davis directs as well as stars as that freedom fighter whose life is endangered by a white mercenary colonel, apparently in the employ of some insidious multinational corporation, and by his own spendthrift nephew. However, one of his key followers, a glamorous, fiery, dedicated revolutionary (Ruby Dee), aided by a black American musician (Greg Morris) on an African tour, save the day.

Shakily plotted, thinly characterized and routinely directed, *Countdown at Kusini* nonetheless gets across some important ideas, mainly the need for solidarity between black people everywhere in the struggle for freedom and dignity . . .

However, for all its pertinent rhetoric--and rich locales--*Countdown at Kusini* is pretty much hack Hollywood formula stuff, suggesting that its American makers weren't all that culturally assimilated themselves.

Morris is ingratiating, Davis has plenty of presence as always, but Miss Dee is unusually flamboyant. Other performances range from adequate to amateurish . . ."

© Los Angeles Times, 1976

Ms., 6/76 (p. 45)
Alice Walker

" . . . a production to be happy about, to learn from, and--with its irrepressible music and nonstop action--to enjoy . . .

The movie is often painful: ideals are betrayed, friends of the revolution are murdered. But it is basically an upbeat, joyous film, with incredible vistas of Africa (filming was done entirely in Nigeria, many of the actors are African), and African ceremonies, music, and customs. One leaves the theater ready to join the next revolutionary battle, not in dejection over how much there is to be done, but in awe of the possibilities for change once an oppressed people decide to rise.

Nearly all the flaws in *Kusini* are both obvious and instructive: Ossie Davis, as Motapo (a composite of Patrice Lumumba, Amilcar Cabral, and Martin Luther King), is essentially detached from the character . . .

Ruby Dee's Leah, Motapo's tough, beautiful corevolutionist, is often distractingly overdressed for her role in a poor, embattled country. Otherwise she is superb, so real as a woman determined to get oppressors off her back that one is moved to reach out and take her hand.

The film's major flaw is the casting of Greg Morris . . . "

© Ms., 1976.

New York Post, 4/8/76 (p. 24)
Archer Winsten

"*Countdown at Kusini* . . . is an African adventure-romance, cum politics, that has the unique distinction of having been produced by the largest black sorority in the world, Delta Sigma Theta. Sad to say, there the distinction ends, for it is not outstanding in other respects, though it does achieve professional standards in the photography of Lagos in Nigeria and in its shoot-'em-down action sequences . . .

. . . This one is not hard to understand. The essentials are almost too easy, the stencil outlines of character and plot being recognizable at all distances from a foot to a mile."

Reprinted by Permission of New York Post.
©1976, New York Post Corporation.

Film Information, 5/76 (p. 6)
Unsigned

"This film presents a serious African issue, the fight for independence against the colonialists, but fails to deal with this issue except on a superficial and banal level.

Ossie Davis directs and stars as Motapo, revered guerrilla leader and liberator who is being hunted by a mad, cigar-chomping mercenary (Tom Aldredge). Ruby Dee is Leah, a loyal revolutionary who enlists the aid of an Afro-American jazz pianist, Red Salter (Greg Morris) to help Motapo escape from the country. A reluctant participant at first, Red's growing attachment to Leah forces him to take a stand for a cause he had not had to fight for before. Routine plot machinations slow down the pace of the film, and the climactic 'countdown' at Kusini is totally without suspense . . . "

© Film Information, 1976.

COUSIN, COUSINE

Director: *Jean-Charles Tacchella*. Screenplay (French with English subtitles): *Mr. Tacchella*. Producer: *Bertrand Javal*. Photography: *Georges Lendi*. Editor: *Agnes Guillemot*. Music: *Gerard Anfosso*. Distributor: *Libra Films*. Running time 95 minutes. New York opening July 25, 1976, at the Paris Theatre. Classification: None. Origin: France.

Marthe: *Marie-Christine Barrault*. Ludovic: *Victor Lanoux*. Karine: *Marie-France Pisier*. Pascal: *Guy Marchand*. Biju: *Ginette Garcin*. Diane: *Sybil Maas*. Sacy: *Jean Herbert*. Gobert: *Pierre Plessis*. Nelsa: *Catherine Verlor*. Thomas: *Hubert Gignoux*.

Saturday Review, 9/4/76 (p. 54)
Judith Crist

". . . *Cousin, Cousine*, a second film (the first released here) by France's Jean-Charles Tacchella, is one of those rare delights you want to see again and again just to share the sheer joy of living, zest for love, genuine affection, all-too-human absurdity, and pure happiness of all those delicious people on screen. Tacchella's is a love story with a twist, a family film about an extensive and extended family,

continued on next page

continued from previous page

a zany comedy that holds firm to its realities—and a complete refreshment for the movie-jaded spirit . . .

Tacchella has captured the mood of the aberrant family that Hollywood once knew so well in such comedies of the thirties as *You Can't Take It With You* and *The Young in Heart* . . .

Tacchella tells their story in novelistic terms, concerned far more with the oddities of character than with the extravagances of the camera, though he is as ready for the trivial sight gag as for the introspective moment. His cast is delightful, with Marie-Christine Barrault, whom you may remember from *Ma Nuit Chez Maude*, a captivating Marthe, and Victor Lanoux, endearing as Ludovic. Marie-France Pisier as Karine, Guy Marchand as Pascal, and Ginette Garcin as the gay grandmother offer fine support . . ."

©Judith Crist, 1976.

Village Voice, 8/9/76 (p. 93)
Andrew Sarris

"Jean-Charles Tacchella's *Cousin, Cousine* seems to have captivated many of my more captious colleagues almost in spite of themselves. I can understand the problem. Even as one is in the process of being enchanted, one begins to sniff suspiciously at the sentimental contrivances of the film. One wants to believe that life and love and sex can be so painlessly civilized even in the midst of a grabby, grubby, middle-class consumer-goods society. One wants to believe also that two nice, sincere, modest unassuming lovers can liberate themselves from all the hypocrisies of family and society. What makes us want to believe these happy fantasies is partly the engagingly plump realism of Marie-Christine Barrault and Victor Lanoux as the blessed lovers, and partly the extraordinary cleverness of writer-director Tacchella's second film in thrusting the two lovers into each other's arms without their having to take the initiative . . ."

Reprinted by permission of The Village Voice.
Copyright © The Village Voice, Inc., 1976.

New York Post, 7/26/76 (p. 9)
Frank Rich

". . . Of course, *Cousin, Cousine* could not function were its stars not sublime—and sublime they are. Miss Barrault (the niece of Jean-Louis Barrault) is a pale, shy beauty, with cornsilk hair and the softest of blue eyes; she metamorphoses from a beleaguered wife into a full-blooded human being in small and amazingly subtle stages.

As Ludovic, Lanoux (who looks not unlike an attractive Paul Sorvino) is a major find. He's not brash—that would turn the hesitant Marthe off—and instead tempers his high-spirited independence with a fetching touch of awkwardness that betrays his own buried vulnerability. Together he and Miss Barrault create a romance that is no less powerful for existing at a modest, human scale. When Marthe and Ludovic fall into each other's arms their love may blind you not only to the essential slightness of *Cousin, Cousine*, but to just about any other care you might have on a summer afternoon."

Reprinted by Permission of New York Post.
©1976, New York Post Corporation.

New York Magazine, 8/2/76 (p. 58)
John Simon

". . . There may be something in the basic mismatedness of the two main couples that is a trifle schematic and improbable; there may be also something oversimplified about the ending, though it is wisely enveloped in ambiguity. But everything in between is both totally believable and freshly observed, down to the very looks of the actors . . .

. . . Nothing could be more filmic than Tacchella's extraordinary pacing made up of those discreet rubatos and accelerandos that help convey the exquisite little eccentricities of *Cousin, Cousine*, and here the expert editing of Agnes Guillemot was of paramount help. Even the interiors and landscapes seem free of premeditation, and Georges Lendi, the cinematographer, uses his often unconventional-seeming subdued or back lighting not because it is unusual, but because that is the way things often are lit, if only we stopped to consider. Gerard Anfosso's music is prankish without being coy, and generally uninsistent. In its least utterances, gestures, or silences, the film is saying something; nothing goes to waste . . ."

©1976 by the NYM Corp. Reprinted with
the permission of NEW YORK Magazine.

Christian Science Monitor, 5/11/76 (p. 22)
David Sterritt

". . . *Cousin, Cousine* has a lot of characters, most of whom belong to a large family that keeps getting larger through marriage and the resulting annexation of cousins. Two of these not-so-near relations meet and fall in love. They decide to keep the affair platonic. Then they throw caution to the wind, since their spouses suspect them anyway. There is no real conclusion to the story, just an insistence that love—the *latest* love—ought somehow to conquer all.

Despite this violation of traditional family values, there's no gainsaying the sparky central performances by Marie-France Pisier and Victor Lanoux. Director Jean-Charles Tacchella keeps the pace fast . . ."

Reprinted by permission from The Christian
Science Monitor © 1976.
The Christian Science Publishing Society.
All rights reserved.

Women's Wear Daily, 7/29/76 (p. 9)
Howard Kissel

". . . Throughout the film, children by chronological definition are constantly warned by their chronological elders to behave. It is the elders, however, who constantly display the irresponsibility, the defiance one expects of bad children. What gives the film its appeal are the marvelous performances. Barrault moves and speaks as exquisitely, as enchantingly as she looks—her face has the delicate features of Catherine Deneuve and sometimes the delicate strength of Liv Ullmann. Lanoux, though a fairly heavy man, is an actor of surprising grace and tenderness—he and Barrault make a beautiful pair. Pisier is the most original comedienne the French have had in years—her wild laugh, her intense but somehow disoriented gaze and the gift she has for delivering funny lines in a way so deadpan that you're thrown completely off balance makes her a riveting actress to watch. The film is directed with a light touch by Jean-Charles Tacchella . . .''

©Women's Wear Daily, 1976.

Newsweek, 8/9/76 (p. 69)
Janet Maslin

''. . . lightweight but very likable new film is a double-edged affair—on the one hand devoted to chronicling adulterous romance, and on the other to having fun with the boisterous silliness of bourgeois family gatherings . . .

Cousin, Cousine is most entertaining when it is a comedy of free-for-all manners, when the families of both couples get together for their regular melees. Pisier, a marvelous comedienne, is the life of every party, whether she is sulking, making announcements like 'I'm only happy in hypnotherapy,' or attempting to slash her wrists in a moment of despair but suddenly finding it more important to fix her lipstick. Tacchella is superb at orchestrating chaos . . . Everyone in the cast seems afflicted with a fine madness. When Tacchella lets the 'man who takes nothing seriously' take full control, *Cousin, Cousine* is fetchingly loony and great fun.''

©Newsweek, Inc. 1976
reprinted by permission.

Film Information, 9/76 (p. 3)
David Bartholemew

''Writer-director Jean-Charles Tacchella gives us a wry, subtly detailed look at a large, provincial French family in *Cousin, Cousine*. The title refers to an extramarital love affair carried on by two cousins, newly, quite distantly related by a marriage that opens the film, and which provides the framework for the story . . .

. . . the film is often very funny, skillfully alternating its moods, sometimes brusquely, as the characters weave into and out of the story and central relationship. Although Tacchella indicates that he is celebrating less-than-perfect human behavior, and he fills his film with children whose emerging cynical knowledge of life is hardly appealing, dis-

criminating mature viewers will find much to appreciate in this keenly observed, excellently acted French view of life.''

©Film Information, 1976.

Films in Review, November 1976 (p. 568)
Marsha McCreadie

''In this movie for today's coupling couples, French director Charles Tacchella's clever *Cousin, Cousine* gives the nod, albeit under special circumstances, to adultery. Fooling around seems both elegant and right, due clearly to the charm of the lead couple: Marthe (Marie-Christine Barrault), a graceful icy-cool blonde with only one ostensible vice—pastry; Ludovic (Victor Lanoux), a beefy type whose only instability (not a bad one) is a propensity to change jobs every three years . . .

The film is partly French bourgeois family drama with a sharp eye for family foibles. The surprise is that the backdrop of normality allows the build-up of a terrific sexuality between Marthe and Ludovic: a relief to see adult sensuality with little sturm and drang! Sequences of passion are intercut by editor Agnes Guillemot with scenes of tender domesticity . . .''

©Films in Review, 1976.

Monthly Film Bulletin, December 1976 (p. 249)
Sue Scott-Moncrieff

''A charming and polished French comedy, *Cousin, Cousine* lightly skims the surface of social comment without venturing into deeper waters. It takes a glancingly satirical look at French middle-class family life, notably in the sequence where the wedding photos taken by Ludovic's daughter, Nelsa, are hurriedly suppressed when it is discovered that she has captured on film the more embarrassing and socially unacceptable aspects of the occasion . . . Hypocrisy is dealt several satirical blows, but Marthe and Ludovic float through untouched. Such a rosy and detached treatment of their relationship becomes a trifle dull in its single-mindedness, not helped by the repeated playing of the carnival mood music. Inevitably, as Marthe and Ludovic ride off into the figurative sunset, one's interest tends to linger with those they have left behind, for all their imperfections and weaknesses.''

©Monthly Film Bulletin, 1976.

The Sunday Times (London), 12/12/76 (p. 35)
Alan Brien

'' 'Family Entertainment' is a phrase to strike torpor into the heart of any parent. But Jean-Charles Tacchella's *Cousin, Cousine* . . . gives the words a new meaning for I can't imagine anyone over the age of 12 being anything but usefully and harm-

continued on next page

continued from previous page

lessly entertained by it. It is about an extended family, a great, warm, greedy, generous, quarrelsome, randy nest of cousins, stepchildren, relations by intermarriage . . .

Most of the plot concerns two couples, recently baptised into the circle, who swap partners. The wicked-looking pair, Guy Marchand, a commercial traveler out to beat Casanova's sales record, and Marie-France Pisier, a narcissistic, self-conscious eccentric, disappear into the bushes, shake hands and end their affair. The two nice ones, Marie-Christine Barrault and Victor Lanoux, both good-looking, sly and slightly overweight, strike up a deep platonic affection driving everyone wild by their proudly guiltless intimacy.

It's a bit of a cheat at the end, for Tacchella's lovers abandon their experiment in extending the boundaries of communal living and depart together. But no one seems overly concerned.''

©The Sunday Times, 1976.

New Leader, 9/27/76 (p. 21)
Robert Asahina

''. . . The universe of the petite bourgeoisie in *Cousin, Cousine* revolves around family weddings, funerals and parties that generate ever larger and more complex networks of involvements. The title and film coyly suggest that adult men and women who instantly become 'cousins' when their families are joined by a marriage can succumb to the temptations of 'incest' without suffering any of its unhealthy consequences . . .

The only way to make sense of *Cousin, Cousine* is to deny that its portrayal of the lovers is at all 'realistic,' and to speculate that audiences are responding to cinematic conventions that differ little from those of American genre films. Admittedly, the film avoids American sexual reductionism and its equally artificial flip side, shallow sentimentalities . . . But its 'realism' is wrought by plot contrivances and caricatures that appear fresh to us merely because they are foreign . . .''

Reprinted with permission from
The New Leader, 1976.
©The American Labor Conference
on International Affairs, Inc.

CRIME AND PASSION

Director: *Ivan Passer*. Screenplay: *Jesse Lasky, Jr., Pat Silver*. Producer: *Robert L. Abrams*. Photography: *Denis C. Lewiston*. Editors: *John Jympson, Bernard Gribble*. Music: *Vangelis Papathanassiou*. Production: *Samuel Z. Arkoff-Gloria Films*. Distributor:

American International Pictures. Running time 92 minutes. New York opening April 22, 1976, at several theatres. Classification: R.

Players: *Omar Sharif, Karen Black, Joseph Bottoms, Bernhard Wicki*.

Film Information, 4/76 (p. 5)
Bea Rothenbeuchner

''Here is a film that might have delivered a biting satirical comment on big business' international financial manipulations and contemporary sexual mores. Instead, *Crime and Passion* is confused and heavy-handed, descending at times to slapstick interlaced with lovemaking of the kind that not so long ago belonged in the ambiance of soft-core porno films.

Considering that Czech director Ivan Passer gave us the highly praised *Intimate Lighting* and the interesting *Born to Win*, one wonders what went wrong during the shooting of this film. One publication noted that a decision to improvise grew out of script inadequacies. This, coupled with editing done after AIP acquired the property, might account in part for the film's unevenness . . .

Unfortunately, Mr. Sharif cannot carry off the embarrassing scenes he is required to play. But, then, not even a David Niven could have saved this film in which *nothing* works . . . except perhaps, a few skiing sequences . . .''

© Film Information, 1976.

Village Voice, 6/7/76 (p. 107)
Andrew Sarris

'' . . . The James Hadley Chase plot is not much to write home about, and Omar Sharif is not the most fashionable leading man these days. Actually, the movie starts in midstream and plunges to its denouement at breakneck speed thereafter. Hence, the exposition has to be sneaked in along the way as the characters flit in and out amid intimations of crooked Swiss banking and kinky sex. Karen Black, Joseph Bottoms, and Bernhard Wicki have a merry old time bedeviling Sharif, but he survives with all the doggedness of a red-eyed, oversexed cocker spaniel . . . For once, Passer's long-suppressed baroque sensibility has a suitable outlet, as *Crime and Passion* turns out to be his greatest exercise in exile to date . . . In his lyrical treatment of consumer-society characters disporting themselves in the sensuous flow of snow and water, in his offhand observation of rococo settings and furnishings, in his light touch with Germanic horror, Passer reveals himself finally as that rarity of rarities: a Continental director . . .''

Reprinted by permission of The Village Voice.
Copyright © The Village Voice, Inc., 1976.

New York Post, 4/22/76 (p. 22)
Archer Winsten

" . . . Passer, in the past a film-maker of serious
intentions, is here running the scales of international thriller-killer nonsense while he has a couple
of major stars, Sharif and Black, at his beck and
call. Nobody emerges with credit, unless you want
to sink yourself into the huge close-ups of Karen's
penetrating eyes and luscious lips.

The scenery and snow rate credits as an assist,
but Passer's descent into the region of the pot-
boiler can only be considered disastrous. Writers
Jesse Lasky, Jr., and Pat Silver probably knew what
they were doing, which is to say, writing to order
and throwing in everything but the kitchen
sink . . ."

Reprinted by Permission of New York Post.
© 1976, New York Post Corporation.

DAGUERREOTYPES

Documentary. Director, Producer: *Agnes
Varda*. Screenplay (French with English subti-
tles and English narration): *Ms. Varda*.
Photography: *Nurith Aviv*. Editor: *Gordon
Swire*. Production: *Cine-Tamaris*. Running
time 80 minutes. New York opening Sep-
tember 14, 1976, at the second International
Festival of Women's Films, at the Cinema
Studio. Classification: None. Origin: France.

Note: There is no cast in this film.

Village Voice, 9/29/76 (p. 91)
Molly Haskell

"The title, *Daguerreotypes*, like much of the film,
is a play on words, with the 'types' of the Rue
Daguerre where Agnes Varda lives comprising the
subject of her affectionate tribute, to them, Paris,
and the inventor of the 'photo-portrait.' It is a slight
but lovely and evocative work, in which one enters
into Varda's feelings and understands precisely
what appeals to her about the musty store window
with old corsets and beauty aids and an inventory
that hasn't been changed since the '50s; the proprietor of the perfume store who makes his own
scents; and especially his mesmerizing old wife
whom some would call senile but is actually halfway
into another realm of existence . . ."

Reprinted by permission of The Village Voice.
Copyright © The Village Voice, Inc., 1976.

DAWNS ARE SO QUIET HERE, THE

Director: *Stanislav Rostotsky*. Screenplay:
Boris Vassilyev, Mr. Rostotsky. Photography:
Vyacheslav Shumsky. Music: *Kirill Molchanov*.
Distributor: *Gorky Film Studio*. Running time
180 minutes. Los Angeles opening November 13, 1976, at several theatres. Classification: None. Origin: U.S.S.R.

Players: *Irina Dolganova, Elena Dropero,
Yetkaterina Markova, Andrei Martynov,
Olga Ostrovmova, Irina Shevchuk*.

Los Angeles Times, 11/12/76 (Pt. IV, p. 26)
Linda Gross

"*The Dawns Are So Quiet Here* . . . is a wonderful Russian movie about heroines during World
War II.

It is the story of five young women gunners (who
are between the ages of 17 and 21) stationed far
from the front in Northern Russia near the Finnish
border in a thick forest, where only an occasional
enemy plane or their own reveries interrupt the
peaceful dawns.

Then, one of them spots footprints in the snow,
and . . . the five spot and intercept a contingent
of 16 German paratroopers who plan to blow up a
railway bridge. All of the women die in battle while
confounding the Nazis . . .

What makes this film a singular achievement is
the very cold and effective contrapuntal imagery in
photography, music and characterization. Vyacheslav Shumsky's photography alternates between
harsh black-and-white war sequences and shimmering memory images. The music by Kirill Molchanov also balances between epic resonance and
sweet songs. During the film, the characters develop from ordinary people into heroines in what
seems to be a most natural progression.

As a director, Rostotsky captures the intimate
intensity and unity of people whose lives depend
on each other.

The five women are fine actresses, as is Martynov as their superior . . ."

©Los Angeles Times, 1976.

DAY THAT SHOOK THE WORLD, THE

Director: *Veljko Bulajic*. Screenplay: *Paul Jar-
rico*. Photography: *Jan Curik*. Editor: *Roger*

continued on next page

continued from previous page

Dwyre. Music: *Juan Carlos Calderon, Libus Fiser.* Production: *An Oliver A. Unger Presentation of a Mundo Film Production.* Distributor: *American International Pictures.* Running time 111 minutes. New York opening January 23, 1977, at the Festival Theatre. Classification: R.

Archduke Ferdinand: *Christopher Plummer.* Duchess Sophie: *Florinda Bolkan.* Djuro Sarac: *Maximilian Schell.* Gavrilo Princip: *Irfan Mensur.*

Film Information, March 1977 (p. 3)
David Bartholemew

"This small-looking, uneven film recounts the events in June 1914 leading up to the assassination of Austrian Archduke Ferdinand (Christopher Plummer) and his wife (Florinda Bolkan), which brought on World War I and marked, as a narrator sternly informs us, 'the end of the Austro-Hungarian Empire and Russian czarism and the beginning of the 20th century.'

The film, however, does not give us enough of the historical background, and director Veljko Bulajic . . . quickly puts us on the side of the assassins (led by Maximilian Schell) as the first sequence shows the royalty gleefully shooting a variety of animals as sport. The acting of the three principals manages to sustain some interest, although not enough to allow us to approach that interesting. cosmic-joke potential built into all historical thrillers . . . that perhaps the moviemakers will change history to suit their own dramatic needs . . ."

© Film Information, 1977

New York Magazine, 1/31/77 (p. 74)
John Simon

". . . a model of everything a historical film should not be. It does not make historical or political data sufficiently clear, it does not involve us in the lives of the participants, it invents some cliche figures (like the Bosnian patriot Sarac, named after a legendary horse and showing rather less intelligence) and stereotypical incidents, and it is shot with a dogged literalness and ponderosity that, though the subject is nominally libertarian, should endear it to all authoritarian heads of state. If you want a more informative and believable account of these events (even though it, too, is fictionalized), I can recommend Hans Koning's novel *Death of a Schoolboy.*

Archduke Ferdinand is played very decently under the circumstances by Christopher Plummer; Florinda Bolkan is regal as always as Duchess Sophie; and Maximilian Schell gives one of his more routine performances as the noble Sarac who does not break under the cruelest tortures . . ."

© 1977 by the NYM Corp. Reprinted with the permission of NEW YORK Magazine.

New York Post, 1/24/77 (p. 19)
Archer Winsten

"*The Day That Shook the World* . . . runs through the preliminaries and main event of the assassination of the Archduke Ferdinand (Christopher Plummer) at Sarajevo on that fateful day, June 28, 1914 . . .

There's not much mystery about what's going to happen since it has all been a part of history, but there's good detail about the procedures and arguments of the three assassins and their fellow conspirators. Things go wrong, and there's also an attempt to call off the attempt because it is seen as the inevitable spark for a world war.

But it did happen, and here it must happen too. What's best about the picture is its re-creation of the time and place, those 60-odd years ago. The performances too are far better than adequate with Plummer every inch the supercilious representative of royalty, Schell a dedicated revolutionary and Bolkan wonderfully decorative, as always . . ."

Reprinted by Permission of New York Post.
© 1977, New York Post Corporation.

DAYDREAMER, THE (LE DISTRAIT)

Director: *Pierre Richard.* Screenplay (French with English subtitles): *Mr. Richard, Andre Ruellen.* Photography: *Daniel Vogel.* Editor: *Marie-Joseph Voyotte.* Music: *Vladimir Cosma.* Production: *Gaumont International-La Gueville-Madeleine Films.* Distributor: *Joseph Green Pictures.* Running time 90 minutes. New York opening May, 1976, at the Juliet 2 Theatre. Classification: None. Origin: France.

Pierre Malaquet: *Pierre Richard.* Guiton: *Bernard Blier.* Lisa: *Marie-Christine Barrault.* Glycia: *Maria Pacome.*

New York Post, 5/27/76 (p. 43)
Archer Winsten

"*The Daydreamer* . . . is a French picture directed by its star, Pierre Richard, and partly written by him. He likes to think of himself as a French Jerry Lewis, and he utilizes broad slapstick comedy in similar fashion.

His story here is that of an advertising underling whose work and schemes go awry with awe-inspiring regularity until, of course, there's that unexpected-inevitable reversal to astounding success . . .

. . . Some easy laughers are going to double up as they get with Pierre Richard in his bumbling pratfalls. Others, like this department, are going to sit there quietly, agonizing as the comedy always tries harder with lessening effect . . ."

Reprinted by Permission of New York Post.
© 1976, New York Post Corporation.

DEADLY HERO

Director: *Ivan Nagy.* Screenplay: *George Wislocki.* Producer: *Thomas J. McGrath.* Photography: *Andrzej Bartkowiak.* Editor: *Susan Steinberg.* Music: *Brad Fiedel, Tommy Mandel.* Distributor: *Avco Embassy Pictures.* Running time 102 minutes. New York opening October 15, 1976, at several theatres. Classification: R.

Lacy: *Don Murray.* Sally: *Diahn Williams.* Rabbit: *James Earl Jones.* Mrs. Broderick: *Lilia Skala.* Reilly: *George S. Irving.* Billings: *Treat Williams.* Baker: *Charles Siebert.* Buckley: *Hank Garrett.* D.A. Winston: *Dick A. Williams.* Arco: *Mel Berger.*

Film Information, 2/76 (p. 3)
Paul Coleman

"Diahn Williams . . . plays a talented cellist and avant-garde conductor who lives on New York's upper West Side. After a late concert, she is terrorized in her apartment by enigmatic drifter James Earl Jones. Police officer Don Murray confronts the drifter and his hostage in a hallway and kills him. The cellist signs a statement with the police affirming that the officer had saved her life . . .

. . . But soon the woman begins to think more clearly about what has happened, and she returns to the police station to change her statement.

Now she remembers what we had seen earlier. The policeman, a law-and-order enthusiast with political ambitions, had reacted cruelly and mechanically. He had shot the drifter needlessly and had imperiled her life more than saved her, she explains. The policeman who had been an instant hero and a symbol for an aspiring mayoral candidate now appears a culprit. She has dashed his future, and he is furious.

A stalking drama ensues as the woman feels the policeman's threatening presence wherever she goes . . .

Everyone in the movie sees their action in black

and white, but director Ivan Nagy is fascinated by the areas of gray. The moody interplay of these shadings presents us with a drama that goes beyond the usual 'urban corruption' or 'stalked heroine' cliches . . ."

© Film Information, 1976.

New York Post, 10/18/76 (p. 24)
Archer Winsten

"*Deadly Hero* . . . has a couple of very distinct advantages over the usual 'bad' cop melodrama.

The cop in question, Lacy (Don Murray), is given a fine performance by Murray, and the man he kills, a black, poetic kidnapper, Rabbit (James Earl Jones), is also very impressive.

In addition, the production is set in New York City, and that's where it was directed by Ivan Nagy. This gives it much of the recognizable look, enough to make you think you're getting some of the smell too . . .

What with the strong performances, intrinsic appeal and sensational activity, the picture keeps you on the edge of your seat. It doesn't rise into any neighborhood of artistic great quality, but it does have those bits and glints that make you stop and pay attention."

Reprinted by Permission of New York Post.
© 1976, New York Post Corporation.

DEATH IS NOT THE END

Director: *Richard Michaels.* Screenplay, Producer: *Elroy Schwartz.* Photography: *Alan Stensvold.* Editors: *Larry Heath, Joan Heath.* Music: *Mort Garson.* Production: *Writer First Productions.* Running time 90 minutes. Los Angeles opening April 11, 1976, at Royal Theatre. Classification: None.

Players: *Elroy Schwartz, Wanda Sue Parrott, Jarrett X, Dr. Ken Dallet.*

Los Angeles Times, 4/9/76 (Pt. IV, p. 24)
Linda Gross

"*Death Is Not the End* is an intense, claustrophobic filmatic exploration of the parapsychological concepts of reincarnation and procarnation (life in the future) . . .

continued on next page

continued from previous page

The film concerns the psychic experiences of two persons: a woman reporter (Wanda Sue Parrott) and a black male laborer (Jarrett X) who are both placed in deep hypnotic trances by the screenwriter (Elroy Schwartz) who also produced the movie . . .

Psychic experiences prove to be static dramatic material. The visions are so deeply personal that the viewer often feels like an embarrassed intruder. After having endured the painful lives and deaths of the two subjects, one is not totally convinced that *Death Is Not the End* is such an encouraging possibility."

© Los Angeles Times, 1976.

DEATH PLAY

Director: *Arthur Storch*. Screenplay: *Jeff Tambornino*. Producer: *Norman Cohen*. Photography: *Gerald Cotts*. Editor: *Arthur Williams*. Distributor: *New Line Cinema*. Running time 88 minutes. New York opening September 1, 1976, at the Thalia and Cinema Village Theatres. Classification: PG.

Karen: *Karen Leslie*. Sam: *Michael Higgins*. Steve: *James Keach*. Harry: *Hy Anzel*. Ernie: *James Catusi*. Linda: *Elizabeth Farley*. Arthur: *Don Fellows*.

New York Post, 9/2/76 (p. 21)
Archer Winsten

". . . Taking into account the basic difficulty of making a plot and characters of this sort seem real—it's artifice doubled and redoubled—author Jeff Tambornino accomplished a surprising tour de force. There's something very believable about the sexual musical chairs that harass these people. Their dialogues sound natural.

Reinforcing this quality are several performances that seem distinctly better than you find in middle or low budget films. It could be that director Arthur Storch is showing in his first picture the ability he has maintained in Broadway theatrical shows like *The Owl and the Pussycat*, *The Impossible Years* and *Golden Rainbow*. Equally possible is the fact that Karen Leslie, James Keach, younger brother of Stacy, and Michael Higgins, a star in *Equus*, are able to give performances that stick in the mind . . ."

Reprinted by Permission of New York Post.
(c)1976, New York Post Corporation.

DELUSIONS OF GRANDEUR (LA FOLIE DES GRANDEURS)

Director: *Gerard Oury*. Screenplay (French with English subtitles): *Mr. Oury, Marcel Jullian, Daniele Thompson*. Photography: *Henri Decae*. Production: *Gaumont International; Mars Films; Coreal Produzione; Orion Film*. Distributor: *Joseph Green Pictures*. Running time 85 minutes. New York opening November 6, 1975, at the Trans-Lux 85th Street and Cinema Village Theatres. Classification: None. Origin: France, 1971.

Sallustre: *Louis De Funes*. Blaze: *Yves Montand*. King: *Alberto De Mendoza*. Queen: *Karin Schubert*. Cesar: *Gabriele Tinti*. Dona Juana: *Alice Sapritch*.

See Volume 1 for additional reviews

Los Angeles Times, 10/12/76 (Pt. IV, p. 14)
Kevin Thomas

". . . More frenetic than funny, *Delusions of Grandeur* is a raucous swashbuckler spoof with De Funes playing the greedy minister of finance to a 17th-century Spanish king (Alberto De Mendoza) and Montand cast as De Funes' likeable, goofy, but morally upright valet.

When De Funes receives a summons from the beautiful Bavarian-born queen (Karin Schubert), he assumes she will be offering him the Infanta's hand in marriage. Instead, she announces she intends to have him exiled for having impregnated her lady-in-waiting.

What ensues is a series of hair-brained calamitous schemes on De Funes' part to regain his lofty position of power . . .

None of De Funes and Montand's shenanigans is very inspired or hilarious, but *Delusions of Grandeur* moves fast and offers a laugh every now and then. Photographed by one of the masters, Henri Decae, the film abounds with sumptuous period costumes and settings in ravishing color. De Funes and Montand do their best with what they've been given, which unfortunately isn't much . . ."

©Los Angeles Times, 1976

DERSU UZALA

Director: *Akira Kurosawa*. Screenplay (Russian with English subtitles): *Yuri Nagibin, Mr.*

Kurosawa. Based on a story by Vladimir Arseniev. Photography: *Asakadru Nakai, Yuri Gantman, Fyodor Dobronavov.* Running time 137 minutes. New York opening October 5, 1976, at the New York Film Festival, Ziegfeld Theatre. Classification: None. Origin: U.S.S.R.

Dersu Uzala: *Maxim Munzuk.* Captain: *Juri Solomine.*

Film Information, November 1976 (p. 3)
Peter P. Shillaci

"This Soviet/Japanese co-production takes its name from a wise old Asiatic hunter from the Taiga who becomes friends with a Russian surveyor mapping the wilds of Eastern Siberia . . .

It is difficult to detect the artistic hand of Akira Kurosawa in a film which so strongly resembles a dozen other Soviet proletarian epics. At times the film is an adventure yarn, with wild rivers to ford and wild tigers to face. At other times, it is a weak attempt at wilderness lore. But most of the time it is a slow epic of men at work, focussing upon courage, persistence and bluff good spirits of the soldiers, who occasionally step into stage lighting and break into songs seemingly scored for the Moscow Symphony Choir.

Kurosawa appears to have lost his judgment in the strange settings of Siberia. His photography remains beautiful, and his action sequences crisp and suspenseful, but in between we wander as if lost, because the famous interior drama that is the Japanese director's forte never penetrates the friendship to extend its significance to other levels . . ."

©Film Information, 1976.

Nation, 10/30/76 (p. 443)
Harold Clurman

"Akira Kurosawa's collaboration with the Soviet film industry and with Russian-speaking actors pays tribute . . . to humankind's power to brave and overcome adversity. Dersu Uzala is the name of a hunter in the wilds of Russia close to the Chinese border. Dersu, an Asian of the region, is a figure of heroic valor and integrity . . .

There is a whiff of 'propaganda' in the film, but it is of the healthy kind. The storms of wind, snow, freezing cold, the perilous breakup of the ice floes are rendered with marvelously convincing vividness. It is exciting as 'adventure' and inspirational in implication. As I watched the men fighting the tempest and other inimical forces I could not forbear thinking: such people are not 'lonely.' They are too busy keeping alive . . ."

©The Nation, 1976.

DEVIL WITHIN HER, THE

Director, Producer: *Peter Sasdy.* Screenplay: *Stanley Price.* Based on a story by Nato de Angeles. Photography: *Kenneth Talbot.* Editor: *Keith Palmer.* Music: *Ron Grainer.* Production: *Unicapital.* Distributor: *American International Pictures.* Running time 90 minutes. Los Angeles opening March, 1976, at several theatres. Classification: R. Origin: England.

Players: *Joan Collins, Eileen Atkins, Ralph Bates, Donald Pleasence,Caroline Munro, Hilary Mason, John Steiner.*

Los Angeles Times, 3/12/76
Linda Gross

"*The Devil Within Her* . . . is a scary English horror movie about the demonic possession of a newborn baby via a prenatal curse administered to his mother (Joan Collins).

The film begins with the difficult birth by forceps of a 12-pound baby who doesn't want to be born. (Could *Rosemary's Baby* have asked for a more apt sequel?) The presiding obstetrician (played by Donald Pleasence with his usual aplomb) is distressed by the infant's size, abnormal strength and violent behavior . . .

Stanley Price's screenplay is convoluted but diversionary demonology, which borrows heavily from *Rosemary's Baby* and *The Exorcist* while creating his own allegory of good versus evil in the guise of the decadent nightclub entertainer versus the virtuous nun.

Peter Sasdy directs with suspenseful but monotone hysteria. Performances by Miss Collins and Miss Atkins are excellent. The bustling locales are well photographed by Kenneth Talbot."

© Los Angeles Times, 1976.

New York Post, 6/24/76 (p. 24)
Frank Rich

"*The Devil Within Her* is approximately the 129th *Exorcist* rip-off to appear over the past two years . . .

It is not the best of a bad bunch and may even be the worst . . .

Since director Peter Sasdy isn't capable of finessing a small budget, *The Devil Within Her* never really provides the cheap violent thrills its story promises. We don't see the furniture bang

continued on next page

continued from previous page

around—we just hear it—and when the child starts to graduate into heavy mayhem, murder is accomplished through all-thumbs trick cutting and careless deployments of red finger paint.

Besides, no matter how often the adults in the film remark about how 'big and strong and well-developed' Lucy's son is for his age, you can't help noticing that the baby who plays the part looks as harmless and frail as a kid in a Johnson and Johnson TV commercial . . ."

Reprinted by Permission of New York Post.
© 1976, New York Post Corporation.

DEVIL'S RAIN, THE

Director: *Robert Fuest.* Screenplay: *Gabe Essoe, James Ashton, and Gerald Hopman.* Photography: *Alex Phillips, Jr.* Editor: *Michael Kahn.* Production: *James V. Cullem and Michael S. Glick.* Distributor: *Bryanston Distributors.* Running time 85 minutes. Los Angeles opening August, 1975, at several theatres. Classification: PG.

Corbis: *Ernest Borgnine.* Dr. Richards: *Eddie Albert.* Mrs. Preston: *Ida Lupino.* Mark Preston: *William Shatner.* Sheriff Owens: *Keenan Wynn.* Tom Preston: *Tom Skerritt.* Julie Preston: *Joan Prather.*

Monthly Film Bulletin, 6/76 (p. 122)
Jonathan Rosenbaum

" . . . If there is anything to recommend this confusing horror exercise, then it surely isn't the direction, which veers throughout from the pedestrian to the stilted. Nor is it the script, which raises more questions in a single reel than it can resolve in three, while satanic effects are piled on at every possible juncture, with gore virtually used to plaster over every gaping loophole. The performances are sufficiently uninspired to make one appreciate Eddie Albert's seemingly bemused amusement in relation to the rest of the goings on, and regret the plot machinations that render Woodrow Chambliss' quizzical charms quickly expendable. But the make-up and special effects work are clearly something to behold, even though they achieve their impact through a rather spectacular form of excess that tends otherwise to bend the film grotesquely out of shape. Ernest Borgnine's transformations into a goat-like incarnation of the devil are splendidly realised . . ."

© Monthly Film Bulletin, 1976.

DIAMONDS

Director: *Menahem Golan.* Screenplay: *David Paulsen, Mr. Golan.* From a story by *Mr. Golan.* Producer: *Mr. Golan.* Photography: *Adam Greenberg.* Production: *Noah Films/Diamonds Production/Orta Films.* Distributor: *Avco Embassy.* Running time 108 minutes. Los Angeles opening January 7, 1976, at several theatres. Classification: PG. Origin: Israel.

Players: *Robert Shaw, Richard Roundtree, Barbara Seagull, Shelley Winters, Shai K. Ophir,* **Yosef** *Shiloah, Gadi Yageel, Jona Ellan, Yehuda Efroni, Bomba Zur, Joseph Graber, Arie Moscona.*

See Volume 1 for additional reviews

New York Post, 10/2/76 (p. 22)
Archer Winsten

"The appeal of *Diamonds* . . . is twofold. It takes a good look at its main locations, Tel Aviv and Jerusalem, and it goes into gratifying detail on the methods used to heist that monstrous hoard of diamonds, a billion dollars worth, give or take a million.

Menahem Golan, producer, director, co-author of the screenplay and sole inventor of the plot, which cannot be revealed lest a surprise be ruined, has here made something more akin to a very short story with a twist than the usual comedy or drama . . .

The picture does keep you awake, and might even make you wonder if you too might like to snatch a billion dollars worth of girl's best friend. Then it really turns around with its moral ending that leaves you with the notion that sibling rivalry operates at all levels, even the richest."

Reprinted by Permission of New York Post.
©1976, New York Post Corporation.

DIRTY HANDS

Director, Screenplay: *Claude Chabrol.* Based on the story DAMNED INNOCENTS by Richard Neely. Producer: *Andre Genoves.* Photography: *Jean Rabier.* Editor: *Jacques Gailard.* Music: *Pierre Jansen.* Distributor: *New Line Cinema.* Running time 102 minutes. New York opening November 3, 1976, at several thea-tres. Classification: R. Origin: France, 1975

Julie: *Romy Schneider*. Louis: *Rod Steiger*. Jeff: *Paolo Giusti*. Legal: *Jean Rochefort*. Lamy: *Francois Maistre*. Villon: *Pierre Santini*. Thorent: *Francois Perrot*.

Film Information, December 1976 (p. 6)
Unsigned

"One of French director Claude Chabrol's ea-gerly awaited films, *Innocents With Dirty Hands* (1975), has been shortened and pushed out into the sexy action circuits as *Dirty Hands* by New Line Cinema, who seem to customarily 'Americanise' their foreign acquisitions before releasing them. The film concerns another murderous bourgeois triangle, this one at play on the French Riviera. Based on a Richard Neely pulp novel, the plotting is extremely convoluted, with sleek Romy Schnei-der conspiring with lover Paolo Giusti to do in im-potent husband Rod Steiger. Chabrol's styling and exquisite sense of color (rendered by his cinema-tographer Jean Rabier), which always inevitably ties into theme, is off-key, perhaps through no fault of his own. We are left mainly with the unsatisfac-tory story and the deadening stridency of Steiger's acting . . ."

©Film Information, 1976.

New York Post, 11/4/76 (p. 26)
Archer Winsten

"*Dirty Hands* . . . is a Claude Chabrol view of man's inhumanity to woman told in terms of a who-dunit that rapidly turns into what-happened. But this is not the end of it either . . .

No one emerges unscathed, though it must be said that some emerge who have disappeared, and some who emerge disappear again. In short, Cha-brol had himself an active chore chasing his charac-ters in and out, up and down, all the while permit-ting them to reveal emotional, selfish and violent sides to their characters . . .

The several reversals of plot eventually inspire the spectator to view the entire picture with sus-picion, which seems to be Chabrol's intent . . ."

Reprinted by Permission of New York Post.
© 1976, New York Post Corporation.

DISTANT THUNDER (ASHANI SANKET)

Director: *Satyajit Ray*. Screenplay (Bengali with English subtitles): *Mr. Ray*. Based on the novel by *Bibhuti Bhusan Bannerji*. Executive Producer: *Mrs. Sarbani Bhattacharya*. Photography: *Soumendu Roy*. Editor: *Dulai Dutta*. Music: *Mr. Ray*. Running time 100 minutes. New York opening October, 1975, at the New York Film Festival, Lincoln Center. Classification: None. Origin: India, 1973.

Gangacharan: *Soumitra Chatterji*. Ananga: *Babita*. Chhuki: *Sandiya Roy*. Dinabandhu: *Gobinda Chakravarty*. Biswas: *Romesh Mukeril*.

See Volume 1 for additional reviews

Commentary, October 1976 (p. 78)
William S. Pechter

". . . a film about a world that's full of death, but a world in which death comes not with sudden violence so much as by stealth: stealing up on one in barely perceptible increments.

Distant Thunder has its faults. Though exquisitely delicate when it keeps to the intimate scale of the man and his wife, it can be perfunctory and un-inspired (montages of newspaper headlines) in sketching the larger social movements in the back-ground; and the symbolic presence of a facially disfigured man who waits in the forest to trade rice for sexual favors seems, at times, an uncharac-teristically easy and even callous stroke (though, finally, even this man seems more victim than predator). Moreover, the ending, with its leap into metaphor, verges on not working, though I found myself pulled along by its power . . ."

©Commentary, 1976.

Los Angeles Times, 4/20/76 (Pt. IV, p. 1)
Kevin Thomas

"Of all the films of India's great Satyajit Ray, his latest, *Distant Thunder* . . . is surely the most har-rowing.

Several young women are happily bathing in a pond in a splendid idyllic setting when some planes fly overhead, suddenly . . . wrenching us into the 20th century. More specifically, it's 1943, and al-though those women pay scant attention to the planes, which are something of a novelty to them, they are harbingers of doom. For it is wartime and Bengal will soon be swept over by a largely man-made famine with the already diminished rice sup-ply being reserved primarily for the armed forces . . .

Ray's imagery has always been striking, and never any more so--or more elegantly stylized

continued on next page

continued from previous page

--than here. Key images--a sunset behind an immense banyan tree, a pair of butterflies against parched soil, etc.--are repeated throughout the film. How ironic is the spectacle disintegrating into utter chaos amid so much lush Garden of Eden-like natural beauty.

As always, Ray's actors seem to live rather than to perform before his camera. Chatterjee is an extraordinarily versatile Ray regular, and Babita is as talented as she is exquisite.''

© Los Angeles Times, 1976.

Cineaste, Spring 1976 (p. 38)
Chris Schemering

'' . . . In a fairy tale romance like this nothing much has really changed, not the couple's civic outlook and certainly not their plumply sensual appearance; neither is noticeably thinner by the end. They're still sacred cows. They have awakened only to social passivity. Their cock-eyed optimism--a mixture of empty bravery and political indifference--will see them through.

This is strange and disappointing coming from a director whose best films deal with the evolving social conscience, the psychology of change. Even stranger is the affectation of the art house equivalent of the Hollywood gloss. The horrible realism of hunger, emaciation, and death are eclipsed by the hypnotizing poetry of Ray's camera--the drifting lyricism, the white heat, the slowly changing rhythms, the softly colored images, and the floating, exotic sounds of the countryside. According to the reviewers it's the latest thing in ambiguity, as if ugliness is more threatening and hideous if it comes gift-wrapped. It achieves the same end--they just starve beautifully, making it so much easier for critics in humanist cloak to be seduced by, rave about and forget.''

© Cineaste, 1976.

DIXIE DYNAMITE

Director: *Lee Frost.* Screenplay: *Wes Bishop, Mr. Frost.* Producer: *Mr. Bishop.* Music: *Styner and Jordan.* Distributor: *Dimension Pictures.* Running time 88 minutes. Los Angeles opening September 1976 at several theatres. Classification: PG.

Players: *Stanley Adams, R.G. Armstrong, Wes Bishop, Christopher George, Jane Anne Johnstone, Kathy McHaley, Mark Miller, Warren Oates.*

Los Angeles Times, 10/1/76 (Pt. IV, p. 13)
Kevin Thomas

''*Dixie Dynamite* . . . fizzles out right away.

It's a violent, numbskull action comedy about a pair of backwoods Georgia sisters (Jane Anne Johnstone, Kathy McHaley) taking elaborate revenge upon a local bad guy (Stanley Adams) who's grabbing up all the land because he's discovered natural gas deposits in the area. Although the girls have some Robin Hood leanings, they don't hesitate to repay one killing with another.

. . . *Dixie Dynamite* rambles and shambles along in incredible fashion. Warren Oates is utterly wasted as the girls' ne'er-do-well pal, and Christopher George is a conscience-stricken sheriff in Adams' thrall.

Miss Johnstone and Miss McHaley are strictly starlets, but Oates, George, Adams and others display unyielding professionalism. Playing George's cowardly deputy, Bishop proves a better actor than director . . .''

©Los Angeles Times, 1976.

DOG DAY AFTERNOON

Director: *Sidney Lumet.* Screenplay: *Frank Pierson.* Based on a magazine article by *P. F. Kluge and Thomas Moore.* Producers: *Martin Bregman and Martin Elfand.* Photography: *Vincent J. Klemper.* Editor: *Dede Allen.* Production: *Artists Entertainment Complex, Inc.* Distributor: *Warner Bros.* Running time 130 minutes. New York opening September 21, 1975, at the Cinema I Theatre. Classification: R.

Sonny: *Al Pacino.* Sal: *John Cazale.* Sheldon: *James Broderick.* Moretti: *Charles Durning.* Sylvia: *Penny Allen.* Mulvaney: *Sully Boyar.* Margaret: *Beulah Garrick.* Jenny: *Carol Kane.* Deborah: *Sandra Kazan.* Miriam: *Marcia Jean Kurtz.* Maria: *Amy Levitt.* Howard: *John Marriott.* Edna: *Estelle Omens.* Vi: *Judith Malina.* Angie: *Susan Peretz.* Leon: *Chris Sarandon.* Bobby: *Gary Springer.*

See Volume 1 for additional reviews

Jump Cut, No. 10/11 (p. 3)
Karyn Kay

''. . . Why is *Dog Day Afternoon* so popular in the cities? Perhaps because Lumet, with a vigilant eye to the new sexual consciousness (both real and professed) of the young, liberal urban audience, has taken the opportune cinematic/historical moment to spring a homosexual hero from the closet. In fact, Lumet teases with tempting script references to *all* the *BIG ISSUES* of the seventies—not only gay rights, but police brutality, Attica and Vietnam—they are red herrings, each and every one. Ultimately Lumet throws over sociology for psychology. He turns *Dog Day Afternoon* into heavy melodrama, a long and wearying case history of the beaten, sobbing, despairing and ultimately powerless anti-hero. In place of an important exploration of sexist America, violent America, unemployed America, inflation America, Sidney Lumet spends his directorial energy guiding Al Pacino to a possible Academy Award . . ."

©Jump Cut, 1976

DOGS

Director: *Burt Brinckerhoff.* Screenplay: *O'Brian Tomalin.* Producers: *Allan F. Bodoh, Bruce Cohn.* Photography: *Bob Steadmann.* Editor: *John Wright.* Music: *Alan Oldfield.* Dogs provided by Frank Inn, Inc. Production: *Mar Vista.* Distributor: *R. C. Riddell & Associates.* Running time 90 minutes. Los Angeles opening February 1977 at several theatres. Classification: R.

Players: *Cathy Austin, Larry Darnell, Debbie Davis, Mike Davis, Linda Gray, Barry Greenberg, Russ Greive, Holly Harris, Fred Hice, Lance Hool, Elizabeth Kerr, Sandra McCabe, David McCallum, Frank Paolosso, Dean Santoro, Eric Server, Jom Stathis, Sterling Swanson, George Wyner.*

Los Angeles Times, 2/25/77 (Pt. IV, p. 24)
Kevin Thomas

"*Dogs* . . . is the latest exploitation picture in which beasts turn upon men. Along with the obligatory grisly special effects this efficiently made little film generates a fair amount of tension and is reasonably diverting. It's one of the better efforts in the genre . . .

Does the dogs' behavior have something to do with the college's controversial linear accelerator—whatever that is—or are the dogs reacting to pheronomes, olfactory stimuli that cause insects, fish and other animals to pack and act with a common purpose? If the cause is the latter, what is its source? One wishes that O'Brian Tomalin's script answered these questions or struck a note of genuine

ambiguity in regard to them, but even so, *Dogs* has a lot of fun scoring human folly . . .

Under Burt Brinckerhoff's lively paced direction a largely unfamiliar cast performs competently enough . . ."

Los Angeles Times, 1977

DOMINO PRINCIPLE, THE

Director, Producer: *Stanley Kramer.* Screenplay: *Adam Kennedy.* Based on the novel by Mr. Kennedy. Executive Producer: *Martin Starger.* Photography: *Fred Koenekamp, Ernest Laszlo.* Editor: *John Burnett.* Production: *Sir Lew Grade for Associated General Films.* Distributor: *Avco Embassy Pictures.* Running time 100 minutes. New York opening March 23, 1977, at several theatres. Classification: R.

Roy Tucker: *Gene Hackman.* Ellie Tucker: *Candice Bergen.* Tagge: *Richard Widmark.* Spiventa: *Mickey Rooney.* Ross Pine: *Edward Albert.* General Tom Reser: *Eli Wallach.* Ditcher: *Ken Swofford.* Gaddis: *Neva Patterson.* Captain Ruiz: *Jay Novello.* Ruby: *Claire Brennan.*

Christian Science Monitor, 4/1/77 (p. 30)
David Sterritt

". . . Apparently the idea was to suggest that nameless bad guys with itchy trigger fingers have political clout. In order to make the atmosphere more menacing—and avoid embarrassing questions of fact—the details are left vague, which may strike you as artistic, cagey, or lazy. By the time the 'domino principle' started operating—with one villain toppling another, to save the man at the top—I was in the market for more old-fashioned storytelling, that would fulfill the promise of those fascinating jail scenes at the beginning. But the message is the meaning in movies like this, even when the message is as old as paranoia itself, and has been more precisely stated in pictures before now . . .

Story aside, Kramer's direction is more restrained than it often is, the cinematography is gorgeous, and the performances are generally deft . . ."

Reprinted by permission from The Christian Science Monitor © 1977 The Christian Science Publishing Society. All rights reserved.

Los Angeles Times, 3/23/77 (Pt. IV, p. 1)
Kevin Thomas

". . . *The Domino Principle* is the latest film to

continued on next page

continued from previous page

suggest the possibility of assassination by conspiracy so far-reaching and elusive as to be permanently indefinable. It touches upon the widespread paranoia of our times and deals with those areas of undercover activity where the distinction between legality and criminality has become impossible to ascertain . . .

Hackman is ideally cast as a forceful man of intense, pent-up emotions, and Candice Bergen receives a pleasant change of pace as his beloved, pretty but decidedly ordinary wife . . . one of her best, most sympathetic portrayals to date.

Widmark and Rooney are standouts . . .

Stanley Kramer, who demonstrates an assured flair for action, has probably never been less preachy and more implicit. *The Domino Principle* is a most respectable effort . . ."

© Los Angeles Times, 1977.

New York Magazine, 4/4/77 (p. 97)
John Simon

"Very little need be said about Stanley Kramer's *The Domino Principle*. Terrible movies tend to start with a preposterous premise and then laboriously work their way to an impossible conclusion. This one, however, starts with an arrant impossibility and works its way to whatever lies beyond and below that. The script, by Adam Kennedy from his own novel, is at least as absurd as other New Paranoia movies such as *Executive Action* and *The Parallax View*, with the incremental detriment of Kramer's utterly banal direction . . .

Gene Hackman struggles manfully with a role totally lacking in substance and consistency . . . Most of the others manage to be even a little worse than their parts . . .

. . . there is also Richard Widmark, a true film actor whom it is a joy to watch. Even when he is doing nothing, as here, he exudes credibility, authenticity, and flesh-and-blood presence."

© 1977 by the NYM Corp. Reprinted with the permission of NEW YORK Magazine

DOWN THE ANCIENT STAIRS

Director: *Mauro Bolognini*. Screenplay (Italian with English subtitles): *Raffaele Andreassi, Mario Arosio, Tullio Pinelli, Bernardino Zapponi*. Based on a novel by *Mario Tobino*. Photography: *Ennio Guarnieri*. Production: *Italian International Film; Les Productions Fow Europa*. Distributor: *Twentieth Century-Fox*. Running time 101 minutes. New York opening October 17, 1975, at the Little Carnegie Theatre. Classification: R. Origin: Italy.

Prof. Bonnaccorsi: *Marcello Mastroianni*. Dr. Anna Bersani: *Francoise Fabian*. Bianca: *Marthe Keller*. Carla: *Barbara Bouchet*. Tonio: *Pierre Blaise*. Francesca: *Lucia Bose*. Gianna: *Adrianna Asti*.

See Volume 1 for additional reviews

Monthly Film Bulletin, October 1976 (p. 218)
Jonathan Rosenbaum

"A lugubrious salad of apparent 'good intentions' strained through cliche-ridden dialogue that is delivered in faulty lip-synch: if *Down the Ancient Stairs* (appropriately named) were ten times easier to digest than it is, it still probably wouldn't add up to much nourishment. In a context where one is invited to gaze at lunatics 'artfully' posed much like the concentration camp victims in *The Night Porter*, screaming memorable lines like 'I want love! I want love!' and accompanied by the usual pretentious *Snake Pit* score equating madness with atonality, one is persuaded that whatever allegory about Mussolini's Italy the filmmakers might have had in mind remains so undeveloped that one could easily imagine Ken Russell filling in all the spaces . . ."

©Monthly Film Bulletin, 1976.

DREAM CITY

Director: *Johannes Schaaf*. Screenplay (German with English subtitles): *Mr. Schaaf*. Based on the novel THE OTHER SIDE by Alfred Kubin. Producer: *Heinz Angermeyer*. Photography: *Gerard Vandernberg*. Music: *Eberhard Schoener*. Distributor: *Peppercorn-Wormser*. Running time 96 minutes. New York opening December 5, 1976, at the Festival Theatre. Classification: R. Origin: West Germany.

Florian Sand: *Per Oscarsson*. Anne Sand: *Rosemarie Fendel*. Das Maedchen: *Olimpia*. Frau Lampenbogen: *Eva Marie Meineke*. Dr. Lampenbogen: *Alexander May*.

New York Post, 12/6/76 (p. 51)
Archer Winsten

"*Dream City* . . . is a German import, with English

subtitles, which creates an imaginary city where people are free to indulge every desire without the limitation of having to make a living . . .

. . . The whole place is ticketed for destruction. As it starts exploding and disintegrating, our hero, Florian, rescues the prettiest female still ambulatory. They make a good run for it, but when last seen were doomed like all the rest of the city.

The film's main thesis, that man's desires, if unchecked, lead to chaos, is here illustrated with better graphics and staging than reason. Even in German, and with the convincing Per Oscarsson, and all these sets, costumes and extras of memorable variety and solidity, the project falls flat in what must be considered a minor disaster."

Reprinted by Permission of New York Post.
© 1976, New York Post Corporation.

Film Information, January 1977 (p. 4)
Suzanne Bowers

". . . the citizenry are, for the most part, a moronic and motley bunch. Order begins to break down with too much freedom, and a city-wide orgy of vandalism, killing and destruction is the final result.

German director Johannes Schaaf and cinematographer Gerard Vandernberg have created some striking images in *Dream City*. However, Schaaf's thematic focus is unclear. He hovers between the psychological and social implications of the dream-come-true, and the political and moral climate such a dream city could engender, and never comes to grips with either. We're left with some imaginative but unresolved situations . . ."

© Film Information, 1977

New York Post, 5/27/76 (p. 43)
Archer Winsten

" . . . The picture falls somewhere between a TV soap opera and a country music movie quickie. Its chief advantage is in the fresh faces, mostly from Texas, which are all around, and the accents that have the authentic twang.

What keeps it from complete success is its ramshackle plot of bits and pieces that never quite decides whether to go for slapstick or burlesque. It does contain elements of all, which reminds you of variety shows attempting to touch all bases and entertain every possible taste.

Drive-In doesn't stay in one place or with one section of the plot long enough for you to get tired of it, but it doesn't get into any of the characters sufficiently for you to care much one way or the other . . ."

Reprinted by Permission of New York Post.
© 1976, New York Post Corporation.

Life for young people in a small Texas town is portrayed in **Drive-In**, a movie full of comedy and country music.

DRIVE-IN

Director: *Rod Amateau*. Screenplay: *Bob Peete*. Producers: *Alex Rose, Tamara Asseyev*. Photography: *Robert Jessup*. Editors: *Bernard F. Caputo, Guy Scarpitta*. Distributor: *Columbia Pictures*. Running time 96 minutes. New York opening May 26, 1976, at several theatres. Classification: PG.

Glowie Hudson: *Lisa Lemole*. Orville Hennigson: *Glen Morshower*. Little Bit: *Gary Cavagnaro*. Enoch: *Billy Milliken*. Alabam: *Lee Newsom*. Spoon: *Regan Kee*.

Monthly Film Bulletin, February 1977 (p. 22)
John Pym

"What little sense of unity this free-style comedy possesses derives largely from the juxtaposition of scenes from the fictional *Disaster '76* (a compendium of recent catastrophe movies) and the less calamitous shenanigans on The Alamo lot engineered by an artfully reversed set of movie 'types' (the vigilante who smokes pot, the boy with greater sexual confidence than his older brother, the gang leader who enjoys fighting less than reruns of TV sit-coms) . . . *Drive-In* remains primarily a salad of intermittently amusing one-take gags, its continuity

continued on next page

continued from previous page

dependent on uninspired repetition . . . and its impetus on a strained and frantic crossing of narrative threads . . ."

©Monthly Film Bulletin, 1977.

Los Angeles Times, 8/11/76 (Pt. IV, p. 11)
Kevin Thomas

"*Drive-In* . . . starts with a solid premise, the chronicling of a rowdy Friday night at a small-town Texas drive-in, and carries it to comically exaggerated heights. It's a shrewdly made exploitation picture, undoubtedly indebted to *American Graffiti* but played very, very broadly to reach the most unsophisticated audiences. Yet as corny as it so often gets, it's consistently funny . . .

Bob Peete's script is inventive, loaded with outrageous homey similes . . . and right on target in its running gag spoof of disaster movies. Director Rod Amateau deftly maintains a heightened but actually carefully controlled aura of reality with the increasingly outlandish shenanigans and also gets sharp performances from his first-rate cast . . ."

©Los Angeles Times, 1976.

DRUM

Director: *Steve Carver*. Screenplay: *Norman Wexler*. Based on the novel by Kyle Onstott. Producer: *Ralph Serpe*. Photography: *Lucien Ballard*. Editor: *Carl Kress*. Music: *Charlie Smalls*. Distributor: *United Artists*. Running time 100 minutes. New York opening July 30, 1976, at Loews State 1 and Loews Orpheum Theatres. Classification: R.

Hammond Maxwell: *Warren Oates*. Mariana: *Isela Vega*. Drum: *Ken Norton*. Regine: *Pam Grier*. Blaise: *Yaphet Kotto*. Bernard De-Marigny: *John Colicos*. Augusta Chauvet: *Fiona Lewis*. Rachel: *Paula Kelly*. Zeke: *Royal Dano*. Lucretia Borgia: *Lillian Hayman*. Calinda: *Brenda Sykes*.

Los Angeles Times, 8/4/76 (Pt. IV, p. 13)
Kevin Thomas

". . . more trash from the same barrel *Mandingo* came from, having been adapted from another of

Kyle Onstott's novels about the bad Old South.

Like *Mandingo*, *Drum* ostensibly condemns slavery but actually uses it as an excuse for salacious miscegenation-inspired sex fantasies. And like *Mandingo*, *Drum* has been lavishly produced yet is hilarious—hopefully therapeutically so—because of its unstinting excesses.

Only vaguely a sequel to *Mandingo*, with Warren Oates taking over Perry King's role as the master of the infamous slave-breeding plantation Falconhurst . . .

If possible, Norman Wexler's script for *Drum* is even more ludicrous than for *Mandingo*, and director Steve Carver, who took over from Burt Kennedy with only four days' preparation, probably had no recourse but to play it for laughs, and at least he keeps things moving at a lively pace.

However, as hilarious as some sequences undeniably are, neither slavery nor the film's Get Whitey message are amusing in the least . . ."

©Los Angeles Times, 1976.

New York Post, 7/31/76 (p. 15)
Frank Rich

". . . The most fascinating aspect of the movie is that it doesn't even have the courage of its scurvy convictions: While designed as a get-whitey picture, *Drum* is just as anti-black as De Laurentiis' *Death Wish*. There's hardly a single black stereotype that doesn't turn up somewhere along the movie's way—and you begin to wonder if the producer might not be trying to accomplish the incredible feat of making a movie that can prey equally on the prejudices of black and white racists. I shudder to think what would happen were the movie's two separate but equal audiences to converge on this potentially incendiary film in the same theater at the same time.

For the record, it should be noted that Paramount Pictures, the distributor of *Mandingo* and originally set to release this film, refused to accept the first, X-rated . . . *Drum* it received from De Laurentiis. Would that United Artists had shown a similar restraint and not picked up the movie for distribution in its current, R-rated form . . ."

Reprinted by Permission of New York Post.
©1976, New York Post Corporation.

The Times (London), 9/10/76 (p. 8)
David Robinson

"*Drum*, directed (more or less) by Steve Carver, is a spinoff of *Mandingo*, pastiche of parody of Deep South costume melodrama. Shamelessly it exploits the factors which explain the success of the prototype: a feeble pretence at outraged historical expose of the abuses of the slave trade provides the excuse for an orgy of wish dreams, and sadism, flagellation, domination, sexuality of all tastes, popular fantasies of negro potency. The racist implications become most complex in the character of the hero Drum (Ken Norton), with his white mother. 'You can't trust a nigger,' concludes Warren Oates as a slave stud farmer, 'when he gets *human* blood in him.' I might comprehend the Whitehouse-Longford lot better if they ever turned their purifying zeal to this kind of thing, which looks fairly pernicious, even when the melodrama dialogue and playing are at their most ludicrously comical . . ."

©The Times, 1976.

Monthly Film Bulletin, October 1976 (p. 212)
Verina Glaessner

". . . painfully apparent that Carver has failed to lend his haphazard selection of key scenes from the novel any kind of perspective. Such themes as the pathological fear of, and fascination with, miscegenation and sexual degeneracy, and the evolution of the primitive capitalism of the first Falconhurst generation into something more veiled but just as nasty, are signalled but never allowed to develop. It is almost as if the sins generally attributed to *Mandingo* were visited threefold upon the hapless *Drum* . . . Further, the sense of a tortured inner life that raised Fleischer's characters so decisively above their pot-boiler origins is evidently lacking in *Drum*, particularly from Warren Oates' Hammond Maxwell. The sole convincing performance comes from Rainbeaux Smith as Hammond's perverse daughter Sophie."

©Monthly Film Bulletin, 1976.

DUCHESS AND THE DIRTWATER FOX, THE

Director: *Melvin Frank*. Screenplay: *Mr. Frank, Barry Sandler, Jack Rose*. From a story by *Mr. Sandler*. Producer: *Mr. Frank*. Photography: *Joseph Biroc*. Music: *Charles Fox*. Distributor: *Twentieth Century-Fox*. Running time 105 minutes. New York opening April 7, 1976, at several theatres. Classification: PG.

Charlie Malloy: *George Segal*. Amanda Quiad: *Goldie Hawn*. Gladstone: *Conrad Janis*. Widdicombe: *Thayer David*. Trollop: *Jennifer Lee*. Bloodworth: *Roy Jenson*.

See Volume 1 for additional reviews

Newsweek, 4/19/76 (p. 94)
Jack Kroll

"Truly mindless entertainment is more rare than you might think, which makes *The Duchess and the Dirtwater Fox* a rarity. It's producer-director-writer Melvin Frank's 33rd movie, and he seems a bit tuckered out in the inspiration department . . . His story (co-written by Barry Sandler and Jack Rose) about a cute little hooker (Goldie Hawn) and a cute little card sharp (George Segal) has a curious hiccupy quality, as if it were written on cocktail napkins and some of them got lost. For example, a gang of bank robbers abducts Segal because he is a smooth ladies' man in a country of hairy stinkpots, and they want him to charm a key away from a banker's fat wife. But all we see is Segal going through the fat lady's bedroom window . . .

Segal is much better than the material Frank gives him, and this is even truer of Goldie Hawn. As the dance-hall floozie high-kicking her way through the fleshpots of the Barbary Coast, she's like a Lautrec that's wandered into a comic strip. Hawn is a natural comedienne, she can really sing and dance, and with her adorable tropical-fish face and sexy body she splendidly updates the mythic figure of the dizzy blonde . . ."

© Newsweek, Inc. 1976
reprinted by permission

Saturday Review, 5/15/76 (p. 52)
Judith Crist

"For old-fashioned mindless comedy-shticks and bits bound together by an erratic story and given gloss and moments of sheer delight by two talented stars--there's Melvin Frank's *The Duchess and the Dirtwater Fox*. Frank serves as producer, director, and co-author with Jack Rose, his longtime collaborator, and Barry Sandler . . . but he, and his cast, are hopelessly hampered by a clumsily obvious chase-story line.

The triumph is in the performances of Goldie Hawn, as the Duchess, a raunchy music-hall performer in search of a better life, and of George Segal, as an inept and greedy gambler. Hawn, allowed at long last to display her song-and-dance talents along with her gift as actress and her irresistibility as a thoroughly delicious sexpot, is just a joy to watch. Segal, relaxed enough to let the talent show through the charm, partners her delightfully . . .'"

© Judith Crist, 1976.

New York Magazine, 5/3/76 (p. 70)
John Simon

" . . . George Segal is not bad at all as a two-bit

continued on next page

continued from previous page

gambler, but Goldie Hawn always comes across as if she were just a little too adorable to be touched by human hands, which is, to say the least, peculiar for the character of a chanteuse cum floozie. Conrad Janis and Thayer David contribute nice bits as unsavory Mormons . . . but there is remarkably cliched cinematography from Joseph Biroc, and hackneyed music by Charles (presumably Cleanwater) Fox, to which Frank and another veteran, Sammy Cahn, have supplied lyrics full of clean dirty jokes. Finally let me warn you that the script is by Barry Sandler, who wrote *Gable and Lombard*, and the shooting script by Sandler, Frank, and Jack Rose––a perfect example of a young Los Angeles filmschool product and two heavy old hands seamlessly joined for the manufacture of unmitigated tripe."

© 1976 by the NYM Corp. Reprinted with the permission of NEW YORK Magazine.

Monthly Film Bulletin, 5/76 (p. 98)
Caroline Lewis

"An impish comedy which apes a variety of styles as it satirizes a profusion of Western stereotypes, with a 'Bluebird of Happiness' whore who poses as a duchess, a bungling gambler who aspires to the tearaway style of more dashing Western rogues, and a faithful steed who continually forgets his cues. But except when they are scoring points off the more obvious cliches, the visual and verbal puns seem rather unsure of their targets, and the film fails to sustain the pace set by a few hilarious scenes. It eventually picks up a maudlin love theme, in earnest demonstration of the multiple ways people may be transformed through love or greed (as the whore and the gambler are accidently sanctified by participating in a Jewish wedding); but as soon as character solidifies into solemnity, the mockery sweeps away and scenes fall flat. The film is at its best when at its zaniest . . . "

© Monthly Film Bulletin, 1976

New York Post, 4/8/76 (p. 23)
Frank Rich

" . . . In keeping with the low humor of the occasion, director Melvin Frank usually aims his camera at Miss Hawn's thighs. Indeed the director is so fixated by his leading lady's legs that he hardly seems to have gotten around to directing his film. The post-production dubbing is often of the quality of a Kung-Fu picture, the stunt men only vaguely resemble the actors they're doubling for: Richard A. Harris' editing gives us a cornucopia of mismatched shots and sudden variations in lighting. This is not professional film making, and it shouldn't be tolerated by a paying audience.

Frank also requires that his stars be too broad for their or his own good––though Miss Hawn, much in the manner of Burt Reynolds when he's in a clinker, finds a way to disassociate herself from the film even as she's trapped within it . . . "

Reprinted by Permission of New York Post.
© 1976, New York Post Corporation.

The Times (London), 4/9/76 (p. 13)
Philip French

" . . . the saddle of Melvin Frank's *The Duchess and the Dirtwater Fox* scarcely smoulders let alone blazes, despite the presence of two gifted comic actors, George Segal and Goldie Hawn . . . The scriptwriters get Miss Hawn off to a good start with a mouthful of cod-German and provide George Segal with an excellent opening line, even if it is one the quotation books usually attribute to Damon Runyon ('The race is not always to the swift nor the battle to the strong, but that's the way to bet'). Thereafter their speech is largely witless and obsessively scatological. The relentless vulgarity of the enterprise suggests that Mr. Frank, having for so long been constrained by the Hollywood Production Code while churning out innocuous comedy vehicles for Bob Hope and Danny Kaye, is still making up for lost time . . . "

© The Times, 1976.

The Sunday Times (London), 4/11/76 (p. 37)
Dilys Powell

" . . . What, one asks oneself, have the Americans got that we haven't got?

For one thing they have got George Segal, and Melvin Frank, who did well with him in *A Touch of Class*, employs him again in *The Duchess and the Dirtwater Fox*; there are too many rather seamy closeups of Mr. Segal, but one can't expect moderation all the time. I call the film a joke because it is a spoof Western––not spoof enough to repel a Western addict, not another *Blazing Saddles*, just a sly look at the cliches of the genre. Goldie Hawn (again America has the advantage; we are low on young and pretty entertainers) plays the dancehall girl to Mr. Segal's card-sharper; and the background is filled in with stage coach staff, hotel clerks and hard-riding pursuers.

There is also a horse; in fact a horse restored to the ancient status of horse-hero. I had an anxious moment when, in one of the charges which I find more and more disturbing in the Western, he (or his stand-in) fell heavily. I hope he was unhurt, for he gave us some of the best anti-heroic passages in Mr. Frank's jape."

© The Sunday Times, 1976.

Film Information, 5/76 (p. 4)
Paul Coleman

"A western with George Segal and Goldie Hawn
practically needs no synopsis. Segal is the
charming heel, as always, and this time around he's
made off with $40,000 in bank robbery loot. Goldie
dithers on the surface and schemes in secret, as
usual, and in this scenario she plays a dance hall
girl out to make a quick fortune. Their paths cross,
natch, and they quickly find plenty of reason to be
on the lam together.

Director Melvin Frank (*A Touch of Class*) plays
each scene to parallel *Butch Cassidy and the Sundance Kid*, and the talents of his two stars hold
together a script that would discourage less daunt-
less performers. George and Goldie bring clever
timing to a gibberish conversation in a stagecoach,
an elaborate Jewish wedding on the frontier, and a
desert chase with desperadoes . . ."

© Film Information, 1976.

Women's Wear Daily, 4/8/76 (p. 12)
Howard Kissel

" . . . *Duchess* is a takeoff on Westerns. It owes
more than a little to the influence of Mel Brooks, but
it has none of the inspiration, the outrageous lunacy
of *Blazing Saddles* . . . *Duchess* gives us mostly
stock stuff--except for a Wild West Jewish wedding, which again seems to reflect the influence but
not the brilliance of Brooks. It is as if somebody did
market research and found if you put in something
Jewish, people will laugh . . .

Duchess is a well-paced film. Frank has directed
his story with more skill than he has written it. He
gets two strong funny performances from George
Segal and Goldie Hawn--but the things they have
to do, however well they do them, are really so ordinary it is awfully hard to get excited about the
movie. Yes, there are millions of people out there
who want nothing more than a relaxing evening with
popcorn and easy laughs--of course they'll like it,
but why should they make a special effort to see it
when, in less than six months, it might be on Home
Box Office?"

© Women's Wear Daily, 1976.

DUELLE

Director: *Jacques Rivette*. Screenplay: *Eduardo
de Gregorio, Marilu Parolini*. Producer:
Stephane Tchalgadjieff. Photography: *William
Lubtchansky*. Editor: *Nicole Lubtchansky*.
Music: *Jean Wiener*. Running time 120 min-
utes. New York opening October 13, 1976, at
the New York Film Festival, Lincoln Center.
Classification: None. Origin: France.

Viva, Sun Goddess: *Bulle Ogier*. Leni, Moon
Goddess: *Juliet Berto*. Pierrot: *Jean Babilee*.
Lucie: *Hermine Karagheuze*. Jeanne/Elsa:
Nicole Garcia. Sylvia Stern: *Claire Nadeau*.

New York Post, 10/13/76 (p. 19)
Frank Rich

". . . a spectacularly empty-headed plea for pure
cinema, but it doesn't even have the full courage
of its convictions: Rivette may think he's made
an honest-to-God anti-narrative movie, but what
he's really done is make a narrative film, which
he's then scrambled haphazardly into chic-looking
incoherence . . .

. . . If *Duelle* were told straightforwardly, it would
be at least twice as boring as it already is.

And, believe me, it's more than boring enough:
De Gregorio's script is a series of determinedly
cryptic conversations written in a style that sounds
like a parody of Girardoux written by Ionesco . . .

The director has tried to create both a 'film noire'
mood piece and an elliptical, metaphysical thriller
out of his material—and he's failed miserably at
both tasks.

Duelle's creepy atmosphere is primarily a function of William Lubtchansky's high-quality cinematography . . ."

Reprinted by Permission of New York Post.
©1976, New York Post Corporation.

EAGLE HAS LANDED, THE

Director: *John Sturges*. Screenplay: *Tom Mankiewicz*. Based on the novel by Jack Higgins.
Producers: *Jack Wiener, David Niven, Jr.* Photography: *Anthony Richmond*. Editor: *Anne V.
Coates*. Music: *Lalo Schifrin*. Production: *Sir
Lew Grade for Associated General Films*. Distributor: *Columbia Pictures*. Running time 123
minutes. New York opening March 25, 1977,
at several theatres. Classification: PG.

Colonel Kurt Steiner: *Michael Caine*. Liam
Devlin: *Donald Sutherland*. Colonel Max Radl:
Robert Duvall. Molly Prior: *Jenny Agutter*.
Heinrich Himmler: *Donald Pleasence*. Admiral
Wilhelm Canaris: *Anthony Quayle*. Joanna
Grey: *Jean Marsh*. Captain von Neustadt:
Sven-Bertil Taube. Pamela Verecker: *Judy
Geeson*. Sergeant Brandt: *Siegfried Rauch*.

continued on next page

continued from previous page

Father Verecker: *John Standing*. Captain Harry Clark: *Treat Williams*. Colonel Clarence E. Pitts: *Larry Hagman*.

Los Angeles Times, 3/25/77 (p. 17)
Kevin Thomas

"*The Eagle Has Landed* . . . with a thud. Yet another World War II action caper, it brings together John Sturges, who directed the highly entertaining *Great Escape*, and writer Tom Mankiewicz, who had a hand in the recent and dreadful *Cassandra Crossing*. Unfortunately, despite all of Sturges' experience and efficiency with handling complicated military logistics, this film is lots closer to *The Cassandra Crossing* than to *The Great Escape* . . .

Handsomely produced on a large scale and involving various locales, including a charming English village, this Columbia presentation is pretty dull business . . .

Mechanical and boring, *The Eagle Has Landed* suggests more than anything else that the World War II action-adventure film may have had its day. After all, as good as it was, *The Great Escape* was made 14 years ago."

©Los Angeles Times, 1977.

New York Post, 3/26/77 (p. 35)
Frank Rich

". . . The particularly crazy thing about Sir Lew's movies is that they all have the same flaws and idiocies; this man is not one who learns from experience . . . *Eagle* is a multi-star pseudo-epic in which all the stars are miscast and in which almost nothing happens . . .

Tom Mankiewicz, who wrote *Cassandra*, also wrote *Eagle*—and a numbing piece of handiwork it is. The film's 'story' is about a group of German paratroopers who, in 1943, attempt to kidnap Winston Churchill—but, of course, Churchill never even appears in the movie . . .

For all the big name actors in *Eagle*'s cast, acting is beside the point here. There are too many characters crammed into the film to allow any actor to develop a sustained characterization . . ."

Reprinted by Permission of New York Post.
© 1977, New York Post Corporation.

The Times (London), 4/1/77 (p. 21)
David Robinson

"The year 1943 is far enough away to be costume period; and if *The Eagle Has Landed* doesn't really look like the reality of the time, at least it recalls vividly the films of 30 years ago. So much so that you are positively startled when someone, in suggesting a rather unmilitary form of punishment, suddenly takes off into seventies' style obscenity.

The film is based on Jack Higgins' novel about a plot to snatch Churchill from a Norfolk weekend and spirit him off to Berchtesgaden to cheer up Hitler, who is facing the prospect of certain defeat.

Even if you allow such a tall story, the film calls for a fairly effortful suspension of disbelief . . ."

©The Times, 1977.

Monthly Film Bulletin, March 1977 (p. 41)
John Pym

". . . That all this falls resoundingly flat is due almost entirely to the mechanical performances of the principals and the unbelievable incidentals of the lavish production: gardens in full bloom in deepest November; John Standing's caricature of a Roman Catholic priest whose early wisecracks render his righteous indignation peculiarly inappropriate; Mrs. Grey (Jean Marsh) far too young to have lived through the Boer War in which she was supposed to have developed her hatred of the British; the implausibility of Devlin, the trained assassin, 'falling in love' and then drawing attention to himself by engaging in a slugging match with his rival Seymour in the village churchyard; the ranting Colonel Pitts, who carelessly sends his men to their death not to save the Allies but to exorcise his mock-comic fury at being posted to Georgia."

©Monthly Film Bulletin, 1977.

EAT MY DUST!

Director, Screenplay: *Charles Griffith*. Producer: *Roger Corman*. Photography: *Eric Saarinen*. Editor: *Tina Hirsch*. Music: *David Grisman*. Distributor: *New World Pictures*. Running time 90 minutes. New York opening May 28, 1976, at the Victoria and UA Columbia 1 Theatres. Classification: PG.

Hoover: *Ron Howard*. Darlene: *Christopher Norris*. Harry Niebold: *Warren Kemmerling*. Big Bubba Jones: *Dave Madden*. Bud: *Robert Broyles*.

Los Angeles Times, 5/6/76 (Pt. IV, p. 20)
Kevin Thomas

"*Eat My Dust!* . . . is a mindless attempt to cross *American Graffiti*--it even stars one of that film's principal players, Ron Howard--with a chase plot. For that matter, this New World release is virtually nothing but a chase. Clean-cut Howard is a small-town youth who, bugged by his overbearing sheriff father (Warren Kemmerling) and infatuated with sexpot Christopher Norris—that's a girl—steals the elaborately customized race car of champion driver Dave Madden that catches Miss Norris' eye at a local competition. Very quickly Howard's joyride with Miss Norris takes on marathon proportions.

It also takes on some very ugly aspects, as Howard tears over the country with his father and his men in hot pursuit. For *Eat My Dust!* suggests that all cops are morons, that anyone over 21 is a hypocrite or fool or both and, above all, that everything—but everything— is for the taking . . ."

© Los Angeles Times, 1976.

ECHOES OF A SUMMER

Director: *Don Taylor*. Screenplay, Producer: *Robert L. Joseph*. Photography: *John Coquillon*. Editor: *Michael F. Anderson*. Production: *Sandy Howard, Richard Harris*. Distributor: *Cine Artists*. Running time 99 minutes. New York opening May 14, 1976, at the Columbia 2 Theatre. Classification: PG.

Eugene Striden: *Richard Harris*. Ruth Striden: *Lois Nettleton*. Deirdre: *Jodie Foster*. Sara: *Geraldine Fitzgerald*. Dr. Hallet: *William Windom*. Philip Anding: *Brad Savage*.

New York Post, 5/15/76 (p. 15)
Frank Rich

" . . . The only honest thing about this movie is its desire to make a buck . . .

The cast is full of high-grade actors, but only Miss Foster manages to survive with her personality intact (despite the fact that the film's lighting makes her look so pasty faced that at any given moment it's difficult to tell whether she's still among the living). Geraldine Fitzgerald, of all people, is stuck with the Godawful role of a God-fearing, nononsense governess, and Miss Nettleton has a crying scene that shouldn't happen to Betsy Wetsy.

Harris walks through *Echoes of a Summer* in a state of moody drear, though whether he's trying to fight off tears of nausea I couldn't say; he also co-produced the film, and while love may mean never having to say you're sorry, I think he owes an apology to anyone who has the misfortune to wander into a movie house where this slow-motion funeral is flickering across the screen."

Reprinted by Permission of New York Post.
© 1976, New York Post Corporation.

Los Angeles Times, 5/21/76 (Pt. IV, p. 16)
Kevin Thomas

" . . . the film impresses through the obvious spirit of commitment and dedication with which it was made. What's more, it does get over its point that parents can be so obsessed with doing the right thing—even when they disagree over what that might be—that they can unwittingly entomb a child while she is still very much alive and even capable of some enjoyment of life. In this instance it takes a 9-year-old boy (Brad Savage), Jodie's only playmate, to make her parents realize that the important thing is simply to live for the here and now, which is of course at base something that most of us should do more of.

Writer-producer Robert L. Joseph's script is highly theatrical, and both children are fiercely, even at times insufferably precocious. But Don Taylor's direction, intense and graceful, draws the best from his fine small cast . . ."

© Los Angeles Times, 1976.

EDVARD MUNCH

Director, Screenplay: *Peter Watkins*. Photography: *Odd Geir Saether*. Distributor: *Norsk Rikstringkasting/Sveriges Radio AB Production*. Running time 167 minutes. New York opening September 12, 1976, at the Festival Theatre. Classification: None. Origin: Norway.

Edvard Munch: *Geir Westby*. Mrs. Heiberg: *Gro Fraas*. Dr. Christian Munch: *Johan Halsbog*. Laura Catherine Munch: *Gro Jarto*. Aunt Karen Bjolstad: *Lotte Teig*. Inger Munch: *Berit Rytter Hasle*. Peter Andreas Munch: *Gunnar Skjetre*. Christian Krohg: *Knut Christiansen*. Vilhem Krag: *Haakon Gundersen*. Hans Jaeger: *Kars Stormark*. August Strindberg: *Alf-Kare Strindberg*. Dagny Iveli: *Isetin von Hanne Bast*. Stanislau Przybyszewski: Ladislaw Reznicek.

Christian Science Monitor, 9/22/76 (p. 22)
Diana Loercher

" . . . Peter Watkins' film *Edvard Munch* is a major advance in the art of depicting artists. It provides a

continued on next page

continued from previous page

model, though flawed, for future films.

Munch, who pioneered the expressionist movement, was born in Norway in 1863, the second of five children in a puritannical bourgeois family. The film focuses on the first half of Munch's life, the childhood and adolescent years which scarred his early manhood with memories of humiliation, sickness and death.

Throughout the narrative the film keeps cutting back to scenes of physical suffering, to confrontations with his stern, repressive father, and to wrenching disappointments in love, which form the leitmotivs in the composition of Munch's intensely emotional paintings . . .

. . . The achievement of the film is that it presents Munch as an authentic human being, not as a romantic stereotype, and thus partly unveils the mysterious transformation of life into art.

To be sure, the film has its defects. The analysis of Munch's creative drive seems at times too facile or contrived, the flashbacks too redundant, and the tone too mordant . . .''

Reprinted by permission from The Christian Science Monitor © 1976. The Christian Science Publishing Society. All rights reserved.

New York Magazine, 9/13/76 (p. 89)
John Simon

''. . . *Edvard Munch* becomes simultaneously a biography, psychography, and iconography of Munch, as well as a kind of *monologue interieur*, verbal and pictorial, of what went on inside the painter's mind.

An undertaking of such boundless, such manic magnitude is clearly doomed to failure, even if spread across the considerable canvas of a 167-minute film. But even if the work is ultimately a failure, it is the most magnificent failure I have seen in years, and one that nobody interested in any aspect of artistic creation can afford to miss.

For this failure comes nearer than any film I have seen to the impossible task of conveying what it means to be a painter, an artist; what creating feels like, and how it is done . . .''

© 1976 by the NYM Corp. Reprinted with the permission of NEW YORK Magazine.

Women's Wear Daily, 9/10/76 (p. 11)
Howard Kissel

''. . . Watkins attempts to answer the questions about how Munch's life and his profoundly disturbing art are related by using an unusual approach—the film uses actors and creates some fictional scenes, but it also uses a narrator, who gives sound, perceptive observations about Munch's technique and development, the complications of his life and relevant sociological data that give us a deeper understanding of seemingly placid Norway.

The film is thus a cross between fiction and documentary. Its goal seems to be not so much to dramatize Munch's career as to understand it. The result is that *Edvard Munch* does not have as great an emotional charge as some lesser biographies do, but it gives one a greater understanding of the subject, which may indeed be a more important objective.

The film is beautifully photographed. Watkins often makes use of the kind of composition he discerns in Munch's work—people in intimate relations with one another adopt poses of alienation or deliberate honcommunication. Though Watkins has kept the 'dramatic' material limited, he gets solid work from his actors . . .''

©Women's Wear Daily, 1976.

New York Post, 9/13/76 (p. 18)
Frank Rich

''It's hard to recall a film as madly—and maddeningly—uneven as *Edvard Munch* . . . For almost three hours, this film whips you back and forth between the sublime and ridiculous: While there are times when *Edvard Munch* illuminates the creative process as few films ever have, there are just as many instances when the movie is so inane as to be laughable . . .

The triumphs of *Edvard Munch* all belong to Watkins—for it is in the film's editing, camera movements and pictorial compositions that its substance is put across. There are few dramatic scenes in the traditional sense, and the cast members (including Geir Westby as Munch) are exploited more for their visual properties than their acting abilities.

And some of what Watkins achieves is amazing, indeed . . .''

Reprinted by Permission of New York Post. ©1976, New York Post Corporation.

Newsweek, 9/27/76 (p. 90)
Jack Kroll

''. . . Peter Watkins' *Edvard Munch* is a welcome event, the cinema's most intelligent attempt to probe and dramatize the mind and methods of a great artist.

Not that it's a total success. England's Peter Watkins is a highly political director who tries to fuse documentary and fiction techniques to illuminate the social forces behind his subjects . . . A certain doctrinaire oversolemnity flaws his vision, and *Edvard Munch* is not entirely free from this. Watkins' ambitious attempt to sketch in the total social, ideological, psychological and esthetic fabric behind the work of Munch is fascinating, but it falls into bathos . . .

The film is sometimes shaky in its overview of art: Munch's work was hardly the 'first rendition of feeling in the history of Western art.' But *Edvard Munch* is the best film I've seen in its depiction of the artistic process—you believe this is really an artist work-ing with real materials under a real creative impulse . . ."

©Newsweek, Inc. 1976 reprinted by permission.

Film Information, October 1976 (p. 1)
Bea Rothenbeuchner

"The creative process has rarely, if ever, been re-created successfully on the screen. But Peter Watkins' filmic portrait of the great Norwegian painter Edvard Munch (1863-1944), one of the founders of Expressionism, is remarkable, not only for its beauty and sensitivity, but also for evoking in the viewer a sympathy for the artist's efforts and an understanding of his work . . .

The cinematography of Odd Geir Saether brilliantly reproduces Munch's outer world and the artist's work, his paintings, etchings, lithographs and woodcuts.

Edvard Munch should be of interest to many people—movie buffs, of course, and artists, anyone even remotely concerned with the definition of artistic creativity."

©Film Information, 1976.

Los Angeles Times, 12/21/76 (Pt. IV, p. 9)
William Wilson

". . . Peter Watkins' *Edvard Munch* . . . is a milestone among feature-length artists' biographies. It scrupulously avoids errors of Hollywood films that act as if artistic obsession can be explained by sticking Jose Ferrer's knees in his shoes.

Watkins . . . uses a quasidocumentary style, with a mixture of professional and amateur performers to try to build a film whose substance is a cinematic parallel of Munch's personal and aesthetic obsessions.

It is the only film I've ever seen about an artist that reflects what actually goes on in the process of artistic creation . . .

The film is a model of rectitude, its structure an excellent parallel of Munch's mind. Watching this worthy exercise, however, is a 167-minute ordeal.

The obsessive repetition of suffocating closeups begins to feel like a money-saving device to reuse footage. The careful re-creation of Munch's activities gives us the feeling Watkins was paralyzed by a bad attack of cultural reverence.

Munch falls into knee-jerk postures of aesthetic awe. The resulting cliches are no less than Hollywood's just because they are the errors of the intelligentsia . . ."

©Los Angeles Times, 1976.

Films in Review, November 1976 (p. 566)
Deirdre Mack

"Illness, insanity and death are the background for *Edvard Munch*, a dance of death called in the film 'a dance of life.' Munch is the Norwegian artist who became famous as a champion of expressionism at the turn of the century in Germany. Geir Westby as Munch and Gro Fraas as Fru Heiberg, the mysterious woman whom Munch loved, an extraordinary influence on his painting, are non-professional actors who give splendid performances.

The biographical film was written, directed and narrated by Peter Watkins. Its running time is 215 minutes, an indication of the loving attention Watkins has given his subject as well as Watkins' inability to be firmer in his editing . . .

Despite the editing limitations, *Edvard Munch* is a major film about a major modern artist . . ."

©Films in Review, 1976.

EMBRYO

Director: *Ralph Nelson*. Screenplay: *Anita Doohan, Jack W. Thomas*. Based on a story by Mr. Thomas. Producer: *Arnold H. Orgolini, Ms. Doohan*. Photography: *Fred Koenekamp*. Editor: *John Martinelli*. Music: *Gil Melle*. Distributor: *Cine Artists*. Running time 104 minutes. New York opening May 26, 1976, at several theatres. Classification: PG.

Dr. Paul Holliston: *Rock Hudson*. Martha: *Diane Ladd*. Victoria: *Barbara Carrera*. Riley: *Roddy McDowall*. Helen: *Anne Schedeen*. Gordon: *John Elerick*. Dr. Wiston: *Jack Colvin*. Dr. Brothers: *Dr. Joyce Brothers*.

Los Angeles Times, 4/28/76 (Pt. IV, p. 22)
Kevin Thomas

"Approaching his home on a stormy night, Los Angeles researcher Rock Hudson accidentally strikes a dog with his car. Carrying the animal into his lab, Hudson discovers the dog is pregnant. He can't save the mother, but he administers a growth hormone to a tiny fetal pup and Zap!—instant dog. What next but to try the stuff on a human fetus?

What happens is revealed suspensefully in

continued on next page

continued from previous page

Embryo . . . a sleek, ingenious sci-fi thriller that is OK until it reaches a gratuitously grisly climax and then goes completely awry in its finale. Along the way, however, it is a reasonably provocative, contemporary variation on the Frankenstein theme . . .

Last seen in *The Master Gunfighter*, the ravishing Miss Carrera makes convincing and finally tragic this exquisite creature who sees herself as a sort of 'nonperson' but who desperately wants to live and attain her rightful sense of identity.

In the most demanding part since the not dissimilar *Seconds* Hudson sustains the film in a far-ranging, demanding role . . .

Embryo . . . is quite a few notches above routine exploitation horror fare . . .''

© Los Angeles Times, 1976.

END OF THE GAME

Director: *Maximilian Schell*. Screenplay: *Mr. Schell, Friedrich Duerrenmatt*. Based on the novel THE JUDGE AND HIS HANGMAN by Mr. Duerrenmatt. Producers: *Mr. Schell, Arlene Sellers*. Photography: *Ennio Guarnieri, Roberto Gerardi, Klaus Koenig*. Editor: *Dagmar Hirtz*. Distributor: *Twentieth*

Century-Fox. Running time 106 minutes. New York opening May 12, 1976, at the Little Carnegie Theatre. Classification: PG.

Walter Tschanz: *Jon Voight*. Anna Crawley: *Jacqueline Bisset*. Hans Baerlach: *Martin Ritt*. Richard Gastmann: *Robert Shaw*. Von Schwendj: *Helmut Qualtinger*.

Film Information, 5/76 (p. 3)
David Bartholemew

'' . . . an obtuse tale of an aging, and dying, police commissioner (Martin Ritt) who has been trying for thirty years to nail a suave, all-powerful criminal (Robert Shaw). The situation is complicated, then brought to a fatal head, when Jon Voight comes into the case as Ritt's assistant.

Like most puzzle or game films, there are few underpinnings to the story to root it in a comfortable or recognizable reality, and part of what is included (especially a character played by Jacqueline Bisset, who moves from man to man) is misjudged in its melodrama and out of place. The film's mystery is not really a mystery (at least not one that plays fair with the audience) and we're left with an air of absurdism which is a bit too studied and smothered in nameless menace . . .

Schell's direction is at times intriguing; the acting is watchable, particularly Shaw, film director Ritt ––returning to the other side of the camera where

Jacqueline Bisset and Jon Voight get involved in **End of the Game**, a murder thriller directed by Maximilian Schell.

he started—and Donald Sutherland, playing a corpse via photograph and tape recording . . ."

© Film Information, 1976.

Christian Science Monitor, 5/20/76 (p. 15)
David Sterritt

" . . . primarily the work of movie star Maximilian Schell, who directed from his own screenplay (written with Duerrenmatt). Schell handles images deftly—the look of the movie is muddy and moody, as it should be.

He fares less well with sound than with pictures, however. The soundtrack is hoarse and careless, marred by unmodulated dubbing and an overall dearth of atmosphere. The script itself makes fuzzy what the novel makes crisp and clear, and throws in bits of sensationalism (some sexual) that are needless and distracting.

The acting is uneven. Voight never gets inside his role as an overzealous criminologist. Filmmaker Martin Ritt (who directed Voight in *Conrack*) looks right in his first on-screen assignment, but shows an unsure grasp of acting niceties. Robert Shaw, by contrast, is absolutely chilling as the evil mastermind, and Jacqueline Bisset makes a lovely foil for all the characters.

All this adds up to a diverting but roughly hewn movie . . ."

Reprinted by permission from The Christian
Science Monitor © 1976.
The Christian Science Publishing Society.
All rights reserved.

Saturday Review, 5/15/76 (p. 51)
Judith Crist

" . . . It's not all luck . . . that *End of the Game* is a very special kind of thriller—pure Duerrenmatt in its sophisticated ironies, chess-game plot, and black undertones, but very much Schell in its introversion, its absurdist and almost surreal scattering of clues, the high style and deep drama of its imaginative evolution. Schell, after all, proved his filmmaking potential as co-producer, co-author, and director of *First Love* in 1970, and fulfilled it with excellence as producer, director, and author of *The Pedestrian* in 1974. Although he appeared as an actor in his first two films, in this one, except for a small, non-speaking role, he has remained behind the camera as director—and put another director in front of it, with superb results.

That director is Martin Ritt, a stage and TV actor whose career was cut short by the McCarthy-era blacklist . . . and who turned to directing . . . But what a glorious on-screen debut he makes as Commissioner Hans Baerlach of the Berne police, an aging, bulging, craggy-faced criminologist with a mortal deadline to meet, but only after a rendez-vous with his lifelong nemesis . . ."

© Judith Crist, 1976.

New York Post, 5/13/76 (p. 22)
Archer Winsten

"*End of the Game*, which boasts it was shot in Berne, Lausanne, Istanbul, Rome and Munich, finds fog and shadowy murder everywhere in this film version of Friedrich Duerrenmatt's 1950 novel, *The Judge and His Hangman* . . .

Directed by Maximilian Schell with strong emphasis on the jump cuts that startle when they occur and add to suspense when they are anticipated, the picture has a good cast to support its rather incredible series of murders . . .

Actually the picture turns into one long mystification with atmosphere galore and . . . good performances by Shaw, Ritt and Voight. Bisset provides a pretty face and figure to make the sex scenes plausible . . ."

Reprinted by Permission of New York Post.
© 1976, New York Post Corporation.

Los Angeles Times, 5/5/76 (Pt. IV, p. 16)
Charles Champlin

" . . . A more addled, overreaching, misjudged, ill-made, wasteful, posturing, uninteresting and tedious little epic has not toddled into town in years.

The biggest applause during the final credits at the press preview was for Donald Sutherland, who is heard but who is seen only as a floppy corpse, which is one way to survive. The only other survivor is Robert Shaw and he appears to have made his own rules of the 'Game,' as it were, and played through.

There are no other survivors—not Martin Ritt (acting, not, alas, directing), not Ms. Bisset, not Voight, not Maximilian Schell (directing, not, alas, acting). Not Friedrich Duerrenmatt, who wrote the originating novel and co-wrote the script with Schell and who makes a cameo appearance as himself . . ."

© Los Angeles Times, 1976.

New York Magazine, 5/31/76 (p. 76)
John Simon

"Another thoughtful and urbane director has come a cropper; I refer to Maximilian Schell with *End of the Game* . . .

Schell . . . has made a film bursting with in-jokes, medium-high camp, obvious melodramatic effects, fancily befogged and deliquescent cinematography—bagfuls of tricks of every kind. He even drags in symbols from other Duerrenmatt works, such as the panther from *The Visit*, here turned into a cheetah—not the only cheater around. Worse, by way of fleshing out a spare novella, he has dreamed up no less than two love stories, one more trite and blatant than the other. No one gives a

continued on next page

continued from previous page

decent performance, and Martin Ritt, a question-able director, proves unquestionably bad as a lead-ing actor. Finally, the film was so poorly post-synched that everyone in it sounds like a talking automaton from which issues a disembodied voice.''

© 1976 by the NYM Corp. Reprinted with the permission of NEW YORK Magazine.

Films in Review, June/July 1976 (p. 379)
Elinor Malone

''. . . Based on Friedrich Duerrenmatt's novel, *The Judge and His Hangman*, this Maximilian Schell-directed film presents most of the weaknes-ses and strengths we're accustomed to from Duer-renmatt: the forthright confrontation between good and evil: the look into the dark corners in the minds and hearts of men: the stilted dialog: the outra-geous formalism of the plot's development, and the loose ends which I suppose are meant to add to the 'mystery.'

No one gives a convincing performance, with Bisset coming closest to that desideratum. Shaw is a paper tiger: Ritt's voice is all wrong: Voight sheds his identity in trying to lose his American twang. Duerrenmatt, as chess player and author, evidently plays himself—a kind of windbag. Schell's direction is overpowered by his respect for the author.''

©Films in Review, 1976.

ENFORCER, THE

Director: *James Fargo*. Screenplay: *Stirling Silliphant, Dean Reisner*. Based on a story by Gail Morgan Hickman and S. W. Schurr. Producer: *Robert Daley*. Photography: *Charles W. Short*. Editors: *Ferris Webster, Joel Cox*. Music: *Jerry Fielding*. Distributor: *Warner Bros*. Running time 96 minutes. New York opening December 22, 1976, at several the-atres. Classification: R.

Harry Callahan: *Clint Eastwood*. Lieutenant Bressler: *Harry Guardino*. Captain McKay: *Bradford Dillman*. DiGeorgio: *John Mitchum*. Bobby Maxwell: *DeVeren Bookwalter*. Mayor: *John Crawford*. Kate Moore: *Tyne Daly*.

Village Voice, 1/24/77 (p. 45)
Andrew Sarris

''. . . the basic thematic thrust of *The Enforcer* re-mains cynical, right-wing individualism, directed both at vote-grubbing politicians and thrill-seeking punks. And there is always the feeling that East-wood has ridden in from the deserts or the moun-tains or the valleys to bring frontier justice to San Francisco, and this most beautiful of cities has never looked more beguiling than it does in *The En-forcer*. It is as if a yearning for purity and innocence had infiltrated every frame of the film. It is the yearn-ing, unfortunately, of a man, not of the city . . . Harry glorifies the victories of the lone avenger who seems to ride off into the sunset even when he is driving a squad car . . .''

Reprinted by permission of The Village Voice. Copyright © The Village Voice, Inc., 1977.

Films in Review, February 1977 (p. 118)
DeWitt Bodeen

''A Clint Eastwood film is not only always loaded with action, but it has the advantage of having in Eastwood the best re-actor in the business. His new feature, *The Enforcer*, is another exploit in the vio-lent, dangerous life of that intrepid San Francisco law officer named Harry Callahan, who may be driven to taking the law into his own hands, but you cannot deny that the justice he wrenches from his action is not only morally right but socially benefi-cial . . .

Eastwood has selected some extremely good players to act with him: Harry Guardino, Bradford Dillman, John Mitchum, DeVeren Bookwalter (a baby-faced killer). Tyne Daly, an earnest and tidy young lady, is his partner in law enforcement. *The Enforcer* is a money winner, and for fast-moving entertainment, look Eastwood's way.''

©Films in Review, 1977.

Ms., March 1977 (p. 32)
Marjorie Rosen

''. . . As for Inspector Kate Moore, screenwriters Stirling Silliphant and Dean Reisner and director James Fargo may have doomed her, but they have at least doomed her to 'die like a man'—coura-geously. And for the space of her life, they have fashioned a heroine of steel and gut and innocence. In a film dominated by the long, tall, silent, craggy, tough self-sufficient Eastwood machismo, Kate Moore is the central element that fascinates. She of-fers him a unique screen partnership, one without romance, without sexual tradeoffs or even innuen-dos. Kate Moore invades masculine turf and insists on playing by the established rules.

Actress Tyne Daly gives us a heroine who's both earnest and mischievous. Like Glenda Jackson or Katherine Hepburn, she stubbornly remains her-self—streamlined, substantial, and unadorned; in short, refreshing. In a medium which dishes women out like holiday confection, Daly presents a heady and uncompromising alternative to the usual drivel . . ."

©Ms., 1977.

Monthly Film Bulletin, February 1977 (p. 23)
Richard Combs

"This second carbon of the Dirty Harry story is faint to the point of invisibility and although James Fargo, directing his first feature, dutifully builds the film around Eastwood's unyielding macho presence, Harry now looks as if he might be just one of the blue-coated legion from the box. The outrageousness of the figure on his first appearance—as both conductor and expiator of the varieties of urban alienation, of impotence and paranoia on many levels—was turned into the simpler stuff of myth for *Magnum Force*, and in clearing the decks for 'his epic version of cops and robbers, John Milius seems unthinkingly to have pushed Harry into the Establishment corner, as a common, fascistic organisation man. His position there is solidified, not to say calcified, by *The Enforcer* . . ."

©Monthly Film Bulletin, 1977.

The Sunday Times (London), 1/2/77 (p. 36)
Alan Brien

". . . Dirty Harry, the West Coast cop . . . once again turns out to be a one-man, anti-crime wave in *The Enforcer* . . . Eastwood tramples through San Francisco like a clean-shaven, foreshortened King Kong.

Harry's idea of freeing hostages from a commandeered liquor store is to smash his police vehicle into the frontage and erupt shooting through the windshield—writing off car, shop, hostages and holdup men, leaving the City to meet several million-dollar damage suits . . .

Director James Fargo whips us along in Harry's picturesque wake, through many breathlessly staged scenes of callous bloodshed by either side. Everywhere that Harry goes—the phrase is from the notably salty, bitter-tongued script by Stirling Silliphant and Dean Reisner—he is 'as welcome as a turd in a swimming pool.' Right-wing vigilante or radical undercover terrorist (there are clues pointing both ways), Dirty Harry is as exciting to watch as he would be appalling to encounter."

© The Sunday Times, 1977.

Newsweek, 1/10/77 (p. 64)
Janet Maslin

". . . The gore has now become so gratuitous that Harry has begun to look like a trigger-happy fool.

One of the movie's early sequences, in which Harry jeopardizes the hostages held by three armed robbers by crashing a car into the liquor store where they are holed up, makes it painfully clear that he's not as clever as he used to be. Later his work gets sloppier and his politics grow ever more strident . . .

. . . The movie is laced with jokes about Harry's humiliation at having to work with a broad, but his prejudice is made to seem so Neanderthal that the routine backfires enough to be funny . . ."

© Newsweek, Inc. 1977
reprinted by permission.

Los Angeles Times, 12/22/76 (Pt. IV, p. 15)
Kevin Thomas

"*The Enforcer* . . . is Clint Eastwood's third and arguably best 'Dirty Harry' movie. To be sure, Eastwood's Harry Callahan, veteran San Francisco Police Department homicide inspector, is just as tough and ornery as ever, but this time he's been presented with unprecedented humor . . .

Written by various hands, *The Enforcer*, which boasts an exceptionally fine Jerry Fielding jazz score, marks a terrific directorial debut for James Fargo, who has been Eastwood's first assistant on several films. Eastwood never stints on quality, so San Francisco's photogenic locales are utilized to full advantage, and he is backed by a good cast . . ."

©Los Angeles Times, 1976.

Film Information, January 1977 (p. 2)
William F. Fore

"A new low in mindless violence is reached in this film, which is so bad that it would be funny if it were not for the gut-thumping killings from beginning to end.

Clint Eastwood is Harry Callahan, a San Francisco cop who . . . shows . . . how the law should be enforced, and along the way we encounter some of the most brutalizing violence yet to come to the screen. There is not even a decent plot to relieve the gore.

The Enforcer is particularly objectionable because the filmmakers consciously put the viewer in the role of the murderer . . ."

© Film Information, 1977.

EVERY MAN FOR HIMSELF AND GOD AGAINST ALL (JEDER FUR SICH UND GOTT GEGEN ALLE)

Director: *Werner Herzog.* Screenplay (German with English subtitles): *Mr. Herzog.* Photography: *Jorg Schmidt-Reitwein.* Editor:

continued on next page

continued from previous page

Beate Mainka-Jellinghaus. Production: Werner Herzog Filmproduction. Running time 110 minutes. New York opening September 28, 1975, at the New York Film Festival, Lincoln Center. Classification: None. Origin: Germany.

Kaspar: Bruno S. Daimer: Walter Ladengast. Kathe: Brigitte Mira. Unknown man: Hans Musaus. Circus director: Willy Semmelcogge. Lord Stanhope: Michael Kroecher. Captain: Henry van Lyck.

See Volume 1 for additional reviews

Los Angeles Times, 12/8/76 (Pt. IV, p. 26)
Charles Champlin

" . . . Herzog opens and closes his film on an undulating meadow of tall grass, billowing in a strong wind like the face of the sea. It is a perfect impressionist image—ambiguous, timeless, pastoral, threatening—for the haunting but often surprisingly funny story. (Hauser was a natural man, earthy and direct, in one scene demolishing a pompous theological pedant with an incisive stroke of common sense.)

Much of the film's sympathetic power stems from Herzog's inspired casting of Hauser. He is a non-actor identified only as Bruno S. and his own story is in its contemporary way as troubling as Hauser's. He is the illegitimate son of a prostitute who placed him in a mental institution when he was 3, evidently not because he was disturbed or retarded but because she couldn't take care of him and the asylum would . . .''

©Los Angeles Times, 1976.

EXHIBITION

Director: Jean Francois Davy. Photography: Roger Fellaus. Editor: Christel Micha. Production: Contrechamp. Running time 118 minutes. New York opening October 5, 1975, at the New York Film Festival, Lincoln Center. Classification: None. Origin: France

Players:Claudine Beccarie, Benoit Archenoui, Frederique Barrat, Beatrice Harnois, Michel Dauba, Patrick Segalas, Ellen Coupey, Mandarine, Didier.

See Volume 1 for additional reviews

Cineaste, Spring 1976 (p. 42)
Doris Toumarkine

" . . . If Jean-François Davy's documentary does not always seem to be telling us the truth, then can his documentary style save the integrity of the film? Technically, Exhibition is competent, well-shot, fairly well-edited and well-recorded. The blow-up from 16mm to 35mm is superb . . . The inexcusable problem of the film as a documentary is its structure. There is too much gratuitous hard-core footage grafted onto the cinema-verite elements. The overlong and too frequent sex scenes interfere with the film's momentum and with the illumination of its main character . . . Some of this footage is justifiable, of course. After all, Claudine makes a living performing sex. Nonetheless, when too much hard-core is splashed on the screen, one begins to doubt the film-maker's motives. Is Exhibition supposed to be a study of Claudine Beccarie or is Claudine's story just an excuse for another hard-core film?

If we do accept the fact that Exhibition fails as both pornography and documentary, at least the film suggests one direction that hard-core footage in films could go . . . ''

© Cineaste, 1976.

The Sunday Times (London), 12/12/76 (p. 37)
Alan Brien

"Jean-Francois Davy in his Exhibition . . . attempts to extricate himself from the sexploitation rut by posing as a serious investigator setting out to find why people appear in pornographic films. This venture all too soon runs aground on several rocks—not least of which is M. Davy's hopelessness as an interviewer. Appearing occasionally in his own shot, a fuzzy bulk knitted head to toe from wire wool on heavy-duty needles, he is omnipresent on the soundtrack, resolutely steering away the dialogue whenever it becomes truly revealing. His main source is Claudine Beccarie, most renowned of all porno-stars in France . . . ''

©The Sunday Times, 1976.

Monthly Film Bulletin, October 1976 (p. 213)
Jill Forbes

"Opponents of censorship are in the embarrassing position of having to go to the stake for *Exhibition*, which may be, as has been claimed, a 'social and historical' document, though not at all because it is 'a documentary on the public and private life of France's premier sex-film actress.' If the documentary label helps the film to escape censorship, then it does so dishonestly. Claudine's life as portrayed here is one of relentlessly petty bourgeois banality, and this 'intimate psychological study' has been directed with an evident degree of patronising snobbery. If Claudine really is such a pathetic creature, it would have been tactful to spare the details; if she is not, then *Exhibition* works, like most sex films, by realising its audience's fantasies . . .''

©Monthly Film Bulletin, 1976.

F FOR FAKE

Director: *Orson Welles.* Screenplay: *Mr. Welles.* Photography: *Christian Odasso and Gary Graver.* Production Coordinator: *Francois Reichenbach.* Editors: *Marie-Sophie Dubus and Dominique Engerer.* Music: *Michel Legrand.* Production: *Janus Films / Les Films de l'Astrophore.* Running time 90 minutes. New York opening September 28, 1975, at the New York Film Festival, Lincoln Center. Classification: None.

Players: *Orson Welles, Clifford Irving, Oja Kodar, Elmyr de Hory, Edith Irving, Francois Reichenbach, Joseph Cotten, Richard Wilson, Paul Stewart, Sasa Devcic, Gary Graver, Andres Vicente Gomez, Julio Palinkas, Christian Odasso, Francoise Widoff.*

See Volume 1 for additional reviews

Monthly Film Bulletin, January 1977 (p. 12)
Richard Combs

''. . . *F for Fake* is truly a 'centreless labyrinth,' in which the alleged credit-hogger, accused of doing down Herman Mankiewicz to claim *Citizen Kane* as totally his own creation, parodies the very notion of 'pure' creativity and autonomous (and attributable) authorship. The ribbing of the experts continues, even in those sections which seem like the most reliable autobiography . . . 'The fake is old as the

Eden tree,' intones Welles; and clearly, in answer to the critics who have deduced the dissipation of his own genius from the undisguised element of sham in his work, he holds up men like De Hory and Irving as his ideal of the creator-jesters at the court of art, who have demonstrated that the practitioners are not entirely their own men, nor are their works definitively tested by the names attached to them . . .''

©Monthly Film Bulletin, 1977.

Nation, 3/12/77 (p. 316)
Robert Hatch

''. . . If only the principals of Welles' little excursion into chicanery were more attractive, or at least more engrossingly peculiar, all this jiggery-pokery with flashbacks, stop photography, montage and slow motion might be worth some attention. But his pals on Ibiza look and talk like members of the jet set who've had their credit cards voided. They lounge around in suntan oil and keep their spirits up by giving parties for one another, while they wait for the mythical cargo ship to steam in. It must have looked to them as though it had done so when Welles steamed in with the idea of showing the world what fabulous frauds they are, but it costs $3 to watch them scramble for the best camera angles and fake money will not fool the cashier.''

©The Nation, 1977.

Los Angeles Times, 3/30/77 (Pt. IV, p. 8)
Kevin Thomas

''With *F for Fake* . . . Orson Welles stretches his material and his legend just about as thin as possible in this tedious treatise on truth and illusion . . .

In essence, Welles has deployed his fabulous technique on a mishmash of material, some of it little more than travelogue footage, that is not strong enough to sustain it . . .

More than anything else, *F for Fake* is simply sad. It's sad to see Welles involved in so minor a project. And since the film was made the puckish and obviously gifted De Hory has committed suicide, the Irvings have met fates that are scarcely amusing, and Howard Hughes is dead. Even Jack E. Leonard, whose name appears on a marquee in front of an oft-repeated shot of Hughes' Desert Inn, is no longer among us.''

©Los Angeles Times, 1977.

New York Magazine, 3/7/77 (p. 76)
John Simon

''. . . *F for Fake* could have been both fascinating and important. But it is, right off, rather like the Holy Roman Empire: It is not new, having kicked around

continued on next page

continued from previous page

for a couple of years already; it is not nonfiction, having a lot of mystification in it; and it is not quite a film, having been made for television. What makes it particularly fake, though, is that about 40 minutes' worth of material has been stretched to almost three times that length, and that at least one of the purposes seems to have been the launching of an attractive but, on the available evidence, not especially talented young woman, Oja Kodar, the nature of whose usefulness to Welles may be worth some short speculation . . .''

©1977 by the NYM Corp. Reprinted with the permission of NEW YORK Magazine.

Film Quarterly, Summer 1976 (p. 42)
William Johnson

''. . . Welles' approach to film making involves many risks. Even at his best, the critical praise he earns is often qualified by such terms as 'showy' or 'bravura.' And any weaknesses are likely to be spotlighted by the hyperesthetic effect. This certainly happens in *F for Fake*, where the confusion as to who or what is the central subject is compounded by stylistic diversity (readymade documentary footage, narrative scenes, semi-documentary sequences, fictional sequences, film clips and stills) and continual shifts of tone (ironic observation, reminiscence, speculation, mystification, humor). In addition, a few lengthy sequences reach the point of tedium all the sooner because Welles has accustomed the viewer to expect rapid changes . . .''

©Film Quarterly, 1976.

The Times (London), 11/19/76 (p. 15)
David Robinson

''The basis of Welles' film was a documentary made in 1968 by Francois Reichenbach, about the celebrated art forger Elmyr de Hory. A shadowy figure in the background of de Hory's sunlit world at Ibiza at that time was his biographer, one Clifford Irving . . .

Welles has cunningly reworked the original to bring Clifford Irving and his wife into the foreground; and presents the whole thing with the kind of mischievous, enchanting legerdemain that must have ·characterized his days as the infant prodigy of radio. Majestic in floppy hat and flowing cloak, Welles presides in person over the whole, bringing the puppets to life with a magic pass here and there, and capping it all with a better joke and bigger fake than any of the rest, which it would be improper to reveal.

The whole thing is irresistible . . .''

©The Times, 1976.

FACE TO FACE

Director, Producer: *Ingmar Bergman*. Screenplay (Swedish with English subtitles): *Mr. Bergman*. Photography: *Sven Nykvist*. Editor: *Siv Lundgren*. Production: *Dino De Laurentiis* Distributor: *Paramount Pictures*. Running time 136 minutes. New York opening April 5, 1976, at the Beekman Theatre. Classification: R. Origin: Sweden.

Dr. Jenny Isaksson: *Liv Ullmann*. Dr. Thomas Jacibi: *Erland Josephson*. Grandpa: *Gunnar Bjornstrand*. Grandma: *Aino Taube-Henrikson*. Maria: *Karl Sylwan*. Elizabeth Wankel: *Sif Ruud*. Dr. Erik Isaksson: *Sven Lindberg*. Lady: *Tore Segelcke*. Dr. Helmuth Wankel: *Ulf Johansson* Veronica: *Kristina Adolphson*. Mikael Stromberg: *Gosta Ekman*. Concert pianist: *Kabi Laretei*. Man: *Birger Malmsten*. Another man: *Gorman Stangertz*. Jenny's mother: *Marianne Aminoff*.

See Volume 1 for additional reviews

Sight and Sound, Winter 1976/1977 (p. 55)
Philip Strick

''. . . As a case-history, it isn't too unusual. Bergman rests nearly its entire weight on the performance by Liv Ullmann, who pulls all the stops out for what must have been exhausting scenes to play before a camera disinclined to blink, but remains a little too dry-eyed throughout. For those unable to work up much enthusiasm for Miss Ullmann, it's a long haul to the unremarkable explanation that she's like she is because of childhood traumas. But being face to face with Bergman is never comforting, nor wholly predictable, and the story of Jenny has nothing cosy in its conclusion. In a film of shocks, nothing is more chilling than Jacibi's revelation, at the end, that he is going abroad, unlikely to return . . .''

©Sight and Sound, 1977.

Monthly Film Bulletin, December 1976 (p. 247)
Tom Milne

''Originally made as a four-part TV series and tailored to its present length for cinema purposes, *Face to Face* is a portmanteau untidily packed with all the familiar Bergman impedimentia (from traumatic childhood memories of being locked in a cupboard to dreams of anguished inadequacy) which starts with several strikes against it: not the least the fact that the anguish loses much of its intensity through being dubbed into a limbo of

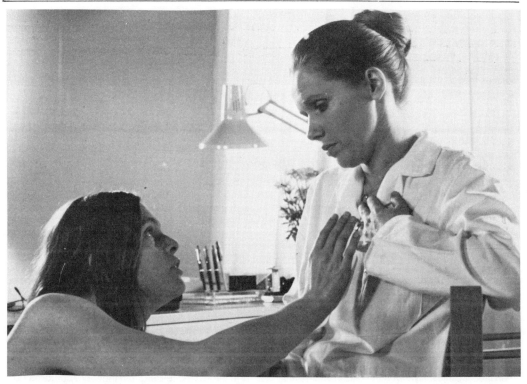

In Ingmar Bergman's **Face to Face**, Liv Ullmann portrays a troubled psychiatrist, here with a patient, Kari Sylwan.

Swedish-tinted English, in some cases evidently by the original cast. Paradoxically, however, the sense of deja vu aroused by both themes and characters tends to work in favour of the film, rather as though the nightmarish terrors had now been tamed, through repeated exposure of their lair in the dark at the top of the stairs, into familiar—even rather friendly—old ghosts . . ."

©Monthly Film Bulletin, 1976.

Take One, October 1976 (p. 40)
Diane Jacobs

". . . Too many things are left unstated or un-defined in *Face to Face*. Important scenes have been deleted, and often the narrative is confusing. Liv Ullmann beautifully enacts the symptoms of physical hysteria, but for the breakdown to be com-pelling thematically we must understand its meta-physical basis. What exactly went wrong with Jenny's marriage, and was her view of the world warped by her parents' premature death? . . . It's too easy to see Jenny as the victim of inhibition, and downright embarrassing to be informed in an addendum that she resolved her problems by breaking up her marriage and taking off to do re-search in the U.S. The dreams, integral parts of the film, look even less dream-like than those of

Persona, and this persistence of reality mitigates against even mystery as the salvation of the human soul . . ."

©Take One, 1976.

The Sunday Times (London), 12/12/76 (p. 35)
Alan Brien

"Both the faces in *Face to Face* . . . Ingmar Bergman's case history of a woman psychiatrist divided against herself, belong to the extraordinary Liv Ullmann. But the face we see most of the time is extraordinary only in being so ordinary. Even dolled up for a party, this successful doctor, com-fortably married with an understanding lover on the side, looks as plain and wholesome as a home-baked tea-cake.

It is when she begins to crack up, racked by emotional anguish like a woman in labour, that we glimpse the beauty that transcends the writhing lips, sweat-dabbled hair and panicky stares . . .

. . . it seems too easily put together, while at the end there are pieces left over which do not fit and arrive too late. And the film, rare for Berg-man, includes some sloppy overplaying in minor

continued on next page

91

continued from previous page

roles, notably a shrill parasitic gay couple, while the dubbing, though technically impeccable, burdens everyone with Swedish accents and intonations as though the cast were foreigners not only to us but to each other."

©The Sunday Times, 1976.

The Times (London), 10/22/76 (p. 15)
Philip French

"At the center of Ingmar Bergman's latest, and longest, movie, *Face to Face*, is a compelling and remarkably detailed performance by Liv Ullmann as a Stockholm psychiatrist breaking down one unhappy summer and attempting suicide. Through her hallucinations (in which she revisits her past, clothed in what appears to be a long dress from one of Miss Ullmann's ghastly Hollywood costume flicks), an association with a homosexual doctor (Erland Josephson), and the loving example of her aged grandparents, she gains the strength to live, and possibly to overcome the frigidity that prevents her building a bridge of love in the cosmic loneliness that engulfs us all.

In effect, *Face to Face* is a reworking in Bergman's later clinical style of that major masterpiece in his late Fifties expressionist mode, *Wild Strawberries* . . . I much prefer *Wild Strawberries* . . ."

©The Times, 1976.

Saturday Review, 5/1/76 (p. 41)
Judith Crist

"Bergman's *Face to Face* is one of his finest films, the most humanistic and thereby the most accessible, perhaps because it is the most personal. The metaphysician, the mystic, the symbol-laden searcher for spiritual surcease have given way to the man in search of self, of an understanding of the universal experiences that enable us to survive . . .

Bergman's compassion has never before been focused so intently on the female psyche, and no 'Bergman woman' has been so thoroughly realized as Ullmann's is here. This is the step beyond the emotional intuitions of *Cries and Whispers*, beyond the pragmatic authenticities of *Scenes From a Marriage*. Fittingly, Ullmann is again complemented, as in *Scenes*, by Erland Josephson. His Thomas is a man whose bridge to understanding is his own bisexuality, his willing submersion in another's pain. The entire cast, Bergman's repertory company, is equally fine in the clear focus of familiar scenes and in the strangeness of the extended realities of dreams––all created through Sven Nykvist's camera eye, all underlined by Kabi Laretei's exquisite piano variations on the theme of Mozart's fantasy in C Minor. Bergman has probed the universal soul and led us to face ourselves, at last, with love and comfort."

© Judith Crist, 1976.

Commonweal, 5/21/76 (p. 333)
Gerald Weales

"It must become unbearable to be Ingmar Bergman. Judging by his movies, he feels our peculiarly modern emotions more urgently and emphatically than any other artist. Nowhere is the solipsism of modern life––the loneliness, isolation and inability to communicate with others––more intense than· in his films . . .

. . . At times Bergman must feel as if he is about to suffocate, as if he himself will scream or go mad if he does not escape from the endless cycle of living and portraying such modern angst.

The only release modern man has for these feelings is in his dreams, and the only release a modern artist has from portraying such feelings is in history. In *Face to Face* Bergman tries to take both ways out at once. Historical dramas have always been attractive to him because they can provide a holiday not only from the modern condition, but from the symbolic bleakness of modern life as well. In *Face to Face* Bergman therefore contrives to get Jenny into historical dress. Time comes unhinged in the film in a way that allows Jenny's memories of her past to become as real as present realities for her, and also allows the historical past to mix with modern life in Jenny's dreams . . .

. . . Jenny's dream is opaque, its imagery a private and seemingly arbitrary one. The fact is that Bergman is much better when he disciplines himself to symbolic gestures made by the camera rather than indulging in those that can be made by the script . . . "

© Commonweal, 1976.

Films in Review, 5/76 (p. 314)
Charles Phillips Reilly

" . . . Miss Ullmann's part has heroic dimensions, to which she is equal. She successfully captures her mental and psychical disintegration within her dream sequences and in her conversations with Josephson while recuperating in the hospital. Her re-enactment of her terror at being shut up in a closet as a child by her grandmother is hair-raising. Gunnar Bjornstrand couldn't be better as the senile grandpa facing death like a scared child; Josephson is believable, though at times remote as the bisexual whose final decision is to go to Jamaica where 'one can lead such a wonderful life of vice.'

But we must come back to Bergman. In his original script, in lines deleted from the film, Jenny's attempted suicide is explained as a result of 'broken connections.' This brings Bergman close to a Dostoievskian view of life, saying that without the grace of love, no matter what one's talents, life is not worth living. A tough, provocative, imperfect and absorbing movie."

© Films in Review, 1976.

Film Information, 5/76 (p. 1)
Dave Pomeroy

" . . . *Face to Face* (with death, with oneself—the title reflects the many levels of a Bergman film) is also a melange of many previous Bergman motifs. Time and age—symbolized by Jenny's close-to-death grandfather (Gunnar Bjornstrand) depress Jenny's sensibilities—reminiscent of the same effect in *Wild Strawberries*. A death image in the form of an old woman (Tore Segelcke) comes frequently into Jenny's psychic consciousness (a la *The Seventh Seal*). Repressed sexuality and uninhibited passion clash in the relationship of Jenny to a psychotic patient, Maria (Kari Sylwan). As among the sisters of *Cries and Whispers*, the color red as an indicator of passion is also important here. And dream sequences play a major role as they have in many Bergman works. In other words, Bergman is bringing much of his previous film genius to bear on an individual's psychic illness . . .
. . . *Face to Face* is good but not great Bergman—still a strong recommendation among the ordinary run of films. It is powerful, frightening in its images (especially in the dream sequences), and demanding of its audience . . . "

© Film Information, 1976.

Nation, 4/17/76 (p. 475)
Robert Hatch

"Ingmar Bergman's *Face to Face* is, as you would expect, a meticulously crafted film, but in the end it failed to enlist me. In a way it resembles *The Exorcist,* being the melodramatic account of the collapse and salvation of a woman possessed, but it is a less easy picture to evaluate. That is, though I am firm in my belief that the Devil does not take up squatter's rights in the bodies of innocent maidens, I am less sure of my opinion about Bergman's account of a personality at the end of its wits . . .
As in its predecessor, *Scenes From a Marriage,* Bergman employs in *Face to Face* a television intimacy that seeks to convince the viewer that absolutely nothing is hidden. And with Liv Ullmann, that most open and malleable of actresses to serve his purpose, he produces an effect which at the time is hypnotic. It is afterward that one may be struck less by what is shown than by what had to be omitted. Who is Jenny Isaksson that we should be concerned about her brainstorm? . . . Bergman opened her up to display her soul, and there was

only a set of ill-meshing wheels. If he hadn't declared that she was working in America, I would have thought that she had been boxed away in a closet, safely stored until needed again."

© The Nation, 1976.

FALLING

Director, Screenplay: *Elly Kenner.* Producers: *Bruce Bartoo, Ralphi Migrom, Constance Richardson, Mr. Kenner.* Photography: *Alan J. Ritsko.* Music: *Misha Segal.* Distributor: *Dover Films.* Running time 87 minutes. Los Angeles opening December 3, 1976, at the Kinsey Auditorium, California Museum of Science and Industry. Classification: None.

Players: *Robert Duggan, Debbie Franco, David Lang, Marilyn Patch, Ginger Tiger.*

Los Angeles Times, 12/2/76 (Pt. IV, p. 26)
Linda Gross

". . . The film tells the story of the friendship between three college roommates, two men and a woman (David Lang, Debbie Franco and Robert Duggan) living in the transition period of the early '70s when cool was more hip than commitment . . .
Kenner's scenario rambles slightly but vividly conveys a slice of student life in the '70s. The three-way camaraderie is very well drawn.
As a director Kenner is both slick and sensitive, able to elicit winning performances from actors as well as nonprofessionals. One monologue, in which a girl brings a birthday cake to her ex-boyfriend and finds him in bed with another, is a gemlike merger of improvisation and directorial skill.
Miss Franco is vulnerable and poignant as the girl caught between stereotypical female roles. Lang is convincing . . . Miss Patch is very good . . . and Duggan is perfect . . ."

©Los Angeles Times, 1976.

FAMILY PLOT

Director: *Alfred Hitchcock.* Screenplay: *Ernest Lehman.* Based on the novel THE RAINBIRD PATTERN by *Victor Canning.* Photography:

continued on next page

continued from previous page

Leonard J. South. Editor: *J. Terry Williams.* Music: *John Williams.* Distributor: *Universal Pictures.* Running time 120 minutes. New York opening April 9, 1976, at several theatres. Classification: PG.

Fran: *Karen Black.* Lumley: *Bruce Dern.* Blanche: *Barbara Harris.* Adamson: *William Devane.* Maloney: *Ed Lauter.* Julia Rainbird: *Cathleen Nesbitt.* Mrs. Maloney: *Katherine Helmond.* Grandison: *Warren Kemmerling.* Mrs. Clay: *Edith Atwater.* Bishop: *William Prince.*

See Volume 1 for additional reviews

Cineaste, Fall 1976 (p. 40)
Al Auster

". . . Harris and Dern are so good that it would take a major effort to dislike them. Dern's eye-popping, nostril-flaring indignation would be the envy of any silent clown . . . Barbara Harris as the merry medium does some of her best mugging in a long time . . .

Even less convincing than the lack of locale and manipulation of class, however, are Hitchcock's attempts at sexual humor. His jokes about crystal balls and Dern ogling Harris' behind are superfluous. He has told us too many times, in this film and others, that danger is the ultimate aphrodisiac. But Hitchcock never really nods. His style and craftsmanship prevent that. Virtuoso shots—an Olympian view of a graveyard scene, comic byplay, Blanche asking for a double shot of anything after a spiritualist's imitation of Jimmy Durante—all show an eye and ear that haven't yet hazed over . . ."

©Cineaste, 1976.

Sight and Sound, Summer 1976 (p. 188)
Jonathan Rosenbaum

". . . Thanks to the precision of Ernest Lehman's script, the movie proceeds like an immaculately polished mechanism that continually bears witness to the fact and wit of its own operations. Eliminating not only murder from his formula (and from the pedestrian Victor Canning novel *The Rainbird Pattern*, which serves as his starting point), Hitchcock has pared down his devices to the point where whole areas of his expertise can be covered in single, functional shorthand notations . . . Best of all is a hair-raising sequence with Blanche and George in a car without brakes barreling down a steep mountain road. An ultimate expression of Hitchcock's storyboard technique—clearly devised at a desk rather than during shooting or at an editing table—its suspense derives from algebraic essentials, where the purest kind of 'musical' variations can be played on the threats of passing cars, culminating in a wonderfully timed procession of passing motorcyclists . . ."

©Sight and Sound, 1976.

Monthly Film Bulletin, 7/76 (p. 146)
Richard Combs

"*Family Plot* is in many ways the perfect Hitchcock conundrum. Its plot dovetails so smoothly with its themes, its implausibilities and illogicalities are flourished with such triumphant sleight of hand, and the familiar Hitchcock motifs (death, the couple, the double, the church) slipped so snugly into the viewer's lap that the work of critical commentary might have been mapped out as carefully as the plot in the director's legendary pre-production phase. In other words, the perverse metaphysician no longer needs to be decoded from the sly storyteller—both seem to be persistently turning into the other . . . Even more clearly than *Topaz* or *Frenzy*, *Family Plot* is an 'old man's film' in which the normal and the abnormal have become cheerfully relative concepts, and the director juggles openly and knowingly with both his moral and narrative materials. The latter is evident in the uncanny simplicity and literalness with which plot tactics become theme . . . it is wholly appropriate that after the consistently unsympathetic performances Hitchcock has elicited in recent films, *Family Plot* features Bruce Dern and Barbara Harris in a delightfully nuanced comic duet, and finds in William Devane a smiling villain of wonderfully tetchy and toothy urbanity."

©Monthly Film Bulletin, 1976.

The Times (London), 8/20/76 (p. 7)
David Robinson

"Seventy-seven last Friday, Alfred Hitchcock has yielded to age none of his mastery as a storyteller. He still possesses the supreme gift of suspense, in the sense of sustaining, at every moment, curiosity about what comes next. Because it's played for light comedy going on farce, *Family Plot* risks being pigeon-holed as a frolic, a minor work in the old master's canon. Time, I guess, may well accord it a central place. It has the geometric ingenuity of the later American work, along with the delight in quirky character that marked Hitchcock's British period . . .

. . . what is most characteristic and charming in the film is a show-off relaxation, an easy demonstration of how it all should be done. Hitchcock this time builds a thriller without ever showing a killing . . . he

94

makes the relationship of the two couples vibrantly sexy without so much as showing a bed or naked elbow . . . It's all a very jolly affair."

©The Times, 1976.

The Sunday Times (London), 8/22/76 (p. 28)
Philip Mackie

"Good news for gerontophiles, and a message of hope for all of us who don't feel as young as we used to. Alfred Hitchcock, born when Victoria was on the throne and the Empire was a musichall, has made a film called *Family Plot* . . . with a sense of excitement and a sense of fun that are exhilaratingly youthful.

Impossible to believe that the monstrous silhouette on the Registrar's window can be the man himself: this film was obviously directed by a slim young athlete. That is, a slim young athlete with fifty years' experience of film-making. The handling of the narrative has all the confidence of absolute mastery. Nothing is accidental: when he points the camera at an inanimate object, the image is held on the screen exactly long enough to register that object in your mind, because it's an essential part of the story . . ."

©The Sunday Times, 1976.

Commonweal, 5/7/76 (p. 305)
Colin L. Westerbeck, Jr.

" . . . a pleasant spoof, but a strictly conventional one. The sort of virtuosity of the direction that has made many other Hitchcock films unique just doesn't occur this time. In *Psycho* a whole series of shots of circular forms--blinding headlights, a peephole in a wall, water swirling down a toilet, a spraying shower nozzle, a tub drain, etc.--culminates in the murder scene in a tight close-up of the victim's dead, visionless eye. These manipulated images are what give *Psycho* its power both to terrify and delight, but *Family Plot* doesn't accumulate imagery like this with which to affect us. In *Shadow of a Doubt* Hitchcock's long shots done from a boom isolate the heroine at just those moments when some increased certainty of her uncle's crimes has further isolated her from her family. In *Family Plot*, no equivalent resource of technique makes the characters matter to us in a comparable way.

The potential for such effects is there, but it remains only a potential. *Family Plot* stays nothing more than a plot . . . "

© Commonweal, 1976.

Saturday Review, 5/1/76 (p. 43)
Judith Crist

" . . . immaculate unfolding of plot and counter-

plot that Hitchcock provides us in the grand style, offering us the monsters in mundane guise, the sunlit terrors, the eccentrics on the sidelines, the red herrings, and the tongue-in-cheek thrills that are his hallmarks. At times he seems to verge on self-satire, but actually it is a master's relish, a crafty craftman's joy in his craft. And his cast is inspired in selection and performance . . .

It is a grand entertainment in the grand tradition, the dialogue is as sprightly as the pace, the giggles as frequent as the gasps, the scene as realistic as the action, the people as credible as the plot. Above all, you find yourself relaxing from the start, intuitively aware that you are in the hands of The Master. And those hands have not lost their touch--it is as deft as ever, mature, tempered with that self-awareness which is the mark of the true sophisticate."

© Judith Crist, 1976.

Nation, 5/8/76 (p. 572)
Robert Hatch

" . . . pure and, for all its interlacing threads, simple fun. Only one person dies and he was so completely without redeeming qualities that his widow's distress quite surprised me. There is some wickedness, but it is tripped by the heels; and there is some rascality, which carries off the prize. In the end all the pieces fit, and justice has been meticulously done to everyone. Exemplary.

The plot-screenplay by Ernest Lehman, from a novel, *The Rainbird Pattern*, by Victor Canning --concerns two couples whose paths intersect at cross purposes. As in many well-motivated fairy stories, one couple is 'good,' and the other is 'bad' . . .

. . . Harris and Dern are young, agile and fresh-faced, and all four principals play the preposterous game in dead earnest. *Family Plot* is not a Hitchcock masterpiece; it is more a bit of skillful foolishness for television, where it will probably appear in a year or so . . ."

© The Nation, 1976.

New York Post, 4/10/76 (p. 39)
Frank Rich

" . . . Hitchcock eats actors for breakfast--that's part of his style--and here he seems to have eaten one of his leads, Karen Black, for breakfast, lunch and dinner; by the time he's finished with her, her part might just as well have been played by a broom. Dern, as a crooked cabbie, and Miss Harris, as a good-naturedly fraudulent medium, mount a broad comic attack on their roles. They are fitfully amusing but they often overemphasize Lehman's flat jokes in the process. Devane works hard as the

continued on next page

continued from previous page

major heavy, but he's a trifle too thin-blooded in a part that James Mason, Joseph Cotton or Claude Rains once would have lit with flaming nastiness.

The real humor and pleasure of *Family Plot* arrive when Hitchcock has the strength to overwhelm the script, as well as the trashy production values that often give the film the look of an assembly-line studio production . . ."

Reprinted by Permission of New York Post.
© 1976, New York Post Corporation.

Film Information, 4/76 (p. 3)
Paul Coleman

" . . . *Family Plot* begins with a pun for a title and ends with a wink. Its modern humor unfurls far away from contemporary cynicism and proves clearly that wry sophistication still delivers a thrill . . .

Barbara Harris and Bruce Dern are unsung treasures among modern movie performers, and their comic pacing is keenly tuned to Hitchcock's themes. Karen Black and William Devane play their icy sophisticates with easy flair but without their usual distracting mannerisms. But the day belongs to Hitchcock in his most peculiarly Christian film.

His theme is the paranoia that arises from guilt unconfessed, one he has treated in such classics as *Rebecca*, *Spellbound*, and *I Confess*. The guilt results from a long buried secret of family death and disappearance. Just when the two plot strains interweave, as innocence confronts paranoia, Hitchcock makes an ecclesiastical joke . . ."

© Film Information, 1976.

New York Magazine, 4/19/76 (p. 84)
John Simon

" . . . In *Family Plot*, much goes very wrong, starting with the overlong initial expository scenes. Hitchcock, in a press conference, explained this as making the audience comfortable at the beginning, so that 'you can then become purely cinematic and tell the story with pictures.' Well, the audience seems to take longer than before, in Hitchcock's view, to become comfortable; though he denies it, he appears to have less faith than of yore in its perspicacity. For similar reasons, I suspect, his actors––Barbara Harris, William Devane, and especially Bruce Dern––are encouraged to italicize every expression and inflection to the point where the customarily unsubtle Karen Black seems to be positively underacting. Dern is particularly worrisome: an actor who can be extraordinary when a part fits or pleases him, as in *Smile*, he can become crudely excessive in meanness, as in *The Great Gatsby*, or in thickness, as here. His mugging now reaches a new low . . ."

© 1976 by the NYM Corp. Reprinted with
the permission of NEW YORK Magazine.

Village Voice, 4/19/76 (p. 122)
Andrew Sarris

" . . . The very varied role-playing of the two couples makes *The Family Plot* at least partly a comedy about the problem of directing actors. Barbara Harris, of course, is a subtextual sensation in her own right, and one senses that Hitchcock directed her with a very loose rein. Her part is reminiscent of Shirley Maclaine's zany widow in *The Trouble With Harry*, a lushly autumnal dark Hitchcockian comedy of two decades ago. Strangely, the more brightly the sun shines in a Hitchcock film, the more darkly does the spirit seem to lurk. Ernest Lehman's dialogue, like Ben Hecht's for *Notorious*, often strikes a coarse note at variance with Hitchcock's visual elegance. Actually, the director's moral determinism seems to resist the greater behavioral freedom in today's cinema without restricting it. Ultimately, his viewpoint is lofty enough to be infinitely merciful, and he is such a gifted teller of filmic fables that though *The Family Plot* is not perfect Hitchcock, and perhaps not even major Hitchcock, I hope he can keep on making movies forever."

Reprinted by permission of The Village Voice.
Copyright © The Village Voice, Inc., 1976.

Los Angeles Times, 4/9/76 (p. 11)
Charles Champlin

" . . . It is atmospheric, characterful, precisely paced, intricately plotted, exciting and suspenseful, beautifully acted and, perhaps more than anything else, amusing. It is not as traumatically scary as *Psycho* nor as gruesomely violent as *Frenzy*. It is a suspense comedy that is probably closest in spirit to *The Trouble With Harry*.

The particular rewards of *Family Plot* include the most extensive and appropriate movie role that the richly talented Barbara Harris has yet had. After her tantalizing moments in *Harry Kellerman*, *Nashville* and points between, it is nice to see her at full length.

She is teamed with Bruce Dern, an able actor who often seems a whole lot better than his parts, but who here has a large opportunity of which he makes the most.

The match play is against William Devane as a suavely psychopathic jewel thief and murderer and Karen Black as the helpmate who hadn't realized quite what a weirdo she has on her hands . . ."

© Los Angeles Times, 1976.

Films in Review, 5/76 (p. 313)
DeWitt Bodeen

" . . . The principal role of Blanche, the medium, has been handed to Barbara Harris, often a charming comedienne, who's simply lost in the dead ends of this unfunny maze.

There is no suspense, surprise, or shock in this picture, nor is there any of the wit and wisdom Hitchcock has heretofore been willing to share. The picture bogs down in one talky, undramatic sequence after another, and the plot, with all its exposition and loose ends, is involved beyond belief.

Nor do Karen Black and Bruce Dern, also interred in this cast, have any of the stylish charisma one associates with actors playing in a Hitchcock film: they are flawed, and don't even have the sparkle to shine. Only William Devane, who may well be Hollywood's next big movie star, has that kind of insolent menace which one associates with the true Hitchcock villain."

© Films in Review, 1976.

Take One, 5/21/76 (p. 21)
John Russell Taylor

" . . . The screenplay Ernest Lehman has fashioned out of Victor Canning's enjoyable but rather silly book, *The Rainbird Pattern,* skillfully plays down the melodrama and extravagance in the conception of the characters . . .

. . . some stunning set pieces. There is, for instance, the sequence in which Blanche and George, lured to a mysterious rendezvous on a mountaintop, find themselves returning empty-handed in a car whose brakes have been drained. You would not think anyone could come up with new variations on that one, but the sheer brio of the subjective shooting and the believable but very funny reactions of the car's occupants, pushed boldly far over towards farce and yet not at all abating the suspense of the scene, make this a classic.

Then again there is the scene which was, I suspect, the nugget from which the whole film was spun: the kidnapping of the bishop in the middle of the mass . . .

Though the film was not without its problems in the shooting, the end result makes it all look as easy as falling off a log. Hitchcock taking it easy, Hitchcock enjoying himself, Hitchcock making just another movie on an idea that takes his fancy, sublimely unconcerned about whether it turns out to be a culminating masterpiece or not. And what, after all, could be nicer or more enjoyable than that? . . ."

© Take One, 1976.

FARMER, THE

Director: *David Berlatsky.* Screenplay: *George Fargo, Janice Colson-Dodge, Patrick Regan, John Carmody.* Producer: *Gary Conway.* Photography: *Irv Goodnoff.* Editor: *Richard Weber.* Music: *Hugo Montenegro.* Production:

Milway. Distributor: *Columbia Pictures.* Running time 98 minutes. New York opening March 9, 1977, at several theatres. Classification: R.

Kyle Martin: *Gary Conway.* Betty: *Angel Tompkins.* Johnny O': *Michael Dante.* Passini: *George Memmoli.* Weasel: *Timothy Scott.* Gumshoe: *Ken Renard.* Conners: *John Popwell.*

New York Post, 3/10/77 (p. 26)
Archer Winsten

"Utilizing a very long arm of coincidence and structuring the rest of the plot with assorted violences, four writers have made *The Farmer . . .* into a wild melodrama of revenge . . .

Naturally your sympathies are with Kyle, and they are not misplaced. It takes a bit of doing, but he manages to kill all the baddies in appropriate ways, one with a wire, garrotting him, one out the window, another with a burst of gunfire, and the fourth in a long pistol duel.

Oddly, the Georgia State Police and local authorities are never permitted to show their faces or automobiles, thus avoiding any credits to cooperating state agencies. These, and other unlikely sequences, reduce *The Farmer* to its lowly artistic status as a mere peg on which to hang all these highly justified killings . . ."

Reprinted by Permission of New York Post.
©1977, New York Post Corporation.

FEAR OF FEAR
(ANGST VOR DER ANGST)

Director: *Rainer Werner Fassbinder.* Screenplay (German with English subtitles): *Mr. Fassbinder.* Producer: *Peter Marthesheimer.* Photography: *Jurgen Jurges, Ulrich Prinz.* Editors: *Liesgrett Schmitt-Klink, Beate Fischer-Weiskirch.* Music: *Peter Raben.* Distributor: *Westdeutscher Rundfunk* (Cologne). Running time 88 minutes. New York opening October 15, 1976, at the New York Film Festival, Lincoln Center. Classification: None. Origin: West Germany.

continued on next page

continued from previous page

Margot: *Margit Carstensen*. Kurt: *Ulrich Faul-haber*. Mother: *Brigitte Mira*. Lore: *Irm Her-mann*. Karli: *Armin Meier*. Dr. Merck: *Adrian Hoven*. Mr. Bauer: *Kurt Raab*. Edda: *Ingrid Caven*. Mrs. Schall: *Lilo Pempeit*.

Film Information, November 1976 (p. 2)
Robert E. A. Lee

". . . a strong cast is . . . greatest asset. Mar-git Carstensen portrays the neurotic hausfrau who has a creeping awareness that she is not in control of her emotions. Every time she looks in a mirror, which she often does in this picture, she feels she is going mad. Her student husband (Ulrich Faul-haber) is too busy and too preoccupied with himself to notice anything wrong. But her self-righteous mother-in-law and sister-in-law upstairs notice everything and deride the sick woman merci-lessly . . .

American filmgoers may well get impatient with the trite optical effects—incessant fade-outs and fade-ins and rippled distortions—as well as the corny music cues signalling each melodramatic moment . . .

But *Fear of Fear* does manage to make us care about some of the characters and get angry at others. It also raises important questions of how to deal with those around us who may be emotionally distressed."

©Film Information, 1976.

New York Post, 10/15/76 (p. 26)
Frank Rich

". . . If Fassbinder hadn't so overstacked the forces pitted against his protagonist, *Fear of Fear* might be somewhat more involving than it is. But he doesn't have any perspective on Margot at all. He just uses her as a pawn to make his same old point—that the social outcasts of his films are bet-ter human beings than the nominally 'normal' mem-taken this familiar plot, enlisted Jeanne Moreau as his star, and together they have brought it up to date with a women's liberation sensibility. The result is a quirky, skittish comedy-drama, written with an American, Marilyn Goldin, that shows off Miss Moreau to great advantage in a major role, her first to be seen in America in far too long . . .

While Techine admirably rings in a whole new set of reactions to a very traditional saga, his seeming offhandedness sometimes is too casual for his own good . . .

Not all the film's various whimsical moments come off convincingly, but Miss Moreau, credibly progressing from sensual if prematurely ravaged laborer to chic executive, comes through . . ."

Reprinted by Permission of New York Post.
©1976, New York Post Corporation.

FELLINI'S CASANOVA

Director: *Federico Fellini*. Screenplay: *Bernar-dino Zapponi, Mr. Fellini*. Producer: *Alberto Grimaldi*. English Dialogue Consultant: *An-thony Burgess*. Photography: *Giuseppe Ro-tunno*. Editor: *Ruggero Mastroianni*. Music: *Nino Rota*. Sets and Costumes: *Danilo Donati*. Distributor: *Universal Pictures*. Running time 165 minutes. Los Angeles opening December 31, 1976, at the Avco Cinema Center. Classi-fication: R.

Players: *Clara Algranti, Sandra Elaine Allen, Tina Aumont, Daniel Emilfork Berenstein, Cicely Browne, Olimpia Carlisi, Margareth Clementi, Silvana Fusacchia, Daniela Gatti, John Karlson, Adele Angela Lojodice, Reggie Nalder, Clarissa Mary Roll, Carmen Scarpitta, Donald Sutherland, Dudley Sutton, Hans van den Hoek, Luigi Zerbinati.*

Newsweek, 1/24/77 (p. 60)
Jack Kroll

"Behind the fantasy, the opulence, the hippo-drome ego of Federico Fellini's work has always dwelt a dark and gnawing terror, and this terror finally explodes in his astonishing and depressing epic, *Fellini's Casanova*. Fellini has spent around $10 million and a couple of years to produce a huge spectacle that's the climax of the apocalyptic nihilism of his other two 'signature' films—*Fellini's Satyricon* and *Fellini's Roma* . . .

This could have been the most honest and brood-ingly powerful of Fellini's films if he had portrayed Casanova frankly as a kind of Fellini—an all-too-human blend of genius and charlatan, a man with a natural sense of life as theater, an explosive com-pound of epicure and moralist. But the film is made static and irresolute by Fellini's ambivalence toward Casanova. It's the first Fellini movie in which there's absolutely no joy at all . . .

. . . the overall effect of the film is a turnoff—chilling and funerary, a catatonic carnival in a mausoleum. *Fellini's Casanova* is really a horror movie: it scared the daylights out of me with its de-piction of human beings as hysterical corpses who don't have the sense to lie down and molder . . ."

Newsweek, Inc. 1977
reprinted by permission.

Nation, 2/26/77 (p. 252)
Robert Hatch

". . . It is strange—Fellini fails here with a much lesser book as he failed with the superb *Satyricon*. He seizes upon everything in it that is sordid and unclean; he overlooks the vivacity and insight that make it all worth consideration. Even the passages

that are surely meant to be comic, or at least laughably grotesque (notably those in which Casanova
struggles to arouse his abused virility), are made
leaden by a seemingly morose distaste for the behavior under review. If he is so incapable of being
entertained by human folly, why does Fellini spend
so much energy on it? He seems to work himself
up as he goes along. In its early passages, the
movie retains a certain tongue-in-cheek appreciation of naughtiness, but as Casanova, like an aging
whore moving away from the bright lights of the
boulevards, travels from France to Switzerland and
then into the German principalities, manners become more uncouth, drunkenness more obsessive,
faces more repellent, and Casanova seems more
and more an object bottled in formaldehyde for display at a temperance lecture. His last bedding is
with a life-sized mechanical doll, the creation of
some German clockmaker—the moral is too
pat . . .''

© The Nation, 1977.

Saturday Review, 2/19/77 (p. 40)
Judith Crist

''. . . what emerges in that most brilliant camera-
eye of the Italian filmmaker is a glowingly detailed
caricature of the eighteenth-century society through
which history's most notorious amorist traveled, his
primary vehicle his sexual reputation. It is a stunning studio creation, a fascination for the eye, a be-
musement for the intellect, and a void for the
heart . . .

Removed though he may be from his protagonist,
even in an 'exercise' Fellini proves himself the
genius of the cinematic vision, his fantasy so deeply
textured that it counteracts the director's alienation.
The auteur's affection may not be with Casanova,
but his wit and wisdom are at work to enthrall his
audience. The work is long—165 minutes—but
never self-indulgent, with the confident hand of a
master artist in control. It's better when his heart is
with his hero—but we'll settle for his intellectual en-
gagement this time around.''

© Judith Crist, 1977.

Christian Science Monitor, 3/2/77 (p. 22)
David Sterritt

''. . . Donald Sutherland plays the title character
as a walking and talking gargoyle, hinting at but deliberately withholding a hidden humanity deep
inside the rogue . . . the film is full of sexual encounters. Yet none are realistic. It's all etched boldly and
superficially. The only personality consistently on
view is Fellini's, for only he is responsible for the
cosmic canvas of sights, sounds, colors, and (it
seems) smells that are the movie's real reason for
being.

Casanova is a reverse 'rake's progress,' a dream,
an immense yet empty vision where the waves in
the sea are made of billowing plastic, the star's face
is molded into an odd new shape, and every mole-

cule of detail springs directly from the filmmaker's
turbulent imagination. It is alternately exhilarating
and exhausting, but rarely satisfying . . .''

Reprinted by permission from The Christian
Science Monitor © 1977.
The Christian Science Publishing Society.
All rights reserved.

Village Voice, 2/28/77 (p. 39)
Andrew Sarris

''. . . The continuity is so ragged and gratuitous
that the present film seems to have been hacked
out of a much longer version with all the vital thematic connections severed. Except for Sutherland's
performance, there is no acting worthy of the name,
only primping and posing in the most self-
consciously Satanic tradition. There is no particular
insight into—nor even much information about—
either Casanova or the 18th century. There is no
eroticism or sensuality, and no good conversation.
One must see the film, though more for Fellini's
sake than Casanova's, and . . . more for Sutherland's sake than Fellini's. Yet I can't help feeling
that Fellini has been wrestling with his own demons
for so long that he has lost sight of the real world
with its changing tastes and obsessions . . .''

Reprinted by permission of The Village Voice.
Copyright © The Village Voice, Inc., 1977.

New York Post, 2/12/77 (p. 17)
Frank Rich

''. . . We get the Satyricon Fellini at his absolute
worst: Casanova, which is loosely based on the
memoirs of the fabled 18th-century lover, is mean-
spirited, egomaniacal, flatulent, mindless and gross.
It is also an unconscionable bore that is likely to
drive audiences out of the theater only halfway into
its two-and-a-half-hour length . . .

The hero is played by Donald Sutherland, who
has the most thankless role of his or any other actor's career. Fellini has shaved Sutherland's head,
elongated his jaw and nose with putty and dressed
him in layers of baroque white underwear. In the
end, the actor looks like a drag queen impersonating Marisa Berenson in Barry Lyndon—and even
so, he isn't allowed to act. (Not that acting could
penetrate the movie's badly dubbed English soundtrack anyway.) Fellini just wanted an empty shell of
a man—and that's what he got all right . . .''

Reprinted by Permission of New York Post.
© 1977, New York Post Corporation.

Take One, March 1977 (p. 11)
Gideon Bachmann

''. . . One would have thought that promiscuity
without emotion would have been an ideal subject
for Fellini—and he may have thought so himself—
but this does not turn out to be a film about women.
As they were for Casanova so they now serve

continued on next page

continued from previous page

Fellini: women are vessels and instruments for the expression of a personal problem. The sweating, labouring grimace of the heaving love Stakhanovite is the recurrent image punctuating the narrative. We do not see the women below, but we recognize the victim above . . .

. . . As a whole, the film, like most recent Fellinis, is a work of arithmetical progression. It is added, strung, episode per episode, a magnificent necklace, not multiplied geometrically to create a mounting dramatic effect. It is, in this sense, pure Fellini: heaped impressionism, assailing, stunning to the eye, but finally a shell, exorbitant as only great art or pure charlatanism can be . . ."

©Take One, 1977.

New York Magazine, 2/21/77 (p. 57)
John Simon

". . . This film, lasting over two and a half hours, may well be the most ponderous specimen of imaginative vacuity ever devised. Particularly offensive and depressing is that Fellini has taken a fascinating protagonist and very rich story only to make them as hollow and aimless as he himself must have become. If this artistic fiasco were not accompanied by boundless arrogance in Fellini's behavior and recorded utterances, one could feel profoundly sorry for the man; as it is, one can only feel revulsion . . .

There is very little acting from the cast here: from some because they are amateurs, or because they have no decent parts; from Casanova because he is Donald Sutherland. The Canadian actor is not helped, of course, by Fellini's having succeeded in making him look even less prepossessing than usual . . ."

©1977 by the NYM Corp. Reprinted with the permission of NEW YORK Magazine.

Film Information, March 1977 (p. 2)
Peter P. Shillaci

". . . What little unity there is in this parade of isolated episodes is provided by Donald Sutherland, fighting gamely against the script to inject some subtle humanity into the tragic figure of Casanova. The Venetian lover created by Sutherland is a man of refinement and culture, a staunch defender of women who fancies himself a connoisseur among lovers. If one could isolate his portrayal from the human grotesqueries, scenic excesses, and audiovisual cacophony of the rest of the film, one might have an interesting drama. As it is, there are only flashes of brilliance, like a guttering candle struggling to keep its flame alive . . ."

©Film Information, 1977.

Los Angeles Times, 1/1/77 (Pt. II, p. 10)
Charles Champlin

". . . Fellini is quoted . . . as having said he chose Donald Sutherland for the role because of the anonymity of his 'erased face.'

That must have warmed Sutherland's heart, but the fact is that under hard and uncomfortable circumstances, he has created the portrait Fellini surely dreamed of. It seems a thankless but hugely skilled piece of acting. His Casanova is a pompous and posturing ass, vain, stupid, obsessed, prattling on about love but incapable of receiving or transmitting anything but gross physical sensations.

Fellini places Casanova beyond our sympathies, but in the end Sutherland generates our pity for the rheumy, peevish and disappointed old man, recognized by the world for the fool he was, that Casanova turned into at the end of his days.

The telling of it is all Fellini, all done on sound stages in the manner of surrealist paintings sprung to life . . ."

©Los Angeles Times, 1977.

The Times (London), 1/20/77 (p. 13)
Gideon Bachmann

". . . We are left with an image of a sad sexual athlete, caught in the web of his cultural aspirations, but exposed as a dilettante not unlike the Latin Lover of today's Roman summer streets.

There are other contemporary dimensions to the film. The image of an upstart in a world that applauds only success, and its master only as long as that lasts; of the purveyor of entertainment collecting acclaim but not love; of the ever-failing narcissist felled by his own social strife, discarded and derided, aging, by the society that feigns complicity only to see him strut and finally stumble . . .

Certainly this is Fellini's most splendid film. Incredible expenses were chalked up to create, around the Cinecitta' pool, a Venice as splendid as the Maritime Republic could never have been, peopled by masks and costumes that defy the imagination . . ."

©The Times, 1977.

FIGHTING MAD

Director, Screenplay: *Jonathan Demme*. Producers: *Roger Corman, Evelyn Purcell*. Photography: *Michael Watkins*. Editor: *Anthony Magro*. Music: *Bruce Langhorne*. Production: *Santa Fe Productions*. Distributor: Twentieth Century-Fox. Running time 88 minutes. Los Angeles opening July 1976 at several theatres. **Classification: None.**

Players: *Peter Fonda, Lynn Lowry, John Doucette, Philip Carey, Scott Glen, Kathleen Miller, Harry Northup, Ted Markland, Gino Franco, Noble Willingham, Peter Fain, Allan Wyatt, Laura Wetherford, Gerry Wetherford.*

Los Angeles Times, 7/28/76 (Pt. IV, p. 11)
Kevin Thomas

"In *Fighting Mad* . . . Jonathan Demme, one of the most promising young writer-directors in exploitation pictures, has allowed violence to outweigh ideas to such a degree that the picture becomes a turnoff, little more than a blatantly obvious play to the yahoo mentality.

It's a shame, because technically the picture is terrific and its story could have sustained considerably more development . . .

There are lots of potent ingredients here: nostalgia for a simpler though endangered way of life vs. rapacious industrialization, a concern for ecology and despair over the corrupt politicians that allow men like Carey to prevail and flourish. But the Niagara of violence unleased when Fonda decides to fight back after Carey has Glen and his wife (Kathleen Miller) savagely murdered finally drowns out everything . . ."

©Los Angeles Times, 1976.

Monthly Film Bulletin, 8/76 (p. 165)
Tom Milne

"Another dose of vigilante justice, not made any more palatable by sporadic attempts to fabricate a conservationist image for Peter Fonda's routine hero . . . With a silly script which spends far too much time on interminable scene setting and far too little on giving the background of absurd legal and political machinations anything approaching credibility, *Fighting Mad* in fact never begins to get off the ground; and even its parade of violence is constantly undermined by laboriously 'stylish' crosscutting which intersperses (for instance) the murder of Charlie and Carolee with shots of the increasingly anxious family group awaiting their arrival for a celebration."

©Monthly Film Bulletin, 1976.

New York Post, 10/9/76 (p. 21)
Archer Winsten

". . . It is unthinkable that our hero will succumb to his many wounds, including a lung shot that makes him cough. On the other hand, he had to be riddled with all those professional gunmen shooting at him.

I'm not going to tell you how it turns out, except

to suggest that from the very beginning Peter Fonda is presented as a very fast man in rough-and-tumble, or anything else, even a bed.

The director-writer of this film, Jonathan Demme, himself once an NYC publicity man, knows well on which side of plotting the butter is laid for popular sympathy. He's done a good job. It's a long bow he pulls, but it has a lot of emotion going for it. Nobody's really in favor of murder, strip mining, and paving over beautiful horse-pasture country with macadam shopping centers. Down with bulldozers! Up the old country virtues, and some open sex, too."

Reprinted by Permission of New York Post.
©1976, New York Post Corporation.

The Times (London), 10/12/76 (p. 35)
Alan Brien

"*Fighting Mad* . . . has Peter Fonda, like his father before him, driven out of the old homestead by the greed of vested interest. But in the Oklahoma plains of *Grapes of Wrath*, Henry Fonda underwent a revolutionary education and joined the ranks of organised labour. In the Arkansas mountains, Peter Fonda, glum and stick-like as a bespectacled grasshopper, opts for the old Western solution of the lone avenger, relying on the shaky assumption that the good guy, simply by virtue of his goodness, must always be faster on the trigger than the baddies . . .

. . . What could have been a serious indictment turns into just another sensation-packed, corpse-filled fairy tale with an improbable happy ending."

©The Times, 1976.

FINDHORN

Documentary. Director: *Peter Werner*. Producers: *Randi Johnson, Victoria Mudd*. Photography: *Rhodan Streeter, Rowena Pattee*. Editor: *Lisa Fruchtman*. Music: *Hans Poulson*. Distributor: *Moving Pictures, Inc.* Running time 62 minutes. Los Angeles opening September 5, 1976, at the Royal Theatre. Classification: None.

Note: There is no cast in this film.

Los Angeles Times, 9/3/76 (Pt. IV, p. 24)
Linda Gross

". . . In 1962, when Peter Caddy, a soft-spoken

continued on next page

continued from previous page

and proud man, was fired from his job as manager of a Scottish luxury hotel, he and his wife Eileen moved to a desolate 5-acre trailer park near an Air Force base and a public dump on a bleak bay along the North Sea. For five years Caddy unsuccessfully tried to find work. When his unemploy-ment money was cut off, the couple accepted it as a sign from God and began growing an unlikely garden on sandy soil.

Today, 15 years later, Findhorn is a thriving set-tlement of 200 persons who live and work together in cooperation among themselves and in commun-ion with plants and elements around them.

Documentary film-makers Randi Johnson and Victoria Mudd spent 10 weeks with a seven-member crew living at Findhorn. The resulting film is a charming portrait of a community which is both contemporary and archaic—a kind of Scottish Brook Farm without the intellectual thrust. Resi-dents are into meditation, group sharing, veg-etarianism, pantheism and a fey Scottish accept-ance of assistance from other-world creatures . . ."

©Los Angeles Times, 1976.

FIST-RIGHT OF FREEDOM—FOX (FAUSTRECHT DER FREIHEIT)

Director: *Rainer Werner Fassbinder.*
Screenplay (German with English subtitles): *Mr. Fassbinder, Christian Hohoff.* Executive Producer: *Mr. Hohoff.* Photography: *Michael Ballhaus.* Editor: *Theat Eymesz.* Music: *Peter Raben.* Production: *Tango Film.* Running time 123 minutes. New York opening September, 1975, at the New York Film Festival, Lincoln Center. Classification: None. Origin: Germany.

Fox: *Rainer Werner Fassbinder.* Eugen: *Peter Chatel.* Max: *Karl-Heinz Bohm.* Philip: *Harry Baer.* Mother: *Ulla Jacobson.* Father: *Adrian Hoven.* Hedwig: *Christiane Maybach.*

See Volume 1 for additional reviews

Film, 4/76 (p. 8)
Lesley Robinson

"Fassbinder's films show an awareness and sympathy for the plight of the outsider, the op-pressed and underprivileged. In his view the exist-ing social structure precludes any real reciprocity in relationships. There will always be the victims

and the oppressors and even the most well-intentioned relationship has a dominant/submissive, guru/disciple element . . .

Fassbinder frequently appears in his own films and here in the role of Franz he gives his most outstanding performance. Certainly not the ar-chetypal Romantic Lead, he has a strange sullenly sensual presence and his portrayal is unerringly observed, understated but at the same time power-ful. Peter Chatel as Eugen is magnificently urbane and sneering and the talented Adrian Hoven, as the choleric and alcoholic factory owner, provides one of the most superb cameos in the film.

One of the film's few faults is the director's too frequent use of the cinematic sledgehammer . . ."

© Film 1976.

Cineaste, Spring 1976 (p. 44)
Ruth McCormick

" . . . The plot in *Fox* is important in that it serves as the skeletal structure upon which the whole story of a society and its contradictions is built. The dialogue is natural, at times almost banal, and peo-ple reveal themselves with the most casual com-ments, as they do by their clothes, their homes, their meeting places . . .

In a world dominated by the market, nothing, and nobody, is free, as Fox learns. Death is the only immediate freedom he can hope for. Eugen, who understands money doesn't come easy and that one must always pay, puts a price upon, as he exacts a price from, not only others, but also him-self. Freedom itself has a price and when the money runs out, any illusions we might entertain about independence are lost. Whether we accept the existing oppressive state of affairs or want to change it, we have to realize our dependence on others––whether, in the first instance, to take *from* them, or, in the second, to work *with* them. *Fox* makes this point very well."

© Cineaste, 1976.

FOOD OF THE GODS, THE

Director, Screenplay: *Bert I. Gordon.* Based on a portion of the novel by H. G. Wells. Ex-ecutive Producer: *Samuel Z. Arkoff.* Photog-raphy: *Reginald Morris.* Editor: *Corky Ehlers* Music: *Elliot Kaplan.* Distributor: *American International.* Running time 88 minutes. Los Angeles opening June, 1976, at several theatres. Classification: PG.

Players: *Marjoe Gortner, Pamela Franklin, Ralph Meeker, Jon Cypher, Belinda Balaski, Tom Stovall, Ida Lupino, John McLiam.*

Los Angeles Times, 6/16/76 (Pt. IV, p. 14)
Kevin Thomas

" . . . Based on a portion––a very small portion, surely––of an H.G. Wells novel, this penny dreadful has a humble country couple (Ida Lupino, John McLiam) discovering a flow of what looks like pancake mix gushing near their island wilderness cottage. Since it didn't prove to be oil––as if it could ever be mistaken for that!––Miss Lupino and McLiam decide, with impenetrable logic, to feed it to the chickens. Wowee! Instant giant hens, caterpillars, wasps and, worst of all, rats . . .

Veteran low-budget producer Bert I. Gordon's special effects, though grisly, aren't much better than his dialogue, and his direction is undetectable. As a result, the cast fares pretty badly. *The Food of the Gods* quickly proves unpalatable."

© Los Angeles Times, 1976.

Monthly Film Bulletin, October 1976 (p. 213)
Tom Milne

"A truly appalling piece of s-f horror in which the cretinous dialogue, hopefully illuminating the follies of human greed and tampering with nature, poses more of a hazard to the cast than the crudely animated giant wasps or the monster rat and cockerel heads stiffly manipulated from the wings, and in which the process work (on the rare occasions when the giant creatures are not simply shown crawling over miniature sets and dinky toy cars) is so wobbly that an earthquake seems the most likely outcome. Although some attempt has been made at updating (Pamela Franklin, in particular, is saddled with what passes for contemporary idiom), the whole thing looks and sounds so antediluvian that the minatory ending seems almost appropriate as the last two jars of the mysterious food are ponderously traced . . . to a kindergarten."

©Monthly Film Bulletin, 1976.

Christian Science Monitor, 7/26/76 (p. 22)
David Sterritt

" . . . most of the movie is taken up in battles between the heroes and giant wasps and rats. (Giant wasps and rats are present in Wells, but easily dispatched in the opening chapters.) They become giant by gobbling some stuff called the Food of the Gods, which seems to be made of pancake mix and is kept by Ida Lupino in jars conveniently labeled 'F.O.T.G.' . . .

The special effects range from repellent to silly. There is lots of violence, but none of it is convincing enough to make a giant ostrich bury its head in the sand. Producer-director-writer Gordon has come up with a neat beginning and an evocative ending, but botched almost everything in between, including the screenplay, which has more plot-holes than any movie in recent memory, and enough dopey lines to make a Saturday-night audience howl in all the wrong places . . . "

Reprinted by permission from The Christian Science Monitor © 1976. The Christian Science Publishing Society. All rights reserved.

New York Post, 7/17/76 (p. 17)
Archer Winsten

" . . . First inkling that something is amiss comes when Morgan (Marjoe Gortner), a football player visiting an island off British Columbia with a couple of friends, has one of them bitten to death by huge wasps.

Next, some caterpillars happen into the stuff and the next thing that you know they're trying to eat an arm off Mrs. Skinner (Ida Lupino), wife of the man who discovered the growth material which he would like to market.

And that's not the worst of it. Some rats eat up and turn into rats the size of dogs and twice as vicious . . .

H.G. Wells himself had the original idea. Reduced to film and equipped with producer-director-screenwriter Bert I. Gordon's dialogue it comes up pure goose-pimpler with a bit of revulsion thrown in for good measure."

Reprinted by Permission of New York Post. ©1976, New York Post Corporation.

New York Magazine, 7/26/76 (p. 56)
John Simon

" . . . I wish I hadn't seen the movie, so that I could avoid it like the plague. It offers a not very generous portion of Wells, but abundant food for thoughtlessness and a good many raucous, albeit unintended, laughs. 'The story,' to quote the program notes, 'deals with the terrifying events caused when [sic] a farmer feeds his normally harmless animals a mysterious substance he finds seeping from the ground. Almost overnight it causes them to grow abnormally large and vicious.' The rest is the usual . . .

None of this, however, is nearly as funny as the dialogue, which contains passages like: 'You're the most selfish man in the world.' 'So why do you work for me?' 'Because jobs for female bacteriologists aren't that easy to find.' And there is plenty more where that came from . . . "

©1976 by the NYM Corp. Reprinted with the permission of NEW YORK Magazine.

FRAMED

Director: *Phil Karlson*. Screenplay: *Mort Briskin*. From the novel by *Art Powers and Mike Misenheimer*. Producers: *Mort Briskin and Joe Briskin*. Photography: *Jack A. Marta*. Editor: *Harry Gersted*. Distributor: *Paramount Pictures*. Running time 106 minutes. New York opening October 1, 1975, at several theatres. Classification: R.

Ron Lewis: *Joe Don Baker*. Susan Barrett: *Conny Van Dyke*. Vince Greeson: *Gabriel Dell*. Sal Viccarrone: *John Marley*. Sam Perry: *Brock Peters*. Haskins: *Roy Jenson*. Bundy: *John Larch*. Morello: *Warren Kemmerling*. Andrew May: *Joshua Bryant*. Senator Tatum: *Walter Brooke*. Frank: *Paul Mantee*.

See Volume 1 for additional reviews

Take One, 12/2/75 (p. 37)
George Morris

"Phil Karlson's *Framed* is unequivocally the finest American film I have seen so far this year (1975). Discarded by Paramount at Manhattan showcase theaters during the New York Film Festival, *Framed* nevertheless consolidates Karlson's reputation as one of the foremost action directors in the cinema. Most of Karlson's films project a unique and personal vision of a universe controlled by organized evil and corruption, but few of them acknowledge the halftones and moral shadings which must penetrate such a world, no matter how dissolute its inhibitants or corrosive its values. *Framed*, like Karlson's very best movies--e.g. *Kansas City Confidential* (1952), *99 River Street* (1953) and *The Brothers Rico* (1957)--successfully creates a macrocosm of undefined morality, where one man's idea of evil is the next man's concept of good . . .

Through the hulking presence of Joe Don Baker's central performance, the staccato rhythms of its action sequences, the visceral force of its violence, and the moral contradictions and implications which Karlson has realized in his *mise-en-scene*, *Framed* approaches that sublime level where form and content, continually reinforcing one another, become virtually indistinguishable. It just may be Phil Karlson's masterpiece."

© Take One, 1975.

FREAKY FRIDAY

Director: *Gary Nelson*. Screenplay: *Mary Rodgers*. Based on the book by Ms. Rodgers. Producer: *Ron Miller*. Photography: *Charles F. Wheeler*. Editor: *Cotton Warburton*. Music: *Al Kasha, Joel Hirschhorn*. Distributor: *Buena Vista Distribution Company*. Running time 95 minutes. New York opening January 28, 1977, at several theatres. Classification: G.

Players: *Iris Adrian, John Astin, Kaye Ballard, Ruth Buzzi, Fritz Feld, Jodie Foster, Barbara Harris, Patsy Kelly, Marc McClure, Sparky Marcus, Marie Windsor*.

Village Voice, 4/4/77 (p. 41)
Andrew Sarris

". . . Actually, *Freaky Friday*, like many supposedly wholesome family films I have encountered, presents a more hellish view of American life than that promoted by the fear-mongers. Here, Daddy (John Astin) bluffs at the office, bullies at home, and is about to fall apart at any moment. The mandatory Disney car chase seems to revel in destructiveness and irresponsibility for their own sake, and existence is one unpleasant embarrassment after another. And yet there are the two leads played by Barbara Harris and Jodie Foster. Barbara Harris and Jodie Foster! Fellini should have such luck and skill in casting his female roles. The playing of Harris and Foster here in this age-reversal situation is more than perfect; it is positively uncanny. Harris, the adult with the childlike eyes and feelings, and Foster, the child with the grown-up eyes and manner, switch roles as if they were switching souls, and neither ever makes a false move or displays a false emotion."

Reprinted by permission of The Village Voice
Copyright © The Village Voice, Inc., 1977.

Newsweek, 2/28/77 (p. 72)
Janet Maslin

"*Freaky Friday* is about a mother and daughter who magically exchange bodies for a day, but the movie's neatest trick has less to do with supernatural forces than with inspired type-casting . . .

Foster's role is the narrower of the two, and when she begins seeing things from her mother's point of view, she becomes not so much a 'grownup' as a wiseacre. Harris is a delight: when she slouches around the house or winces when she has to kiss her tiny son ('What a nerd!'), she's not just playing a kid but giving a letter-perfect Jodie Foster imitation. Harris is funniest when performing the redoubtable turn of acting like a young girl *trying* to act like her mother so that the neighbors, the repairmen and the cleaning lady won't catch on. Harris has been affecting the mannerisms of an aging adolescent for years—but she has never before deployed them under such devilishly appropriate circumstances.''

©Newsweek, Inc. 1977
reprinted by permission.

Los Angeles Times, 12/20/76 (Pt. IV, p. 15)
Kevin Thomas

''. . . *Freaky Friday* has the stuff of a stronger, more sophisticated film but has been processed to fit into the bland, synthetic Disney formula. Even so, both Miss Harris and Miss Foster make the most of their offbeat opportunity . . .

Miss Harris is so special in her antic charm that it's always worth seeing her, even though her rather infrequent screen appearances are usually in family entertainments. Once again Miss Foster, here a typical healthy adolescent, astonishes in her versatility . . .

No Disney film is complete without several favorite veteran players. Besides Patsy Kelly there are Fritz Feld as Miss Foster's band instructor, Marie Windsor as her typing teacher and Iris Adrian as a lady on a bus perplexed by Miss Foster's antics . . .''

©Los Angeles Times, 1976.

New York Post, 1/29/77 (p. 21)
Archer Winsten

''. . . Outwardly they remain the same, but inside Annabel's body is her mother, and inside Mrs. Andrews resides the reckless spirit of Annabel.

The wildest slapstick emerges when Mrs. Andrews, really the unlicensed, untutored Annabel, drives the family Volks Bug, and when Annabel, really her mother, is forced to perform waterskiing heroics followed by a flight in a towed hang-glider.

This kind of Disney family comedy has been proven popular with easy laughers, and this film is no exception. Jodie Foster is an accomplished youngster and Barbara Harris suffers her predictable predicaments with a skill that comes with long practice and an amiable face . . .''

Reprinted by Permission of New York Post.
©1977, New York Post Corporation.

Films in Review, January 1977 (p. 57)
Tatiana Balkoff Lipscomb

''Like a wholesome, unpretentious sweet, a Disney film is predictable in flavor, but still agreeable to taste. *Freaky Friday*, a slight and 'kooky' farce, has Jodie Foster playing Annabel, a 13-year-old on the brink of growing up, with good support from Barbara Harris (Annabel's mother), John Astin (the father), Sparky Marcus (a 6-year-old brother) and an able cast including Patsy Kelly, Kaye Ballard, Ruth Buzzi and Marc McClure to make the 'situations' work . . .

Ron Miller's concept of the Mary Rodgers script

is apt, and Gary Nelson's direction is paced nicely. If uncomplicated laughter is your dish, *Freaky Friday* will be a feast.''

©Films in Review, 1977.

Film Information, February 1977 (p. 3)
Robert E. A. Lee

''. . . A very interesting point remains unarticulated although implied in this film . . . And that point is that the husband/father (John Astin) is self-centered, if well-meaning, and at every point takes advantage of them both; if unknowingly, the demands he makes of them are unfair. And the film cutting back and forth between the daily routines of both women increasingly becomes a well-aimed softly feminist statement. Of course, the movie is played mostly for laughs and one could very well sit through it and not notice the inherent social criticism. But it is there, and it makes *Freaky Friday* one of Disney's most relevant films.

The difficult casting is excellent, although Jodie Foster, with much varied screen experience behind her, seems at times much too old as the 14-year-old daughter (however, it is her true age), and Barbara Harris, at times too young to be her mother . . .''

©Film Information, 1977.

Christian Science Monitor, 2/14/77 (p. 18)
David Sterritt

''. . . The results hit close enough to home to keep parents and older kids interested, with enough sheer slapstick to cheer viewers as young as my five-year-olds, who loved it (especially the wrecked cars that proliferate near the end).

Much of the credit goes to Gary Nelson, who directed with more sophistication and visual wit than most of the Disney regulars show. *Freaky Friday* is no pillar of family-film art, and the finale is much too pat, but sly touches are tucked sneakily in the corners, and extra chuckles creep in when you least expect them. Though things do get too talky, there's a quiet sophistication here that the Disney folks don't usually find these days, lurking amid some cleverly constructed laughs.

The cast also deserves plenty of commendation, especially Jodie Foster . . . and Barbara Harris . . .''

Reprinted by permission from The Christian
Science Monitor © 1977.
The Christian Science Publishing Society.
All rights reserved.

FRENCH PROVINCIAL
(SOUVENIRS D'EN FRANCE)

Director: *Andre Techine*. Screenplay (French with English subtitles): *Mr. Techine and Marilyn Goldin*. Photography: *Bruno Nuytten*. Editor: *Anne-Marie Deshayes*. Music: *Philippe Sarde*. Production: *Stephan Films*. Running time 91 minutes. New York opening October 9, 1975, at the New York Film Festival, Lincoln Center. Classification: None. Origin: France.

Berthe: *Jeanne Moreau*. Hector: *Michel Auclair*. Regina: *Marie-France Pisiec*. Prosper: *Claude Mann*. Augustine: *Orane Demazis*. Pedret: *Aram Stephan*. Lucic: *Helene Surgere*. Victor: *Julien Guilomar*.

See Volume 1 for additional reviews

Los Angeles Times, 10/12/76 (Pt. IV, p. 1)
Kevin Thomas

"Remember those Joan Crawford-Bette Davis-Barbara Stanwyck movies about the strong women who step in and save the family business from disaster?

Young French writer-director Andre Techine, in his feature debut, has in *French Provincial* . . . taken this familiar plot, enlisted Jeanne Moreau as his star, and together they have brought it up to date with a women's liberation sensibility. The result is a quirky, skittish comedy-drama, written with an American, Marilyn Goldin, that shows off Miss Moreau to great advantage in a major role, her first to be seen in America in far too long . . .

While Techine admirably rings in a whole new set of reactions to a very traditional saga, his seeming offhandedness sometimes is too casual for his own good . . .

Not all the film's various whimsical moments come off convincingly, but Miss Moreau, credibly progressing from sensual if prematurely ravaged laborer to chic executive, comes through . . ."

©Los Angeles Times, 1976

Take One, October 1976 (p. 39)
Joe Blades

". . . *Souvenirs d'en France* (U.S. title *French Provincial*) satisfies, initially, due to its story line. Its texture is that of a fine novel. In content, but in content only, it is the most Faulkner-like film I've seen . . .

Ultimately, however, the film's source is the nou-veau roman tradition of Duras, Robbe-Grillet, Sarraute, and, in America, Susan Sontag. In Parisian literary circles these writers are lumped together as *l'ecole du regard* because of their concentration on minute detail . . .

On the surface, everything appears scaled down, skeleton-bare. This literary school is a natural for the movies, where the order (or disorder) of the human mind can be conveyed in purely pictorial terms. Indeed, the nouvelle roman has breathed screen life long before now, most notably in *Hiroshima, Mon Amour* and *Last Year at Marienbad*; but never has the result been so compelling. What *Souvenirs d'en France* does with cinema form is a major achievement . . ."

©Take One, 1976.

FROM NOON TILL THREE

Director, Screenplay: *Frank D. Gilroy*. Based on the novel by Mr. Gilroy. Producers: *M.J. Frankovich, William Self*. Photography: *Lucien Ballard*. Editor: *Maury Weintrobe*. Music: *Elmer Bernstein*. Distributor: *United Artists*. Running time 99 minutes. Los Angeles opening October 20, 1976, at several theatres. Classification: PG.

Graham Dorsey: *Charles Bronson*. Amanda Starbuck: *Jill Ireland*. Buck Powers: *Douglas V. Fowley*. Ape: *Stan Haze*. Boy: *Damon Douglas*. Mexican: *Hector Morales*. Sheriff: *Bert Williams*. Rev. Cabot: *William Lanteau*. Edna: *Betty Cole*.

Los Angeles Times, 10/20/76 (Pt. IV, p. 16)
Charles Champlin

". . . The movie, written and directed by Frank D. Gilroy (author of *The Subject Was Roses*) from his own novella, is a curious piece of business, even farther off-trail than most off-trail westerns.

It is not so much a demythologizing of the old and cherished West as it is a very contemporary satire on the world's eagerness to build romantic legends out of pieces of string, circumstantial evidence, white and gray lies and ruthless, efficient promotion . . .

In a real sense, the movie is not Bronson's but Jill Ireland's, who is Mrs. Bronson. It is a lovely chance to evolve from the sad and straitlaced widow to the sensuous woman to the greedy living legend with innards by National Cash Register and a script by Ned Buntline, and she brings it off attractively and competently.

It is all, for better or worse, a fable, improbable to begin with and escalating to and beyond the preposterous . . ."

©Los Angeles Times, 1976

Film Information, October 1976 (p. 3)
Suzanne Bowers

". . . *From Noon Till Three* is a welcome and surprising change of pace. In it, Bronson deftly mocks his familiar macho screen persona, giving one of his most realistic and human portrayals to date . . .

Bronson, who at first seems out-of-place and uncomfortable with the put-on comedy of the first scenes, settles into the character of Graham Dorsey. What could have been a cardboard caricature becomes an all-too-human man caught in a situation not of his own making. Ireland, though saddled with a less sympathetic character, is warmer and less stilted than in previous films with her husband. Frank D. Gilroy . . . elicited versatile and natural performances from them. His screenplay, based on his own novel, although not totally believable in its Western ambience, captures the mentality and ironies of a time in our history when legends could become 'truth.' . . ."

©Film Information, 1976.

New York Post, 1/29/77 (p. 21)
Frank Rich

". . . The main thing—hell, the only thing—really worth noting about *From Noon Till Three* is that it is profoundly weird, which is not quite the same thing as being good. The weirdness, though, isn't immediately apparent, because the film's first half is devoted to a conventional and tedious rendition of standard Western plot No. 29a . . . Then the funny business begins: We suddenly discover that the film's first 45 minutes were nothing but an elaborate buildup for a joke whose unraveling takes up *From Noon Till Three*'s tolerable second half . . .

. . . Unfortunately, there's no depth to the filmmaker's spoofing, and 45 minutes is a terribly long time to wait for the fun, such as it is, to begin . . .

The acting doesn't help. Charles Bronson may be all things to many men and women, but a comedian he is not . . ."

Reprinted by Permission of New York Post.
©1977, New York Post Corporation.

Films in Review, February 1977 (p. 120)
Steve Swires

"*From Noon Till Three* wants desperately to be taken for a sardonic Western, demonstrating the

consequences of the classic John Ford line: 'When the legend becomes fact, print the legend.' There may well be a clever idea in this story about a bank robber who spends three idyllic hours with a lonely widow renewing her zest for life, only to suffer an ironic retribution, but it has been completely sabotaged by the heavy-handedness of writer-director Frank D. Gilroy. Gilroy has no visual sense whatsoever, and even though he utilized the considerable talents of veteran cinematographer Lucien Ballard, his film still has the flat, monotonous look of a made-for-TV movie . . .

Most damaging of all, Gilroy has burdened himself with the somnambulant screen presences of Charles Bronson and his wife Jill Ireland . . ."

©Films in Review, 1977.

FRONT, THE

Director, Producer: *Martin Ritt*. Screenplay: *Walter Bernstein*. Executive Producer: *Charles H. Joffe*. Photography: *Michael Chapman*. Editor: *Sidney Levin*. Music: *Dave Grusin*. Distributor: *Columbia Pictures*. Running time 94 minutes. New York opening September 30, 1976, at the Coronet Theatre. Classification: PG.

Howard Prince: *Woody Allen*. Hecky Brown: *Zero Mostel*. Phil Sussman: *Herschel Bernardi*. Alfred Miller: *Michael Murphy*. Florence Barrett: *Andrea Marcovicci*. Hennessey: *Remak Ramsay*. Meyer Prince: *Marvin Lichterman*. Delaney: *Lloyd Gough*. Phelps: *David Margulies*. Sam: *Joshua Shelley*. Howard's Attorney: *Norman Rose*. Committee Counselor: *Charles Kimbrough*. Committee Chairman: *M. Josef Sommer*.

New York Times,10/1/76 (p. C 7)
Vincent Canby

". . . As much as an entertainment film can be, *The Front* is about what it was like when to be a member of the Communist Party, or to have been a member at some earlier time, or to have associated with people who might have been members, or to have had left-wing sympathies, or to have been sympathetic to people who might have had such sympathies, was enough to destroy one's career, to

continued on next page

continued from previous page

turn old friends into stool pigeons, to humiliate the codes by which men professed to live morally.

The film's inspiration is the casting of Woody Allen in the pivotal role of Howard Prince, a quintessential Woody Allen rat, an unsuccessful, amateur bookmaker who works in a bar as a cashier and has absolutely nothing on his mind except small schemes doomed to fail.

The Front looks at the McCarthy period through the eyes of this epically self-absorbed coward, who, as is the way of cowards in such comedies, slips upon his finest hour as if it were a banana peel and slides to unexpected nobility . . .

Mr. Ritt and Mr. Bernstein tell the basically comic story of Howard Prince's rise, fall and rise against an authentically grim background of deceit, blackmail, injustice and personal tragedy . . .

Mr. Allen, Michael Murphy (who plays his blacklisted friend), Mr. Mostel, Andrea Marcovicci (the girl Howard Prince lusts after), are all fine . . ."

©1976 by the New York Times Company.
Reprinted by permission.

Saturday Review, 10/2/76 (p. 38)
Judith Crist

". . . Bernstein and Ritt provide a detailed tapestry of those Dark Ages during the golden age of television, from the 'liberal' producer turned hypocritical hatchet man to the network president kowtowing to sponsors and self-styled investigators; from the cold-blooded interrogators to the terrorized victims. The filmmakers' careful balance and cool approach let the viciousness and sweetness of humans speak for themselves. The casting is impeccable, with Allen's completely unmannered and utterly winning Howard; Mostel's monstrously comic and heartbreakingly hopeless clown; Herschel Bernardi's futile producer; Michael Murphy's sophisticated scriptwriter; and Andrea Marcovicci's beautiful and passionate script editor. Incidentally, Mostel, Bernardi, and two supporting players were also blacklist victims. Fittingly, it is the survivors who, in recalling a terrible past, provide us with hope for our present survival and do so by way of one of the year's best films."

©Judith Crist, 1976.

Newsweek, 10/4/76 (p. 89)
Jack Kroll

"*The Front* is Woody Allen as Howard Prince, a quiet little schlemiel in 1953 who works as a restaurant cashier and loses all his money playing the horses. His fronthood comes about when a writer friend (Michael Murphy), who has been blacklisted by the television networks in the McCarthyite hysteria of those days asks Howard to pretend to be the author of his scripts. Soon Howard Prince is the big new name in TV drama, fronting for no fewer then three blacklisted writers, living in a snazzy new apartment on his 10 per cent of the fees and making it with a script editor (the stunning and delightful Andrea Marcovicci) who thinks the shnook is a genius.

Funny? Yes. Improbable? Very. True? Mostly. Yes, Virginia, there really was a blacklist in those gutless '50s when movie studios and TV networks knuckled under to professional patriots and their lists of 'subversives'—alleged Communists and fellow travelers, who were promptly fired and couldn't get jobs anywhere in the entertainment business. Those were shameful and tragic years, strewn with the wreckage of careers and lives. But there was also something 'gruesomely funny' about that time, as Walter Bernstein, who wrote *The Front*, puts it. Bernstein was a blacklisted writer in the '50s, and *The Front* is a kind of grimly laughing elegy for those days by Bernstein and some other survivors of the blacklist—director Martin Ritt, Zero Mostel, who plays a blacklisted performer, and actors Herschel Bernardi, Joshua Shelley and Lloyd Gough . . ."

©Newsweek, Inc. 1976
reprinted by permission.

New York Post, 10/1/76 (p. 16)
Frank Rich

"Up until it falls apart before your very eyes, *The Front* . . . is a genuine rarity among American movies—a light comedy forged out of dark and authentic pain. The men responsible for this picture, director Martin Ritt and screenwriter Walter Bernstein, were victims of the show business blacklist of the Joe McCarthy era, and *The Front* is their attempt to exorcise the ghosts of that time—both for themselves and for a mass audience . . .

The tragedy of *The Front* is that Ritt and Bernstein . . . squander their brightly conceived movie in the most mundane fashion imaginable: When *The Front* fails, it is not, as you might expect, from a lack of guts or intelligence, but from sloppy errors of direction, writing and casting . . .

. . . the filmmakers' most crucial mistake is the casting of Woody Allen as Howard. While Allen is his usual wonderfully funny self during the movie's first half, he can't handle the serious acting demanded of him in the second . . .

. . . even so there's much to admire—including the superb performances by Murphy as the blacklisted writer and Mostel as the TV comic who's reduced to groveling before right-wing inquisitors and opportunistic Catskills resort owners to get work . . . Had *The Front* successfully maintained the desperate tension we see in these performances, it would have been the great movie about the McCarthy era we've long been waiting for; as it stands, it will more than do until that great movie comes along."

Reprinted by Permission of New York Post.
©1976, New York Post Corporation.

Women's Wear Daily, 9/20/76 (p. 18)
Howard Kissel

". . . The preposterous situations the McCarthy years created are things we can laugh at with a certain discomfort now, but in themselves they are, of course, in no way funny. The uneasy tone of *The Front* reflects this state of affairs beautifully. At times the pace of the film seems disjointed, even frenetic, but the moods Ritt creates are clearly dictated by the difficult material. The film has been perfectly cast. Woody Allen as the central character conveys both the nebbishness and the laughable braggadocio of a man on his way up from a restaurant cashier and bookie to a media literary hero. One can't help but be impressed by his ability to make this farcical character believable, particularly in his puzzled response to the unctuous Congressmen.

Zero Mostel plays a blacklisted actor with his usual bravura and occasional overzealousness— but his painful scene of humiliation in the Catskills resort is one of overpowering genuineness . . .

The Front is both a powerful, sardonic reminder of ugly times and a monument to those who were able to survive them."

©Women's Wear Daily, 1976.

Film Information, 9/76 (p. 1)
Bea Rothenbeuchner

"*The Front* is about a shy little man, an everyday guy, Howard Prince (Woody Allen), who wants very much to get ahead in the world. A restaurant cashier and occasional bookie, he unwittingly achieves celebrity status when he agrees to do a friend a favor. His decision not only brings him fame and fortune but also forces him to confront a moral dilemma of immense proportions. For this is in the 1950s and Howard Prince is swept into the horrors of the McCarthy era—particularly, those involving the broadcast industry . . .

For the pivotal role of Howard Prince, Ritt chose Woody Allen. Woody is the catalyst that makes the film work as well as it does. More than any other element, it is his characterization that bridges the distance between today's audience and a time that many might prefer to forget. His portrayal of the little man who manages to transcend his own venality, or greed, depending on how you look at it, to emerge a 'hero' (and is human enough to enjoy his moment of glory, even as he is being taken off to prison) is a characterization few contemporary actors could match . . ."

©Film Information, 1976.

Village Voice, 10/4/76 (p. 121)
Andrew Sarris

". . . Ritt and Bernstein do not make the three writers wronged innocents on the rack of the inquisition, but rather committed Communists who never retreat from their convictions. *The Front* therefore diverges from the purely libertarian point of view of the recent *Fear on Trial*, based on the real-life clearing of radio entertainer John Henry Faulk of all the charges brought against him by the blacklisters. Through the recalcitrant writers in the movie, Ritt and Bernstein seek to make opposition to America's role in the Cold War in the late '40s and early '50s ideologically consistent with later opposition to the war in Vietnam, thus bridging the gap between the Old Left and the New Left. It is a hard-nosed approach to the subject, and one that raises more questions than it resolves . . .

It is so easy to imagine that that was another time and another place as if each age did not breed its own scrapegoats. There are perhaps fewer victims at the moment, but I have not detected a great rush to the side of Daniel Schorr and Harry Reems in their recent encounters with the enemies of the Bill of Rights. Ritt and Bernstein and Allen have restaged an Old War with a falsely optimistic ending. It's a shame because the Woody Allen character had the comic potential of a truly Brechtian character. Like Dr. Johnson's dog on its hind legs, however, *The Front* deserves a great deal of credit for having been done at all."

Reprinted by permission of The Village Voice.
Copyright © The Village Voice, Inc., 1976.

Christian Science Monitor, 10/1/76 (p. 22)
David Sterritt

". . . Naturally, Woody Allen's presence dominates the movie clear through. His character is a weasel of a man, chiseling and procrastinating and generally stumbling through life until his unexpected 'front' assignment pushes him into a major decision that reveals unexpected depth. It is essentially a low-key comic part despite the film's serious theme—you don't know whether to laugh or cry during the amazing scene when he explains to his girlfriend that he isn't *really* a brilliant writer—but Allen makes it work on every level. Bravo for this most versatile talent.

Others have shaped the film too, of course. As you watch *The Front* you can almost feel the powerful emotions of the blacklist victims who helped to make it. Walter Bernstein's screenplay commands attention and credibility even when its events and characters seem overdrawn or caricatured (such as the police figures). Only at the end does it falter badly . . .

Mostel comes on too strong in some scenes; as a character observes in Saul Bellow's novel *Humboldt's Gift*, Zero is 'a comedian of genius. But if he isn't restrained, he runs away with everything.' His sad farewell scene is delicate and touching, however."

Reprinted by permission from The Christian
Science Monitor © 1976.
The Christian Science Publishing Society.
All rights reserved.

continued on next page

continued from previous page

Sight and Sound, Winter 1976/1977 (p. 58)
Geoff Brown

". . . Mostel's performance as usual seems designed to reach the back row of the theatre balcony, and his extravagant displays of self-pity weigh the film down heavily . . .

They also clash with the nervous, intimate style of Woody Allen, who turns Howard Prince into an ingenious variation on his usual screen persona . . . Yet Allen's lightweight presence never seriously sabotages the character of the film. When the script manoeuvres him into serious situations . . . his performing skills support him admirably . . .

Ritt's direction is typically measured and meticulous, with no stylistic jiggery-pokery intruding on the conflicts or emotions of the scenes . . . yet to some extent it works against the film. Without any visual camouflage, the patterning of scenes is frequently revealed as baldly melodramatic and conventional; there is little sense, too, of paranoid nightmare . . ."

ⓒ Sight and Sound, 1977

The Times (London), 1/7/77 (p. 6)
David Robinson

". . . *The Front* is wise, literate, witty, intelligently played (notably by Woody Allen in an impressive debut as a straight man, and by the graceful Andrea Marcovicci); yet it is melancholy and muted where it should, even today, be angry. The role played by Zero Mostel seems symptomatic. Blacklisted in 1950, Mostel was celebrated for the belligerence of his resistance. (At his hearing in 1955 he wiggled five fingers to indicate he was invoking the Fifth Amendment and at the conclusion of his televised testimony formally thanked the committee 'for making it possible for me to be on television, since I've been blacklisted from it for the past five years.') In the film, however, Mostel plays the comedian, a lachrymose political innocent.

There is about the film, despite the boldness of its attempt to treat the tragedy from this off-centre and slightly absurdist situation . . . a prevailing sense of pain too much contained . . .''

ⓒ The Times, 1977

The Sunday Times (London), 1/9/77 (p. 37)
Alan Brien

". . . This is not the classic I have been looking for—nevertheless it remains an extraordinary, individual, inventive entertainment . . .

Zero Mostel I find personally icky, like the notorious leaning tower of pizza. But here, as the all-enfolding star you'd hate to love, we follow him, reluctant and enslaved, through humiliations and deprivations, to an elegant, even spry suicide.

The Front also pictures several writers, notably Michael Murphy, who incredibly look and sound like writers; TV producers, notably Herschel Bernardi,

who talk and behave as if they are in the business; and a heroine, Andrea Marcovicci, who like a real girl manages to seem sometimes both horse-faced and beautiful . . .''

ⓒ The Sunday Times, 1977

Cineaste, Winter 1977 (p. 44)
Peter Biskind

"*The Front* is an Old Left wet dream, where the hero gets to say 'Fuck You' to HUAC, and is rewarded w'th a big kiss from his beautiful girlfriend. It's Hollywood's version of those bumper stickers common in the pre-feminist days of the peace movement which said: 'Girls say yes to guys who say no.' Director Martin Ritt and writer Walter Bernstein wanted to make a film without polemics, but they have made one without politics as well . . .

The Front is a pious reminder that it did happen here, but it furthers our understanding of the period not an iota. If it works at all, it does so as a black comedy about Making It, propped up by a brilliant performance by Woody Allen and an occasionally very funny script by Walter Bernstein . . .''

ⓒ Cineaste, 1977

Films in Review, November 1976 (p. 566)
Charles Phillips Reilly

". . . In making the film, director Martin Ritt has brought together some people who, with him, were on the blacklist: scripter Walter Bernstein, and actors Zero Mostel and Herschel Bernardi, all of whom do a good job here.

Memorable is the performance of Allen as a part-time bookie and cashier, a man uninterested in the law, on the fringes of society, out of communication with the kind of world his brother Meyer (Marvin Lichterman), successful furrier and family man, inhabits . . .

Right and Left will dislike some of this film, but Allen is superb in his first dramatic part. *The Front*, despite slow moments, is one of the better films of '76 . . .''

ⓒ Films in Review, 1976

Nation, 10/16/76 (p. 378)
Robert Hatch

". . . *The Front* is utterly devoid of ideology. It doesn't lecture about civil liberties, belabor the point that the Red scare was invented by evil men for base advantage, or declare in righteous anger that the true champions of the American way of life were those caught by the witch hunt. It deals in simple terms with attractive people who find themselves in a dreadful fix . . .

The Front is full of laughs, full of tears, keeps you cheering for the home team. It doesn't tell you how bigotry gets a hold on this country from time to time, but what it does, which more serious discussions never quite seem to do, is make you sense how it would feel to be played with by jackals. And, being entertainment, it ridicules evil. That, of course, is not the only way to fight it, but laughter is a useful tool in the cause of virtue."

©The Nation, 1976.

Monthly Film Bulletin, December 1976 (p. 251)
Richard Combs

". . . the film is rather undercut by its bland sincerity of tone (one can imagine how Paddy Chayefsky would at least have invested it with more venom), or rather by its confusion of tone, since the presence of two very distinctive comedians in leading roles occasionally suggests the makings of a black farce, which Ritt's po-faced style does nothing to accommodate. In effect, the two leads make over their portions of the movie to their own purposes. Zero Mostel is grandiloquently pathetic as the victimised comedian, while Woody Allen is apologetically pathetic as the inadvertent celebrity, although effectively allowing his usual put-upon persona to acquire overtones of the little man as political opportunist. More frequently, especially in his scenes with Andrea Marcovicci, the old Allen routines and phobias seem merely to be struggling to find a more flexible, and directly funny, format."

©Monthly Film Bulletin, 1976.

New Leader, 10/25/76 (p. 23)
Robert Asahina

". . . *The Front* is not at all what its makers promise, and given the degree of personal experience that went into it, since both men were themselves blacklisted, this is surprising and disappointing. Instead of the mixture of tragedy and farce that would have been appropriate, the film offers empty moralism, the cheapest of ironies and little bitterness—or, indeed, any other genuine feeling. It is a hash of pathos and low humor that turns 'the plague years' into a laughing matter: What comes off as ludicrous is the movie's own foolishness, not the time of the blacklist. If *The Front* is successful at all, it is as a snidely ingratiating comic vehicle for its star, Woody Allen . . ."

Reprinted with permission from
The New Leader, 1976.
©The American Labor Conference
on International Affairs, Inc.

New York Magazine, 10/11/76 (p. 78)
John Simon

". . . *The Front* is all facade, posturing, cliches, and cutenesses; it might as well have been made by people whose information about McCarthyism came from a couple of magazine articles, and whose knowledge of human beings from Earl Wilson's column . . .
Martin Ritt has directed with some skill in moving his actors about, and the film is not deficient in rhythm, to which Sidney Levin's editing must have

made its handsome contribution. But Ritt's directorial vision is no more complex than Walter Bernstein's scenaristic one: The film is a congeries of skits rather than a credible organic development. Among the performers, Michael Murphy as Alfred Miller and Charles Kimbrough as an odious congressional counsel come off best . . ."

©1976 by the NYM Corp. Reprinted with
the permission of NEW YORK Magazine.

FUN WITH DICK AND JANE

Director: *Ted Kotcheff.* Screenplay: *David Giler, Mordecai Richler, Jerry Belson.* Based on a story by Gerald Gaiser. Producers: *Peter Bart, Max Palevsky.* Photography: *Fred Koenekamp.* Editor: *Danford B. Greene.* Music: *Ernest Gold.* Distributor: *Columbia Pictures.* Running time 95 minutes. New York opening February 9, 1977, at Loews State 1 and Loews Tower East Theatres. Classification: PG.

Dick Harper: *George Segal.* Jane Harper: *Jane Fonda.* Charlie Blanchard: *Ed McMahon.* Doctor Will: *Dick Gautier.* Loan Company Manager: *Allan Miller.* Raoul Esteban: *Hank Garcia.* Jane's Father: *John Dehner.* Mr. Weeks: *Walter Brooke.* Billy Harper: *Sean Frye.* Jane's Mother: *Mary Jackson.* Immigration Officer: *James Jeter.* Charlie's Secretary: *Maxine Stuart.* Bob: *Fred Willard.*

New York Times, 2/10/77 (p. 48)
Vincent Canby

". . . *Fun With Dick and Jane* . . . is a deceptively sunny, sometimes uproariously funny comedy about the bad taste, vulgarity and awful aimlessness of a certain kind of middle-class American affluence.
Buried not very deeply within the film, there is a small flaw. We are asked to like and to sympathize with Dick and Jane, played by Mr. Segal and Miss Fonda with a fine, earnest kind of intensity I associate with good screwball comedy of the past, and we do like them enormously, even though the char-

continued on next page

continued from previous page

acters are completely dedicated to maintaining all-wrong values. In this respect, the film seems to want to stand on both sides of the fence at once, to take credit for having a social conscience while not really honoring it. It's not enough for us to be told that Dick and Jane are really ripping off the system. They aren't that believably cynical.

This may be taking the film more seriously than anyone intended, though I doubt it . . .

I never have trouble remembering that Miss Fonda is a fine dramatic actress but I'm surprised all over again every time I see her do comedy with the mixture of comic intelligence and abandon she shows here . . ."

©1977 by the New York Times Company.
Reprinted by permission.

Newsweek, 2/21/77 (p. 91)
Janet Maslin

". . . Ted Kotcheff, who directed *The Apprentice-ship of Duddy Kravitz*, clearly intends this as a movie with a message, and David Giler, Jerry Belson and Mordecai Richler's script contains at least one too many tepid truisms about the decline and fall of the bourgeoisie. But the film is so eloquent in its garishness—every piece of furniture in Dick and Jane's compulsively overdecorated house looks brand new—that the polemics fade comfortably into the distressed woodwork. What emerges is a delightfully comic fusion of innocence and intelligence, broad yet carefully detailed, without a hint of the condescension that might have soured the whole thing. Both Segal and Fonda manage to scale themselves down to fit the film's simplest comic predicaments without losing any of the bogus sophistication that makes them sympathetic.

The role is tailor made for Segal, who is fine but unsurprising. Fonda has never before seemed such a guilelessly attractive comedienne . . ."

(©)Newsweek, Inc. 1977
reprinted by permission.

Village Voice, 2/21/77 (p. 49)
Molly Haskell

". . . the message seems to be that it's okay to rob blind as long as the money is for its own sake and not for a heated swimming pool, and as long as you do it in style . . .

Given this by now standard and ugly caper philosophy and the fact that Kotcheff's direction is more of a liability than an asset, it's amazing that *Fun With Dick and Jane* averts disaster and exudes charm as often as it does. For this, I think there is one big and one little reason, and their names are Fonda and Segal: together they generate sparks reminiscent of the sexy-romantic screwball comedy partners of the '30s.

Segal gives an unusually restrained performance. Without the superciliousness that has marred his recent movie roles, he is downright attractive, and Fonda is outrageously, deliciously, effortlessly wonderful. From the moment she appears, we know that she has not only grown in talent, timing, and beauty, but has acquired that nth power that great movie actresses have—a way of going about their business without looking over their shoulders because they assume you are there with them . . ."

Reprinted by permission of The Village Voice.
Copyright © The Village Voice, Inc., 1977.

New York Post, 2/10/77 (p. 42)
Frank Rich

". . . Amusing and pointed as the film's premise may sound, it is systematically dismantled in the script. The screenwriters—who include such notables as novelist Mordecai Richler (*The Apprenticeship of Duddy Kravitz*) and TV alumnus Jerry Belson (of the original "Dick Van Dyke Show")—just don't have any respect for human truth, and without some grounding in truth, comedy can't be funny.

The writers don't even accomplish their most fundamental task—they don't give us characters we can care about or identify with. Dick and Jane aren't credible as people—he's a grinning Pollyanna and she's a wisecracking suburban doxy—and they're about as three-dimensional as stick figures. When Dick loses his job, we never see either him or Jane suffer any real anguish—and if that anguish isn't dramatized, even in comic terms, we can't believe that the couple would take the drastic step of resorting to crime . . ."

Reprinted by Permission of New York Post.
©1977, New York Post Corporation.

Christian Science Monitor, 3/4/77 (p. 19)
David Sterritt

". . . The message is cynical but apparently heartfelt: In an atmosphere of bribes, slush funds, and capitalistic hysteria, misdeed breeds until there's scarcely a moral in sight.

Director Ted Kotcheff's past work has ranged from biting to wheezing, and *Dick and Jane* contains some unnecessary vulgarisms. But the filmmaker strikes many clever and telling notes, sympathizing with his protagonists' plight while never losing sight of the materialistic mania that spurs them on. Though you have to dig a little to see it, *Fun* wears a frown beneath its smile—a frown directed at all the Dicks and Janes whose standards are dictated by cravings.

The cast, including Ed McMahon as a fat-cat boss, is more than capable, and Miss Fonda demonstrates some first-rate comic gifts . . ."

Reprinted by permission from The Christian
Science Monitor (©)1977.
The Christian Science Publishing Society.
All rights reserved.

New York Magazine, 2/28/77 (p. 54)
John Simon

". . . the entire film looks like several months' worth of TV situation comedy by various hands, excerpted and slapped together. And not merely the highlights—quite a few lowlights, too . . .

. . . Fonda is by far the most irresistibly smart-alecky wife since Myrna Loy's Nora in the *Thin Man* series, and more womanly to boot; as Dick, George Segal works hard and not ineffectually, but, as usual, without the apparent effortlessness that is the sine qua non of true comedy . . .

Most astonishing about the film is the amateurish cinematography by the usually accomplished Fred Koenekamp. He seems to have had special trouble with how to make the Harpers' front yard look sun-drenched in studio shots, and ended up with an effect that is like lemon juice in your eye . . ."

© 1977 by the NYM Corp. Reprinted with the permission of NEW YORK Magazine.

Los Angeles Times, 2/9/77 (Pt. IV, p. 1)
Charles Champlin

"There may be better comedies than *Fun With Dick and Jane* made this year, and I certainly hope so.

This dull-edged satire on middle-class unemployment may catch some trade from audiences said to be starved for laughs but, ranked alongside the historic movie jollities, *Fun With Dick and Jane* is short, stale stuff, a good chance badly missed . . .

. . . It is a slapdash structure erected on an awkward and unattractive premise. The script is by several hands, and sounds like it. The direction is without discernible style, and some attractive people are wasted on forced jokes masquerading as satiric barbs (jokes defined loosely enough to include armed robbery and vital bodily functions performed publicly) . . .

The underuse of the charm and intelligence of Segal and Fonda is disappointing, to say it calmly . . ."

© Los Angeles Times, 1977.

Film Information, February 1977 (p. 2)
Thomas O. Bentz

"'See Dick run.' So goes the prologue/punchline in a film whose opening cartoon characters prove to be more engaging—and more fun—than the human embodiments that follow. It is a movie that runs but doesn't move—its couple romps through the pages of life without reflection on its moods or meanings . . .

George Segal is equally unbelievable as an engineer, a father, or an outlaw. He flails his lines like the unloaded gun he carries, calling attention to himself, but then finding himself unable to follow through."

The worst follow-through, however, falls to Jane Fonda, the antiwar realist who a few years ago vowed to do only 'significant' films. After commendable and emotionally gripping performances in *Klute* and *They Shoot Horses, Don't They?* she slipped right back to Barbarella with this sexist and escapist waste . . ."

© Film Information, 1977.

Saturday Review, 2/19/77 (p. 41)
Judith Crist

"*Fun With Dick and Jane* is a funny and promising movie that unfortunately reneges on its promise halfway. Written by David Giler, Jerry Belson and Mordecai Richler, this Peter Bart-Max Palevsky production promises to be the first film to deal with downward mobility in America via the plight of the mortgaged middle class en route to becoming the nouveau poor. The idea, dreamed up by Ted Kotcheff, the film's director, is a dandy, but it is not, alas, the stuff of box-office appeal, and so there's a switch midway to the trite and true path of Watergate-era morality (i.e. turn crook in a crooked system) and the Cinderella-story ending in the comedy tradition . . .

. . . Segal is perhaps the most relaxed of 'light' performers and Fonda, as *Period of Adjustment*, *Cat Ballou*, and other vehicles have demonstrated, has a graceful sense of comedy . . . They lend a sprightly humor to the plight of the children of affluence brought face-to-face with economic necessity. That the scriptwriters failed them midway with an abrupt switch from realistic social comedy to pure caper-plotting is regrettable . . ."

© Judith Crist, 1977.

FUTUREWORLD

Director: *Richard T. Heffron*. Screenplay: *Mayo Simon, George Schenck*. Producers: *Paul N. Lazarus III, James T. Aubrey*. Executive Producer: *Samuel Z. Arkoff*. Photography: *Howard Schwartz*. Editor: *James Mitchell*. Music: *Fred Karlin*. Distributor: *American International Pictures*. Running time 104 minutes. New York opening August 1976 at several theatres. Classification: PG.

Chuck Browning: *Peter Fonda*. Tracy Ballard: *Blythe Danner*. Duffy: *Arthur Hill*. Gunslinger: *Yul Brynner*. Schneider: *John Ryan*. Harry: *Stuart Margolin*.

continued on next page

continued from previous page

New York Post, 8/14/76 (p. 15)
Frank Rich

". . . this thing is a joke. In *Futureworld*, the robots, under the leadership of a mad scientist (John Ryan) who politically and phonically resembles Henry Kissinger, want to take over the world—and that's the kind of sci-fi movie cliche that went out with the Eisenhower era.

At least Richard Benjamin and James Brolin, the cloying leads of *Westworld*, are not back this time. But Brynner—even though he was destroyed at the end of the previous picture—is. He appears in an 'erotic' dream sequence dreamt by heroine Blythe Danner—but don't ask me to explain what the dream sequence is doing in the movie, or why Brynner is in it, or why the dream looks like a cross between an Agnes De Mille ballet and a TV commercial for the Burlington Look . . .

. . . Let's just dispense with *Futureworld* altogether: It's an easy film to forgive and even easier to forget."

Reprinted by Permission of New York Post.
©1976, New York Post Corporation.

Los Angeles Times, 8/18/76 (Pt. IV, p. 1)
Kevin Thomas

". . . *Futureworld* is that extreme rarity, a sequel that's a decided improvement over the original. Filmed largely at NASA's Manned Flight Center in Houston and featuring smashing special effects devised by Brent Sellstrom, an alumnus of *Westworld*, this handsome entertainment is downright spectacular.

What's more, it sounds good, with a script by Mayo Simon and George Schenck that offers not only a plot twist that's as ingenious as the original premise, but also bright, even witty dialogue. For a movie with so far-out a plot, *Futureworld* draws remarkably few unintended laughs. Briskly directed by Richard T. Heffron (who it is said had a lot to do with injecting more humor into the story), this AIP presentation is a lot easier on the eyes and ears than *Logan's Run* . . ."

©Los Angeles Times, 1976.

Film Information, 9/76 (p. 6)
Unsigned

"This is a weak-kneed sequel to *Westworld*. Peter Fonda and Blythe Danner play investigative reporters given a chance to tour and do features on the rebuilt and enlarged entertainment resort which was partially destroyed in *Westworld* when the robots ran amuck. Fonda sniffs out some strange goings-on masterminded by host Arthur Hill and villainous scientist John Ryan, who plot to take over the world by replacing prominent businessmen and political figures with look-alike robots . . . strong on its emphasis on computer technology and has used NASA facilities as sets to good effect. The same cannot be said for the story line—it is quite superficial and uninteresting . . ."

©Film Information, 1976.

The Times (London), 10/22/76 (p. 15)
Philip French

". . . In *Futureworld*, the simple frontier town in which most of the action took place in *Westworld* has been replaced by a space exploration section where holidaymakers can ski on Mars and bed spaceship hostesses. Peter Fonda and the delightful Blythe Danner play a pair of Brad-and-Janet-style reporters, who discover that the masters of Delos, using their army of robots, plan to take over the world. Like the recent *Logan's Run, Futureworld* is all flashy hardware and fancy modern interiors (what Kingsley Amis might call new maps of Heal), and hasn't an idea in its head or a good word in its mouth, even falling back on 'That sounds like a line from an old movie.' *Logan's Run* is being advertised with the splendidly ambiguous slogan, 'It begins where imagination ends'; *Futureworld* begins where thinking ends."

©The Times, 1976.

Monthly Film Bulletin, October 1976 (p. 214)
John Pym

"*Westworld*—the less whimsical predecessor of this uncertain comic fantasy—was spoilt by a script which failed to follow up the one interesting question it posed (namely, why did the robots turn on the humans?). *Futureworld* is similarly underdeveloped, though here the implications of the narrative are not so much ignored as submerged by a relentlessly self-conscious display of hardware . . . if the conclusion of *Futureworld* is intended to suggest that the robots of *Westworld* have taken over Delos and are now programming themselves, this intriguing possibility is given little play by the Mayo Simon-George Schenck script. Having apparently decided not to take their premise seriously, they seem content to do little more than lead the players through the standard diversions of a caper movie . . ."

©Monthly Film Bulletin, 1976.

The Sunday Times (London), 10/24/76 (p. 35)
Alan Brien

"Richard Heffron's *Futureworld* . . . is a sequel to *Westworld*, and I foresee, with pleasant anticipation, even more followups, as with the *Planet of the Apes* series . . .

Naturally, behind it all is a mad scientist, a good low-key performance by John Ryan, though he seemed quite sane to me. All he wanted to do was remove the egomaniacs controlling the world today and replace them by rational, humane, cooperative doubles run up in his lab. Fonda strides along as ever, like a man in diving boots and lead gloves, just smart, and brave, and inventive enough to foil the plan, with Blythe Danner scrabbling prettily a step behind. There's plenty of suspense, some good jokes, and lots of lovely, intricate hardware . . ."

©The Sunday Times, 1976.

Films in Review, October 1976 (p. 506)
Steve Swires

"*Futureworld* is a post-Watergate science fiction adventure in which two investigative reporters uncover a sinister conspiracy lurking behind the deceptively benign exterior of 'Delos,' the computer complex responsible for the earlier and inferior *Westworld* . . .

Location filming at NASA's Manned Space Flight Center in Houston provides a more varied scope than was possible with MGM's broken-down backlot, and since director Richard T. Heffron has a more imaginative visual sense than Michael Crichton, he has replaced the two-dimensional sterile look of the first movie with a luster which takes full advantage of Brent Sellstrom's inventive special effects . . . Along with Britain's Douglas Hickox, Heffron's name on a picture is now a virtual guarantee of a master craftsman at work in a genre too long taken for granted."

©Films in Review, 1976.

GABLE AND LOMBARD

Director: *Sidney J. Furie*. Screenplay: *Barry Sandler*. Producer: *Harry Korshak*. Photography: *Jordan S. Cronenweth*. Editor: *Argyle Nelson*. Music: *Michel Legrand*. Distributor: *Universal Pictures*. Running time 131 minutes. New York opening February 11, 1976, at several theatres. Classification: R.

Clark Gable: *James Brolin*. Carole Lombard: *Jill Clayburgh*. Louis B. Mayer: *Allen Garfield*.

Ivan Cooper: *Red Buttons*. Rita Gable: *Joanne Linville*. Dixie: *Melanie Mayron*. Noreen: *Carol McGinnis*.

See Volume 1 for additional reviews

Monthly Film Bulletin, November 1976 (p. 232)
Geoff Brown

". . . there is too much distance between the originals and these tame, vulgar re-creations—a distance only accentuated by the wayward impersonations of the stars. James Brolin has Gable's jug-handle ears and bootlace moustache, but the charm is missing—this King of Hollywood is almost a dullard; Jill Clayburgh fares better in capturing Lombard's nervous energy and coarse sense of fun, though she hardly resembles her subject at all. One could believe in the couple more if their environment were created with any plausibility. But Hollywood here is virtually reduced to the presence of Louis B. Mayer (given an enjoyably sly, soft-spoken impersonation by Allen Garfield) who periodically offers parental advice to the erring stars . . ."

©Monthly Film Bulletin, 1976.

GARAGE SALE

Director, Screenplay, Editor: *Norman Yonemoto*. Producers: *Bruce Yonemoto, Mr. Yonemoto*. Photography: *Nikolai Ursin*. Videotape Supervisor: *Larry Nichols*. Music: *Sunset Boulevard and the Dreaded Mr. Twister*. Distributor: *Kyodi Productions*. Running time 92 minutes. Los Angeles opening December 13, 1976, at the Fox Venice Theatre. Classification: None.

Players: *Anastasia, Goldie Glitters, Ruth Hagopian, Bruce Lovern, Steven McGrew, Paul Mathews, Bob Opel, Tom White*.

Los Angeles Times, 12/13/76 (Pt. IV, p. 20)
Kevin Thomas

"*Garage Sale* starts out—after a hardcore prologue—like an Andy Warhol or Jahn Waters drag queen epic with the wraithlike, gaudily costumed

continued on next page

continued from previous page

Goldie (whose real name is Michael Heesy) demanding a divorce from her handsome, blue-eyed, blond young husband Hero (Tom White) because he hasn't made anything of his life. Dimwitted and bewildered by the rejection, Hero spends the rest of the film improbably trying to get Goldie back . . .

Photographed by Nikolai Ursin, *Garage Sale* has a stunning sense of imagery and clear, sharp color. With its far-out sense of humor and several X-rated sequences (none of which features Goldie and Hero), *Garage Sale* is best left to the hip—and also to some extent, to the forgiving. Even though the film attests to its maker's wit and perception it too often lacks pace and energy . . ."

©Los Angeles Times, 1976.

GATOR

Director: *Burt Reynolds*. Screenplay: *William Norton*. Producers: *Jules Levy, Arthur Gardner*. Photography: *William Fraker*. Editor: *Harold Kress*. Music: *Charles Bernstein*. Distributor: *United Artists*. Running time 95 minutes. Los Angeles opening July 27, 1976, at several theatres. Classification: PG.

Players: *Burt Reynolds, Lauren Hutton, Jack Weston, Jerry Reed, Alice Ghostley, Dub Taylor, Mike Douglas, Burton Gilliam, William Engesser, John Steadman, Lori Futch, Stephanie Burchfield, Dudley Remus, Alex Hawkins.*

The Times (London), 5/30/76 (p. 36)
Alan Brien

". . . It begins as an all-out attack on a criminal-dominated county of Georgia, USA, which is to be exposed by a pair of undercover agents—Burt Reynolds, a handsome, unrufflable, local bootlegger, and Jack Weston, a portly, sweating, Jewish Federal agent from New York. It all swings along, full of menace and decadence, drugged teenage whores and brutalised black barkeeps, until it becomes apparent that, as usual, the good guys cannot win unless the odds are fixed.

And then the second weakness appears. What the hell, it's entertainment, isn't it? So let's have a few laughs. The two crusaders have to enlist on their side a zany lady protestor who refuses to bur-

glarise the city records without bringing along her two cats. And there follows the inevitable comic car chase where the machine is punished but the passengers always emerge unscratched.

In the end, justice and democracy triumph, but don't worry, you don't have to believe it. It's only a film."

©The Times, 1976.

Los Angeles Times, 7/27/76 (Pt. IV, p. 3)
Charles Champlin

". . . This time Reynolds is both star and director. The direction is crisp and competent and as an action melodrama, *Gator* stays active all the way through.

It remains true and evident, however, that the hardest task of the star-director is directing the star. All the performances except Reynolds' own have a start-to-stop consistency (a thin consistency, by the nature of the undertaking, but steady). Reynolds' characterization swings between understatement and flamboyance . . .

On the positive side is Lauren Hutton, looking swell as a local television newsperson bucking to be Barbara Walters. More than looking well, she shows a pleasant touch for droll humor and a likeable casual energy missing from her earlier decorative outings. Reynolds' real gifts may be as a director of women.

Also on the positive side is Jack Weston as an extraordinarily incompetent federal man . . ."

©Los Angeles Times, 1976.

New York Magazine, 9/6/76 (p. 72)
John Simon

". . . It is the kind of movie where a righteous but crazy bookkeeper insists that her pet pussycats be taken along on a perilous break-in to steal the secret ledgers of Bama McCall, and where Burt Reynolds and Lauren Hutton can, while all of Dunston County is after them, spend an idyllic night of peaceful copulation on the beach.

There are two newish performers in the cast: Mike Douglas, the TV host, and Jerry Reed, the country-music star. Even a cameo role proves long enough for Douglas to forget his southern accent; Reed mostly flashes a powerful set of choppers that threaten to burst into song any moment. For supposed belly laughs there are Jack Weston and Alice Ghostley, but their frantic overacting is less humorous than Reynolds and Hutton's efforts at being Bogart and Bacall . . ."

©1976 by the NYM Corp. Reprinted with
the permission of NEW YORK Magazine.

Women's Wear Daily, 8/25/76 (p. 25)
Howard Kissel

". . . The story has possibilities but it seems to

have been developed as if the major guideline was, 'Is there a way we can do it sleazier?' The villain, for instance, not only destroys a lot of property and terrorizes poor people, but also enslaves young adolescent girls with drugs, and, as if this weren't enough, he kills both nebbish Weston, who has been the comic relief all the way through, and the poor old lady, who runs into a burning house to save her cats. The cheapest way to make a character a villain has always been to have him kick a dog—clearly it wasn't cheap enough for *Gator*. The film (scripted by William Norton) makes many jokes about Weston's being a New York Jew—the fact that one of the producers is named Levy is probably supposed to mitigate the crudeness of such humor.

The acting is as coarse as the material, and the camera photographs the action as if the film were an exercise in seeing how many cliches could be incorporated in one film . . ."

©Women's Wear Daily, 1976.

The Times (London), 5/28/76 (p. 11)
Philip French

". . . Once again the Reynolds screen person—a gentle sadist to whom a quip and a laugh come as naturally as a kick and a snarl—is unleashed upon a world so crudely viewed as to make him the upholder of virtue. The relentless violence, the sentimentality, the raucous stag-party humor, the inability to cut off a scene once it's made its point, attest to the influence of Robert Aldrich, a one-time Losey assistant, who directed Reynolds in his best recent movie, *The Mean Machine*, and his most expansively indulgent, *Hustle*. Reynolds' girlfriend, a TV reporter who leaves him to take up a network reporting job, is played by . . . Lauren Hutton, who seems set to become the late 1970s notion of a classy dame, the role Grace Kelly had in the fifties."

©The Times, 1976.

Village Voice, 9/13/76 (p. 108)
Molly Haskell

". . . Reynolds is made for certain types of comedy—romantic comedy, musical comedy, lightweight adventure, sex farce—a flair to which he is turning more and more as he takes his career in hand. He has always been more aware of his strengths and limitations than he has been given credit for . . .

Gator marks his directorial debut, but in name only. Like Eastwood, Redford, and many of today's studioless stars, he has managed, consciously or unconsciously, to develop his own persona through various forms of control—of projects, of directors, and of direction—previously uncredited.

Structurally, *Gator* is a bit of a mess, largely because of the civilizing and romantic influence Reynolds has brought to the randy domain of the redneck action film . . ."

Reprinted by permission of The Village Voice.
Copyright © The Village Voice, Inc., 1976.

New Leader, 9/13/76 (p. 24)
Robert Asahina

". . . While it is difficult to dislike Reynolds, who also makes his directorial debut with *Gator*, it is indeed easy to belittle his adolescent and self-conscious posturing, and his rather severe limitations as an actor. Critics often disparagingly claim that he merely 'plays himself' in his pictures. Yet we admire John Wayne or Marlon Brando precisely because each 'plays himself'—that is, brings the force of his personality to bear on all of his roles. Reynolds' likeableness consists precisely in this ability to establish instant recognition and contact with the viewer. This is a power grounded less in acting skill than in cinematic presence, and he has been especially successful in such small-town pictures as *Gator* . . ."

Reprinted with permission from
The New Leader, 1976.
©The American Labor Conference
on International Affairs, Inc.

Monthly Film Bulletin, 7/76 (p. 147)
Richard Combs

"It would be tempting to put *Gator* down as a case of too many cooks spoiling the broth, if it were not for the fact that Burt Reynolds seems to have so many different ideas about the kind of film he was making that he might actually have leased it out in parts to various performers and technicians . . . Reynolds . . . presents his own character as a series of disconnected numbers, from shambling funny man (there is an excruciatingly ill-timed bit of business with two small boys and a large dog as Gator tries to phone for help) to romantic hero. The choppiness of the material is further emphasized by Reynolds' rather graceless handling of his lush, blockbursting format, except when he turns the film over to specialists, with particularly fine photography throughout by William Fraker . . ."

©Monthly Film Bulletin, 1976.

Film Information, July/August 1976 (p. 6)
Bea Rothenbeuchner

". . . *Gator* is one of those productions that Hollywood cranks out with mind-numbing technical facility. The chase sequences contain precision timing, the fights are tough and realistic, the girls are pretty and non-individualistic—except for the mo-

continued on next page

continued from previous page

ment at the end when the heroine (Lauren Hutton, who is a top fashion model most of her time) tells the hero (Burt, of course) that she'd rather carry out an assignment as a TV reporter than go off into the sunset with him. This is, apparently, Hollywood's idea of changing sex roles in film.

Called a sequel to *White Lightning*, *Gator* has Reynolds continuing the adventures of Gator McCluskey, Moonshiner . . . The flimsy story line is full of cliches that crop up with B-movie-like inevitability. So we see the debasement of teenage girls; Reed's freakish bodyguards enjoying their sadistic work; Reynolds and Hutton making love on a beach. Ms. Hutton, TV reporter, and Alice Ghostley, cat lover and former civil servant turned crusader, help the good guys catch the bad guys . . ."

©Film Information, 1976.

New York Post, 8/26/76 (p. 14)
Archer Winsten

". . . A plot of uncommon crime logic brings in opportunities for Reynolds to enter a lion's den of hazard in Bama McCall's (Jerry Reed) corrupted county and emerge reasonably intact. The odds are slightly terrific, the color compelling and some of the southern pathos impenetrable. What you do feel very consistently is that these 'good ole southern boys,' criminals all, have the real feeling and accent. It is to be expected of Reynolds, but that he could choose and handle his cast with such skill is gratifying . . .

What stands out, however, is the fact that Reynolds threads his way through the badinage of violence with a certitude that has become his very own trademark. It works, and he is not slow to appreciate the talents of such supporting characters as Jack Weston . . ."

Reprinted by Permission of New York Post.
© 1976, New York Post Corporation.

Christian Science Monitor, 10/7/76 (p. 22)
David Sterritt

". . . Too much of *Gator* is explicitly ugly stuff, tame enough for a PG (parental guidance) rating but unengaging anyway. However, in between bouts of punching and killing—some of them annoyingly calculated to provoke titters instead of shudders—there are scenes of odd power. One has Gator trying to help a teen-age girl whose life is being wrecked by a Chopin-playing music box containing an assortment of mind-destroying drugs. Another finds Gator himself helplessly at bay in the bad guy's clutches.

Perhaps Reynolds' next film will have more such potent touches, make even better use of cinema-

tographer William A. Fraker's ironic long shots, and get more consistent acting from such able cast members as Jack Weston, Alice Ghostley, Lauren Hutton, and Mike Douglas."

Reprinted by permission from The Christian Science Monitor © 1976.
The Christian Science Publishing Society.
All rights reserved.

GENERAL IDI AMIN DADA

Documentary. Director: *Barbet Schroeder*. Producers: *Jean-Pierre Rassam, Charles-Henri Favrod*. Photography: *Nestor Almendros*. Editor: *Denise de Casablanca*. Production: *Mara Film, TV Rencontre* and *Le Figaro*. Running time 90 minutes. New York opening August 31, 1976, at the RKO 59th Street Twin 1 Theatre. Classification: None. Origin: France, 1974.

Newsweek, 9/6/76 (p. 65)
Janet Maslin

". . . The dictator clearly prefers the role of buffoon to that of bully. The film depicts none of his celebrated tantrums, but it does include his boasts about his country's naval prowess, even after Schroeder gently reminds him that Uganda is landlocked. Some of the humor here is surely unintentional, but Amin is so frequently made to look foolish, by sequences he both staged and approved, that the viewer is forced to weigh the dictator's naivete against his guile. The grinning, often inarticulate Amin of this study demonstrates none of the cunning that must have helped him to rise to power. And the film's unrelenting emphasis upon his amiability, honesty and humanity may be its most perversely effective contrivance of all. Propaganda so transparent becomes revealing.

Schroeder conveys a vivid sense of this terrifyingly enigmatic tyrant, but the filmmaker's contributions should not be overestimated; even if the crew set out to use Amin as part of some larger statement about African politics or the nature of dictatorship, his interference ultimately denies them a point of view . . . The editing often seems random, and the cinematography (by Nestor Almendros, who did such delicate work on *The Story of Adele H.*) is frantic . . ."

©Newsweek, Inc. 1976
reprinted by permission.

Village Voice, 9/20/76 (p. 125)
Andrew Sarris

". . . Ultimately, it is not clear that Schroeder has exploited Amin more than Amin has exploited Schroeder. There are many moments when the viewer's mind shifts from the gruesome political contexts of Amin's rule to a contemplation of a strange, exotic man with a flair for dramatizing his links with the tribe and the jungle. Even in his business suit he manages to beguile us as he clutches a spear and feigns throwing it—for a moment we enter his mind to meditate on what modern leader would stand a chance against Amin in single armed combat. He is not ascetic like his ideological ally Qaddafi of Libya. Apart from his four wives and 18 children, there are the rumours of prodigious excesses of carnality.

Amin's boisterous competitiveness in a swimming pool is alone worth the price of admission. And as our friendly tour guide, he is not ashamed to talk to the crocodiles and the elephants on the shore. What his screen image does not tell us is what further bloody deeds he has in store for us."

Reprinted by permission of The Village Voice.
Copyright © The Village Voice, Inc., 1976.

Saturday Review, 10/2/76 (p. 39)
Judith Crist

". . . an almost mesmerizing session with a dangerous despot—and a dangerous documentary for those unaware of the facts of Amin's bloody rule, since his statements are unchallenged and his primitive charm and humor are all too evident. Unfortunately, the filmmakers cannot risk updating the material or adding commentary. But in one respect Amin traps himself. Declaring that his dreams provide him with clairvoyance, he predicts the end of Israel by the end of 1975. Then, announcing his support of Black Septembrists and terrorists, he declares Palestinian hijackers welcome. As for the hijackers' hostages, he suggests that they book their flights wisely, avoiding high-risk airlines, like El Al or TWA: 'You must fly Air France or East African Airways.' The Entebbe affair was apparently beyond his dreams."

©Judith Crist, 1976.

New York Magazine, 9/13/76 (p. 91)
John Simon

". . . It's no use trying to describe this film; it has to be seen and heard as it is proffered by Amin to the eyes and ears of the camera, with his intonations and facial expressions. The general is an odd mixture of monstrousness and charm, shrewdness and stupidity, arrogance and eagerness to captivate. He is both a liar and a visionary, sordid and grandiosely unhinged, a man of many talents: mur-derous, hilarious, some even likable. That the Israelis scored so brilliantly off him at Entebbe should not blind us to his continuing menace; that his risibility is a fairly close real-life equivalent to the uproarious fiction of Evelyn Waugh's *Black Mischief* should not make us forget the thousands of lives the man has taken and will, no doubt, go on taking . . ."

©1976 by the NYM Corp. Reprinted with
the permission of NEW YORK Magazine.

Christian Science Monitor, 9/20/76 (p. 21)
David Sterritt

". . . The movie is never ferocious; it is calm and ironic. Judging from his face, gestures and speech, President Amin seems most of the time to be enjoying some immensely funny private joke. This would be all right if he weren't running a country . . .

In the picture, President Amin himself is likely to respond with uproarious laughter rather than reasoned defense when confronted with some of his past practices and statements. And some of those acts and words seem astonishing . . .

Some viewers find all this highly amusing, others find it deeply upsetting. Both reactions are appropriate. Though this film is a documentary authorized by its subject, it reveals and alludes to more quirks, flaws and horrors than most self-portraits would dream of allowing."

Reprinted by permission from The Christian
Science Monitor © 1976
The Christian Science Publishing Society
All rights reserved

New York Post, 8/1/76 (p. 12)
Sylviane Gold

"As far as Idi Amin is concerned, Barbet Schroeder is just the 'victim of a Zionist plot' . . . that was organized by the producers of the film *Idi Amin Dada*. And the 35-year-old director has a standing invitation to Uganda's presidential palace any old time.

He doesn't plan to go.

Schroeder, who started his career as a film critic and graduated to producer, director and sometime actor, directed the remarkable 'self-portrait' of the Ugandan dictator during a two-week break between other projects. It follows the erratic ruler from less than proficient displays of military might to a cabinet harangue to a Nile boat trip in which he cheerfully waves at elephants along the bank and sees them waving back.

In retrospect, Schroeder wonders why he wasn't more nervous while in Uganda—even if it was before the Entebbe raid that inspired the film's belated release here . . ."

Reprinted by Permission of New York Post.
©1976, New York Post Corporation.

continued on next page

continued from previous page

Women's Wear Daily, 8/27/76 (p. 8)
Howard Kissel

"Like Chaplin, Idi Amin Dada not only stars in *General Idi Amin Dada*, but directed much of the film and composed music for it. The documentary (in which Amin received some assistance from French filmmaker Barbet Schroeder, who is credited with the direction), while nowhere near as funny as *The Great Dictator*, at least has greater consistency of tone.

The tone is set by Amin himself, who rarely lets the camera stray very far from him. We watch Amin take a boat trip down the Nile, waving at crocodiles and elephants . . .

This spirit of low farce is enhanced by Amin's music, which is an amalgam of Western-type melodies, incompetently harmonized, set to African rhythms . . .

The self-portrait was filmed in 1974. Before it was shown in Paris, Amin insisted on certain cuts—one has to assume he considers the resulting version flattering. In some ways it is—we are apt to find Amin so absurd that we might forget this is the man, on learning from one of his children that students in the university were making fun of him, sent soldiers onto the campus, killing 50 students . . ."

©Women's Wear Daily, 1976.

Film Information, October 1976 (p. 2)
Thomas O. Bentz

"The theology—or self-deification—of Idi Amin on the screen looks like a dream sequence. This close-up documentary of the man who runs Uganda is revealing, like seeing through a keyhole . . .

His dreams-come-true are others' nightmares. He spins disdain for the men of his cabinet and the women of his countryside: 'Tell women to get up at dawn, pull up their socks, and open up the markets.' He kicks out three of his four wives because they are not revolutionary enough.

His racist view of Jews is a Third World echo of the Third Reich. This odd self-portrait, well worth seeing, is true to life as the General interprets it—a Strangelove letter to himself. It is touched with humor, and heavy with a dangerous hand of arbitrary force that is a sin against the God he would be and an offense against the people he should serve and defend."

©Film Information, 1976.

GET CHARLIE TULLY

Director: *Cliff Owen*. Screenplay: *John Warren, John Singer*. Producer: *E. M. Smedley*

Aston. Executive Producers: *Frank Launder, Sidney Gilliat*. Photography: *Ernest Steward*. Running time 97 minutes. New York opening January 16, 1977, at the Fine Arts Theatre. Classification: PG. Origin: Great Britain.

Charlie Tully: *Dick Emery*. Sid Sabbath: *Derren Nesbitt*. Reggie Campbell Peek: *Ronald Fraser*. Libby Niven: *Pat Coombs*. Arnold van Cleef: *William Franklyn*. Jo Mason: *Cheryl Kennedy*.

New York Post, 1/17/77 (p. 22)
Archer Winsten

"*Get Charlie Tully* . . . is a fanciful British excursion into the misadventures of a couple of con artists . . .

This is the sort of elaborate comedy the British find laughable and we usually don't. As plot, it's at once complicated and obvious, which undermines that as a source of interest. Two distinguished names from the past, Frank Launder and Sidney Gilliat, are listed as executive producers. Perhaps one can attribute to them the good locations in London and the tolerable performances. But it is more likely that this picture represents the weak echo of a kind of British comedy that married local types to international movie gangsters, substituting farcical excess and odd character for basic humor . . ."

Reprinted by Permission of New York Post.
© 1977, New York Post Corporation.

GIANT SPIDER INVASION, THE

Director: *Bill Rebane*. Screenplay: *Robert Easton, Richard L. Huff*. Producers: *Mr. Rebane, Mr. Huff*. Photography: *Jack Willoughby*. Running time 82 minutes. Los Angeles opening February 27, 1976, at several theatres. Classification: PG.

Players: *Steve Brodie, Barbara Hale, Leslie Parrish, Alan Hale, Robert Easton, Bill Williams*.

See Volume 1 for additional reviews

Monthly Film Bulletin, March 1977 (p. 43)
Tom Milne

"'Did you ever see the movie *Jaws?*' says the awestruck sheriff gazing at the giant spider. 'It makes that shark look like a goldfish!' Brave words, but compared to that pneumatic monster, this one looks like something left over from a joke shop sale. More mileage was obviously to be had out of the real spiders, but apart from one genuinely edgy scene where Ev is menaced in bed by a horde of the venemously hairy little creatures, the film chooses to bank on its risibly unconvincing monster . . . Meanwhile the cast, plodding through 'psychological' subplots of supreme banality, all respond with stilted embarrassment."

©Monthly Film Bulletin, 1977

GIVE 'EM HELL, HARRY!

A film of a play. Play Director: *Peter H. Hunt.*
Playwright: *Samuel Gallu.* Play Producers:
Mr. Gallu and Thomas J. McErlane. Film
Director: *Steve Binder.* Film Producers: *Al
Ham, Joseph E. Bluth.* Photography: *Ken
Pallus.* Music: *Milton P. Larsen.* Production:
TheatroVision. Running time 104 minutes.
New York opening September 24, 1975, at
several theatres. Classification: None.

Harry S. Truman: *James Whitmore.*

See Volume 1 for additional reviews

Film Information, 4/76 (p. 4)
John McClurken

"Any remembrance of presidents past is immediately open to a host of problems. Behind most of the difficulties is the basic reality that an objective historical perspective is hard to achieve on the stage or screen—or anywhere else, for that matter. *Give 'Em Hell, Harry!* manages to avoid the problem by not pretending to give us a massive dose of history. Instead it provides an American actor with a tour de force role. The events become secondary to the vehicle of one James Whitmore. He is brilliant and deserves his Oscar nomination.

With a few minor costume changes and a clever display of outright unabashed guile, Whitmore moves around the stage as Harry Truman in the White House, at home in Independence, Missouri, in Kansas City and campaigning. The production at times seems to be a collection of Truman's finest

moments without any particular attempt at objectivity. It can be said that what results, however, is not just Harry Truman at his best, but at his most revealing . . . "

© Film Information, 1976.

GO FOR IT

Director: *Paul Rapp.* Screenplay: *Neil Rapp.*
Producers: *Paul Rapp, Richard Rosenthal.*
Photography: *Rick Robertson, Pat Darren.*
Editor: *John O'Conner.* Music: *Dennis Dragon.*
Production: *Wilt Chamberlain-Hal Jepson.* Distributor: *World Entertainment.* Running time 90 minutes. Los Angeles opening August 1976 at several theatres. Classification: PG.

Los Angeles Times, 8/26/76 (p. 18)
Linda Gross

"*Go for It* . . . is an arrogant and exploitative ode to adventure. The dazzlingly photographed documentary about skate-boarding, surfing, hang-gliding and other high risk sports is a cakewalk for cultists but redundant for regular movie audiences.

The film contains glorious fugal footage of surfing in Waimea, hang-gliding and skateboarding in Malibu, mountain climbing in the Rockies, and snow skiing in the Caribou mountains . . .

The script by Neil Rapp tries to incorporate a heady psychological analogy between permissive modern society and the inherent death-risk motivating these sportsmen, but fails to sustain its premise by providing any additional insight other than the age-old adage that a mountain climber climbs a mountain because it's there.

The nature of the material is extremely repetitious, but director Paul Rapp maintains high-speed, unabated enthusiasm and reverence throughout . . ."

©Los Angeles Times, 1976.

GOALIE'S ANXIETY AT
THE PENALTY KICK, THE

Director: *Wim Wenders.* Screenplay (German with English subtitles): *Peter Handke, Mr. Wenders.* Based on the novel by Mr. Handke. Photography: *Robbie Mueller.* Editor: *Peter*

continued on next page

continued from previous page

Przygodda. Music: *Jurgen Knieper*. Distributor: *Bauer International*. Running time 101 minutes. New York opening January 13, 1977, at the Film Forum. Classification: None. Origin: West Germany.

Josef Bloch: *Arthur Brauss*. Hertha Gabler: *Kai Fischer*. Gloria T.: *Erika Pluhar*. Anna: *Libgart Schwarz*. Maria: *Marie Bardischewski*. Salesman: *Michael Toost*. Girt: *Edda Koch*. Idiot: *Ruediger Vogler*.

New York Post, 1/14/77 (p. 20)
Frank Rich

". . . it's about a professional soccer goalie who leaves his team after muffing a big play. The protagonist, Bloch (Arthur Brauss), travels from his home in Vienna to the Austria-Hungary frontier to try to put himself together again—but there is nothing to put together . . .

What makes the movie work is the way it's shot: The fractionalized editing and the Ozu-like objectivity of the camera placement combine with Robbie Mueller's metallic color cinematography to present a gripping view of a psychically exhausted world. As Wenders reminds us in a final, ingenious sequence, we're looking at life as a goalie does—from a lonely vantage point, away from the action. It's such an arresting vision that, for anyone who really cares about film, *Goalie's Anxiety* easily transcends the sum of its other, mundane parts."

Reprinted by Permission of New York Post.
© 1977, New York Post Corporation.

GOD TOLD ME TO

Director, Screenplay, Producer: *Larry Cohen*. Photography: *Paul Glickman*. Editors: *Arthur Mandelberg, William J. Waters, Christopher Lebenzon, Mike Corey*. Music: *Frank Cordell*. Production: *Larco*. Distributor: *New World Pictures*. Running time 90 minutes. Los Angeles opening November 1976 at several theatres. Classification: R.

Players: *Harry Bellaver, Jo Flores Chase, Sandy Dennis, Robert Drivas, John Heffernan, Mike Kellin, Sam Levene, Tony Lo Bianco, Richard Lynch, George Patterson, Deborah Raffin, Lester Rawlins, William Roerick, Sylvia Sidney, Walter Steele, Sammy Williams*.

Los Angeles Times, 11/19/76 (Pt. IV, p. 30)
Kevin Thomas

"In *God Told Me To* . . . Manhattan is struck by a series of murders in which all the perpetrators explain their seemingly motiveless killings by uttering the phrase that gives this violent and tedious penny-dreadful its title . . .

Anyway, it seems that not only was the incandescent hermaphrodite (Richard Lynch), who had ordered all those killings, born of a virgin, so was the dedicated, religious New York cop (Tony Lo Bianco) trying to track him down. Indeed, Lo Bianco discovers that his mother (Sylvia Sidney), who gave him up for adoption at birth, had been sucked into a flying saucer and somehow impregnated while on her way home from the 1939 New York World's Fair in Flushing Meadows.

To put it bluntly, it's beyond the abilities of writer-director-producer Larry Cohen to pull off such far-out material . . ."

©Los Angeles Times, 1976.

GODZILLA VERSUS MEGALON

Director, Screenplay: *Jun Fukuda*. Based on a novel by Chinuchi Skezawa. Executive Producer: *Tomoyuki Tanoka*. Production: *Toho Eizo Company*. Distribution: *Cinema Shares International Distribution Corporation*. Running time 85 minutes. New York opening July 21, 1976, at several theatres. Classification: G. Origin: Japan.

Players: *Katsuhiko Sasaki, Hiroyuki Kawase, Yutaka Hayashi, Mori Mikita*.

New York Post, 7/22/76 (p. 14)
Archer Winsten

". . . a Japanese brainstorm which imagines that a nuclear blast in the Aleutians may have conjured up from Seatopia some long-vanished creatures resembling the famed Tyrannosaurus of geological memory.

The monsters take off, intercontinental-missile-style, for Japanese targets where the Army and its tanks, missiles and planes are prepared to do puny battle. They're no match for the mighty prehistoric reptiles.

Luckily for Japan, old Godzilla, a saurian of Japanese movie antecedents, has been waiting in the wings. So Hippity-hop, comes Godzilla ready to emit a blue light with its destructive power of a laser beam.

It's a tough battle, folks, for Godzilla has to contend with not only Megalon but also his twin, Gigan. Godzilla is assisted by the Robot Man . . .''

Reprinted by Permission of New York Post.
©1976, New York Post Corporation.

GOIN' HOME

Director, Screenplay, Producer, Editor: *Chris Prentiss*. Photography: *Sloan Nibley III, Mr. Prentiss*. Music: *Lee Holdridge*. Distributor: *Prentiss Productions*. Running time 100 minutes. Los Angeles opening December 1976 at the Plitt Century Plaza Theatre. Classification: G.

Players: *Della Bradford, Todd Christiansen, Marion Forbes, Kevin Oliver, Robert Dale (Dusty) Poole, Melvin Ruffin, Bernard Triche.*

Los Angeles Times, 12/25/76 (Pt. IV, p. 17)
Linda Gross

''*Goin' Home* . . . is an offbeat and sincere film odyssey about a Florida boy who runs away from home to save his dog who has been wrongly accused of seriously wounding a small child.

Romantically photographed and epically scored by Lee Holdridge, the movie provides a dazzling visual tour of the United States but also contains some disturbingly harsh and scary moments when the characters are hunted down by the forces of evil. This kind of relentless persecution seems out of place in a G-rated movie.

Fear is present from the first few moments when a tough redneck sheriff goes after the dog (Crash) and his teen-age owner (Todd Christiansen). The boy and dog escape with the sheriff and his armed posse in pursuit . . .

It is very much the labor of love of Chris Prentiss . . . The story, often hard to follow, is a dark and fragmented mood poem. Prentiss creates a strong nostalgic atmosphere which is more conducive to allegory than to film.

Still, there are sound emotional moments and engrossing natural performances . . .''

©Los Angeles Times, 1976.

GREAT SCOUT AND CATHOUSE THURSDAY, THE

Director: *Don Taylor*. Screenplay: *Richard*

Shapiro. Producers: *Jules Buck, David Korda*. Executive Producer: *Samuel Z. Arkoff*. Photography: *Alex Phillips, Jr*. Music: *John Cameron*. Distributor: *American International*. Running time 102 minutes. New York opening June 23, 1976, at several theatres. Classification: PG.

Sam Longwood: *Lee Marvin*. Joe Knox: *Oliver Reed*. Jack Colby: *Robert Culp*. Nancy Sue: *Elizabeth Ashley*. Cathouse Thursday: *Kay Lenz*. Billy: *Strother Martin*. Mike: *Sylvia Miles*.

New York Post, 6/24/76 (p. 24)
Archer Winsten

'' . . . a slapsticked burlesque of the latter-day West with sex interludes that are almost embarrassing in their crudity. I mean they aren't funny, and they don't achieve pornographic appeals, and they seemingly don't intend a serious approach to romance.

It's just a bunch of happy, frolicking whores being rescued, fondled or otherwise handled . . .

I won't say that Lee (*Cat Ballou*) Marvin doesn't sustain his established character as a white-haired brawler, or that the others don't fill their roles successfully. My feeling is that it's an action comedy that operates on a level so simple that only the least discriminating audiences will find it laughable. And if it isn't laughable, it isn't anything . . .''

Reprinted by Permission of New York Post.
© 1976, New York Post Corporation.

Los Angeles Times, 9/15/76 (Pt. IV, p. 15)
Kevin Thomas

''The problem with *The Great Scout and Cathouse Thursday* . . . besides its gimmicky derivative title, is writer Richard Shapiro's crass sense of humor. It would take lots more talent than Shapiro possesses to find laughter in VD, in a young prostitute trying to escape the clutches of her rampaging lesbian madam or in the repeated slugging of women.

The Great Scout and Cathouse Thursday has lots of good people and a not-bad premise; it just isn't nearly as funny as it thinks it is.

Displaying much verve and amiability, Don Taylor directs as if the material were hilarious instead of merely juvenile (and rather strongly sexist). If this isn't *Cat Ballou*— if only it were—Lee Marvin is every bit as good as he was in that film . . .''

©Los Angeles Times, 1976.

continued on next page

continued from previous page

New York Magazine, 7/19/76 (p. 85)
John Simon

". . . Although there is comic potential in a Western that takes place in 1908 against an electioneering background . . . when the motorcar already encroaches on the horse and the villain has turned big-time promoter, a concept alone is not enough . . . this would require more courage and skill than Richard Shapiro, the writer, and Don Taylor, the director, can muster.

The acting is undistinguished when not downright embarrassing (which, for once, includes even the usually delicious Elizabeth Ashley). Least culpable are Robert Culp as a charismatic crook, and Oliver Reed as the Indian . . . Kay Lenz, as the runaway whore with a heart of—let's say out of deference to William Jennings Bryan—silver, is even sub-double standard. In the tiny role of a grotesque madam with lesbian and homicidal proclivities, Sylvia Miles finally gets a part worthy of her talents. The cinematography by Alex Phillips, Jr., is no better here than it was in *Man Friday* . . ."

©1976 by the NYM Corp. Reprinted with the permission of NEW YORK Magazine.

Newsweek, 7/12/76 (p. 69A)
Janet Maslin

"Even its title bespeaks desperation: *The Great Scout and Cathouse Thursday* sounds as though it's the latest in the cute-twosome series launched by *Butch Cassidy and the Sundance Kid*. In fact, this movie features not just two but seven wacky wild Westerners, who all seem addicted to stealing, hee-hawing, falling into puddles and punching one another in the privates . . .

The plot has something to do with a $60,000 robbery and the kidnapping of Elizabeth Ashley . . . Ashley seems hardly present, but Robert Culp does nicely as the smoothie husband . . . As a whore inexplicably called Thursday, Kay Lenz, who looks like a young Raquel Welch without the heavy artillery, stays calmer than anyone else, so her scenes come as a welcome relief. Lee Marvin (as the Scout), Sylvia Miles (as a prairie madam of dubious Bronx charm) and Strother Martin as Marvin's raunchy old pal seem to be feeling no pain in what should have been moments of acute embarrassment. But Oliver Reed gives an amusing performance, perhaps because he has the movie's only really curious role . . ."

©Newsweek, Inc. 1976 reprinted by permission.

Film Information, July/August 1976 (p. 5)
Peter P. Shillaci

"*The Great Scout and Cathouse Thursday* is a feeble Western farce designed to capitalize on the success of *Cat Ballou* and *Blazing Saddles*. Unfortunately, it has neither the novelty of the former or the vulgar wit of the latter. The film takes an over-the-hill hero, Sam Longwood, 'Injun fighter' and cavalry scout, and places him with two bizarre buddies in Serenity, Colorado, 1908. The result is a massacre, of which the principal victims are comic invention and the Western legend . . .

Director Don Taylor is provided with many comic situations by writer Richard Shapiro, but he blows most of them with clumsy pacing. As a result, the working humor is chiefly verbal in the *Blazing Saddles* galloping anachronism style. In between verbal exchanges and sight gags, there are assorted chases, pratfalls, and a caper-type robbery . . .

The paradox of a film such as *Great Scout* is that it managed to lure so many name stars into roles . . ."

©Film Information, 1976.

GREAT TEXAS DYNAMITE CHASE, THE

Director: *Michael Pressman*. Screenplay: *David Kirkpatrick, Mark Rosin*. Producer: *David Irving*. Photography: *Jamie Anderson*. Editor: *Millie Moore*. Music: *Craig Safran*. Distributor: *New World Pictures*. New York opening March 1977 at several theatres. Classification: R.

Candy Morgan: *Claudia Jennings*. Ellie Jo Turner: *Jocelyn Jones*. Slim: *Johnny Crawford*. Jake: *Chris Pennock*. Pam Morgan: *Tara Strohmeier*.

New York Post, 3/12/77 (p. 17)
Frank Rich

". . . It's not a picture that can be taken seriously. The car chases are routine, the bank heists perfunctory, but the blood and violence flow in Bonnie & Clyde style. And finally the girls ride away from all this carnage, crossing the Mexican border on horseback, and living happily ever after in Mexico City and Brazil.

. . . director Michael Pressman has given the picture the headlong pace of senseless action, more action. The girls, Claudia Jennings and Jocelyn Jones, seem more at home stripped and sexually engaged than in those action sequences, but the cars do screech and the dynamite explodes often enough to make a big bang at climactic moments. It'll keep you awake, even if dissatisfied."

Reprinted by Permission of New York Post.
©1977, New York Post Corporation.

GREY GARDENS

Documentary. Directors: *David Maysles, Albert Maysles, Ellen Hovde and Muffie Meyer*. Photography: *Messrs. Maysles*. Editors: *Ms. Hovde, Ms. Meyer and Susan Froemke*. Production: *Messrs. Maysles*. Running time 94 minutes. New York opening September 27, 1975, at the New York Film Festival, Lincoln Center. Classification: None.

Mother: *Edith Beale*. Daughter: *Edith Beale*. Handyman: *Jerry Torre*. Birthday guest: *Lois Wright*. Birthday guest: *Jack Helmuth*. Gardener: *Brooks Hires*.

See Volume 1 for additional reviews

Los Angeles Times, 7/2/76 (Pt. IV, p. 1)
Charles Champlin

". . . The new Maysles documentary, *Grey Gardens*, is an incredible piece of eccentric Americana, and it exists and succeeds because its principals choose to perform for the cameras. The equipment is not only not concealed, it is glimpsed, and we hear the Beale ladies commenting on it and talking to the Maysles brothers and their associates (Ellen Hovde, Muffie Meyer and Susan Froemke).

The Beales, Edith Bouvier Beale, about 78 as the film was made, and her daughter, Edith Bouvier Beale, Jr., about 56 as the film was made, are aunt and cousin to Jacqueline Bouvier Kennedy Onassis . . .

The world of *Grey Gardens* looks not least to be miserably uncomfortable. But that conceivably is the price for being able to sustain a self-contained sanctuary as distant from the madding crowd as anyone gets this side of a Tibetan cave . . ."

© Los Angeles Times, 1976.

Nation, 3/13/76 (p. 317)
Robert Hatch

". . . *Grey Gardens* is not a documentary; it is a happening, and speculation as to whether the Maysles 'intruded' on the Beale women, or that their presence as witnesses may have distorted the situation they were filming, is beside the point. Of course they intruded and distorted the situation—or rather they made the situation, for *Grey Gardens* is essentially an account of how this strangely reclusive mother and daughter responded to the novel experience of being filmed . . .

What an audience gets from all this is a little hard to say. There is something ghoulish about the eagerness with which the Beale women expose themselves, and that has a fascination. It is warm-ing to observe the affection growing between the film people and their subjects, and one likes the idea that for months these forlorn women had an object in life (to be 'stars') and for months to come will relish the memory of it . . . I felt oddly altruistic at being a part of the audience for the Beales, that somehow I meant more to them than they meant to me. They are not very interesting women, and I doubt that they ever were. They were just representative examples of American wealthy society who by accident fell down a well and might never have emerged again, except that the Maysles discovered them."

© The Nation, 1976.

GRIZZLY

Director: *William Girdler*. Screenplay, Producers: *Harvey Flaxman, David Sheldon*. Photography: *William Anderson*. Editor: *Bob Anderson*. Music: *Robert O. Ragland*. Distributor: *Film Ventures International*. Running time 92 minutes. New York opening May 12, 1976, at several theatres. Classification: PG.

Kelly: *Christopher George*. Don: *Andrew Prine*. Scott: *Richard Jaeckel*. Allison: *Joan McCall*. Kittredge: *Joe Dorsey*. Corwin: *Kermit Echols*.

Los Angeles Times, 5/14/76 (Pt. IV, p. 14,
Linda Gross

"*Grizzly* is a graphic PG-rated adventure movie about a massive, carnivorous grizzly on the loose in an unspecified national park. Like *Jaws*, the film is also about the bear's relationship with the three men who track him down.

A national park, which ordinarily only shelters herbivorous bears already taken north for the winter, is suddenly terrorized by a 2,000-pound, 18-foot grizzly who savagely attacks, murders and mutilates two unsuspecting girls and later attacks park rangers, more tourists, hunters and a mother trying to save her small son . . .

Lingeringly photographed sequences which precede the grizzly attacks flaunt the victim's vulnerability in a pretty but uncomfortable fashion. Harvey Flaxman and David Sheldon have written some inane dialogue but also provoke terror. Director William Girdler sustains scariness but is

continued on next page

continued from previous page

heavyhanded in handling scenes with crowds. Andrew Prine brings depth and dimension to his character."

© Los Angeles Times, 1976.

Film Information, 6/76 (p. 4)
Unsigned

"A company called Film Ventures International has been gaining a reputation as one of the industry's foremost rip-off businesses . . . Now they have fashioned *Grizzly*, a grotesquely violent film that has a blatant similarity to *Jaws*.

Two girls camping in a national park are mutilated and devoured by a 18-foot, two-thousand-pound grizzly who has strayed from the high country. While the park supervisor refuses to close the area to tourists, the bear murders again and again. Ranger Christopher George, helicopter pilot Andrew Prine, and wildlife specialist Richard Jaeckel, desperately try to locate and kill the carnivorous monster. Cheaply made, with poor direction (William Girdler) and script, and inanely acted, *Grizzly* is a horrific experience in every regard."

© Film Information, 1976.

New York Post, 5/13/76 (p. 24)
Archer Winsten

"*Grizzly* . . . is an unsuccessful attempt to capitalize on two events: the enormous success of *Jaws* and the death of two girl campers in a national park a few years ago in a grizzly attack . . .

Not to keep you in suspense, for this picture is too weak in detail of action, characterization and dialogue to deserve extra attention, they eventually do get the bear. A gun doesn't have any effect. It takes a torpedo launcher and this looses a blast practically atomic which burns the villainous bear down to a mere black grease spot on the ground.

Sic semper ursa Terriblis, or something like that. If you could believe it, it would be a thrill. But don't count on this as much more than a quickie equivalent to the big thriller."

Reprinted by Permission of New York Post.
©1976, New York Post Corporation.

Monthly Film Bulletin, February 1977 (p. 24)
Richard Combs

"William Girdler seems set to corner the market in low-yield spin-offs, following his dismal re-creation of *The Exorcist* (*Abby*) with this poor man's version of *Jaws*. The primaeval scourge in this version is of-fered not just one but four young women, in various states of undress, to whet his (and the audience's) appetite within the first forty minutes—a distinctive eating habit that is even remarked on in the film. Otherwise, the inevitable clash of principle between the kindly ranger, who wants to close the park until the danger is over, and his career-minded supervisor, who alternates between a high-handed brusqueness in trying to sweep the matter under the carpet and an opportunistic yen to invite in the media, is thickly written and obtusely motivated . . ."

©Monthly Film Bulletin, 1977.

GUERNICA

Director, Screenplay: *Fernando Arrabal*. Producers: *Harry N. Blum, Federico Mueller*. Photography: *Ramon Suarez*. Editor: *Renzo Lucidi*. Running time 110 minutes. New York opening May 21, 1976, at the 68th Street Playhouse. Classification: None.

Vandale: *Mariangela Melato*. Goya: *Ron Faber*. Count Cerralbo: *Bento Urago*. Raphael: *Cosimo Clinieri*. Onesimo: *Franco Ressel*. Ramiro: *Mario Novelli*. Angel: *Cyril Spiga*. Antonio: *Rocco Fontana*.

Newsweek, 6/14/76 (p. 90)
Jack Kroll

"The Spanish playwright-poet-filmmaker Fernando Arrabal is obsessed with the civil war that tore his country's heart apart. A passionate anti-Fascist still living in exile, he has made in *Guernica* a blazing hymn to the Spain that died in 1936 . . . Arrabal is both surrealist and realist, and *Guernica* doesn't quite succeed in blending them both. But it's one of the most personal and fiery films you'll ever see, filled with real love and real hatred coming from a real human heart. It's also filled with buckets of blood––in a climactic scene Arrabal shows the triumphant Fascists holding a mock bull-fight in which the 'bulls' are several dwarfs who fought for the Loyalist side, who are slain by a soldier dressed as a matador. Made in Italy, the film uses as its central symbol of Spain Mariangela Melato (Lina Wertmuller's favorite actress), whose savagely beautiful face is as close to the Furies as human features can get."

© Newsweek, Inc. 1976
reprinted by permission.

New York Post, 5/22/76 (p. 15)
Archer Winsten

"*Guernica* . . . deals with the Spanish Civil War in terms that are both documentarily realistic and then, in contrast, wholly in keeping with the artistic past of Fernando Arrabal, the playwright and co-founder of the Theater of Panic. This creates effects as powerful as they are weird, enigmatic and mysterious . . .

The picture has the usual eloquence of Spanish Loyalists, plus those special images of Arrabal who utilizes the bullfight, religion and rites of blood and lust to emphasize his hatred of the Fascists and his admiration for those who fought against them.

Mariangela Melato of the huge eyes is hauntingly eloquent. Ron Faber suffers outrageous torture. Fernando Arrabal has made a picture that is a scream of protest by an avant-garde poet-playwright. This means inevitably that few moviegoers of the standard brand will appreciate it, but among the few who are willing to study it there will be praise for its flamboyant visual quality. Arrabal has done it again, in blood and hatred. It is a memorial that writhes."

Reprinted by Permission of New York Post.
© 1976, New York Post Corporation.

New York Magazine, 6/7/76 (p. 74)
John Simon

" . . . This unspeakable phony, whose plays and movies are equal garbage, thinks that his anti-Franco politics is enough to excuse sordid perversions masquerading as poetic metaphors, inane dialogue posturing as eccentric profundity, and the most inept filmmaking carrying on like avant-garde originality. Actually, that must be what his defenders think; Arrabal manifestly fancies himself an unqualified genius. He does manage, however, to make the noble cause of antifascism look like some ghastly disease. Mariangela Melato should know better than to appear in such trash, but actors and actresses, I guess, seldom do."

© 1976 by the NYM Corp. Reprinted with
the permission of NEW YORK Magazine.

Film Information, July/August 1976 (p. 3)
Jackson Ferry

"Fernando Arrabal's *Guernica* is the first film made by a Spaniard about the Civil War. Arrabal, exiled by the Franco regime, has created a film brutal and uncompromising. His imagery is startling, sometimes shocking, but never sophomoric or offensive. For it is clear from the onset that this film is about the human passion for freedom, and Arrabal's effort is fueled by the universal hope for justice. Mixing romantic, religious, and political imagery, *Guernica* is, in the end, a spiritual film . . .

. . . Arrabal's taste for the absurd is surpassed only by the beauty with which he is able to depict it.

Arrabal fuses religious and political imagery throughout. His political statements are definitive and easily identifiable: the peasants represent the democratic and communistic elements, the soldiers and the elite, the fascistic. If each co-opts religion and religious symbols for their own purposes, in the long run, it is not religion which is the loser . . ."

© Film Information, 1976.

GUMBALL RALLY, THE

Director, Producer: *Chuck Bail*. Screenplay: *Leon Capetanos*. From a story by Messrs. Bail and Capetanos. Photography: *Richard C. Glouner*. Editors: *Gordon Scott, Stuart H. Pappe, Maury Winetrobe*. Music: *Dominic Frontiere*. Production: *First Artists*. Distributor: *Warner Bros*. Running time 93 minutes. Los Angeles opening August 1976 at several theatres. Classification: PG.

Players: *Michael Sarrazin, Raul Julia, Norman Burton, Gary Busey, John Derren, Susan Flannery, Harvey Jason, Steven Keats, Tim McIntire, Joanne Nail, J. Pat O'Malley, Tricia O'Neil, Lazaro Perez, Nicholas Pryor, Vaughn Taylor, Wally Taylor.*

Los Angeles Times, 8/5/76 (Pt. IV, p. 14)
Kevin Thomas

". . . of the various destruction derby films, *The Gumball Rally* . . . is the most enjoyable to date. That's because stylish, inventive writer-producer-director Chuck Bail, whose last picture was *Cleopatra Jones and the Casino of Gold*, and his cowriter Leon Capetanos actually play more for humor than violence.

Since nobody really gets hurt, the film serves as a release through fantasy, allowing the viewer the vicarious pleasure of experiencing the total freedom of all-out speeding without any of the deadly consequences that should normally ensue. What's more, the people involved are all likeable enough and intelligent enough to make it possible to identify with them rather than to be repelled by them. In

continued on next page

continued from previous page

short, by not becoming the usual vicious blood-bath, *Gumball Rally* can be lots of fun for those who like all-out racing pictures . . ."

©Los Angeles Times, 1976.

Drivers and fans celebrate in **The Gumball Rally**, a movie about the illegal race from New York to Los Angeles.

New York Magazine, 9/6/76 (p. 73)
John Simon

"*The Gumball Rally*, concerning the illegal car race from New York York to Los Angeles (which, alas, actually exists), is about as witless and crass as a comedy concerning an illegal car race can get. Written by Leon Capetanos and Chuck Bail, the latter of whom also directed, this is the kind of movie where a policeman refers to his 'stakeout' outside Gallagher's steak house, the two women racers hail from Beaver Falls, Pennsylvania (*beaver* being the CB-radio term for woman), a burning car careers into a fireworks factory, and a motorcyclist goes crashing through a billboard bearing the slogan 'Next Time Take the Train.' Roughly 96½ percent of the movie consists of cars racing past one another—or over, under, and preferably, into things. The quantity of supposedly hilarious wrecks is enough to outfit a better automobile graveyard . . .

A cast of relatively unknown players is headed by Michael Sarrazin, who, if he continues heading in this direction, may end up equally unknown . . ."

©1976 by the NYM Corp. Reprinted with the permission of NEW YORK Magazine.

New York Post, 8/21/76 (p. 15)
Archer Winsten

". . . After a fair amount of mystification as the project gets under way, we're off to the brrrump,

brrrump! of racing motors and the crash-bang as this or that competitor generates dozens of traffic pile ups among innocents. Hair whips in the wind of an open car, and the law hides at vantage points which will turn out to be one more frustration . . .

The action grows progressively wilder, slapsticky and unlikely.

The characters stop developing, the film deteriorates into tremendous face-making and ever noisier engine roars . . .

By this time the picture has been reduced to pure sound and fury and mechanics. I don't know who will enjoy it, outside of Jersey and Quebec drivers who may pick up a few pointers for speeding on the N.Y. Thruway."

Reprinted by Permission of New York Post.
©1976, New York Post Corporation.

Monthly Film Bulletin, October 1976 (p. 214)
Carol Howard

"In an inept attempt to parody the overworked 'zany car-chase' format, *The Gumball Rally* is tiresome enough to turn the most avid motor fanatic into a pedestrian. 'In this country you ain't no-one if you ain't got wheels,' remarks one of the characters, summing up the ethos of car-as-status-symbol/alter-ego/love-object. Unfortunately, if the 'wheels' are propelled by cardboard characters in an incoherently edited succession of crashes, smashes, stunts and explosions, freely borrowed from other sources, they lose all sense of direction . . . The banality of the script is summed up by the toast raised at the start of the rally: 'Here's to internal combustion and wind in your face.' "

©Monthly Film Bulletin, 1976

GUS

Director: *Vincent McEveety*. Screenplay: *Arthur Alsberg, Don Nelson*. Based on a story by Ted Key. Producer: *Ron Miller*. Photography: *Frank Phillips*. Editor: *Robert Stafford*. Music: *Robert F. Brunner*. Production: *Walt Disney Productions*. Distributor: *Buena Vista Distribution Company*. Running time 96 minutes. Los Angeles opening July 7, 1976, at several theatres. Classification: G.

Players: *Edward Asner, Don Knotts, Gary Grimes, Tim Conway, Liberty Williams, Dick Van Patten, Ronnie Schell, Bob Crane, Johnny Unitas, Dick Butkus, Harold Gould, Tom Bosley, Dick Enberg, George Putnam, Stu Nahan, Iris Adams.*

Film Information, 9/76 (p. 5)
Suzanne Bowers

"The Walt Disney studios continue to crank out feature films with great regularity. While there's nothing offensive about their newest movie, *Gus*, it is obvious that their standard formula is wearing thin and some new ideas are sorely needed . . .

The Disney brand of 'realism' has become predictably one-sided. Villains are always clumsy buffoons with two left feet and subzero mentalities who throw a monkey wrench into the proceedings, but never pose any serious threat. The 'good guys' are clean-cut, upstanding characters . . . all black-and-white delineations with no shades of gray. We still need Disney escapist entertainment, but a little more honesty . . . would help to give 'family films' a good name again."

©Film Information, 1976.

Los Angeles Times, 7/6/76 (Pt. IV, p. 13)
Linda Gross

". . . a funny and loveable, though familiar Disney live-action fantasy film for football families about a mule from Yugoslavia who salvages a sagging L.A. gridiron by kicking 100-yard field goals . . .

In the Disney tradition, Gus is loveable and wise—one step ahead of humans in agility and intelligence. The film relies too heavily on this gimmick and makes the ending in which an underachiever becomes a hero, predictable but not entirely satisfactory in terms of plot or character development.

The script by Arthur Alsberg and Don Nelson, from a story by Ted Key, includes some hilarious gags, slapstick and spoofs. The teams' cheerleaders are plump and platinum klutzes who fall from their fancy formation into the band's drum. Gus eludes the bumbling heavies, Bosley and Conway, in a zany, madcap supermarket chase . . ."

©Los Angeles Times, 1976.

New York Post, 7/10/76 (p. 18)
Archer Winsten

"*Gus*, a Walt Disney studio item in the comic tradition of their talking horses, this time a Yugoslavian mule who can kick a football 100 yards, can be sampled . . .

I don't know why you would want to, but that's a matter of taste.

At the beginning of the film there are a couple of giggles as the California Atoms, a professional football team impersonated by the Rams and other NFL individuals, act out a scenario of utter futility.

Later Johnny Unitas pretends to be a football announcer whose high-powered thrilla-minute co-announcer hogs all the air time. That too is good for a giggle, low-grade. The rest is hardly worth a synopsis . . ."

Reprinted by Permission of New York Post.
©1976, New York Post Corporation.

Films in Review, August/September 1976 (p. 440)
Tatiana Balkoff Lipscomb

"In the current comedy climate, when humor so often hinges on some four-letter word or its lengthier variant, a light-hearted football game spoof is a breath of fresh air.

The hero, Gus, a talented, field-goal-kicking mule, and his modest devoted owner, a farm boy from Yugoslavia, give Super Bowl football a wild super-twist. Director Vincent McEveety paced this unpretentious Disney (Ron Miller) production with a deft touch. The gags in the screenplay (based on a Ted Key story) by Alsberg and Nelson were managed with *taste*. Brunner's music suited the script.

The cast (Edward Asner, Don Knotts, Gary Grimes & Tim Conway) does a uniformly fine job . . ."

©Films in Review, 1976.

HARLAN COUNTY, U.S.A.

Documentary. Director, Producer: *Barbara Kopple*. Photography: *Hart Perry, Kevin Keating, Phil Parmet, Flip McCarthy, Tom Hurwitz*. Editors: *Nancy Baker, Mary Lampson, Lora Hays, Mirra Bank*. Music: *Hazel Dickens, Merle Travis and others*. Running time 103 minutes. New York opening October 15, 1976, at the New York Film Festival, Lincoln Center. Classification: None.

Newsweek, 11/1/76 (p. 83G)
Janet Maslin

". . . Kopple's debut feature can be faulted on several counts: its delineation of strike issues is sketchy, its history of the United Mine Workers is almost casual and its picture of life in Harlan County is perhaps incomplete. But Kopple was less interested in being thorough than she was in getting to the heart of the matter—and to the extent that her film captures the spirit of a place, a people and an insoluble predicament, it is a brave effort that succeeds magnificently.

The strike, precipitated by the mine owners' refusal to sign a UMW contract and by the miners' complaints about unsafe conditions, is the event around which this unabashedly pro-miner film revolves . . ."

©Newsweek, Inc. 1976
reprinted by permission.

continued on next page

continued from previous page

Nation, 11/6/76 (p. 475)
Harold Clurman

"*Harlan County, U.S.A.* is by no means perfect. Experts on the matter of documentary film may find reason to carp. It is nonetheless a moving, noble and most important picture. Its young director, Barbara Kopple, spent four years in its making. It is the record of a strike which endured that long in the coal fields of Kentucky.

We see the miners at their fearsome work; their homes, wives and children; the bosses and their representatives; the town sheriff; the intrepid women on the picket lines . . .

. . . Through the film we become intimate with the doughty participants—the bereaved mothers, the rough, hardy men, the tough, the scruffy, the scrappy—and we (or perhaps more precisely I) feel embarrassed for having been so long apart from them, though in a sense we all live off them . . ."

©The Nation, 1976.

New York Post, 10/15/76 (p. 15)
Frank Rich

". . . one can only applaud Miss Kopple for venturing where others haven't dared.

Unfortunately, that's about all that one can applaud Miss Kopple for: *Harlan County, U.S.A.* is an ineffectual mess, both as a movie and a social document, and it doesn't begin to be worthy of the miners whose lives it aspires to record . . .

. . . Miss Kopple's approach to documentary filmmaking is so unimaginative and slapdash that even ABC News might find her methods substandard. *Harlan County, U.S.A.* is just an incoherent (and somtimes inaudible) stew of 'talking heads' into which newsreel footage, explanatory title cards, repetitive film records of strikers' meetings and superficial digressions about important matters (black lung disease, mine disasters, etc.) have been inserted willy-nilly. Instead of being a film equivalent fo Agee's *Let Us Now Praise Famous Men* or Dos Passos' Harlan County reportage of the '30s, this movie looks like the film version of an inexperienced cub reporter's raw notes . . ."

Reprinted by Permission of New York Post.
©1976, New York Post Corporation.

Nation, 2/5/77 (p. 158)
Robert Hatch

"*Harlan County, U.S.A.* documents a dark subject, but it is far from being a dark picture. Barbara Kopple's record of the year and more struggle whereby the coal miners, and notably their wives and mothers, won a United Mine Workers contract from the Brookside mine (parent company, Duke Power) is, among other things, a celebration of human excellence. The mining families of Harlan County are a deprived and abused people—you have only to see their teeth to know it. But a sad or beaten people they are not; on the contrary, they are vivid, eloquent, quick of body and mind, and witty. Needless to say, they are ill-educated, but by force of intelligence they go an astonishing way to overcome the lack . . .

. . . *Harlan County* attains its main goal—to honor a segment of our society which the rest of America has been willing to write off as underdogs, victims sacrificed to the imperatives of an industrial nation. It is a shock to discover that these expendable, burrowing creatures are in fact as splendid a people as the country can show. Ms. Kopple found a great cast; she has made a film worthy of her company and their story."

©The Nation, 1977.

New York Magazine, 1/24/77 (p. 83)
John Simon

". . . What a chasm there is between a great documentary by, say, Marcel Ophuls and Miss Kopple's *Harlan County, U.S.A.* Yet the latter is not a total loss. After all, when people are trodden down to the point where their naked humanity is stepped on—when they at last take cognizance of the need to band together and fight against great and brutal odds—there are bound to be moments of courage and dignity, of warmth and suffering and even humor begotten of suffering, that cannot help moving and sternly shaking us. All the filmmaker need do is be there . . .

Such an enterprise should not be underrated, however. It takes vision and determination to conceive, shoot, and put together a *Harlan County, U.S.A.*, even if it is not done particularly well. There are sequences here as tragic or heartwarming as anything ever seen on film . . ."

©1977 by the NYM Corp. Reprinted with
the permission of NEW YORK Magazine.

Film Information, February 1977 (p. 1)
Robert E. A. Lee

". . . The most dramatic moments are those when the people argue the conscience questions of what to do when the other side meets them at the picket line armed with guns. Persuasive voices push the normally nonviolent miners toward counterviolence. Several of the outspoken women reveal themselves to have characters that are almost prototypically the stuff of legends. The company foreman emerges as 'the enemy' to the miners and their families, yet we see him also as a worried loyalist brave enough to defend the power establishment against the insurgents who are his neighbors . . .

Harlan County, U.S.A. must be seen by all of us Americans who tend to reduce the energy crisis to economic formulae instead of understanding it as a profoundly human and moral question linked to the universal issue of freedom.''

©Film Information, 1977.

Commonweal, 3/4/77 (p. 149)
Colin L. Westerbeck, Jr.

''. . . At one point Kopple is interviewing an old woman who was once made to evacuate her house when a nearby mine exploded. 'They said it was because the house was in danger I had to leave,' she sneers. 'But it wasn't that at all: it was because they didn't want me to see what they was doing there.' As she reaches this conclusion the words crowd quicker and quicker into her throat and the breath between them becomes ever more compressed, until we see that the explosion in the mine was nothing compared to the explosion of insight and realization that has been building in her over the years. All the women in Kopple's film give this impression—the impression of a subterranean rage bursting forth at last . . .''

©Commonweal, 1977.

Saturday Review, 3/5/77 (p. 39)
Judith Crist

''. . . a work as passionate as it is insightful, as partisan as it is informative . . .
There is laughter and sorrow and a tremendous exhilaration in Kopple's work, its fulfillment the transmission of concern and involvement. The film's power goes beyond the specific subject of the miners, so vital a one, so rarely touched upon by Hollywood . . . Kopple's major accomplishment is her revitalization of social juices long dormant for those of us who were radicals and unionists in our youth, only to become cynics and conservatives in our middle age. Hers is a reminder that there cannot be neutrals—anywhere.''

©Judith Crist, 1977.

HARRY AND WALTER GO TO NEW YORK

Director: *Mark Rydell*. Screenplay: *John Byrum, Robert Kaufman*. Based on a story by Don Devlin and Mr. Byrum. Producers: *Mr. Devlin, Harry Gittes*. Executive Producer: *Tony Bill*. Photography: *Laszlo Kovacs*. Editors: *David Bretherton, Don Guidice*. Music: *David*

Shire. Lyrics: *Alan Bergman, Marilyn Bergman*. Distributor: *Columbia Pictures*. Running time 123 minutes. New York opening June 17, 1976, at Radio City Music Hall. Classification: PG.

Harry Dighby: *James Caan*. Walter Hill: *Elliott Gould*. Adam Worth: *Michael Caine*. Lissa Chestnut: *Diane Keaton*. Rufus T. Crisp: *Charles Durning*. Gloria Fontaine: *Lesley Ann Warren*. Chatsworth: *Val Avery*. Mischa: *Jack Gilford*. Lewis: *Dennis Dugan*. Florence: *Carol Kane*. Barbara: *Kathryn Grody*. Ben: *David Proval*. Billy Gallagher: *Michael Conrad*. Warden Durgom: *Burt Young*. Guard O'Meara: *Bert Remsen*.

Women's Wear Daily, 6/18/76 (p. 32)
Howard Kissel

''*Harry and Walter Go to New York* is a period 'caper' picture, an involved story about two seedy vaudevillians who undergo an arduous apprenticeship in bank robbery in an effort to enter the glittering, snobbish world of the criminally successful. Set at the turn of the century in Boston and New York . . . *Harry and Walter* is high on period charm and somewhat less fussy about making sure its complex plot is air-tight.
The tone is breezy. Elliott Gould, a generally obnoxious actor usually cast as a groovy contemporary neurotic, is much more enjoyable playing a nervous innocent of a less frenetic era. He and James Caan make a good 'couple,' as male couples go these days . . . Michael Caine plays the 'doyen' of the upper-crust criminal set with proper finesse, and Diane Keaton is properly hysterical as a young crusading reporter.
Obviously the intent was to create something on the order of *The Sting*, but *Harry and Walter* is not as conscientious about fashioning its complicated story to build tension. As a result, the film lacks charge but is good summer entertainment.''

© Women's Wear Daily, 1976.

New York Magazine, 6/28/76 (p. 69)
John Simon

''*Harry and Walter Go to New York* is an attempt at crossbreeding a number of genres: slapstick, romantic comedy, the caper film, the straight musical, the operetta parody. It might just barely have worked in the hands of an expert, but not with scenarists like John Byrum (*Inserts, Mahogany*)

continued on next page

continued from previous page

and Robert Kaufman *(Getting Straight, I Love My Wife)*. Although they manage a few mildly funny throwaway lines, what really should have been thrown away is their entire script. Mark Rydell has directed at a curious double pace: an underlying leadenness that is sporadically interrupted by furious spasms--rather like an old dog occasionally twitching in his sleep.

Elliott Gould, more subdued than usual and playing a goofball, is better than he has been lately; Michael Caine is a past master at smoothness edged with menace. Charles Durning, too, is good as a pompous banker, but James Caan seems not quite at home in this kind of farce. At least he is never so embarrassing as Diane Keaton, who goes through her meager bag of tricks for the umpteenth time, and is totally out of sync with the period . . .''

© 1976 by the NYM Corp. Reprinted with the permission of NEW YORK Magazine.

Newsweek, 6/28/76 (p. 77)
Janet Maslin

''*Harry and Walter Go to New York* brings out the worst in every one of its principals, and therein lies the secret of its lightweight success. Elliott Gould (Walter), childishly hammy in even the gravest of roles, is perfectly suited to the part of a fleabag, turn-of-the-century vaudevillian. James Caan (Harry), who has never before revealed a flair for musical comedy, makes Gould an ideal no-talent foil. Marilyn and Alan Bergman, who may well be the worst cornball lyricists that Hollywood has ever spawned, crank out just the right brand of treacle to explain why the Gould-Caan duo will never strike it rich in their ill-chosen field . . .

Mark Rydell is the ideal director for such meringue; he neither takes it unduly seriously nor forces it to be Fun. *Harry and Walter* is long enough to go slack in spots and more expensively turned out than it needed to be . But it exudes more than its share of bumbling charm . . .''

© Newsweek, Inc. 1976 reprinted by permission.

Christian Science Monitor, 6/24/76 (p. 30)
David Sterritt

''*Harry and Walter Go to New York* is a noisy farce with lots of jokes about vaudeville, safecracking, restaurants, jail, crusading journalists, and the turn of the century. The plot is more complicated than clever, the humor is more punchy than funny, but it is innocuous enough and should suffice if you are that desperate for a few laughs . . .

Director Mark Rydell keeps the pace fast and the atmosphere pleasant, while coming up with too few genuinely witty moments. The screenplay comes from Robert Kaufman and John Byrum . . .

Top honors in *Harry and Walter* go to the actors, who work very hard. Mr. Gould has not performed so convincingly or likably in ages, and Mr. Caan shows a flair for the flat comic inflections. Mr. Caine has the class he carries so well, and Miss Keaton provides a lovely energy. Bert Remsen, Charles Durning, and the gifted Carol Kane head a large and colorful supporting cast.''

Reprinted by permission from The Christian Science Monitor © 1976. The Christian Science Publishing Society. All right reserved.

New York Post, 6/18/76 (p. 28)
Frank Rich

'' . . . This film fails to work as light comedy, as a period piece, as a jigsaw puzzle . . . Mainly, it just sits there and dies.

The reason it dies is that you can't make a stylish entertainment if you have no sense of style. And virtually no one connected with this film has a stylish conception of either his own work or the overall direction of the entire project.

The anything-goes script . . . is rooted neither in period nor human reality nor the rudiments of basic comedy writing . . . photographed by Laszlo Kovacs in a manner that doesn't so much recall *The Sting* as suggest how *Hester Street* might have looked if it had been swept by a dust storm. David Shire's cluttery rinkytink score makes one long for Scott Joplin--or even Marvin Hamlisch.

Then there's the contribution of director Rydell . . . *Harry and Walter Go to New York* is almost a case-book study in what happens when a weak director loses control over his film . . .''

Reprinted by Permission of New York Post. © 1976,New York Post Corporation.

Monthly Film Bulletin, 9/76 (p. 192)
Geoff Brown

'' 'It's a Laurel and Hardy film with real people,' Mark Rydell declared, when interviewed during the production of this nine-million-dollar frolic, but the remark is revealed as nonsense once the finished product is inspected, for Stan and Ollie had ten times the reality of Harry and Walter, the bumbling duo who at one point directly evoke the pair with a childish bout of hat-stomping and nose-tweaking. They also had a great deal of warmth and humanity—qualities conspicuously lacking in this banal, mechanical concoction, which relentlessly pursues a coarse line of humor, gracelessly put over by a starry cast. The pitch is unpleasantly frenetic: Michael Caine and Diane Keaton do a lot of shouting, and in the criss-cross exchanges between Gould and Caan speed easily outdistances wit . . .''

©Monthly Film Bulletin, 1976.

Saturday Review, 7/24/76 (p. 42)
Judith Crist

"*Harry and Walter Go to New York*, written by John Byrum and Robert Kaufman and directed with intermittent style by Mark Rydell, is . . . a thing of bits and pieces . . . there's a near-embarrassment of rich acting talents on hand, with little to activate them. James Caan and Elliott Gould play two Gay Nineties vaudeville performers who, as someone aptly says, 'would need practice to be oafs.' . . . Caan and Gould are appealing despite their desperate attempts to take on a Laurel and Hardy air. Caine is smashing as the matinee-idol crook, and Keaton is a joy as the passionate crusader who decides to rob a bank 'in the name of decency.' But they, unlike the shrewdies in *The Sting*, are never sure who's kidding whom. The David Shire score gives a vaudeville air to the goings-on that Rydell's direction only sporadically justifies—with shades of *The Night They Raided Minsky's* and *The Great Bank Robbery* all too evident. There's small sense of period or style beyond the lush Nineties sets, which we have much too much time to admire."

©Judith Crist, 1976.

Los Angeles Times, 7/28/76 (Pt. IV, p. 13)
Kevin Thomas

". . . This $8 million Columbia production has everything money can buy—James Caan, Elliott Gould, Michael Caine and Diane Keaton, glorious period settings and costumes given a nostalgic golden glow by cinematographer Laszlo Kovacs, a beguiling score by David Shire . . . and good natured direction by Mark Rydell.

But then there's the matter of the screenplay, written by John Byrum and Robert Kaufman from a story by the film's co-producer Don Devlin and Byrum: It's so relentlessly silly and puerile that cutting 12 minutes out of an unconscionable 123 minutes hasn't helped it a bit. *Harry and Walter Go to New York* is strictly for those who'll laugh at anything . . ."

©Los Angeles Times, 1976.

Film Information, July/August 1976 (p. 5)
William F. Fore

"Harry (James Caan) and Walter (Elliott Gould), a bumbling song-and-dance team of the 1890s, steal the plans of master thief Adam Worth (Michael Caine) to rob the First National Bank of Lowell, Mass., and together with a motley crew of reformers headed by lovely Lissa Chestnut (Diane Keaton), they race Worth's gang for the money, one group drilling from above, the other from below.

All this is served with a few sight gags, some zany antics, a couple of songs and long stretches of ho-hum. The story is predictable, the pacing slow, and except for a funny sequence where Caan and Gould take over a melodrama musical in order to make it last an extra fifteen minutes (and thereby defeat the crooks), the routines are routine . . ."

©Film Information, 1976.

HAWMPS

Director, Producer: *Joe Camp*. Screenplay: *William Bickley, Michael Warren*. Photography: *Don Reddy*. Editor: *Leon Seith*. Music: *Euel Box*. Distributor: *Mulberry Square Productions*. Running time 127 minutes. New York opening May 27, 1976, at the Guild 50th Theatre. Classification: G.

Howard Clemmons: *James Hampton*. Uriah Tibbs: *Christopher Connelly*. Naman Tucker: *Slim Pickens*. Colonel Hawkins: *Denver Pyle*. Hi Jolly: *Gene Conforti*. Jennifer Hawkins: *Mimi Maynard*. Bad Jack Cutter: *Jack Elam*.

Los Angeles Times, 5/27/76 (Pt. IV, p. 20)
Kevin Thomas

"Back in 1855 Secretary of War Jefferson Davis, subsequently the one and only Confederate President, actually persuaded Congress to spend $30,000 for importing camels to be introduced into the cavalry . . .

. . . it took Joe Camp, the Texas-based producer-director who scored such a hit with *Benji,* to make a movie about it . . .

. . . it's a pretty funny picture, its humor very broad but unfailingly good-natured. Consequently, it's able to overcome its excessive length—2 hours, 7 minutes—by sheer amiability.

Chubby, a wistful-eyed James Hampton, always so stalwart in supporting roles, attains star status as an inept Army lieutenant sent out West from Washington, D. C., to take charge of the camel experiment at a fort commanded by artillery veteran Denver Pyle . . .

. . . Camp has a feel for what is cinematic and has genuine affection for his actors. The better part

continued on next page

continued from previous page

of the film's undue length is at least spent in allowing us to get to know and care about the
people . . .''

© Los Angeles Times, 1976.

Film Information, 6/76 (p. 3)
William C. Winslow

'' . . . The idea of making a funny film about
camels wandering around in the American Southwest with soldiers desperately trying to learn how to
manage such seemingly ungainly beasts is a good
one. Unfortunately, *Hawmps* (Texan for humps)
doesn't make it. And it doesn't make it because this
movie (made by Mulberry Square, producers of
Benji) tries to be a comedy Western for the *entire*
family. The plot does not adapt easily to such a
broad audience, even though the story line is simple and predictable. It chronicles the bumbling efforts of Lt. Clemmons (James Hampton of TV's *F
Troop*) to command the Camel Corps and prove
their worth. To remind the audience that this is a
comedy Western, every joke, pratfall, and sight gag
is pounded home with sledgehammer emphasis.
Good actors like Slim Pickens seem to have their
talents reined in by the need to appeal to that broad
family audience. Some of the other characters are
cardboard figures right out of Central (Texas) Casting. Actually, many are office employees of Mulberry Productions. This is good family entertainment only if your idea of a good time is to watch
reruns of *Hee Haw* . . .''

© Film Information, 1976.

New York Post, 5/28/76 (p. 24)
Archer Winsten

"Having hit the jackpot with a sentimental dog
picture, *Benji*, last year, the Texas-based Mulberry
Square Productions, which is a guy named Joe
Camp, has tried again with *Hawmps* . . .

This time they're camels, and to say they haven't
the charisma of that dog is putting it in another
county.

To take up the slack they have used every old
slapstick device known to man or beast, utilized
painfully obvious comic characters, and whipped
out a plot that moves fast but not fast enough to
avoid either the telegraphing or the punches that
miss . . .

If Joe Camp can parlay this picture into a smash,
he'll have to be the promotion genius of the decade. My guess is he's riding for a hard fall.''

Reprinted by Permission of New York Post.
© 1976, New York Post Corporation.

Christian Science Monitor, 5/28/76 (p. 23)
David Sterritt

'' . . . a good-natured farce for young and old
alike. I suspect that older children will be its biggest
audience, since jaded adults will find its slapstick
repetitious, while its two-hour-plus running time is
much too long for the youngest set. But its heart
and its humps are in the proper place, and I think
any open-minded viewer will find something to
enjoy.

Hawmps are camels, of course, in cowboy slang.
The comical cavalrymen of Joe Camp's movie are
downright furious at the idea of riding such exotic
beasts, especially after expecting their new 'Arabian mounts' to be splendid foreign horses. And
imagine the ribbing from the other guys on the
base!

This is the kind of humor that children seem to
enjoy heartily, and producer-director Camp makes
the most of it. The climax of the movie is an epic
race between horsemen and camelmen, the winners to determine army policy toward 'hawmps.'
Throw in a few bad guys, some unexpected twists,
and a water shortage, and you have a situation
alternately sprightly, exciting, and harrowing--a
blend of effects not often encountered in the bland
kiddie-movie market . . .''

Reprinted by permission from The Christian
Science Monitor © 1976.
The Christian Science Publishing Society.
All rights reserved.

HEARTS OF THE WEST

Director: *Howard Zieff.* Screenplay: *Rob
Thompson.* Producer: *Tony Bill.* Photography:
Mario Tosi. Editor: *Edward Warschilka.*
Music: *Ken Lauber.* Production: *Metro-
Goldwyn-Mayer.* Distributor: *United Artists.*
Running time 103 minutes. New York opening
October 4, 1975, at the New York Film Festi-
val, Lincoln Center. Classification: PG.

Lewis Tater: *Jeff Bridges.* Howard Pike:
Andy Griffith. A. J. Nietz: *Donald Pleasence.*
Miss Trout: *Blythe Danner.* Kessler: *Alan
Arkin.* Stout crook: *Richard B. Shull.* Polp:
Herbert Edelman. Earl: *Alex Rocco.* Pa Tater:
Frank Cady. Lean crook: *Anthony James.*

See Volume 1 for additional reviews

Monthly Film Bulletin, 6/76 (p. 126)
Jonathan Rosenbaum

" . . . A modest if charming lark of a movie,
Hearts of the West--inexplicably retitled *Hollywood
Cowboy* for English consumption--treats the Western myth exclusively as an occasion for celebrating
the gentle innocence of a Midwesterner's appreciation of it . . . What keeps the film happy and
hopeful . . . apart from a successfully muted sense
of period decor--are its quieter virtues, all geared
around cheerful connections between characters
and performances: a rusty old-timer sporting his
'true' Western profile in a flush of bashful vanity; a
campy barber protesting when Lewis orders his
hair to be cut exactly like Zane Grey's; Alan Arkin,
as the excitable director, jerking the chair he's
seated on across an office floor in a kind of pro-
longed manic stutter. But more essentially, the
movie belongs to its two stars, who can come up
with delightful surprises regardless of what the
script throws at them: Jeff Bridges, mouthing his
cowboy cliches with a relish that makes them inde-
lible; and Blythe Danner, triumphing over a conventional Girl Friday part so that she not only looks
entirely different from the way she did in *Lovin'
Molly*--slimmer, smarter, sharper and cooler--but
takes on a fresh aspect in each successive scene,
a chameleon running changes around the equally
likeable stasis of Bridges."

© Monthly Film Bulletin, 1976.

The Times (London), 5/16/76 (p. 37)
Dilys Powell

" . . . Set in the early days of the talkies and accompanied by the soft-footed songs of the period, it
is about an Iowa farm boy ambitious to write Western novels and scarcely capable of opening his
mouth without letting some ripe Western cliche escape. A job as a Western extra provides some
horse-satire, never too smart, and some horse-
instruction: How does it feel after jumping from a
roof to land astride on the waiting animal?
   But the point of this entertaining film is its lack of
strain. The cinema repeatedly makes jokes about
the Western; I sit through them frozen-faced. But
this time there is a shade of affection. The boy takes
the Western as well as himself completely seriously:
no guying, just the natural absurdity of the cinema's
methods of faking. Jeff Bridges plays the role with
the right touch of gullibility."

© The Times, 1976.

Sight and Sound, Summer 1976 (p. 191)
Richard Combs

" . . . Bridges makes such disarming work of the

dedicated writer as simple farm-boy, capable of
flourishing in the tawdriest circumstances. And as a
picture of Thirties' Hollywood, the film largely takes
its tone from the hero's pragmatic enthusiasm. An
advertising mural for *Anna Christie* ('Garbo talks')
decorates one city wall, but all the show-biz
dreamers here have entered through the back door
of the factory, and the poverty-row production line
serves Lewis as usefully—as a place 'to soak up a
little Western atmosphere'—as it does the quickie
director Kessler (one of the best excuses yet for
Alan Arkin's exercise in dynamic irascibility and
grandiloquent insecurity). But the presiding spirit is
clearly Howard Pike (Andy Griffith), the aging bit-
player who had his own day as a Western writer,
and who tutors Lewis in the economics and group
ethics of this new line of work . . ."

©Sight and Sound, 1976.

HEDDA

Director: *Trevor Nunn.* Screenplay: *Mr. Nunn.*
Based on the Henrik Ibsen play, *Hedda
Gabler.* Executive Producer: *George Barrie.*
Producer: *Robert Enders.* Photography:
Douglas Slocombe. Editor: *Peter Tanner.*
Music: *Laurie Johnson.* Art Director: *Edward
Tester.* Costumes: *John Napier.* Production:
*The Royal Shakespeare Company; Brut
Productions.* Running time 104 minutes. Los
Angeles opening December, 1975, at the UA
Cinema Center Theatre. Classification: PG.
Origin: Great Britain.

Players: *Glenda Jackson, Peter Eyre, Timothy
West, Jennie Linden, Patrick Stewart,
Constance Chapman, Pam St. Clement.*

See Volume 1 for additional reviews

Monthly Film Bulletin, February 1977 (p. 24)
Brenda Davies

" . . . The weakness of Trevor Nunn's version is its
tendency to underplay the social aspects of the
text, so that attention is concentrated on personalities and personal relationships. No doubt this was
inevitable since his Hedda, played with tigerish
venom and razor-sharp intelligence by Glenda Jackson, could never for a moment be taken for a highly
sensual woman trapped by her own rigid social

continued on next page

continued from previous page

conformity . . . The compliant conspiratorial laxity that would attract the womanising Brack is quite outside her range, and she becomes the dominant, aggressive partner in all their exchanges . . . There is one important bonus from this attacking attitude—one is able to believe for the very first time in Hedda's suicide. But the play has been stood on its head to justify this final coup . . ."

©Monthly Film Bulletin, 1977

HIDING PLACE, THE

Director: *James F. Collier*. Screenplay:*Allen Sloane and Lawrence Holben*. Based on the book by *Corrie ten Boom and John and Elizabeth Sherrill*. Producer: *Frank R. Jacobson*, Photography: *Michael Reed*. Editor: *Ann Chegwidden*. Production: *World Wide Pictures*. Running time 145 minutes. Los Angeles opening October 1, 1975, at several theatres. Classification: PG.

Players: *Julie Harris, Eileen Heckart, Arthur O'Connell, Jeannette Clift, Robert Rietty, Pamela Sholto, Paul Henley and Richard Wren.*

See Volume 1 for additional reviews

Monthly Film Bulletin, 9/76 (p. 192)
John Pym

"*The Hiding Place*, a lavish product of Billy Graham's evangelical organisation, is an unusual brand of inspirational story-telling which, judging from its pre-publicity, is to be marketed primarily as a star-packaged commercial vehicle. It becomes unmistakeably obvious, however, that the film is no more than a Bible-thumping tract once the ten Booms' tranquil life (represented by sepia-tinted stills, raising expectations of another *Godfather)* is perfunctorily interrupted by the Nazis (whose main representative, it seems, is a bewildered young soldier with a keen interest in clocks), and the cloak-and-dagger concealment of the Jews gives way to a desultory storyline repeatedly punctured by assertions of the power of the Christian faith . . ."

©Monthly Film Bulletin, 1976.

HOLLYWOOD BOULEVARD

Directors: *Joe Dante, Allan Arkush.* Screenplay: *Patrick Hobby.* Producer: *Jon Davison.* Photography: *Jamie Anderson.* Editors: *Amy Jones, Mr. Arkush, Mr. Dante.* Music: *Andrew Stein.* Distributor: *New World Pictures.* Running time 83 minutes. Los Angeles opening April 28, 1976, at several theatres. Classification: R.

Players: *Candice Rialson, Mary Woronov, Rita George, Jeffrey Kramer, Dick Miller, Richard Doran, Tara Strohmeier, Paul Bartel, John Kramer, Jonathan Kaplan, Commander Cody and the Lost Planet Airmen.*

Los Angeles Times, 4/28/76 (p. 17)
Kevin Thomas

"At least as far back as *Merton of the Movies* (1924) Hollywood has been turning its cameras on itself, generally with satirical and often savage intent.

But there's never been anything quite like *Hollywood Boulevard* . . . an outrageous, often hilarious spoof of the zany world of low-budget exploitation film-making. And what better company to produce such an effort than Roger Corman's New World Pictures?

To be sure, New World knows its audience too well to attempt anything like an authentic glimpse of the actual hectic, often ruthless and desperate existence of aspiring young talent. Rather, it has played everything very, very broad, making certain there's plenty of fast action and above-the-waist nudity to satisfy the fans of the very films it's making fun of. Yet it is also sufficiently maginative and knowledgeable to amuse film buffs . . ."

© Los Angeles Times, 1976.

Take One, 5/21/76 (p. 65)
Tim Onosko

"*Hollywood Boulevard* . . . may very well be mistaken by general audiences as another R-rated semi-porn pic destined for drive-in and grind houses. Mostly, though, it is the end result of seeing too many movies and then attempting to make one's own—and should be an enjoyable lesson for all aspirants to film production. This is not to say that it is bad. In fact, it is quite good considering it was reportedly made for *under* $60,000. But it is eccentric.

Briefly, it is the loosely constructed story of a series of mishaps (read murders) involving four budding actresses working for a 'B' movie studio . . . The plot is just an excuse to indulge in the ambience of traditional Hollywood 'B' forms, the Gangster film, the War film and the Science-Fiction and Horror film . . .

. . . Davison, Arkush and Dante will be heard from again. They have created the ultimate drive-in movie––one that need not sustain levels of attention or, even, pander to the audience's insatiable desire for good, wholesome entertainment. There is enough machine-gun fire, semi-clad female form, and what *Mad* editor Harvey Kurtzman called 'eyeball kicks' to last a lifetime . . . ''

© Take One, 1976.

HOT POTATO

Director, Screenplay: *Oscar Williams*. Producers: *Fred Weintraub, Paul Heller*. Photography: *Ronald Garcia*. Distributor: *Warner Brothers*. Running time 87 minutes. New York opening April 28, 1976, at several theatres. Classification: PG.

Players: *Jim Kelly, George Memmoli, Geoffrey Binney, Irene Tsu, Judith Brown, Sam Hiona, Ron Prince, Hardy Stockman, Metta Rungrat, Supakorn Songsermvorakul.*

Los Angeles Times, 5/7/76 (p. 27)
Linda Gross

"*Hot Potato* . . . is a stylish and visually exotic Kung-Fu movie, shot in Thailand, which stars the kinetic Jim Kelly as a cool soldier of fortune.

A U.S. Senator hires a trio of American mercenaries (Kelly, George Memmoli and Geoffrey Binney––along with a local police sergeant, Irene Tsu) to rescue his kidnapped daughter (Judith Brown). The daughter is being held hostage to stop a foreign aid bill by a treacherous warlord (Sam Hiona), who owns a tank of pet tigers who eat trespassers . . .

The affable and appropriately hip script by Oscar Williams suggests how the American presence in Asia can complicate local politics. Williams also directs with wit, though he occasionally lapses into colloquial cuteness. The golden pagodas, wedding ceremonies and musical parades are authentically photographed by Ronald Garcia.

The film is enhanced by the intelligent and versatile presence of Jim Kelly, as well as the engaging and attractive performances of Memmoli, Binney, Miss Tsu, Miss Brown, Miss Rungrat, and Supakorn . . .''

© Los Angeles Times, 1976.

New York Post, 4/29/76 (p. 27)
Archer Winsten

"*Hot Potato* . . . puts in a strong bid as the most ridiculous movie of the year, and possibly the most wasteful, too.

Both in plot and action it achieves an ultimate worst. The plot takes three American heroes, Jones (Jim Kelly), Rhino (George Memmoli) and Chicago (Geoffrey Binney), into a very colorful southeast Asia to rescue the daughter of a U.S. Senator (Judith Brown) who is being held captive by the arch villain, Rangoon (Sam Hiona).

Their behavior is an absurd combination of Oriental karate chops and kicks with personalities taken from the Three Stooges . . .

. . . It's the kind of picture you walk out on unless you're curious to find out how much worse it can get.''

Reprinted by Permission of New York Post.
© 1976, New York Post Corporation.

HOUSE OF EXORCISM, THE

Director: *Mickey Lion*. Screenplay: *Albertto Cittini, Alfred Leone*. Producer: *Mr. Leone*. Music: *Carlo Savino*. Production: *Alfred Leone International Production*. Distributor: *Peppercorn-Wormser*. Running time 91 minutes. Los Angeles opening October 1976 at several theatres. Classification: R.

Players: *Robert Alda, Sylva Koscina, Kathe Leone, Telly Savalas, Elke Sommer, Alida Valli.*

Los Angeles Times, 10/15/76 (Pt. IV, p. 28)
Linda Gross

"In the tradition of *Beyond the Door* and *Abby*— only much worse—*The House of Exorcism* . . . is a revolting rip-off of *The Exorcist*. However, this dubbed, ghastly, gothic-demonic movie boasts the added attraction of Telly Savalas starring as a white-gloved, lollipop-licking, radish-serving butler-devil who makes puppet-corpses and converses with them a la Edgar Bergen and Charlie McCarthy . . .

The nudity, murder and gore are clear, only the plot in this creaky and confusing script by Albertto Cittini and Alfred Leone is murky and implausible.

Director Mickey Lion seems to be confused between camp and other styles, so he lets each actor play it his own way. Elke Sommer looks bewildered, Robert Alda is sincere, and Telly Savalas plays Kojak . . .''

© Los Angeles Times, 1976.

HOW FUNNY CAN SEX BE?
(SESSO MATTO)

Director: *Dino Risi*. Screenplay (Italian with English subtitles): *Ruggero Maccari, Mr. Risi.* Photography: *Alfio Contini*. Music: *Armando Trovaioli, Alberto Gallitti*. Production: *Dean Films, Cinetirrena*. Distributor: *In-Frame Films*. Running time 97 minutes. New York opening September 28, 1976, at the Trans-Lux East Theatre. Classification: R. Origin: Italy.

Butler, Executive, Groom, Laborer, Donor, Provincial Man, Corpse, Employee: *Giancarlo Giannini*. Rich Woman, Ignored Wife, Bride, Laborer's Wife, Nun: *Laura Antonelli*. Gilda: *Alberto Lionello*.

Women's Wear Daily, 9/28/76 (p. 20)
Howard Kissel

"Dino Risi's *How Funny Can Sex Be?* is a collection of what must be the Italian equivalents of farmer's daughter stories. The eight sketches in the film all deal with quickly recognizable types—the man who presents a Casanova image in public and is incapable of living up to it in private; the young man who has a passion for older women . . .

Each type is set in an anecdote that doesn't really deal with his sexual plight, but ends in farce . . .

There would have to have been a lot of brandy and cigars for these stories to have been successful on the after-dinner circuit. What makes them agreeable as film is that Giancarlo Giannini is adroit at exploiting the farcical potential in each of the situations, and Laura Antonelli makes an extremely attractive object for his often bizarre lust . . ."

©Women's Wear Daily, 1976.

New York Post, 9/29/76 (p. 43)
Archer Winsten

"What *Le Sex Shop* was for France, the funniest and wittiest, *How Funny Can Sex Be?* is for Italy. It's a Rabelaisian series of eight sketches that show the passionate male animal, played by the inimitable Giancarlo Giannini in a marvelous variety of postures . . .

First, he's a butler drooling over the very noticeable charms of his employer (Laura Antonelli), next a bridegroom promising his bride (Laura again) a great first night, but failing . . .

Director Dino Risi has made the most of his two popular stars, turning out what is unquestionably the funniest, bawdiest sex comedy of the month and probably the year."

Reprinted by Permission of New York Post.
© 1976, New York Post Corporation.

Los Angeles Times, 10/29/76 (Pt. IV, p. 1)
Charles Champlin

"*How Funny Can Sex Be?* is not a movie that will get mentioned in a lot of letters to the folks back on the farm. It is bawdy, vulgar and foolish and it tangoes right up to the edge of tastelessness. It is also bizarrely funny and, if not precisely innocent, at least healthily unsalacious and pleasantly nonprurient.

It is a series of nine sketches, united by the exceedingly expert presences of Giancarlo Giannini (the sad-eyed star of most of Lina Wertmuller's movies) and Laura Antonelli, who blends a face of heavenly beauty, a body of earthly delight and the disciplined intelligence of a very able comedienne . . ."

©Los Angeles Times, 1976.

New York Magazine, 10/11/76 (p. 80)
John Simon

". . . there are two irresistible performers. Giancarlo Giannini proves yet again what a varied and delicious comedian he is, switching faces, voices, and accents as you or I might change underwear; he has, besides, more charm than a barrelful of kittens. As for his equally role-changing leading lady, Laura Antonelli, she is a more than competent actress with an incomparable loveliness that is both ribald and innocent enough to turn saints into fiends and vice versa. Armando Trovaioli's music is his usual claptrap, and the cinematography by Alfio Contini, another Antonioni discovery, is workmanlike. There is, moreover, a tremendous performance by Alberto Lionello as a transvestite . . ."

© 1976 by the NYM Corp. Reprinted with the permission of NEW YORK Magazine.

Film Information, October 1976 (p. 3)
Jackson Ferry

". . . what this movie lacks is subtlety. There is a sense, particularly in the segments entitled 'A Difficult Case' and 'Wild Gooseberries,' that Risi and his players are trying to make funny a situation that really is not funny, at least in the context in which they present it. People with traditional moral principles will probably find these two sequences, which deal with homosexuality and artificial insemination, overdone and offensive. In fairness, much of the humor may be lost in the translation to English . . . always a risk for foreign language comedies.

The film's best sequences are the first and the last, 'Eight O'Clock Madame' and 'The House Guest' . . ."

©Film Information, 1976.

HUMAN FACTOR, THE

Director: *Edward Dmytryk.* Screenplay: *Tom Hunter, Peter Powell.* Photography: *Qusama Rawl.* Editor: *Alan Strachen.* Music: *Enrico Moriconi.* Distributor: *Branston Films.* Running time 96 minutes. New York opening November, 1975, at several theatres. Classification: R.

John Kinsdale: *George Kennedy.* Mike McAllister: *John Mills.* Dr. Lupo: *Raf Vallone.* General Fuller: *Arthur Franz.* Janice: *Rita Tushingham.* Kamal: *Frank Avianca.* Pidgeon: *Haydee Politoff.* Taylor: *Tom Hunter.* Edmonds: *Barry Sullivan.*

See Volume 1 for additional reviews

The Sunday Times (London), 6/20/76 (p. 37)
Dilys Powell

". . . The hero of this unedifying tale is a computer expert (George Kennedy) who drives home one evening to find his wife and children cold under blood-soaked sheets: the terrorists have been at work. Aided by murmurs of Old Chum by a colleague (John Mills) and by unauthorized use of NATO equipment, the middle-aged widower plans to play executioner. And indeed computers, though in private life their function seems to be to get one's bank balance wrong, appear to be quite a help in criminal investigation. At any rate, Mr. Kennedy, panting over rooftops and up and down flights of Neapolitan stone steps, is enabled to strangle one of the killers with a length of heavy chain.

Then, while NATO and the Italian police (Raf Vallone) stand around helplessly, he takes on the whole gang in a supermarket . . ."

©The Sunday Times, 1976.

The Times (London), 6/18/76 (p. 9)
David Robinson

". . . The reactionary sentiments of the film are extreme. 'Radical' becomes not merely a wholly derogatory term but synonymous with 'terrorist.' There is a disturbing emphasis on the fact that the terrorists are all well educated (we are told several times that the leaders were at Berkeley) and from rich backgrounds. The man from the embassy whimpers that one of the victims is 'not some fat-cat industrialist—just a lousy little accountant' (it seems irrelevant that the accountant was living in a palace). Had there been books around, Kennedy and his NATO friends, you feel, would have conformed to precedent and made a bonfire of them . . ."

©The Times, 1976.

HUMAN TORNADO, THE

Director: *Cliff Roquemore.* Screenplay: *Jerry Jones.* Producer: *Rudy Ray Moore.* Photography: *Bob Wilson.* Music: *Arthur Wright.* Production: *Comedian International.* Distributor: *Dimension Pictures.* Running time 98 minutes. Los Angeles opening October 1976 at several theatres. Classification: R.

Players: *J.B. Bart, Glorya de Lani, Herb Graham, Howard Jackson, Java, Jerry Jones, Jimmy Lynch, Rudy Ray Moore, Lady Reed.*

Los Angeles Times, 10/9/76 (Pt. IV, p. 10)
Linda Gross

"*The Human Tornado* . . . is a sequel to last year's *Dolemite.* It's a frenetic, technically terrible, run-of-the-mill blaxploitation movie with lots of sex, sadism, racism, car chasing and karate chops that look like pratfalls.

Like its predecessor, *Human Tornado* stars entertainer Rudy Ray Moore, who runs around in the raw uttering raucous, raunchy rhymes and participating in a series of comedy routines and nightclub acts.

Because *Human Tornado* doesn't take itself seriously, it is vulgar, silly and sometimes hilarious . . .

The screenplay by Jerry Jones has absolutely no continuity and leaps from one incident to another with no explanation or transition. The script also boasts dreary dialogue and some explicit, exploitative and kinky scenes of sadism.

Director Cliff Roquemore handles the sex scenes with imagination.

Rudy Ray Moore, who also produced the movie, is a bawdy, low-brow comedian with appropriate irreverence . . ."

©Los Angeles Times, 1976.

HURRY TOMORROW

Documentary. Director: *Richard Cohen.* Photography: *Kevin Rafferty.* Editors: *Mr. Cohen, Mr. Rafferty.* Sound, Additional Camera Work: *Joshua Morton.* Production Assistant: *Richard Davis.* Additional Camera Work: *Richard Wedler.* Additional Soundwork: *Marie Consiglio, Wolf Seberg.* Production: *Halfway House Films.* Running time 80 minutes. Los Angeles opening December 14, 1975, at the Royal Theatre. Classification: None.

continued on next page

continued from previous page

Los Angeles Times, 12/5/75
Unsigned

"*Hurry Tomorrow* . . . is a shocking, 80-minute documentary about forced drugging of mental patients in state institutions, made by two young film-makers, Richard Cohen and Kevin Rafferty, who spent five weeks filming in one of the locked men's wards at Metropolitan State Hospital in Norwalk.

The film implies that in 1975 the arbitrary misuse of chemotherapy (specifically such drugs as Thorazine and Prolixin) has replaced the abuses of shock treatment and lobotomies that Ken Kesey cursed in *One Flew Over the Cuckoo's Nest* 15 years ago . . .

. . . *Hurry Tomorrow* is a crucifying indictment of ward conditions, drug companies and the violation of present laws. The film is an act of courage and a warning about mind control, told with compassion and rage."

© Los Angeles Times, 1975.

New York Post, 5/6/76 (p. 25)
Archer Winsten

" . . . from the Metropolitan State Hospital in Norwalk, Calif., *Hurry Tomorrow* is a lot of raw footage and poorly recorded conversations that tell you it's bad, but slip a cog somewhere between situation and solution.

Young Richard Cohen, 27, director and editor, was intending to make a documentary about a halfway house when he was invited by a resident psychiatrist to train his cameras on this ward and these patients . . .

The picture loads its case against hospital procedures against . . . drugs, citing horrible side effects listed by the drug concerns as possibilities.

One minute it's saying no one should be forced to take injections without his own consent.

The next, the doctor contends everything would be worse without the drugs. He also says that he doesn't oversedate, the way they do elsewhere.

This picture doesn't give you the information that would complete your knowledge of the pros and cons. It leaves you up in the air . . ."

Reprinted by Permission of New York Post.
© 1976, New York Post Corporation.

Cineaste, Fall 1976 (p. 36)
Phil Brown

" . . . Mental patients' liberation and the related prisoner movements against psychosurgery and behavior modification have brought to light another form of bourgeois repression. *Hurry Tomorrow* goes far in documenting that repression in an aver-

age ward and is thus of service to those working in mental health institutions. *Hurry Tomorrow* may not speak specifically to the fact that state hospitals are a social control mechanism against the working class and the poor, but at least it avoids the anti-worker and anti-woman attitude of *One Flew Over the Cuckoo's Nest* . . . *Hurry Tomorrow* does, however, show the potential for organizing and certainly points out the broader social breakdown evidenced in the psychiatric hospital."

©Cineaste, 1976.

I WILL, I WILL . . . FOR NOW

Director: *Norman Panama.* Screenplay: *Mr. Panama, Albert E. Lewin.* Producer: *George Barrie.* Photography: *John A. Alonzo.* Editor: *Robert Lawrence.* Music: *John Cameron.* Distributor: *Twentieth Century-Fox.* Running time 107 minutes. New York opening February 18, 1976, at several theatres. Classification: R.

Les Bingham: *Elliott Gould.* Katie Bingham: *Diane Keaton.* Lou Springer: *Paul Sorvino.* Jackie Martin: *Victoria Principal.* Dr. Magnus: *Robert Alda.* Steve Martin: *Warren Berlinger.* Sally Bingham: *Candy Clark.* Dr. Williams: *Madge Sinclair.* Maria: *Carmen Zapata.* Dr. Morrison: *George Tyne.* Miss Ito: *Koko Tani.*

See Volume 1 for additional reviews

Film Information, 4/76 (p. 5)
Thomas O. Bentz

"Director Norman Panama (the producer of *A Touch of Class*) has lost touch in this throwaway nonmarriage manual. *The Joy of Sex* appears on the coffee tables of the plasterboard cast. But, although Elliott Gould says, 'I swear on a stack of sex manuals,' not even he lives the creed. When he and Diane Keaton repair to a sex clinic, there is no joy, no touch, only the question: Why are these people laughing?

This film is funny only if incompatibility and suicide are enjoyable. It begins with a broken marriage and unsatisfying affairs, and works down from there. When ex-husband Elliott comes back for her body, Diane demands a contract that will guarantee that he dó half of the housework and take time to talk to her. The fact that the latter demand proves to be unbearable brings the sad discovery that there is nothing to hold these two people or this movie together . . ."

© Film Information, 1976.

The Times (London), 11/26/76 (p. 11)
David Robinson

"*I Will, I Will . . . for Now*, taken at its face value, is a dispiriting commentary upon the sexual fixations and sexual immaturity of the American bourgeoisie. Written and directed by Norman Panama, it is about a divorced couple (Elliott Gould and Diane Keaton) whose mutual sexual attraction still survives and who therefore, rather than remarry, settle for a renewable and conditional contract to cohabit. When they still cannot cope with the relationship, they go to a sex clinic—straight out of a porno movie—where the prescribed treatment is to play infant games of doctor and patient.
Even a touch of satire might have redeemed the film; but it is consistently written and handled at the witless level of flaccid soft-core . . ."

© The Times, 1976.

Monthly Film Bulletin, November 1976 (p. 233)
John Pym

"A relentless flow of innuendo, limp wisecracks and an attempted tone of sexual sophistication (buttressed by a series of ludicrously opulent sets) suggest that *I Will, I Will . . . for Now* was derived from some rejected Doris Day-Rock Hudson script of the Fifties. Norman Panama seems to be attempting a kind of soft-core reworking of contemporary sex manuals (Les at one point puts his back out attempting a new position from *The Joy of Sex*), although *I Will, I Will . . . for Now* attempts nothing more visually risque than shots of a soapy Les and Katie splashing in a tub discreetly hidden up to their necks in water. Some sort of humorous low is reached in the clinic scene where the whooping Les is reduced to chasing the decorously clad Jackie with her padded brassiere wrapped around his forehead . . ."

©Monthly Film Bulletin, 1976.

ILLUSTRIOUS CORPSES (CADAVERI ECCELLENTI)

Director: *Francesco Rosi*. Screenplay (Italian with English subtitles): *Tonino Guerra, Lino Januzzi, Mr. Rosi*. Based on the novel THE CONTEXT by Leonardo Sciascia. Producer: *Alberto Grimaldi*. Photography: *Pasquale De Santis*. Editor: *Ruggero Mastroianni*. Music:

Divorced couple Katie (Diane Keaton) and Les (Elliott Gould) share a drink but little else in **I Will, I Will . . . for Now**.

continued on next page

continued from previous page

Piero Piccioni, Astor Piazzola. Distributor: *Produzioni Europea Associate* (Rome), *Les Artistes Associes* (Paris). Running time 121 minutes. New York opening October 6, 1976, at the New York Film Festival, Lincoln Center. Classification: None. Origin: Italy.

Inspector Rogas: *Lino Ventura.* Procura Varga: *Charles Vanei.* Minister of Security: *Fernando Rey.* Chief Justice: *Max Von Sydow.* Police Chief: *Tino Carraro.* Unemployed Man: *Marcel Bozzuffi.* Dr. Maxia: *Paolo Bonacelli.* Judge Rasto: *Alain Cuny.* Mrs. Cres: *Maria Carta.* Cusan: *Luigi Pistilli.* Prostitute: *Tina Aumont.* Police Commissioner: *Renato Salvatori.* Galano: *Paolo Graziosi.*

New York Post, 10/6/76 (p. 61)
Frank Rich

". . . *Cadaveri Eccellenti* could be unfolding in modern Italy, in pre-coup Chile or even in an America of recent memory: Wherever it is, this place is hell.

And it's a hell that Rosi makes extraordinarily vivid. While *Cadaveri Eccellenti* is a terribly uneven movie, its depiction of a nation going mad with political unrest is powerful stuff. Without even clubbing an audience over the head with melodramatic political spectacle, Rosi paints a portrait of a sleek modern civilization—neither fascist nor communist—that is collapsing under the strain of unfathomable conspiracies and unspeakable injustices . . .

. . . Rosi tends to view his characters much as he views his story; he doesn't feel compelled to color them in. Except for the hugely talented Ventura, who's on screen so much he can give shading to the thin characterization of the detective, the other members of the fine cast . . . are used exclusively as pawns against the film's richly detailed landscape . . ."

Reprinted by Permission of New York Post.
© 1976, New York Post Corporation.

IN CELEBRATION

Director: *Lindsay Anderson.* Screenplay: *David Storey, based on his stage play.* Producer: *Ely Landau.* Executive Producer: *Otto Plasckes.* Photography: *Dick Bush.* Editor: *Russell Lloyd.* Production: *American Film Theatre.* Distributors: *Ely Landau Organization and Cinevision,*

Ltd. Running time 131 minutes. New York opening March 17, 1975, at selected theatres. Classification: PG.

Andrew Shaw: *Alan Bates.* Colin Shaw: *James Bolam.* Steven Shaw: *Brian Cox.* Mrs. Shaw: *Constance Chapman.* Mrs. Burnett: *Gabrielle Daye.* Mr. Shaw: *Bill Owen.*

See Volume 1 for additional reviews

The Times (London), 6/11/76 (p. 9)
David Robinson

"The collaboration of David Storey as writer and Lindsay Anderson as director has been the British theatre's most fruitful creative partnership in recent years; and the enterprise of the British Film Theatre (originally the American Film Theatre) in filming notable stage productions would be vindicated if only for providing a record of their first stage collaboration, *In Celebration* . . .

In Celebration appears more centrally autobiographical than David Storey's other plays . . . dealing as it does with a Yorkshire mining family, like Storey's own, and with the psychic problems of the children whom education and aspiration remove from the socio-economic situation of their parents. It is also more obviously literary, depending on a dense, poetically compressed text . . .

British directors tend to certain shibboleths about adapting stage material to the screen, which mostly result in the 'opening out' and consequent dissipation of the original. Predictably, as the most cinematic-minded of theatre directors, Anderson, far from falling into any such trap, uses all the means the cinema offers for heightening the claustrophobic concentration of the play . . ."

© The Times, 1976.

The Sunday Times (London), 6/13/76 (p. 37)
Dilys Powell

" . . . David Storey, writing his own script, has left his play very little altered: no widening of the view, no looking out, except to warn of an arrival or watch a departure, beyond the walls of the old miner's cramped house. One character has been omitted; thus any changes have been to restrict rather than enlarge . . . it is a text in which one is aware of careful design. Everything happens in twenty-four hours in that confined space, everything is argued and shockingly disclosed.

Mr. Anderson is directing the cast he directed in the theatre; they play splendidly together. Nevertheless one observes the isolation of the individual . . . Looking back I recall the cast grouped in scenes of gaiety or discord. But I think still more of single players framed by the screen . . . And thinking of that framing of a face, a figure which is a conspicuous success of Mr. Anderson's film, I feel that for once the effect of cinema on theatre has been constructive."

© The Sunday Times, 1976.

IN SEARCH OF DRACULA

Documentary. Director, Producer, Music: *Calvin Floyd*. Screenplay: *Yvonne Floyd*. From a book by Raymond McNally and Radu Florescu. Photography: *Tony Forsberg, Anders Bodin, Gunnar Larsson, Anna Tyron*. Production: *Aspekt Films*. Distributor: *Independent-International Pictures, Far West Films*. Running time 83 minutes. Los Angeles opening September 1976 at several theatres. Classification: PG. Origin: Sweden.

Los Angeles Times, 9/24/76 (p. 16)
Linda Gross

"*In Search of Dracula* . . . is a Swedish-made documentary that tells you all you have ever wanted to know about that nocturnal, blood-sucking, coffin-sleeping undead count from Transylvania . . .

The documentary is weakened by limp dramatizations and a very bogus case history of a strange young man from South Carolina who gets depressed when the moon is full and is shown drinking his own blood.

The script by Yvonne Floyd lacks dramatic structure and abuses the book's more grisly anecdotes.

Director Calvin Floyd rambles and uses rickety technique.

In Search of Dracula is a definitive primer on how to recognize and destroy vampires. It is also a curious exploration of the religious, erotic, psychological and atavistic human longings that perpetuate the shadowy belief in prenatural beings, which are somehow linked to the fear of death and the desire for eternal life."

©Los Angeles Times, 1976.

IN SEARCH OF NOAH'S ARK

Director: *James L. Conway*. Screenplay: *Charles Sellier, Jr.;   Mr. Conway*. Based on a book by David Balsiger and Mr. Sellier. Producer: *Mr. Sellier*. Photography: *George Stapleford*. Editor: *Sharron Miller*. Narrated by Brad Crandall. Distributor: *Sunn Classic Pictures*. New York opening December 24, 1976, at several theatres. Classification: G.

Los Angeles Times, 1/14/77 (Pt. IV, p. 12)
Linda Gross

". . . The film includes photos, film clips, testimonies and eyewitness reports. But the most compelling bits of evidence that the huge wooden vessel is lurking within the glacial mountain have been pieces of wood planks retrieved from the treeless mountain . . .

The screenplay by James L. Conway and Charles E. Sellier, Jr., has been stacked to substantiate their suppositions. At times, they disregard the views of other archaeologists and theologians who aren't entirely convinced that the ark is at home on Ararat.

In Search of Noah's Ark is narrated by Brad Crandall with conviction. Director Conway has assembled a vast amount of research into a cohesive and entertaining movie . . ."

©Los Angeles Times, 1977.

Film Information, January 1977 (p. 4)
Paul Coleman

". . . Quickie production values account for a slipshod retelling of the original flood narrative. And the producer's insistence upon publicizing this tale as the 'first and greatest of all disasters' may add a touch of irony. The film's assertion that the story of Noah is the 'greatest Bible story of them all' is questionable, but then serious treatments of biblical materials are hardly common in commercial films.

The film's trivial elements aside, it does present wide-ranging evidence to suggest a) that such a flood could have occurred, b) that existence upon an ark such as the Bible describes could be possible and even reasonably comfortable, c) that the actual vehicle may be preserved in the glacial ice of Ararat . . ."

©Film Information, 1977.

IN THE REALM OF THE SENSES (L'EMPIRE DES SENS)

Director: *Nagisa Oshima*. Screenplay (Japanese with English subtitles): *Mr. Oshima*. Producer: *Anatole Dauman*. Photography:

continued on next page

continued from previous page

Kenichi Okamoto, Hideo Ito. Editor: *Keiichi Uraoka*. Music: *Minoru Miki*. Production: *Arges Films/Oshima Productions*. Running time 115 minutes. Previewed at the New York Film Festival, Lincoln Center, September 1976, before seizure by United States Customs officials. Classification: None. Origin: Japan.

Sada: *Eiko Matsuda*. Kichizo: *Tatsuya Fuji*. Tramp: *Taiji Tonoyama*.

Los Angeles Times, 5/21/76 (Pt. IV, p. 1)
Charles Champlin

". . . It is the story of a love affair between a geisha and her boss, ending as she kills him—with his blessing. It was drawn from a famous case that took place in Tokyo in 1936, and it is a continuously and spectacularly erotic work—hard-core by the technical definitions of the form, yet far from prurient and not likely to appeal to the regular customers of hard-core stuff.

L'Empire des Sens is about sexuality in the way that the best of Peckinpah's violent works are about violence. His couple—attractively and intelligently played by Eiko Matsuda and Tatsuya Fuji—are in a sense willingly enslaved by their responses . . .

The film will be a sensation in the United States, whatever the auspices under which it is shown. It will be rated X (if not Y and Z as well) but it is unmistakably a pioneering work of the movie arts, the first by a major international talent to deal with eroticism in personal and nonexploitational terms and to comprehend the extent of the pleasures and the deadly extent of the dangers when the pleasures grow to be an unslakable obsession . . ."

©Los Angeles Times, 1976.

The Times (London), 5/20/76 (p. 13)
David Robinson

". . . Since the action of the film is almost uninterrupted copulation for most of its 115 minutes, climaxing with an orgasmic death by strangulation and the ultimate amputation of the man's sexual member, it is unlikely to be seen by a very large international public. This much said, it must be stated that it is a work quite without prurience, as direct and pure in its expression as an erotic drawing by Utamaro or Hokusai (who are inevitably recalled by the insistent use of close-ups of the lovers' ecstatic faces).

Complex, rigorous, obsessive, the film traces the course of an all-consuming love, which demands its fulfillment at all times and in all places . . . Astounding in its virtuosity . . . unique in the cinema as the expression of a total erotic passion."

©The Times, 1976.

New York Post, 10/2/76 (p. 38)
Frank Rich

"*In the Realm of the Senses*, Nagisa Oshima's explicit account of an obsessional sado-masochistic love affair . . .

. . . doesn't begin to merit all the fuss that has surrounded it. This movie is merely a stultifying failure by a somewhat less than first-rate Japanese director, and it isn't worthy of extended discussion by serious people . . .

The movie's story is based on an actual 1936 incident, and it has to do with a gangster . . . and a geisha girl . . . whose passion for each other is so great that it literally consumes them.

During most of the film, we watch the couple conduct marathon copulation bouts that leave them little time for routine human activities (such as sleeping)—and, as the film and their affair progress, the protagonists' love-making becomes insistently more baroque. For these lovers, sexual love is everything: Their bizarre connubial pyrotechnics are a natural and inevitable expression of their intense feelings for each other—even when their sexual pleasure takes the form of pain, and, finally, death . . .

. . . Within a year, I'm sure, Oshima's movie (in a dubbed version) will take its place alongside the other recent s-m exploitation films (from *Snuff* to *The Story of Joanna* to *Drum*) on Broadway.

After that, this movie—like such past hot properties as *I Am Curious (Yellow)*, *Dear John*, and Hedy Lamarr's *Ecstasy*—will be but an item for a trivia quiz."

Reprinted by Permission of New York Post.
©1976, New York Post Corporation.

Film Information, November 1976 (p. 3)
Dave Pomeroy

"Based on an actual 1936 case in Japan in which a former prostitute strangled her lover and then castrated him, *In the Realm of the Senses* purports to utilize explicit sex as a means of conveying a significant story. The trouble is that the film itself is so obsessed with the sexual activity of its protagonists that we learn nothing of them outside this realm . . . and thus the shocking denouement is bereft of its context.

Sada (Eiko Matsuda) is the prostitute-cum-geisha who becomes the mistress of Kichizo (Tatsuya Fuji). We learn nothing of him . . . Images of death pervade the film. Also a kind of voyeurism is omnipresent, as servants and others observe their love-making with attitudes ranging from disgust to emulation, but basically with a sense of detachment.

In the end, *Realm* as a case study of possessive/obsessive love cannot overcome the benumbing effect on an audience of constant sexual exposure, and thus the film's somewhat interesting pretensions are defeated by dulled, rather than heightened senses."

©Film Information, 1976.

Take One, March 1977 (p. 10)
Bruce Berman

". . . Throughout the film (at least on the surface) Sada, it should not be forgotten, remains a geisha, a prostitute, a whore. Under such apparently unconclusive circumstances it is difficult to imagine that she can 'truly' love any man, let alone her mistress's master. However, *In the Realm of the Senses* there are enough moments where Sada's very enslavement seems to be alternately and even concurrently reinforced and transcended. (Specifically when and why is the film's unsettling essence.) . . .

In the Realm of the Senses' answers are not to be read like the information conveyed by some reassuring subtitle. It is a difficult film which takes one in with a subtle force seldom accomplished in even the most intelligent Western films. It takes one to the very bowels of the paradoxically fantastic and frightening 'realm' which, I sense, all intense involvements must to some extent traverse. Needless to say, this is a film rich in probing associations: and one as boldly unpornographic as its shocking confiscation in the name of 'public decency' is despicable . . ."

©Take One, 1977.

Cineaste, Winter 1977 (p. 33)
Ruth McCormick

". . . In this film, we witness a relationship between two people, who neither put on an exhibitionistic show for us, nor make us feel embarrassed that we may be spying on them. This, to my mind, is a major breakthrough in the depiction of eroticism on film. There is no fetishism of parts of the body; the sex scenes between the two, photographed from every conceivable angle, are never voyeuristic, and neither partner is objectified by the camera. In each scene, Oshima creates a total gestalt; the shots, mostly long and static, are composed so as to place the two protagonists at the center of simple, stunning settings, realistic without ever ceding to the puerile naturalism of most porno films . . ."

©Cineaste, 1977.

Film Quarterly, Winter 1976/1977 (p. 58)
Michael Silverman

". . . Oshima's project would seem to involve the narrowing of sensational and empathic response for the purpose of furthering ideological enquiry, or, at least, posing social questions . . . Ostensibly, it can be seen as a fuck film; indeed, it is so explicit that it may never be shown in 'respectable' art houses or at festivals subject to discreet censorship. Its spectacle inheres in the unremitting display of sexuality, so that an occasional exterior shot seems a lapse in concentration. As the film progresses, the director eliminates establishing shots as the lovers eliminate foreplay; simply, the penis is in the vagina, and the investigation continues . . . Oshima's persistent narrowing denies any romantic or metaphysical gesture the opportunity of replacing the physical fact . . ."

©Film Quarterly, 1977.

INCREDIBLE SARAH, THE

Director: *Richard Fleischer*. Screenplay: *Ruth Wolff*. Producer: *Helen M. Strauss*. Photography: *Christopher Challis*. Editor: *John Jympson*. Music: *Elmer Bernstein*. Distributor: *Reader's Digest Films Limited*. Running time 106 minutes. New York opening November 5, 1976, at the Festival Theatre. Classification: PG.

Sarah Bernhardt: *Glenda Jackson*. Sardou: *Daniel Massey*. Montigny: *Douglas Wilmer*. Duc De Morny: *David Langton*. Hendi De Ligne: *Simon Williams*. Damala: *John Castle*.

Newsweek, 11/8/76 (p. 107)
Janet Maslin

"*The Incredible Sarah* was produced by the film division of Reader's Digest, and it treats the great Bernhardt as if she were one of those lovable loons who populate the Digest's most-unforgettable-character section. Playing the legendary actress up to the age of 35 (although Bernhardt's career spanned more than half a century), Glenda Jackson goes through 40 costume changes and almost as many temper tantrums, surrounded by a menagerie that grows to include a puma, a monkey, several leading men and an illegitimate child . . . she engages in each of the actress's favorite stunts

continued on next page

continued from previous page

exactly once, thus making the film a prime exemplar of the slide-show approach to biography.

Director Richard Fleischer and screenwriter Ruth Wolff are at some pains to sugar-coat their subject . . .

. . . Glenda Jackson performs with her usual authority, but Fleischer's camera shoots her at such close range that the Divine Sarah's legendary charisma is absolutely unfathomable."

©Newsweek, Inc. 1976
reprinted by permission.

Monthly Film Bulletin, November 1976 (p. 232)
Richard Combs

"An incredible hodge-podge, which never achieves an intellectual grip on its subject or her significance, but does maintain a rigid directorial distance—thus missing out as well on all the usual excitements of the biopic . . . the one fleetingly formal notion holding this ramshackle structure together is that Sarah's theatre was somehow the fulfillment not only of her own morbid fantasies—from such early self-dramatisation as composing herself in a coffin to later creating her own theatre when no one else would employ her—but also her audience's (emphasised mainly by cutting between shots of agog spectators and dull snippets of classical plays in which the dry, clipped, thoroughly modern Miss Jackson struggles to be flamboyantly Bernhardt) . . . on all levels, the film's sensitivity to varieties of artifice and their significance is fairly disastrous, ranging downwards from Sarah's triumphant appearance at the end in *Joan of Arc*, when Fleischer pulls the film audience into the euphoria of the scene by making the on-stage burning impossibly realistic . . ."

©Monthly Film Bulletin, 1976.

Films in Review, December 1976 (p. 635)
Rob Edelman

"If it weren't for Glenda Jackson, *The Incredible Sarah* would be an incredible fiasco . . . Ruth Wolff's lifeless screenplay never explores what in fact made the actress tick.

Richard Fleischer's direction is plodding, with little attempt at dramatic subtlety or creative camera movement. Glenda Jackson is so talented she could put life in a tree stump, yet the camera continually cuts away from her at the wrong moment Jackson does as well as she can under the circumstances. Ultimately *The Incredible Sarah* is too much a caricature of an eccentric actress rather than a portrait of an extraordinary human being."

©Films in Review, 1976.

Christian Science Monitor, 11/29/76 (p. 23)
David Sterritt

"*The Incredible Sarah* is so old-fashioned it creaks. Yet it's not bad fun if you can still work up an appetite for a flamboyant 'biopic' that spins legend upon myth until facts don't seem to matter any more . . .

Miss Jackson brings off most of this convincingly, with assists from some capable supporting players—among others you'll spot David Langton and Simon Williams from TV's 'Upstairs, Downstairs.' Ruth Wolff's script oozes preposterous romanticisms, but at least it takes itself seriously, so we might as well get in the spirit . . .

The director of *The Incredible Sarah* was the prolific Richard Fleischer, under whose guidance the movie comes off something like a corny stage piece, complete with broad portrayals and hammy lines . . ."

Reprinted by permission from The Christian
Science Monitor © 1976.
The Christian Science Publishing Society.
All rights reserved.

Los Angeles Times, 11/5/76 (Pt. IV, p. 1)
Charles Champlin

". . . Jackson gives *The Incredible Sarah*, which was written by Ruth Wolff and directed by Richard Fleischer, a large and untidy vitality. It is all the more welcome because the movie is otherwise unbelievably unmussed—well-lit, clean, rich, tidy and disappointingly bloodless, as if she were the sole life-force in a tableau of mannequins.

There are some crackling good moments—Jackson as Bernhardt as Camille, dying with scary conviction, Sarah enraged and laying waste to a whole roomful of bric-a-brac, Sarah as Joan of Arc facing the stake but also facing down a hostile mob of an audience that has been pelting her with vegetables.

They are all Glenda Jackson's and they reveal all that there may have been to reveal about Bernhardt, which is on this evidence that there was passion and there were appetites but perhaps less mind and depth . . ."

©Los Angeles Times, 1976.

Film Information, September 1976 (p. 3)
Peter P. Shillaci

". . . Glenda Jackson does an often convincing job of portraying Sarah. From her outrageous attempt to liven up the stodgy staging of Moliere at the Comedie Francaise, to her classical case of stage fright at the Odeon, Sarah is shown to possess an absolute genius, not so much for acting as for drawing attention to herself.

When Glenda does get to act Sarah, we are treated to vignettes of her famous roles, among them Camille, Phaedre and Joan of Arc. One cannot tell whether these episodes work because of

the power of the roles (Bernhardt loved them because the characters died so gloriously—a posture
she cultivated by keeping a coffin in her bedroom)
or because of Miss Jackson's acting . . . Director
Richard Fleischer seems to have trouble controlling
his star's dramatic exuberance. Her acting style is
at times that of the stage, convincingly broad for
the period, but at other times in close-up she re-
verts to a cinematic style with a 'Method' flavor
that carries too much interiorization for Bernhardt.
As a result, we find her tantrums more interesting
than her performances."

©Film Information, 1976.

New York Magazine, 11/22/76 (p. 92)
John Simon

"*The Incredible Sarah* is as bad as only *Reader's
Digest*, which produced it, can make a film. The
climax has Sarah Bernhardt as Saint Joan, by way
of an onerous comeback, apparently immolating
herself on what looks like a very authentically flaming stake built stage center in what looks like
a very inauthentic Theatre Sarah Bernhardt. The
direction, by Richard Fleischer, is appalling; there
is, for instance, no sense of place, or of genuine
progression from one real locale to another. The
acting, even from competent British performers,
is no better than the film deserves.
As Sarah, Glenda Jackson acts either bored
with everything or in the grip of a terrible, all-
embracing, downright metaphysical rage. Miss
Jackson is well on her way to fabricating an acting
style out of cosmic fury, heavily laced with snarling
mockery, and the film duly allows her not one but
two scenes in which she smashes everything
around her . . ."

©1976 by the NYM Corp. Reprinted with
the permission of NEW YORK Magazine.

Saturday Review, 11/27/76 (p. 41)
Judith Crist

". . . it is Glenda Jackson's portrait of Bernhardt
that makes *The Incredible Sarah* indeed the tale of
a woman worthy of the legends surrounding her
career. The screenplay, by Ruth Wolff, is admittedly
'a free portrayal of events in her early tempestuous
career,' but the resultant film, richly produced by
Helen M. Strauss and tightly directed by Richard
Fleischer, is given total credibility. It takes the risks
run by film biography and conquers all . . .
It takes the remarkable Jackson, in bits and
pieces of classical drama, to convince one of the
power of the performer and make the legendary
quality emerge therefrom. While the woman of
whim and temperament and personal appetite is
there, she is rounded out with the convictions of
a woman liberated before her time and given quick-

silver beauty that is so much Jackson's own and
so becoming to Sarah. She gets good support
from an outstanding British cast . . ."

©Judith Crist, 1976.

The Sunday Times (London), 11/14/76 (p. 39)
Alan Brien

". . . Richard Fleischer's version has Glenda
Jackson, a superb actress in her own range, but
contemporary in style, flat of figure and flat of
accent, snub of nose and snub of manner. The
extracts from Racine and other classical plays give
us no hint of how Bernhardt lit up the stage. Indeed,
the only time she is flamboyant is when she goes
up in improbably real flames as Joan of Arc. The
film is overblown and under-researched, full of
silliness, such as the Bernhardt troupe arriving by
train in London at a station called in large letters
just 'LONDON,' or when we are shown her Capu-
chin monkey, a present from a royal lover, grown
up, in defiance of all zoology, into a chimpan-
zee . . ."

©The Sunday Times, 1976.

The Times (London), 11/12/76 (p. 9)
David Robinson

"Presented by Reader's Digest, Richard Fleischer's screen biography of the early years of
Sarah Bernhardt (or Sairer Burnhart as everyone
in the film calls her) respects the old biopic tradition of making even historical incident seem quite
unlikely—which is possibly why they called it
appropriately *The Incredible Sarah* . . .
. . . Unkindly it must be said that the ultimate
improbability is Glenda Jackson as the actress
who electrified the nineteenth-century theatre.
Every effort is made to sustain the illusion by surrounding her on stage with dummies, and by having
her speak each word individually, with a separate
and distinct glare of defiance for each. But it is
still old Glenda, doing her nut."

©The Times, 1976.

Village Voice, 11/29/76 (p. 53)
Andrew Sarris

"*The Incredible Sarah* is an incredibly old-fashioned movie full of the most unforgettable moments
you have ever tried to forget. Richard Fleischer
directs every scene as if it were a coming attraction
for a forthcoming extravaganza on the gaudy, glorious life and career of Sarah Bernhardt. It seems
to be dedicated to the proposition that Glenda
Jackson can do anything on the screen. The irony

continued on next page

continued from previous page

is that Bernhardt in any version is just about the last project the cool, controlled, intelligent Miss Jackson should undertake . . .

Not that I can think of any actress to play Bernhardt under the best of conditions—a young Garbo, perhaps, or a young Arletty, or a young Irene Worth, for the tingling timbre of her voice.''

Reprinted by permission of The Village Voice.
Copyright ©The Village Voice, Inc., 1976.

INFINITE TENDERNESS, AN

Director: *Pierre Jallaud*. Screenplay: *Mr. Jallaud*. Producer: *Claude Lelouch*. Distributor: *United Artists*. Running time 93 minutes. New York opening January 14, 1976, at the Film Forum. Classification: None. Origin: France, 1972.

Players: *José Guerra, Jean Christophe, Jeanne Lenox, Noelle France, and the children and staff of "an unnamed French hospital."*

See Volume 1 for additional reviews

Los Angeles Times, 6/18/76 (Pt. IV, p. 18)
Linda Gross

" . . . *An Infinite Tenderness* . . . is a particularly special achievement because it deals with the friendship between two brain-damaged children who are unable to walk, talk or feed themselves.

The documentary, written and directed by Pierre Jallaud, took a year to film within an unnamed French hospital where the boys live. The result is an exhilarating and heartbreaking affirmation that even the most limited lives can be alleviated by love and friendship.

The movie has been conceived, silently, from one of the boys' points of view. The children appear to be about 10, but their age and the specific nature of their illness is not disclosed . . .

Produced by Claude Lelouch, *An Infinite Tenderness* is finely made and fragilely photographed in an impressionistic style which is simultaneously lyrical and clinical . . . "

© Los Angeles Times, 1976.

INSERTS

Director: *John Byrum*. Screenplay: *Mr. Byrum*. Producers: *Davina Belling, Clive Parsons*. Photography: *Denys Coop*. Editor: *Mike Bradsell*. Distributor: *United Artists*. Running time 99 minutes. New York opening February 27, 1976, at several theatres. Classification: X. Origin: Great Britain, 1975.

Boy Wonder: *Richard Dreyfuss*. Cathy Cake: *Jessica Harper*. Big Mac: *Bob Hoskins*. Harlene: *Veronica Cartwright*. Rex: *Stephen Davies*.

See Volume 1 for additional reviews

New Leader, 4/12/76 (p. 26)
Robert Asahina

" . . . The ludicrous plot and the painfully obvious symbolism—the phallic image of the title, the joint metaphors of the condemned mansion and the Hollywood Freeway, the link between sexual and artistic potency—make it tempting to interpret *Inserts* as a comedy. Yet to assume that a bad movie about the making of a bad movie is somehow good by virtue of its badness is to be guilty of a kind of mimetic fallacy. Moreover, the acting ranks with the worst I have ever seen, and bad actors portraying bad actors simply magnify whatever is wrong to begin with.

In the case of *Inserts*, everything is wrong. The script is utterly devoid of dramatic tension: Most of the plot developments are telegraphed . . . The staging is nonexistent . . . A New York University Film School graduate, Byrum nevertheless appears to have learned little about moviemaking . . . ''

Reprinted with permission from
The New Leader, 1976.
© The American Labor Conference
on International Affairs, Inc.

Film Information, 4/76 (p. 6)
Unsigned

"This film is about five characters in Hollywood, circa 1930. It is a small budget production (one set, etc.) and looks it. Richard Dreyfuss portrays a once famous director reduced to cranking out stag movies. So good in *The Apprenticeship of Duddy Kravitz* and *Jaws*, Dreyfuss' performance here is an embarrassment because it is so bad. Veronica Cartwright's depiction of the degradation of an ex-star turned porno actress is an embarrassment because it is so good. When she dies from an overdose of heroin, her body is dragged off by the male stag actor (Stephen Davies) with whom she had just performed, assisted by the crass producer (Bob Hoskins), whose only thought is to finish the picture. Jessica Harper plays a shrewd society girl intent on getting into the movies, even if it means taking up where the dead girl left off. Twenty-eight-year-old John Byrum wrote and directed . . ."

© Film Information, 1976.

The Times (London), 3/11/77 (p. 9)
David Robinson

". . . John Byrum, who wrote and directed the film (apparently on a tiny budget, and in Britain), has been responsible for two of the more awful screenplays of recent years, *Mahogany* and *Harry and Walter Go to New York*; and here too he's encumbered himself with a lot too many words. They don't altogether obscure a clean underlying dramatic line, a good deal of wit, and the ingenuity with which the gestures and language of pornography are used as the means of psychological revelation. The five-person ensemble—as well as Dreyfuss, Veronica Cartwright and Stephen Davies as the 'meat' and Bob Hoskins and Jessica Harper as the moneybags and his mistress—play impeccably in their single set, a gone-off art deco studio."

©The Times, 1977.

The Sunday Times (London), 3/6/77 (p. 37)
Alan Brien

"John Byrum, author-director of *Inserts*, sets his Hollywood anecdote 20 years on, at the beginning of the Thirties. This is a very curious work—wordy, stagy, meticulously contrived with a cast who vanish from the action whenever they exit the mock baronial ballroom of a Beverly Hills mansion of the period, now used as a studio for home-made skin-flicks. But the resemblance to filmed theatre vanishes as the lens pursues the five characters like an entomologist's killing bottle. Somehow we have been trapped along with them in a timeslip or space warp where Noel Coward is trying to talk his way out of an Andy Warhol situation . . .

An odd, unusual, Janus-faced film, indelibly acted in several different styles, stirring ambiguous feelings in its audiences . . ."

©The Sunday Times, 1977.

ISLANDS IN THE STREAM

Director: *Franklin J. Schaffner.* Screenplay: *Denne Bart Petitclerc.* Based on the novel by Ernest Hemingway. Producers: *Peter Bart,*

Max Palevsky. Photography: *Fred Koenekamp.* Editor: *Robert Swink.* Music: *Jerry Goldsmith.* Distributor: *Paramount Pictures.* Running time 110 minutes. New York opening March 9, 1977, at the Coronet Theatre. Classification: PG.

Thomas Hudson: *George C. Scott.* Eddy: *David Hemmings.* Captain Ralph: *Gilbert Roland.* Lil: *Susan Tyrrell.* Willy: *Richard Evans.* Audrey: *Claire Bloom.* Joseph: *Julius Harris.* Tom: *Hart Bochner.* Andrew: *Brad Savage.* David: *Michael-James Wixted.* Helga Ziegner: *Hildy Brooks.* Andrea: *Jessica Rains.* Herr Ziegner: *Walter Friedel.* Constable: *Charles Lampkin.*

Saturday Review, 3/19/77 (p. 40)
Judith Crist

". . . George C. Scott, crew-cut and bearded to bear striking resemblance to Hemingway, gives one of the finest of his fine performances as the superficially macho man unconscious of the depths of his relationships, but ready to deal honestly with them as they surface. There is a constant awareness of others, a sensitivity that cannot be denied; he offers a decency that makes a mockery of heroics, retaining that appreciation of the elementals that was Hemingway's hallmark. His crew of buddies are familiar Hemingway characters . . . Under Franklin J. Schaffner's leisurely but disciplined direction, however, each achieves a distinctive personality; each becomes meaningful in Hudson's emergence into a community of feeling . . . And if the final moments of recognition are overdrawn, with sentiment stretching into sentimentality, it is somehow forgivable, a minor indulgence after the major sharing of honest emotions."

©Judith Crist, 1977.

Women's Wear Daily, 3/7/77 (p. 16)
Howard Kissel

". . . Franklin Schaffner has generally struck me as a very square director. It may be the very squareness, the simplicity of this approach that makes *Islands* such a strong emotional experience. Schaffner doesn't play games. He just puts George C. Scott in front of the camera and lets him give one of the deepest, most honest performances of his career, playing not just the character in the book, but a man very easy to identify with Hemingway himself. Scott's last few screen roles have been overblown heroes, and the solidity of his act-

continued on next page

continued from previous page

ing has given the parts greater credibility than they deserved—here the work is much harder because the emotions are too direct to convey with anything but genuine emotions, and Scott does it. He is surrounded by sensitive performances . . ."

©Women's Wear Daily, 1977.

New York Magazine, 3/14/77 (p. 70)
John Simon

". . . Franklin J. Schaffner, the director, rates somewhere between 'deserving' and 'plodding' on my scale. Sometimes he inclines more toward the one, sometimes more toward the other. Here he is distinctly plodding, albeit in the best Book-of-the-Month Club or Literary Guild style. Be it said, though, that in his defense, that he gets little support from the script . . .

George C. Scott is an actor always interesting to watch, and though his characterization of Thomas Hudson is unlikely to add an iota to his artistic stature, it is solid craftsmanship with enough gusto to keep the movie at least half alive. In the supporting cast, only David Hemmings has anything like a real part, and he makes Eddy as nearly believable as the writing allows, thus turning in his best performance in years. Claire Bloom, even when she has nothing to do, does it with class; and the three boys are at least inoffensive . . ."

©1977 by the NYM Corp. Reprinted with the permission of NEW YORK Magazine.

Film Information, March 1977 (p. 1)
William F. Fore

". . . one of the better films-from-literature made in a long time . . .

. . . it is George C. Scott as Thomas Hudson who brings the Hemingway feel to the screen: the elements of macho, virility, compassion and self-doubt are all there. A talented and proud man who has elected to be a loner, he discovers that he cannot escape his past, present or future. He realizes he still loves his first wife but cannot return to her. He learns that it is almost unbearable to live without his three attractive sons after they have vacationed with him one summer. He finds that he is inextricably drawn into the war as refugees pour in from Europe and German submarines torpedo ships within sight of the Bahamian coast.

It is an old Hemingway theme: you have to get off your island and into the stream. Scott and company have given it life and reality . . ."

©Film Information, 1977.

Newsweek, 3/14/77 (p. 95)
Jack Kroll

". . . the fight with the marlin is as flat as a flounder, in part due to a shockingly bad intermix of real and process shots. The Hawaiian location is skimpy and vague, a postcard cliche totally lacking Hemingway's crucial poetry of place. Hudson's pivotal confrontation with his ex-wife after their son is killed in World War II is high grade soap opera, despite the haunting beauty of Claire Bloom. Worst of all, Denne Bart Petitclerc's screenplay tries to solve the problem of the disjointed novel by moving into a shameless rehash of *To Have and Have Not* . . .

'I know now that there is no one thing that is true,' says the wounded Hudson. 'It is all true.' Hemingway's whole life was an attempt—often noble—to breathe life into that tautology. Once again a movie has turned it into malarkey. Poor Papa."

©Newsweek, Inc. 1977
reprinted by permission.

Village Voice, 3/28/77 (p. 41)
Andrew Sarris

". . . One either loves the film or loathes it, and I must say that I am much closer to the lovers than to the loathers. Honest sentiment has always been very precious to me, and never more so than now, when all is alienation and anomie. People complain that there are no feelings in contemporary movies, and then when a relatively grown-up tearjerker like *Islands in the Stream* comes along they hang back for fear of being caught up in something that lacks chic and funk. Not that the film is without faults. Quite the contrary. In their loving celebration of the Hemingway hero, director Franklin Schaffner, scenarist Denne Bart Petitclerc, and actor George C. Scott are swimming gallantly but hopelessly against the tide of cultural history . . .

. . . the movie, like the book, is as much if not more about places than about people, and Franklin Schaffner is nothing if not loyal to the spirit of the last locales of Hemingway's Homeric wanderings . . .

I must add that *Islands in the Stream* is a beautiful, elegant movie, and a thoughtfully ennobling entertainment. If it should fail I would have to suppose that both Hemingway and Scott are commonly perceived to be passe, and that the Hemingway hero has outlasted his welcome . . ."

Reprinted by permission of The Village Voice.
Copyright © The Village Voice, Inc., 1977.

New York Post, 3/10/77 (p. 24)
Frank Rich

"There is nothing particularly brilliant or terrible about *Islands in the Stream*, the new film that's been adapted from Ernest Hemingway's final, posthumously published novel. The movie's director, Franklin J. Schaffner, and its screenwriter, Denne Bart Petitclerc, aspire only to be pedantically faithful to their source material—and they've achieved this goal by producing what is essentially an illustrated version of the book. Like the book, the movie is anecdotal, rambling and sentimental, but it lacks the commitment of Hemingway's prose. Instead of the commitment, we get oodles of bland good taste—as if good taste alone were synonymous with good art . . .

. . . to me the only truly inspiring aspect of the movie is the casting of George C. Scott in the central role. Scott plays Thomas Hudson, an expatriate, middle-aged sculptor who is an unabashed Hemingway stand-in—and what actor do we associate more with Hemingway than Scott . . ."

Reprinted by Permission of New York Post.
© 1977, New York Post Corporation.

Los Angeles Times, 3/18/77 (Pt. IV, p. 1)
Charles Champlin

"*Islands in the Stream* . . . is pure Hemingway. As such it is a source of great interest and also of a kind of double melancholy.

Its essential material is in itself immensely affecting—a father's relationship with his sons, seen with tenderness and pride and touched with the pain of loss. The mood of the film is melancholy, an elegy for the life and career of the artist Tom Hudson who is Hemingway's central figure.

But Hudson also seems, more openly than any other Hemingway character, an alter ego for the author himself at the moment of writing . . .

The melancholy beyond the material is that the Ernest Hemingway of *Islands in the Stream* seems so much a part of his time—another, earlier and now closed time—in the same sense that Dickens and Hugo and Dreiser and Galsworthy can be seen with a particular finality as having belonged to their times . . .

Scott's performance stands with his best, which is very, very good, and his mixture of arrogance and tenderness, sadness without self-pity, is impressive to watch . . ."

©Los Angeles Times, 1977.

Christian Science Monitor, 3/25/77 (p. 21)
David Sterritt

"*Islands in the Stream*, based on Ernest Hemingway's last published novel, takes on the theme of sadness in its most basic and intimate forms. It is preoccupied with partings, endings and deaths; its incidents flow from the end of a vacation to the end of a life. It is an affecting film, yet it lacks the intellectual or emotional strength that might have deepened it into a thorough examination or dignified it as a study. It is an exercise, as brisk and somber as an evening walk visited with unhappy memories . . .

Director Schaffner . . . builds a mood so intense and introspective as to become claustrophobic. He seems too interested in the externals of the Hemingway persona to want to strip away the trappings, truly revealing the personality underneath. Thus, the introspection falls short of its final destination. What we do find out about this weather-beaten hero is touching and sometimes instructive. His deeper

secrets stay hidden from us, though, as they do from Schaffner and Scott, and perhaps as they did from Hemingway himself."

Reprinted by permission from The Christian Science Monitor © 1977. The Christian Science Publishing Society. All rights reserved.

J.D.'S REVENGE

Director, Producer: *Arthur Marks*. Screenplay: *Jaison Starkes*. Photography: *Harry May*. Editor: *George Folsey, Jr*. Music: *Robert Prince*. Distributor: *American International Pictures*. Running time 96 minutes. Los Angeles opening June 1976 at several theatres. Classification: R.

Players: *Glynn Turman, Joan Pringle, Lou Gossett, Carl Crudup, James Louis Watkins, Alice Jubert, Stephanie Faulkner, Fred Pinkard, Fuddie Bagley, Jo Anne Meredith, David McKnight*.

Los Angeles Times, 7/1/76 (Pt. IV, p. 18)
Kevin Thomas

". . . Promising young writer Jaison Starkes, in what is his first produced script, and producer-director Arthur Marks keep us involved and intrigued from start to finish. Like the majority of today's films, especially those that fall into the exploitation category, *J.D.'s Revenge* is overly violent but fortunately not to a ruinous degree. It's possible to care about Starkes' well drawn people, particularly Turman's likeable Ike, who begins to think he's losing his mind as he becomes increasingly haunted by the vision of those terrible deaths. Ike develops into a very showy part for Turman, the talented and dynamic star of *Cooley High* and one of the best young actors on the screen.

Lou Gossett is a phony evangelist who has begun to believe in himself, Fred Pinkard his wary brother and Joan Pringle Ike's lovely distraught wife . . ."

©Los Angeles Times, 1976.

Film Information, 9/76 (p. 5)
Paul Coleman

"Possession by the spirit of a dead person is one

continued on next page

continued from previous page

of the movie's oldest and most reliable saws. But the spirits of *Rebecca* and *Laura* cry far from the up-to-date black hipness of *J.D.'s Revenge*. Glynn Turman, very good in *Cooley High* and *The River Niger*, is a young actor to watch. He plays a law student possessed by the vengeful spirit of an underworld gangster killed over thirty years earlier in New Orleans. Lou Gossett portrays a revivalist preacher who is somehow connected to the original murder. In a role most actors would disdain, he develops the colorful dramatics of fire-and-brimstone preaching and, at the same time, presents a sincere and troubled character of genuine dimension. Turman and Joan Pringle as his puzzled wife overcome the hurdle of the script's fragmented characterizations to present moments of insight and even grace . . ."

©Film Information, 1976.

New York Post, 8/26/76 (p. 14)
Archer Winsten

"*J.D.'s Revenge* . . . undertakes the triple chores of its black characters, explicit sexuality and the occult. This is a large bite, and though Glynn Turman works hard as Ike, possessed at times by the angry spirit of J.D. Walker, the long-dead gangster, it's all uphill. I mean you have to be open to that kind of psychic hipper-dipper not to feel they're pulling a make-up switcheroo.

Lou Gossett impresses with his portrait of a fire-and-brimstone preacher while Joan Pringle, Ike's long-suffering wife who bears the brunt of his character-changes, takes a lot of punishment as if it's real.

Location in New Orleans keeps the picture visually alive.

Director-producer Arthur Marks handles his cast and action with such confidence that one wishes he had chosen a story less far out on those fringes of psychic disorder . . ."

Reprinted by Permission of New York Post.
©1976, New York Post Corporation.

JACKSON COUNTY JAIL

Director: *Michael Miller*. Screenplay: *Donald Stewart*. Producer: *Jeff Begun*. Photography: *Bruce Logan*. Editor: *Caroline Ferrol*. Music: *Loren Newkirk*. Distributor: *New World Pictures*. Running time 85 minutes. New York opening June 11, 1976, at several theatres. Classification: R.

Dinah Hunter: *Yvette Mimieux*. Coley Blake: *Tommy Lee Jones*. Bobby Ray: *Robert Carradine*. Hobie: *Frederic Cook*. Sheriff Dempsey: *Severn Darden*. David: *Howard Hesseman*. Deputy Burt: *John Lawlor*. Bartender: *Britt Leach*. Allison: *Nan Martin*. Shaw: *Gus Peters*. Cassie Annie: *Patrice Rohmer*. Poquitta: *Amparo Mimieux*. Pearl: *Mary Woronov*.

New York Times, 6/12/76 (p. 13)
Vincent Canby

" . . . *Jackson County Jail* is film making of relentless energy and harrowing excitement that recalls the agit-prop melodramas of the 30's. It's not exactly in a class with Lang's *You Only Live Once*, but it possesses the kind of fury that can breathe life into a melodrama even when the point of view is simple-minded.

The film was directed by Michael Miller and written by Donald Stewart, neither of whom I'd heard of before. Roger Corman, sometimes called the king of the B's, was the executive producer, and it has the drive, movement and economy of narrative that are the marks of Corman films, good and bad.

Jackson County Jail shows how someone as self-aware, self-assured and secure as its middle-class heroine can, literally overnight, find herself in a landscape where nothing she has ever known or believed still holds . . .

Miss Mimieux is excellent in a role that subjects her to as many bruises, humiliations and indignities as she might get in the boxing ring. All of the performances are fine and to the point. I hesitate to say too much, thus to oversell a movie that is best come upon without great expectations. I would suspect that Mr. Miller and Mr. Stewart are new film makers to watch."

© New York Times, 1976.

Los Angeles Times, 6/9/76 (Pt. IV, p. 10)
Kevin Thomas

" . . . The film . . . is loaded with surprises. An example of exploitation picture-making at its most creative, it turns back all the obligatory genre requirements--sex, violence and action--to produce a harrowing image of Bicentennial America that doesn't just touch a contemporary raw nerve here and there but a complex network of sensitivities, further revealing a dark underside in our national psyche . . .

So strong are its characterizations and so rich is it in ideas and emotions that *Jackson County Jail* not only sustains its sensational plot elements but also makes them a part of its comment. In short, a rape, a wild car chase and a bloody shootout--the staples of exploitation movies--are conceived and executed to tell us something about ourselves.

How ironic it is that Yvette Mimieux, in a genteel career that hasn't been as major as it has deserved to be, should find her best screen role to date in a movie called *Jackson County Jail*. She is most effective in a demanding, far-ranging part and is well matched by Jones, a massive, brooding type who brings to mind Robert Forster . . . "

© Los Angeles Times, 1976.

New York Post, 6/12/76 (p. 12)
Archer Winsten

"*Jackson County Jail* . . . is a modern melodrama subjecting a civilized creative woman to a rural underworld violence she has never known. Basically it's the kind of cheap sensationalism that isn't taken seriously, and yet, it has a quality that lifts it above its class . . .

Partly, no doubt, it is the superior performance of Yvette Mimieux in the star role. It might also be that a newcomer, Tommy Lee Jones, sporting backgrounds as disparate as Texas, football and Harvard, is also rather impressive as Coley Blake, a criminal by choice.

Director Michael Miller, another not too well-sung name, has injected a degree of realism into this film that augurs well for his future . . .

Jackson County Jail, though not a big one, is a small-time winner that you can watch without suffering a dull moment."

Reprinted by Permission of New York Post.
© 1976, New York Post Corporation.

Village Voice, 6/28/76 (p. 135)
Andrew Sarris

" . . . the dignity and maturity with which Miss Mimieux confronts her extraordinary ordeal lifts the film way up in class. The rape sequence, particularly, is shown so uncompromisingly from the woman's point of view that it never becomes a voyeuristic turn-on like the rapes in *Straw Dogs* and *Lipstick*. There is no coming to terms with the outrage, no lip-smacking complicity with the sensuality. For once, the 'triumph' of the rapist tumbles down into whimpering guilt, self-hatred, and psychological degradation. Seeking pity from his victim, the rapist encounters only violent revulsion. This is very strong stuff, and unusually perceptive for this level of filmmaking . . . It would have helped some if the character acting and bit playing did not set out to be a series of showstoppers. Severn Darden, for example, is no more convincing as a Deep South sheriff than Theodore Bikel was in *The Defiant Ones* nearly two decades ago. Also, Tommy Lee Jones plays the drop-out felon somewhat too nobly and compassionately for my taste . . . "

Reprinted by permission of The Village Voice.
Copyright © The Village Voice, Inc., 1976.

Cineaste, Fall 1976 (p. 36)
Peter Biskind

" . . . Well, what does it all add up to? When freedom is outlawed, only outlaws will be free. Cops are pigs, women alone are subject to violent sexual assault, the South is little better than a jungle, 'the whole goddam country is a rip-off,' as Yvette's companion tells her. All well and good. But the film hammers home its message so crudely, employs such two-dimensional stereotypes, strikes out at such easy targets, that it auto-destructs in the process . . .

Jackson County Jail could have been a liberal riposte to *Walking Tall*, but it misses the mark. It is too simpleminded to do more than cartoon the ideas it pretends to take seriously."

©Cineaste, 1976.

JACOB THE LIAR
(JAKOB DER LUGNER)

Director: *Frank Beyer*. Screenplay: *Jurek Becker*. Photography: *Gunter Marczinkowsky*. Editor: *Rita Hiller*. Music: *Joachim Werzlau*. Distributor: *DEFA Film-Fernsehen*. Running time 95 minutes. Los Angeles opening March 10, 1977, at Filmex. Classification: None. Origin: East Germany.

Players: *Vlastimil Brodsky, Erwin Geschonneck, Henry Hubchen, Blance Kommerell, Manuela Simon.*

Los Angeles Times, 3/9/77 (Pt. IV, p. 14)
Kevin Thomas

"*Jacob the Liar* is much like other films of the Holocaust—there's a little girl Jacob tries to care for, a pair of star-crossed young lovers, flashbacks to happier times—but it is tinged with a wry, absurdist humor.

Brodsky is a wonderfully expressive actor, capable of much woebegone deadpan, and is well-balanced by Geschonneck as Jacob's brave, finally tragic comrade.

Jacob the Liar was directed with much passion by Frank Beyer from a script by Jurek Becker, who spent his childhood in a ghetto and later in a concentration camp. *Jacob the Liar* represents 10 years of persistence on the part of Beyer and Becker, who in the interim reworked his script into a novel that has been translated into 27 languages."

©Los Angeles Times, 1977.

JAMES DEAN:
THE FIRST AMERICAN TEENAGER

Documentary. Director: *Ray Connolly.* Producers: *David Puttnam, Sandy Lieberson.* Photography: *Peter Hannan, Mike Molloy, Robert Gersikoff.* Editor: *Peter Hollywood.* Research: *Valerie Wade, Adrian Bales, Sandra Wake, John Howlett.* Narrated by *Stacy Keach.* Distributor: *ZIV.* Running time 83 minutes. Los Angeles opening June, 1976, at the UA Cinema 1. Classification: PG.

Players: *Corey Allen, Carroll Baker, Leslie Caron, Sammy Davis, Jr., Dennis Hopper, Kenneth Kendall, Jack Larson, Sal Mineo, Adeline Nell, Malla Nurmi, Jean Owen, Hal Owen, Nicholas Ray, Leonard Rosenman, Capt. E. Tripke, Cristine White, Peter Witt, Natalie Wood.*

Los Angeles Times, 6/9/76 (Pt. IV, p. 1)
Kevin Thomas

" . . . earnest, fairly comprehensive, occasionally superficial and evasive documentary that includes generous portions of the three films he completed before his death in 1955 in a car crash at the age of 24.

The quality that makes an actor a star is perhaps inevitably finally elusive, but Dean projected a vulnerability combined with an intense magnetism that held his generation in thrall . . . documentarian Ray Connolly has rounded up plenty of people who knew him well enough to offer some insight into what made him tick. (There are some intriguing absences, however, beginning with *East of Eden*'s director, Elia Kazan.)

The impression we receive, one that confirms what most people already have, is that of a young man of more talent than discipline, with much ambition and many insecurities, possessed of both a gift for self-dramatization and a streak of self-destructiveness . . . "

© Los Angeles Times, 1976.

New York Post, 11/19/76 (p. 30)
Archer Winsten

"*James Dean—The First American Teenager* . . . is a documentary about the legendary cult hero whose survival for these 21 years after death may seem mysterious to some. They need wonder no longer, for this picture, drawing material from his three biggest films, *East of Eden, Rebel Without a Cause* and *Giant* as well as his first screen test

for Elia Kazan, and clips from four television plays, a road safety commercial, ironically, and a newsreel of him in his racing car, repeats his magical effect . . .

This is a picture you should see if Jimmy Dean means anything at all to you, pro or con. Ray Connolly put it together. David Puttnam and Sandy Lieberson produced it."

Reprinted by Permission of New York Post.
© 1976, New York Post Corporation.

JEWISH GAUCHOS, THE
(LOS GAUCHOS JUDIOS)

Director, Producer: *Juan Jose Jusid.* Screenplay (Spanish with English subtitles): *Oscar Viale, Alejandro Saderman, Ana Maria Gerchunoff, Mr. Jusid.* Based on a novel by Alberto Gerchunoff. Photography: *Juan Carlos Desanzo.* Music: *Gustavo Beytelmann.* Choreography: *Lisa Jelin.* Distributor: *Julio Tanjeloff Productions.* Running time 92 minutes. Los Angeles opening January 1977 at the Westland II. Classification: None. Origin: Argentina.

Dr. Naum: *Pepe Soriano.* Maria: *Ginamaria Hidalgo.* Brane: *Maria Rosa Gallo.* Rabbi Simon Liske: *Osvaldo Terranova.* Rachel Kelner: *Dora Baret.* Gabriel: *Victor Laplace.*

Los Angeles Times, 1/19/77 (Pt. IV, p. 12)
Linda Gross

"As unlikely as it sounds, *The Jewish Gauchos* . . . is a sweet and ironic musical that dramatizes the true story of Russian Jews who migrated to Argentina in the 1890s, settled in agricultural colonies and became cowboys under the tutelage of Baron de Hirsch . . .

The film is full of sympathetic though thinly drawn characters . . .

The screenplay by Juan Jose Jusid, Oscar Viale, Alejandro Saderman and Ana Maria Gerchunoff combines folksy reminiscences, picturesque tableaux, dark drama, songs and dance. It's a conglomeration that doesn't always gel. Characters and situations are presented in fantasy fashion without realistic details, which is fine during musical numbers but jarring during a fairly lengthy birth sequence or in scenes with ironic nightmarish overtones.

Director Jusid handles the material with loving enthusiasm, but some kind of connection is missing and the movie lacks lust and coherence . . . "

© Los Angeles Times, 1977.

Film Information, July/August 1976 (p. 4)
Suzanne Bowers

"*The Jewish Gauchos* is an Argentine film which depicts the culture shock of Jews who, fleeing against Russian pogroms in the 1890s, had to adapt to life in gaucho territory.

The focus is upon the interactions and relationships among these emigrants, rather than their adjustment to their new country and neighbors. In anecdotal form, many scenes are vividly portrayed: a frail woman (played by Argentina's international singing star, Ginamaria Hidalgo) determines to have her baby despite doctor's warnings; the reaction to the fire that destroys their first crop; a young girl is married off to a man she doesn't love, but rides off with her true love after the ceremony.

The film has a disturbing aspect. A father, wishing to restore his family's honor, murders his own son because he feels his behavior in a fight was cowardly. The son, however, is innocent of the charges that got him into the fight in the first place. This fact makes the father's actions even more difficult to understand from our present-day point of view . . ."

©Film Information, 1976.

JONAH WHO WILL BE 25 IN THE YEAR 2000

Director: *Alain Tanner*. Screenplay (French with English subtitles): *John Berger, Mr. Tanner*. Producers: *Yves Gasser, Yves Peyrot*. Photography: *Renato Berto*. Editor: *Brigitte Sousselier*. Music: *Jean-Marie Senia*. Production: *Action Films*; *Citel Films*; *Societe Francaise de Production*; *SSR-Swiss Television*. Distributor: *New Yorker Films*. Running time 115 minutes. New York opening October 2, 1976, at the New York Film Festival, Lincoln Center. Classification: None. Origin: Switzerland.

Max: *Jean-Luc Bideau*. Mathilde: *Myriam Boyer*. Marco: *Jacques Denis*. Marcel: *Roger Jendly*. Marguerite: *Dominique Labourier*. Madeleine: *Myriam Meziere*. Marie: *Miou-Miou*. Mathieu: *Rufus*. Old Charles: *Raymond Bussieres*.

Film Information, November 1976 (p. 2)
Frederic A. Brussat

"Alain Tanner and co-writer John Berger accomplished what few Marxist moviemakers have been able to achieve—they made a political movie that is thoroughly entertaining and believable. It is what the director calls a 'didactic comedy.' We look at

the lives of eight idiosyncratic individualists whose lives have been touched and in varying degrees transformed by the political events of 1968 in Switzerland . . .

All of these people are flexible and capable of flying in the direction of surprise and the unknown. The 1968 revolution gave them a sense of possibility. And when their lives intertwine, Jonah (the child of the ex-typesetter and his wife) becomes the symbol of their hopes for the future. They have tempered their beliefs from political revolution to cultural evolution . . .

Jonah Who Will Be 25 in the Year 2000 is one of the best films at this year's festival with its excellent ensemble acting and literate script. Tanner reveals an ability to sensitively depict the awkward but endearing nature of woman."

©Film Information, 1976.

New York Post, 10/22/76 (p. 21)
Frank Rich

". . . On paper this movie looks like an engaging, lyrical and sophisticated comedy about contemporary politics, but on screen it never gets a rhythm going: It's not as funny as it should be, and it often refuses to come alive.

There's no denying, though, that Tanner fails in a most unusual fashion. While other directors fritter away fine material through sloppines or stupidity, he defeats himself by being overly meticulous and a little too smart. *Jonah* . . . is in such damn tight control that it forgets to let loose and enjoy itself.

The movie's script—written by Tanner and his frequent collaborator, the art critic and novelist John Berger—positively bristles with potential. Set in the present, it deals with eight extraordinarily appealing protagonists, men and women who are in their 30s and who are haunted by the political upheavals that convulsed Europe and America in the late 1960s . . .

. . . by describing these people's idiosyncratic personalities and their brief, shared adventures, Tanner and Berger mean to illuminate the process of social change in uncommonly human and comic terms . . ."

Reprinted by Permission of New York Post.
©1976, New York Post Corporation.

Christian Science Monitor, 10/21/76 (p. 26)
David Sterritt

". . . The eight major characters—not counting Jonah, who is born halfway through—represent a cross section of Swiss (and presumably West European) life.

continued on next page

continued from previous page

Tanner considers these people to be 'metaphors on two legs.' He examines them ironically from his socialist perspective, caring more for their traits and foibles than for traditional storytelling techniques.

Jonah can be extremely engaging, as when the friends get together to celebrate Jonah's arrival and the screen warms with their conviviality . . .

. . . Tanner's technique of 'working with a big eraser,' eliminating much connective and explanatory material, will leave an empty feeling in the hearts and minds of many who want to respond fully to the film's numerous positive elements.

Jonah emerges as a flawed but often merry work, socially aware but rarely propagandistic, disjointed but energetic. It could be Tanner's most widely liked film so far."

Reprinted by permission from The Christian
Science Monitor © 1976.
The Christian Science Publishing Society.
All rights reserved.

New York Magazine, 11/15/76 (p. 119)
John Simon

"*Jonah Who Will Be 25 in the Year 2000* is, as customary with Tanner and Berger, composed of rambling episodes from the lives of eight good people, more or less left-oriented Genevans or French from across the border, all of whom will act as mentors to Jonah, who is about to be born to two of them . . .

Typical of the invention of the film is that each character's name begins in *Ma* (e.g., Max, Mathilde, Marco, etc.), which may be a tribute to Marx and Mao or to mania and mannerism. The film is riddled with quotations from and references to everyone from Diderot to Piaget, from Rousseau to Neruda, without, however, appreciably enlivening the routinely capricious proceedings. There are a few pleasing performances, notably from Jacques Denis, Raymond Bussieres, and the incomparable Miou-Miou . . ."

© 1976 by the NYM Corp. Reprinted with
the permission of NEW YORK Magazine.

Take One, March 1977 (p. 14)
Michael Tarantino

". . . The central character of the film is Max, who, for all intents and purposes, has remained standing still for the last seven years. Jean-Luc Bideau imparts to Max a weariness which dominates each scene he is in. He sees '68 as the year in which modern history played itself out, advancing to the edge, only to retreat. Throughout the film, Tanner uses black and white to illustrate the fantasies each character must resort to in the face of a dull or meaningless vocation. However, we rarely see Max at his job—the elements of black and white are reserved for his 'memories,' i.e. political involvement. He has equated his memories with finality, thus imparting to them a surrealistic edge which increases as they move back in time . . ."

© Take One, 1977.

JUVENILE LIAISON

Documentary. Directors: *Joan Churchill, Nicholas Broomfield.* Production: *British Film Institute.* Running time 101 minutes. New York opening March 25, 1976, at the Film Forum. Classification: None. Origin. Great Britain.

See Volume 1 for additional reviews

Monthly Film Bulletin, 6/76 (p. 127)
Verina Glaessner

"In 1968, juvenile liaison sections were attached to a number of local police departments to function as a kind of bridging operation between young offenders, their homes and their schools in an effort to keep the youngsters out of court. Nick Broomfield and Joan Churchill's film follows the day to day working of one such section, attached to the Lancashire police, and specifically the activities of two officers, George Ray and Lilian Brooks. It is an admirably modest film in many respects: working as a self-contained unit . . . shooting over a seven-week period using available light and allowing sequences, for the most part, to occur in real time without use of cut-aways or commentary, the two filmmakers have refrained from generalizing from the specific situations they show . . . As the film progresses, it makes devastatingly clear that the police are probably the least appropriate body to handle the kinds of social problem presented to them in the course of their juvenile liaison work."

© Monthly Film Bulletin, 1976.

KASEKI

Director: *Masaki Kobayashi.* Screenplay (Japanese with English subtitles): *Shun Inagaki.* Based on a story by Yasushi Inoue. Producer: *Masayuki Sato.* Photography:

Kouzo Okazaki. Music: *Touru Takemitsu*. Distributor: *New Yorker Films*. Running time 213 minutes. New York opening September 1976 at the New Yorker Theatre. Classification: None. Origin: Japan, 1974.

Tajihei Itsuki: *Shin Saburi*. Mme. Marcelin: *Keiko Kishi*. Funazu: *Hisashi Igawa*. Kishi: *Kei Yamamoto*. Mrs. Kishi: *Orie Sato*. Itsuki's Daughters: *Komaki Kurihara, Mayumi Ogawa*. Kihara: *Shigeru Kouyama*. Itsuki's Stepmother: *Haruko Sugimura*. Itsuki's Brother: *Ichiro Nakatani*. Itsuki's Friend: *Jukichi Uno*. Sakagami: *Yuusuke Takita*. Narrator: *Goh Kato*.

The Times (London), 9/14/76 (p. 8)
Derek Prouse

"*Kaseki* . . . is a long film which needs to be approached in a mood of serenity; it flows like an unhurried river, equally concerned with its tributaries as with its mainstream. It is also a film of great subtlety. Inevitably, it will invite comparison with Kurosawa's fine film *Living* (1952), which dealt with a minor bureaucrat's realization that he had only six months to live, and with his subsequent search for a meaning to his life. But in the new film the middle-aged man is an eminently successful businessman who has devoted his life exclusively to his career. His quest is, perhaps, even more labyrinthian . . .

. . . this is filmed with the kind of simplicity that conceals consummate technique. This artistic economy is impeccably matched by the performance of the leading actor, Shin Saburi; restrained both in his irascibility and in his private agony—and in the depiction of his most baffling dilemma, when he undergoes an operation and finds himself facing another, almost unwelcome span of life. He has come to terms with death and now finds his old way of life tawdry . . ."

©The Times, 1976.

New York Magazine, 9/27/76 (p. 85)
John Simon

". . . It is hard to evoke the loveliness of a film where still lifes of the most mundane objects are composed with the delicacy of Japanese flower arrangement. The texture of things is embraced by the camera until those things yield up their essences to it. And the acting is no less purposive than the camera: No intonation or expression is extended by a single unnecessary second. Shin Saburi is most affecting as he makes Itsuki deepen from toughness into fineness, always avoiding easy sympathy; Keiko Kishi is equally appealing as vi-

sion and woman, in gentle wisdom or buoyant vivacity. The supporting cast is equally fine. And always there is that marvelous rhythm of the film: slow and stately in its overall progression but often quite nervously agitated in the individual sequences. The score, by the distinguished modernist Touru Takemitsu, aptly harks back to the chamber music of Faure and Debussy, and is used sparingly for emotional heightening. Even if it falls short of ultimate greatness, the film fails us neither artistically nor humanly."

©1976 by the NYM Corp. Reprinted with the permission of NEW YORK Magazine.

Sight and Sound, Summer 1975 (p. 190)
Philip Strick

"When Masaki Kobayashi tells a story, he tells it in painstaking detail, piling up actions and consequences to create a solid structure of events. With *Kaseki* . . . his determination to leave nothing unsaid results in a film of just over three-and-a-half hours . . . The story is of a lonely widower preparing to die of inoperable cancer in his late fifties after a long and successful business career, a theme without novelty, glamour or comfort. We may be forgiven for approaching with caution.

In Kobayashi's films, however, nothing is quite as it seems. Exterior and interior realities can differ alarmingly, as with the episode in *Kwaidan* when a man awakens from a night with his wife fo find her corpse embracing him. Itsuki (Shin Saburi), the melancholy businessman of *Kaseki*, is in similar clutches, the imminence of his own death forcing him to observe his surroundings with new and unexpected meanings . . .

. . . it would seem that Kobayashi is no longer interested in granting the romantic fiction of a proud and memorable suicide, even to illustrate the pointlessness of the society that would interpret it in such terms. Today's samurai, working himself into his grave behind an office desk, is challenged to find good reason for his sacrifice, and to find it while he's still in a position to change his mind . . ."

©Sight and Sound, 1975.

The Sunday Times (London), 9/12/76 (p. 10)
David Robinson

". . . The length (3½ hours) and range of *Kaseki* reveal its dual origin. Based initially on a novel, the film is an adaptation of an eight-part television serial. From time to time the episode links and serial recapitulations can be detected; and certainly for a Western audience the film is weakened by diffuseness. This leisure nonetheless enables Kobayashi to develop his portrait through various levels of detachment from the central, essentially subjective problem. A commentary over the film (which sets

continued on next page

continued from previous page

off by telling us exactly what is about to happen to Mr. Itsuki); Itsuki's conversations with the phantom lady; his own private thoughts and behaviour; the interaction with family, friends, colleagues and subordinates maintain a continually varying viewpoint on Isuki's meeting with death . . ."

©The Sunday Times, 1976.

Monthly Film Bulletin, 6/75 (p. 138)
Tony Rayns

". . . This film version of *Kaseki* is Kobayashi's reduction (to the form he originally intended) of his popular 8-part serial made for Japanese TV, and although its style couldn't be further removed from the aggressive close-ups of American made-for-TV movies, its genesis remains clear enough in the sprawling, episodic construction and the necessarily leisured pace. At the same time, though, such qualities are conventionally more suggestive of literature than cinema, and their presence here is doubtless traceable back to Yasushi Inoue's novel; the same is presumably true of the film's ambitious thematic range, which draws a broad association between a Japanese reaction to European culture and religion and a more purely Japanese questioning of material values . . . If the results are more fascinating for their exploration of the territory between film and literature than for their contribution to existentialist philosophy, then Kobayashi's endeavor is none the less for that."

©Monthly Film Bulletin, 1975.

New York Post, 9/9/76 (p. 19)
Archer Winsten

". . . such is the quality of the photography and the seriousness of the subject, aided by Saburi's performance, that one maintains a good level of interest. As travelogue alone it has value.

More than that, as an example of a movie which is less an entertainment than an exploration of life's proper meaning, it demonstrates again the high seriousness of a director like Kobayashi. For those who value the best of the Japanese films, *Kaseki* becomes a worthy, if ponderous, item, not to be missed in this run which will doubtless be one of the few and also of modest duration."

Reprinted by Permission of New York Post.
©1976, New York Post Corporation.

Film Information, October 1976 (p. 1)
Herbert F. Lowe

"*Kaseki* (Fossil) is a deceptively complex film. It is reminiscent of the earlier work of Sweden's Ingmar Bergman, the later works of Senegal's Ousmane Sembene, and the classic films of India's Satyajit Ray . . .

The Japanese way of dealing with the truth is to cover it with many layers. Such interwoven layers are the fabric of *Kaseki* . . .

In *Kaseki*, director Masaki Kobayashi has given us a Japanese film with a universal theme. The title, *Kaseki*, means 'fossil.' The unique fossil-mural, on the wall of Itsuki's war buddy's office, gives Itsuki an insight into creation and a perspective from which he can relate his own life to past, present and future . . ."

©Film Information, 1976.

KEETJE TIPPEL

Director: *Paul Verhoeven*. Screenplay (Dutch with English subtitles): *Gerard Soeteman*. Based on the writings of Neel Doff. Producer: *Rob Houwer*. Photography: *Jan de Bont*. Editor: *Jane Speer*. Music: *Rogier van Otterloo*. Distributor: *Cinema National Corporation*. Running time 104 minutes. New York opening September 26, 1976, at the 68th Street Playhouse. Classification: None. Origin: Holland.

Keetje Tippel: *Monique van de Ven*. Mother: *Andrea Domburg*. Father: *Jan Blaaser*. Sister Minna: *Hannah De Leeuwe*. Andre: *Eddie Brugman*. Hugo: *Rutger Hauer*. George: *Peter Faber*.

New York Magazine, 10/4/76 (p. 87)
John Simon

". . . a series of cliches from the lives of the poor and oppressed, and particularly the upward-mobile poor, female division. These lives are sad and touching, but, alas, not impervious to platitudinous treatment. What may have worked as a three-volume novel full of detailed and fresh observation, compressed into 104 minutes of a passing parade of novelistic and cinematic commonplaces—predictable disasters and no less predictable moments of respite—emerges amateurish and ludicrous on screen . . .

Keetje-Neel is played by Monique van de Van with a saucy charm and the face of an indomitable urchin, but without histrionic depth. The other parts are inconsequential; only the role of the mother escapes total superficiality in one or two scenes. The virtues of the film, such as they are, are the cinematography of Jan de Bont, somewhat arty but still impressive; and the many views of Amsterdam, one of the world's most watchable cities."

©1976 by the NYM Corp. Reprinted with the permission of NEW YORK Magazine.

Film Information, October 1976 (p. 3)
Ellen Clark

"In Amsterdam in the 1870s, Keetje (Monique van de Ven), a young beauty, is determined to escape employers who financially exploit and sexually abuse her, and her cruel mother who forces her into prostitution to feed the impoverished family.

Pretensions of feminism and socialist politics cling to the movie through the epilogue, which announces that the story and the 'indomitable spirit' of the Cinderella heroine are true.

Striking color photography and a lively and fascinating re-creation of life in nineteenth-century Holland atone for the pat plot and contrived ending, but only up to a point. The characters are one-dimensional, except the heroine, who is two-dimensional . . ."

©Film Information, 1976.

Christian Science Monitor, 10/7/76 (p. 22)
David Sterritt

". . . realism is director Verhoeven's justification for the sexual and scatological explicitness that starts before the opening credits have finished and shows up intermittently until nearly the end. In between learning how Keetje was raped and forced into prostitution and so on and so forth, we get an apparently plausible picture of what probably happened all the time to poverty-stricken late-19th-century families who migrated to big cities with no money and little idea of what would happen to them or how to comport themselves.

Monique van de Ven gives an attractive and capable performance as Keetje, though she has a disappointing tendency to lapse into cute-little-girl overacting. Mr. Verhoeven's directing is well thought out and carefully executed . . ."

Reprinted by permission from The Christian Science Monitor © 1976. The Christian Science Publishing Society. All rights reserved.

KILLER ELITE, THE

Director: *Sam Peckinpah*. Screenplay: *Stirling Silliphant*. Producers: *Martin Baum, Arthur Lewis*. Executive Producer: *Helmut Dantine*. Photography: *Phil Lathrop*. Editor: *Garth*

Craven. Music: *Jerry Fielding*. Distributor: *United Artists*. Running time 123 minutes. New York opening December 17, 1975, at several theatres. Classification: PG.

Mike Locken: *James Caan*. George Hansen: *Robert Duvall*. Cap Collis: *Arthur Hill*. Laurence Weyburn: *Gig Young*. Yuen Chung: *Mako*. Miller: *Bo Hopkins*. Mac: *Burt Young*. O'Leary: *Tom Clancy*. Tommie Chung: *Tiana*. Amy: *Katy Heflin*.

See Volume 1 for additional reviews

Sight and Sound, Spring 1976 (p. 121)
Richard Combs

" . . . *The Killer Elite* (United Artists) has already been condemned for a . . . set of sins––the stereotyped commercialism of its thick-ear ingredients, and its hand-me-down plot about the dirt that clings to the hands of anyone who messes with modern power politics. Unmistakably, however, the melancholia . . . filters through the material, etching the political cynicism more deeply than *Three Days of the Condor* and other recent, muddle-headed exponents of the genre have done, and casting a regretful aura of wasted lives behind each of the characters, even while encasing them in self-sufficient eccentricity. The result is a strangely dissonant and compelling entertainment, an unsettling criss-cross of Chinatown Nights' fantasy and dyspeptic meditation on figures set firmly in their contemporary landscape . . ."

© Sight and Sound, 1976.

KILLING OF A CHINESE BOOKIE, THE

Director: *John Cassavetes*. Screenplay: *Mr. Cassavetes*. Producer: *Al Rubin*. Photography: *Fred Elmes, Mike Harris*. Editor: *Tom Cornwell*. Music: *Anthony Harris*. Distributor: *Faces Distribution Corporation*. Running time 130 minutes. New York opening February 15, 1976, at the Columbia I and II Theatres. Classification: R.

Cosmo Vitelli: *Ben Gazzara*. Mort Weil: *Seymour Cassel*. Flo: *Timothy Carey*. Phil:

continued on next page

continued from previous page

Robert Phillips. John-the-Boss: *Morgan Woodward.* Eddie-Red: *John Red Kullers.* Marty Reitz: *Al Rubin.* Rachel: *Azizi Johari.* Betty: *Virginia Carrington.* Mr. Sophistication: *Meade Roberts.* Sherry: *Alice Friedland.* Margo: *Donna Gordon.* Waitress: *Trisha Pelham.* Chinese Bookie: *Soto Joe Hugh.*

See Volume 1 for additional reviews

Films in Review, 4/76 (p. 243)
Charles Phillip Reilly

"This film is basically a simple story of a night club owner (Ben Gazzara) who can't pay his gambling debts to the mob, who then demand he kill a Chinese bookie. Gazzara commits the murder, only to find his life forfeit. Instead of a direct action suspenser its director John Cassavetes has chosen to make *The Killing* an exercise in often unrelated dialogue, camera shots so distorted as to give us torsos when heads or feet are called for, plot lines that lead into blind alleys, and people about whom one doesn't care.

Gazzara's role finds him in love with a Black girl (Azizi Johari), working in his nightclub's sleazy revue, headed by a fat, unentertaining entertainer (Meade Roberts). Both the girl and the entertainer mean something to our hero, but what isn't clear. Gazzara's performance is the best he's done on screen though it's hampered by the director's framework which purposely beclouds most of Gazzara's actions . . ."

© Films in Review, 1976.

Sight and Sound, Winter 1976/1977 (p. 61)
Richard Combs

"In its diffuse, freakish way, *The Killing of a Chinese Bookie* . . . may be John Cassavetes' most infuriating, unclassifiable and intriguing project to date. A black thriller, about the owner of a struggling Los Angeles strip club who gets into debt with the Syndicate and must buy his way out with murder, the film's drive towards bloody mayhem and double-cross is constantly diverted by the behavioural complexity Cassavetes allows his characters and the generosity he extends to his actors. The tension between the two in fact seems to be responsible for the strangely unrealised, half-formed ambience of the film . . ."

© Sight and Sound, 1977.

Take One, 8/76 (p. 35)
W. S. Di Piero

". . . With *The Killing of a Chinese Bookie*, Cassavetes ends his brief infatuation with 'meaning' and returns to the messy, homely, open-ended details of recognizable human behavior. Here, as in *Husbands* and *Faces*, improvised filmmaking embodies raw, improvised life . . .

Cassavetes' visual style is not as anecdotal as some would have us believe. The apparently vagrant movements of his camera inevitably result in a fierce concentration on character . . .

Although *The Killing* ought to be a kind of *film noir*, it has few of the pictorial conventions of the genre. It's a gangster film, to be sure, but rather than dramatize the bizarre moral zones of gangster behavior the film bears down on the banal and embattled quality of Cosmo's life. The actual killing of the bookie, filmed with breathtaking ellipses, elicits no thrills, no fear: it evokes instead a feeling of humiliation and muffled pain. Violence fuses with shame. When Cosmo confronts his victim—a shrivelled, harmless-looking old man—he sees in him a version of his own embarrassment. Anyone who lives an improvised overreaching life (like Cosmo, the bookie, and the punk Cosmo later kills), runs the risk of being fatally trapped by his own ambitions, haunted by his own mean aspirations."

© Take One, 1976.

KING KONG

Director: *John Guillermin.* Screenplay: *Lorenzo Semple, Jr.* Based on a story by Edgar Wallace and Merian C. Cooper. Producer: *Dino De Laurentiis.* Photography: *Richard H. Kline.* Editor: *Ralph E. Winters.* Music: *John Barry.* Special Effects: *Carlo Rambaldi, Glen Robinson, Rick Baker.* Distributor: *Paramount Pictures.* Running time 135 minutes. New York opening December 17, 1976, at several theatres. Classification: PG.

Jack Prescott: *Jeff Bridges.* Fred Wilson: *Charles Grodin.* Dwan: *Jessica Lange.* Captain Ross: *John Randolph.* Bagley: *Rene Auberjonois.* Boan: *Julius Harris.* Joe Perko: *Jack O'Halloran.* Sunfish: *Dennis Fimple.* Carnahan: *Ed Lauier.* Garcia: *Jorge Moreno.*

New York Post, 12/17/76 (p. 31)
Frank Rich

". . . *King Kong*, the $24 million remake of the

classic 1933 ape film, is a clumsy, pallid and often listless movie that fails on its own terms and almost any other terms that could reasonably be applied to it . . .

To me, the most shocking aspect of this *Kong* is how tacky it looks. Richard H. Kline's color cinematography is washed out in the daytime scenes; in the crucial nighttime scenes (on Kong's island and, at the end, in New York), the lighting is so flat that colors, and even images, lose clear definition.

. . . the writing sabotages *Kong* at every turn. The profusion of oneliners keeps us from taking anything seriously . . . and reminds us we're watching a movie; *Kong* becomes a campy in-joke instead of a tale of horror and romance . . ."

Reprinted by Permission of New York Post.
©1976, New York Post Corporation.

Women's Wear Daily, 12/17/76 (p. 8)
Howard Kissel

"The wonderful news about *King Kong* is that it lives up to everything you imagined about it— Jessica Lange is as stiff as you heard she would be as Kong's would-be consort; Lorenzo Semple's screenplay is as full as you thought it would be of lines to groan at ('My horoscope said today I'd meet somebody big,' Lange says as an expeditionary crew takes off for Kong's island); John Guillermin's reaction maximizes the groan-potential in the screenplay—but who would want it any other way?

My original fear, when I saw the posters, was that this Kong was not designed as humanly as his predecessor. But, if the earlier Kong had the looks, this one at least is all heart. Visually he may not be for all tastes, but emotionally he sure grows on you . . ."

©Women's Wear Daily, 1976.

Christian Science Monitor, 12/24/76 (p. 14)
David Sterritt

". . . Well, the Dino De Laurentiis rehash doesn't seem to care much about improving. But it does have a wonderful time imitating, embellishing, and spoofing. It's a rousing entertainment in its silly way, and I had a surprising lot of fun watching it . . .

What lends this nonsense a breath of new life is the self-deflating approach of John Guillermin's direction. The screenplay, by Lorenzo Semple, Jr., goes too far with campy irony . . . But Guillermin, an action specialist, allows his actors just the right amount of distancing during the most effective scenes, replacing suspense (everyone already knows the plot, except the youngest) with humor and the self-conscious sense of adventure that greets the beginning of a roller-coaster ride . . ."

Reprinted by permission from The Christian
Science Monitor ©1976.
The Christian Science Publishing Society.
All rights reserved.

The Times (London), 12/23/76 (p. 9)
David Robinson

". . . Worst of all, great Kong, who is so pure in the original version, who forces on you respect for his nobility and his tragedy despite his unkind habit of breaking the backs of natives in his teeth, or hurling white men down canyons, is now played for easy sympathy. Instead of eyes like a cartoon character his are as appealing as Rita Tushingham's. Sometimes he even looks like Lord Olivier as the tragic Moor . . .

. . . Technically, there is no doubt that the Kong of 1976 represents 43 years of advance over the old one; but—and it is certainly not just nostalgia speaking—as a character, the new monster is altogether dwarfed by his predecessor."

©The Times, 1976.

Village Voice, 12/27/76 (p. 13)
Molly Haskell

". . . Kong, defanged and adorable and the real love object, is the antithesis of macho. Although he gives out a few lusty roars, it is with his kittenish smiles, sad eyes, and poet's sensibility that the movie is concerned. Instead of seeing him in a terrifying long shot when he first appears to seize Fay Wray at the stake, it is his face that fills the screen. Most of the ads are facial close-ups of Kong, and it is into the construction and manipulation of this face—that could sink a thousand ships and a major film company too—that a major portion of the $24 million must have gone. He is permitted a far greater range of expressions than the rest of the cast together, and most of the time they are easy to read . . ."

Reprinted by permission of The Village Voice.
Copyright ©The Village Voice, Inc., 1976.

Newsweek, 12/20/76 (p. 103)
Jack Kroll

". . . This bathetic clunk from the sublime to the ridiculous is characteristic at almost every point of comparison between Kongs I and II. Even the ballyhooed 40-foot, 6½-ton monster with its hydraulic system is a good deal of a cheat: it turns out that for certain key scenes (such as Kong hammering through the natives' giant protective wall) what looks like marvelously supple animation is only a man in an ape suit . . . Although their basic ape is well conceived, with the tartar of centuries on his teeth and a roar like the flushing of a thousand industrial toilets, in moments of deep feeling his features skew themselves into a remarkable re-

continued on next page

continued from previous page

semblance to Jack Nicholson's Satanic tenderness.

Even with color, the settings of Kong II are no match for the rich black-and-white chiaroscuro of Kong I, with its echoes of artists like Gustave Dore and Max Ernst and its sensitivity to the emotional values of tone and texture . . ."

©Newsweek, Inc. 1976
reprinted by permission.

New Leader, 1/17/77 (p. 25)
Robert Asahina

". . . the new *King Kong* doesn't provide much entertainment even for those with addled brains. This $24 million spectacle has been billed as 'the most exciting original motion picture event of all time.' That it is not original scarcely needs emphasizing; that it is not particularly exciting is apparent from the rather clumsy and unthrilling special effects. The producers employed a variety of sophisticated techniques, but the patently phony miniature sets and painted backgrounds cast a pall of sleaziness over the entire proceedings . . .

. . . Charles Grodin occasionally mugs shamelessly and Jeff Bridges is often a trifle too hip and hirsute as a Princeton professor of primate paleontology, yet both bring an air of professional solidity to this otherwise gas-filled epic. Not so, however, with John Guillermin, whose direction is pedestrian where it is not obtrusive, or John Barry, whose ponderous score deadens the ear almost as much as

Semple's tinny dialogue does. In all, *King Kong* is probably De Laurentiis' most expensive flop . . ."

Reprinted with permission from
The New Leader, 1977.
©The American Labor Conference
on International Affairs, Inc.

Saturday Review, 2/5/77 (p. 41)
Judith Crist

". . . the one and original lovable monster is lost amid all the hydraulic manipulations in what now emerges as the story of a dumb blonde who falls for a huge plastic finger.

For those who have not seen the original film, the new version can be a foolish entertainment, made that way because of a total lack of viewpoint on the part of De Laurentiis (the kind of producer who makes mention of his director, John Guillermin, and screenwriter, Lorenzo Semple, Jr., literally academic). To cater to cynics, he starts out with one-liners and cheap self-mockery, totally vitiating, for anyone above the age of eight, the emotional and sentimental impact he so openly demands in the second half of the movie. What comes clear—and he has made no secret of it—is that this is a money-making project, with the big sell pointed to surpassing the $100 million *Jaws* has amassed . . ."

©Judith Crist, 1977.

Film Information, January 1977 (p. 3)
Paul Coleman

". . . a film that dares not acknowledge the feelings that made the original work so well.

Newcomer Jessica Lange plays Dwan in Dino De Laurentiis' multimillion-dollar remake of the 1933 classic, **King Kong**.

The point of a savage, dominating beast acquiring the human virtues of love and trust must be developed gingerly but coherently. The affection that arises in both the zoologist and the starlet for the ape, even when he has killed their comrades, even when he threatens a whole city, is difficult to make believable, especially when modern audiences shy away from such feelings, even in human characters. The Kong scenes concentrate instead on technical wizardry. (We can thank the engineers who assembled the ape on display, and the make-up man who 'plays' him in closeups.)

Apart from Mr. Grodin's satiric characterization, the cast seems uninspired . . .''

©Film Information, 1977.

Monthly Film Bulletin, February 1977 (p. 26)
Jonathan Rosenbaum

''. . . Dino De Laurentiis' expensive piece of mischief is visibly designed to obliterate the past with a tidal wave of arch modishness. Its value as an expression of liberal morality can be easily gauged by noting that the film's most glaringly racist statement is uttered by the hero, an erudite bearded hippie with a credit card who, after remarking Kong's importance for the natives ('He was the terror and the mystery of their life, their magic'), goes on to say that, without him, they are bound to turn into alcoholics—a notion that appears to add redskins to an already crowded melting pot. The silliest lines, however, are accorded to Jessica Lange, a likable Tuesday Weldish ingenue whose range is regrettably not broad enough to encompass fear . . .''

©Monthly Film Bulletin, 1977.

Commonweal, 2/4/77 (p. 86)
Colin L. Westerbeck, Jr.

''. . . the new film will never have the same sway with us that the old one has. De Laurentiis' version is limited in this respect by its own financial resources and spectacularity. The one place where De Laurentiis has shown neither wit nor restraint is in the promotion of his film, which began over a year in advance. In all the ads, for example, far from being shot down by a couple of helicopters, Kong is shown crumpling up a whole jet fighter in one hand like a beer can. With an advertising blitz like this, De Laurentiis' film is perhaps too central a document of our time to become a genuine legend. Great myths come, like Kong himself (or Christ), out of nowhere. They begin in some hinterland and take us by surprise . . . To have made the film the first time required real inspiration. To have made it a second time, maybe even to have made it better in some ways, required only intelligence.''

©Commonweal, 1977.

New York Magazine, 12/27/76 (p. 79)
John Simon

''The remake of *King Kong* rates very high on my list of unnecessary films. The new version tries hard to come up with things the original lacked: Freud, feminism, ecology, social satire, spoofing of astrology, and above all, sympathy for the ape. In fact, the romance is now much more between beast and girl than between boy and girl, and the film can barely restrain itself from providing a Liebestod for the sweetly simian protagonist and the clearly zoophilic heroine. But for all this, nothing substantial has been added and something considerable has been forfeited . . .

. . . The cinematography of *KK II*, by Richard H. Kline, is just about the worst I have seen in so expensive a movie in years: Kline's lighting (which, as everyone knows, is what cinematography is mostly about) is downright primitive, and makes large chunks of the movie garish or washed-out. And Guillermin's direction is consistently uninteresting throughout . . .''

©1976 by the NYM Corp. Reprinted with the permission of NEW YORK Magazine.

The Sunday Times (London), 1/2/77 (p. 36)
Alan Brien

''. . . Whoever King Kong is today, his current biopic, directed by John (*Towering Inferno*) Guillermin, turns out to be a mammoth, gripping, two-and-a-quarter-hour fairy tale.

A few customers will mourn the old anarchic Kong of 1933, reintroduced to a new generation on TV this Christmas, for his unpredictable changes of size, his jerky clockwork movements, his indiscriminate gnawing of adoring natives, even for Fay Wray's incessant steam-whistle screaming. But they can be reassured that Lorenzo Semple, Jr.'s, screenplay sticks closely to the original storyline, sometimes almost shot for shot. Very soon, it is impossible to resist this gargantuan, 40 foot, pet giant, especially his dopey, moping face . . .''

©The Sunday Times, 1977.

Films in Review, February 1977 (p. 116)
William K. Everson

''. . . it is a *lot* better than we had a right to expect. The original property is treated with reverence, and there's a non-campy approach to the updating, some of which is quite intelligent. The arrival on the island is particularly well done, and the best sequence of all is original in this version: Kong going on a rampage in his ship-hold prison, and being calmed by the girl. This relatively unspectacular sequence also has some of the film's best art direction. And Jessica Lange, as the girl, is a delight—an unlikely but most winning combination of Marilyn Monroe and Grace Kelly, and giving a surprisingly

continued on next page

continued from previous page

relaxed performance for the first time out as an actress.

There, unfortunately, the purely plus factors end . . .

There's no doubt about it, if the original *Kong* didn't exist, this would be a well-above-average adventure yarn. But it does exist, and the best of the new *Kong*, including its score, owes its qualities to that original . . ."

©Films in Review, 1977.

Film, February 1977 (p. 12)
Peter Cargin

"In the new version of *King Kong*, Jeff Bridges could be the scientist character from *Jaws* who has wandered into another blockbuster and faces up to oil vulgarian Charles Grodin. The latter has told him the natives on the island will be glad to get rid of Kong, their forty-foot monkey God. He comments, 'Kong was the magic, the mystery, the terror in their lives. Without him they'll be a nation of helpless drunks within a year.' It could be someone reproaching Dino De Laurentiis for what he's done to movie enthusiasts . . .

The original *Kong* had its limitations as a feat of artistry or engineering. The playing was in a style that the movies had already abandoned by 1933 and the effects were often obvious or crude. However, nothing could take the edge off the fight on the top of the Empire State Building with the attacking biplanes . . . But there is no doubt that even with its limitations, the first film outclasses the remake . . ."

©Film 1977.

KINGS OF THE ROAD

Director, Screenplay, Producer: *Wim Wenders.* Photography: *Robbie Mueller, Martin Schaefer, Peter Przygodda.* Music: *Axel Linstadt.* Running time 176 minutes. New York opening October 3, 1976, at the New York Film Festival, Lincoln Center. Classification: None. Origin: West Germany.

Bruno: *Ruediger Vogler.* Robert: *Hanns Zischler.* Cashier: *Lisa Kreuzer.* Robert's Father: *Rudolph Schuendler.* Man Who Lost His Wife: *Marquard Bohm.*

New York Post, 10/5/76 (p. 51)
Archer Winsten

". . . an agonizingly long (176 minutes) semi-mute dialogue between two men in a bus. The bus owner and driver is Bruno (Ruediger Vogler), a mechanic who works on small-town movie projectors. The companion, Robert (Hanns Zischler), found when he drives his VW bug at high speed into a river, is eventually revealed as having left his wife in Genoa eight years ago. Typical of this picture, he is still suffering . . .

The main trouble with *Kings of the Road* is having to wait so long for the men to say something, even a little. They suspect they have been 'colonized' by the Americans, listening to American music and occasionally speaking English. It is, of course, a horrible fate, but not one this reviewer was willing to share. One must add that it is well photographed and very real in its very own, tedious way."

Reprinted by Permission of New York Post.
©1976, New York Post Corporation.

Christian Science Monitor, 10/22/76 (p. 27)
David Sterritt

"Wim Wenders' *Kings of the Road* is a slow three-hour ride down bumpy highways along the border between West and East Germany . . . it is largely about time—the audience shares in the boredom and lack of energy that plagues the main characters . . .

Though the film is almost devoid of female characters, Wenders has made it known the real subject is women—as they exist in the minds of the protagonists. We learn the men's attitudes gradually and indirectly, by watching the repairman avoid and the intellectual flee. It is a fascinating idea for a movie, boosted by striking, black-and-white photography and bluesy music.

One wonders, though, why everything has to happen so slowly, why the story is so diffuse . . ."

Reprinted by permission from The Christian
Science Monitor ©1976.
The Christian Science Publishing Society.
All rights reserved.

The Times (London), 2/18/77 (p. 11)
David Robinson

". . . It's not easy to convey the peculiar attraction of the film, which lies in Wenders' gift for highlighting the oddity of a chance roadside incident, and his ability to provide a landscape for his lost souls. The setting he has chosen—the dispirited lands along the East-West border; the wastes of sand dunes and quarries, with their abandoned and inexplicable industrial structures; above all the mausoleum world of once-prosperous cinemas now empty and dirty—seems a proper background for the spiritual disorientation of men in retreat, like Bruno and Robert . . .

. . . Wenders' view of his Germany is not an encouraging one."

©The Times, 1977

The Sunday Times (London), 2/20/77 (p. 38)
Alan Brien

"Towards the end of Wim Wenders' *Kings of the Road* . . . a small boy squats by the bus stop writing up a project in his exercise book. In the badlands of the border with East Germany, his task today is to record everything—the stones on the road, a paper floating by, a man with a black eye, the train speeding through the vacant landscape. It seems perhaps a metaphor for the film. Wenders is as laconic in his script as Chayefsky is prolix . . .

But at the end of our three hours, which could be a lifetime or ten seconds of an instant dream, all we have seen is gathered into meaning, sometimes too much meaning, overarticulated and superfluously symbolic. It is the sort of film a critic wants to write essays about, yet is best seen without any preconceptions . . ."

©The Sunday Times, 1977.

KNOTS

Director, Screenplay: *David I. Munro*. Based on the book by R. D. Laing and the play by Edward Petherbridge. Producer: *Simon Perry*. Photography: *Mike Berwick*. Editor: *Norman Wanstall*. Running time 62 minutes. Los Angeles opening April 25, 1976, at the Royal Theatre. Classification: None. Origin: Great Britain, 1975.

Players: *Caroline Blakiston, Paola Dionisotti, Sharon Duce, Edward Petherbridge, Robert Eddison, Tenniel Evans, Mark McManus, Robin Ellis, Matthew Long, Juan Moreno, Sheila Reid, R. D. Laing.*

Los Angeles Times, 4/23/76 (Pt. IV, p. 21)
Linda Gross

"The theatricality of life and the reality of make-believe are deftly demonstrated in *Knots* . . .

The film is an ingenuous enactment of the book by R. D. Laing, the psychiatrist who is spiritually in step with Sartre, Dostoevsky, Beckett and Lewis Carroll . . .

With wit and wisdom, the script by David Munro exposes the game playing, double entendres and absurdities inherent in everyday conversation. The Actors Company is an engaging ensemble which is remarkably able to mime, instruct and entertain. Particularly noteworthy in the troupe is the Laingian everyman (Matthew Long), a ventriloquist who ambivalently hates the woman he loves.

Director Munro skillfully translates Laing's sad relevance into a moving and revealing theatrical experience . . ."

© Los Angeles Times, 1976.

Monthly Film Bulletin, 7/75 (p. 156)
Verina Glaessner

"Based on the play devised from R. D. Laing's book *Knots* by Edward Petherbridge, a founder member of the Actors Company, David I. Munro's film explores a variety of double-bind situations through a series of verbal and logical 'knots' (Laing's term)—gnomic utterances which build into sharp mini-sketches. Far from indulging the kind of breast-and-brow-beating psychodrama of various recent filmic explorations of the 'new psychiatry,' Munro's film is restrained to the point of schematisation by the text itself, and is further helped by the Company's disciplined, brisk and precise performances. Inevitably, some sketches are more successful than others . . . Munro handles his difficult material fluidly and with some finesse . . . Laing himself is sighted from time to time presiding over events from the stalls, shrouded it seems more in self-satisfaction than in mystery."

© Monthly Film Bulletin, 1975.

Film, 9/75 (p. 3)
Variety de Toledo

"A bus drives slowly down the road; inside a dozen people silently look out of the windows, suddenly one of them starts speaking: the game has begun.

When the bus stops, it is in front of a stage door, the new play is opening the next day, but for the actors it is already happening . . .

The actors find themselves 'knotted' into their insidious game; exposed and more vulnerable but still protected by the amusing aspect of it.

Based on R.D. Laing's book, the show itself comes last in the film. It is by far the best part of it as the 'knots' are treated here in a light hearted, humorous way. The actors enjoy it and give a brilliant performance. The pace is fast, the sketches witty and the general mood remains ironical enough to give the whole a certain depth."

© Film 1975.

LAST HARD MEN, THE

Director: *Andrew V. McLaglen*. Screenplay: *Guerdon Trueblood*. From the novel by Brian Garfield. Producer: *William Belasco*. Photography: *Duke Callaghan*. Music: *Jerry Goldsmith*. Distributor: *Twentieth Century-Fox*. Running time 98 minutes. New York opening April, 1976, at several theatres. Classification: R.

Sam Burgade: *Charlton Heston*. Zach Provo: *James Coburn*. Susan Burgade: *Barbara Hershey*. Cesar Menendez: *Jorge Rivero*. Sheriff Noel Nye: *Michael Parks*.

Film Information, 6/76 (p. 2)
Paul Coleman

" . . . Heston remains the center of attention when he is on screen, as he has for twenty-five years. His performances in themselves offer little (his Oscar notwithstanding), but his features carry a solid dignity that no other actor achieves so effortlessly. Coburn becomes more animated as an actor each year, and the villainies of this characterization provide him with an ideal showcase. Notable in support are Michael Parks (the much touted successor to James Dean of a few years ago) as the laconic and ambivalent sheriff and Christopher Mitchum as the Harvard trained agriculturalist who helps Heston find his daughter. The music of Jerry Goldsmith . . . underlines the strong effect of the action.

The most essential difficulty with *The Last Hard Men* is the haphazard direction of Andrew V. McLaglen *(Shenandoah, Fool's Parade)* who has a penchant for padding his films with sweeping vistas when he could well profit by clarifying the action. Occasionally his symbolism is laughably obvious. None of these quirks is damaging in themselves, but as the film gathers momentum from its actors and the script, it loses the focus only a strong director can provide . . ."

© Film Information, 1976.

The Sunday Times (London), 6/20/76 (p. 37)
Dilys Powell

"*The Last Hard Men* . . . takes what has now become a fashionable theme, the end of the old romantic West, and sets a retired lawman (Charlton Heston) against an outlaw (James Coburn) just escaped with a party of cut-throats from Yuma jail . . .
. . . in the past decade or so an alien ferocity has taken the Western over. In fairness it must be said that Mr. Heston gives a very reasonable impersona-

tion of an agitated father—and that the film often looks beautiful, its sunny landscapes finely framed. But the Western is traditionally beautiful. The composition of its movement in space has given it great possibilities from the black-and-white days onwards, and for over thirty years now colour has added to what was always an aesthetic experience. But only Sam Peckinpah has been able, and he only rarely, to draw aesthetic satisfaction from the patterns of death. *The Last Hard Men* gives us just the savagery—rape, stabbing, the body plummeting down the cliff."

© The Sunday Times, 1976.

The Times (London), 6/18/76 (p. 9)
David Robinson

"*The Last Hard Men*, which like *The Human Factor* quotes the biblical tag of 'eye for eye, tooth for tooth,' has a more traditional, elementary and endemically reactionary context—untamed Arizona territory in the early century. James Coburn plays a half-breed killer whose excess of pearly white teeth have remarkably survived the rigours of train robbing and a spell in Yuma gaol, to be able to snarl and snarl again.
Breaking gaol with a group of other desperadoes, he sets out to wreak vengeance on the lawman who captured him and in the process accidentally killed his pregnant Indian wife . . . (no trick, you perceive, is missed: the official synopsis hastens primly to explain 'Heston deplores this tragic mishap') . . ."

© The Times, 1976

Monthly Film Bulletin, 8/76 (p. 166)
Richard Combs

" . . . McLaglen, predictably, no more has the temperament for a revenge Western than he does for graceful celebrations of the pioneer spirit or Fordian canvases. The action proceeds slackly from one set-piece shoot-up to the next, barely providing the voltage for the two leads to turn their stock roles into displays of star power: James Coburn is an effortlessly smooth and smirking villain, but his Indian parts seem to be missing, and Charlton Heston is more whiskery than usual, but otherwise his personification of the grizzled veteran is limited to a stiff delivery of a perfunctory script. For the most part, though, the acting does provide a kind of haphazard charm . . ."

© Monthly Film Bulletin, 1976.

LAST TYCOON, THE

Director: *Elia Kazan*. Screenplay: *Harold Pinter*. Based on the novel by F. Scott Fitzgerald. Producer: *Sam Spiegel*. Photography: *Victor Kemper*. Editor: *Richard Marks*. Music: *Maurice Jarre*. Distributor: *Paramount Pictures*. Running time 125 minutes. New York opening November 17, 1976, at the Cinema I Theatre. Classification: PG.

Monroe Stahr: *Robert De Niro*. Rodriguez: *Tony Curtis*. Pat Brady: *Robert Mitchum*. Didi: *Jeanne Moreau*. Brimmer: *Jack Nicholson*. Boxley: *Donald Pleasence*. Kathleen Moore: *Ingrid Boulting*. Fleishacker: *Ray Milland*. Red Ridingwood: *Dana Andrews*. Cecilia Brady: *Theresa Russell*. Wylie: *Peter Strauss*. Popolos: *Tige Andrews*. Marcus: *Morgan Farley*. Guide: *John Carradine*. Doctor: *Jeff Corey*. Stahr's Secretary: *Diane Shalet*. Seal Trainer: *Seymour Cassell*. Edna: *Angelica Huston*.

Saturday Review, 12/11/76 (p. 77)
Judith Crist

"There are, as filmmakers have demonstrated over the years, countless ways to kill a classic. *The Last Tycoon*, F. Scott Fitzgerald's unfinished Hollywood novel, has been killed with reverence.

This long-awaited, much-fanfared film arrives with almost awesome cachet: produced by Sam Spiegel, whose hallmark has been intelligence and taste; directed by Elia Kazan, a man of remarkable accomplishment on stage and screen; written by Harold Pinter, the British playwright, who has earned well-deserved praise for his work in film. And in the title role we have Robert De Niro, one of the most versatile of the newer stars. Among them, they have made a faithful, lavish, and bloodless transcription to film of Fitzgerald's literary fragment and reduced what has endured as an insightful study of a man and an industry into an insipid little love story . . ."

©Judith Crist, 1976.

Los Angeles Times, 11/18/76 (Pt. IV, p. 1)
Charles Champlin

". . . It was unusually important that *The Last Tycoon*, Fitzgerald's unfinished but superb Hollywood novel, should have been filmed very well. It is unusually disappointing and angering that it turns out to be such a swollen and tiresome mishmash.

It betrays at every turn an unfine mismating of adapter, director and material. Subtlety has never been Elia Kazan's style as a director. Bodies on meat hooks and unbridled lust amidst the chickweed, power and raw emotions displayed in the operatic and poster-colored film-making of an earlier time have characterized his most effective work. But Fitzgerald, all too clearly, demanded alternate or additional gifts . . .

Pinter's cryptic and measured silences are famous and they exist in *The Last Tycoon*, but now they are hollow, listless and inappropriate, as if neither Pinter nor anyone else could think of anything to say because they had nothing on their minds.

Robert De Niro as Monroe Stahr, Fitzgerald's Thalberg, tough and introspective, sensitive and headstrong, romantic and ruthless, is the movie's most successful element. He looks the part and delivers the man . . .''

©Los Angeles Times, 1976.

New York Post, 11/18/76 (p. 27)
Frank Rich

". . . *The Last Tycoon* . . . burrows right to the heart of the writer's last, uncompleted novel and spreads Fitzgerald's vision across the screen. It's a startling achievement.

Not that *The Last Tycoon* is a perfect film; it isn't. But it's relentlessly smart and uncompromising—so uncompromising that at first it's hard to know what to make of it. At this point we're so used to vulgarized adaptations that when the real thing comes along, it looks puzzling . . .

Elia Kazan, who directed the film and at last seems to be back in touch with his talent, has given the movie a look that is the visual equivalent to Pinter's script. *Tycoon* has the appropriate period detail, but the overall feel is one of spareness and loneliness . . .

The director also has the good fortune to have Robert De Niro as his star: As always, this actor is remarkable—he even convinces us of Stahr's New York/Jewish origins—and his performance embodies the entire film . . ."

Reprinted by Permission of New York Post.
©1976, New York Post Corporation.

Village Voice, 11/15/76 (p. 51)
Andrew Sarris

". . . In my capacity as a consumer consultant, I consider *The Last Tycoon* eminently worth supporting if we are to preserve a literate cinema in the English language.

At the very least, the combined talents of Elia

continued on next page

continued from previous page

Kazan, Harold Pinter and Robert De Niro can be credited with having brought Fitzgerald's Monroe Stahr to life (and imminent death) without defacing his portrait of the man. Much of the irony, subtlety, and ambiguity of the book finds its way into the movie, with none of the flagrant editorializing that characterized the recent version of *The Day of the Locust* and none of the fussy embalming of *The Great Gatsby* . . .

It is all De Niro's show, and Kazan's and Pinter's, as they transform *The Last Tycoon* into a sustained Hollywood hallucination. The audience is drawn into the spectacle by a modern frankness about moment-to-moment existence coupled with an absurdist elusiveness about ultimate meanings . . ."

Reprinted by permission of The Village Voice.
Copyright ©The Village Voice, Inc., 1976.

Newsweek, 11/22/76 (p. 108)
Jack Kroll

". . . It's an exceptionally well-made movie. But something is missing.

What's missing is a certain vital heat, an incandescent fusion of style and feeling, Fitzgerald's gallant pain and the graceful poignance of his reach to the stars. The movie has to round off both in character and action what Fitzgerald never lived to complete, and it doesn't quite do this. De Niro captures Fitzgerald's vivid sketch of Stahr—the street-smart Jewish kid from the Bronx who never went beyond a night-school course in stenography, a romantic, a practical businessman, a sleepless worker who's driving himself to death, a benevolent despot who's threatened by the new corporate Hollywood. But we don't feel the driving force of Stahr that catapulted him on his short, doomed flight over star-struck America . . .

Fitzgerald can tell us about this vision; the film has to show it to us, and it never quite does . . ."

©Newsweek, Inc. 1976
reprinted by permission.

Film Information, December 1976 (p. 2)
William F. Fore

". . . What turned the silk purse into a sow's ear? First, the purse itself leaves much to be desired. Fitzgerald's manuscript was only half completed when he died in 1940. His own notes indicate considerable dissatisfaction with it ('Chapter I: Has become stilted with rewriting. Rewrite from mood.') and he planned to cut several thousand words. Fully half of the novel remained to be written. Unfortunately, a good deal of the novel's own dialogue is used—which may account for some of the awkward moments on the screen. Furthermore, Fitzgerald chose to alternate between two different points-of-view, using both third person and first.

The second problem lies with the creative triumvirate . . . Between them, Kazan, Spiegel and Pinter allowed scenes from the book into the film which have no reason to be there. Conversely, they omitted elements in the book that are necessary to understanding the story. It is almost as if they assumed that the film audience had as much familiarity with the novel as they themselves had . . ."

©Film Information, 1976.

Women's Wear Daily, 11/15/76 (p. 18)
Howard Kissel

". . . Elia Kazan's direction is no less impressive than the screenplay. Kazan keeps the satiric elements of the work in check. He is not doing a period piece. He doesn't let production values run away with the picture. The stress is on human values. The honesty of the acting makes most of what I have seen and even liked in the last year seem conventional and superficial. Robert De Niro has everything Monroe Stahr had—authority, vulnerability—and a quiet sensuality. The scenes between him and Ingrid Boulting, who has a restrained English sexiness, have an electric charge. Robert Mitchum is in his very presence threatening, but he seems subdued here . . ."

©Women's Wear Daily, 1976.

New York Magazine, 11/29/76 (p. 70)
John Simon

"The movie version of Fitzgerald's *The Last Tycoon* is an honorable failure. Honorable because it tries to serve its version of the original faithfully; a failure because that vision falls considerably short of Fitzgerald's . . .

. . . Kazan has directed with a technical solidity his recent undertakings, like *The Arrangement* and *The Visitors*, had made me think he had lost. The camera is always in a suitable place; the occasional bravura touch does not stridently call attention to itself; and even Pinter's obligatory long and sinister silences are dealt with intelligently . . .
Even so, a pall of slowness enshrouds the movie.

Kazan also gets good work from a large cast . . .
. . . Robert De Niro's Stahr is perfection itself. Here is that terrible soft-spoken irresistibility of the steamroller that can gracefully and speedily convince its victims that flat is not only beautiful but also necessary . . ."

© 1976 by the NYM Corp. Reprinted with
the permission of NEW YORK Magazine.

Films in Review, December 1976 (p. 634)
DeWitt Bodeen

". . . Only occasionally . . . and thanks then to
director Elia Kazan's sympathetic interpretation,
does the picture come to life and glow with movie
magic. The love scenes, as acted by Robert De
Niro and the lovely Ingrid Boulting, are lyrical. Not
only is De Niro in top form as the luckless Stahr,
especially in the writers' conference scene, but
there is a stunning performance by Robert Mitchum,
beautifully cast against type as a hypocritical, ruthless mogul, and Jack Nicholson contributes an
arresting characterization as the rebellious, Commu-
nist-minded agitator. And there is also an unforgettable, almost entirely pantomimic cameo by
Morgan Farley, playing a very old Adolph Zukor-like
producer, so frail that he has to be carried in and
out of board meetings . . .

A fascinating film, *The Last Tycoon* commands
your attention and is one of this year's best from
Hollywood."

©Films in Review, 1976.

New Leader, 12/20/76 (p. 23)
Robert Asahina

". . . Unfortunately, this confluence of talents
has failed to create anything but a big-budget bore.
Recalling the MGM spectacles of the '30s, *The Last
Tycoon* reeks of 'quality,' of the best that money
can buy, yet in its failure reveals perhaps more
about Hollywood than the novel did.

What is missing most is the tragic scope of the
book. In part, this is the result of some spectacular
miscasting by Spiegel that seems to have been
motivated mostly by the desire to land big-name,
big-dollar stars, regardless of their suitability . . .

But Pinter, who also appears to have been hired
less for his skill than for his name, must bear most
of the blame for the perversion of Fitzgerald's intent . . ."

Reprinted with permission from
The New Leader, 1976.
© The American Labor Conference
on International Affairs, Inc.

Christian Science Monitor, 11/18/76 (p. 35)
David Sterritt

". . . Pinter and Fitzgerald make an odd couple
in any case, and it is interesting that their 'collaboration' on the movie version of *Tycoon* is for
the most part a resonant, provocative success . . .

. . . Happily, the talents involved in Paramount's
venture are major ones. Pinter is an expert at probing ambiguous depths of character, while director
Elia Kazan is an accomplished veteran of the movie
dream factory that Fitzgerald studied first-hand.
And the cast is a roster the tycoon himself could
have been proud of . . .

. . . Stahr is a potentially impressive and moving
hero. Though Pinter and Kazan treat him more as
a metaphor than as a breathing man, De Niro's
taste and skill make him seem real and reachable,
if rather more mysterious than necessary . . ."

Reprinted by permission from The Christian
Science Monitor © 1976.
The Christian Science Publishing Society.
All rights reserved.

Cineaste, Winter 1977 (p. 45)
Leonard Quart and Barbara Quart

"*The Last Tycoon* is a literate, intelligent, but uneven film, one which frequently strikes a chord of
deep romantic yearning while at other times it
seems almost embalmed, without any movement or
resonance . . .

The most profound ingredient in the romance and
the film is De Niro's performance, for he is able to
make his silences significant, drain every nuance
out of an emotion, and convey both the mythic and
finite Stahr. He makes Fitzgerald's concluding
aphorism to the novel's notes—'action is character'
—come alive, evoking a Stahr who can be under-
stood only through the sum of his movements and
choices, not through dialogue or exposition . . ."

©Cineaste, 1977.

The Times (London), 2/25/77 (p. 11)
David Robinson

". . . The film, in the end, has most of the weaknesses of the novel and not many of the excel-
lences. Rejecting Fitzgerald's own intentions for the
end (except to bring forward the ousting of Stahr, to
provide a neat finale), it still appears uncomfortably
as half a structure . . .

There is no visual charge to compensate for the
charge of Fitzgerald's exact and poetically weighted
words. Between the lines of dialogue, which Harold
Pinter leaves reverentially intact, you are only
aware of gaping spaces.

The sensation is not helped by the leading performances. Required to seem laconic and reserved,
Robert De Niro seems simply to have lost his ordinary interior energy. Ingrid Boulting plays with a
strange, sapped and zombie quality which has very
little to do with Fitzgerald's Kathleen . . ."

©The Times, 1977.

The Sunday Times (London), 2/27/77 (p. 35)
Alan Brien

". . . Fewer than a handful of players, all of them
male, emerge uncrushed from the weighty crassness of the exercise. Robert De Niro, the psychotic
avenger of *Taxi Driver*, is a brilliant Monroe Stahr,
the fighting cock whose comb is bloody but un-
bowed, his veins pumping 100-degree-proof charis-

continued on next page

continued from previous page

ma, a self-made artisto with the instincts of a street-brawler. Tony Curtis, whose own screen career has shown how to climb hand-over-hand from pretty boy to middle-aged character actor, turns in a concentrated, highly self-critical portrait of an Errol Flynn superstar with hardening arteries. And the film comes suddenly alive in a short, late scene between De Niro, movieland's feudal lord, and Jack Nicholson, the businesslike, Communist spokesman for the revolting serfs . . .

The Last Tycoon is an unintentional disaster movie, a Titanic vehicle which goes down with almost all hands, taking with it the reputations of director Kazan and scriptwriter Pinter, both of whom have been long overrated as filmmakers . . ."

©The Sunday Times, 1977.

LAST WOMAN, THE

Director: *Marco Ferreri*. Screenplay (French with English subtitles): *Mr. Ferreri, Rafael Azcona*. Producer: *Edmondo Amati*. Photography: *Luciano Tovoli*. Editor: *Enzo Menicone*. Music: *Philippe Sarde*. Production: *Productions Jacques Roitfeld* (Paris)—*Flaminia Produzioni* (Rome). Distributor: *Columbia Pictures*. Running time 111 minutes. New York opening June 6, 1976, at the Fine Arts Theatre. Classification: X. Origin: France.

Gérard: *Gérard Depardieu*. Valerie: *Ornella Muti*. Pierrot: *David Biffani*. Michel: *Michel Piccoli*. Rene: *Renato Salvatori*. Gabrielle: *Zouzou*. Benoite: *Giuliana Calandra*. Anne-Marie: *Carole Lepers*. Nathalie: *Nathalie Baye*. Michel's Friend: *Daniela Silverio*.

New York Post, 6/7/76 (p. 17)
Frank Rich

"*The Last Woman*, the new film by Marco Ferreri, the director of the dull but determinedly shocking *La Grande Bouffe*, is a very dull domestic drama in which an engineer (Gérard Depardieu, God forgive him) and his lover (Ornella Muti, a zombie) sit around in the nude, have sex and conduct an intellectually primitive debate about the evolving roles of men and women in a modern world. By the end, the hero realizes that his macho habits are socially obsolete, but rather than have his consciousness

raised he takes an electric carving knife and commits a graphically depicted act of self-castration.

Do you want to hear any more? No, I really don't think you do . . ."

Reprinted by Permission of New York Post.
© 1976, New York Post Corporation.

Newsweek, 6/14/76 (p. 90)
Jack Kroll

" . . . Ferreri may be the first filmmaker to have his mind destroyed by women's lib. His movie is about a young engineer (Gérard Depardieu) whose wife has left him with their year-old son. He shacks up with a girl (the supernally lovely Ornella Muti) who objects to his macho ways, and so in despair he—well, he does something that's as stupendously silly as it is shocking, something that's obviously bedeviled French male minds since Abelard was punished for loving Héloise. Libertarians will applaud the film's equal-time nudity for both sexes, but Ferreri's use of the adorable baby is close to exploitative."

© Newsweek, Inc. 1976
reprinted by permission.

New York Magazine, 6/21/76 (p. 74)
John Simon

" . . . whenever characters in a film have the same names as their portrayers (Gérard-Gérard Depardieu; Michel-Michel Piccoli; Nathalie-Nathalie Baye; Rene-Renato Salvatori), we should know that we are in for misery. For it means that the filmmakers could not even be bothered to imagine original names for their creatures, so little were they interested in conceiving genuine people. What they were after was merely a new, modish thrill and, of the few modish thrills still left over, they happened to seize on castration. It need not be in the least clear whether Gérard performs it to spite himself, Valerie, or women in general; or whether the act is to be viewed as a triumph or a defeat. Real people and convincing actions have long since become expendable; what is needed is a suggestive background of evil capitalism, idling factories, soulless high rises, men and women simultaneously at one another's genitals and throats, and oodles of suburban despair . . ."

© 1976 by the NYM Corp. Reprinted with
the permission of NEW YORK Magazine.

Cineaste, Winter 1977 (p. 40)
Cobbett Steinberg

"In much of Marco Ferreri's *The Last Woman*,

Gerard Depardieu—a horny, young engineer whose liberated wife has left him and their infant son— walks around his modern French apartment quite naked. After a night of particularly active sex, he applies medicine to his all-too-sore member and winces in pain. Bathing with his infant son, he playfully compares their bodies, delighted by the obvious differences. About to have sex with his latest mistress (wonderfully played by Ornella Muti), he turns in profile to show his proud erection.

The attention to Depardieu's body is more casual than sensational, and it's an important casualness in the history of film sexuality. It completely reverses all those other erotic movies in which an entire group of naked women are 'serviced' by a solitary man still wearing (nervously?) his undershorts and socks. In previous erotic films the camera promiscuously explored the feminine anatomy while modestly avoiding the masculine, but in *The Last Woman* men as well as women most definitely possess bodies.

It's an important change, more important than first thoughts might suggest . . ."

©Cineaste, 1977.

Film Information, July/August 1976 (p. 6)
Unsigned

"Several years ago Marco Ferreri directed the unappetizingly graphic *La Grande Bouffe*, the story of four bored men who decided to commit suicide by eating themselves to death. With *The Last Woman*, Ferreri proves he hasn't lost his ability to shock and disgust. Gerard Depardieu, promising actor from *Going Places* and *The Wonderful Crook*, gives an agonized, Brando-like performance as a man unable to understand the women in his life or to make a fulfilling commitment to a new woman who has moved in with him and the baby he adores. His lack of sensitivity increasingly alienates him from those around him, and eventually he is driven to commit a desperate, horrifying act. He castrates himself with an electric meat carver. Ferreri demonstrates that controversial climaxes cannot redeem a boring, vapid film . . ."

©Film Information, 1976.

Films in Review, August/September 1976 (p. 443)
Marsha McCreadie

"*The Last Woman*, directed by Marco Ferreri (*La Grande Bouffe*), is the latest, and one might hope, the last word in screen violence. The film's climax is what we remember, the hero's self-mutilation and castration. The apparent realism of this conclusion, accomplished by extraordinarily clever editing, is nearly too much to bear . . .

. . . *The Last Woman* means to raise provocative questions about individuals whose training allows them no place in a world of changing relations between men and women. But we're not interested in these characters: a young mistress (Ornella Muti) who does little but prettily pout her dissatisfaction; and a strutting, constantly nude hero. Surely there must be a more effective way of conveying the male ego than by showing protruding stomachs, beer-swilling, and bellowing . . .

. . . What may be the most compelling issue of our time—the reorganization of sexual roles—is glossed over to despair and sensationalism."

©Films in Review, 1976.

Monthly Film Bulletin, November 1976 (p. 237)
Jonathan Rosenbaum

". . . it is on the physical rather than the intellectual plane that the film achieves something; on the sheer tactile level of settings (plastic French suburbia in a high-rise wasteland) and characters (man, woman and child), it carries a raw assertiveness that is rare in modern cinema, a kind of candour whose ultimate expression can only perhaps be found in Pasolini's remarkable *Salo*. Ironically, this physicality in both films is permitted to exist only by assuming the form of a parable in a world defined by its isolation from the one we usually know: Gerard is significantly never seen at work, and the various time ellipses suggest that the narrative follows an inner logic not bound by the usual requirements of plot . . ."

©Monthly Film Bulletin, 1976.

The Sunday Times (London), 10/10/76 (p. 35)
Alan Brien

"With *The Last Woman* . . . we are again in a foreign country, the Land of Machismo, and among humans who behave like quite separate species, men and women. Or rather one man, several women, for this is a naked, close-up anatomy of a chauvinist pig driven to frenzy by the new breed of young females who seem to him to have turned from shrinking violets into Venus Flytraps . . .

Behind the sex, there is love, but behind that, hate, envy and fear. Even his devotion to his 13-month-old son is toward a part of his own body, temporarily cut off. *The Last Woman*, written by the director Marco Ferreri with Rafael Azcona, is not what is usually termed entertainment, more therapy perhaps than art, but a collector's piece for all that."

©The Sunday Times, 1976.

LATE SHOW, THE

Director, Screenplay: *Robert Benton.* Producer: *Robert Altman.* Photography: *Chuck Rosher.* Editors: *Lou Lombardo, Peter Appleton.* Music: *Ken Wannberg.* Distributor: *Warner Bros.* Running time 94 minutes. New York opening February 10, 1977, at the Sutton Theatre. Classification: PG.

Ira Wells: *Art Carney.* Margo: *Lily Tomlin.* Charlie Hatter: *Bill Macy.* Ron Birdwell: *Eugene Roche.* Laura Birdwell: *Joanna Cassidy.* Lamar: *John Considine.* Mrs. Schmidt: *Ruth Nelson.* Sergeant Dayton: *John Davey.* Harry Regan: *Howard Duff.*

Los Angeles Times, 2/25/77 (Pt. IV, p. 1)
Charles Champlin

". . . *The Late Show*, which Benton wrote and directed and Robert Altman produced, is an appreciation, a kind of rolling into one of the principal ingredients of all the private-eye flicks that ever played the Late Show (and the Morning, Noon, Matinee and Early Shows as well) . . .

An appreciation . . . an artful and affectionate original, lively and enjoyable on its own self-sufficient terms, which catches the spirit and reflects the structure of previous private-eye pleasures . . .

. . . For all its obvious and careful make-believe, *The Late Show* works, as the best of the private detective stories have always worked, because there is a vivid and sympathetic central character to root for.

Like Spade and Marlowe, Carney's Ira Wells is a man of honor, left battered and nearly broke by an indifferent and ungrateful world . . .

Lily Tomlin . . . creates a comical character but stops well short of being a grotesque and in the end generates a sympathy to match Carney's own . . ."

©Los Angeles Times, 1977.

Saturday Review, 3/19/77 (p. 41)
Judith Crist

". . . *The Late Show* is a tightly structured, over-plotted pastiche in the Hammet-Chandler private-eye tradition—but not one, alas, in a class with Altman's *The Long Goodbye*. Written and directed by Robert Benton, long teamed as a writer with David Newman (*Bonnie and Clyde, There was a Crooked Man, What's Up, Doc?, Bad Company*), it's the story of an aging detective . . . teamed up . . . with a very kooky young woman. Art Carney is the detective, and you are thereby guaranteed the total pleasure of his company as an ailing, irascible, decent, courageous, literal-minded man of no mean intelli-

gence. The very kooky young woman is Lily Tomlin, and you are thereby guaranteed some intermittent pleasures . . .

Benton has managed to encompass most of the plot cliches of the Spade-Marlowe-Archer action . . . But his direction, as noted in *Bad Company*, with which he made his directorial debut in 1972, is as uneven in tone as his script is in mood . . ."

©Judith Crist, 1977.

Nation, 3/12/77 (p. 315)
Robert Hatch

". . . I confess I enjoyed this exercise in innocent manslaughter. The script . . . involves adultery, stolen goods, blackmail and a cat that is being held as a hostage. It is not entirely plausible (for one thing, the police show a surprising lack of interest in the bodies pouring into the morgue), but that is somewhat offset by the fact that it is not entirely comprehensible, partly because the characters are of the sort who do not enunciate very clearly and partly because a considerable number of them are dead before the plot catches up with them. I find it difficult to keep the corpses straight in my mind; sprawled or economically packed away, they all look very much alike. But against these deficiencies, the moment-to-moment action is crisply staged, the villains are sufficiently repulsive that one can cheer their abrupt extinction with a good conscience and Carney plays the deceptively inoffensive nemesis as well as it has been done since Spencer Tracy stepped off the train at Black Rock . . ."

©The Nation, 1977.

Film Information, March 1977 (p. 3)
Robert E. A. Lee

". . . The best thing about *The Late Show* is its touches of local color revealing the unglamorous side of Hollywood—the dingy rooming houses, the garish motels, the laundromats and cheap bars.

The worst thing about *The Late Show* is its imposition of violence into the plot for the sake of 'decoration' instead of honest character development. Sometimes it pretends to be a comedy and at other times serious melodrama. It doesn't fit either category and it doesn't quite work as a standard 'whodunit' either . . .

But the characters do give us some insight into lonely people and the hesitancy or eagerness of their reaching out for new relationships. Art Carney is excellent . . .

Lily Tomlin . . . is convincing as an inane and freaky female whose need for activity gets fulfilled when she can team up with a private eye . . ."

©Film Information, 1977.

New York Magazine, 2/14/77 (p. 66)
John Simon

". . . Lily Tomlin, whom I have never previously liked, is totally winning as an absurd, aging hippie with solid instincts well hidden under layers of bizarre clothing, parlance and behavior; there is also first-rate supporting work from Bill Macy, Eugene Roche, and Ruth Nelson. Only Joanna Cassidy continues to be a washout. And then there is Art Carney. This basic nonactor tries very hard, and manages to avoid obvious errors, but still fails to convince me. It may be that he is a little too successful at being as common as dirt even while he thinks he is charmingly matter-of-fact; whatever it is, Carney always makes me feel slightly unclean just watching him. Chuck Rosher's cinematography is unimpressive, but the art direction and set direction make up for what it lacks. If only this entire genre, complete with its own brand of nostalgia, did not strike me as hopelessly juvenile!"

© 1977 by the NYM Corp. Reprinted with
the permission of NEW YORK Magazine.

Take One, March 1977 (p. 9)
James Monaco

". . . *The Late Show* isn't really about revenge, double crosses and figuring out whodunit. It's about Ira and Margo. It's not a romance, really . . . it's more of an essay in lifestyles. That the thirty-year-old actress/agent/dress designer/fence's helper/dealer/psychoanalysand develops such a strong feeling for the sixty-year-old macho/loner private eye is honestly moving. Carney and Tomlin make it so . . .

Margo and Ira would be enough by themselves to make *The Late Show* a landmark of sorts, but they're not alone. They are surrounded by a carefully crafted group of supporting characters . . .

These . . . actors work together as if they'd been playing ensemble for years, and much of the pleasure of *The Late Show* is due to their precisely calculated performances: every gesture is perfect, every line delivered with genius, the choices are inspired. In the background you can hear the true electric hum of talent. But the ultimate success of *The Late Show* depends on Benton's overall conception. He knows where we've been, he knows where we are, and he has a lot that's true to say about the connection between the two . . ."

© Take One, 1977.

New Leader, 3/14/77 (p. 23)
Robert Asahina

". . . director Benton's self-indulgent hommage is at least partially foiled by writer Benton's straightforward thriller: We are quickly plunged into a vintage mystery. Wells' old pal, Harry Regan (Howard Duff), arrives with a .45-caliber bullet lodged in his gut, and dies before revealing the name of his killer . . .

The most complex characters, however, the two

leads, are the least well played. The part of Margo —the self-dramatizing has-been actress, would-be dress designer, part-time drug dealer, and full-time nonstop talker—would be a plum for any talented actress. But Tomlin does not so much act as impersonate, a throwback to her shtick from the "Laugh-In" days. Superficially vivid as her performance is, it

Art Carney (top), Lily Tomlin, and Bill Macy star in **The Late Show**, a tribute to great old private-eye flicks.

lacks any real conviction. One need only contrast it with her work in *Nashville* . . .

As for Ira Wells, while Carney—a careful and competent actor—tries hard, he is just not equal to the task . . . his characterization, like Tomlin's, is almost wholly external . . ."

Reprinted with permission from
The New Leader, 1977.
© The American Labor Conference
on International Affairs, Inc.

Newsweek, 2/21/77 (p. 88)
Jack Kroll

". . . *The Late Show* is Benton's second film as a director. It doesn't have the touch of pretentiousness that [Alan Rudolph's] *Welcome to L.A.* does but it's not quite as satisfying. You don't believe it when Carney beats up Considine or when Tomlin outdrives the bad guys in a car chase. Benton and

continued on next page

continued from previous page

Rudolph are smart, sophisticated types who are still focusing their visions. But Rudolph is an out-and-out esthete, and it's safer that way—if you grasp form, you'll grasp some kind of truth . . . Benton wants to be both hip and straight. Both celebrating and satirizing Ira and Margo as a tattered rear guard of honor, his movie fuzzes its fun—it's a thriller that's not quite a thriller, a comedy that's not really a comedy. Carney and Tomlin are fine performers, but they get caught in this double bind . . .''

©Newsweek, Inc. 1977
reprinted by permission.

New York Post, 2/11/77 (p. 24)
Frank Rich

''. . . *The Late Show* just doesn't resonate as much as it should; it never gives us enough of its characters because the writing is too doggedly tied to the detective genre's conventions. The film's directorial style is too meticulous as well, and yet, on its own terms, it's perfectly executed: The squalid settings stink of decay, the spare pacing captures the tough style of Hammett prose, and the stylized use of blood puts some sting into murder.

The director also has assembled a superb supporting cast—but the movie really belongs to Tomlin's Margo and Carney's Ira. When this woman who could 'never play the Hollywood game' gets together with the tired detective who's made a career of playing that game 'by the hard rules,' *The Late Show* rises above its apocalyptic title and deathly pallor to give us an original and invigorating slice of life.''

Reprinted by Permission of New York Post.
© 1977, New York Post Corporation.

Christian Science Monitor, 1/16/77 (p. 22)
David Sterritt

''. . . Hollywood borrows its ancient characters and conventions right back again, spiking them with some '70s-style violence while mellowing the stew with a humane performance by the gifted Art Carney. The result might have been ordinary and old-fashioned but for Carney's continual presence, coupled and counterbalanced with the mordant wit of writer-director Robert Benton . . .

It's an odd mix of characters, each strangely out of kilter, yet given depth and conviction by the actors on hand: Lily Tomlin as the partner, talented Eugene Roche as the crook, Bill Macy (far outdoing his Walter role on TV's ''Maude'') as the friend, Joanna Cassidy as the wife, and others. In their mouths even the script's satirical dialogue rings true —as with the villain's endless bribes of name-brand suits and stereos, or the wife's delicate admission that her endless lies have been 'untruths' . . .''

Reprinted by permission from The Christian
Science Monitor © 1977.
The Christian Science Monitor Publishing Society.
All rights reserved.

Village Voice, 2/21/77 (p. 47)
Andrew Sarris

''. . . My own feeling is that *The Late Show* is a very good movie in which the lyricism prevails over the drama. It will never supplant the teeming '40s classics that inspired it, but people made more movies in those days, made them quicker, and allowed more margin for error. By contrast, Benton has had to walk a tightrope over an abyss of posturing nostalgia and asshole paranoia. It is so hard to make a good little picture in this age of colossal claptrap that Benton's own efforts strike me as heroically dedicated. But he could never have pulled it off if Carney, and particularly Tomlin, had not performed above and beyond the call of duty. Consequently, *The Late Show* glows with the good spirits of a fun movie felt from within.''

Reprinted by permission of The Village Voice.
Copyright © The Village Voice, Inc., 1977.

Women's Wear Daily, 2/8/77 (p. 18)
Howard Kissel

''*The Late Show*, a low-key comedy about a semi-retired private eye and an aging faddist solving a crime with his skills and her highly developed instincts, has the warm, relaxed, somewhat melancholy spirit of '40s jazz.

Robert Benton, who wrote and directed the film, has a wonderful feeling for offbeat characters. What makes gumshoe pictures continually attractive are their portraits of people on the seamy fringes of society . . . The most interesting of the characters in *The Late Show* is the detective's former partner, pretty much of a louse, whose eye for 'the angle' in everything is sometimes helpful, sometimes dangerous. The part is played beautifully by Bill Macy.

As the detective, Art Carney gracefully combines weariness, disillusion and underlying strength. Lily Tomlin is properly annoying as his spaced-out colleague. Ruth Nelson as his landlady is an evocation of all the innocence and charm of Southern California before the freeway era.''

©Women's Wear Daily, 1977.

LE MAGNIFIQUE

Director: *Philippe De Broca*. Screenplay (French with English subtitles): *Mr. De Broca*. Producers: *Alexandre Mnouchkine, Georges Dancigers*. Photography: *Maurice Chapiron*. Music: *Thomas Sosa*. Production: *Les Films Ariane*. Distributor: *Cine III*. Running time 86 minutes. New York opening July 7, 1976, at the Fine Arts Theatre. Classification: None. Origin: France.

Bob St. Claire, Francois Merlin: *Jean-Paul Belmondo*. Tatiana Christine: *Jacqueline Bisset*. Karpof Charron: *Vittorio Capriolo*.

New York Post, 7/8/76 (p. 13)
Frank Rich

". . . *Le Magnifique*, the new De Broca film . . . is, like the director's 1963 *That Man From Rio*, a James Bond spoof with Jean-Paul Belmondo in the central role; as you might imagine, it is as tired and irrelevant as its predecessor was fresh and timely . . .

The only genuine energy in *Le Magnifique* comes from the performers. Jacqueline Bisset, who plays the woman in both St. Claire and Merlin's lives, is so beautiful that she can blind you to any movie's inadequacies for at least the first 15 minutes she's on screen. The same applies to Belmondo's charm: The actor has no less energy than he did in his last collaboration with De Broca and he plays superhero St. Claire . . . with such irrepressible relish that you almost feel guilty that you're not having as much fun with *Le Magnifique* as he is."

Reprinted by Permission of New York Post.
©1976, New York Post Corporation.

Christian Science Monitor, 7/30/76 (p. 22)
David Sterritt

"Philippe De Broca's latest farce, *Le Magnifique*, manages to take off both *Jaws* and *La Dolce Vita* within the first couple of minutes. Then the going really gets crazy, as hero Bob St. Claire races against time, danger and his own sanity to defeat various villains and win (every time) the pretty girl.

But wait. Bob St. Claire isn't Bob St. Claire at all. He is the fantasy, the alter ego, the secret Mitty of a miserable French author named Merlin . . .

Le Magnifique bounces back and forth between this poor guy's harassed day-to-day and the rich adventures of his make-believe counterpart (both played with might and main by Jean-Paul Belmondo). The hinge is the girl upstairs, the gorgeous sociology major (Jacqueline Bisset) who enters the author's life to study his dreadful novels, becomes willy-nilly the object of Bob St. Claire's imaginary affections and saves the day by loving our protagonist . . .

We expect fun and romance from the filmmaker who gave us *Cartouche* and *That Man From Rio* and *King of Hearts*, and *Le Magnifique* has plenty of both . . ."

Reprinted by permission from The Christian
Science Monitor © 1976.
The Christian Science Publishing Society.
All rights reserved.

Village Voice, 8/23/76 (p. 117)
Michael McKegney

"The protagonist of Philippe De Broca's new film *Le Magnifique* is a self-confessed hack writer of '42 potboilers with five or six good pages in each.' As Francois Merlin, Jean-Paul Belmondo cranks out sexy superspy fantasies about an alter ego named Bob St. Claire (also Jean-Paul Belmondo), which he visualizes as some poor French cousin of E. Howard Hunt. Reality keeps breaking in on fantasy, of course, but only intermittently, and De Broca switches back and forth between reality and fantasy with a succession of devices which flaunt their cleverness only to reveal their clumsiness, and which recall less the spirit of Bunuel than the spirit of Danny Kaye . . .

. . . De Broca's justification-by-surrogate of his own career won't wash, and we get not even one good minute in this witless and washed-out parody of Bondery . . ."

Reprinted by permission of the Village Voice.
Copyright © The Village Voice, Inc., 1976.

New York Magazine, 7/19/76 (p. 88)
John Simon

". . . This current take-off on James Bond movies . . . is bestially stupid, most humorless when brutishly reaching out after cheap laughs, as obvious as anything devised by a five-year-old lover of the worst kinds of movies. And though its gore is meant to be farcical it is explicitly and viciously gory enough to make the movie unsuitable even for the small, unbright children it seems intended for.

Jean-Paul Belmondo, the hitherto always at least desirable Jacqueline Bisset, and the previously no less oafish Vittorio Capriolo play the leading parts as badly as they deserve to be played. If your choice is, say, between *Le Magnifique* and the bubonic plague, you'd do better with the plague."

©1976 by the NYM Corp. Reprinted with
the permission of NEW YORK Magazine.

Los Angeles Times, 3/2/77 (Pt. IV, p. 12)
Kevin Thomas

". . . Written by Francis Veber (who had his name taken off the picture because he felt too many liberties had been taken with his script), *Le Magnifique* is as light as a souffle, and De Broca never allows it to fall flat. Indeed, De Broca's graceful, buoyant direction and Belmondo's engaging, energetic virtuosity sustain the film through some very thin sections.

continued on next page

continued from previous page

As both the comically heroic St. Claire and the seedy, wistful Merlin, Belmondo exudes an unfailing charm, and he is well-matched by Miss Bisset, equally irresistible as either Christine or Tatiana. Possibly *Le Magnifique* may be saying something about the role of fantasy, both good and bad, in our lives but above all it is good escapist fun . . .''

©Los Angeles Times, 1977.

LEADBELLY

Director: *Gordon Parks*. Screenplay: *Ernest Kinoy*. Producer: *Marc Merson*. Executive Producer: *David Frost*. Photography: *Bruce Surtees*. Editor: *Harry Howard*. Music: *Fred Karlin*. Leadbelly vocals: *HiTide Harris*. Distributor: *Paramount Pictures*. Running time 126 minutes. New York opening May 28, 1976, at Loews State 2 and Loews Cine Theatres. Classification: PG.

Huddie Ledbetter: *Roger E. Mosley*. John Lomax: *James E. Broadhead*. Tom Pruitt: *John McDonald*. Guard: *Leonard Wrentz*. Margaret Judd: *Dana Manno*. Wes Ledbetter: *Paul Benjamin*. Sally Ledbetter: *Lynn Hamilton*. Miss Eula: *Madge Sinclair*. Gray Man: *Timothy Pickard*. Blind Lemon Jefferson: *Art Evans*. Gov. Pat Neff: *John Henry Faulk*.

Women's Wear Daily, 5/28/76 (p. 8)
Christopher Sharp

'' . . . *Leadbelly* portrays the black experience against a rural setting. Parks absorbs his central character into a colorful fabric of country scenes. It is possible to see in this cinematography how the poetry within the landscape of the Deep South could be translated into the Leadbelly music. As we hear some of the music and the lyrics against the backdrop of Parks' scenes, we feel assured that the genesis of Leadbelly's inspiration has been detected.

Roger Mosley plays Leadbelly in a physical manner. He draws out an intuitive intelligence that seems to be equally distributed across his muscular body. Leadbelly wrote some of his best songs while he was serving a prison term for murder, and in this film we see how the desire for perfection in both chain-gang chores and composition enhanced his survival. The final scene deals with

Leadbelly breaking rocks on his chain gang and declaring, 'You're not going to break my spirit.' Parks has prefaced this last note so poetically that it comes to us as a revelation. It is a beautiful film that has been built on a simple foundation.''

© Women's Wear Daily, 1976.

The Sunday Times (London), 6/6/76 (p. 36)
Dilys Powell

'' . . . in spite of a shape in general conventional, the film is adventurous. It is about one of the celebrated Black folksingers, and the role is played by an unfamiliar actor, Roger E. Mosley. The director is Black, the production crew from assistant directors to stunt coordinator are Black. It's true a few white players appear. There are the penitentiary guards, displaying the cruelty with which the cinema has acquainted us; but the others, dressed in pale, washed out white, are made to look distinctly wan . . .

. . . one must be content with a decently played biographical musical. Mr. Mosely doesn't give us a particularly endearing Leadbelly, but the performance is convincing and powerful. The blending of songs with action is notably skillful; these really are work-songs, travel-songs, the authentic Blues . . . I should like to point also to the playing, controlled and sorrowful, of Paul Benjamin as the father, and to the myopic submarine appearance of Art Evans as Blind Lemon Jefferson.''

© The Sunday Times, 1976.

The Times (London), 6/4/76 (p. 9)
David Robinson

'' . . . As a black folk hero, Leadbelly has remained a somewhat equivocal figure. On the one hand he represented an incorruptibly pure strain of black music, and as a human being survived incredible hardships with monumental physical fortitude and spiritual resistance intact. At the same time, his life story as long-time convict, brothel singer, bar-room gambler, brawler, and two time murderer was an image which made black people uneasy . . .

Made by Gordon Parks, a black director whose own personal recollection of Leadbelly's era contributes to the impressive period feeling of the film, *Leadbelly* elevates the hero, but does rather less than justice to the man. Covering the period from 1907 to 1932, it is a very sanitized account of Leadbelly's convict years. Noble and innocent, he is seen purely as the victim of Southern racism. The two murders are forced upon him. Even the songs, performed by HiTide Harris, have been robbed of the gritty strength of Leadbelly's own original recordings. It is a tribute to Roger E. Mosley's performance that something of a human being still survives all the disinfection.''

© The Times, 1976.

New York Magazine, 6/14/76 (p. 66)
John Simon

''In *Leadbelly*, Gordon Parks tries to tell the story of the black singer who spent years of his life on Southern chain gangs in a way that is one part moralizing primer for black children, and one part unpleasant facts transmuted into striking pictures for white coffee-table books. It is calculated . . . to disturb without upsetting, which means that the protagonist's seamy side must be prettified, and suffering must be represented in artfully staged images, as if it were Washington Crossing the Delaware. There must always be reaction shots of black faces in picturesque groupings, and whenever possible, misty out-of-focus landscapes or sunsets turning the world into a place inhabited solely by blood oranges. I admire Parks' purpose and his fight to get the film made and exhibited, but I can react to the actual movie only with polite uninvolvement.''

© 1976 by the NYM Corp. Reprinted with the permission of NEW YORK Magazine

Los Angeles Times, 4/28/76 (Pt. IV, p. 1)
Charles Champlin

'' . . . Gordon Parks, the *Life* photographer turned film-maker (*The Learning Tree, Shaft*), has used Leadbelly's spoken autobiography as the basis for a vivid entertainment, a melodrama rich with music and with the feeling of a folk myth. The emotions, laughter included, come through loud and clear.

Leadbelly was larger than life; that's the way he saw himself, that's the way he told it and that's the way it happens in Ernest Kinoy's fast-moving script . . .

The performances are strong and affecting with special honors to Mosley and newcomer Art Evans, Loretta Greene as a woman who knows better than to hope big and Madge Sinclair as the madam in good times and poor.

The events have a folk-tale quality, primary and powerful, because Parks lets us see them in the spirit Leadbelly told them . . . ''

© Los Angeles Times, 1976.

Saturday Review, 5/29/76 (p. 48)
Judith Crist

''Good intentions and good music are the hallmarks of *Leadbelly*, Gordon Parks' biography of the great folksinger. The film is intended as an inspiring story of a man who, confident of his artistry, found himself and his individuality in a chaingang world of savage injustice and eventually attained freedom to pass on a brilliant musical heritage before his death in 1949. As such, with an intelligent script by Ernest Kinoy based on what material is available, and with a handsome production saturated in the Louisiana-Texas locales, it details the picaresque young manhood and sobering maturity of the musician in engrossing terms. Better yet . . . the film is filled with music. The Leadbelly classics . . . pour forth in charm and glory . . .''

© Judith Crist, 1976.

Newsweek, 4/19/76 (p. 95)
Katrine Ames

'' . . . In spite of rich raw material, both factual and fanciful, the movie falls a little flat. It moves, but never jumps; what's missing is the sort of energy that might have been supplied by James Earl Jones, who was originally scheduled to play the title role. Ernest Kinoy's screenplay is only adequate. Director Gordon Parks gets good but not memorable performances from his actors, and though he concentrates on what should be the film's greatest asset, the music, he fails to do it justice. Leadbelly's guitar sounds as if it's hitched up to a rock-concert amplifier. HiTide Harris, who does the vocal behind Mosley's engaging manner, does fine with the high pitched 'Green Corn,' but misses on 'Goodnight Irene' and other classics. Visually, the movie is magnificent: Parks and cinematographer Bruce Surtees capture the look and feel of the old rural South . . . ''

© Newsweek, Inc. 1976 reprinted by permission.

Film Information, 4/76 (p. 4)
Annette Samuels

''The light of the sun temporarily blinds you. Music, movement, life are captured momentarily. Soft and romantic, tinged with violence, Gordon Parks' latest film, *Leadbelly*, is another testament to the talents of the renowned photographer turned director. But the film doesn't quite measure up to the excitement, anger, pride and lust for life that the Black folk singer, Huddie 'Leadbelly' Ledbetter exhibited during his lifetime.

Gordon Parks, a man who has learned to control his anger, or better yet, to subdue it, has directed a film that says more about his ability to adjust to a harsh world of racism than about his protagonist's inability to do so . . .

Leadbelly is not a heartrending film, nor is it par-

continued on next page

continued from previous page

ticularly exciting. But the film is worth seeing, if for no other reason than to hear the music of Leadbelly . . . "

© Film Information, 1976.

Christian Science Monitor, 2/5/76 (p. 23)
David Sterritt

" . . . His real name was Huddie Ledbetter, and he was both a singer and a killer. Notorious for his mercurial moods, he spent years in prison as a convicted murderer. Loved by millions for his songs––now hard-hitting, now lyrical––and for his diesel-whistle delivery, he spent the latter part of his life in concert halls and recording studios, establishing himself as one of America's great natural artists. He was a contradictory man, but uniquely gifted . . .

Director Parks seems to feel deeply about the movie and its themes. Though the first half moves too jumpily, undercutting its own leisurely atmosphere, the plot and images mesh smoothly most of the way, creating a warm and credible portrait of a genuinely mythical personality. Aimed at amateurs rather than folky purists, and easily transcending racial barriers, *Leadbelly* is a meaningful achievement despite the slick celluloid surfaces that don't quite jibe with the rough-styled Leadbelly spirit."

Reprinted by permission from The Christian Science Monitor © 1976. The Christian Science Publishing Society. All rights reserved.

Films in Review, 1/76 (p. 56)
Michael Buckley

"Superbly directed . . . written . . . and photographed . . ., *Leadbelly* is the nickname for and story of Huddie Ledbetter, whose legacy of memorable songs (including *Goodnight Irene*, *Cotton Fields at Home*, *Rock Island Line*) belied his lack of education and many years on a chain gang. Told in flashback, it ends six months prior to his final release from prison (in '34, fifteen years before his death): and much of the music is sung over the action.

In the title role, Roger E. Mosley gives an impressive first starring performance (with vocals dubbed by HiTide Harris) . . .

Most audiences should respond favorably to this study of a man's survival through his art."

© Films in Review, 1976.

New York Post, 5/29/76 (p. 17)
Archer Winsten

" . . . To put it bluntly, this is a remarkable and true story, acted by a cast that is notably better than that found in most such black films, and directed by Gordon Parks with a knowledge, feeling and restraint that represents a distinct step up for him. I am referring specifically to the immense dignity of Huddie's mother (Lynn Hamilton) and father (Paul Benjamin), or the women in Huddie's life, or the white prison guards. There is an absence of caricature in the latter, or sentimental exaggeration in the former Gordon Parks, working with complete knowledge, is not lured into missteps of too much or too little.

The key, of course, is the casting of Roger E. Mosley, a muscular comparative unknown, in the Ledbetter role. He is wholly convincing in both extremes of his rare character, the singer and the fighter . . ."

Reprinted by Permission of New York Post. © 1976, New York Post Corporation.

Monthly Film Bulletin, 7/76 (p. 149)
Michael Grossbard

" . . . a stiff and lifeless portrait of the black blues singer, with Roger E. Mosley too soft-looking, and his arrogantly puckered face too pretty, for the swashbuckling braggart who learnt the blues the hard way—breaking rocks. Leadbelly's life does indeed have mythological proportions, and his influence is vast. The songs used here to punctuate the drama with rhythm and verve are among the finest popular poetry of our century; they are, as Leadbelly says, himself. Unfortunately, they are rendered in an adequate but less than inspired fashion by HiTide Harris, while the film as a whole seems to have little sense of the idiom and style of the songs—and the black way of life they express—as the cultural antithesis of everything white. Art Evans as Blind Lemon Jefferson perhaps gets closest to a feeling for this kind of jive . . ."

©Monthly Film Bulletin, 1976.

LEGACY

Director: *Karen Arthur.* Screenplay: *Joan Hotchkis.* Producer: *Ms. Arthur.* Photography: *John Bailey.* Editor: *Carol Littleton.* Music: *Roger Kellaway.* Original stage production directed by *Eric Morris.* Running time 90 minutes. Los Angeles opening November 8, 1975, at the Los Feliz Theatre. Classification: None.

Players: *Joan Hotchkis, George McDaniel, Dixie Lee, Sean Allen, Richard Bradford III, Sarah Hotchkis.*

See Volume 1 for additional reviews

Film, 5/76 (p. 4)
Lesley Robinson

"This sombre film chronicles a day in the life of a middle aged American housewife, Bissie Hapgood. On this particular day her husband is away on a business trip, her three children are at camp and she is left alone with enough time on her hands to indulge in reminiscences which leave her in a state of near hysteria . . .

Karen Arthur's debut as a director does little to further the cause of women's lib, and Bissie Hapgood, with her affluent life style and morbid self-preoccupation, doesn't elicit very much sympathy, either. However, the film is saved by Joan Hotchkis' performance—a tour de force by any standards . . ."

© Film 1976.

Film Information, 5/76 (p. 5)
Bea Rothenbeuchner

" . . . During the course of one day, an upper-middle-class matron reveals her life--present and past--through stream-of-consciousness exposition and flashbacks. A brief morning visit to her senile mother conjures up ugly thoughts of old age, her own; indecision about the table setting for a planned dinner party brings on near hysteria; a lazy afternoon bath in a sunken tub provokes masturbation. Shown to be living in a *House Beautiful* environment where even the teacups match the pastel flowered upholstery, dependent on her psychiatrist for guidance in her daily life, sexually unfulfilled-- apparently because of her husband's insensitivity-- this self-absorbed woman appears to be suffering from a form of alienation not unlike that depicted in *A Woman Under the Influence*. Then suddenly, at day's end, she is shown to be insane . . . not just disturbed, but totally mad in a way that is unconvincing in terms of her previous actions. This is a serious flaw in a film that provides interesting insights into women's sexuality.

The direction is competent and the cinematography by John Bailey is appropriately lush . . ."

© Film Information, 1976.

New York Post, 5/3/76 (p. 22)
Frank Rich

"If a movie is going to devote its entire length to a rambling monologue by a single character, that character had better be a hell of a lot more fascinating than the neurotic Beverly Hills housewife who dominates *Legacy* . . .

When she isn't overdoing it for the camera, Miss Hotchkis suggests that she may be a better actress than she is a screenwriter. Miss Arthur, who uses percolating music, zoom shots and primitive flashbacks to underscore the movie's heavy dramatic moments, has no discernible talent at all--unless sheer gall counts as such. If I were she, I'd be embarrassed to death to have made a film that says less about the plight of the American housewife in 90 minutes of phony emotional fireworks than TV's *Mary Hartman* does in two minutes of throw-away jokes."

Reprinted by Permission of New York Post.
© 1976, New York Post Corporation.

Women's Wear Daily, 5/3/76 (p. 18)
Howard Kissel

"*Legacy*, a film about an upper-class woman going mad, was first performed as a play by Joan Hotchkis, who wrote the film and stars in it. If *Legacy* were a monologue on the order of Ruth Draper's one could regard it as a theater piece and admire its opportunities for an actress to hold the stage with pantomime and skillful movement. As a film, however, since our minds are not busy *imagining*, we have to concentrate on the *ideas*, which are, in fact, nothing more than the usual dreary recital of Woman's Grievances . . .

The film, produced and directed by Karen Arthur, is well made, and Hotchkis' performance has a ring of shrill authenticity. But it is hard to look at *Legacy* as anything but a *movement* film and an unsympathetic one at that."

© Women's Wear Daily, 1976.

Christian Science Monitor, 5/12/76 (p. 29)
David Sterritt

"A vivid, energetic, and introspective performance by Joan Hotchkis dominates every frame of the dark drama called *Legacy* . . .

Legacy was developed as a theatrical monologue, and theatricality becomes its major flaw in Miss Arthur's screen version. A voice-over narration would have presented its own problems, but cinematic credibility is shaken by a character who mutters obsessively to herself for 90 minutes and shrieks through closed doors to other people never glimpsed by the cameras.

Still, Miss Arthur has lent a unique visual dimension to her film by literally hazing the images as her protagonist sinks farther into depersonalized desperation, and both filmmakers deserve credit for laboring sincerely under obvious and amazing limitations of time and budget. Their *Legacy* is a troubled and troubling document."

Reprinted by permission from the Christian
Science Monitor © 1976.
The Christian Science Publishing Society.
All rights reserved.

LES ZOZOS

Director, Editor: *Pascal Thomas*. Screenplay (French with English subtitles): *Roland Duval, Mr. Thomas*. Producer: *Albina du Boisrouvray*. Photography: *Colin Mounier*. Music: *Vladimir Cosma*. Distributor: *Bauer International*. Running time 105 minutes. New York opening March 24, 1977, at the Jean Renoir Cinema. Classification: None. Origin: France, 1972.

Frederic: *Frederic Duru*. Francois: *Edmond Railard*. Paringaux: *Jean-Marc Chollet*. Venue: *Jean-Claude Antezack*. Uncle Jacques: *Daniel Ceccaldi*. Elisabeth: *Annie Cole*. Martine: *Verginie Thevenet*. Nelly: *Caroline.Cartier*. Jacqueline: *Michele Andre*. French Teacher: *Serge Rousseau*. Vice Principal: *Jacques Debary*.

New York Post, 3/25/77 (p. 36)
Archer Winsten

"*Les Zozos* . . . is the first film in which the new young French film director, Pascal Thomas, sets about exploring adolescent sex among schoolboys and girls. That was 1972, and he chose 1960 as the period to be inspected. The current Algerian war was making little impression on these youths who studied little, resisted the disciplines of their teachers and spent most of their leisure moments planning seductions or lying about successes they'd never had . . .

Thomas and Roland Duval wrote the screenplay, and Thomas himself displays complete ease in handling the hesitations of young men and women together in their first semi-serious relationships . . .

. . . a minor picture of very perfect elements, thoroughly entertaining for those who can view the natural frustrations of inexperience without the impatience of those who have been there before and don't want to return."

Reprinted by Permission of New York Post.
© 1977, New York Post Corporation.

LET'S DO IT AGAIN

Director: *Sidney Poitier*. Screenplay: *Richard Wesley*. From a story by *Timothy March*. Producer: *Melville Tucker*. Photography: *Donald M. Morgan*. Music: *Curtis Mayfield*. Distributor: *Warner Bros*. Running time 110 minutes. New York opening October 6, 1975, at several theatres. Classification: PG.

Clyde Williams: *Sidney Poitier*. Billy Foster: *Bill Cosby*. Biggie Smalls: *Calvin Lockhart*. Kansas City Mack: *John Amos*. Beth Foster: *Denise Nicholas*. Elder Johnson: *Ossie Davis*. Bootney Farnsworth: *Jimmie Walker*. Dee Dee Williams: *Lee Chamberlin*.

See Volume 1 for additional reviews

Monthly Film Bulletin, 8/76 (p. 166)
Jonathan Rosenbaum

"Despite a frankly nonsensical plot full of formula antics and an unnecessarily protracted running time, *Let's Do It Again* is a healthy reminder of the relative energy and talent to be found nowadays in the so-called 'black exploitation' film . . . Modestly directing himself as a straight man for much of the time, Sidney Poitier gives most of the show over to the ebullient Bill Cosby, and the latter takes every advantage of the opportunity . . . Poitier for the most part keeps things moving lightly on the strength of his enjoyable cast, with a nicely handled chase thrown in for good measure. But a few happy moments are occasionally offered by lines in Richard Wesley's script . . ."

©Monthly Film Bulletin, 1976

LET'S TALK ABOUT MEN

Director, Screenplay: *Lina Wertmuller*. Producer: *Pietro Notarianni*. Photography: *Ennio Guarnieri*. Music: *Louis Enriquez Bacalov*. Distributor: *Allied Artists*. Running time 93 minutes. New York opening August 4, 1976, at Loews Tower East. Classification: PG. Origin: Italy.

The Man: *Nino Manfredi*. The Wife (in each episode): *Luciana Paluzzi, Milena Vukotic, Margaret Lee, Patrizia de Clara*.

Women's Wear Daily, 8/2/76 (p. 9)
Howard Kissel

". . . The release of one of Lina Wertmuller's earliest films, *Let's Talk About Men*, gives one insights into what her strengths are and how they have been spoiled in her transition from simple filmmaker to philosopher. *Let's Talk About Men* is simply a collection of four anecdotes about selfish, dishonest, arrogant husbands.

The vignettes center on obvious ironies. In one, a wealthy man scolds his wife for stealing her friends' jewelry—she does it quite innocently out of boredom. But when his fortunes are reversed he pretends to be the butler and phones her friends to urge them to wear their best pieces for dinner at his house the next night . . .

All these ideas are broad. They are acted superbly by a cast headed by Nino Manfredi, who plays all the men. The sketches work partly because they are short, partly because they are abstract. We learn just enough about the characters to find them funny . . .

Let's Talk gives us a marvelous look at Wertmuller's gifts as a comic writer. What has happened in the intervening years is that she has become a spokesman for the point of view of wealthy Northern Italians, who seem to be flirting with radical chic the way we did some years back . . ."

©Women's Wear Daily, 1976.

Village Voice, 9/27/76 (p. 107)
Andrew Sarris

"Some of Lina Wertmuller's admirers (and she is admired more in America than anywhere else) have complained that it is bad form to release her bad early films and thus discredit her overrated later ones . . .

Actually, *Let's Talk About Men* is consistent with her later work in its obviousness, clumsiness, shrillness, and garrulousness. The only interesting episode in this multi-episode mish-mash is the one which parodies Fellini's *La Strada* but the premise of even this skit is superior to its execution . . .

. . . I have seen many of these skit films, and Wertmuller's is clearly one of the weakest. Her male star, Nino Manfredi, has been brilliant with other directors; here he is barely passable . . ."

Reprinted by permission of The Village Voice.
Copyright © The Village Voice, Inc., 1976.

New York Post, 8/5/76 (p. 18)
Frank Rich

". . . simply and unequivocally awful.
Let's Talk About Men cannot, however, be held against Miss Wertmuller too strenuously. She made the film—in black and white and on a seemingly tacky budget, in 1965—well before she found herself artistically and directed the movies that are responsible for her currently lofty reputation. My guess is that she finds this film every bit as embarrassing as those audiences who have the misfortune to sit through it—but, happily, the embarrassment will be short-lived. Once the word-of-mouth starts to spread, *Let's Talk About Men* will beat a hasty retreat back into the can from which it has so unceremoniously sprung . . .

. . . In *Let's Talk About Men*, the sexual and class conflicts that are Miss Wertmuller's stock-in-trade are dealt with at the most primitive intellectual level imaginable, and there's nothing else in the movie to hold on to . . ."

Reprinted by Permission of New York Post.
©1976, New York Post Corporation.

Film Information, 9/76 (p. 4)
Bea Rothenbeuchner

". . . Made in 1965, in black-and-white, with sets that appear to be furnished with left-overs from a tag sale, *Men* is obviously a low-budget production. But it is not without interest. Whatever it may lack in cinematic style it makes up for by showing signs of the keen wit and sense of urgency that mark Ms. Wertmuller's later works.

Nino Manfredi plays the lead in four stories, vignette form, all dealing with man's debasement of women . . . True, Ms. Wertmuller revels in exaggeration when dealing with relationships between the sexes and here the results are at times ludicrous . . ."

©Film Information, 1976.

Christian Science Monitor, 8/12/76 (p. 22)
David Sterritt

". . . Unfortunately, a flatness spoils much of *Let's Talk*. There is little Wertmuller energy in the story of 'a good man' who stumbles through a useless peasant existence with no notice of his wife's unfailing work and worry. Neither the 'man of honor' nor his odd spouse wins much laughter or sympathy.

Yet there are foreshadowings of future Wertmuller savagery in the vignette about a 'superior man' who dresses his wife in degrading costumes and puts her through the stages of a murder plot (shades of Pasqualino in *Seven Beauties*) that backfires on everyone in turn. And bittersweet echoes of Fellini's *La Strada* waft through the 'old knife thrower' episode in which a male chauvinist literally destroys the woman who loves him—but not until the screen has filled with sad-lovely images of two lovers joining in a mutually destructive romantic fantasy . . ."

Reprinted by permission from The Christian
Science Monitor © 1976.
The Christian Science Publishing Society.
All rights reserved.

Saturday Review, 9/18/76 (p. 41)
Judith Crist

". . . There are flashes of Wertmuller's wit and ample evidence of her saving grace—humor and humanism save her from the man-hating sump of libbers—in seeing clearly the stupid, vapid, near-neurotic, and cowlike women who accept their status. But Manfredi and the four attractive women

continued on next page

continued from previous page

assigned to him are so self-consciously cute in each of their roles, and Wertmuller's directorial concept so similar in each episode, that the bits and pieces of a burgeoning talent and its potential are hard to find under the cumulative didacticism and monotony. But they are there for seekers."

©Judith Crist, 1976

Los Angeles Times, 8/25/76 (Pt. IV, p. 1)
Charles Champlin

". . . *Let's Talk About Men* is in black and white, which is curiously exciting to see—and curiously credible—in our color-saturated later days. Ennio Guarnieri was the photographer of the shifting moods and Louis Enriquez Bacalov's music, circus-flavored at start and finish, has an edgy and ironic flavor well-matched to Ms. Wertmuller's lacerating *Talk* about the hypocrisy, arrogant pride, assertive chauvinism and more generalized incompetence and uselessness of men.

It is enough to make a chap demand a recount.

This 1965 work was obviously done on a tight budget with limited physical resources, but admirers or students of the later Wertmuller *Seven Beauties* et al. will be fascinated to see these early evidences of her social concerns and attitudes, her ability to generate emotional power and her skill as a story teller and provoker of performances . . ."

©Los Angeles Times, 1976.

New York Magazine, 8/23/76 (p. 61)
John Simon

"There is not much to be said for Lina Wertmuller's decade-old *Let's Talk About Men* beyond that it shows a playwright and stage director making her uneasy transition to film (when have four unrelated episodes, perfectly acceptable as one-act plays, ever come together into a good movie?), and that it contains some of the themes and devices that Wertmuller was to elaborate into such efficacious cinema later on. There is racy acting from Nino Manfredi, occasionally verging on excess; and there are pleasant flashes of wit, as when a bankrupt husband tells his spoiled wife who bravely announces that they can be happy in a garret, 'All you know about garrets is what you saw in a production of *La Boheme* by Zeffirelli.' . . ."

©1976 by the NYM Corp. Reprinted with the permission of NEW YORK Magazine.

Cineaste, Winter 1977 (p. 48)
David Bartholemew

". . . Despite its thematic strengths and accom-

plished acting, *Let's Talk About Men* is a disappointment. Only the last story, with some notion of applying camera movement and mis-en-scene to theme, looks ahead to the sleek styling of later Wertmuller. The stories are all set bound, talky and roughly edited; later, Wertmuller will be able, perhaps with more time and money at her disposal, to begin to conceptualize her ideas in strongly visual terms and cutting rhythms. The last story in the film is evidence that Wertmuller's talent needs only the shaping of experience.

Seen in retrospect, this early film remains one of Wertmuller's most pessimistic expressions of her constantly warring individuals, played out with little hope of appeasement or understanding on a grid of sex, politics, tradition and economics. Unlike in the later films, the lines of good and evil are split along surprisingly morbid sexual boundaries alone . . ."

©Cineaste, 1977.

LIES MY FATHER TOLD ME

Director: *Jan Kadar.* Screenplay: *Ted Allan.* From a story by *Mr. Allan.* Producers: *Anthony Bedrich, Harry Gulkin.* Photography: *Paul van der Linden.* Editors: *Edward Beyer, Richard Marks.* Music: *Sol Kaplan.* Distributor: *Columbia Pictures.* Running time 103 minutes. New York opening October 12, 1975, at the Paris Theatre. Classification: None. Origin: Canada.

Grandfather: *Yossi Yadin.* Father: *Len Birman.* Mother: *Marilyn Lightstone.* David: *Jeffrey Lynas.* Mr. Baumgarten: *Ted Allan.* Mrs. Tannenbaum: *Barbara Chilcott.* Mrs. Bondy: *Mignon Elkins.* Uncle Benny: *Henry Gamer.* Edna: *Carole Lazare.* Cleo: *Cleo Paskal.*

See Volume 1 for additional reviews

The Sunday Times (London), 5/9/76 (p. 35)
Dilys Powell

" . . . The setting is Montreal in the 1920's, the characters are an immigrant Jewish family; Jeffrey Lynas plays a little boy whose allegiance is to the idealistic old grandfather who drives a rag-and-bone cart rather than to the father who wants to belong to the go-ahead modern world and dreams of making a fortune from indestructible trouser-creases.

Nowadays all child players are resourceful; the boy shows vivacity as well as resource. There is a performance of some sensibility by Marilyn Lightstone as the mother, and as the grandfather, Yossi Yadin, benignly dispensing fairytale wisdom, does all that could possibly be asked of such a role. There are occasional knots of good sense in the dialogue; there are one or two jokes in the narrative; the attitude towards the old white cart-horse is decently humane. But the whimsicality which even in *The Shop on the High Street* creeps into Kadar's work is pervasive here. I find the film too cosy for comfort."

© The Sunday Times, 1976.

The Times (London), 5/7/76 (p. 9)
David Robinson

" . . . This is sentiment by numbers, given in a Jewish ghetto in Montreal in the Twenties; a lovable child awakening to discovery of the world; a lovable, whimsical old grandfather; a lovable ne'er-do-well father; a lovable, long-suffering mother; a lovable broken down horse; lovable neighbours; a lovable whore across the way. It all strives so hard to be lovable that you want to scream, not least when lovable old granddad suddenly takes off into a lovable Fiddler-on-the-Roof-type musical number, or reappears, persistent to the last, as a sepia ghost. It was directed by Jan Kadar, one of that group of Czech exiles in the New World which includes Milos Forman and Ivan Passer. Kadar was half of the team of Kadar and Klos which made the admired and prize-winning *The Shop on the High Street*."

© The Times, 1976.

LIFEGUARD

Director: *Daniel Petrie*. Screenplay: *Ron Koslow*. Producer: *Ron Silverman*. Photography: *Ralph Woolsey*. Editor: *Argyle Nelson, Jr*. Music: *Dale Menten*. Songs: *Paul Williams*. Distributor: *Paramount Pictures*. Running time 96 minutes. New York opening July 23, 1976, at several theatres. Classification: PG.

Rick: *Sam Elliott* Cathy: *Anne Archer*. Larry: *Stephen Young*. Chris: *Parker Stevenson*. Wendy: *Kathleen Quinlan*. Machine Gun: *Steve Burns*. Tina: *Sharon Weber*. Mrs. Carlson: *Lenka Peterson*. Mr. Carlson: *George D. Wallace*.

Christian Science Monitor, 8/9/76 (p. 23)
David Sterritt

". . . Daniel Petrie directed this quintessentially Californian minicomedy about a man in his mid-30s who refuses to leave his beach-bound way of life, despite his friend's offer to put him in the money as a car dealer and despite his parents' puzzlement over what he'll do when he 'grows up.'

A lot of emphasis is put on his sex life, and some of the language is as salty as the Pacific. In terms of intelligence, the movie as a whole is no deeper than a drainage ditch. But the water looks wonderful, there are some nicely empathetic touches in the most joyless class-reunion scene of the year, and a solemn-faced actress named Kathleen Quinlan gives a refreshing performance. Sam Elliott and Anne Archer head the cast, competently."

Reprinted by permission from The Christian Science Monitor © 1976. The Christian Science Publishing Society. All rights reserved.

New York Post, 7/24/76 (p. 15)
Frank Rich

". . . the funny thing about *Lifeguard* is that you don't want to see what's beneath its fog, even if you could. Screenwriter Ron Koslow establishes Rick's growing malaise by marshalling a series of dramatic moments so mechanical, predictable, and interchangeable that you never believe the character exists; it's as if the writer were taking his hero through a mathematical equation rather than a traumatic change of life . . .

Petrie also has the annoying habit of hyping each of the script's self-conscious curtain lines by dissolving into a shot of the sea and flooding the soundtrack with some remorseful music (by Paul Williams) that sounds like a cross-fertilization between the Carpenters and the Beach Boys. After a while, *Lifeguard*'s misty seaside imagery becomes so thick that you feel as if you're getting salt water up your nose . . ."

Reprinted by Permission of New York Post. ©1976, New York Post Corporation.

Newsweek, 8/2/76 (p. 78)
Janet Maslin

". . . *Lifeguard* is photographed in the manner of a low-budget travelogue and padded with truisms on the order of: 'Only place joggin's gonna getya is right back where you started.' But the film is also extremely well acted by a cast of little-known players who deserve to go on to better things. As Rick, Sam Elliott is loaded not only with muscles, but charm, which he lays on as thickly—and protectively—as Sea & Ski. As his former sweetheart, Anne Archer is relaxed and attractive, and as a lifeguard-in-

continued on next page

continued from previous page

training, Parker Stevenson has a particularly winning moment when he can't bring himself to reprimand a flasher because the man looks like his father. But *Lifeguard*'s real discovery is Kathleen Quinlan as a sweetly flirtatious piece of jail bait who knows how to capitalize on Rick's devotion to the line of beach duty. 'I want to make love with you,' she murmurs to him in one of the film's few dramatic moments. 'I've wanted to ever since you bandaged my finger.' "

©Newsweek, Inc. 1976
reprinted by permission.

Film Information, July/August 1976 (p. 6)
Unsigned

". . . a cut above the usual beach movie we've been seeing for the past fifteen years. An over-30 lifeguard has to come to a decision about his future. Should he succumb to family and social pressures and become a Porsche salesman, or should he continue his carefree existence as a lifeguard? What's wrong with being a lifeguard the rest of your life is the touchy question the film asks. Viewers may be divided about the outcome, but the film doesn't cop out or leave the question unanswered. Sam Elliott is physically perfect as the unsure lifeguard, and Kathleen Quinlan is appealing in her film debut as a teenager who falls in love with him. Director Daniel Petrie has a sure touch, and he gives us an authentic, colorful look at the Southern California beach scene."

©Film Information, 1976.

New York Magazine, 8/16/76 (p. 61)
John Simon

". . . Ron Koslow, whose scriptwriting debut this is, spent his adolescent summers on the beaches of Southern California, then five further, presumably adult, 'hanging around with ocean lovers and [Los Angeles] lifeguards,' and the results seem to be this movie and water on the brain. The humorless persistence with which he worries his hero's existential dilemma makes me wonder whether the movie isn't more Kierkegaard than *Lifeguard*. It is, at any rate, studded with inadvertently uproarious lines . . .

Daniel Petrie has directed with veteran shlockiness, Ralph Woolsey's camera work is irritatingly picturesque or moodily washed-out, and the performances are unremarkable except for that of Sam Elliott as the protagonist. Elliot is so perfect as a befuddled beach Galahad, all mustache and suntan, as to make me worry about whether he could play any other part at all . . ."

©1976 by the NYM Corp. Reprinted with
the permission of NEW YORK Magazine.

Monthly Film Bulletin, 8/76 (p. 167)
Peter Markham

". . . The choice between accruing wealth as a car salesman and remaining comfortably affluent as a lifeguard is a peculiarly diluted and nondescript crisis . . . generally the comedy seems complacent rather than corrosive, consisting of tired double entendres and stock shots of married men eyeing lovelies. Rick's rebellion itself is as inoffensive as the antics of the dapper old man who 'flashes' at sunbathing females, and flounders in a disconnected plot, a profusion of minor characters . . . who remain on the level of makeshift caricature, and a prosaic visual texture that removes all mystery from the sea at which the hero continually gazes."

©Monthly Film Bulletin, 1976.

Jump Cut, Winter 1977 (p. 1)
Ernest Larsen

". . . Middle-class teenagers are fated to act out their parents' values or their reaction to them in the same arena in which they attempt to define their sexuality. In *Lifeguard*, as in life, both values and sexuality appear as limits rather than possibilities. The "Beach Party" pictures depicted the agonies of the double standard in their blandest form. *Lifeguard* spices the action, but the double standard still operates as the social merger of sexual expression and bourgeois values. In the heyday of Doris Day we knew the way Annette was supposed to behave, and luckily (for the sanctity of Annette's 'reputation'), so did Annette. Popularizers of the sexual revolution have encouraged us to believe that things have changed. More significantly, the advent of the feminist movement demonstrated the necessity for change.

The message of *Lifeguard* is that the more things change, the more they stay the same . . ."

©Jump Cut, 1977.

LINDA LOVELACE FOR PRESIDENT

Director: *Claudio Guzman.* Screenplay: *Jack S. Margolis.* Producers: *David Winters and Charles Stroud.* Photography: *Robert Birchall.* Editor: *Richard Greer.* Production: *J. J. Ltd.* Distributor: *General Film Corporation.* Running time 83 minutes. Los Angeles opening September, 1975, at several theatres. Classification: R.

Players: *Linda Lovelace, Fuddie Bagley, Val Bisoglio, Jack De Leon, Mickey Dolenz, and Joey Forman.*

See Volume 1 for additional reviews

Monthly Film Bulletin, 8/76 (p. 167)
John Pym

"A barrage of racial insults and relentless double entendres will not, one assumes, compensate British patrons for their disappointment at seeing Linda Lovelace, in the first of her films to be released here, perform no more than three simulated acts of sexual intercourse. Although occasionally brightened by moments of supreme bad taste . . . Jack Margolis' screenplay generally works on a level of witless contrivance which confines the players to back-slapping caricature. The tedium of this indulgent prankishness is unalleviated even by the curiosity value of Ms. Lovelace's exuberant unwholesomeness."

©Monthly Film Bulletin, 1976.

LIPSTICK

Director: *Lamont Johnson.* Screenplay: *David Rayfiel.* Producer: *Freddie Fields.*
Photography: *Bill Butler.* Editor: *Marion Rothman.* Music: *Michel Polnareff.* Production: *Dino De Laurentiis.* Distributor: *Paramount Pictures.* Running time 90 minutes. New York opening April 2, 1976, at Loews State 2 and Loews Cine Theatres. Classification: R.

Chris McCormick: *Margaux Hemingway.*
Carla Bondi: *Anne Bancroft.* Gordon Stuart: *Chris Sarandon.* Steve Edison: *Perry King.* Nathan Cartright: *Robin Gammell.* Martin McCormick: *John Bennett Perry.* Kathy McCormick: *Mariel Hemingway.* Francesco: *Francesco.* Sister Margaret: *Meg Wylie.* Sister Monica: *Inga Swenson.*

See Volume 1 for additional reviews

The Times (London), 7/9/76 (p. 9)
David Robinson

"The credits of *Lipstick* acknowledge the assistance of a number of solemn social organizations. That should not fool anyone into giving much credence to the pretensions, as an essay on the legal implications of rape, of this sleek and sleazy exploitation of the beauty-and-the-beast theme. The victim is a glamorous and provocative photographic model; the rapist is a nice-mannered young music teacher . . .
Lamont Johnson directs this with all the brio of a television commercial. The principal actors are Chris Sarandon (the transvestite in *Dog Day Afternoon*) and Margaux Hemingway, granddaughter of Ernest. Her sibilants are defective, but the film amply reveals compensating assets. Her real-life sister Mariel, who plays her sister in the film, is a better actress though."

©The Times, 1976.

Films in Review, June/July 1976 (p. 378)
Marsha McCreadie

"*Lipstick* is every bit as lurid and obvious as its advertising campaign. Though the movie cries out against rape (and who's for it?) the real message is the sensationalistic use of Margaux Hemingway (model, pop personality, and Ernest's granddaughter) as the glamorous victim.
Director Lamont Johnson makes shameless use of the Hemingway connection . . .
The only twist in *Lipstick*'s otherwise banal plot is that the rapist (efficiently played by Chris Sarandon) is, unaccountably, a new music aficionado. There are good performances by Anne Bancroft as a feminist lawyer, and by young Mariel Hemingway 'playing' sister to Margaux: the acting talents of the heroine haven't yet emerged.
One of *Lipstick*'s points is that voyeurism encourages senseless crime, but it unfortunately ignores its own lesson."

©Films in Review, 1976.

Monthly Film Bulletin, 8/76 (p. 168)
Caroline Lewis

". . . never develops beyond a clumsy presentation of how sex becomes just one more commodity in a consumer society, how the lure of rape is pervasive, and how, when it occurs, the woman can be held responsible for her role as temptress, and the man acquitted for being male enough to respond sexually. In the process, the film converts what could have been informed advocacy into an unconvincing hard-sell campaign against the way American society treats the crime, and constructs a sociological montage which seems as contrived as

continued on next page

continued from previous page

the world of cosmetics advertising . . . Margaux Hemingway's real-life sister Mariel is the only actor who makes any headway against the stilted script . . ."

©Monthly Film Bulletin, 1976.

New York Magazine, 4/26/76 (p. 73)
John Simon

"*Lipstick* is a meretricious shocker based on a California case in which a woman shot the man who raped her. Any intelligent discussion of rape and its consequences would, of course, be very welcome, but this movie, aside from various other exploitative atrocities, has the victim's kid sister raped by the same man later on to justify big sister's shooting him dead. This cravenly evades the principal issue, besides being an excuse for further cheap thrills. Margaux Hemingway is good on the eye, terrible on the ear, and somewhere in between as a performer, but her real-life little sister, Mariel, is a genuine find. Lamont Johnson has directed flashily; Bill Butler has photographed sometimes brilliantly, sometimes only splashily; and there is a trashy score by Michel Polnareff that violates your sensibility . . ."

© 1976 by the NYM Corp. Reprinted with the permission of NEW YORK Magazine.

Village Voice, 4/26/76 (p. 149)
Molly Haskell

" . . . Here the solid talents of Lamont Johnson, a coolly energetic director whose association with films *a these* (*The Execution of Private Slovik*) has mistakenly won him identification as a socially conscious director, can do little to salvage *Lipstick* from its untalented star, and a screenplay (by David Rayfiel) that is a muddle of motives and metaphors, pretending--but not too hard--to be concerned with the problem of rape while exploiting to the hilt its sensationalism.

Margaux plays a high-fashion model . . .

Johnson does what he can with her, which is to say he does without her whenever possible, cutting away from her when the script will permit. But occasionally she must speak . . .

Chris Sarandon brings a slimy attractiveness to the role of Gordon Stuart, music teacher and electronic composer who comes calling with his tape and stays to rape . . ."

Reprinted by permission of The Village Voice. Copyright © The Village Voice, Inc., 1976.

Film Information, 5/76 (p. 3)
David Bartholemew

"A dog in sheep's clothing, *Lipstick* is doubly irritating in that it piously purports to study women in contemporary society and deal with a deeply rooted social/criminal problem in rape. However, it is clear almost immediately that the filmmakers are more interested in the grimy joys of genre thrills than in serious examination of the important issue they flippantly play around with . . .

Supermodel Margaux Hemingway plays a supermodel who is raped. As an actress, she is a disaster; she has no voice, does not move well, has eyebrows like two advancing caterpillars, and should have seen an orthodontist many years ago. Her younger sister Mariel plays the supermodel's younger sister, who is also raped by the same crazed cartoonish villain (Chris Sarandon), all of which leads to a *Death Wish*-y revenge finale. Mariel walks away with the movie in a difficult role.

This sordid enterprise traps some talented people, including Sarandon, Anne Bancroft, and director Lamont Johnson."

© Film Information, 1976.

Ms., 7/76 (p. 39)
Marjorie Rosen

" . . . despite claims that the film's producers consulted with the National Organization for the Prevention of Rape and Assault and the Rape Squads of the Los Angeles and New York Police Departments, *Lipstick*, essentially a vigilante film on the order of *Death Wish*, manages to play up the complexity of the rapist and to shortchange the trauma of the victims . . .

. . . Apparently, this tale of an adult woman's sexual violation was not judged compelling, weighty, or horrifying enough in itself by the movie's producer, Freddie Fields, director Lamont Johnson, and screenwriter David Rayfiel. Rather than show us how the experience *really* affected Chris or her impressionable younger sister, Kathy (Mariel Hemingway), they've chosen to make Chris' rape the prelude to the *real* injustice, the *real* violation --child-rape. And so Kathy is ravaged by the same music teacher only days after this busy man is acquitted for crimes against her sister . . .

Imbalancing the film even further is the fact that Sarandon's Gordon Stuart is the best-written, most complex and interesting character in the film. And Sarandon is a consummate actor playing against amateurs--sisters Margaux and Mariel Hemingway . . . "

© Ms., 1976.

LITTLE SERPENT

Director: *Yoshihiro Kawasaki.* Screenplay (Japanese with English subtitles): *Toshiro Ide, Makire Aoi.* Based on a novel by Yasuko Harada. Photography: *Hiroshi Murai.* Editor: *Sachiko Yamachi.* Music: *Shiroichi Mashino.* Distributor: *Toho.* Running time 90 minutes. Los Angeles opening January 1977 at the Kokusai. Classification: None. Origin: Japan.

Players: *Kumiko Akiyoshi, Mitsuko Kusabue, Makoto Miyata, Takenori Murano, Tatsuya Nakadai, Ko Nishimura, Ken Tanaka.*

Los Angeles Times, 1/14/77 (Pt. IV, p. 19)
Kevin Thomas

". . . Adapted by Toshiro Ide and Makire Aoi from a novel by Yasuko Harada, *Little Serpent* is strongly literary in flavor, indulging in a lot of symbolism involving swans, especially dead ones. Directed by Yoshihiro Kawasaki—this is only his second feature —this lushly photographed Toho release is very much a young man's film, as revealed in its unrelieved solemnity in dealing with grand passions. But Kawasaki has a strong cinematic flair and a sure way with actors that suggests he may be embarking on an important career.

What ensues is terrifically familiar but expressed with a redeeming eloquence . . .

Nakadai and Miss Kusabue are among the most distinguished players in Japanese films, and they emerge as figures of sympathy and dignity . . ."

©Los Angeles Times, 1977.

LITTLEST HORSE THIEVES, THE

Director: *Charles Jarrott.* Screenplay: *Rosemary Anne Sisson.* Based on a story by Burt Kennedy and Ms. Sisson. Producer: *Ron Miller.* Photography: *Paul Beeson.* Editor: *Richard Marden.* Music: *Ron Goodwin.* Production: *Walt Disney.* Distributor: *Buena Vista Distribution Company.* Running time 104 minutes. New York opening March 31, 1977, at the Radio City Music Hall. Classification: G.

Lord Harrogate: *Alastair Sim.* Mr. Sandman: *Peter Barkworth.* Luke: *Maurice Colbourne.* Violet: *Susan Tebbs.* Miss Coutts: *Geraldine*

McEwan. Dave Sadler: *Andrew Harrison.* Tommy Sadler: *Benjie Bolgar.* Alice: *Chloe Franks.* Mrs. Sandman: *Prunella Scales.* Bert: *Joe Gladwin.* Carter: *Leslie Sands.*

Los Angeles Times, 3/31/77 (Pt. IV, p. 16)
Charles Champlin

"Despite a slightly syrupy title which hints of a Shirley Temple remake, *The Littlest Horse Thieves* is by several lengths the best movie to carry the Disney label in years . . .

. . . this tale of pit ponies in a Yorkshire coal mine in 1909 and of the children who try to save them is fresh, ambitious, richly atmospheric, beautifully photographed with a naturalism which is quite different from the well-lit make-believes of the Burbank studio product, and sensitively acted by a generally unfamiliar but gifted cast . . .

The movie, in fact, joins that still relatively small body of classic family literature of the screen which both engrosses and entertains, reasserts the civilized virtues, and opens the mind to distant lands and lives . . ."

©Los Angeles Times, 1977.

LOGAN'S RUN

Director: *Michael Anderson.* Screenplay: *David Zelag Goodman.* Based on the novel by William F. Nolan and George Clayton Johnson. Producer: *Saul David.* Photography: *Ernest Laszlo.* Editor: *Bob Wyman.* Music: *Jerry Goldsmith.* Production: *Metro-Goldwyn-Mayer.* Distributor: *United Artists.* Running time 120 minutes. New York opening June 23, 1976, at the Loews Astor Plaza and Loews Orpheum Theatres. Classification: PG.

Logan: *Michael York.* Francis: *Richard Jordan.* Jessica: *Jenny Agutter.* Box: *Roscoe Lee Browne.* Holly: *Farrah Fawcett-Majors.* Doc: *Michael Anderson, Jr.* Old Man: *Peter Ustinov.*

Women's Wear Daily, 6/22/76 (p. 17)
Howard Kissel

" . . . The nightmare world described in a new, intriguing science fiction, *Logan's Run*, is one built

continued on next page

continued from previous page

on our obsession with age. It is a world where all one's physical and sensual needs are supplied gratis. The only drawback is that one seems to have no choice but to die and disintegrate at 30. *Logan's Run* describes the flight of Michael York and Jenny

Michael York, as Sandman-turned-Runner Logan, faces capture with Jenny Agutter in the sci-fi **Logan's Run**.

Agutter out of this electronically self-sufficient world into, for lack of a better term, the real world. There they discover such things as the sun, night and the ruins of a city dominated by three distinctive landmarks--a tall obelisk, a dome-shaped building and a weed-covered rectangular building with classical columns on the outside and, on the inside, an imposing statute of a bearded august man who has clearly managed to live past 30. In the ruins of the dome-shaped building York and Agutter discover another man with a beard, this one alive, who actually remembers his parents (an unheard of thing in a society where babies are produced in laboratories), who knows about an old custom called burial and who recites snippets of poetry about cats, dozens of which share his home. Deliciously played by Peter Ustinov, the old man convinces his two confused visitors that they really need not fear age or even death . . .

The film, of course, is most alive in the delightful scenes with Ustinov and his cats--given the premise of the story, this is entirely appropriate. If the various catastrophes science has enabled us to envision do come to pass, there is some comfort imagining a devastated, weed-encrusted Washington inhabited only by a simple old eccentric who amuses himself reciting *Old Possum's Book of Practical Cats*."

©Women's Wear Daily, 1976.

New York Post, 6/24/76 (p. 23)
Archer Winsten

"*Logan's Run* . . . is science fiction jumping us forward 300 years to an elaborately domed city where everyone is 30 years of age or younger.

At precisely 30 they're put into a Carousel, where they are told they have a chance of renewal, but where, in actuality, it's their Last Day.

Some who try to avoid this fate are known as Runners. They are chased and ruthlessly killed by Sandmen.

Sandman Logan (Michael York) is given a special assignment when he's only 26. He is to become a runner in order to find out where some escapees go--a place called Sanctuary.

He in turn makes his run with the assistance of a younger girl, Jessica (Jenny Agutter) who has previously resisted his advances. He has learned that she has some kind of contact with the Sanctuary people . . .

In the end, when they finally make it to the surface of the old enduring earth . . . who do they meet but Old Man, very bearded, white-haired and wrinkled (Peter Ustinov) . . .

The ensuing dialogues are less than inspiring, but what can you expect in science fiction? . . .

The main point is, you've become involved. The ending turns out to be reasonably happy even if it is 2274 and the world very different and deserted."

Reprinted by Permission of New York Post.
© 1976, New York Post Corporation.

New York Magazine, 7/5/76 (p. 75)
John Simon

"*Logan's Run* is a piece of science fiction about which the most interesting thing is whether it fails more as science or as fiction. It is yet another of those tiresome world-after-the-holocaust bits of futuristic woolgathering, trying to differ from its mates by combining the technological-over-development-with-spiritual-underdevelopment and total-devastation-with-lone-survivors subgenres. The apparent assumption is that two has-beens equal one is. The film has a script by David Zelag Goodman, who has done better in the past, and direction by Michael Anderson, who is down to his usual level. It would be idle to detail the self-contradictions of a movie that is all frame-to-frame inconsistency, paradigmatic nonsense . . . Michael York and Jenny Agutter are gifted and winning performers who overcome deadly preposterousnesses almost as easily as mortal dangers, and there is creditable supporting work from Richard Jordan and a bit of genius from Peter Ustinov . . . "

© 1976 by the NYM Corp. Reprinted with the permission of NEW YORK Magazine.

Los Angeles Times, 6/22/76 (Pt. IV, p. 1)
Charles Champlin

" . . . the movie is a close call, threatening to disintegrate halfway through, but it saves its best stuff for the last (rare in a time when nobody seems to know how to finish movies). A richly hammy turn by Peter Ustinov, the most spectacular of the visuals and an amusing and touching commercial for geriatrics make the lingering impression of *Logan's Run* positive . . .

You surrender to the mumbo-jumbo make-believe of science fiction/fantasy or you don't––and if you don't, you are in some kind of trouble with *Logan's Run.*

If you do it's a bright, untroubling ride. But as usually happens when the logistics of a movie are as complicated and demanding as they were here, the live acting suffers. The performances director Michael Anderson took from York and Agutter are so solemn and stolid that *Logan's Run* initially takes on a dread severity it neither needs nor wants . . .

Jerry Goldsmith's score is right on, scary, eerie, electronic in part, entirely futurish. The veteran Ernest Laszlo did the demanding photography, and the real stars, assembled by producer Saul David, are the visualists . . . "

© Los Angeles Times, 1976.

Christian Science Monitor, 7/15/76 (p. 22)
David Sterritt

" . . . *Logan's Run* usually makes sense on its own terms, which is a first requisite for successful sci-fi.

Michael York is strong and likeable as Logan, a Sandman (killer of rebels) who is assigned to locate and destroy a nest of runners (fugitives from the mandatory deathday), but becomes a convert to the idea of freedom and natural life. Jenny Agutter is energetic and convincing as his fellow runner. Richard Jordan gives one of his strongest performances as Logan's adversary, an unregenerate Sandman . . .

Director Michael Anderson has worked in many formats, from *Around the World in 80 Days* artifice to *Conduct Unbecoming* theatricality. His current venture into science fiction is fairly logical and imaginative, though his city of the future looks too much like a miniature model in long-shot (which it is) and a new-fangled commercial building in close-up (which it is). Also, certain episodes are poorly integrated into the plot . . . "

Reprinted by permission from The Christian
Science Monitor © 1976.
The Christian Science Publishing Society.
All rights reserved.

Film Information, July/August 1976 (p. 4)
Frederic A. Brussat

" . . . Bad sci-fi tales stress the setting and hard-ware over any concern with meaning, or the complicated marvel of human nature. *Logan's Run* is an example . . .

Waste characterizes this sci-fi spectacular on all levels. First and foremost, there's a watering down of William F. Nolan and George Clayton Johnson's dandy novel into a low calorie screenplay by David Zelag Goodman. The interesting turns of character and ideas in the story have been junked for a tedious chase format. Millions of dollars have been wasted on futuristic sets of the city, an ice cavern, and the vine-covered ruins of Washington, D.C., but it all has a tacky look. The acting, too, is a waste, especially Peter Ustinov . . .

Director Michael Anderson (*Pope Joan, Shoes of the Fisherman*) has no sense of pace, which emphasizes the boring story line . . . "

©Film Information, 1976.

Village Voice, 7/12/76 (p. 116)
Andrew Sarris

" . . . Since the technology and architecture are nine-tenths of the fun, I shall not describe them in detail. In the book there is an actual Sanctuary to which runners can escape. It is on an abandoned space station on the dark side of the moon. In the movie there is no Sanctuary, only a return to Life as we have known it. According to the movie, we must escape from the planners (even the ecological planners) and return to a state of nature in which all age groups are welcome. Science is the big villain, and Family the ultimate salvation. We are back in Baron Frankenstein's infernal castle, from which the only plausible escape is God's mysterious ways. No longer is it a matter of averting nuclear war, or of respecting the environment, but rather of reverting to our cuddly animal instincts. For this reason, Michael Anderson's direction of the chase lacks tension. Sanctuary has been reduced to Homily and Platitude."

Reprinted by permission of The Village Voice.
Copyright © The Village Voice, Inc., 1976.

Monthly Film Bulletin, October 1976 (p. 216)
Richard Combs

" . . . Michael Anderson handles this toy-town concept with a kind of squint-eyed concentration on getting his wafer-thin characters from A to B, thus never bothering to indicate just when Logan ceases to be an undercover fink and becomes a genuine 'runner.' The film is a sluggish succession of expensive but banal designs, as though the art director were having a restless night of unpleasantly pastel dreams, and reaches a nadir of tiresomeness when hero and heroine reach the world outside, and find Peter Ustinov presiding over a brood of cats in the

continued on next page

continued from previous page

ruins of Washington (and presumably reasserting the maturing principle, though as inane in his second childhood as everyone else is in their first). *Logan's Run* heralds a rash of new s-f films, but augurs far less for its genre than for the future."

©Monthly Film Bulletin, 1976.

Films in Review, October 1976 (p. 507)
Steve Swires

"*Logan's Run* is Hollywood's idea of science fiction. Based on a wildly inventive, extremely cinematic novel by William F. Nolan and George Clayton Johnson, David Zelag Goodman's screenplay waters down complex and provocative ideas so as to make them accessible to an audience which considers science fiction to be 'The Six Million Dollar Man' and 'The Bionic Woman.' . . .

While Joseph Losey and Val Guest have demonstrated that expense is not necessarily a factor in making a compelling science fiction film, director Michael Anderson has here emphasized the visual splendor at the almost total expense of content . . . When you consider that writer-director L. Q. Jones was able to shoot his high-quality film version of Harlan Ellison's *A Boy and His Dog* for about one-eighth the cost, you recognize *Logan's Run* for what it truly is—entirely superfluous."

©Films in Review, 1976.

The Sunday Times (London), 10/3/76 (p. 35)
Dilys Powell

". . . The special effects are impressive: too impressive, perhaps, for the players, who—possibly to keep up the appearance of an advanced society—are persuaded to act very woodenly indeed. (Mr. Ustinov, of course, carries on outside the glass domes and exudes charm and idiosyncrasy.)

Occasionally somebody tries to give the aerial ballet a miss; somebody runs, only to be shot down by the police. Hence the title; Logan the runner is played by Michael York, who has Jenny Agutter as his partner in escape. There is plenty of fantasy-adventure, and just to show that violence hasn't been quite forgotten the finale indulges in the usual explosions and crashing masonry."

©The Sunday Times, 1976.

LOOSE ENDS

Directors, Screenplay, Producers: *David Burton Morris, Victoria Wozniak*. Photography: *Gregory M. Cummins*. Music: *John Paul Hammond*. Production: *Fat Chance Productions*. Running time 100 minutes. New York opening May 18, 1976, at the Whitney Museum of American Art. Classification: None.

Billy: *Chris Mulkey*. Eddie: *John Jenkins*. Jen: *Linda Jenkins*.

New York Post, 5/19/76 (p. 51)
Archer Winsten

"*Loose Ends*, a character study of two young men who work in a garage, Billy (Chris Mulkey) and Eddie (John Jenkins), the former divorced, the latter still married to Jen (Linda Jenkins), the mother of his four-year-old and mother-to-be, brings quality if no great popular appeal . . .

The marriage and the relationship with his friend Billy proceed along predictable lines, but with an accuracy of expression, dialogue and feeling that improves on a lot of big-time fiction films. Mulkey, Jenkins and Linda Jenkins deliver extremely good and true performances under the writing, producing and directorial guidance of David Burton Morris and Victoria Wozniak.

Music by John Paul Hammond becomes an integral part of feelings that expand inexorably and finally explode.

It's a picture that proves its quality in not seeming overlong despite a length of 100 minutes and a minimal plot . . . "

Reprinted by Permission of New York Post.
© 1976, New York Post Corporation.

LOST HONOR OF KATHARINA BLUM, THE (DIE VERLORENE EHRE DER KATHARINA BLUM)

Directors: *Volker Schlondorff and Margarethe von Trotta*. Screenplay (German with English subtitles): *Mr. Schlondorff and Ms. von Trotta*. Based on the novel by Heinrich Boll. Executive Producer: *Eberhard Jundersdorf*. Photography: *Jost Vacano*. Editor: *Peter Przygodda*. Music: *Hans Werner Henze*. Production:

Bioskop Film. Running time 102 minutes. New York opening October 3, 1975, at the New York Film Festival, Lincoln Center. Classification: None.

Katharina Blum: *Angela Winkler.* Belzmenne: *Mario Adorf.* Werner Totges: *Dieter Laser.* Dr. Blorna: *Heinz Bennent.* Trude Blorna: *Hannelore Hoger.* Moeding: *Harald Kuhlmann.* Alois Straubleder: *Karl Heinz Vosgerau.* Ludwig Gotten: *Jurgen Prochnow.*

See Volume 1 for additional reviews

Los Angeles Times, 9/23/76 (Pt. IV, p. 1)
Kevin Thomas

". . . Schlondorff and Miss Von Trotta (who does not appear in the film) are terrific, endlessly provocative storytellers who work in a clear-cut traditional style . . .

The Schlondorffs present a very broad spectrum of society, generate a wealth of incident yet take care to come up with the most subtle and revealing details. For example, of all the people connected with Katharina, only her uncle seems to have escaped scrutiny in the press. 'Perhaps it's just because I'm an old Nazi,' he says smiling, touching upon the truth that the West German past generally avoids dealing with the Third Reich.

What's more, *The Lost Honor of Katharina Blum* carries on the Schlondorffs' concern for women's liberation, for in a very real sense Katharina is as much a victim of rampant, dirty-minded male chauvinism as anything else.

As in all good films, the actors become the people so totally they don't seem to be acting. Angela Winkler's Katharina is terribly brave yet vulnerable and very naive. Visually stunning and superbly crafted in all aspects, *The Lost Honor of Katharina Blum* is a political thriller with much the excitement of *Z*."

©Los Angeles Times, 1976.

LOVE UNDER ONE UMBRELLA

Director: *Yoji Yamada.* Screenplay: *Yoshitaka Asama, Mr. Yamada.* Based on a story by Mr. Yamada. Producer: *Kiyoshi Shimazu.* Photography: *Tetsuo Takaba.* Editor: *Iwao Ishii.* Music: *Naozumi Yamamoto.* Distributor: *Shochiku.* Running time 90 minutes. Los Angeles opening August 1976 at the Kokusai Theatre. Classification: None. Origin: Japan.

Players: *Kiyoshi Atsumi, Chieko Baisho, Ruriko Asaoka, Eiji Funakoshi, Masami Shimolo, Chieko Misaki, Gin Maeda, Hayato Nakamura, Hisao Dazai, Gajiro Sato, Chushu Ryu.*

Los Angeles Times, 8/20/76 (Pt. IV, p. 15)
Kevin Thomas

"In a time when movies that actually lift spirits are so few and far between, the next Tora-san picture is always something to look forward to. The latest, *Love Under One Umbrella,* . . . is yet another delight, full of compassionate warmth and humor based on human frailties.

Tora-san (Kiyoshi Atsumi) is that feckless, kindhearted itinerant peddler who from time to time returns home to his loving, forgiving relatives in Tokyo . . .

As usual, the very gifted writer-director Yoji Yamada, who created the Tora-san series 14 pictures earlier, eschews plot to concentrate on the interactions between his people. What emerges is Yamada's characteristically Japanese acceptance of life as it is, extolling the family as the enduring source of sustenance in the face of life's disappointments.

The force of Yamada's eloquent expressiveness lifts the Tora-san series above its serial genre conventions and gives it genuine emotional impact rather than mere sentimentality . . ."

©Los Angeles Times, 1976.

LOVERS AND OTHER RELATIVES

Director: *Salvatore Samperi.* Screenplay (Italian with English subtitles): *Ottavio Jemma, Alessandro Parenzo.* Producer: *Silvio Clementelli.* Distributor: *Crystal Pictures, Inc.* Running time 98 minutes. New York opening August 1976 at the Little Carnegie Theatre. Classification: R. Origin: Italy.

Young Wife: *Laura Antonelli.* Sandro: *Alessandro Momo.* Renzo: *Orazio Orlando.* Mother: *Lilla Brignone.* Giustino: *Tino Carraro.* Contessa: *Monica Guerritore.* Beachboy: *Lino Toffolo.*

continued on next page

continued from previous page

Women's Wear Daily, 8/16/76 (p. 12)
Howard Kissel

". . . In *Lovers*, directed by Salvatore Samperi, everything coyly leads up to a teen-ager's rape of his brother's wife.

Samperi's previous film shown here, *Malizia*, was similarly obsessed with the sexual initiation of a teen-age boy by an older woman—in that case it was the family maid. The innocence and adolescence of this obsession . . . make the analogy with old nudist movies appropriate—only the most ingenious can find anything resembling a frisson in this material. The only erotic moments in the film are some closeups of women on the beach rubbing suntan lotion on their inner thighs.

Laura Antonelli, whose face is too expressive, too evocative for such a dumb part, does her assignment as the sister-in-law well. Alessandro Momo, who played the young boy in *Malizia*, and who was killed in a car crash, is fine again. There is also an excellent character performance by a small, white, unidentified dog."

©Women's Wear Daily, 1976.

New York Post, 8/16/76 (p. 14)
Archer Winsten

". . . brings Italian high spirits to a family sex farce which pounds the obvious to a pulp . . .

The main event turns on a mistaken identity in which Renzo is encouraging Sandro to seduce that unidentified married lady of his lusts, never realizing that it's his own wife. Actually Sandro, the virgin, makes such slow and uncertain progress that his own father has come to the tragic conclusion that his son is homosexual.

Since young Momo is a handsome youth and Laura Antonelli very pretty, and each is able to project the appropriate emotions of desire, fear and decency, the picture is never too far from success. Unfortunately plotmakers Ottavio Jemma and Alessandro Parenzo . . . seem unable to resist a once-over-heavily to any sex notion that occurs . . ."

Reprinted by Permission of New York Post.
©1976, New York Post Corporation.

LOVES AND TIMES OF SCARAMOUCHE, THE

Director: *Enzo G. Castellari.* Screenplay: *Mr. Castellari, Tito Carpi.* Producer: *Federico Alcardi.* Distributor: *Avco Embassy.* Running time 90 minutes. New York opening March, 1976, at several theatres. Classification: PG. Origin: Italy.

Players: *Michael Sarrazin, Ursula Andress, Aldo Maccione, Michael Forest, Giancarlo Prete, Sal Borgese.*

See Volume 1 for additional reviews

Films in Review, June/July 1976 (p. 380)
Michael Deskey

"In this witlessly haphazard film, the screenwriters have ignored the Sabatini story of an aristocratic lawyer who disguises himself as a clown with a traveling theater group during the Revolution, and instead made Scaramouche (Michael Sarrazin) a bumbling lout who divides his time bed-hopping with available wives, and brawling in countless duels, in which, in the ninety-six long minutes of the picture, there is not a drop of blood . . .

The movie is loud and raucous with an intrusive music score and badly dubbed dialogue. The director (Enzo Castellari) has, however, filmed some fairly impressive battle scenes (in Yugoslavia) which look as if they belong to another film. There are several light, grin-provoking lines that are unexpected: Napoleon, sacking Italy, glimpses the 'Mona Lisa.' 'Put that in my baggage,' he orders."

©Films in Review, 1976.

Los Angeles Times, 4/28/76 (p. 15)
Linda Gross

"*The Loves and Times of Scaramouche* is a silly, slapstick spaghetti spoof of swashbuckling adventure movies starring Michael Sarrazin as the havoc-provoking rogue . . .

The script by Tito Carpi and Enzo G. Castellari is an anachronistic and gimmicky melange of action, farce, cliches like bathtub scenes and caricatures.

Sarrazin is a bland Scaramouche, who doesn't equal the dashing earlier portrayals of Ramon Navarro in 1922 or Stewart Granger in 1952. Maccione plays a broad, comic version of Napoleon and Miss Andress' nude Josephine seems inappropriate. Prete is an amiable sidekick and Mejorsek is winning as the lost Cossack.

The Loves and Times of Scaramouche is a badly dubbed hodge-podge, grandiosely shot in Yugoslavia by Italian filmmakers. The film lacks a deft historical perspective so even the artful battle footage by photographer Giovanni Bergamini looks like it belongs in another kind of movie."

© Los Angeles Times, 1976.

LUMIERE

Director: *Jeanne Moreau*. Screenplay (French with English subtitles): *Ms. Moreau*. Producer: *Claire Duval*. Photography: *Ricardo Aronovich*. Editor: *Albert Jurgenson*. Music: *Astor Piazzola*. Distributor: *New World Pictures*. Running time 95 minutes. New York opening November 14, 1976, at the Beekman Theatre. Classification: R. Origin: France.

Sarah: *Jeanne Moreau*. Julienne: *Francine Racette*. Laura: *Lucia Bose*. Caroline: *Caroline Cartier*. Gregoire: *Francois Simon*. Heinrich Grun: *Bruno Ganz*. Thomas: *Francis Huster*. Nano: *Niels Arestrup*. David: *Keith Carradine*. Saint-Loup: *Jacques Spiesser*.

Newsweek, 11/29/76 (p. 115)
Janet Maslin

"*Lumiere*, the film that marks Jeanne Moreau's directorial debut, is a sweetly self-absorbed look at four Parisian actresses who are close friends . . .

Moreau's antidote to the prevailing anomie of the four women is to present their friendship as idyllic. And she has made every scene look as pretty as possible. *Lumiere* is most memorable for the striking symmetry of its compositions and for the innocent sensuality Moreau's Sarah brings to her supportive encounters with the others. One night, she visits the troubled, sleeping Laura in her bedroom and pensively smooths the slightly rumpled silk sheets into elegant order. *Lumiere's* dramatic strategy is similar—so delicately covert that its characters' underlying anguish, however palpable, remains obscure."

©Newsweek, Inc. 1976
reprinted by permission.

Christian Science Monitor, 12/9/76 (p. 26)
David Sterritt

". . . *Lumiere* rarely invites the kind of active audience involvement demanded by more story-oriented films. The spectator meanders through its fragments and fabrics as the camera does, lingering with great fascination one moment, moving restlessly on the next. The picture would not succeed were it not for Miss Moreau's visual imagination, which can be disappointingly cool or shiveringly sensitive and exquisitely pretty—as when light glints off the personality-revealing artifacts in a character's room. or the camera catches a warmly festive mood by peeking through the windows of a happy house in a long and marvelously executed tracking shot.

Credit goes to stars Francine Racette, Lucia Bose, and Caroline Cartier for carrying the movie's

rhythm through some of the bare spots when Miss Moreau's directorial momentum falters . . .''

Reprinted by permission from The Christian
Science Monitor ©1976.
The Christian Science Publishing Society.
All rights reserved.

New York Magazine, 12/6/76 (p. 124)
John Simon

". . . *Lumiere*, a film that offers us Miss Moreau as scenarist, director, and star, and disappoints us to a greater or lesser degree on all counts . . .

The cause of feminism receives a few perfunctory obeisances such as Laura's *cri de coeur*, 'I'm sick of being my father's daughter, my husband's wife, my children's mother. I am Laura!' But the old order also gets its due when Sarah glues her ear to Laura's pregnant belly and asks, 'And the baby, how is it?' 'It's fine.' 'That's the main thing.' . . .

No point in adducing further absurdities and pretensions. There are three authentic scenes: the one where a laconic Gregoire learns that he is doomed by leukemia, the one where a demure Julienne goes to see her ex-husband, and the one where a rejected lover clumsily proposes to Sarah. Otherwise, despite some good performances, especially from Francine Racette, there is not much to recommend this film, unless one takes the position that any film made from the feminine point of view is something to cheer about. And so it might be if it were made better, as was, for instance, Antonioni's *Le amiche*."

©1976 by the NYM Corp. Reprinted with
the permission of NEW YORK Magazine.

Films in Review, December 1976 (p. 634)
Jane Morgan

"Jeanne Moreau debuts as a director with *Lumiere*, writing the screenplay and acting the lead. This film about women might have been an important milestone for women in filmmaking. Unfortunately it merely reverses the usual sexual roles, treating men as appendages to women. The women are manipulative and self-centered, with Moreau failing to portray them with the irony we find in Claude Sautet's *Vincent, Francois, Paul and the Others* . . .

In a prologue, Sarah (Moreau) recalls a time in Paris when everything changed in her life. We switch back to incidents in the lives of Sarah and three other actresses . . .

Moreau has given the film some poignant moments, eliciting good performances from her cast, but the tempo of the film is choppy."

©Films in Review, 1976.

continued on next page

continued from previous page

Film Information, December 1976 (p. 3)
Ellen Clark

". . . Though no feminist manifesto, *Lumiere*
is very much a woman's film. Women who are
not lesbians caress each other, care for each other
in their loneliness—a nice change after so many
male 'buddy' films. The friendship of the four actresses cuts across the boundaries of age, achievement and acclaim, a feminist vision.

Jeanne Moreau gives a fine performance as
the aging star Sarah and elicits sensitive portrayals
from the others. Her film is beautifully made and
directed. The main weakness stems from the insignificant screenplay. Miss Moreau's women are
shallow, unsympathetic, and their conversation
trivial. In one scene they sit around recalling early
sexual encounters. (Candid sex talk presumably
merits the 'R' rating.) They share intimacies but
not serious introspection. In an important film by
and about women, we want more than that."

©Film Information, 1976

New York Post, 11/15/76 (p. 22)
Archer Winsten

"*Lumiere* . . . is a first and rather brilliant directorial effort by Jeanne Moreau, the long-time French
star who here joins three other French actresses
in acting out an impressionistic rendition of feminine
sensibility in their relationships to men and each
other . . .

Ultimately the picture reduces itself to a kind
of recollection of the way these women, these
actresses, respond to their very French world of
movie-making. All the portraits are good and believable, rising to a peak with Moreau's presentation of what one assumes to be herself. If this very
feminine world is within your personal realm of
understanding, it can be a memorable assembly
of the velleities."

Reprinted by Permission of New York Post.
© 1976, New York Post Corporation.

Commonweal, 2/18/77 (p. 114)
Colin L. Westerbeck, Jr.

". . . at the same time that *Lumiere* is about a
world of total illusion, a dream world, it is also a
documentary. This is what gives it its density and
singularity as a film. For it not only stars Jeanne
Moreau, but it is about her as well, and was written
and directed by her. In the French filmmaking of the
last twenty years, especially that of the New Wave
in which Moreau rose to stardom, there is an acute
awareness of the paradox by which all filmmaking
is a documentary of a fantasy, a record and realiza-

tion of someone's imaginings. This paradox hasn't
been lost on Moreau either, having participated in it
so often. Like that old friend of Sarah's who commits suicide, Gregoire (Francois Simon), a cancer
researcher who discovers that he too is now in-
fected with cancer, Moreau's film studies the very
sensibility with which she herself is afflicted . . ."

©Commonweal, 1977.

Los Angeles Times, 1/12/77 (Pt. IV, p. 1)
Kevin Thomas

". . . The very contemporary milieu that Miss
Moreau takes us into so knowingly and so percep-
tively is one of luxury, glamour and success.
Amidst constant activity and excitement—and a lot
of hard work—her women strive for happiness and
fulfillment . . .

In every way *Lumiere*, with its gleaming, lyrical
camerawork and spare but effective score, is outstanding and deeply affecting. Besides Miss
Moreau, Miss Racette and Simon, best remembered
as the comically cadaverous waiter in the Swiss
film *L'Invitation*, are especially impressive. Miss
Moreau had hoped to get Bibi Andersson or Gunnel
Lindblom (another Bergman favorite) or Audrey
Hepburn to star instead of herself, but her failure
was our gain. A *Lumiere* without Jeanne Moreau's
on-screen presence could never have been so
radiant—or meaningful."

©Los Angeles Times, 1977.

MAD DOG

Director, Screenplay: *Philippe Mora*. Based on
the book MORGAN THE BOLD BUSHRANGER by
Margaret Carnegie. Producer: *Jeremy
Thomas*. Photography: *Mike Molloy*. Editor:
John Scott. Music: *Patrick Flynn*. Distributor:
*Cinema Shares International Distribution
Corporation*. Running time 93 minutes. New
York opening September 22, 1976, at several
theatres. Classification: R.

Daniel Morgan: *Dennis Hopper*. Billy: *David
Gulpilil*. Superintendent Cobham: *Frank
Thring*. Detective Manwaring: *Jack
Thompson*. Macpherson: *Wallas Eaton*.
Sergeant Smith: *Bill Hunter*.

New York Post, 9/23/76 (p. 24)
Frank Rich

"Although nothing else is right about *Mad

Dog . . . its title is woefully appropriate. This film has rabies and unless you've been properly inoculated—with, say, sodium pentathol—you'd be smart to keep your distance.

Mad Dog is about a 19th-century Australian outlaw, Daniel Morgan (Dennis Hopper) who stole from the rich, gave to the poor, smoked opium and generally antagonized the cruel colonial prison officials who ran his country at the time. Philippe Mora . . . apparently thinks Morgan's saga can serve as a political statement of contemporary relevancy—hence the casting of Hopper, our movies' most persistent professional anti-hero and dope enthusiast—but the only real energy in Mad Dog can be found in the film's vicious violence . . .

If Mora had made Mad Dog in the late '60s—and made it with some narrative spunk—maybe he would have gotten away with it. In 1976, this film is about five dozen anti-Westerns too late, and, besides, we're past the point when a filmmaker can give the audience the finger in the form of violent shock effects and expect to be taken as a hip anti-authoritarian . . ."

Reprinted by Permission of New York Post.
©1976, New York Post Corporation.

Los Angeles Times, 10/27/76 (Pt. IV, p. 10)
Kevin Thomas

". . . All this is the familiar stuff of many a legend of the American frontier, and Mad Dog unfolds against majestic unspoiled locales much in the manner of a superior western. It is a classic tale of tragic injustice, and Hopper expresses eloquently the pain, frustration and longing beneath Morgan's bravado. Jack Thompson is the shrewd policeman who wants to bring in Morgan alive, David Gulpilil (of Walkabout) is Morgan's aborigine companion and Frank Thring is a dastardly police superintendent.

Mora combines a broad, sweeping style with an eye for revealing, ironic detail that gives Mad Dog's familiar themes a quality of individuality . . ."

©Los Angeles Times, 1976.

MADAM KITTY

Director, Editor: Tinto Brass. Screenplay: Ennio De Concini, Maria Pia Fusco, Mr. Brass. Producers: Giulio Sbarigia, Ermanno Donati. Photography: Silvano Ippoliti. Music: Fiorenzo Carpi. Distributor: Trans-American Pictures. Running time 111 minutes. New York opening January 1977 at several theatres. Classification: X. Origin: Italy.

Wallenberg: Helmut Berger. Kitty: Ingrid Thulin. Margherita: Teresa Ann Savoy. Hans: Bekim Fehmiu. Biondo: John Steiner. Dino: Stefano Satta Flores. Rauss: Dan van Husen. Clift: John Ireland. Herta Wallenberg: Tina Aumont.

Los Angeles Times, 1/20/77 (Pt. IV, p. 14)
Charles Champlin

"The ads and billboards cry 'Depraved Decadent Damned!' and if that's your cup of drool, be advised that for once the goods are fairly described.

Madam Kitty, rated X for want of a more eloquent alphabet, is a roughed-up exploitation piece involving some talented people who, you can only hope, didn't really know what they were getting into . . .

The production design . . . is rich and stunning, and the performances by Ingrid Thulin as the madam and Helmut Berger as a Nazi officer have a kind of degenerate power, possibly recalled from their teaming in The Damned.

But the handling by Brass is so heavy handed, and heavy lidded, so voyeuristic and so deliberately campy by turn, that what you feel is neither historical horror nor present arousal but only a restless and embarrassed discomfort . . ."

©Los Angeles Times, 1977.

New York Post, 1/22/77 (p. 33)
Archer Winsten

". . . Made by the Italians, with Tinto Brass, an appropriate name, as director and a distinguished international cast in the lead roles, the picture becomes a curious combination of truth-in-porn.

Ingrid Thulin, the Swedish star, plays Madam Kitty, singer and proprietress of Berlin's most distinguished and kinky whorehouse, and she does it with beautiful overtones of Marlene Dietrich in The Blue Angel. Helmut Berger, the Austrian actor who made his distinguished start under Visconti, plays Wallenberg, an SS officer of brutal personal ambition . . .

It may be argued that the picture is simplistic, wholly lacking in subtleties and kicking the Nazis around with what amounts to caricature. The fact remains, however, that much of the Nazi pomp and ceremony lends itself to that interpretation. This picture has much to recommend it if you can view it without revulsion and with some memory of the time, place and people involved."

Reprinted by Permission of New York Post.
©1977, New York Post Corporation.

MAHLER

Director, Screenplay: *Ken Russell*. Producer: *Roy Baird*. Photography: *Dick Bush*. Music: Mahler, played by the Amsterdam Concertgebouw Orchestra, directed by Bernard Haitink. Running time 126 minutes. New York opening April 4, 1976, at the D.W. Griffith Theatre. Classification: None. Origin: Great Britain.

Mahler: *Robert Powell*. Alma Mahler: *Georgina Hale*. Max: *Richard Morant*. Bernard Mahler: *Lee Montague*. Hugo Wolfe: *David Collings*. Cosima Wagner: *Antonia Ellis*.

See Volume 1 for additional reviews

Films in Review, June/July 1976 (p. 378)
Page Cook

". . . The film is mainly flashback revolving about Mahler's return to Vienna several months before his death. Incidents trigger his memory to reveal facets of the composer's persona. There's little attempt made at creating an historical document: Russell seeks the *essence* of his subject. There are fine scenes (Mahler's country retreat at Mainernigg evoking the early 20th century ravishingly), and there are shoddy passages (the dance to a pastiche of the 3rd movement from Mahler's 7th Symphony and the First movement to the Ninth). Memorable is Mahler, with his two children beating out the third Kindertotenlieder song.

The performances range from Robert Powell's complex and fascinating Mahler to Georgina Hale's vulgar Alma . . .

Russell's utilization of the Bernard Hiatink interpretations of the Mahler symphonies is disturbing. Though satisfactory, they can't compete with Leonard Bernstein's monumental performances . . ."

©Films in Review, 1976.

Film Information, 5/76 (p. 2)
Frederic A. Brussat

" . . . Whether considering *The Music Lovers* (Tchaikovsky), *Lisztomania* (Liszt), or *Mahler*, one comes away with divergent feelings for what Russell has achieved: (1) a respect for those moments when he penetrates through to the essence of the music and achieves a filmic epiphany commemorating the composer and his vision of life, and

(2) an antithetical feeling of revulsion when Russell's florid symbolism does a terrible disservice to the artist and his art . . .

Russell finds the clue to Mahler's music in the composer's wrestling with the images of death and eternal life. He justifies a very shocking dream sequence where Alma does an erotic dance on Mahler's coffin with the following thought, 'I treat death as he did in his music . . . I treat it sometimes as a joke, sometimes as a terror, a fear that haunted him throughout his life. He was totally preoccupied with death . . .

Robert Powell as Mahler is very good in catching the tyrannical, mean and sensitive sides of this musical genius. Georgina Hale is excellent as his wife, a woman who endures much pain to find out at last that Mahler's music is his love for her. The cinematography by Dick Bush is exquisite, and selections from Mahler's works are well performed by Amsterdam's Concertgebouw Orchestra under Bernard Haitink's direction."

© Film Information, 1976.

MAIDS, THE

Director: *Christopher Miles*. Screenplay: *Robert Enders and Mr. Miles*. Based on the Minos Volanakis translation of Jean Genet's French play. Producer: *Mr. Enders*. Executive Producer: *Bernard Weitzman*. Photography: *Douglas Slocombe*. Editor: *Peter Tanner*. Production: *Robert Enders Films and Cine-Films, Inc*. Distributor: *The American Film Theatre*. Running time 95 minutes. New York opening April 21, 1975, at several theatres. Classification: PG.

Solange: *Glenda Jackson*. Claire: *Susannah York*. Madame: *Vivien Merchant*.

See Volume 1 for additional reviews

The Sunday Times (London), 4/4/76 (p. 37)
Dilys Powell

" . . . The parable needs outsize performance, thunder, the electric shock of personality; and at first thought there seems no reason why such elements should not be possible in the cinema. But then one comes up against the difference in the sense of reality between the stage and the screen. Curious how one accepts the coloured shadows of a film as real creatures while the stage with its real flesh and blood and bone can appear an artificial medium. I have never seen *The Maids* in the theatre. I suppose that there its irrationality and its huge artifice suit the medium. But they conflict with the realities of the screen. The film . . . has three splendid performers, Glenda Jackson and Susannah York as the sisters, Vivien Merchant as the mistress. But even with this extraordinary trio one comes away not so much alienated as never from the start having been concerned."

© The Sunday Times, 1976.

MAITRESSE

Director: *Barbet Schroeder*. Screenplay (French with English subtitles): *Paul Voujargol, Mr. Schroeder*. Photography: *Nestor Almendros*. Editor: *Denise de Casablanca*. Music: *Carlos d'Alessio*. Production: *Les Films du Losange-Gaumont*. Distributor: *TINC Productions*. Running time 112 minutes. New York opening November 4, 1976, at the Baronet Theatre. Classification: X. Origin: France.

Olivier: *Gerard Depardieu*. Ariane: *Bulle Ogier*. Mario: *Andre Rouyer*. Lucienne: *Nathalie Keryan*. Man in Cage: *Roland Bertin*. Emile: *Tony Taffin*. Gautier: *Holger Lowenadler*. Secretary: *Anny Bartanovsky*.

Village Voice, 12/20/76 (p. 57)
Andrew Sarris

"Barbet Schroeder's *Maitresse*, like his *More* of some years ago, is almost too knowing for its own good. It is the old problem of the sophisticate being too bored to explain his own sophistication. Ostensibly *Maitresse* is concerned with the subterranean world of sadomasochism . . . The couple never really becomes integrated with the clients, and the sadomasochism becomes increasingly literal. There is a provocative role reversal worthy of Genet when the Depardieu character begins participating in his mistress' revels, but this promising ploy is quickly discarded. The denouement is so disconcertingly conventional that it makes one appreciate the surrealist rigor of Bunuel's *Belle de Jour* . . ."

Reprinted by permission of The Village Voice.
Copyright © The Village Voice, Inc., 1976.

New York Post, 11/5/76 (p. 25)
Frank Rich

"In *Maitresse*, his first film since *Idi Amin Dada*, filmmaker Barbet Schroeder tries awfully hard to be serious and thoughtful about sadomasochism, and increasingly trendy subject that most filmmakers invoke only for exploitation purposes. While Schroeder's cool stance toward this hot topic is admirable, I wish he hadn't been quite so relentlessly high-minded—that he'd allowed himself to be a bit more trashy . . .

The problems begin (but do not end) with a terribly arch and disconnected script . . . that tends to throw away most of its intellectual conceits and dramatic strategies before they begin to be resolved. *Maitresse* has a provocative first 20 minutes, but then drops dead—and its static demeanor is further heightened by Schroeder's direction (which confuses uninventiveness with stylistic objectivity) and by the excessively spaced-out performances of the two talented stars, Gerard Depardieu and Bulle Ogier . . ."

Reprinted by Permission of New York Post.
© 1976, New York Post Corporation.

New York Magazine, 11/15/76 (p. 119)
John Simon

"Barbet Schroeder, whose *Idi Amin Dada* was a gruesomely fascinating documentary, now gives us *Maitresse*, a grisly and unabsorbing tale about a professional dominatrix and her well-to-do clients who come to her to be subjected to bondage and torture, and with whom she lives in a peculiar symbiosis . . .

Now, the intention seems to be to show some sort of parallel between so-called normal and so-called abnormal relationships, but this does not come off for two sovereign reasons. The 'story' part of the film is superficially conceived and jerkily executed, and we never find out much more about the lovers (mechanically played by the able Bulle Ogier and Gerard Depardieu) than that they favor more or less kinky forms of lovemaking. But the 'sadomasochist documentary' part of the film is told in copious detail yet without any sort of directorial inventiveness or moral or intellectual passion . . ."

© 1976 by the NYM Corp. Reprinted with
the permission of NEW YORK Magazine.

continued on next page

continued from previous page

Los Angeles Times, 11/20/76 (Pt. IV, p. 10)
Charles Champlin

". . . In Schroeder's *Maitresse* . . . he examines a Krafft-Ebing notebook's worth of sexual aberrations, finds them sad, tedious and disgusting, and ends with a rousing celebration of free-wheeling heterosexual normality.

The material is not really exploited (it is about as erotic as a long walk through a sleet storm after dark) but there it is, and you do ask yourself, was this whip necessary? Despite its traditionalist attitudes and even some laughter early on, *Maitresse* remains a downer because its echoing images are of its sordid half-world of joy through humiliation . . ."

©Los Angeles Times, 1976.

MALE OF THE CENTURY

Director: *Claude Berri*. Screenplay (French with English subtitles): *Mr. Berri, Jean-Louis Richard*. Based on an idea by Milos Forman. Producer: *Pierre Grunstein*. Photography: *Jean-Pierre Baux*. Music: *Claude Morgan*. Production: *Renn Productions-Les Films Christian Fechner*. Distributor: *Joseph Green Pictures*. Running time 95 minutes. New York opening June 2, 1976, at the Juliet 2 Theatre. Classification: None. Origin: France.

Isabelle: *Juliet Berto*. Claude: *Claude Berri*. Hubert: *Hubert Deschamps*. Ganster: *Laszlo Szabo*. Louis Maboui: *Yves Afonso*. Son: *Julien Langmann*. Claude's Mother: *Mme. Langmann*. Isabelle's Mother: *Denise Provence*. Isabelle's Father: *Jacques Bebary*. Nurse: *Bernadette Robert*.

Nation, 6/19/76 (p. 765)
Robert Hatch

"Claude Berri's *Male of the Century* in which Berri himself plays opposite Juliet Berto as his wife, is not the French domestic comedy of the century. Its humor occasionally turns coarse in a way that disputes the frothy nonsense of the situation, and so too the violence sometimes looks mean . . .

. . . Claude, the dominant male at 5 feet 4 and short of breath, is a figure of fun. He is also a figure of some weight because he gives off so strongly the flavor of the French working class. Compared to him, the American working-class hero of Cassavetes's *Woman Under the Influence* seems no more substantial than an actor demonstrating the repertory of hysterical mannerisms. What it comes down to is that for social drama-comedy or tragedy––you need a society solid enough and long enough established to supply the norms on which fiction can play its variations . . ."

© The Nation, 1976.

New York Magazine, 6/21/76 (p. 74)
John Simon

" . . . The film is 'based on an idea by Milos Forman,' which isn't an idea at all, only an old Jewish joke that has been kicking around Eastern Europe for ages. It's no wonder Forman gave it away; the question is why anyone––even Berri––would want it. As Berri has developed it, with the help of Jean-Louis Richard, it concerns a pants merchant in Lyons whose faithful, long-suffering wife, on whom he freely cheats, finally has a fling of her own . . .

Our director is as fond as John Cassavetes of casting himself and members of his family in his movies, and so here we are exposed to his own progeny playing his progeny, and his own mother, Mme. Langmann (Berri's real name), playing his mother. Their services could, no doubt, be had for free, but, considering their performances, that may have been an overpayment. There is also mediocre photography and worse music; however, Juliet Berto plays the wife. Mlle. Berto is well on her way to becoming a very considerable actress; she performs with intelligence and economy––a certain melancholy incisiveness––more eloquent in one shot than Berri in his entire output."

© 1976 by the NYM Corp. Reprinted with the permission of NEW YORK Magazine.

New York Post, 6/3/76 (p. 26)
Archer Winsten

"Not content with having made *Le Sex Shop*, the funniest semi-porn picture of the period, Claude Berri has now addressed himself to the changing roles of men and women in modern society. In *Male of the Century* . . . he has directed a theme suggested by Milos Forman, namely, that bank robbers seize someone's handsome wife as hostage and that the irate husband vacillate between fear for his wife's life and fury that she may be losing her virtue.

It's not a bad idea to be studied in these days of equal rights . . .

These are the same old questions. What makes them fresh here is the quality of character and performance, the French setting, and Claude Berri's personal touch. He makes it seem very alive, and funny, too. Man's inconsistency is well argued, his troubled psyche laid bare. But since this is a comedy, not a tragedy, no lives are lost, no marriages shattered. Better, more tranquil days are coming . . . maybe.

Reprinted by Permission of New York Post.
© 1976, New York Post Corporation.

Los Angeles Times, 7/22/76 (Pt. IV, p. 14)
Kevin Thomas

". . . In short, the film's fatal flaw is that while we're subjected continually to Berri's marathon ranting and raving we're never allowed to see what it is about this often physical, brutal man that makes his very attractive wife love him no matter what. And since we never really get to know Miss Berto we're left to wonder whether she isn't some sort of sick masochist.

Now Berri is very adept at wittily staging the robbery and its aftermath and showing the police gleefully meeting the challenge it presents, yet he can't seem to make up his mind whether the film really is the comedy it ostensibly is . . . it swings almost nonchalantly between humor and pathos. However, that Berri's hero (or anti-hero) is so singularly unappealing makes what the film means to be beside the point . . ."

© Los Angeles Times, 1976.

Film Information, July/August 1976 (p. 4)
Jeffrey Weber

"Can one person successfully write, direct and star in the same motion picture? Perhaps, but it certainly isn't a winning combination for Claude Berri in his new film, *Male of the Century*.

A self-described soap opera, *Male of the Century* traces the jealous fears and fantasies of Claude (Claude Berri) after his wife Isabelle (Juliet Berto) has been taken hostage in a bank robbery—an event Claude first learns about while watching the evening news. Throughout Isabelle's four-day sequestration, Claude's brooding suspicions convince him that his wife is willingly submitting to the robber's sexual seduction. In Claude's mind her well being becomes equated with her fidelity. And the double standard becomes a unilateral right of all men . . .

. . . moviegoers will be reminded of the amateur robbery portrayed in *Dog Day Afternoon*. Some of that film's humor is present in *Male of the Century*, but this satire of antedated male chauvinism, despite moments of insightful characterization, never quite makes it."

© Film Information, 1976.

MAN FRIDAY

Director: *Jack Gold*. Screenplay: *Adrian Mitchell*. Inspired by Daniel Defoe's novel *Robinson Crusoe*. Producer: *David Korda*. Photography: *Alex Phillips*. Editor: *Anne V. Coates*. Music: *Carl Davis*. Distributor: *Avco Embassy*. Running time 123 minutes. Los Angeles opening December 25, 1975, at Mann's Westwood Theatre. Classification: PG.

Players: *Peter O'Toole, Richard Roundtree, Peter Cellier, Christopher Cabot, Joel Fluellen, Sam Seabrook, Stanley Clay.*

See Volume 1 for additional reviews

Saturday Review, 4/17/76 (p. 44)
Judith Crist

". . . Adrian Mitchell's *Man Friday* manages to do in Robinson Crusoe . . . Mitchell has chosen to turn Defoe's marvelous tale into a presumptuous and pretentious Third World primer, with Peter O'Toole the pompous product of a false-value civilization and Richard Roundtree the noble savage who attempts to teach his master the true values of ignorance and simple-mindedness. O'Toole, a dandy Crusoe until the plot mucks him up, and Roundtree, as dopey a Friday as farce could manufacture, seem embarrassed by the whole thing—or maybe that's wishful thinking. Mitchell and director Jack Gold do manage to make a classic story boring: that, after all, is no simple accomplishment."

© Judith Crist, 1976.

MAN WHO FELL TO EARTH, THE

Director: *Nicolas Roeg*. Screenplay: *Paul Mayersberg*. Based on the novel by Walter Tevis. Producers: *Michael Deeley, Barry Spikings*. Photography: *Anthony Richmond*. Running time 158 minutes. New York opening May 28, 1976, at the Cinema I and Cinema II Theatres. Classification: R.

Thomas Jerome Newton: *David Bowie*. Nathan Bryce: *Rip Torn*. Mary Lou: *Candy Clark*. Oliver Farnsworth: *Buck Henry*. Peters: *Bernie Casey*.

continued on next page

continued from previous page

Christian Science Monitor, 6/23/76 (p. 22)
David Sterritt

"*The Man Who Fell to Earth* is Nicolas Roeg's latest excursion into mod fantasy. Unfortunately, it lacks the coherence, mystery, and excitement that marked some of Roeg's former work. Many viewers will also be put off by the savage sexuality flaunted in a couple of perverse passages.

English rock singer David Bowie gives a strong and inventive performance as Thomas Jerome Newton, who begins the film as a strange visitor from another planet, becomes a capitalist tycoon, slips into a kind of suburban doldrum, and ends up as an English rock singer . . .

What a pity that Roeg seems to have forgotten that an audience would be out there watching his artful dodges. *The Man Who Fell to Earth* veers among wildly disconnected episodes, some fascinating, some repulsive, some lovely, some incomprehensible. They are linked by a melancholy atmosphere, a pensive attitude, a musing on loneliness. By they never quite form a tale. Nor do they quite come together on the 'poetic' level toward which Roeg seems to strive. Eventually we feel like the main character, whose hobby is watching a dozen TV programs at the same time. Roeg probably intended this effect, but from a spectator's eye-view it looks like ordinary self-indulgence . . ."

Reprinted by permission from The Christian Science Monitor © 1976. The Christian Science Publishing Society. All rights reserved.

Saturday Review, 7/10/76 (p. 63)
Judith Crist

" . . . one of the most interesting science-fiction films of recent years has been derived from Walter Tevis' 1963 novel, *The Man Who Fell to Earth*. The focal point of the interest, to fascinate even non-sci-fi enthusiasts, is the casting of rock star David Bowie in the title role. His impersonation of the extraplanetary visitor goes beyond the physical to a magnetism of personality and persona that is remarkable . . .

Roeg, a cinematographer-turned-director who dealt with mystery with flashes of inspiration and heavy-handed explicitness in *Don't Look Now*, is governed by mood rather than matter, and the coherence of his story suffers as he devotes himself to wonderfully earthy encounters between Newton and his warmhearted shoddy little mistress and to unnervingly beautiful flashes of Newton's previous life. But Bowie tempts one to yield on the pragmatics of plot and to accept the film as the story of a mysterious outsider who is doomed by a venal and suspicious society, betrayed by all with whom he permits himself to be human. And, as such, Bowie makes the film work, simply through his own performance. He gets excellent support from Candy Clark as the mistress and Buck Henry as the patent attorney. Rip Torn, after a tasteless and irrelevant introductory sequence of lechery, proves interesting as a chemist who moves from campus to corporation to find cynical success. But the film is Bowie's—and, we hope, it will only be his first cinematic achievement."

© Judith Crist, 1976.

The Times (London), 3/19/76 (p. 12)
David Robinson

" . . . you feel finally that all that has been achieved has been to impose a haze and aura of mystery and enigma where essentially there is none; to turn a simple tale into the sort of fragmented accumulation of sensations that has become fashionable . . .

The surfaces are beguiling, of course. Roeg is as accomplished and inventive a meteur-en-scene as Britain possesses, a master of arresting images and haunting sound effects. Working with a sympathetic director of photography, Anthony Richmond, he has given the film a visual aura of Caspar David Friedrich Romanticism: and a special luminosity produced out of city lights, of shimmering water, of reflections in spectacles or eyes.

It was a happy inspiration to cast David Bowie, whose androgynous features, frail body, gentle, insolent eyes and slight, fearful facial tremors exactly embody the Anthean of Tevis' book . . ."

© The Times, 1976.

The Times (London), 3/21/76
Dilys Powell

" . . . it is one of the virtues of the performance of David Bowie in *The Man Who Fell to Earth* . . . that the actor can be taken as belonging to both an alien planet and our own. He has the wan, almost ethereal aspect of the figures he sees in waking dreams of his home world. But he still looks ordinary. Ill, but ordinary.

Probably it is the reversal of the normal in science fiction which has drawn Nicolas Roeg to this theme . . .

. . . The technical achievements are extraordinary —the mysterious object streaming through the atmosphere, the violent descent. And Paul Mayersberg's script and Nicolas Roeg's direction, all through the actions of the visitor and his relations with everyday people, discreetly maintaining the sense of the abnormal lurking behind the normal . . ."

© The Times, 1976.

New York Magazine, 6/14/76 (p. 63)
John Simon

" . . . it is, like all of Roeg's films, the blowing up of something simple or simpleminded to arrogantly bloated dimensions and purporting to be chock-full of hermetic truths merely awaiting their interpreters . . .

I defy anyone to come up with a coherent synopsis of this film, let alone an explication of the individual scenes and resolution of the inconsistencies, contradictions, and preposterous non sequiturs that litter it from the very start . . .

The cinematography, by Roeg himself, is expert, and a few effects are quite exciting. The performances are mostly routine, with people like Rip Torn and Buck Henry going through their standard motions . . . The one serious performance comes from Candy Clark as Mary Lou, and though it is often affecting, it is, for that very reason, out of keeping with the rest of the film. As always in a Roeg film, there is a good deal of sexual intercourse, which gets intercut with something else. Here it is intercut with more intercourse––spatial intercourse, which differs from the terrestrial kind in that it is more boring to watch. There is also some interracial nudity, fantastic gadgetry, and opulent interior decoration. What is most on display, though, is Roeg's third-rate sensibility desperately aspiring to the second-rate."

© 1976 by the NYM Corp. Reprinted with the permission of NEW YORK Magazine.

Film, 5/76 (p. 8)
Douglas McVay

"Nicolas Roeg's new movie is, for me, a more seductive, exciting and moving work than either *Performance* or *Don't Look Now*, although it also shares one or two of the faults of those films (a tendency towards thematic obscurity and visual pretentiousness). In both subject and technique, *The Man Who Fell to Earth* reflects many of its director's earlier preoccupations: the obsession with time, space and mortality, the juggling of cinematic tenses . . .

. . . Roeg's general pictorial approach is often very meaningful: his zoom-shots annihilate the space-time continuum, just as his extra-terrestrial hero annihilates it by his ultra-sensitive ocular powers: similarly, Roeg's slow panning-shots rhyme with the curving surfaces of our planet and the planet from which the central figure comes . . . "

© Film 1976.

Nation, 6/19/76 (p. 765)
Robert Hatch

" . . . The one point that *The Man Who Fell to*

Earth manages to make explicit is that strangers to the white man's ways fall easy victims to his vices; Newton proves susceptible to gin, to which he is introduced by the amorous chambermaid. His sexual prowess appears to be considerable and that perplexed me a bit. For beneath his Bowie disguise Newton is no mammal, being a kind of bifurcated sea anemone, and I should have thought the species gap too wide for dalliance. That's quibbling, I suppose, but I wouldn't quibble if the film had given me anything more pertinent to talk about. All in all, it's a witless venture, tritely sardonic and covering its unresolved implications with outer-space photographic swirls. It reminds me of that little black box which, when you wind it up, opens its lid so that a spooky little hand can reach out and close the lid. People even used to buy them; maybe they'll buy *The Man Who Fell to Earth*."

© The Nation, 1976.

Village Voice, 6/14/76 (p. 135)
Andrew Sarris

" . . . I can report only that the movie seemed choppy and vague at many points, but in these days of fashionable ellipsis, one is never sure whether one is the victim of abbreviation or affectation . . . The biggest problem, however, is that the picture produces puzzlement without involvement, and hence, fantasies without feelings. In this respect, it is decisively inferior to Kubrick's *2001* and *A Clockwork Orange*; that is, if one is into science fiction in the first place . . .

. . . in its present form, the picture fails to present an adequate artistic structure for its ultimate mood of abject, drunken despair. The thinking is there, but not the feeling. As for David Bowie's fans, my own hunch is that they will find the going heavy rather than flashy."

Reprinted by permission of The Village Voice. Copyright © The Village Voice, Inc., 1976.

Women's Wear Daily, 5/28/76 (p. 8)
Christopher Sharp

" . . . what can you say about a man from another planet trying to make enough money through business adventures to pay for a trip home?

This Nicolas Roeg film has more pretensions than we can deal with in a limited space. There is an impression here that a screenplay was not written for the show: It looks as if the actors were trying to embody vague ideas that the director had about a story. It is certainly not clear why Bowie left his planet for Earth in the first place, since he spends almost every minute of the film plotting to go back.

continued on next page

201

continued from previous page

Roeg does suggest that people from outer space are generally more humane and sensitive than we are. But I am hard put to know what to do with this insight."

© Women's Wear Daily, 1976.

Newsweek, 6/14/76 (p. 89)
Jack Kroll

" . . . Roeg, formerly a superb cinematographer, has become one of the most interesting and mysterious filmmakers anywhere . . .

. . . You could call Roeg a pretentious director, but he is a gifted one, and many of his pretensions pay off in beauty, tension and a mysterious, unsettling power.

The Man Who Fell to Earth has enough of these qualities to offset a sometimes maddeningly oblique style and a pulsating vein of moral sentimentality--including hints that the story (written by Paul Mayersberg from a novel by Walter Tevis) is meant to be an allegory of the life of Christ. Roeg's images have the metaphysical quality of painters like Magritte or Max Ernst--their reality seems to shimmer with a hidden pathos. He seems to have a special insight into the perverse, childlike utopianism of the androgynous rock idol. Bowie is a sweet, sad, touching space-saint with his unisex face and body, his nutty pomegranate hair and lynx eyes over which he pastes earthling's orbs. If all space visitors are as gentle and meek as this, the CIA and the KGB have nothing to worry about."

© Newsweek, Inc. 1976
reprinted by permission.

Los Angeles Times, 7/7/76 (Pt. IV, p. 1)
Charles Champlin

". . . A lot of time passes and the makeup jobs on Henry, Clark and Torn are impressively realistic. (Bowie stays the same since he has masked the way he really looks, which is one of the film's large jolts.)

Bowie, flat-voiced and impassive, pale and soft like an elongated child, is perfect casting— otherworldly even as he tries to feign worldliness. (His planet receives earthly television, mostly the BBC, to judge by his accent.)

The score by John Phillips is its own jolty and useful mixture of what you might call 'here' sounds and 'there' sounds, bluesy and spacey by turn . . .

. . . The suspension of ordinary reality is what Roeg aims for a lot of the time and when it succeeds it is transporting in a magical sense.

The rest of the time you jolt from bright image to bright image, awaiting the grand cohering shape, the payoff to the dazzlings. There is a punch line to *The Man Who Fell to Earth*, but it takes forever and great expectations slump away."

© Los Angeles Times, 1976.

Commonweal, 7/16/76 (p. 463)
Colin L. Westerbeck, Jr.

". . . Like travelling through space to another country, travelling through time to another century defeats its objective because when we arrive we only impose our own meanings on what we find. Speculation of this kind—expanding our imaginations into other eras and other galaxies— disappoints us every time because it turns out to be such a self-centered activity. The only way to make a good science fiction movie, in fact, is to make one that is about this very incapacity in ourselves. That's essentially what Stanley Kubrick did in *2001* and in a less ambitious fashion it is what Nicolas Roeg has done in his new sci-fi film, *The Man Who Fell to Earth*. It is not really the recesses of the universe that these films are about, but rather the limits of our own imagination . . ."

© Commonweal, 1976.

Films in Review, August/September 1976 (p. 442)
Jane Morgan

". . . Paul Mayersberg's screenplay (based on Walter Tevis' novel), Roeg's direction, and the generally fine acting give even the minor characters some depth—unusual for science fiction movies (though not for science fiction). Roeg knows how to use the medium fully. Anthony Richmond's photography is often spectacular, one reason the 118 minutes seem short. John Phillips' musical background comments on characters (the lawyer listens to cool jazz) and broadens the action ('The moon stood still on Blueberry Hill' becomes science fiction). A major flaw is too much emphasis on Bowie as rock star, making a joke of the ending. Bowie's acting is appealing enough without winking at his fans."

© Films in Review, 1976.

Film Information, July/August 1976 (p. 2)
Eugene A. Schneider

". . . Director Nicolas Roeg (who was a famous cameraman—*Petulia*—before turning to directing—*Walkabout*, *Don't Look Now*) continues to use striking visuals as an integral part of his work. They are particularly suited to this latest film. Even the choice of David Bowie to play the leading role seems to have been made on the basis of appearance. Here, Bowie's unisex charisma derives in part from his intense pallor, bright red dyed hair, black-rimmed yellow eyes, and emaciated body. He *looks* like an extraterrestrial being.

Bowie's cool, almost detached characterization of the innocent creature who succumbs to earthly corruption—mainly gin, television and sex—complements Roeg's filmmaking style. Some viewers may find Roeg a bit too metaphysical, oblique, mannered. But youth will find he speaks their language and will make of *The Man Who Fell to Earth* a cult film . . ."

©Film Information, 1976.

New York Post, 5/29/76 (p. 15)
Frank Rich

". . . It's a movie that Roeg never should have made, for it's loaded with plot, characters and ideas (bad and borrowed ideas, to boot)—and these conventional elements are like mines that explode in the director's face all along the way . . .

Probably the mainstay of Roeg's cinematic style is his ability to create disorientation through fractionalized editing. As he's demonstrated amply in the past, this cutting style has its erotic uses as well, and the new movie contains a blisteringly hot sequence where a lewd sex scene is intercut with a samurai sword fight. This time, though, the splintered look of the movie as a whole never forms an abstractly coherent design; the visual images often seem forced, and eventually Roeg throws in outer-space tableaus and time dislocations for no apparent reason other than to keep the audience awake.

Given the limitations, the performances aren't bad . . ."

Reprinted by Permission of New York Post.
©1976, New York Post Corporation.

Take One, October 1976 (p. 38)
Will Aitken

". . . Until *The Man Who Fell to Earth*, we've shared Roeg's mordant glee. We've enjoyed watching the brutalities of contemporary dislocation because it's famous well-paid actors falling through the cracks in civilization's sidewalks instead of us.

The Man Who Fell to Earth wanted to imply these earthly pitfalls must be doubly jarring to one from another planet; this implication, though, is quickly contradicted by Newton—after he's been kidnapped, imprisoned and tortured—telling an earthling, 'We'd probably have treated you the same if you'd come over to our place.'

For a film as gimmicked up (to borrow from the script, 'technologically overstimulated') as this one, there are fewer and fewer distractions to ease the viewer along the way . . ."

©Take One, 1976.

MAN WHO SKIED DOWN EVEREST, THE

Screenplay: *Judith Crawley*. Based on the diary of Yuichiro Miura. Producers: *F. R. Crawley, James Hager, Dale Hartleben.* Photography: *Mitsuji Kanau.* Editors: *Bob Cooper, Millie Moore.* Narrated by *Douglas Rain.* Production: *Can/Am Ltd. Production.* Distributor: *Specialty Films.* Running time 86 minutes. New York opening May 27, 1976, at the D. W. Griffith and Regency Theatres. Classification: G.

Note: There is no cast in this film.

New York Magazine, 6/7/76 (p. 73)
John Simon

"There is a poem by the contemporary Japanese poet Saijo Yaso in which the 'hills . . . blaze/Savage and red' with 'a single red leaf.' So, too, Mount Everest blazes with the solitary red patch of Miura Yuichiro, the Japanese skier in his crimson Windbreaker, schussing down the highest, most dangerous, most inaccessible slope of all. It is the last of the many wonders of *The Man Who Skied Down Everest*, but not necessarily the greatest, for this delicate, awesome, and humane film is brimful of miracles.

Only the Japanese could have realized this project. Miura, in conceiving and executing it, proves himself a combination Kamikaze in the service of peace, athlete of the sort Pindar celebrated, Oriental philosopher, and Japanese poet fusing epic and filigree . . ."

© 1976 by the NYM Corp. Reprinted with the permission of NEW YORK Magazine.

Christian Science Monitor, 8/2/76 (p. 27)
David Sterritt

". . . we are given an overblown technicolor adventure, deserving of its Academy Award for Best Documentary only because, in spite of all untoward circumstances, they somehow managed to keep the cameras rolling. And some of the footage is truly spectacular. But the immensity of the undertaking makes a farce of the simplicity of the · Japanese philosophy that is interspersed here and there as a sort of defense. It is an ill-fated marriage of the excesses of modern technology (one sequence shows the group watching video tapes of the old *Bonanza* TV series amid the soundless snows of the Himalayas), and a sort of 15th century superstition . . .

continued on next page

continued from previous page

. . . Miura's quest was nobody's dream but his own. And so the film remains merely a private moment that has gone public."

Reprinted by permission from The Christian
Science Monitor © 1976.
The Christian Science Publishing Society.
All rights reserved.

Newsweek, 7/26/76 (p. 73)
Janet Maslin

"In 1970, the Japanese ski champion Yuichiro Miura set out to surpass himself in a spectacular fashion: having once set the world's speed record on skis and having raced down Mount Fuji, he decided to try the world's highest mountain on for size. *The Man Who Skied Down Everest*, which won this year's Oscar for the best documentary but is only now being widely distributed, is an account of that singularly presumptuous adventure . . .

. . . The film opens with a curious shot of the mountain, its peak and base clearly visible but a fine mist obscuring everything in between. Miura's perspective—his diary supplies the movie's narration—is quite aptly encapsulated by this single striking image. Covering the distance between ground and summit, between the absolutes of failure and success, was his original driving goal. But later on, reaching a middle ground becomes more important . . . Miura neither succeeds nor fails in his original ambition, but he achieves something more profound—a sense of his place in nature and an appreciation of the order of things. What begins as an act of supreme arrogance becomes a gesture of respect.

This is a moving chronicle, structured by the events themselves rather than a superimposition of the filmmakers' attitudes . . ."

©Newsweek, Inc. 1976
reprinted by permission.

MAN WHO WOULD BE KING, THE

Director: *John Huston*. Screenplay: *Mr. Huston, Gladys Hill*. Based on the short story by Rudyard Kipling. Producer: *John Foreman*. Photography: *Oswald Morris*. Editor: *Russell Lloyd*. Music: *Maurice Jarre*. Production: *Persky-Bright/Devon*. Distributor: *Allied Artists*. Running time 129 minutes. New York opening December 17, 1975, at the Loew's Astor Plaza and Coronet Theatres. Classification: PG.

Daniel Dravot: *Sean Connery*. Peachy Carnehan: *Michael Caine*. Rudyard Kipling: *Christopher Plummer*. Billy Fish: *Saeed Jaffrey*. Kafu-Selim: *Karroum Ben Bouih*. District Commissioner: *Jack May*. Ootah: *Doghmi Larbi*. Roxanne: *Shakira Caine*.

See Volume 1 for additional reviews

Sight and Sound, Spring 1976 (p. 122)
Geoff Brown

" . . . lively, totally assured, and certainly one of Huston's more bracing movies, though inevitably the story emerges much expanded, with different emphases. Kipling told the bulk of the narrative via the idiosyncratic reported speech of Carnehan, in which descriptions are pared down to the occasional flash of homely imagery—'We starts forward into those bitter cold mountainous parts, and never a road broader than the back of your hand.' Huston fills out the picture: the 'bitter cold mountainous parts' become beautiful landscapes of snow so desolate that one half expects the travellers to tumble upon the smiling lamas of Shangri-La . . .

Christopher Plummer—dressed in Kiplingesque glasses and a baby walrus mustache—gives a delightfully sober performance. Caine and Connery are equally fine (and Caine gives further proof of his unsung comic talents), but the script's bantering elaboration of the adventurers' pasts and personalities hinders their viability as symbolic figures—two matching alter egos venturing into dangerous new realms."

© Sight and Sound, 1976.

Jump Cut, Winter 1977 (p. 17)
Robert L. Greene

" . . . *The Man Who Would Be King* is a well-made film, a fact which makes its politics all the more unfortunate. Directed and coscripted by Huston from a story by Rudyard Kipling, featuring strong performances by Michael Caine and Sean Connery and grand production values, the film does succeed on the level of an exciting and often witty adventure story. It portrays the rise and fall of two ambitious scoundrels . . .

. . . the ideology underlying *The Man Who Would Be King* reinforces racist, imperialist, sexist and acquisitive beliefs. Although at times it gently pokes fun at Carnehan, Dravot, militarism and the British Empire, basically the film glamorizes Carnehan and Dravot and suggests that these rugged, macho comrades are true heroes and that the Asiatics, on the other hand, are barbaric, often laughable and essentially stupid . . ."

©Jump Cut, 1977.

MARATHON MAN

Director: *John Schlesinger*. Screenplay: *William Goldman*. Based on the novel by Mr. Goldman. Producers: *Robert Evans, Sidney Beckerman*. Photography: *Conrad Hall*. Editor: *Jim Clark*. Music: *Michael Small*. Distributor: *Paramount Pictures*. Running time 125 minutes. New York opening October 6, 1976, at the Loews State 1 and Loews Tower East Theatres. Classification: R.

Babe: *Dustin Hoffman*. Szell: *Laurence Olivier*. Doc: *Roy Scheider*. Janeway: *William Devane*. Elsa: *Marthe Keller*. Professor Biesenthal: *Fritz Weaver*. Karl: *Richard Bright*. Erhard: *Marc Lawrence*. Babe's Father: *Allen Joseph*. Melendez: *Tito Goya*. Szell's Brother: *Ben Dova*. Rosenbaum: *Lou Gilbert*. LeClerc: *Jacques Marin*. Chen: *James Wing Woo*.

New York Times, 10/7/76 (p. 62)
Vincent Canby

". . . Lord Olivier, one of the great ornaments of the English-speaking theater and cinema, helps to make John Schlesinger's *Marathon Man* a film that you won't want to miss, given a strong stomach for bloodshed and graphic torture that includes dental interference of an especially unpleasant sort.

In addition to Lord Olivier's superb performance, *Marathon Man* has several other superior things going for it: Dustin Hoffman as a moody, guilt-ridden, upper-West Side New Yorker, a haunted innocent obsessed with running, pursued by an unknown evil; Roy Scheider and William Devane as members of some sort of super-super Central Intelligence Agency, and the direction of Mr. Schlesinger, who has made a most elegant, bizarre, rococo melodrama out of material that, when you think about it, makes hardly any sense at all . . .

When the explanations do start coming, you may feel that *Marathon Man* is a kind of thriller that has run its course. High-level conspiracies really aren't that interesting unless we can get a fix on who is doing what to whom, which is never clear here. Yet the individual details of *Marathon Man*, the performances, and the attention given to its physical settings—in New York, Paris and South America—keep one's belief willingly suspended by a wickedly thin thread . . . "

©1976 by the New York Times Company.
Reprinted by permission.

Women's Wear Daily, 10/5/76 (p. 16)
Howard Kissel

"John Schlesinger's *Marathon Man* is rather like a well-trained athlete whose performance is hampered by psychological and ideological concerns that have very little to do with his sport. At heart, *Marathon Man* is an effective suspense picture somewhat overladen with Significance . . .

Even those of us who admire Schlesinger have to admit subtlety is not his strong suit. At times the film seems unusually heavyhanded, so much so that instead of heightening the tension, a grisly moment actually relieves it. The sequence in which Hoffman is tortured with a dentist's drill is obviously one everybody in the audience will identify with, but when Schlesinger gives us a closeup of a drill advancing toward us, the effect is less chilling than it is comic. A few times Schlesinger lets Hoffman get out of control, building into emotional moments that are deeply, honestly felt, but out of proportion to the rest of the picture. Still, Hoffman's work is impressive—he seems the only actor around who could carry the weight of all the excess ideological baggage without losing credibility as a man of action. Laurence Olivier does a superb job in the unlikely role of the Nazi dentist. Roy Scheider and William Devane are convincing as agents of The Division, and Marthe Keller is fine as the complex 'romantic interest.'. . . "

©Women's Wear Daily, 1976.

Films in Review, December 1976 (p. 636)
William Bernard

"Written by William Goldman, *Marathon Man* is a violently bloody thriller. Its protagonists are Christian Szell (Lord Laurence Olivier), ex-Nazi dentist who tortured patients at Auschwitz and now the owner of the key to a fortune in diamonds in a box in a NYC bank, and Babe (Dustin Hoffman), history graduate student who must outwit Szell to avenge the murder of his brother . . .

As directed by John Schlesinger, photographed by Conrad Hall and skillfully edited by Jim Clark, *Marathon Man* will hold your interest and upset your stomach during its running time. It's in recalling the film that the absurdity of the plot surfaces, and you see the introduction of the problems of city and national life as an attempt to give 'meaning' to what is basically only a good-versus-evil confrontation.

Olivier is coolly vicious in the use of a dentist's drill. Hoffman fails to explain what he's running from or to, while Scheider and Devane succeed in representing that Orwellian world of intrigue we have come to associate with super-governmental agencies."

©Films in Review, 1976.

continued on next page

continued from previous page

Saturday Review, 10/30/76 (p. 54)
Judith Crist

"The seductive powers of the thriller are epitomized by *Marathon Man*. It is, in fact, a film of
such rich texture and density in its construction,
so fascinatingly complex in its unfolding, so engrossing in its personalities, and so powerful in
its performance and pace that the seduction of the
senses has physical force . . .

Hoffman's persona is perfection for the young
man enmeshed in the affairs of his brother, a
double agent . . . These involvements lead to the
runner's confrontation with the White Angel of
Auschwitz, a surviving embodiment of the Nazi
torture horror. That horror is given full satanic force
by Laurence Olivier, who brings a soul-cringing
credibility to evil. Roy Scheider as the brother,
William Devane as his colleague, Marthe Keller
as a lovely pawn, and the minor players who have
their moments in the deadly race are all brilliantly
cast . . ."

©Judith Crist, 1976.

Village Voice, 10/18/76 (p. 60)
Molly Haskell

"Director John Schlesinger seems to have carved
a career out of making New York look even worse
than it is, and that takes some doing. In fact, it takes
so much doing that *Marathon Man* fairly reeks with
the sweat of Schlesinger's labors and those of the
panting and grunting postgraduate marathon runner
played by Dustin Hoffman. The muggings and murders, the decapitations and cavities and dental
depravities about which you have surely heard,
are the least of it. It's the random but unrelenting
nastiness of New York that adds insult to injury
and does violence to the soul, creating an uneasi-
ness that hovers overhead like a climatic inversion, and induces in the viewer the cold queasiness
of a nausea that owes more to Sade than Sartre . . ."

Reprinted by permission of The Village Voice.
Copyright ©The Village Voice, Inc., 1976.

New York Post, 10/7/76 (p. 26)
Frank Rich

"*Marathon Man*, the new John Schlesinger film
starring Dustin Hoffman, is a staggering but Pyrrhic
victory of slick filmmaking know-how and high-
powered acting over sleazy, piddling material.
Schlesinger, the British director of *Darling* and
Sunday, Bloody Sunday, knows how to grab an
audience, and he'll hit you with anything to keep
your attention—illogical emotional histrionics, baffling plot gimmicks, disorienting editing and, most
of all, extravagant violence.

By the time you leave *Marathon Man*, you feel
as if you've been put through the ringer a dozen
times—and yet, to what end? This movie doesn't
have a good (or even coherent) thriller story, it
rarely touches the heart or mind. It's just a stomach
churner—albeit one of the most luxuriously out-
fitted stomach churners of recent years . . ."

Reprinted by Permission of New York Post.
©1976, New York Post Corporation.

New York Magazine, 10/18/76 (p. 80)
John Simon

". . . Incremental gloss derives . . . from fancy
foreign locales, an international cast, and the presence of Laurence Olivier in a role for which any
number of Hollywood actors would have been
sufficient. Certainly Olivier's Nazi, a combination
of petty shrewdness, stolidity, and querulous self-
pity, is refreshingly different from the usual arrogant
demon . . .

A very fine performance, too, is Dustin Hoffman's
Babe . . . played by Hoffman with a perfect blend
of agony and comic absurdity that characterizes
nightmares, and falls not a whit short of Olivier's
marvelous mix of menace and preposterousness.
The stock part of Doc is enlivened with extraordinary authenticity by Roy Scheider . . .

The rest of the cast is defeated by the material,
most sadly Marthe Keller . . ."

©1976 by the NYM Corp. Reprinted with
the permission of NEW YORK Magazine.

Monthly Film Bulletin, December 1976 (p. 252)
Tom Milne

". . . Schlesinger's film proposes a sort of sub-
Watergate atmosphere of murky political conspiracy
and self-seeking supranational secret agentry. Unfortunately . . . what is left is simply a slick thriller,
fashionably violent (blood spurts everywhere), distinctly self-conscious (a girl agent walks into the
darkness, a soft thud is heard, a child's ball rolls
slowly into view in imitation of Lang's *M*), conventionally moralistic (Babe pointedly does *not* kill
Szell), and absolutely devoid of resonance. With
Dustin Hoffman coasting through a part evidently
written with his mannerisms in mind, and Olivier
doing the star-in-heavy-makeup bit, the best performances come from Roy Scheider and (though
repeating his *Family Plot* characterisation) William
Devane."

©Monthly Film Bulletin, 1976.

The Sunday Times (London), 12/19/76 (p. 27)
Alan Brien

". . . So long as Schlesinger sticks to New York
—the grubby Fulton Fish Market, the uneasy alternation of day and night activities in Central Park,

the chases on foot across the layered East Side motorways—plot and image coalesce. But in opening up the narrative to pile on the cosmopolitan glitter of James Bondery, director and scriptwriter let much of the murky fog of mystery leak away.

In an attempt to revitalise the now somewhat familiar mechanics of cross and double-cross, they carry us off into picture-postcard grandiosity, travel exhibitionism and waxwork gore. What read as mildly improbable now looks wildly incredible . . .

The performances are all professional and competent, though Hoffman seems rather insecurely spliced in between flashbacks and TV clips of the Olympics, while Olivier fills out a hollow role by switching a trifle arbitrarily between businesslike, executive tetchiness and senile snapping and spitting . . .''

©The Sunday Times, 1976.

The Times (London), 12/17/76 (p. 15)
David Robinson

''. . . Only by reading Schlesinger's intentions . . . as aiming at a dreamlike unreality is it possible to explain the garish overcolouring of the urban scene, the flamboyant inclination to stage set-pieces in extremely public and spectacular locations (as well as Lincoln Center, there is the Paris Opera and the Champs Elysees), the emphasis on blood, the recurrent subjective memory images.

It is strongly played by Laurence Olivier (always at his best in roles that call for him to be seedy or nasty or both), Dustin Hoffman, looking convincingly youthful and athletic in a role very evidently tailored to him, and Roy Scheider, a character actor of sinewy tough style . . .''

©The Times, 1976.

Christian Science Monitor, 10/27/76 (p. 23)
David Sterritt

''. . . Laurence Olivier delivers a gripping performance as the Nazi fugitive who comes out of hiding to chase after the contents of a mysterious tin box. Roy Scheider is coolly efficient as the hero's undercover brother, while Marthe Keller makes a properly fetching but disconcerting girl friend (and contributes to the movie's one sex scene), Fritz Weaver stands out as a teacher who wants to probe Babe's feelings.

William Goldman's screenplay, based on his novel, betrays his latter-day preference for calculation over conviction. Like Schlesinger's directing, everything is snappily put together, but little seems deeply felt or thoroughly thought out. Audiences will thrill to *Marathon Man* but will learn little from it and be stimulated little by it . . .''

Reprinted by permission from The Christian Science Monitor © 1976. The Christian Science Publishing Society. All rights reserved.

Newsweek, 10/11/76 (p. 111)
Jack Kroll

''. . . *Marathon Man* is an intelligently and largely satisfying thriller, written by William Goldman from his own novel, directed by John Schlesinger and photographed by Conrad Hall. But the most satisfying element is the work of Olivier, one of the few who turn acting into one of the great humane professions of Western civilization. It's wonderful to see how Olivier invests everything he does, no matter how small a role, with the same care, preparation and resourcefulness that he gives to *Othello* or *Long Day's Journey into Night*.

Olivier shows us that a great actor is the sculptor of his self, turning his body into a sign, a symbol and a force that jolts us into a higher consciousness. As Szell, he recharges Hannah Arendt's banality of evil' by restoring the primacy of evil in that all-too-familiar phrase . . . ''

©Newsweek, Inc. 1976 reprinted by permission.

Nation, 10/23/76 (p. 413)
Robert Hatch

''. . . the moral of the story seems to be that, whereas it is fine patriotic work to trot around the world killing people whom the Secret Service, 'say' (that must be a tacit reference to the CIA), is incompetent to eliminate, it is probably unwise to peddle diamonds for an old Nazi with a knife up his sleeve —and certainly foolish to cheat him in the process . . .

The presentation of this nonsense is as elegant as its content is fatuous, with some fine, hyper-realistic photography of New York and Paris, elegant wardrobes and instructive 007 prattle about vintage wine. Dustin Hoffman does again his impersonation of a homicidal mouse, and Olivier, with the help of a pair of very thick lenses, attains the final pinnacle of the master criminal cliche. Sir Laurence is not only one of the age's most eminent actors but, I begin to suspect, one of the most cynical.''

©The Nation, 1976.

Film Information, November 1976 (p. 5)
Paul Coleman

''. . . How . . . protagonists come together, amid flashes of gore and anguish, is the focus of the film before us. At film's end, if you have followed the series of double and triple crosses, braved the torture scenes, and still don't know what it was all about, you're bound to have company.

As with his previous films, director John Schlesinger has mounted scenes of intensity, pacing and

continued on next page

continued from previous page

verve. He has an uncanny knack for triggering moments of personal identification with the audience—the budding love relationship between Hoffman and Keller, the competition between the two brothers, the antics of two men in a street argument. What he cannot provide is a unified style that not only connects the moments but carries the plot over the rough spots where credibility and motive have departed.

The torture scenes provide an illustration of the film's fragmentation. Technically, they are magnificent. But their function in the plot is at best secondary . . . a gratuitous distraction. Those who die here generally experience much pain, and at no particular service to God, country, flag, or themselves. Such cynicism may be Schlesinger's preoccupation, but assembling one of the most appealing and talented casts of recent years to illustrate it seems to be wasteful . . .''

©Film Information, 1976.

Sight and Sound, Winter 1976/1977 (p. 56)
Richard Combs

''. . . In one respect at least, Goldman and Schlesinger have extended the catchpenny devices of the novel by refusing to allow their hero to become a simple, brutalised avenger, taking satisfaction for his father's hounding to suicide and his brother's slaying by adopting a ruthless vigilante ethic in pursuing Szell. Here Babe retains a certain moral ambiguity, sentimental to a degree (he is conveniently not required to execute Elsa), but at least in keeping with the vague religious notions of absolution and atonement that float through the film. The fountain in which Babe and Elsa bathe each other's wounds after the assault in the park is conceivably the same one in front of which Doc is later killed. And the cleansing motif is neatly clinched by the ending . . .''

©Sight and Sound, 1977.

MARQUISE OF O . . . , THE
(DIE MARQUISE VON O . . .)

Director: *Eric Rohmer*. Screenplay (German with English subtitles): *Mr. Rohmer*. Based on the story by Heinrich von Kleist. Photography: *Nestor Almendros*. Editor: *Cecile Decugis*. Production: *Janus Films* (Frankfurt), *Artemis* (Berlin), *Les Films du Losange* (Paris), *Gaumont* (Neuilly). Distributor: *New Line Cinema*.

Running time 102 minutes. New York opening October 17, 1976, at the New York Film Festival, Lincoln Center. Classification: None. Origin: Germany.

Marquise: *Edith Clever*. Count: *Bruno Ganz*. Father: *Peter Luhr*. Mother: *Edda Seippel*. Brother: *Otto Sander*. Midwife: *Ruth Drexel*. Doctor: *Eduard Linkers*. Porter: *Hesso Huber*. Russian Officer: *Richard Rogner*. Russian General: *Erich Schachinger*. Courier: *Thomas Straus*. Priest: *Volker Prachtel*.

Films in Review, December 1976 (p. 636)
Charles Phillips Reilly

''Adapted by director Eric Rohmer from the Heinrich von Kleist story, *The Marquise of O . . .* begins with a young widow and her children caught up in a minor battle skirmish. Threatened with rape by the soldiers, she is rescued by a Count. Exhausted, her maid gives her a sleeping potion. When the Count views her sleeping form, he cannot resist temptation . . . How she, the Count and her family react to this 'impossible' pregnancy is the heart of the matter.

Rohmer has delightfully spun out this tale, often using von Kleist's dialogue verbatim, but through the eye of Nestor Almendros' splendid camera. The costumes and sets convey the period faultlessly.

Witty and urbane, *The Marquise of O . . .* is most fortunate in its cast, particularly Edith Clever (the Marquise); Bruno Ganz (the Count); Peter Luhr (a stern, soldierly father); Edda Seippel (an astonished mother). For its sophistication of language and image *The Marquise of O . . .* confirms that Eric Rohmer ranks among today's best directors.''

©Films in Review, 1976.

The Times (London), 5/20/76 (p. 13)
David Robinson

''. . . Rohmer finds in Kleist, with his precise and objective descriptions of the outward expression of his characters' sentiments, a perfect scenarist, and he has followed him meticulously, risking the absurdities of lachrymose romantic sentiment, letting Kleist's own ironic distance provide its own commentary and comedy.

'To rejuvenate the work we did not attempt to modernize it, but to restore it to its own times.' The period sentiments are unadulterated and uncompromised. Nestor Almendros' impeccable photography and the design capture the luxurious austerity of Empire dress and decoration. Given the sentiments and the setting, the actors seem naturally to become creatures of the time and of Kleist's anecdote, in every posture and intonation . . ."

©The Times, 1976.

Monthly Film Bulletin, December 1976 (p. 253)
Jonathan Rosenbaum

". . . Widely and justifiably praised for its immaculate direction, acting and visual sophistication, it can none the less be regarded as a Jamesian rewrite of the novella that dims the passions of the latter with a form of delicate detachment quite in keeping with the tenor of Rohmer's *Contes Moraux* . . . There are many things to marvel at: the painterly compositions (beautifully shot by Nestor Almendros, with actions often charted along diagonal paths which evoke the director's long-term interest in Murnau's *Faust*), the gentle eroticism and emotional charge of Edith Clever as the Marquise (who figures to best advantage in her two long scenes with the equally impressive Edda Seippel, playing her mother), the ingenious blocking out and compression of the physical action itself . . ."

©Monthly Film Bulletin, 1976

The Times (London), 10/22/76 (p. 15)
Philip French

". . . Rohmer tells this funny and painful story with the same fastidiousness that he brought to the *contes moraux*, unravelling the various strands of the philosophical dilemmas with wit, clarity and precision, yet relating them closely to the specific milieu from which they emerge. He is assisted by a fine German cast, and by his gifted Spanish cinematographer Nestor Almendros, who has worked with Rohmer since leaving Cuba in 1964, and did such a remarkable job of naturalistic lighting on his *La Collectionneuse* and *Claire's Knee* . . . Again finding a style suited to the subject, Almendros has photographed the exquisitely dressed sets in high definition and deep focus, and while the film clearly evokes neoclassical painting (and many of the images look like animated pictures by David or Ingres), the characters are most assuredly inhabiting their world, and the audience—standing at a slight distance—is consciously and unpatronizingly observing them."

©The Times, 1976.

New York Magazine, 11/8/76 (p. 79)
John Simon

". . . in turning, however unpreventably, *The Marquise of O . . .* into a proto-comedy from a rigor-

ous study of individual moral growth to heroic dimensions, Kleist's work has been, charmingly and cogently, cheapened. The mindless guffaws of the theater audience with which I saw the film turned my stomach just as they no doubt caused Kleist to turn in his grave.

Rohmer's direction is, as always, theatrical, but that fits in with the major part of this material . . .

The casting is partly inspired—Edda Seippel as the mother, several minor parts, and especially Edith Clever, as the heroine; partly poor—Peter Luhr as the father, Otto Sander as an inappropriately yokelish brother, and, worst of all, Bruno Ganz as the Count . . ."

©1976 by the NYM Corp. Reprinted with the permission of NEW YORK Magazine.

Christian Science Monitor, 12/6/76 (p. 50)
David Sterritt

"*The Marquise of O . . .* is a delicate experiment in literary cinema. Eric Rohmer, one of the most word-conscious filmmakers anywhere, has taken a long story by the German writer Heinrich von Kleist and attempted to transpose it to the screen, word for word and gesture for gesture. The result is an immaculately wrought and justly celebrated excursion into manners, morals, and borderline surrealism . . .

Only a director as civilized as Rohmer could have maintained the exquisite balance that prevails throughout *The Marquise of O . . .* He unfolds the story smoothly and quietly, allowing its absurdisms to erupt so organically from the narrative texture that we don't know whether to laugh, cry, or gasp. So we do some of all three, and at the end we realize that's exactly what Rohmer intended. It's an emotional balancing act of the first order, pulled off with singular wit and grace . . ."

Reprinted by permission from The Christian Science Monitor ©1976. The Christian Science Publishing Society. All rights reserved.

New York Post, 10/18/76 (p. 22)
Frank Rich

". . . *The Marquise of O . . . . . .* is simply above reproach: Every shot is meticulously designed, every irony is brought home with an exquisitely light touch. It's the kind of movie that renders criticism superfluous.

Or almost. While I liked *The Marquise of O . . .* which, by the way, is an adaptation of the 1808 Heinrich von Kleist story—I must confess that it doesn't make me feel like cheering. Yet this movie is more or less perfect (some of the acting is a bit drab), but a price perfection. It seems to me that Rohmer has stopped taking the big risks in his

continued on next page

continued from previous page

work—the risks that can lead to an artistic disaster but that can also lead to artistic growth . . ."

Reprinted by Permission of New York Post.
©1976, New York Post Corporation.

The Sunday Times (London), 10/24/76 (p. 35)
Alan Brien

". . . Throughout the film, Nestor Almendros' camera tends to remain as immobile as an easel. The pictures flash up like slides on a magic lantern, giving the impression of being all coloured by hand.

If this sounds static, then I am doing the film an injustice. There is a good deal of domestic action, fountains of tears and muffled sobbings, and at some time almost everyone sinks to their knees and begs forgiveness of another. But the screen remains, if not a picture frame, certainly the box set of a private theatre, with the players walking off and on as if entering, or leaving the proscenium of an intimate stage . . .

A German anecdote about an Italian scandal, translated to the screen by a French director through German actors, *Die Marquise von O* . . . is likely to divide audiences. Some may find it slow, sentimental, naive and old-fashioned; others leisurely, beautiful, controlled and illuminating. I found it both, often at the same time. Rohmer seems to be saying—here it is, take it or leave it. At the end, I felt I had left it. But, since then, it keeps returning."

©The Sunday Times, 1976.

Newsweek, 11/1/76 (p. 83)
Jack Kroll

". . . Rohmer, whose films (*Claire's Knee*, *My Night at Maud's*) are all about desire chilled in the icebox of custom, has brilliantly reproduced the impact of this rationally irrational story: he captures Kleist's almost surreal effect of a grenade whose exploding fragments somehow arrange themselves into a classically formal pattern . . .

Rohmer and his superb cinematographer Nestor Almendros translate Kleist's famous 'thunderclap' style into lightning-bolt images . . . Rohmer knows how to turn words into actions, and his excellent German actors bring to life those Kleistian conversations whose formality masks a frantic urgency. Best of all, Rohmer finds humane laughter in this story, which shocked the good people of its time with its X-ray vision of the passion beneath the periwig."

©Newsweek, Inc. 1976
reprinted by permission.

Nation, 11/6/76 (p. 475)
Harold Clurman

". . . a clear, classic surface which induces chuckles and yet remains unaccountably disturbing. The French director of *My Night at Maud's*, Eric Rohmer, has literally transcribed the story to the screen and in doing so has wrought his best film . . .

A German critic has found something of Kafka in Kleist. For my part, I find the film's 'surface,' pictorially and dramatically, so direct, burnished and *light* that it eludes explanation while it says all. The acting by the entire company is flawless. Besides the excellence of each of its individual members, all of them have been associated in a permanent theatre ensemble. It shows."

©The Nation, 1976.

Village Voice, 10/25/76 (p. 49)
Andrew Sarris

"Eric Rohmer's *The Marquise of O* . . . which concluded the 14th New York Film Festival with a flourish, is so remarkably faithful to Heinrich von Kleist's short story that it may seem to some that the cinema has been shortchanged in favor of literature. In the early part of the film I began to fear that Rohmer's mise-en-scene was too posed and painterly, and that he had been intimidated by a period subject. But as the plot progressed, the guileless force of the acting began to grip me with an intensity reminiscent of the early Griffith films with Lillian Gish and Mae Marsh. In this story of virtue triumphant and vice repentant, Rohmer's boundless faith in his characters matches Kleist's in a way that is beautiful to behold . . ."

Reprinted by permission of The Village Voice.
Copyright ©The Village Voice, Inc., 1976.

Film Information, November 1976 (p. 2)
Bea Rothenbeuchner

". . . The all-German cast handles the unadulterated classical dialogue with a fine feeling for its mixture of reserve and excess. Edith Clever's Marquise is the personification of maligned innocence while Bruno Ganz is a convincingly remorseful rapist/hero. Peter Luhr and Edda Seippel as the parents portray parental feelings of wrath and joy with skill and aplomb.

Cinematographer Nestor Almendros makes the most of beautiful Empire costumes and settings, his compositions, colors, and lighting reminiscent at times of the paintings of Jacques Louis David.

Eric Rohmer has said, 'We wanted to depict the world of the past with the same care for detail as we observed the world of today in the *contes moraux*.' He has achieved this . . . the recreation of Kleist's masterwork is meticulous throughout.

At the same time Rohmer subtly satirizes the differences between *then* and *now*, reminding us that, after all, human foibles remain comfortably consistent."

©Film Information, 1976.

New Leader, 11/8/76 (p. 25)
Robert Asahina

". . . Remarkably, Rohmer renders the story in a fashion that absolutely refuses to permit our condescension toward a plot and characters in danger of appearing foolish to modern sensibilities. He does so in part by providing a visual counterpoint to Kleist's prose: a precise balance of colors, action and speech that avoids romantic sentimentality as well as easy irony—he gives us cool shades (white dresses and blue-gray interiors), carefully blocked movements and scrupulous enunciation . . . The result is an esthetic distance between the audience and the screen, just as Kleist's exact and succinct phrases distance the readers of his story . . .

The separation, as Rohmer has observed, allows us to appreciate the tension between the outward manifestations of feeling and the equally external moral code binding the characters, on the one hand, and their inner feelings, about which we learn nothing directly, on the other . . ."

Reprinted with permission from
The New Leader, 1976.
©The American Labor Conference
on International Affairs, Inc.

Sight and Sound, Winter 1976/1977 (p. 54)
Tom Milne

". . . Articulating his film through a melodic alternation of fades and direct cuts (respectively demarcating the moments of baffled impasse and the sudden rushes toward decision or supposed resolution), Rohmer exactly captures the breathless gravity of Kleist's style: a classical serenity stirred by a fierce undertow of agitation as the injured innocent suffers proudly, resignedly, and for all the absurdity of the situation, very movingly. Although Kleist kept his story at arm's length as a legend of another (not so very distant) time and place, a kind of reality keeps breaking through the surface . . ."

©Sight and Sound, 1977.

MARTYR, THE

Director: *Aleksander Ford*. Screenplay: *Joseph Gross*. Based on a story by Alexander

Ramati. Producer: *Artur Brauner*. Photography: *Jerzy Lipman*. Editor: *C. O. Bartning*. Music: *Moshe Wilensky*. Production: *CCC-Filmkunst*. Distributor: *Joseph Green Pictures*. Running time 90 minutes. New York opening June 16, 1976, at the Juliet 1 Theatre. Classification: None. Origin: Israel/West Germany.

Dr. Janusz Korczak: *Leo Genn*. Stefa: *Orna Porat*. Ruth: *Efrat Lavie*. Yakov: *Ohad Kaplan*. Michael: *Benjamin Volz*. Adam: *Carlos Werner*.

New York Post, 6/17/76 (p. 27)
Archer Winsten

"*The Martyr* . . . tells the harrowing story of a Warsaw doctor, Janusz Korczak (Leo Genn) who chose to take care of 200 Jewish orphans in the doomed Warsaw Ghetto of 1942.

The Germans had made their plans of annihilation. Very detailed.

Word came to Dr. Korczak through a member of the outside Underground who also carried a pass to safety for the doctor. As a widely known writer and humanitarian he was considered worthy of the special effort.

But he cannot bring himself to leave the children behind.

He asks, 'What can I tell them? I have never lied to them.'

The picture has succeeded in personalizing the children for the audience as well as the doctor. His question is not without force . . .

Made as the first Israeli-German co-production and directed by Aleksander Ford, this picture is a very realistic and touching view of this small section of that overwhelming tragedy . . . it is well acted by Leo Genn and the less known supporting players and children."

Reprinted by Permission of New York Post.
© 1976, New York Post Corporation.

MATTER OF TIME, A

Director: *Vincente Minnelli*. Screenplay: *John Gay*. Based on the novel THE FILM OF MEMORY by Maurice Druon. Producer: *Jack H. Skirball, J. Edmund Grainger*. Photography: *Geoffrey*

continued on next page

continued from previous page

Unsworth. Editor: *Peter Taylor.* Music: *Nino Oliviero.* Songs: *Fred Ebb, John Kander.* Distributor: *American International Pictures.* Running time 97 minutes. New York opening October 7, 1976, at Radio City Music Hall. Classification: PG.

Nina: *Liza Minnelli.* The Contessa: *Ingrid Bergman.* Count Sanziani: *Charles Boyer.* Mario Morello: *Spiros Andros.* Valentina: *Tina Aumont.* Jeanne Blasto: *Anna Proclemer.* Antonio Vicaria: *Gabriele Ferzeti.* Pavelli: *Arnolda Foa.* Gabriele: *Orso Maria Guerrini.* Charles Van Maar: *Fernando Rey.* Nun: *Isabella Rossellini.*

Women's Wear Daily, 10/7/76 (p. 10)
Howard Kissel

". . . The songs and their 'interpretations' are symptomatic of the whole film, a dreary attempt at nostalgia and old-fashioned romance in which Liza, as an Italian country girl, takes lessons in life from an aging courtesan, . . . Ingrid Bergman, whose grotesquely mascara-ed eyes make her look like a wraith. Liza's daddy Vincente directed it (nothing in the wretched material requires a director like Minnelli); and Ingrid's daughter by Rossellini, Isabella, an exquisite young woman, plays a nurse, coyly named Sister Pia. (Get it?) All this, I suppose, is to make the film attractive to collectors of Trivia. Well, it's good to know there's something in it for somebody."

©Women's Wear Daily, 1976.

Newsweek, 10/25/76 (p. 107)
Janet Maslin

"*A Matter of Time* recycles every trick in the storybook, except perhaps for the one that says if you click your heels three times you'll go back to Kansas . . .

Vincente Minnelli, who is credited as *A Matter of Time*'s director, has reportedly disowned the finished product, but the movie's most grievous errors were built in at its conception, over which he must have had some control. The film burns up far too much of its limited energy trying both to glorify the Bergman character's eccentricities and to dismiss them as symptoms of senility. It is also wrongheaded in depicting the chambermaid as both daytime innocent and nocturnal coquette, because Liza Minnelli can neither simulate naivete nor seem wholesomely irresistible. Minnelli is at her best when projecting a perverse, even menacing, sensuality—although I'm sure that her father, understandably, would disagree."

©Newsweek, Inc. 1976
reprinted by permission.

New York Magazine, 10/25/76 (p. 91)
John Simon

"*A Matter of Time* is a 97-minute version of Vincente Minnelli's three-hour film based on a novel by Maurice Druon. Since I admire Druon but little, and Minnelli, except for *The Clock*, not at all, I doubt whether much was lost here. What is left is a contemporary Cinderella story set in Rome, and so hackneyed, inept, and stupid as to be almost amusing. Wags are calling it 'Daddy's Revenge,' and certainly daughter Liza Minnelli looks more bug-eyed, blubber-lipped, and untalented than ever. What is remarkable, though, is that Ingrid Bergman, as a daffy fairy godmother of a countess, manages to sink to Liza's level . . ."

©1976 by the NYM Corp. Reprinted with
the permission of NEW YORK Magazine.

Los Angeles Times, 10/8/76 (Pt. IV, p. 22)
Kevin Thomas

". . . Under Minnelli's direction Miss Minnelli in her first major film appearance under her father's guidance and Miss Bergman make this relationship between youth and old age infinitely touching. What's more, Minnelli manages most deftly those shifts between fantasy and reality, as the maid imagines she's the contessa in her prime.

There's no denying that *A Matter of Time* suffers from its tinny, hollow, postsynchronized dialogue, which tends to give the lie to an already fragile whimsy. Fortunately, its stars are allowed their own familiar voices, but the English dubbing of the many Italian supporting players is pretty obvious and stilted. As if the soundtrack weren't enough of a liability, the film has a decidedly murky look despite having been photographed by the celebrated British cinematographer Geoffrey Unsworth.

Yet the spell the film casts holds from start to finish, and there are some stunning moments along the way . . ."

©Los Angeles Times, 1976.

Christian Science Monitor, 10/14/76 (p. 26)
David Sterritt

". . . Miss Bergman is about the best thing about *A Matter of Time.* She hams it up deliciously, spouting the nutty lines of John Gay's screenplay with a dead pan lightened by just a touch of mischievousness. And naturally, she's lovely, even behind the Contessa's spooky makeup.

Miss Minnelli hasn't nearly so much good material—curiously, since her father put the movie together and seems to be trying to look after her best on-screen interests. She sings her three songs strongly, and does lots of wide-eyed mugging, and wears plenty of fancy outfits, but never becomes more than Miss Bergman's second banana. Boyer and Rey are wasted in their tiny roles . . ."

Reprinted by permission from The Christian Science Monitor © 1976. The Christian Science Publishing Society. All rights reserved.

New York Post, 10/8/76 (p. 46)
Frank Rich

"It's only a matter of time before *A Matter of Time*, Vincente Minnelli's first film since *On a Clear Day You Can See Forever*, vanishes forever from this earth, but before it does, attention must be paid. While this film . . . is a catastrophe, it is a catastrophe of an especially high order: It's so bad that it almost becomes good. Certainly only a couple of other movies have made me laugh so hard this year, and unintentional though the laughter provoked by *A Matter of Time* may be, I'm all in favor of taking what you can get . . .

. . . this movie is so spectacularly crazy that if Minnelli could only convince Mel Brooks to put his name on it, *A Matter of Time* might yet be the comedy sleeper of the year."

Reprinted by Permission of New York Post. © 1976, New York Post Corporation.

Film Information, November 1976 (p. 6)
Eugene A. Schneider

"*A Matter of Time* gives two well-known movie stars, Liza Minnelli and Ingrid Bergman, the opportunity to demonstrate their acting talent while doing and saying nothing of significance.

Liza Minnelli plays the role of an Italian peasant girl, Nina, who moves to Rome and becomes a chambermaid in a once-elegant hotel. Ingrid Bergman is the Contessa, one of the hotel's permanent guests. Once the talk of glittering European society, she is now poverty-stricken, living on the sale of her last jewels.

Charles Boyer puts in a cameo appearance as the separated husband who had not seen the Contessa for forty years . . .

The color cinematography, with many fantasy forwards and flashbacks, is intriguing, as are the glamorous costumes and settings—mostly Rome and Venice. But production lushness cannot make up for a basically weak story . . ."

© Film Information, 1976.

MEMORY OF JUSTICE, THE

Documentary. Director, Producer: *Marcel Ophuls*. Photography: *Mike Davis*. Editor: *Inge Behrens*. Sound: *Anthony Jackson*. Produc-

tion: *Max Palevsky* and *Hamilton Fish 3rd*; *Polytel International*. Distributor: *Paramount Pictures*. Running time 278 minutes. New York opening October 5, 1976, at the New York Film Festival, Lincoln Center. Classification: PG.

New York Times, 10/5/76 (p. 54)
Vincent Canby

"Like his earlier *The Sorrow and the Pity*, which examined the behavior of the French during the Nazi occupation, Marcel Ophuls' *The Memory of Justice* expands the possibilities of the documentary motion picture in such a way that all future films of this sort will be compared to it. *The Sorrow and the Pity* and *The Memory of Justice* have set standards and created expectations that even Mr. Ophuls himself may not always meet, as in *A Sense of Loss*, his film about Northern Ireland, that was just as illusive as its subject. Mr. Ophuls doesn't deal in paltry material.

The Memory of Justice is monumental, though not only because it goes on for a demanding 4 hours and 38 minutes, plus an intermission. It also marks off, explores, calls attention to and considers, tranquilly, without making easy judgments, one of the central issues of our time: collective versus individual responsibility.

The starting point is an evocation of the 1946-47 Nuremberg war crimes trials, through newsreels and interviews with surviving defendants, prosecutors, defending attorneys, and witnesses, that leads to a consideration of French tactics in the fight to keep Algeria and America in action in Vietnam . . .

The ethical questions are timeless but the subject is particular, and it's through the accumulation of particularities that *The Memory of Justice* makes its impact . . .

There is absolutely no way to condense this material. Its effect is cumulative . . ."

© 1976 by the New York Times Company. Reprinted by permission.

The Times (London), 5/29/76 (p. 7)
David Robinson

". . . what makes the film so compelling for all its four hours and thirty-eight minutes is the close underlying texture and the brilliance and inevitability with which film and argument are structured. Part One deals specifically with Nuremberg and concludes leaving the spectator disturbed, yet sure of

continued on next page

continued from previous page

his moral position. The second part of the film bit by bit undermines this confidence, as the argument ranges wider, reexamining guilt and justice in the light of Dresden, Algeria, My Lai . . . The strength of the film is that Ophuls refuses any easy journalistic identifications of the Nazi leaders with, say, the French in Algeria or the Americans in Vietnam. He is inclined to favour General Taylor's distinction between the coolly planned genocide of the former and the kind of idiotic cruelties that pressure and fear can produce. The Nazis, anyway, cannot be made scapegoats for all the guilt of the twentieth century any more than the Americans: which of us, the film constantly asks, could look into his own heart and know how he might act under comparable pressures? . . ."

©The Times, 1976.

Women's Wear Daily, 10/5/76 (p. 16)
Howard Kissel

"Toward the end of Marcel Ophuls' *The Memory of Justice*, we see a Frenchwoman who survived a year in Auschwitz testify at the Nuremberg trials about the concentration camp. The women she was with used to talk, she says, about how hard it would be to make people believe what had happened there because even those who were there found it hard to believe . . .

After giving testimony, she walks through the courtroom and stops to look at the men in the defense box, Speer, Goering, and the others. They look like ordinary men, she realizes; but then even the men who ran the camps looked perfectly ordinary. Her bafflement in the face of unimaginable evil mirrors our own. But Ophuls does not stop there. The film is wrenching because it does not place us merely on the side of the woman. We also have things in common with the men in the box. Using Nuremberg as a reference point, Ophuls goes on to weigh notions of collective guilt of the French in Algeria and the Americans in Vietnam . . .

. . . Ophuls' film is not just a documentary—it makes a complex moral quest a passionate, harrowing experience."

©Women's Wear Daily, 1976.

Christian Science Monitor, 10/8/76 (p. 22)
David Sterritt

". . . Ophuls counterposes Nuremberg and My Lai, Dachau and Algeria, Dresden and Hiroshima. He interviews an unregenerate former Nazi in the German countryside, repentant war-crime ex-convict Albert Speer in his comfy living room, and a Nuremberg psychologist who jovially recalls the prisoners' competitiveness about their IQ scores . . .

. . . perhaps most important, he chats at length with Nuremberg chief prosecutor Telford Taylor, whose book *Nuremberg and Vietnam, an American*

Tragedy, initially inspired the film . . .

Ophuls' views . . . become evident as the film progresses. *The Memory of Justice* does not pretend to utter objectivity, but seeks rather a balanced and humane point of view with all options out in the open so the spectator can use his own mind in agreeing or disagreeing.

Nor is the purely human side forgotten in this vigorous exercise . . .

The Memory of Justice is a stunning rarity: a wholly personal documentary that seeks and finds its own sense of justice as it sifts and weighs some of this century's profoundest moral questions. It will enrich the life of anyone who sees it."

Reprinted by permission from The Christian
Science Monitor © 1976.
The Christian Science Publishing Society.
All rights reserved.

The Times (London), 11/5/76 (p. 9)
David Robinson

". . . Ophuls centres his contemplation of the theme of guilt—of nations as of individuals—and of the moral right to judge, upon the Nuremberg tribunals. He sifts again through the old, contrasty newsreels, and confronts the actors in them—judges, counsel, accused and accusers—with their present selves.

Seemingly casual, the argument is in fact brilliantly and purposefully structured. At the end of the first half, concentrated on Nuremberg, the viewer is shaken, but still sure of his moral position. By the end of the second the argument has become wider and more complex; and he is sure of nothing except how elusive are concepts of responsibility, guilt and justice. How do you distinguish responsibility for the concentration camps from responsibility for Dresden or My Lai? . . ."

©The Times, 1976.

Newsweek, 10/25/76 (p. 104)
Jack Kroll

". . . Crosscutting and interweaving more than 40 interviews with varied old footage, Ophuls creates a tissue of images through which morals are made flesh . . .

Ophuls confronts you with unspeakable images of the Nazi death camps and the destruction in Vietnam. The rhythm and pressure of his method explode the easy answers that leap to your mind. You look for yourself in the film: is that you, the self-assured face of Daniel Ellsberg, or the still quizzical and angry face of Col. Anthony Herbert?

At the ethical center of the film are Mrs. Barbara Keating, widow of a Marine officer, and Louise and Robert Ransom, who lost their son in Vietnam. Mrs. Keating stands next to a cupboard filled with her husband's medals: her stance expresses solidarity with her husband and the policy he represented. The Ransoms sit at their table quietly talking about their son, whom 'his country wasted.' Ophuls fixes us in an exquisite dialectical tension between Mrs. Keating and the Ransoms. Our instinct to give the Ransoms higher marks seems cheap—we feel uneasy in our moral complacency . . ."

©Newsweek, Inc. 1976
reprinted by permission.

Saturday Review, 10/16/76 (p. 43)
Judith Crist

". . . The issues of Nuremberg and of German national guilt are primary in the first half of the film. Through these Ophuls explores the difficulties of moral judgments and, perhaps, the frustrations, if not the futilities, also involved. The second half of the film expands to other considerations and becomes, for me, far more diffuse and less interesting. We encounter the more familiar faces and expected reactions of Daniel Ellsberg . . . Barbara Keating, a vengeful Vietnam War widow; Colonel Anthony Herbert, who protested American atrocities in Vietnam; Kent State war protestors; Vietnam deserters; and the parents of GIs killed there. What we are left to ponder goes far beyond the simple judgments of Ellsberg toward the compassionate appreciation of human fallibility that Taylor suggests and Ophuls builds on. There are no absolutes in issues so complex, and the exquisite intelligence Ophuls uses in his search for understanding simply illuminates that complexity . . ."

©Judith Crist, 1976.

New York Post, 10/2/76 (p. 18)
Frank Rich

"If a more important documentary than Marcel Ophuls' new epic film *The Memory of Justice* has been made during my lifetime, I do not know what it is. In this movie . . . Ophuls takes as his subject some of the most crucial moral debates to haunt mankind during the post-World War II era—and not only does he bring those debates to fiery life, but he uses them as the inspiration for a full-fledged work of movie art. This is a movie about history and ideas, real people and real events, that, amazingly enough, has all the urgency, drama, compassion, mystery and esthetic ripeness that we expect from the best fiction films . . ."

Reprinted by Permission of New York Post.
©1976, New York Post Corporation.

Nation, 10/30/76 (p. 442)
Harold Clurman

"The outstanding entry in the New York Film Festival's program was Marcel Ophuls' *The Memory*

of Justice . . . On being asked whether I liked it I could only reply, 'Can one "like" an earthquake or a similar misfortune?' Though artfully made, *The Memory of Justice* is not art; it is the record of a mountain of disasters: the German concentration camps, the war in Vietnam, and their aftermaths. Its 'stars' are Hitler, Goering, Albert Speer, the still living and the dead of Auschwitz and Buchenwald, the judges, the witnesses at Nuremberg, the heroes and martyrs of those days, people of many creeds and nationalities. We do not hold court on them, we *see* them . . ."

©The Nation, 1976.

Film Information, October 1976 (p. 1)
William F. Fore

". . . We realize that the moral issue is universal, that we all have a share in the blame when inhumanity is visited on anyone, anywhere. As much as we initially reject the idea, we are forced to recognize that we are no different from the Germans and that given the circumstances we are capable of acquiescing to atrocities and mass murder by *our* state and we cannot escape the moral implications.

The Memory of Justice cannot possibly become a popular film. It will receive only limited showing in art houses, and we can be grateful that Paramount is willing to place it into commercial release. It is 4½ hours long. It is complex and requires close attention. It presses home moral lessons which are unpalatable. But for the persons who sense that sometime, somewhere, we all have to face the problem of when to keep quiet and when to speak out, *The Memory of Justice* is simply required viewing."

©Film Information, 1976.

Commentary, December 1976 (p. 66)
Dorothy Rabinowitz

". . . There is a side of Ophuls that intrudes on all his better intentions in this film, a side best and briefly described as an impulse toward anti-Americanism. He intended to make a movie that took up the admittedly complicated question of whether the victors in a war may in good conscience judge the vanquished. He fought a hard battle to rescue his film from editing that would have leaned too heavily on Vietnam footage and thus made too much of a parallel between the Nazis in Europe and the Americans in Vietnam. Still, having rescued his own film, it is now what *he* has made it. Ophuls intended a movie exploring the question of whether the victor ought to judge the vanquished and ended up making a movie that is a judgment on the victors. He intended to make a film that would in the end stand as an endorsement of the Nuremberg trials and ended with one that

continued on next page

continued from previous page

denies the legitimacy of Nuremberg at every turn, with every facile cut to Vietnam . . ."

©Commentary, 1976.

New York Magazine, 10/25/76 (p. 90)
John Simon

". . . In *The Memory of Justice* there are five principal ingredients: (1) the old piece of documentary film, used as it was shot, but changed by a new commentary or a new context; (2) the old filmed material crosscut with new footage, usually of the same person or place as he, she, or it is now; (3) film clips from the past, but not directly related to the matter at hand, yet shedding a fascinating oblique light on it; (4) interviews with prominent or obscure people now, who were somehow involved with the events of the past; (5) talks with quite ordinary people uninvolved with the historic events, except by sometimes being in the places where those events occurred.

The results are prodigious . . ."

©1976 by the NYM Corp. Reprinted with the permission of NEW YORK Magazine.

Nation, 11/6/76 (p. 474)
Robert Hatch

". . . I think that from all the evidence that *The Memory of Justice* amasses on the prevalence of wickedness in this world, it might have plucked this one nugget of hope that for man improvement is possible, though justice may ever elude his grasp. It is there in the film, but it is not made to shine. One comes from the theater, or at least I did, depressed by being made to endure once more the smug self-abasement of Speer, the lying truculence of Doenitz, the effective arrogance of Goering, and the latter-day hairsplitting of the legal celebrities who passed judgment on them. Ophuls is a master film editor; it is commonly conceded that he can make four hours or more of taped interviews into a mesmeric film by his genius for timing, his appreciation of the witty, ironic or revelatory possibilities of juxtaposition. He works that magic in *The Memory of Justice*; it is an absorbing film. Nevertheless, I found myself editing it again in my head to create a document which would celebrate the fact that those now-elderly lawyers who sit somewhat complacently for Ophuls' portrait camera did in fact change the basic ethical equation at Nuremberg."

©The Nation, 1976.

Films in Review, November 1976 (p. 565)
Dorothy Dean

". . . Ophuls devises a highly professional amalgam of interviews and news film footage (sources such as *The March of Time*). The interviewees number some 60 'famous or unknown personalities' . . . Unfortunately, as was also true of *The Sorrow and the Pity*, the audience's aural comprehension, even under optimum conditions, is gravely eroded by the use of English-language simultaneous translation (often grotesquely accented) in preference to subtitling or dubbing. Where called for, the English is superimposed on the soundtrack over the original German or French (which remain audible but not intelligible), in such fashion that at times it is impossible to understand the speakers. Nonetheless, for those with patience, *The Memory of Justice* is considerably more than worthwhile."

©Films in Review, 1976.

Cineaste, Winter 1977 (p. 41)
Lenny Rubenstein

". . . Ophuls' film provides . . . a court before which ideal justice, the Platonic 'memory of justice,' can be enacted, the sound condemnation of our guilt as well as that of our opponents. It is an ambitious task, and this $4^1/_2$-hour production does not always succeed.

The film has many of the elements of a trial—there is evidence of crimes in the form of still photographs, newsreel footage and witnesses' testimony, crimes that range from the Nazi concentration camps to the torture of Vietnamese civilians, from the random murder of wounded prisoners to the whimsical shooting of Algerian children . . ."

©Cineaste, 1977.

Ms., February 1977 (p. 38)
Frances Fitzgerald

". . . Through this political essay Ophuls weaves a . . . profound series of questions concerning the limits of moral responsibility, the nature of the human community, and the capacity of human beings—or Western civilization at its current state of development—to learn from history and to control their own fate. These questions are abstract only in the sense that they can be abstracted for the sake of analysis. In the film they emerge from the testimony of people such as Albert Speer, Henri Alleg, Daniel Ellsberg, and a variety of ordinary Germans and ordinary Americans who have faced (or have refused to face) these ultimate questions and who speak in terms of their own personal histories.

Ophuls is in no way clinical or judgmental about these people. He presents them as a novelist would, by—as it were—walking all the way around them. And in every case, what emerges is a kind of miracle . . .''

©Ms., 1977

Sight and Sound, Winter 1976/1977 (p. 58)
Penelope Houston

". . . with his own rather abrasive, stateless voice, Ophuls is a good interviewer, a back of the head presence in his own films, not afraid to ask either the difficult or the obvious questions. His films attempt neither historical neutrality nor partisanship, but a position somewhere between: that perhaps of a man trying to make up his mind through the process of filmmaking, and caught up in the ironies of all situations. And, of course, he has a mastery of how to exploit the medium, including the shifts between the colour of the present and the black and white of the past . . .

In the end, *Memory of Justice* seems bound to leave an impression that memory knows no justice and that justice has little memory . . .''

©Sight and Sound, 1977

MIDDLEMAN, THE (JANA-ARANYA)

Director, Music: *Satyajit Ray*. Screenplay (Bengali with English dialogue): *Mr. Ray*. Based on a story by Shankar. Producer: *Subir Guha*. Photography: *Soumendu Ray*. Editor: *Dulai Dutta*. Production: *Indus Films*. Running time 134 minutes. New York opening October 12, 1976, at the New York Film Festival, Lincoln Center. Classification: None. Origin: India.

Somnath: *Pradip Mukherjee*. Father: Satya *Banerjee*. Brother: *Dipankar Dey*. His Wife: *Lily Chakravorty*. Bishu: *Utpal Dutt*. Mr. Mitter: *Rabi Ghosh*. Kuana: *Sudeshna Das Sharma*. Somnath's Fiancee: *Aparna Sen*.

Nation, 10/30/76 (p. 442)
Harold Clurman

". . . Like all of this artist's work, *The Middleman* speaks eloquently in a low key. There is hardly any stress, no pounding of a message. With its beautiful cast, it is gently humorous, unemphatically sad-

dening. The film depicts the gradual degradation of an innocent and innately decent people.

Ray hardly accuses, never rages, suggests no panacea. He shows with utmost delicacy of compassion a vast population sinking beneath the incalculable burden of economic and historical pressures. Still, under the crushing social behemoth the people remain sentient and loving . . . one thought I found inescapable was that even in total disorder in every phase of human concourse, indestructible vitality may still amazingly exist. Ray's film provides lyric testimony to this wonderful fact.''

©The Nation, 1976.

New York Post, 10/12/76 (p. 52)
Frank Rich

". . . Compared to this Indian filmmaker's masterpieces of the past decade—*Days and Nights in the Forest* and *Distant Thunder*—*The Middleman* is a major disappointment . . .

. . . Once Ray sets up his dramatic situation, we know—and we can even guess the major twist of the denouement well in advance.

That wouldn't make any difference if Somnath's story were told with Ray's usual poetic force, but for the most part it is not. *The Middleman* is pretty much a series of flatout expository scenes well done but rarely carrying us beneath the surface of the action or the characters . . .''

Reprinted by Permission of New York Post.
©1976, New York Post Corporation.

Film Information, November 1976 (p. 4)
Bea Rothenbeuchner

". . . set in Ray's native Calcutta. Against a documentary-like background of the city's overcrowding, poverty, and political tensions, we follow a highly qualified college graduate trying to find work. After months of futile searching, the young man decides to break with his Brahmin heritage and become a businessman—a middleman, buying cheap and selling at the biggest possible profit.

Ray's view of the Indian business world is marvelously satiric and, to us, eye-opening. Apparently, wheeling and dealing has world-wide similarities and is just as dehumanizing in Calcutta as in New York.

Pradip Mukherjee is the protagonist, a sensitive youth, unable to adjust easily to the demands of the marketplace. His form of inertia is not unfamiliar to our average citizen. But as portrayed by Mr. Mukherjee, Ray's hero appears to us a little too passive, too naive.

Like all of Ray's films, *The Middleman* provides a

continued on next page

continued from previous page

vivid, detailed view of contemporary Indian life and customs. But we miss the sustaining warmth we have come to expect of Ray."

©Film Information, 1976.

The Times (London), 2/11/77 (p. 9)
David Robinson

". . . Ray's characters are drawn in terms so essentially human that we can feel an instant identification with them. In his films the unfamiliarity of the features, the costumes, the setting and the situation are unimportant: we are only aware of the problems of fellow human beings as foolish, funny and bothered as the rest of us. The small-time business world of *The Middleman* is as rich in individuals as the village of *Pather Panchali*, from the cross little stationery clerk who orders up Somnath's letter-headings to the PR smoothy who becomes his guide in the necessary arts of corruption . . .

As well as a master of character, Ray is a master of narrative, using old and unfashionable techniques like the montage sequence with such appreciation of their value as storytelling devices that they seem in his hands like new inventions."

©The Times, 1977.

The Sunday Times (London), 2/13/77 (p. 37)
Alan Brien

". . . Ray's strength increasingly lies in his ability to present all the ambiguities of his theme—here a young graduate, of good family but low degree, launched into the alien, bizarre underworld of small business—and yet impose upon them complete harmony and control. For let there be no doubt, Satyajit Ray is one of the master directors of today, not just in some regional ghetto class, but measured against world competition.

At first, we seem to be back in the domain of Dickens and Balzac, Gogol and Mark Twain, the formative years of early capitalism, still in its stage of primitive accumulation, when a lucky beggar could stumble on a fortune. Soon it becomes clear that Ray, who writes and directs, is mirroring for us a reality in modern India with a clarity of etching that must be more disturbing than funny for those who have to live there . . ."

©The Sunday Times, 1977.

Monthly Film Bulletin, March 1977 (p. 43)
Geoff Brown

"This is Ray in *Company Limited* territory . . . Yet

The Middleman is no exact sequel, for Ray's portrait of the sad interrelationship between amorality and success is painted in far greater detail and in darker colours. There is more explicit emphasis on the breakup of India's past traditions, represented by Somnath's father, who becomes so alienated by the progress of his son's career that he retreats into silence . . . The film runs for a little over two hours, and the narrative drifts and drags its feet slightly; a couple of flashback scenes seem curious intrusions. But nothing can detract from the film's overall success and its penetrating charm."

©Monthly Film Bulletin, 1977.

MIDWAY

Director: *Jack Smight*. Screenplay: *Donald S. Sanford*. Producer: *Walter Mirisch*. Photography: *Harry Stradling, Jr.* Editors: *Robert Swink, Frank J. Urioste*. Music: *John Williams*. Production: *Mirisch Corporation*. Distributor: *Universal Pictures*. Running time 132 minutes. New York opening June 18, 1976, at several theatres. Classification: PG.

Captain Matt Garth: *Charlton Heston*. Admiral Nimitz: *Henry Fonda*. Captain Vinton Maddox: *James Coburn*. Rear Admiral Spruance: *Glenn Ford*. Commander Joseph Rochefort: *Hal Holbrook*. Admiral Yamamoto: *Toshiro Mifune*. Admiral Halsey: *Robert Mitchum*. Commander Carl Jessop: *Cliff Robertson*. Lieutenant Commander Ernest Blake: *Robert Wagner*. Rear Admiral Fletcher: *Robert Webber*. Admiral Pearson: *Ed Nelson*. Haruko Sakura: *Christina Kokubo*. Vice Admiral Nagumo: *James Shigeta*. Commander Max Leslie: *Monte Markham*. Captain Miles Browning: *Biff McGuire*. Ensign George Gay: *Kevin Dobson*. Lieutenant Commander Wade McClusky: *Christopher George*. Lieutenant Commander John Waldron: *Glenn Corbett*. Captain Elliott Buckmaster: *Gregory Walcott*. Lieutenant Tom Garth: *Edward Albert*.

Newsweek, 6/28/76 (p. 78)
Janet Maslin

"*Midway* never quite decides whether war is hell, good clean fun, or merely another existential dilemma. This drab extravanganza toys with so many conflicting attitudes that it winds up reducing the pivotal World War II battle in the Pacific to utter nonsense. Like the disaster epic *Earthquake*, *Midway* employs the electronic grumble that is Sensurround--in this case to accompany, all too appropriately, the dropping of bombs. 'The management assumes no responsibility for the physical and emotional reactions of the individual viewer,'' declares an opening title. All the management really need worry about is waking you when it's all over.

The movie features several fine performances, all of them by machines: the aircraft carrier that was cast as two different aircraft carriers deserves a particularly big hand. The leading human players fare less well . . .''

© Newsweek, Inc. 1976
reprinted by permission.

Los Angeles Times, 6/18/76 (Part IV, p. 1)
Charles Champlin

'' . . . *Midway* leaves no doubt of the prides and excitements of war, and while it does not even make a stab at being an antiwar statement--it is a disaster film whose disaster is war--*Midway* also leaves no doubt of the horrifying cost in young lives. The movie is spectacular, but the carnage is part of the spectacle.

As in *Earthquake*, the reverberations of Sensurround rattle your eardrums and your socks; a parade of stars marches past, and the footage. some of it from wartime newsreels, is vivid. With all, I'm saying, responses to *Midway* are bound to be personal and mixed, having relatively little to do with the quality of the movie itself. There are the memories of pride and achievement, and memories of loss and wastage of lives and other treasures . . .

. . . it is the action, the exploding planes, the floating holocausts, the black plumes arcing into the sea, the cannons roaring, which carry the picture for those who care . . .''

© Los Angeles Times, 1976.

New York Post, 6/19/76 (p. 18)
Frank Rich

'' . . . *Midway*, an exercise in World War II jingoism . . .

. . . just as wars aren't as dramatically satisfying as they once were, neither are war movies, and I wouldn't worry that *Midway* might bring about a revival of gung-ho militarism. Indeed, if enough people see this film, it could eliminate war altogether --for *Midway* makes the tumult of battle seem considerably less exciting than a heated UN Security Council debate about international fishing rights . . .

Midway fails in every way a war movie can-- including, most crucially, at the story level. Though

we are constantly shown war-room maps dotted with little boats and arrows and though the film is laced with title cards that repeatedly identify its warring ships, planes and protagonists, only a military historian or a devoted player of board games like *D-Day* and *U-Boat* could begin to fathom what is going on . . .

Even the addition of *Sensurround*, which induces nausea more than anything else, can't bring the grainy air-and-sea theatrics to life . . .''

Reprinted by Permission of New York Post.
© 1976, New York Post Corporation.

Christian Science Monitor, 7/2/76 (p. 22)
David Sterritt

'' . . . *Midway* . . . accomplishes the remarkable feat of taking a major World War II battle, a huge budget, and some of the sturdiest faces in Hollywood, and parlaying them into a crashing bore.

The redoubtable Heston has the biggest role, as an American officer who has to whup the Japanese at Midway and also help his troubled son (Edward Albert) get to first base with pretty Japanese girlfriend (Christina Kokubo) who is being investigated by the FBI.

Most of *Midway* cuts endlessly between war rooms and decks of aircraft carriers and military installations, with an occasional glimpse of the beleaguered island itself. For all the talk about tactics and speeches about strategy, we learn very little about how a battle was actually fought, except for the usual cliches, such as the perennially stupifying moment when someone looks up and says, 'I sense danger out there.' . . .''

Reprinted by permission from The Christian
Science Monitor © 1976.
The Christian Science Publishing Society.
All rights reserved.

Film Information, July/August 1976 (p. 3)
Paul Coleman

"Heroism being in short supply these days, Universal has lavished considerable care on this tribute to the courage of the men on both sides of the Battle of Midway . . .

. . . The battle scenes are unusually effective, helped no little by Harry Stradling, Jr.'s sharp and sweeping cinematography and Robert Swink's and Frank J. Urioste's precise editing that employs both shots of the original battle and graphic recreations of the action.

Director Jack Smight allows little human drama to penetrate the overall sweep of history. Charlton Heston and Glenn Ford are appropriately stoic as always; Cliff Robertson and Hal Holbrook provide momentary flashes of humor and dramatic breadth in their characterizations. But the startling lack of

continued on next page

continued from previous page

personal characterization from such fine actors as Toshiro Mifune, Robert Mitchum, Henry Fonda, James Coburn, and James Shigeta are a clear disappointment . . ."

©Film Information, 1976.

Films in Review, August/September 1976 (p. 439)
Charles Phillips Reilly

"The battle of Midway in which the U.S. bested four Japanese carriers accompanied by more than 200 ships and an occupation force threatening U.S. control of the Eastern Pacific is considered by many naval historians as the greatest battle the U.S. Navy has ever won. The film is a reworking of that battle, the courage of the men involved on both sides, together with the intelligence and the bit of luck which gave us that victory. The acting of the film stars playing the roles of Nimitz, Spruance, Yamamoto, Halsey, Fletcher, Nagumo et al. . . . pales before the excitement of Jack McMaster's special effects, and they are burdened by Donald S. Sanford's script. But for those of us who were in the Armed Forces of W.W. II, *Midway* does recreate some part of the bravery and the dedication of the men who gave their lives for their country."

©Films in Review, 1976.

Saturday Review, 7/24/76 (p. 43)
Judith Crist

"Some of the 'biggies' are big only in the disappointment for expectant moviegoers and deserve mention on that basis . . . *Midway*, with actors who were in the ranks during World War II now elevated to top-brass status (Charlton Heston, Henry Fonda, Robert Mitchum, Toshiro Mifune among them), looks as if it has been glued together from *Tora! Tora! Tora!* outtakes. Written by Donald S. Sanford and directed by Jack Smight, it makes a muddle of the battle, but indicates, as most latter-day World War II movies made with an eye to foreign markets do, that while we may have won the war, those charming, civilized, intelligent Japanese really deserved to."

©Judith Crist, 1976.

New York Magazine, 7/12/76 (p. 74)
John Simon

". . . the movie is mostly high-level strategy discussed in terms that manage to be both folksily simplistic and unclear, commands shouted into intercoms that remain sublimely undecipherable, a sentimental fictional plot that is (in the best tradition of such movies) sheer riches of embarrassment,

and some passable action photography (much of it from newsreels and, we learn, an old Japanese movie) improperly matched with the studio sequences. That there is unwholesome excitement in watching some of the battle footage, it would be dishonest to deny; that the rest of the movie, under Jack Smight's platitudinous direction, is all lumbering stereotypes, is even less deniable. The performances, by guest and host stars alike, are cut from the same old burlap, with one exception: the Admiral Nimitz of Henry Fonda, an actor who instills a gracious, unharried humanity into the most routine acting chores. But this gain is more than offset by Charlton Heston . . ."

©1976 by the NYM Corp. Reprinted with the permission of NEW YORK Magazine.

Jump Cut, Winter 1977 (p. 14)
Norman D. Markowitz

". . . Although it was probably foolish to expect something on the level of such World War II classics as *Guadalcanal Diary* or *Objective Burma* (the blacklists, among other things, wreaked havoc with the writers of the better war films), *Midway* probably could have been much better if the Hollywood movie moguls believed that war films were as commercially attractive as disaster films or that plot and character were as important as gadgets and stars. As it is, *Midway* is a boring hulk of a film, filled with the technological junk of contemporary mass consumer society, even with Japanese officers whose studied monotone reminds one of Nixon White House aides. It is a comment upon a system and a business where technique has replaced substance and even technique is in serious decline.

Sensurround is *Midway*'s big gimmick, its noisy substitute for a coherent and serious motion picture . . ."

©Jump Cut, 1977.

The Times (London), 1/7/77 (p. 6)
David Robinson

"There is no sense of inhibition about *Midway*, another fragment of American history. The stars have turned out to pay their tribute to this moment of Second World War glory. There's Henry Fonda as Admiral Nimitz; Glenn Ford as Rear Admiral Spruance, Charlton Heston as Captain Garth, and Robert Mitchum briefly glimpsed as poor Admiral Halsey, laid up with an itch. The United States, in fact, seems on the evidence of this film to have won the war with a remarkably geriatric naval command . . .

. . . The object of the film is to use the technical marvel of Sensurround . . . to re-create the sense of being present at the battle . . ."

©The Times, 1977.

Monthly Film Bulletin, February 1977 (p. 19)
Richard Combs

". . . *Midway* does not, like *Tora! Tora! Tora!*, turn part of its running time over to the former enemy for his version of events, but it is similarly painstaking in assessing the mistakes and misapprehensions on both sides, and the turns of fortune that determined the outcome. The result is the usual stilted blend of historiography and wide-screen blood and thunder (and, courtesy of Sensurround, realer than real plane and bomb vibrations). The mixture is not helped by the interlacing of footage actually shot during the battle with re-created air-sea combat, nor by the usual guest-starring to impress historical names on the mind's eye . . ."

©Monthly Film Bulletin, 1977.

MIKEY AND NICKY

Director, Screenplay: *Elaine May*. Producer: *Michael Hausman*. Photography: *Victor Kemper*. Editor: *John Carter*. Music: *John Strauss*. Distributor: *Paramount Pictures*. Running time 118 minutes. New York opening December 21, 1976, at the Little Carnegie Theatre. Classification: R.

Mikey: *Peter Falk*. Nicky: *John Cassavetes*. Kinney: *Ned Beatty*. Annie: *Rose Arrick*. Nell: *Carol Grace*. Sid Fine: *William Hickey*. Dave Resnick: *Sanford Meisner*. Jan: *Joyce Van Patten*. Bus Driver: *Emmet Walsh*.

Newsweek, 12/27/76 (p. 56)
Jack Kroll

". . . it's clear that May can't let her material go, a syndrome intensified with *Mikey and Nicky*, which stems from her own early days in Chicago, where she knew some characters in the workaday underworld. Peter Falk and John Cassavetes play Mikey and Nicky, two petty crooks working for Resnick, a syndicate boss (Sanford Meisner). They are childhood friends, and when the syndicate puts out a contract on Nicky, who's stolen some house money, Mikey shows up to help him. It's not giving anything away to say that Mikey turns out to be the finger man who's setting up his old buddy for the kill . . .

Cassavetes and Falk give fine performances, fleshing out with style and pace the crazy paranoid charm that is Elaine May's specialty. Her original script is interesting—it's like her comedy with the pathos tuned way up and the laughs down. But (as was not the case with her earlier films *A New Leaf* and *The Heartbreak Kid*) removing the comic thrust leaves her characters and situation stuck in a viscous sentimentality. Under its often effective surface, *Mikey and Nicky* is conventional . . ."

©Newsweek, Inc. 1976
reprinted by permission.

New York Post, 12/22/76 (p. 19)
Frank Rich

Mikey and Nicky, the new Elaine May film . . . is the work of an artist who's so wrapped up in her personal obsessions that she seems to have lost touch with her audience and, worse, with her talent. While this is undoubtedly a well-intentioned film, and while Miss May could probably explain to us exactly what those intentions were, *Mikey and Nicky* is impossible to decipher on the basis of the evidence on screen. What's on screen is an impenetrable, ugly and almost unendurable mess . . .

All this movie really makes us care about, though, is Elaine May. *Mikey and Nicky* which was years in the making obviously became a creative ordeal for her—and the desperation of the struggle is apparent in almost every frame of the film. Indeed, when you leave this self-destructive movie behind, your first impulse is to find its creator, shake her and say—listen, relax, it's all right . . ."

Reprinted by Permission of New York Post.
© 1976, New York Post Corporation.

Women's Wear Daily, 12/20/76 (p. 5)
Howard Kissel

". . . *Mikey and Nicky* has certain moments that don't seem logical, certain inconsistencies, but it is full of intense, powerful acting—great performances by Peter Falk and John Cassavetes in the title roles, Ned Beatty as the hit man and, in the small role of the gangsters' chief, Sanford Meisner.

We are used to seeing gangster films where the characters are larger than life, men of strong passions and indomitable wills—*Mikey and Nicky* shows us two gangsters who are childish, vulnerable, even pathetic. The more one thinks about it, the more this approach seems very much an Elaine May approach. The acting has the spontaneity, the freshness one associates with the improvisatory style . . ."

©Women's Wear Daily, 1976.

continued on next page

continued from previous page

Village Voice, 1/3/77 (p. 36)
Molly Haskell

". . . Elaine May hasn't come any closer to
mastering the basics of filmmaking or developing a
feeling for the medium, and awkwardnesses that
were incorporated into the daffiness of *A New Leaf*
or partially covered by the professionalism of
Heartbreak Kid here stand exposed, and there is no
humor to redeem them.

Although the story of two childhood friends
turned small-time gangsters—one now being set up
for a gangland killing by the other—has interesting
possibilities, it has become a pretext for Falk and
Cassavetes to indulge in one of those long,
lugubrious Actors' Studio exercises that wore out
its welcome with the last frame of *Husbands* and
before *The Killing of a Chinese Bookie* . . ."

Reprinted by permission of The Village Voice.
Copyright © The Village Voice, Inc., 1977.

Los Angeles Times, 12/25/76 (Pt. IV, p. 1)
Charles Champlin

"In a long lifetime you are not apt to find more
intelligence and good acting expended on a lost
cause than in Elaine May's *Mikey and Nicky*.

The suspicion grows that Ms. May is an excellent
dialogue coach who has not yet got the hang of
making movies: how to see the action, how to pace
the action, how to match the tone of the presentation to the nature of the material.

Despite the chummy title, the story that she wrote
recalls the hard-edge films of the past, and there
are echoes of Hemingway's masterful short story,
The Killers . . .

For most of its length, the film is a slow psychological study, a stripping away of poses to reveal
why it is that Falk so hates Cassavetes' guts. Then,
for the last little while, *Mikey and Nicky* is the cat-
and-mouse thriller it might always have been . . .

Toward the end, the film begins to make good on
its intentions of letting the action flow out of character as revealed (as against imposing action on
characters arbitrarily by the author's hand). But it is
too late to care about the principals or to enjoy
the suspense."

© Los Angeles Times, 1976.

Christian Science Monitor, 12/31/76 (p. 19)
David Sterritt

"Even when she stuck to comedy, Elaine May
had one of the dourest visions in today's movie
world. Now she has left the laughs behind and gone

deadly serious with *Mikey and Nicky*—the most
grimly fascinating, if deliberately unpleasant character study to hit the screen this year . . .

. . . plants Elaine May more firmly than ever on
the map of budding first-class directors. What few
woman filmmakers there are still get suspicious
looks from too many movie-land observers, but
could any man have conceived, written and directed a more penetrating, intelligent—and yes,
sadly sympathetic—vision of macho self-destruction
running amok through gloomy urban watersheds?

Much credit goes also to Falk and Cassavetes
for a pair of astonishing performances . . . Ned
Beatty . . . heads a splendid supporting cast . . . Insight and unstated compassion are the qualities
Elaine May brings to the project, and her stark
film demands the same from its audience every
step of the way."

Reprinted by permission from The Christian
Science Monitor © 1976.
The Christian Science Publishing Society.
All rights reserved.

Saturday Review, 1/22/77 (p. 49)
Judith Crist

". . . *Mikey and Nicky*, four years and close to $5
million in the making, is a two-character drama that
looks like a collection of leftovers from *Husbands*—
and not simply because Peter Falk and John Cassavetes, two of the stars from Cassavetes' 1970 film,
are on hand to improvise and meander their way
through May's script . . .

. . . Before long, as these two actors work their
ways through one Actors Studio-type exercise after
another, with many an impromptu smirk at their
own antics, all thought of liking 'em vanishes. They
are loathsome as petty mobsters given to racism,
woman abuse, and sentimental slobbery, despicable
in their behavior, and worst of all, boring . . . Cag-
ney and Bogart they aren't—and Elaine May is all
too obviously out of her genre, let alone depth . . ."

© Judith Crist, 1977.

Films in Review, February 1977 (p. 119)
William Bernard

"Nicky (John Cassavetes) and Mikey (Peter Falk)
have been friends since childhood and are mixed
up in the rackets. When Nicky calls Mikey from a
sleazy hotel room, it's to beg for help to escape
from a hit man (Ned Beatty). Mikey arrives to face
hysterical abuse from Nicky, which makes Mikey's
patience too good to be true. Who is the real hit
man? The interplay given M & N include a sado-
masochistic relationship which becomes tiresome
instead of interesting in director-scripter Elaine
May's hands, shutting out even so competent a performer as Ned Beatty . . . As M & N push, embrace

John Cassavetes, left, and Peter Falk portray two syndicate hoods in **Mikey and Nicky**, directed by Elaine May.

and excoriate each other, they become hateful so that the well-directed ending brings more relief from tedium than terror."

©Films in Review, 1977.

Film Information, January 1977 (p. 2)
Frederic A. Brussat

". . . Elaine May's film is uneven and disappointing. She seems to have aimed for the equivalent of John Cassavetes' inimitable style of cinema verite with its gritty feeling and magical moments of truth —but she misses the mark. There are a few excellent scenes that have an authentic urban toughness: one when Mikey explodes in a coffee shop and another when Nicky wordlessly terrifies a shop owner. But overall, the film has a dramatic flatness that contradicts its pressure-cooker situation.

Word has it that Elaine May took over eight years to make this movie which cost about $5 million. It has neither the flair of *A New Leaf* nor the punch of *The Heartbreak Kid*, her two other directorial efforts. John Cassavetes (gripped by paranoia) and Peter Falk (edgy in his anger) act well enough given the flimsiness of the story. Ned Beatty provides

some light moments as an incompetent hit man. But it all adds up to very little considering the time and expense put into this movie . . ."

©Film Information, 1977.

New York Magazine, 1/10/77 (p. 55)
John Simon

". . . What truly sets one's teeth on edge . . . is that Miss May cannot forgo that cuteness which, when used aptly in zany, satirical comedy, adds an extra flavor to the zestful brew. Superimposed on this morose and morbid mess, however, it is unendurable—rather like a cloying perfume fighting a losing battle with an acrid body odor.

Now add to this technical analphabetism. Victor Kemper's always rather amateurish cinematography is further undercut by editing and continuity that are thoroughly shocking in a major film. Thus during one scene John Cassavetes is both shaven and glaringly unshaven; or fragments from the same bus ride will appear both before and after a long maudlin cemetery sequence, with the fragments after it not even benefiting from an establishing shot of

continued on next page

continued from previous page

some sort. One becomes acutely aware of Miss May's endless, irresolute editing, of her unhealthy inability to be finished with something, to let go . . .''

© 1977 by the NYM Corp. Reprinted with the permission of NEW YORK Magazine.

Take One, March 1977 (p. 10)
Michael Tarantino

''. . . May has managed the perfect blend, utilizing the improvisatory techniques of her actors in order to reinforce the film's narrative thrust. As disjointed as it may seem, each stray piece of business belongs. Ultimately, the film's 'look' reflects itself, and not the years of production hassles and Stroheim-esque tales of Elaine May's nights in the editing room which preceded its release.

Whereas *A New Leaf* and *The Heartbreak Kid* suggested malaise, *Mikey and Nicky* delivers. It opens with Micky stretched out in a seedy hotel, his ulcers killing him from lack of food. The editing is extremely disjunctive, frustrating the viewer's attempt to define the space . . .

. . . It is the rare American film which defines the event in terms of its own essences . . .''

© Take One, 1977.

MILESTONES

Directors, Photographers, Screenplay: *Robert Kramer, John Douglas*. Producers: *Barbara Stone, David C. Stone*. Running time 195 minutes. New York opening October 8, 1975, at the New York Film Festival, Lincoln Center. Classification: None.

Mama: *Mary Chapelle*. John, blind potter: *John Douglas*. Erika: *Kalaho*. Lou, with beard: *Lou Ho*. Helen, filmmaker: *Grace Paley*. Elizabeth, Helen's daughter: *Tina Shepherd*. Karen: *Sule Solf*. Joe: *David C. Stone*. Peter: *Paul Zimet*.

See Volume 1 for additional reviews

Cineaste, Spring, 1976 (p. 36)
Gina Blumenfeld

'' . . . For all the talk—between mothers and daughters, fathers and sons, friends, lovers—it is remarkable that nothing insightful, either politically or psychologically, is ever said in *Milestones*. While there are interminable conversations, filled with the striving for 'meaningful' expression, the very language used—the counter-culture jargon which once seemed so expressive—now systematically precludes the possibility of communication . . .

The deliberately off-hand construction of *Milestones*, both technically and formally, goes hand in hand with the mystified notions of 'naturalness' expressed in the film. These notions give the impression that the very attempt to make a work aesthetically coherent, much less technically proficient, amounts to calculated deception of the worst sort; only that which is apparently homemade and artless can embody the unvarnished truth. Contrary to all intents, this deliberate ingenuousness must remain no less a matter of style than the most mannered theatricality . . .''

© Cineaste, 1976.

MISSOURI BREAKS, THE

Director: *Arthur Penn*. Screenplay: *Thomas McGuane*. Producers: *Elliott Kastner, Robert M. Sherman*. Photography: *Michael Butler*. Editors: *Jerry Greenberg, Stephen Rotter, Dede Allen*. Music: *John Williams*. Distributor: *United Artists*. Running time 126 minutes. New York opening May 19, 1976, at several theatres. Classification: PG.

Lee Clayton: *Marlon Brando*. Tom Logan: *Jack Nicholson*. Little Tod: *Randy Quaid*. Jane Braxton: *Kathleen Lloyd*. Cary: *Frederic Forrest*. Calvin: *Harry Dean Stanton*. David Braxton: *John McLiam*. Si: *John Ryan*. Hank Rate: *Sam Gilman*. Lonesome Kid: *Steve Franken*. Pete Marker: *Richard Bradford*. Hellsgate Rancher: *James Greene*. Rancher's Wife: *Luana Anders*. Baggage Clerk: *Danny Goldman*.

New York Times, 5/20/76 (p. 45)
Vincent Canby

'' . . . Instead of being elegaic and funny . . . the anachronisms in *The Missouri Breaks* too often seem like camp.

This, I suspect, is principally because of the out-of-control performance given by Mr. Brando. He enters the film hidden behind a horse, which he at last peeks around, and then spends the rest of the movie upstaging the writer, the director and the other actors. Nothing he does . . . has any connection to the movie that surrounds him. He grabs our attention, but does nothing with it.

In their earlier films both Mr. Penn and Mr. McGuane have demonstrated a fondness for eccentric characters whose impulses have a kind of grandeur about them. There's no grandeur to Mr. Brando's character. Nor much mystery. He behaves like an actor in armed revolt.

One has no way of knowing whether *The Missouri Breaks* would have been a good film without this peculiar presence as its center, but there are so many arresting things in the rest of the movie that one can speculate . . .

The film conveys a fine sense of place and period, of weather and mood and the precariousness of life, which are things that Mr. Nicholson responds to as an actor. Yet the plot, along with Mr. Brando, keeps intruding and throwing things out of balance . . .''

© 1977 by the New York Times Company.
Reprinted by permission.

Village Voice, 5/31/76 (p. 131)
Andrew Sarris

'' . . . *The Missouri Breaks* strikes me as over-directed, overwritten, overphotographed, over-edited, and overacted. Still, it remains interesting because all of the people involved are interesting. You really have to see Brando and Nicholson for yourself if only to experience the extraordinary lack of electricity between them.

Brando's is much the more outrageous performance of the two . . . As far as I can recall, Brando's brogue is even more outlandish here than it was in *The Nightcomers*. Its effect is to create the impression that Brando is 'putting on' the rest of the cast, and even Nicholson . . .

By contrast, Jack Nicholson's performance is standard-surly-snarling-antiauthoritarian-angry Jack Nicholson. Unfortunately, the context of his characterisation seems morally confused . . .

One interesting aspect of the cinematography and editing is the relative lack of contact it achieves between Brando and Nicholson. Through most of the film they seem to have been performing in different times and different places . . .''

Reprinted by permission of The Village Voice.
Copyright © The Village Voice, Inc., 1976.

Film Information, 6/76 (p. 1)
Robert E. A. Lee

"Excitement is promised on the screen when Marlon Brando and Jack Nicholson, both Academy Award winners, are billed together and directed by Arthur Penn, who is responsible for many memorable movie images. But Penn doesn't seem sure whether he is making a period piece comedy or a romantic Western or a satire on frontier justice. So the ambitious, would-be blockbuster, *The Missouri Breaks*, for all its promise, is mainly bizarre and ultimately disappointing . . .

Nicholson seems to view the film and his role in it one way and Brando in another. Nicholson plays it straight––he is credible, fascinating, and effective as a sympathetic outlaw who seems on the verge of reform. He seems genuinely weary of crime. Brando, on the other hand, hams it up and plays his part self-indulgently as a rather broad burlesque. He is far too clever, too eccentric, too crudely theatrical. And we don't believe him for a minute.

But Brando is Brando and he gives a good show. He is performing, not acting, and his props and costumes and vocal imitations are of course entertaining in a way that is not particularly related to the story or the picture . . .''

© Film Information, 1976.

Christian Science Monitor, 5/21/76 (p. 23)
David Sterritt

'' . . . It is not a flawless film––it takes too many minutes to tell its tale, and it lapses into inexplicable vulgarity during the manhunt that concludes it. Yet its performances are as vivid as life, its images are composed with painterly affection, and its story says more about loyalty and loneliness than any western epic in ages.

This last element, a rueful humanism, is the film's most poignant asset . . .

Looking past Penn's masterly direction, marred only when the pace sags and when flashes of sadism leap explicitly from the chief villain, top credit goes to the splendid *Missouri Breaks* cast. Nicholson offers another sharp, smart performance as the good bad guy, while Brando––in his brightest movie moment in years––works wonders . . .''

Reprinted by permission from the Christian
Science Monitor © 1976.
The Christian Science Publishing Society.
All rights reserved.

New York Post, 5/20/76 (p. 20)
Archer Winsten

"*The Missouri Breaks* . . . is a Western that has become a classic because it has two of the best actors in the movies riding for a confrontation . . .

The plot designed by Thomas McGuane uses a lot of genuine Montana scenery, probables in the line of action, and dialogue that avoids most of the cliches.

Director Arthur Penn, always front and fore with theatricality, uses this bent to full advantage with these characters and events that lend themselves naturally to the theater of wild action . . .

continued on next page

continued from previous page

. . . the action is always prompt, frequently surprising, and freshly imagined.

What results is a Western that rivets you with its violence and invites you to involve your sympathies on what has to be the losing side. This alone should guarantee its popularity. In addition the performances of Nicholson and Brando are, as expected, superb. Miss Lloyd is surprisingly good, a find. And the supporting players are so consistently satisfactory that one must look to Arthur Penn as the coordinating factor . . . ''

Reprinted by Permission of New York Post.
© 1976, New York Post Corporation.

Women's Wear Daily, 5/17/76 (p. 14)
Howard Kissel

'' . . . *Missouri Breaks* is another nail in the coffin of the myth of the American West. Thomas McGuane's screenplay uses the traditional characters and actions of the frontier to create a highly personal, quirky vision in which no traditional value goes unchallanged. McGuane's mordant vision is aided by the fact his sensibility is not moralistic or bitter but highly theatrical. At one point, for example, someone asks who Thomas Jefferson was. 'A guy back East!' is the reply. At another point a judge tells a criminal, 'Anything you care to say before we pass judgment? We would prefer something colorful, life on the frontier being what it is. This is obviously not verismo, and while it is entertaining, it creates problems for the actors; they are allowed to play with an ironic swagger and a high style that suits the lines, but they aren't permitted to go much below the surface . . .

. . . the film is superbly photographed by Michael Butler and directed by Arthur Penn with an understanding of the style. But despite its many virtues, one's overall impression is less of having seen a drama than having watched a sophisticated essay about the West.''

© Women's Wear Daily, 1976.

Commonweal, 6/18/76 (p. 403); 7/2/76 (p. 436)
Colin L. Westerbeck, Jr.

'' . . . *The Missouri Breaks* is perhaps another bid at originality in the Western, another . . . attempt to break new ground. Certainly Penn fancies himself the kind of marauder who can come in from outside and shake up a genre, as he proved with *Bonnie and Clyde*. *Stagecoach* went beyond the pure-hearted heroes of the silent Western by suggesting that the bad guys—the prostitute, outlaw and drunken doctor—might actually turn out to be the good guys. *Shane* and *High Noon* went further by suggesting that the good guy has to be gotten rid of in the end too. The trend has been away from gun-

fighters who are righteous and heroic toward those who are tragic and self-defeating. Having run the entire moral gamut, it seemed that at last, in the slow-motion sequences of Peckinpah or in the films of Clint Eastwood and Sergio Leone, the violence in the Western might become a purely aesthetic event—a work of visual beauty without any moral content at all.

But clearly Penn's film is an effort to find yet another moral alternative for the Western. In Penn's version what lies beyond the showdown—beyond the duel in the street at high noon or the gunfight at the OK corral—is murder by stealth . . .

Human experience in Penn's film seems finally to conform to the very landscape where the film is set. The breaks of the Missouri River are an area of dry declivities, an area where the prairie floor just falls away suddenly like Clayton's life. It seems a futile landscape, this riverbed with no river in it, but learning to navigate here is largely what Penn's film is about . . . ''

© Commonweal, 1976.

Nation, 5/29/76 (p. 670)
Robert Hatch

''*The Missouri Breaks*, script by Thomas McGuane, is a picture of which it might be said they shouldn't make 'em like that anymore. Arthur Penn is a canny director, and he has taken a lot of pains and spent a lot of money to build intriguing sets and photograph exuberant scenery; his timing is lively and his bit parts are raffish. But virtuoso actors like Brando and Nicholson get out of hand when the material runs thin. Brando gets almost completely out of hand.

The Missouri Breaks (named for a rough section of the river in northern Montana) is a 'mature' Western; i.e., it is spiced with enough casual sex to earn it an interesting rating and contains no single character whom you would want your son or daughter to emulate . . .

. . . *The Missouri Breaks* is a picture that explains very little—including why anyone thought it a work that demanded to be made. Except, of course, to agitate a gullible public with the promise of the Brando-Nicholson match of the century.''

© The Nation, 1976.

Saturday Review, 5/12/76 (p. 48)
Judith Crist

'' . . . The view is of hard men in a harsh landscape, of men forced to extremes they find hard to rationalize; it is a view tempered by ironies, by a self-awareness that tinges its mythology with wit and leavens its melodrama . . .

Brando, without doubt, proves himself master of

every nuance of controlled madness . . . It is a remarkable effect of personality, with his performance evoking an almost reflective revelation from others while keeping his own enigmatic persona intact. And it works, one realizes, primarily in contrast to Nicholson's completely relaxed rationality, to the tenderness that lies beneath the surface bonhomie and manliness . . . It is the ultimate in understatement, overwhelming in its power.

Penn's control of his stars is the film's strength . . . "

© Judith Crist, 1976.

New Leader, 6/7/76 (p. 22)
Robert Asahina

" . . . Penn has not hesitated to present graphic scenes of violence--a stake piercing a man's eye, a slit throat gurgling blood. The mix of excessive gore and forced humor is as unsettling here as it was in Penn's *Bonnie and Clyde*. The earlier movie, with its inventive and dramatic cutting, established the reputation of its editor, Dede Allen. In *The Missouri Breaks* she has pointlessly and mindlessly cross-cut parallel story lines. Penn, we must assume, is responsible for the bizarre and obtrusive camera angles, and for the movie's confused point of view. Together, the direction and editing only compound the inherent weakness of the material.

Sadly, some good acting is wasted. Nicholson and Harry Dean Stanton try for dignity to offset Brando's mugging; Randy Quaid is, for a change, restrained; and Kathy Lloyd turns in a winning performance as a Frontier woman liberated before her time. But it is Brando's flamboyant foolishness that perfectly reflects the stupidity of the entire project . . . "

Reprinted with permission from
The New Leader, 1976.
© The American Labor Conference
on International Affairs, Inc.

New York Magazine, 5/31/76 (p. 73)
John Simon

" . . . What really hurts . . . is the dialogue. It is all studied quirkiness, self-congratulatory cuteness, and insipid pseudopregnancy. No one ever talked like this in the West, East, North, or South . . .

Utterly lamentable, too, is Brando's performance, even more slatternly and self-indulgent than his bloated physique. Starting with a correspondence-school brogue and bits of mannerism left over from his garish performance in *The Nightcomers*, he adds to them an effeteness and smarminess that would keep even the likes of Braxton from hiring him, he comes across as a mixture of Rod Steiger doing *Hennessy* and Tallulah Bankhead doing Tallulah. His cutesy moues in the notorious bathtub scene are matched only by the abject ineptitude of

Kathleen Lloyd as Jane Braxton, who turns what needed to be only a badly written lost soul into a full-fledged driveling idiot . . .

Only Jack Nicholson comes out of this mess well-nigh unscathed, almost succeeding in turning the nullity handed him by the filmmakers into a living character . . . "

© 1976 by the NYM Corp. Reprinted with
the permission of NEW YORK Magazine.

Newsweek, 5/24/76 (p. 103)
Jack Kroll

"Brando vs. Nicholson--obviously a great shoot-out, dominating any film and any director. So it's to Arthur Penn's credit that he doesn't allow their collision to capsize *The Missouri Breaks*, but instead wraps it firmly in the texture of the movie . . .

Brando and Nicholson are great fun to watch and hear. Their rhythms are beautiful--they are antiphonal antagonists who confront each other with irony and respect. Penn and McGuane have made an intelligent, entertaining Western, nicely balanced between the protagonists and the well-woven, colorful tapestry in which they're placed. Penn is in the line of Elia Kazan in his ability to get a round humanity from actors; his good cast includes Randy Quaid as an amiable young rustler, Harry Dean Stanton as an older and grimmer one, John McLiam as the morally twisted rancher and newcomer Kathleen Lloyd as his daughter. The showdown between Brando and Nicholson is an intimate apocalypse, a last spasm of almost quiet violence between two men who know how to behave like myths."

© Newsweek, Inc. 1976
reprinted by permission.

Los Angeles Times, 5/21/76 (Pt. IV, p. 17)
Charles Champlin

"*The Missouri Breaks* is a pair of million dollar babies in a five and ten cent flick.

Nothing involving Jack Nicholson and Marlon Brando can be completely uninteresting, but *The Missouri Breaks* does not miss by much.

Nicholson ambles through the part with a kind of dazed sweetness . . .

Brando is a buckskin Caligula, mad as a ten gallon hatter . . .

Whether it is or not, the whole characterization plays like an improv done without a great deal of relevance to the other goings-on, so that the hand-to-hand battle of skills you anticipate between the two stars never materializes in a crowd-pleasing way. Too much of the time they could have been

continued on next page

continued from previous page

performing in separate states . . .

. . . Some of the scenes have an artful look, and Michael Butler's cinematography is fine. But the prevailing impression is that Brando made his own running and Penn and everyone else played catch up . . . "

© Los Angeles Times, 1976.

The Times (London), 7/9/76 (p. 9)
David Robinson

". . . The world of the Western, with its reassuring moral certainties, is . . . stood on its head. This is, in itself, intriguing; but it takes rather more to make a film; and I am not sure that McGuane's screenplay has so much more to give. Uncertainty on this point is because so much of the dialogue is thrown to the wind, while a lot more is lost because of Brando's insistence (a favourite old ham trick) on talking most of the time with his mouth full.

Brando's extravagant scene-hogging performance, indeed, seems to belong to a rather different film from the more considered playing of Jack Nicholson and Kathleen Lloyd: it is a fatal stylistic rift in no way justifiable by Brando's situation as an outsider in the community.

It is, in all, a rather messy and inconsequential film for Arthur Penn . . . "

©The Times, 1976.

The Sunday Times (London), 7/11/76 (p. 34)
Dilys Powell

". . . Arthur Penn began his career in the cinema with a Western, *The Left-Handed Gun*, in 1967 . . . Now with *The Missouri Breaks* he is back with straight violence, a developing violence. You might say the film was the tale of a thief, leader of a gang, who is opposed to brutality and corrupted by it; he begins by stealing horses and ends by slitting throats. In mid-course he steals money. He robs a train. Conditioned as we are by the cinema we are disinclined to pass any moral judgment, at any rate as long as the action isn't savage, and in fact it is a comic action. Mr. Penn is good at investing tension with absurdity . . .

But something is wrong. The confrontation is wrong. So far as the narrative is concerned the two actors are in opposition. All the same they should play as it were together, each drawing strength from the other. What happens is the opposite. Singly each is memorable; together each is dimmed. It doesn't happen with other players. In his scenes with Randy Quaid, for instance, Brando is all smiling, subterranean threat . . . "

©The Sunday Times, 1976.

Sight and Sound, Summer 1976 (p. 190)
Tom Milne

"According to Marlon Brando, he saw his character in *The Missouri Breaks* (United Artists) as an opportunity for 'a serious study of the American Indian.'. . . In the event, the character he plays has become a sort of camp Buffalo Bill with an Irish accent, who makes his entrance playing peekaboo from behind his horse and at one point stalks his outlaw prey in a poke bonnet and dress . . .

. . . *The Missouri Breaks* is one of the few recent films to have attempted to render the flavour of period lighting (shadowy golden-browns for the oil-lit interiors, echoing the landscape burning up under the Montana sun), while at the same time avoiding the mistake made by nearly all Westerns under the influence of dingy, dusty settings favoured by Ince and Griffith (Penn's little farm towns and mining villages are impeccably ramshackled but constructed out of new, rawly cut planks) . . ."

©Sight and Sound, 1976.

Monthly Film Bulletin, 8/76 (p. 168)
Richard Combs

"With its quirkishly colourful script by Thomas McGuane and a painterly attention to the details of period and setting, *The Missouri Breaks* stands out from Arthur Penn's previously spare Western exercises in social and psychological themes . . . *The Missouri Breaks* piles on detail and eccentric doodles of character, like some rococo decoration of the *Butch Cassidy* formula. That the film remains, for all its razzle-dazzle camouflage, both coherent and likeable is a tribute to its various auteurs (not the least, though the most maligned, of which is Marlon Brando, playing the cold-blooded gun for hire as a tipsy harlequin), who seem to have amiably collaborated while going their own ways . . . *The Missouri Breaks* is a Western about hobbyhorses, about the American Dream writ small as a kind of obsessive tinkering . . ."

©Monthly Film Bulletin, 1976.

Films in Review, August/September 1976 (p. 438)
Marsha McCreadie

"Even the simplest-minded Western has some locus of interest, some conflict upon which to center. But *The Missouri Breaks* puts the entire burden on character, atmosphere, and 'bits.' Luckily for the production, directed by Arthur Penn (*Bonnie and Clyde, Night Moves*) there is enough fine acting and clever dialogue (the screenwriter is Thomas McGuane of *Rancho Deluxe* and *92 in the Shade*) that our interest is, amazingly, sustained . . .

But there's no structure—or uniformity of vision—to unite this bevy of talents. The photography is beautifully elegiac, picking up one of the movie's themes; the music jarringly absurdist, underscoring another. Everyone, including the viewer, is left slugging it out on his or her own. No wonder Brando runs wild, burlesquing his role(s) in a brilliant but out-of-kilter performance. Nicholson struggles heroically with what amounts to a non-part. *The Missouri Breaks* leaves us fascinated, but baffled."

©Films in Review, 1976.

Commentary, 7/76 (p. 61)
William S. Pechter

". . . *The Missouri Breaks* is a bead-stringing succession of striking scenes, full of a willful eccentricity and preening wit, all of which adds up to nothing more than the self-conscious cleverness of some merry prankster, with a blanket scorn for all those who don't share his (and his heroes') flippancy. In the world of McGuane's films, the many exist for the privileged few to humiliate them . . .

Yet, luckily, the script of *The Missouri Breaks* gets a surprising and inestimable lift from one stunning job of rewrite—by Brando . . .

. . . Brando, in the role of a bizarre hired gun, *has* what's essentially a character part, and is able to make of it a creation quite independent of the film's smart-aleck air of meandering game playing . . . what he creates, in *The Missouri Breaks*, is a comic (but disturbing) grotesque, flamboyantly done up with vividly outlandish gesture, accent, and costume: an unsettling combination of steely coldness and infectious charm. And though he's stopped by the materials from creating anything of great depth, one can nevertheless revel in the dazzling theatricality of the surface . . ."

©Commentary, 1976.

Take One, 8/76 (p. 36)
George Morris

"Thomas McGuane is becoming the thinking man's Neil Simon. His script for *The Missouri Breaks* is liberally sprinkled with pungent one-liners, all tinged with that acerbic, anachronistic humor one has come to expect from his writing; but like Simon's manufactured comedies, it is woefully lacking in the development of a cohesive structure, consistent characterizations, and believable situations. Unfortunately for director Arthur Penn, this script—studied and precious as it is—is the root of everything that seems wrong or misguided about *The Missouri Breaks*.

The Missouri Breaks is a particularly disappointing juncture in Arthur Penn's career, coming as it does on the heels of *Night Moves*, one of his very

finest works. Even with its faults and excesses, however, the new film is not without its virtues, the most notable of which recur in almost every Penn film: an uncommonly brilliant group of performances, and the brutal lyricism of the violence . . .

If *The Missouri Breaks* had been blessed with a more tightly controlled formal structure, Brando's performance might be hopelessly out of key, but as it is, he is the propelling force underlying the entire film . . ."

©Take One, 1976.

Film, 8/76 (p. 10)
Lesley Robinson

"For me, the name of Jack Nicholson amounts to a seal of approval. He's an actor of such virility and warmth that his presence seems to act as a catalyst in any movie. And coupled with such an idiosyncratic talent as Brando's, the effect is bound to be explosive . . .

Brando's performance is perhaps a little too mannered for this type of movie and thus puts the whole thing something out of balance, so that it tends to border on grand guignol at times. Nicholson proves yet again what a versatile and perceptive actor he is, and his handling of the scenes with Kathleen Lloyd probably had something to do with this newcomer's promising performance . . ."

©Film 1976.

MOHAMMAD, MESSENGER OF GOD

Director, Producer: *Moustapha Akkad*. Screenplay: *H. A. L. Craig*. Photography: *Jack Hildyard*. Editor: *John Bloom*. Music: *Maurice Jarre*. Running time 180 minutes. New York opening March 9, 1977, at several theatres. Classification: PG.

Hamza: *Anthony Quinn*. Hind: *Irene Papas*. Bu-Sofyan: *Michael Ansara*. Bilal: *Johnny Sekka*. Khalid: *Michael Forest*. Zaid: *Damien Thomas*. Ammar: *Garrick Hagon*.

Newsweek, 3/21/77 (p. 89)
Janet Maslin

". . . Despite its three-hour running time and multi-million-dollar budget, this first international movie

continued on next page

continued from previous page

about the birth and growth of Islam isn't much of an epic. By conventional standards, it is cinematically crude and so reverential toward its subject as to seem mechanical. Its story, of course, has the elements of tremendous drama: a middle-aged merchant in Mecca, prompted by the voice of God, unites a quarrelsome pagan society by preaching brotherhood and taking up arms to vanquish his enemies. But the movie's dramatic force is inevitably undercut because its central figure, Mohammad, can never be shown or even heard—Muslims believe it blasphemy to depict the prophet. His hordes of followers address the camera as if it were their leader, and the movie's ostensible star, Anthony Quinn, playing Mohammad's warrior uncle, is little more than a supporting, grizzled presence to a nonexistent lead . . ."

©Newsweek, Inc. 1977
reprinted by permission.

Los Angeles Times, 3/8/77 (Pt. IV, p. 1)
Charles Champlin

". . . Surprisingly in a work of edification aimed, you might have said, for a whole-family audience, the violence is abundant and graphic: Arrows plunk home, lances impale, blades slash and draw blood, horses fall, bodies litter the darkling plain. None of it may faze the cool kids, but it could give their elders a queasy time . . .

Michael Ansara plays Bu-Sofyan, Mohammad's chief adversary, and Irene Papas is Ansara's wife. Ansara gives an intense and solemn performance, conveying the feelings behind the pageant language. Papas, all snarling revenge, is Lady Macbeth in a burnoose, mightily overacting.

Anthony Quinn is Hamza, Mohammad's uncle and military leader, and Quinn's dignity and stature are right for the role . . ."

©Los Angeles Times, 1977

The Sunday Times (London), 8/1/76 (p. 27)
Dilys Powell

". . . the desert hasn't looked so beautiful since *Lawrence of Arabia*; Jack Hildyard and his camera assistants have caught the frightening purity of the smoothed sand and the knife-edges into which the wind can drive it. Stirring battles, too, the worshippers of one God against the upholders of Mecca's old order and 300 gods . . .

The playing is suitably gallant, with Johny Sekka handsome as the slave who survives torture. The emphasis all through is on the humane tenets of the new faith, as of course has always been in the cinema's Early Christian essays; while in the Old Testament films the Israelites are shown as merely wanting to get out of Egypt alive. Puzzling, isn't it,

that throughout history Christians, Muslims and Jews, peace lovers to a man, should have devoted so much time and energy to exterminating one another."

©The Sunday Times, 1976

New York Magazine, 4/4/77 (p. 96)
John Simon

". . . a long, arid desert of a movie directed by Moustapha Akkad, an authentic Moslem, no doubt, but an equally certifiable no-talent as a director. For well over three hours, this film stumbles, staggers, lurches, and bumbles ahead, without any true rhythm, construction, vision, or even bare minimum of craft. There are battle scenes as boring and uncompelling as the scenes of personal relationships, which are the last word in ponderous platitudes and stilted lifelessness.

The cast comprises mostly second-rate, posturing European actors who, moreover, sound (or are) dubbed ineptly . . . Anthony Quinn plays a feeble replica of his part in *Lawrence of Arabia*—of which film *Mohammad* is, in its entirety, a flimsy replica—and wisely avoids the merest semblance of conviction while delivering his ineptly contrived speeches . . ."

©1977 by the NYM Corp. Reprinted with
the permission of NEW YORK Magazine.

Film Information, February 1977 (p. 1)
Dave Pomeroy

"*Mohammad, Messenger of God* is Islam's *Greatest Story Ever Told*—a filmic, financial and faith-filled flop. Like the De Mille and Stevens Biblical spectaculars, *Mohammad* attempts to convey spiritual meaning via the multimillion-dollar spectacular route, and ends up worshipping its own technical achievements. Moreover, its three-hour length, too long by at least an hour, leads both to boredom and an overemphasis on the violent carnage surrounding religious clashes in 7th century Arabia. The historical Mohammad and contemporary Islam are equally ill-served by *Mohammad*.

Producer/director Moustapha Akkad and screenwriter H. A. L. Craig have taken too reverential a view of their subject. Thus, a sense of awkward historiocity pervades the film . . ."

©Film Information, 1977.

MONDO MAGIC

Documentary. Producers: *Alfredo Castiglioni, Angelo Castiglioni*. Distributor: *Peppercorn-Wormser*. Running time 105 minutes. New York opening December 1976 at the Victoria and Selwyn Theatres. Classification: None.

Note: There is no cast in this film.

New York Post, 12/16/76 (p. 43)
Archer Winsten

"*Mondo Magic* . . . is said by its distributor to be more shocking than *Mondo Cane*.

It is . . .

We travel through Africa's most sensational ceremonies, then on to the Indians in the basin of the Amazon, then to the Philippines, and finally to India. It should be obvious that these sensational aspects of primitive, religious and mystic observances require a special taste and curiosity on the part of the beholder. The photography is explicit to an ultimate degree, matching the events. The acceptance of pornography on the screen has made possible a new approach to sexual organs under scrutiny. I don't know how you can enjoy it, but from the point of view of information it is a heavy load, and possibly not something merely staged for sensation-mongers. It is hard to believe that any performer would do these things for any reason this side of belief, certainly not money."

Reprinted by Permission of New York Post.
©1976, New York Post Corporation.

MONKEY HUSTLE, THE

Director, Producer: *Arthur Marks*. Screenplay: *Charles Johnson*. Story: *Odie Hawkins*. Photography: *Jack L. Richards*. Editor: *Art Seid*. Music: *Jack Conrad*. Distributor: *American International Pictures*. Running time 90 minutes. New York opening December 1976 at several theatres. Classification: PG.

Daddy Foxx: *Yaphet Kotto*. Goldie: *Rudy Ray Moore*. Mama: *Rosalind Cash*. Win: *Randy Brooks*. Vi: *Debbi Morgan*. Player: *Thomas Carter*. Tiny: *Donn Harper*. Jan-Jan: *Lynn Caridine*. Shirl: *Patricia McCaskill*.

New York Post, 12/27/76 (p. 40)
Archer Winsten

"*The Monkey Hustle* . . . takes a fevered look at the Chicago black ghetto and makes it serio-comic hyper-active, purely movie-style.

They use so much jive talk you get the gist but not all the details of conversation.

Daddy Foxx (Yaphet Kotto) is the key-operative, a kindly Fagin teaching a group of fast-moving young men how to cheat the cheaters and where to pass the loot. He has a thing with Mama (Rosalind Cash), the girl with the big smile who is also pursued by Goldie (Rudy Ray Moore), the overlord of local vice . . .

It's a good-natured film . . . striving only to entertain with this hyped-up view of black street society in Chicago. It's simultaneously false and true, real in the talk, performances and perhaps the petty crime too, but virtually musical comedy false in the choreographing of its firecracker plot . . ."

Reprinted by Permission of New York Post.
©1976, New York Post Corporation

Los Angeles Times, 12/27/76 (Pt. IV, p. 16)
Linda Gross

"*Monkey Hustle* . . . is a scrambled but inoffensive series of vignettes about Chicago ghetto life that shows how everybody rallies to save their neighborhood when it is threatened by a freeway project.

The movie doesn't really work because its director, Arthur Marks, is a competent craftsman who exhibited style in *Friday Foster* and intensity in *J.D.'s Revenge* but doesn't know how to blend pathos, humor and ensemble energy . . .

It is disturbing to see actors of the caliber of Yaphet Kotto and Rosalind Cash wasted in a routine blaxploitation film. Newcomers Randy Brooks and Debbi Morgan show promise and fare better . . .

Marks' direction is phlegmatic and uninspired."

©Los Angeles Times, 1976.

MOSES

Director: *Gianfranco De Bosio*. Screenplay: *Anthony Burgess, Vittorio Bonicelli, Mr. De Bosio*. Producer: *Vincenzo Labella*. Photography: *Marcello Gatti*. Editors: *Gerry Hambling, Peter Boita, John Guthridge, Alberto Gallitti, Freddie Wilson*. Music: *Ennio Morricone*. Production: *ITC/RAI*. Distributor: *Avco Embassy*. Running time 141 minutes.

continued on next page

continued from previous page

New York opening March 26, 1976, at the Ziegfeld Theatre. Classification: PG. Origin: Italy.

Moses: *Burt Lancaster.* Aaron: *Anthony Quayle.* Miriam: *Ingrid Thulin.* Zipporah: *Irene Papas.* Dathan: *Yousef Shiloah.* Joshua: *Aharon Ipale.* Eliseba: *Marina Berti.* Jethro: *Shmuel Rodensky.* Princess Bithia: *Mariangela Melato.* Pharaoh Mernetta: *Laurent Terzieff.* Young Moses: *William Lancaster.* Narrator: *Richard Johnson.*

See Volume 1 for additional reviews

Saturday Review, 5/1/76 (p. 44)
Judith Crist

" . . . Originally telecast in six one-hour segments last summer by CBS, the film has been re-edited, some footage added, and the whole epic boiled down to two and a half hours. The result is a talky, plodding, unspectacular pseudo-epic sparked by a magnificent performance by Lancaster but damped down by a plethora of historic details, chubby extras, cheapjack production, uninspired special effects (ah there, C.B.!) and, above all, middle class good taste. The literate script, by Anthony Burgess, Vittorio Bonicelli (one of the writers of *The Bible*) and the director, Gianfranco De Bosio, is over-literalized; De Bosio, a theater-rooted filmmaker, has arranged set-pieces in the endless Israeli desert, appropriate for the small screen but static on the large . . ."

© Judith Crist, 1976.

Film Information, 4/76 (p. 6)
Unsigned

"Burt Lancaster is impressive as the Hebrew Patriarch who leads the Israelites from bondage in Egypt to the Promised Land. This two-hour-twenty-minute-long epic follows Moses from his birth and early life in Egypt, and during the years of wandering in the wilderness, up until he and his weary followers, at long last, come within sight of the River Jordan and their goal, the rich land beyond it.

A literal interpretation of the Bible story, *Moses* gives us filmic re-creations of the ten plagues brought down on the head of Pharaoh Mernetta, the crossing of the Red Sea, the providing of manna in the desert, the orgy of the golden calf.

Two years in the making, this is a handsome film. Obviously, great care has been lavished on all phases of production. The costumes and authentic settings--Jericho, for one, site of the ancient city--add to the film's strong visual impact . . ."

© Film Information, 1976.

MOSES AND AARON

Directors: *Jean-Marie Straub, Daniele Huillet, Klaus Hellwig.* Screenplay: *Mr. Straub, Ms. Huillet.* A filmed version of the opera by Arnold Schoenberg. Executive Producer: *Mr. Hellwig.* Photography: *Gianni Cantarelli, Ugo Piccone, Saverio Diamanti, Renato Berto.* Production: *Austrian Radio, West German Television, Janus Film and Fernsehen, NEF Diffusion, Straub-Huillet, Italian Television, French Television, Taurus Film.* Running time 105 minutes: New York opening October 5, 1975, at the New York Film Festival, Lincoln Center. Classification: None. Origin: Austria.

Moses: *Gunter Reich.* Aaron: *Louis Devos..*

See Volume 1 for additional reviews

Los Angeles Times, 5/14/76 (Pt. IV, p. 12)
Martin Bernheimer

" . . . One approached the film with great optimism. The problems that make *Moses* all but impossible on the stage could disappear on the screen. Cameras, after all, can create illusions beyond even the best equipped opera house . . .

Unfortunately, the Straubs make no effort to capture illusions or expand dramatic impact through cinematic translation. Instead, they seem to aim for stultifying immobility, a primitivism that borders on the amateurish.

Moses and Aaron is even more static on film than it is in its conventional context. The Straubs have treated Schoenberg to a colossal cop-out, an oratorio in a sandlot.

Presumably in the name of stylization, they have reduced the protagonists to bearded statues and frozen all perspectives. When the camera finally moves from Aaron's left profile to his right profile, the effect is thunderous. Visual relief in excelsis. That represents the Straubs' idea of excitement . . ."

© Los Angeles Times, 1976.

MOTHER, JUGS AND SPEED

Director: *Peter Yates*. Screenplay: *Tom Mankiewicz*. Based on a story by Stephen Manes and Mr. Mankiewicz. Producers: *Mr. Yates, Mr. Mankiewicz*. Photography: *Ralph Woolsey*. Editor: *Frank P. Keller*. Distributor: *Twentieth Century-Fox*. Running time 98 minutes. New York opening May 26, 1976, at several theatres. Classification: PG.

Mother: *Bill Cosby*. Jugs: *Raquel Welch*. Speed: *Harvey Keitel*. Harry Fishbine: *Allen Garfield*. Murdoch: *Larry Hagman*. Davey: *L.Q. Jones*. Leroy: *Bruce Davison*. Rodeo: *Dick Butkus*. Barney: *Milt Kamen*.

Los Angeles Times, 5/26/76 (Pt. IV, p. 14)
Charles Champlin

"With a title like *Mother, Jugs & Speed* (Bill Cosby, Raquel Welch and Harvey Keitel respectively) you'd think there was no place to go but up. Wrong.

I'm told that the necrophilia scene has been cut (Larry Hagman had been trying to make it with a dead or dying overdosed drug victim in the back of a speeding ambulance). There is still enough left to award *Mother, Jugs & Speed* the tarnished cup for shrill sludgery.

There are ambulance chasers and there are evidently chaser ambulances, cut-throat commercial carriers preying on the maimed--Stephen Manes and Tom Mankiewicz have fashioned a story and script out of this raw material, making it part low farce, part melodrama--an Emergency in need of surgery.

Cosby gives a strong, coherent and wasted performance . . ."

© Los Angeles Times, 1976.

New York Post, 5/27/76 (p. 43)
Archer Winsten

"*Mother, Jugs and Speed* . . . is a direct descendant of *M*A*S*H* in its lack of respect for humans in extremis.

The subject is a struggling private ambulance service in an outlying section of Los Angeles County.

Its owner-manager flannel-mouth is Harry Fishbine (Allen Garfield), its star driver 'Mother' Tucker (Bill Cosby), its telephone operator Raquel Welch who is known as 'Jugs' for two obvious reasons, and Speed is an unfrocked cop (Harvey Keitel) who has been accused of selling cocaine to the youth of the land. Hence, the title, *Mother, Jugs and Speed* . . .

. . . it's all in good black humorous fun, and Cosby, Keitel, Garfield and Welch give it their best, which turns out good on this occasion.

After all, you do have a director of the caliber of Peter (*Bullitt*) Yates, and a writer of the Mankiewicz family named Tom . . ."

Reprinted by Permission of New York Post.
© 1976, New York Post Corporation.

Village Voice, 6/28/76 (p. 135)
Andrew Sarris

" . . . as bad as everyone else says it is. Bill Cosby has a moment when he does a Stepin Fetchit imitation, Harvey Keitel is hopelessly out of key for this failed dark comedy, and Raquel Welch is pure plastic. The tastelessness of the enterprise is too ineptly executed to be truly offensive. Director Peter Yates seems to have lost his flair even with motor vehicles; he never had any with people."

Reprinted by permission of The Village Voice.
Copyright © The Village Voice, Inc., 1976.

Christian Science Monitor, 10/7/76 (p. 22)
David Sterritt

"*Mother, Jugs and Speed* has been talked up as a comedy, but I found it too grim and cynical to fit that category despite its frequent gallows humor. The main characters are foul-mouthed ambulance drivers sirening their way through a Los Angeles of dark and despair. The comedy centers on anomalous accidents and sex in the back of the rig. The social comment focuses on compassionless hospitals and urban decay and, less seriously, women's lib.

Bill Cosby, Raquel Welch and Harvey Keitel are strong as the trio of the title. Allen Garfield heads a manic supporting cast that includes Larry Hagman and Severn Darden. Peter Yates' direction falls somewhere between *Bullitt* tough and *Hot Rock* cool. *M, J & S* is fierce and sometimes repellent, but it has chosen a path it considers meaningful . . ."

Reprinted by permission from The Christian
Science Monitor © 1976.
The Christian Science Publishing Society.
All rights reserved.

Monthly Film Bulletin, 9/76 (p. 194)
John Pym

" . . . *Mother, Jugs and Speed*, Peter Yates' latest attempt to recast a proven comic format (in this case *M*A*S*H*) is encumbered with not only . . .

continued on next page

continued from previous page

self-conscious effects but also a choppy script which sets off in all directions without deciding its final destination. Tom Mankiewicz's screenplay is based primarily on the comedy of overlapping surprise, and in the opening sequence with the dandified, fast-talking 'Mother' Tucker (Bill Cosby) driving his well-appointed ambulance (complete with beer cooler and cassette player) on a hair-raising round it works well enough . . . Unable to maintain this frenetic pace, however, the movie subsequently lapses into the juxtaposition of mere improbabilities; and the final awkwardly appended shoot-out reveals that its method (by this point, anything startling would have served) has completely taken over from its semi-serious theme about the commercial exploitation of suffering . . .''

©Monthly Film Bulletin, 1976.

Film Information, July/August 1976 (p. 3)
Robert F. Moss

''In *Mother, Jugs and Speed*, audiences have the opportunity to watch a virulent strain of commercialism slowly ravage a promising film. The subject is novel (a private ambulance company), the treatment is exhilarating (free-wheeling satire), some of the actors are excellent (Allen Garfield, Larry Hagman). The first sympton of aesthetic disease is Raquel Welch . . .

The film preserves a look of healthy irreverence throughout, but, underneath, the box office orientation shows through poisonously . . .

Cosby is as mannered and self-indulgent as ever, and he and Ms. Welch provide irritating examples of the old Hollywood practice of casting parts on the basis of celebrity rather than acting ability. The opposite approach is exemplified by Hagman, as a raunchy, opportunistic driver, and Garfield, hilarious as the sleazy pugnacious owner of one of the companies . . .''

©Film Information, 1976.

MOTHER KUSTERS GOES TO HEAVEN

Director: *Rainer Werner Fassbinder*. Screenplay (German with English subtitles): *Kurt Raab, Mr. Fassbinder*. Producer: *Christian Hohoff*. Photography: *Michael Ballhaus*. Editor: *Thea Eymesz.*Music: *Peter Raben*. Production: *Tango Films*. Distributor: *New Yorker Films*. Running time 108 minutes. New York opening

March 6, 1977, at the New Yorker Theatre. Classification: None. Origin: West Germany.

Mother Kusters: *Brigitte Mira*. Corinna Corinne: *Ingrid Caven*. Ernst: *Armin Meier*. Helene: *Irm Hermann*. Journalist: *Gottfried John*. Mr. Thalmann: *Karl-Heinz Bohm*. Mrs. Thalmann: *Margit Carstensen*.

New York Magazine, 3/14/77 (p. 70)
John Simon

''. . . a perfectly serviceable story, but Fassbinder develops it with his customary mixture of heavy underscoring and cavalier offhandedness. Occasionally there is some satiric bite, but more often the film contents itself with facile and predictable observations, which the director now shoots with greater assurance than before, but still without particular distinction. Here the ending happens to be happy; it could just as easily have been otherwise. The acting is generally rudimentary or, in the case of the repellent Irm Hermann and Gottfried John, downright poor; only . . . Bohm and, at times, Ingrid Caven seem to know what they are doing and how to do it. Michael Ballhaus' cinematography is just adequate, and does nothing to counteract the general air of stasis and insignificance. Still, the film is not offensive, which for Fassbinder is pretty good.''

©1977 by the NYM Corp. Reprinted with the permission of NEW YORK Magazine.

New York Post, 3/7/77 (p. 13)
Frank Rich

''. . . *Mother Kusters*—a middling Fassbinder movie—is reasonably representative of his work. It deals with some of the typical Fassbinder themes—alienation, class conflict, the ambiguity of reality and the dehumanizing aspects of industrialized society—but the film's content is never as galvanizing as the director's style. That style, if you've never encountered it before, is utterly unique: Fassbinder mixes the dialectical devices of Godard with old movie camp and avant-garde minimalism to produce a supple and arresting vision . . .

This is, to say the least, a remote kind of filmmaking and though some of the movie is quite funny (Fassbinder puts down radical-chic Communists as well as the self-obsessed Kusters children), it's so dry that at times it's arid. Like so many German artists, this filmmaker is a practitioner of Brechtian alienation—but couldn't he have some of Brecht's showmanship as well? . . .''

Reprinted by Permission of New York Post. ©1977, New York Post Corporation.

MOVING VIOLATION

Director: *Charles S. Dubin*. Screenplay: *David Osterhout, William Norton*. Producer: *Julie Corman*. Photography: *Charles Correll*. Editors: *Richard Sprague, Howard Terrill*. Music: *Don Peake*. Production: *New World Pictures*. Distributor: *Twentieth Century-Fox*. Running time 91 minutes. Los Angeles opening September 1, 1976, at several theatres. Classification: PG.

Players: *Stephen McHattie, Kay Lenz, Eddie Albert, Will Geer, Lonny Chapman, Jack Murdock, Dennis Redfield, Richard O'Brien*.

Los Angeles Times, 9/1/76 (Pt. IV, p. 6)
Chuck Davenport

"*Moving Violation* is a switched-roles chase in which the cops are the unbelievably bad guys going all out to eliminate two innocent witnesses to a police murder. This newest effort from the Roger Corman film works, produced by Mrs. Julie Corman, is a competent delivery of formula action to the drive-in market . . .

. . . Geer is chilling here as the calculating Rockfield, and you remember this veteran actor can do much more than folksy grandpas.

Eddie Albert is the sympathetic and seasoned lawyer who takes the couple in . . .

Lenz and McHattie create a remarkably touching love story amid all the chaos, imparting some depth to the story without the awkwardness that the inevitable drippy words usually generate. The lines are there—but sparingly—and deftly spoken . . ."

©Los Angeles Times, 1976.

MURDER BY DEATH

Director: *Robert Moore*. Screenplay: *Neil Simon*. Producer: *Ray Stark*. Photography: *David M. Walsh*. Editors: *Margaret Booth, John Burnett*. Music: *David Grusin*. Production: *Rastar*. Distributor: *Columbia Pictures*. Running time 94 minutes. New York opening June 23, 1976, at several theatres. Classification: PG.

Tess Skeffington: *Eileen Brennan*. Lionel Twain: *Truman Capote*. Milo Perrier: *James Coco*. Sam Diamond: *Peter Falk*. Bensonmum: *Alec Guinness*. Jessica Marbles: *Elsa Lanchester*. Dick Charleston: *David Niven*. Sidney Wang: *Peter Sellers*. Dora Charleston: *Maggie Smith*. Yetta: *Nancy Walker*. Miss Withers: *Estelle Winwood*. Marcel: *James Cromwell*. Willie Wang: *Richard Narita*.

Los Angeles Times, 6/23/76 (Pt. IV, p. 1)
Charles Champlin

"*Murder by Death* does not quite qualify as an homage to the mystery story. Neil Simon finds mysteries, with their silly sleuths and their timetable solutions, on the foolish side of preposterous.

But they don't infuriate him as they did the late literary critic Edmund Wilson (who never snarled at dear Agatha Christie). Simon takes the form as amusing, as fetishes go, and has some quite tasty sport with it.

In *Murder by Death*, he has written a kind of comedy of mannerisms, a spoofy retirement party for a world's worth of solvers of intricately premeditated slayings . . .

. . . Peter Falk, doing his gruff, dirty-trenchcoat homage to Humphrey Bogart, gives *Murder by Death* its vitality and its funniest moments, and he stalks off with it, trailing cigaret ash . . .

If in the end one feels a certain disappointment (and one did), it may well be the author, the idea and the cast conjured up impossible dreams. As it is, *Murder by Death* is a literate, sophisticated, impeccably and colorfully acted, well-made diversion that is innocent of either sex or gore (and on that ground alone has to be welcomed with prayerful gratitude).

As one of that sleepless army of mystery addicts I wouldn't have missed it, and I laughed a lot . . ."

© Los Angeles Times, 1976.

New York Post, 6/24/76 (p. 22)
Frank Rich

" . . . Satire, used properly, is a sharp comic tool, but Simon turns it into a sledgehammer. Barely have the detectives been firmly established in fond detail than Simon rips their guts out and reduces them to comic-book buffoons who are vague shadows of their original selves. He does so because he knows that the more blurred the detectives are, the more latitude he can have in taking

continued on next page

continued from previous page

pot shots at them—and, sure enough, *Murder by Death* starts to upheave with gags that knock th detectives' virility, insult their intelligence and ma fun of their accents and even their toilet habits

Peter Sellers, Maggie Smith, and David Niven are famous detectives in Neil Simon's comedy, **Murder by Death**.

. . . Simon's satire becomes so hysterical that it cuts itself completely adrift from its subject; it becomes undirected bile that lands equally on the detectives and the movie's audience. After all, no mystery writer, least of all the ones invoked in this film, ever provided red herrings to the exclusion of telling a story, and, by doing so himself, Simon leaves an audience feeling far more cheated than any detective novel or movie ever has.

If you feel any affection for the fictional detectives who are the butts of Simon's practical joke, it's impossible to laugh—and you really can't enjoy the film on any level . . ."

Reprinted by Permission of New York Post.
© 1976, New York Post Corporation.

Village Voice, 7/19/76 (p. 103)
Molly Haskell

". . . Simon brings together his walking legends and then provides them with little more than class insults rather than the deeper antagonisms their differing methodologies might be expected to produce. But the nastiest blow comes when Nancy Walker appears as the deaf-mute cook for hire who sits around while the dinner instructions fall on deaf ears. And thus does the surliness of trying to kill off the guests turn to downright sadism in refusing to give them at least a gastronomic treat to reward

their and our forbearance. As for the 'murder plot,' suffice it to say it has as much substance as the nonmeal.

Other than trying to keep Capote's appearances and closeups to a merciful minimum, it is hard to know what director Robert Moore has done, or could have done, with the Simon material—a classy cheat that makes *The Last of Sheila*, another inverted thriller, look like a gem of comic invention and inner conviction."

Reprinted by permission of The Village Voice.
Copyright © The Village Voice, Inc., 1976.

The Sunday Times (London), 8/29/76 (p. 26)
Dilys Powell

". . . Much of the fun, both visual and audible, comes from Alec Guinness as a blind butler (nice to see him bothering to give a good performance). There is an assortment of shrinking rooms, automatically aimed daggers, poisoned wine, scorpions and doorbells which shriek instead of ringing. Everybody is discredited morally as well as professionally; and such is the profusion of masks, twin rooms and plastic corpses that five minutes after the end I couldn't remember who was who.

It seems to me that if you haven't watched the real Thin Man and the real Bogie in the real *Maltese Falcon* you won't see the joke; and if you have watched them, the joke isn't good enough. But I suppose one must be thankful that Mr. Simon hasn't attempted a Philip Marlowe."

©The Sunday Times, 1976.

Film Information, 9/76 (p. 5)
Bea Rothenbeuchner

"Neil Simon's parody murder mystery contains a great many one-liners delivered by a half-dozen of our favorite stars with fine expertise. The stars obviously relish their roles satirizing some of detective fiction's best-loved sleuths as they appeared both in print and on the screen. No matter that Simon's plot is full of loose ends and crime detection is incidental—it is the flair with which this unsubstantial material is presented that counts . . .

Robert Moore, who has directed for stage and television, makes his feature-film debut with *Murder by Death*. Considering the limited visual possibilities of the film, and given its emphasis on the spoken word, it is difficult to assess his film directorial ability on the basis of this one effort."

©Film Information, 1976.

The Times (London), 8/27/76 (p. 9)
Richard Combs

". . . Unfortunately, this is the kind of theatrical di-

version which looks as if it would make a better par-
lour game than it does a movie. Neil Simon's
screenplay keeps the pastiche moving along
briskly, ringing just the right changes on the
cliches . . . But once his pop-up, mocked-up crew
of detectives has been established, there is little
suspense (and decreasing amusement) in watching them go through the kind of routines which
seem more suitable for party charades or the infinitely extendable manoeuvres of a board game . . .

But even if the film's tactics seem to call out for
audience involvement rather than numb contemplation, it must be admitted that the cast generally fit
their parts like a glove . . ."

©The Times, 1976.

Christian Science Monitor, 7/8/76 (p. 22)
David Sterritt

". . . In the end, *Murder by Death* is a mildly
amusing diversion, packing more chuckles than
guffaws, but generally pleasant and elegant. I ob-
jected to the preponderance of jokes based on
physical disability, and Simon's childish overuse of
leering double entendres. I was captivated by the
best portrayals, though, including Mr. Niven and
Miss Smith as the impeccable Charlestons, Miss
Lanchester as the energetic Miss Marbles (like a
girlish Margaret Rutherford), and Mr. Falk as the raffish shamus in a Columbo raincoat who has no
place among these well-bred colleagues. On the
other hand, not enough is made of the brilliant Mr.
Guinness, and TV fans should be warned that
Nancy Walker is given very little to do.

Special applause to David M. Walsh for chillingly
atmospheric photography . . ."

Reprinted by permission from The Christian
Science Monitor © 1976.
The Christian Science Publishing Society.
All rights reserved.

Commonweal, 7/30/76 (p. 500)
Colin L. Westerbeck, Jr.

". . . Though *Murder by Death* is allegedly a
movie, the five detectives and their host are in fact
six stage characters who've found their author. By
throwing together a bunch of master detectives in a
manor house Simon has provided himself with six
quip artists and concocted a run-of-the-mill drawing room comedy. 'I am number one here,' announces Capote when he joins his guests. 'You
look more like number two to me, if you know what I
mean,' retorts the Sam Spade character. Even leaving aside the overemphasis of 'if you know what I
mean,' this stuff is a pretty pale imitation of Noel
Coward, and pitiful fare for a movie. (Out of respect
for the occasional good work done by the cast, I
won't mention who they are.) . . ."

©Commonweal, 1976.

Films in Review, August/September 1976 (p. 443)
William Avery

". . . Though the one-liners have the Simon seal,
the script occasionally falters to the vulgarly witty,
giving both director Robert Moore and the cast's
professionalism a few uneasy moments. Amid the
array of stars, Eileen Brennan comes close to stealing the picture as Tess Skeffington, Sam Diamond's
girl. Wasted in the plot are Alec Guinness as a blind
butler, Nancy Walker as a deaf and dumb maid,
and Estelle Winwood as a nurse who has to be
nursed.

Truman Capote plays Lionel Twain, the millionaire who has assembled these sleuths in his
Northern California castle. He gives a revolting
caricature of himself.

Charles Addams has done the clever title drawings, and throughout there's an appropriate Simon
slickness, but the movie contains too many plot
twists . . ."

©Films in Review, 1976.

Saturday Review, 7/24/76 (p. 42)
Judith Crist

"Neil Simon's medium is the theater—or so
his original screenplay for *Murder by Death* indicates. The characters, the lines, the scenes, are
there—but where's the movie? The idea is a delicious one: a mysterious character, rib-pokingly
named Lionel Twain, invites five of fiction's greatest
detectives to his electronically gloomed-up mansion 'for dinner and a murder,' with a million-dollar
prize for the one who solves the crime . . .

Each character has a parodic or satiric shtick—
and another, and another. And what Simon seemingly dreamed up on a Friday and tossed off during
a dull weekend has been translated into a richly
produced and sluggishly directed series of mini-
skits that deplete whatever wit and style the performers bring to their impersonations. Once the
characters have been collected, Simon seems at a
total loss as to what to do with them . . . The beginning and the finale, involving an unlayering of suspects with a neatly unexpected last twist, are worth
watching; the director has, mercifully, provided
enough tedium between so that you can doze and
awake refreshed for the amusing ending."

©Judith Crist, 1976.

Nation, 7/17/76 (p. 60)
Robert Hatch

"The gulf between funny and foolish is not so
wide that Neil Simon could not leap it in his screenplay for *Murder by Death*. The picture starts as the
one and soon collapses into the other . . .

continued on next page

continued from previous page

The cast is not only stellar but talented and the impersonations, particularly those of Falk, Niven and Sellers, are entertaining. Capote is a celebrity, not a star, so he impersonates himself, a tiresome exploit, and that is one fault of the picture. A more serious one is that Simon is a gag writer, not a mystery plotter. As a result, once the guests have been gathered, under various slap-stick circumstances, into the dark house, the picture begins to stutter, and the players, given nothing cogent to do, begin to impersonate like crazy . . . These, however, are specialties that do not become more endearing in the absence of substance, and the substance runs from comic exaggeration to improbability to hysteria in a breakneck descent to chaos. Parody implies wit; gags are not enough . . ."

©The Nation, 1976.

New York Magazine, 7/12/76 (p. 77)
John Simon

"*Murder by Death* . . . can be described fairly accurately in terms of certain stock phrases such as 'a hilarious spoof of classic detective novels and movies,' 'vintage Neil Simon comedy,' and 'fun-filled ensemble acting by a distinguished cast.' I say *fairly* accurate because the hilarity does take some serious dips here and there, because what Simon writes best (as he does here) is farce rather than comedy, and because the otherwise good to excellent cast has inflicted on it the worse than amateurish presence of Truman Capote. Hitherto I thought that Zsa Zsa Gabor was unique among 'performers' in not even being able to play herself on screen; now Capote has snatched those sorry laurels from her. Though a good many of the film's jokes fall flat, Capote is the only one that is offensive . . ."

©1976 by the NYM Corp. Reprinted with
the permission of NEW YORK Magazine.

Monthly Film Bulletin, October 1976 (p. 216)
John Pym

"As the credits of this distended and tortuous parody come up, the camera moves along a line of Charles Addams caricatures, introducing the viewer to each of the well-known detectives. These cut-out, pop-up drawings, are, in a way, a model for the film: neat, witty, but strictly two-dimensional . . . Simon's wit is as sharp as ever—and with the exception of the sibilant Truman Capote, he is well served by the players; his fiction within a fiction is perfectly signalled by Stephen Grimes' set designs (Twain's oil paintings are undeniably tacky). But the insubstantial plot cannot, finally, support Simon's self-congratulatory pyrotechnics . . ."

©Monthly Film Bulletin, 1976.

MY FRIENDS (AMICI MIEI)

Director: *Mario Monicelli*. Screenplay (Italian with English subtitles): *Pietro Germi, Piero De Barnardi, Leo Benvenuti, Tullio Pinelli*. Producer: *Carlo Nebiolo*. Photography: *Luigi Kuveiller*. Editor: *Ruggero Mastroianni*. Music: *Carlo Rustichelli*. Production: *Rizzoli Films*. Distributor: *Allied Artists*. Running time 113 minutes. New York opening July 18, 1976, at the 68th Street Playhouse. Classification: PG. Origin: Italy.

Mascetti: *Ugo Tognazzi*. Melandri: *Gastone Moschin*. Perozzi: *Philippe Noiret*. Necchi: *Duilio Del Prete*. Sassaroli: *Adolfo Celi*. Righi: *Bernard Blier*. Donatella: *Olga Karlatos*. Mascetti's Wife: *Milena Vukotic*. Tutti: *Angela Goodwin*.

Newsweek, 8/2/76 (p. 78)
Janet Maslin

". . . The four friends in this wickedly funny boy's-night-out farce lead miserable lives most of the time, but every so ofteh they get the urge to become 'gypsies.' They drive into isolated villages, chalk-mark a few buildings for demolition, explain to the dumbfounded residents that a superhighway will be coming through and drive away. One of them is lovesick, and the others help him win the madonna of his dreams—along with her children, their governess, a St. Bernard and a canary. Then they just as jovially make friends with her husband (Adolfo Celi), and break up the affair. They pull up to a hospital in the dead of night unaccountably mangled after some unseen catastrophe, demand 'a room for four,' and end up in bandages, casts and traction. When a nun catches one of them flexing his arm in an obscene gesture, he pre-empts her indignation by inquiring, 'Injection, sister? I'm all ready.'
It's the poverty—mostly emotional—of their lives that makes their escapades so irresistible . . ."

©Newsweek, Inc. 1976
reprinted by permission.

Saturday Review, 9/4/76 (p. 54)
Judith Crist

". . . It is a very funny and shrewd low comedy about five grown men who relieve their bleak provincial-backwater lives by going 'gypsying,' taking off on a series of practical jokes that range from gate-crashing parties to elaborate charades . . . On the surface it is a hilarious account of their wooing of a woman with obscene phone calls; their providing for the count with respect for his pride; their turning a town topsy-turvy posing as highway engineers; and their hoaxing a stingy pensioner into thinking he's in on a Mafia drug deal. But underneath the fun and games there's a devastating picture of men behaving on a small-boy level, prone to declare, 'It sure is great to be with men—why weren't we born fags?' A good time is one 'like when we were kids'; the refuge from being nobodies, they can from scorning and using women, from the joylessness of the lives they've made, lies in infantile clowning. Both Germi and Monicelli are masters of the surface hilarity that glosses the nastiness of little lives. This collaboration embodies their craft and the bitter truths beneath the comedy."

© Judith Crist, 1976.

Women's Wear Daily, 7/19/76 (p. 9)
Howard Kissel

"*My Friends* is about a group of middle-aged provincial Italian men who love to abandon their work and their wives to go off in search of adventure or merely pranks. The film is episodic, and the success of the humor varies from episode to episode. The high point for this viewer was a practical joke the gang loves to play at the railroad station, where they bounce up and down slapping the faces of people leaning out the windows of departing trains . . .

The unevenness, in fact the down-right unfunniness of much of *My Friends* stems perhaps from the fact that Pietro Germi, who conceived the project, became too sick to execute it. As a result much of the humor comes across as heavyhanded and forced—it does not have the deft touch Germi displayed even in one of his lesser films, *Alfredo, Alfredo* . . ."

©Women's Wear Daily, 1976.

New York Magazine, 8/2/76 (p. 59)
John Simon

". . . The problem, aside from the tendency of the humor to flag, is a certain lack of rhythm and form. Though the death of one of the practical jokers provides a kind of ending—albeit an open one—there is no beginning or middle, what with flashbacks within flashbacks and a time sequence not artfully enough scrambled, so that instead of a wonderful, crazy continuum, we actually get confusion and anticlimax. Moreover, the minor characters do not come sufficiently alive; not only are they merely pawns, they also fail to add up (as they so richly do in *I Vitelloni*) to a panorama of the society against which our anarchic 'gypsies' play out their madcap games, rebelling not so much against conformity as

against the process of aging.

Furthermore, the film is deficient in emotional shading . . ."

©1976 by the NYM Corp. Reprinted with
the permission of NEW YORK Magazine.

Village Voice, 9/27/76 (p. 107)
Andrew Sarris

"*My Friends*, the oddly premised Italian film (begun by the late Pietro Germi, and completed by Mario Monicelli after Germi's death), is reminiscent of Ring Lardner's classic short story, *Haircut*. But whereas Lardner's story bitterly condemns the practical joker as a familiar American type, the Italian movie sentimentalizes its aging practical jokers as if they were poignant sufferers from the human condition. The film is so openly misogynous that it seems to come out the other side into at least a suggestion of auto-critique. But the practical jokes themselves are singularly witless and unfunny, occasionally disgusting, and almost invariably sadistic. After one of the practical jokers dies of a heart attack, the surviving pranksters continue to revel at his funeral . . ."

Reprinted by permission of The Village Voice.
Copyright © The Village Voice, Inc., 1976.

Film Information, 9/76 (p. 3)
Bea Rothenbeuchner

"*My Friends* is mostly about male camaraderie . . . Gallant toward each other, and protective, their attitude toward women is something else. Women will find their moronic vulgarity offensive, and their 'middle-aged' philosophizing—Should life be taken seriously or as a big joke—too superficial to gain them any sympathy . . .

It is interesting to consider the causes that may be behind *My Friends*' 'shortcoming.' The cast is certainly blameless. Philippe Noiret (to be seen currently in the critically acclaimed *The Clockmaker*), Ugo Tognazzi, Bernard Blier, Adolfo Celi, are outstanding actors. And their performances are unquestionably competent. They speak the lines given to them in the script and do what they've been told to do by the director. Should Monicelli have interpreted the script differently? Possibly . . ."

©Film Information, 1976.

New York Post, 7/19/76 (p. 10)
Archer Winsten

"*My Friends* . . . is told in the form of a reminiscence dealing with four Italian men who had been companions in devilment almost from childhood.

continued on next page

continued from previous page

See Volume 1 for additional reviews

And a fifth who joins them later . . .

As an example of the work of one of Italy's most distinguished directors, Mario Monicelli, the picture is distinctly minor and light-minded. The humor that reached its all-time Italian high with *The Big Deal on Madonna Street* is here closer to the practical joker level. The humanity remains, but in a limited way. These men go off on a bachelor trip together to raise hell as if they were still young and irresponsible.

The performances of one and all are excellent, memorable."

Reprinted by Permission of New York Post.
© 1976, New York Post Corporation.

Los Angeles Times, 10/13/76 (Pt. IV, p. 12)
Kevin Thomas

"*My Friends* . . . is a lovingly crafted but terrifically tedious and long-winded Italian comedy-with-pathos about a group of middle-aged men who've known each other since childhood and who frequently get together to indulge in elaborate pranks that more often than not seem silly and cruel rather than funny. Indeed, so puerile are their shenanigans that there's no incentive to pay attention to their drawn-out unfolding.

Clearly director Mario Monicelli (who took over from Pietro Germi, who died only a week into production) and his colleagues mean for us to see the interminable practical joking of these grown men as a form of protest against their dismal lives. Unfortunately, since their sense of humor is pretty dismal too, *My Friends* seems doubly sad . . ."

©Los Angeles Times, 1976.

MY MICHAEL

Director: *Dan Wolman*. Screenplay (Hebrew with English subtitles): *Mr. Wolman, Ester Mor*. Based on a novel by *Amos Oz*. Producer: *Shlomi Cohen*. Photography: *Adam Greenberg*. Music: *Alex Cagan*. Distributor: *Alfred Plaine*. Running time 90 minutes. New York opening March 17, 1976, at the Festival Theatre. Classification: None. Origin: Israel.

Michael: *Oded Kotler*. Hanna: *Efrat Lavie*. Aunt: *Dina Roitkof*. Student: *Moti Mizrachi*. Landlord: *Israel Segal*. Duba: *Lliza Loria*.

Film Information, 5/76 (p. 3)
Eugene A. Schneider

"*My Michael* is a sensitive interpretation of the controversial novel by Amos Oz. The setting is Jerusalem in the 1950's when, as a result of the 1948 war, the city is divided into two separate parts--Jewish and Arab. People are uprooted, friendships and attachments disrupted. Hanna and Michael, students at the university, meet by accident and fall in love. They marry and have a son.

Beneath the superficial peacefulness of the couple's life, tension mounts, complementing the mood of the city. Unable to communicate with her husband, Hanna's alienation grows. She has sexual fantasies about two Arab men she knew as boys when Jerusalem was an undivided city.

My Michael is an interesting study of human loneliness, suitable for late teenagers and adults."

© Film Information, 1976.

Village Voice, 5/1/76 (p. 126)
Michael McKegney

"*My Michael* . . . is set in Jerusalem around the time of the 1956 Israeli-Arab war, but consistently attends to the very private lives of an attractive young couple whose marriage is slowly disintegrating.

The boy (Oded Kotler) is a geology student, hardworking and diligent, 'all for my father, so that one day he can address an envelope to me as a Ph.D.' . . . His is a virtually unplayable part-- certainly an unrewarding one. Mr. Kotler's character is supposed to be as dull as humanly possible, and I guess you could say he 'succeeds' in being so. In these circumstances, our attention naturally gravitates to his wife (Efrat Lavie), and she manages to absorb it adequately for the film's brief running time. *My Michael* is thus an actress's vehicle, and even when its heroine is displaying some rather perverse symptoms of her own, we have to sympathize with her spiritual revolt against the emotionally and intellectually empty environment in which she is enclosed . . .

Unfortunately . . . abrupt cutting turns aesthetically destructive through most of . . . the film . . ."

Reprinted by permission of The Village Voice.
Copyright © The Village Voice, Inc., 1976.

Los Angeles Times, 10/14/76 (Pt. IV, p. 20)
Linda Gross

". . . Hanna, the troubled Jewish heroine, whose acute sense of loss and ambivalent attraction toward the Arabs reflect the conscience of Jerusalem and of the film, is brought to life by Efrat Lavie. Her performance as the sulky, maddeningly listless, emotionally fragile and pathetically unhappy woman is extraordinarily intense, delicate and complex. As Michael, Oded Kotler is affectingly plodding and poignant.

In his low-keyed film, director Dan Wolman creates an internal memory of a troubled marriage that is also a metaphor for a city, evoking a strong sense of Jerusalem and subtly conveying the drab, negative aspects of a people at the dawn of their independence—still shell-shocked and waiting for the Messiah.

Adam Greenberg's golden autumn photography of Jerusalem enriches this memorable, chilling film of intellectual depth and psychological perceptiveness . . ."

©Los Angeles Times, 1976.

MYSTERIOUS MONSTERS, THE

Documentary. Director, Screenplay: *Robert Guenette*. From a story by Frances Guenette and Mr. Guenette. Producers: *Charles Sellier, Jr., Mr. Guenette*. Photography: *David Meyers, Eric Darstart*. Editors: *Earle Herden, Robert Lambert*. Music: *Rubin Rasin*. Narrator: *Peter Graves*. Production: *David L. Wolper Organisation*. Distributor: *Sun Classics Pictures*. Running time 84 minutes. Los Angeles opening July 1976 at several theatres. Classification: G.

Note: There is no cast in this film.

Los Angeles Times, 7/30/76 (p. 15)
Linda Gross

"*The Mysterious Monsters* . . . which purports to document the existence of primitive zoological aberrations like Bigfoot, the Loch Ness Monster and the Abominable Snowman, is a fascinating example of failed documentary film-making.

Produced by the Wolper Organisation (*Chariots of the Gods, The Hellstrom Chronicle* and *The Outer Space Connection*), the movie unsuccessfully merges scientific evidence, psychic observations and the dramatized encounters of eyewitnesses who recall their confrontations with the hairy, foul smelling, gigantic, man-like anthropoid.

Unfortunately, when people who aren't professional actors recreate dramatic moments in their

past, they do so with the flat earnestness of actors giving testimonials for margarine, whereas Bigfoot reconstructed resembles actors costumed for roles in *Planet of the Apes* . . .

The Mysterious Monsters explores the evidence of these weird creatures with reverence and dignity, but since it lacks insightful editing, the arguments it states are inconclusive."

©Los Angeles Times, 1976.

NASTY HABITS

Director: *Michael Lindsay-Hogg*. Screenplay, Producer: *Robert Enders*. Based on THE ABBESS OF CREWE by Muriel Spark. Executive Producer: *George Barrie*. Photography: *Douglas Slocombe*. Editor: *Peter Tanner*. Music: *John Cameron*. Distributor: *Brut Productions*. Running time 91 minutes. New York opening March 18, 1977, at the Cinema II Theatre. Classification: PG.

Alexandra: *Glenda Jackson*. Gertrude: *Melina Mercouri*. Walburga: *Geraldine Page*. Winifred: *Sandy Dennis*. Mildred: *Anne Jackson*. Geraldine: *Anne Meara*. Felicity: *Susan Penhaligon*. Hildegarde: *Edith Evans*. Priest: *Jerry Stiller*. Maximilian: *Rip Torn*. Monsignor: *Eli Wallach*. Bathildis: *Suzanna Stone*. Baudouin: *Peter Bromilow*. Officer: *Shane Rimmer*. Ambrose: *Harry Ditson*. Gregory: *Chris Muncke*.

Christian Science Monitor, 3/30/77 (p. 21)
David Sterritt

"*Nasty Habits* is Watergate via novelist Muriel Spark and a cabal of very unorthodox nuns.

An odd mix, you say? Quite right . . .

It's fun to watch these able performers do their sundry specialities, and diverting to figure out the 'tragicomedy a clef' plot in which each character has a real-life counterpart familiar to anyone who paid attention during the Nixon years. *Nasty Habits* might have broadened its appeal and deepened its interest by offering some new insight into the nature of political gamesmanship, but for the most part newsy entertainment is the order of the day . . .

Director Michael Lindsay-Hogg handles his material in all the obvious ways, neither strengthening nor weakening its inherent jokes and dull stretches. He seems to have allowed his actors freedom to

continued on next page

continued from previous page

handle their interpretations as they saw fit, which results in some uneven ensemble work and overdrawn portraying (especially Miss Dennis in spots),
but should please fans who seek a lighthearted evening peopled by popular favorites."

Reprinted by permission from The Christian
Science Monitor © 1977.
The Christian Science Publishing Society.
All rights reserved.

Saturday Review, 4/2/77 (p. 41)
Judith Crist

". . . the screen is set aglow by so brilliant a series
of performances by outstanding actresses, so
marked by droll actions and sparked by true wit and
high style . . . that one hesitates to examine too
closely the lack of overall imagination and the
pedestrianisms that keep the movie earthbound,
with slightly heavy-handed scriptwriting to supple-
ment the uninspired direction provided by Michael
Lindsay-Hogg, whose style was so admirable in the
Beatles' *Let It Be*.
The pure gold is provided by the women, starting
with the late Dame Edith Evans in a feisty introductory cameo . . .
. . . Jackson is no less than superb as the master
planner aglow with self-righteousness . . . Page and
Jackson are the ultimate Erlichman-Haldeman convinced sycophants; Anne Meara is dandy as a
meat-and-potatoes assistant; Melina Mercouri's
world-traveling missionary is more than a Greek
chorus . . . and Susan Penhaligon is a pretty little
rebel. But it is Sandy Dennis, as the loud-voiced,
simpleminded tool given to rendezvousing with the
blackmailers in the ladies' room at Wanamaker's or,
in drag, in the men's room of a public lavatory, who
steals the show right out from under the others
while proving herself a thoroughly original comedienne of first rank . . ."

©Judith Crist, 1977.

Newsweek, 3/28/77 (p. 86)
Janet Maslin

"The ads for *Nasty Habits*, featuring a curvaceous
nun with a recording device strapped to her thigh,
are more vulgar than the movie itself—which is too
bad. Once the producers decided to throw good
taste to the winds by filming Muriel Spark's *The Abbess of Crewe*, which ingeniously set the Watergate
in a convent, they should have been willing to go
for broke. Instead, the movie is almost perversely
refined: the power-mad nuns curse moderately ('Oh,
Christ!'), study Machiavelli and sip vintage wine, but
they never capture the hoodlum mentality of the figures on whom they're based . . .
Anne Meara, who makes such funny radio commercials that she seems miscast in longer roles,
plays each scene as if it were an isolated sketch;
her performance has a fragmented vitality that
might, in larger doses, have rescued the movie.

Glenda Jackson endows the abbess with so much
of her own brittle hauteur that she is able to
broaden the role into deliberate—and very effective
—self-parody. But the rest of the players are relegated to reciting unfunny lines mechanically and
simulating wickedness with very little conviction.
Nasty Habits may be based on Watergate, but the
only thing faintly scandalous about it is its title."

©Newsweek, Inc. 1977
reprinted by permission.

New York Post, 3/19/77 (p. 17)
Frank Rich

". . . This dumb, dreary and amateurish movie actually manages to take all the fun out of hating
Richard Nixon; it's the Watergate junkie's equivalent
of Methadone.
Nasty Habits has been crudely adapted from
novelist Muriel Spark's slender 1974 allegorical
novel *The Abbess of Crewe*, in which the Watergate saga is reenacted in a convent. In place of
Nixon and his dirty tricks, we get a tyrannical nun
(Glenda Jackson) who turns to third-rate burglaries
and illegal wiretapping to assure her election as Abbess of Philadelphia . . .
. . . Maybe *Nasty Habits* perpetrators thought
they could squeak by on sheer offensiveness—but
this film doesn't offend in any way that counts; it
never effectively attacks Nixon or even the Catholic
Church. If *Nasty Habits* makes any moviegoers
angry, it will only be because they feel—rightfully—
that they're being ripped off."

Reprinted by Permission of New York Post.
©1977, New York Post Corporation.

Village Voice, 4/4/77 (p. 41)
Andrew Sarris

". . . The movie, like the book, is full of disclaimers on the issue of anti-Catholicism . . .
As it happens, however, the movie is funnier than
it has any right to be. For one thing, the ensemble
acting is just short of extraordinary with Glenda
Jackson, Sandy Dennis, and Geraldine Page particularly skillful in confronting one outrageous contrivance after another without flinching. Even so, the
single get-Nixon-to-a-nunnery joke begins to wear
thin less than halfway through the picture. Yet the
laughs continue. Why? I suspect the cause of the
merriment to be not Nixon, but the nuns. Hence, despite all the disclaimers, a very nervous anticlerical-
ism is about all that *Nasty Habits* has going for
it . . ."

Reprinted by permission of The Village Voice.
Copyright © The Village Voice, Inc., 1977.

New York Magazine, 3/28/77 (p. 60)
John Simon

"*Nasty Habits* is a nasty little piece of goods over

which it would be kindest to pass in silence, if only it deserved kindness, and if our most eminent woman critic had not waxed dithyrambic about it. Actually, I think, this most tasteless of movies deserves every kick it can get . . .

. . . The language is rowdy throughout, the goings-on licentious or sacrilegious, and convent life is turned into an ugly, unfunny travesty. What justification is there for all this? . . .

. . . what is particularly offensive is the transposition of the Nixon gang into a Roman Catholic convent. What is the relevance, desirability, or justification for this? One reason, I suppose, is that Catholics lack the vigilante organizations that other minorities—blacks, Jews, women—so vociferously enjoy. And if you are prejudiced, vulgar, infantile, or stupid enough, you can always get a cheap laugh out of nuns using four-letter words, tumbling in the hay with priests, or even just munching a pizza on a bus. And judging by the less than steady but more than sporadic laughter I heard at the screening I attended, there may be a sufficiency of such prejudiced, vulgar, infantile, or stupid people to constitute an audience for this muck . . .''

©1977 by the NYM Corp. Reprinted with the permission of NEW YORK Magazine.

New Leader, 3/14/77 (p. 24)
Robert Asahina

". . . Regrettably, the movie is as long as the novel was short, and as blatant as the book was allusive. Moreover, whatever shock value the film starts out with is cynically and tiresomely exploited in pointless repetitions . . .

. . . Glenda Jackson (as the Nixon-nun), Melina Mercouri (as Henry Kissinger, unintentionally hilarious in her Greek-accented attempt to mimic the former Secretary's Germanic English), Geraldine Page (as H. R. Haldeman), Anne Jackson (as John Ehrlichman), Anne Meara (as Gerald Ford), and Sandy Dennis (as John Dean) are permitted—nay, encouraged—to make fools of themselves by director Michael Lindsay-Hogg. It is especially disheartening to see Glenda Jackson gradually turning into the next great harridan of the screen, a fate that formerly befell Bette Davis . . .

There is little else to say about this wretched movie . . .''

Reprinted with permission from
The New Leader, 1977.
©The American Labor Conference
on International Affairs, Inc.

NETWORK

Director: *Sidney Lumet.* Screenplay: *Paddy Chayefsky.* Producer: *Howard Gottfried.* Photography: *Owen Roizman.* Editor: *Alan Heim.*

Music: *Elliot Lawrence.* Production: *Metro-Goldwyn-Mayer.* Distributor: *United Artists.* Running time 120 minutes. New York opening November 14, 1976, at the Sutton Theatre. Classification: R.

Diana Christensen: *Faye Dunaway.* Max Schumacher: *William Holden.* Howard Beale: *Peter Finch.* Frank Hackett: *Robert Duvall.* Nelson Chaney: *Wesley Addy.* Arthur Jensen: *Ned Beatty.* Great Ahmed Kahn: *Arthur Burghardt.* Bill Herron: *Darryl Hickman.* Edward George Ruddy: *William Prince.* Helen Miggs: *Sasha von Scherler.* Louise Schumacher: *Beatrice Straight.* Laureen Hobbs: *Marlene Warfield.*

New York Times, 11/15/76 (p. 39)
Vincent Canby

". . . *Network* . . . is, as its ads proclaim, outrageous. It's also brilliantly, cruelly funny, a topical American comedy that confirms Paddy Chayefsky's position as a major new American satirist. Paddy Chayefsky? Major? New? A satirist? Exactly.

Mr. Chayefsky, who made his name initially as television's poet of the small and everyday, has evolved through work like *The Latent Heterosexual* and *The Hospital* into one of our very few, card-carrying satirists with access to the mass market . . .

I expect that a lot of people will sniff at the film on the ground that a number of the absurdities Mr. Chayefsky and Mr. Lumet chronicle so carefully couldn't happen, which is to miss the point of what they're up to. These wickedly distorted views of the way television looks, sounds and, indeed, is, are the satirist's cardiogram of the hidden heart, not just of television but also of the society that supports it and is, in turn, supported . . .

Network can be faulted both for going too far and not far enough, but it's also something that very few commercial films are these days. It's alive. This, I suspect, is the Lumet drive. It's also the wit of performers like Mr. Finch, Mr. Holden and Miss Dunaway. As the crazy prophet within the film says of himself, *Network* is vivid and flashing. It's connected into life.''

©1976 by the New York Times Company.
Reprinted by permission.

Newsweek, 11/22/76 (p. 107)
Charles Michener

". . . screenwriter Paddy Chayefsky has now taken a whip to the menace that everyone loves to hate but can't seem to live without—television . . .

continued on next page

continued from previous page

Directed with steely assurance by Sidney Lumet and acted smashingly at all levels by its large cast, *Network* hurts in a way that recalls the great social comedies by Preston Sturges of the 1940s—as a barrage of violently funny shocks of recognition.

Like Sturges, Chayefsky shocks by blending realism with farce, reality with fantasy . . .

. . . Lumet and his cinematographer, Owen Roizman, have shaped, paced and lit the action with the sneakiest sensitivity to shadings and detail— catching the background figure of a programming assistant inhaling breath freshener during a story conference, subtly shifting the movie's look from that of a documentary to that of a TV commercial.

Still, this is, above all, a writer's movie. Researched in the enemy camp, Chayefsky's dialogue crackles with authenticity and never dodges an emotion or idea. Perhaps the most exhilarating payoff of that work is the acting: to watch Finch, Dunaway, Holden, Duvall and a score of minor players attack and fill out their roles is to see a group of gifted actors relishing their first full meals in a long time . . .''

©Newsweek, Inc. 1976 reprinted by permission.

New York Magazine, 11/22/76 (p. 88)
John Simon

". . . *Network* is not only uncertain of tone, floundering between the grim exposé and absurdist kitsch, it does not even play fair on the plot level. We are, for example, given specimens of Beale's radical populist oratory, but no sample of his post-conversion right-wing populism, which must have taxed Chayefsky's ingenuity beyond endurance. The relationship between Max and Diana is psychologically preposterous, an uninterrupted series of reversals in a power play whose emotional basis is never believably conveyed. Even the question of whether their sex is good or bad, discussed repeatedly and at length, undergoes constant revisionist interpretations. Such things may exist in the world; where they do not have true existence is in Chayefsky's pedestrian plotting and shopworn prose . . .''

©1976 by the NYM Corp. Reprinted with the permission of NEW YORK Magazine.

Women's Wear Daily, 11/8/76 (p. 16)
Howard Kissel

". . . *Network* is clearly the screenwriter's movie—Chayefsky's style is a broad one and so are the performances. Faye Dunaway is extremely funny as the ruthless programmer for whom ide-

ology, life, love, and death are all reduced to matters as quantifiable as ratings. Peter Finch is absurdly poignant as the newscaster she makes into a five-night-a-week prophet. The story makes contact with conventional reality only briefly in William Holden's conflict between his fascination with Dunaway and his loyalty to his wife—Holden, one of the most dependable, solid of screen actors, manages this balancing act beautifully, and Beatrice Straight is fine as his wife. The film is full of great performances . . .''

©Women's Wear Daily, 1976.

New York Post, 11/15/76 (p. 22)
Frank Rich

". . . For all the self-consciously deployed 25-cent words in its screenplay, this movie is so heavy-handed and simplistic that a 12-year-old wouldn't find it challenging; its characters are painted in such venomous broadstrokes that you end up feeling that *Network*'s authors have as dim and cynical a view of the human race as the perpetrators of a TV show like 'Charlie's Angels.' . . .

Lumet's direction meanwhile is as disheveled as the script. While he's brought more energy to *Network* than any of his projects since *Serpico*, he never gives the film a consistent tone; part of it looks like *Dr. Stangelove*, part like *Putney Swope*, part like a documentary and part like a Doris Day-Rock Hudson comedy about Madison Avenue . . .''

Reprinted by Permission of New York Post. ©1976, New York Post Corporation.

Christian Science Monitor, 11/15/76 (p. 25)
David Sterritt

"After years of peaceful coexistence, the movies have apparently declared war on TV. *Network*— written and filmed by men who once worked for television—is one of the most ferocious, outspoken, and generally cynical attacks launched by one medium upon another, and on the society that shapes and harbors them both.

Fortunately, the talents involved are significant— notably writer Paddy Chayefsky—so the assault is often as entertaining as it is savage, as meaningful as it is deliberately offensive at times . . .

Network is a fantasy, wildly improbable yet not completely impossible. Certainly it has timely warnings with regard to the sensationalism that often creeps into TV news on a local, if not national, level; and there is bitter truth in its indictment of audiences who respond to such sensationalism . . .''

Reprinted by permission from The Christian Science Monitor ©1976. The Christian Science Publishing Society. All rights reserved.

The Village Voice, 11/29/76 (p. 53)
Andrew Sarris

"*Network* is blessed with three hilarious ideas: 1) an anchorman goes crackers on camera; 2) a workaholic woman television executive 'comes' too soon in bed, and 3) Third World terrorists slide smoothly into the jargon of media contracts. Add a fine nonsuperstar cast of Faye Dunaway, William Holden, Peter Finch, Ned Beatty, and Robert Duvall to articulate Paddy Chayefsky's windiest rhetoric in one of Sidney Lumet's patented urban jungles, and you have the makings of a bright satire. Unfortunately, *Network* ends up as a combination *Meet John Doe* and *A Face in the Crowd* as it goes through the roof with a highly explosive mixture of male menopausal megalomania and apocalyptic assassination . . ."

Reprinted by permission of The Village Voice.
Copyright© The Village Voice, Inc., 1976.

Film Information, December 1976 (p. 1)
Dave Pomeroy

" 'The Arabs are embargoing oil, Patty Hearst is on trial, New York City is about to default—and Howard Beale is all over page one.' Howard Beale, anchorman for 'fourth' network UBS's Nightly News, has achieved that kind of prominence because he announced on network TV that 'I finally just ran out of bulls—.' Paddy Chayefsky/Sidney Lumet's *Network* takes this outrageous, yet crazily plausible premise and builds it into a funny, searching, insightful commentary on us and our culture. It is, in many respects, the most important film of the year.

Chayefsky's genius is to have taken the reality of inner machinations within a network and the way in which these then impinge on all of our lives and blown this reality up to only slightly larger than life. Undergirding his concept is transcendent, Old Testament theology which places the ludicrous excesses of these human actors *sub specie aeternitatis* . . ."

© Film Information. 1976.

Films in Review, December 1976 (p.635)
DeWitt Bodeen

". . . outrageously funny.
Cinematically it has everything working for it: brilliantly directed by Sidney Lumet from a screenplay by Paddy Chayefsky which has just about the sharpest and most blasphemous dialogue to be heard in years, it also has some glittering performances by Faye Dunaway, William Holden, Peter Finch, Robert Duvall, and Ned Beatty, that should bring them nominations for the year's best acting performances.

Chayefsky, our Voltaire for these times, once himself the king of TV writers, knows whereof he writes, and his story has to do with the dog-eat-dog world behind the scenes at a major TV network station, when a bitch goddess moves in on a faltering news-of-the-day department and makes it her own. Not only is *Network* the most brilliant of black comedies, it's also the wisest and, sadly, the truest. One thing for sure: it pulls no punches—it's a knockout hit!"

© Films in Review, 1976.

Nation, 12/4/76 (p. 605)
Robert Hatch

". . . Sidney Lumet, director of *Network*, has encouraged his cast to perform as though everything they know about being men and women they have learned at second hand. They may not be robots, but they sure as hell are hams . . .

So is this a slashing comment on network television and therefore exceedingly bold? Not by a country mile. There is plenty wrong with television, plenty to satirize. But *Network* prudently misses the point, dishing up an outrageous razzle-dazzle stew that will ruffle no network feathers and delight an audience that enjoys being titillated by improbable threats . . ."

© The Nation, 1976.

The Times (London), 2/18/77 (p. 11)
David Robinson

". . . If the overall effect seems diffuse, individual moments have bite. There is a telling scene at the start of the film when Beale's announcement of his impending suicide meets with total absence of response within the studios, where people are so immunized that they are blind and deaf to anything seen or heard on the tube. Faye Dunaway, too, is often funny as the prototypical, viciously charming television career girl, still chattering on about her programmes and ratings even—maybe specially—at the moment of sexual climax.

The two central performances, too, go far to redeem a film of somewhat shattered notions. William Holden plays a television executive, defeated, battered, passed by, betrayed, but still fighting to retain some shred of human feeling and reaction—a lone survivor in a world of Disneyland automata. Peter Finch's obsessed and tormented madman was his last performance, and stands as one of the best of his latter years."

© The Times, 1977.

continued on next page

continued from previous page

Monthly Film Bulletin, January 1977 (p. 9)
Richard Combs

". . . Chayefsky's constant spluttering jeremiads qualify him as much as the Finch character for the tag of a 'strip Savonarola.' His script, further, is so compromised by special pleading—blatantly pandering to middle-aged exasperations, it allows only William Holden to emerge with his dignity and his life-enhancing vote for real emotion and real pain intact—that it never achieves the dispassionate, all-embracing irony of *Strangelove* or Gore Vidal's early essay, *The Messiah*, on the possibility of a religious takeover of the tube. Both the actors and director Sidney Lumet work smoothly into this show-stopping declamatory style, with the result that the characters seem to exist in self-contained pockets of rhetoric . . ."

©Monthly Film Bulletin, 1977.

The Sunday Times (London), 2/20/77 (p. 38)
Alan Brien

". . . *Network* is rare in the commercial cinema in being almost deafeningly literate. Words come first, then images. Character, motive, and performance follow, ruthlessly tailored to the message. Peter Finch's last part is not one of his best, but only because it barely exists in human terms. Like almost all the characters along the TV corridors of power, he is more an emblem than a person.

Nearest to messy, unpredictable, silly humanity are the ill-matched lovers, aging, failed Head of News William Holden and ambitious, aggressive young producer Faye Dunaway, whose wordy, on-the-trot affair sometimes threatens to disrupt the modern-day morality play Chayefsky seems to be staging . . .

Network is an imperfectly outrageous motion picture, but funny, intelligent and often joltingly out of the rut. Lumet claims to regard it as reportage where its main appeal lies in the pugnacity of its satire."

©The Sunday Times, 1977

NEW GIRL IN TOWN

Director: *Gus Trikonis*. Screenplay, Producer: *Peter J. Oppenheimer*. Photography: *Irv Good-noff*. Editor: *Jerry Cohen*. Music: *Kim Richmond*. Distributor: *New World Pictures*. Running time 90 minutes. New York opening March 1977 at several theatres. Classification: R.

Jamie Barker: *Monica Gayle*. Jeb Hubbard: *Glenn Corbett*. Kelly: *Roger Davis*. Johnny Rodriguez: *Himself*. C.Y. Ordell: *Jesse White*. Alice: *Marcie Barkin*.

New York Post, 3/12/77 (p. 17)
Archer Winsten

"*New Girl in Town* . . . goes through the life and hard times, rape by rape, of a 16-year-old Kentucky girl, Jamie Barker (Monica Gayle), who wants to be a country singer in Nashville . . .

It's a long hard road, eventually leading to gold, glitter, autograph hounds and, by golly, still another rape.

I don't want to make light of the sexual aspects, but they do seem to be emphasized by producer-writer Peter J. Oppenheimer beyond what must be average expectancy. Maybe I'm wrong, however, and musicians in Nashville are affected by the emotional heightening of the songs they sing. In any case, Monica Gayle does sing well and behave like a reluctant victim, bravely going into the den of iniquity again and again after each setback."

Reprinted by Permission of New York Post.
©1977, New York Post Corporation.

NEXT MAN, THE

Director: *Richard C. Sarafian*. Screenplay: *Mort Fine, Alan Trustman, David M. Wolf, Mr. Sarafian*. Based on a story by Martin Bregman and Mr. Sarafian. Producer: *Mr. Bregman*. Photography: *Michael Chapman*. Editors: *Aram Avakian, Robert Lovett*. Music: *Michael Kamen*. Production: *Artists Entertainment Complex*. Distributor: *Allied Artists*. Running time 108 minutes. New York opening November 10, 1976, at several theatres. Classification: R.

Khalil Abdul-Muhsen: *Sean Connery*. Nicole Scott: *Cornelia Sharpe*. Hamid: *Albert Paulsen*. Al Sharif: *Adolfo Celi*. Justin: *Marco St. John*. Dedario: *Ted Beniades*. Fouad: *Charles Cioffi*.

Film Information, December 1976 (p. 5)
Dave Pomeroy

". . . With a more literate script, Connery's character might have been elevated to the archetypal tragic 'fool,' conquering through ingenuousness rather than power.

But these authors keep *The Next Man* on the level of political intrigue, as OPEC, with sinister background aid from oil interests in the U.S.A. and U.S.S.R., hire beautiful political assassin Cornelia Sharpe to do in the Minister. Sharpe and Connery become lovers, but their relationship and her conflict over whether to do the deed are never really credible, with predictable results that are as brutal as they are implausible.

Director Richard Sarafian takes forever to set up the film's premise, and then he lingers over interminable street festivals and lush scenery. *The Next Man* has had millions spent on it, with exotic locations from Morocco to Teterboro, N.J., which makes one cringe at the waste . . ."

©Film Information, 1976.

Village Voice, 12/20/76 (p. 57)
Andrew Sarris

"*The Next Man* has received some of the worst notices of the season, and though it is not even a passable movie, it is not so bad as all that. I am particularly struck by the critical overkill directed at Cornelia Sharpe for parading around as a blank-faced clotheshorse. One would think that this was the first big glamour buildup in movie history . . .

As for the picture itself, Sean Connery's enlightened Arabian leader, who proposes peace and partnership with Israel, is mocked by the daily headlines. The scenario's mixture of assassin-oriented paranoia and liberal wishful thinking is too silly to discuss seriously. Still, much of the movie is skillfully directed by Richard Sarafian, as if it were actually going somewhere besides the graveyard."

Reprinted by permission of The Village Voice. Copyright ©The Village Voice, Inc., 1976.

New York Post, 11/11/76 (p. 13)
Frank Rich

"*The Next Man* . . . is, from all appearances, a vanity production that's been designed to make a star out of an actress named Cornelia Sharpe. According to her official bio, Miss Sharpe's 'most widely known credits include Pan Am's 'Girl from C.A.R.G.O.,' The Noxema Mermaid, Woolite and Zest'—and I think it's safe to say that, *The Next Man* notwithstanding, these will continue to be her most widely known credits . . .

. . . the biggest laughs belong to Miss Sharpe, who gets in trouble every time she has to say a line longer than 'I'll drive' or has to express an emotion other than complete and utter boredom.

As the leading lady's straight man, Connery doesn't have the most enviable job in the world— it's hard to play opposite a post—and he executes his chores with charm that is well beyond the call of duty . . ."

Reprinted by Permission of New York Post ©1976, New York Post Corporation.

New York Magazine, 11/22/76 (p. 92)
John Simon

". . . Incredible even on the level of hokum, the movie will, however, supply a number of unintended, unwholesome laughs. My own favorite moment comes when Nicole, predictably in love with her designated victim Khalil, listens to him raptly in the U.N. visitors' gallery as he makes his world-shaking love-Israel speech. Every vaguely Near-Eastern or Near-Eastern-looking actor whom Hollywood could dig up (including at least one Jew) to portray Near-Eastern U.N. delegates exudes amazement or displeasure. At that very instant, a messenger hands an envelope to Miss Sharpe with the laconic instruction 'NOW!!!' scribbled on a pink slip. She must stop romancing and start dispatching her man. NOW. 'The National Organization for Women,' I explained to my companion."

©1976 by the NYM Corp. Reprinted with the permission of NEW YORK Magazine.

Los Angeles Times, 11/10/76 (Pt. IV, p. 1)
Charles Champlin

"*The Next Man* is out of the ransacked file drawer labeled International Intrigue. The usual ingredients have been rounded up: shadowy forces contending for unthinkably high stakes, stalkers stalked by still other stalkers in exotic locations, a lone idealist fighting for honor and peace even as love and evil duly fight for control of a mysterious beauty . . .

So you pay your money and you get your bright but not entirely engrossing diversion, the pleasure of Sean Connery's assured company and a ballady score by Michael Kamen.

Director Sarafian is an able storyteller (here providing a few more fetes, parades and other local colors than seem essential). It is just that the story being told was too labyrinthine for its own interplay of good and evil . . ."

©Los Angeles Times, 1976.

Women's Wear Daily, 11/10/76 (p. 68)
Howard Kissel

"The premise of *The Next Man* is that an Arab leader, in an attempt to bring peace to the Mideast, announced he is going to invite Israel to join OPEC. The plot of *The Next Man* is about as plausible as this premise. What may be noteworthy about it is that we are asked to sympathize with a man of

continued on next page

continued from previous page

peace whose efforts are obviously doomed—in more innocent times a film with as many holes as this would at least have offered us a happy ending; it is a little unsettling to think that now pessimism seems to have more box-office appeal . . .

One nice thing about this competently made film is that it treats New York well. There are some beautiful shots of the city from the air at dawn and an intriguing look at one of the city's forgotten arcana—a railroad station under the Waldorf."

© Women's Wear Daily, 1976.

Films in Review, January 1977 (p. 58)
Michael Buckley

". . . plods through locations . . . and features many . . . murders while attempting to be a political intrigue thriller. The feeling of excitement is not achieved while one gets a touch of jet lag.

The editing by sometimes director Aram Avakian (*Cops and Robbers*, et al.) makes the film appealing to the eye, if not the brain, camouflaging the absence of substance in the shish kebab of a screenplay by Mort Fine, Alan Trustman, David M. Wolf and Richard C. Sarafian, who also directed . . .

. . . Connery looks incongruous as an Arab, but does a competent job. Making her starring debut as the assassin who falls in love with her target (Connery) Cornelia Sharpe is more appealing in appearance than in performance . . ."

© Films in Review, 1977.

NEXT STOP, GREENWICH VILLAGE

Director: *Paul Mazursky*. Screenplay: *Mr. Mazursky*. Producers: *Tony Ray, Mr. Mazursky*. Photography: *Arthur Ornitz*. Editor: *Richard Halsey*. Music: *Bill Conti*. Distributor: *Twentieth Century-Fox*. Running time 110 minutes. New York opening February 4, 1976, at the Cinema I Theatre. Classification: R.

Larry Lapinsky: *Lenny Baker*. Mom: *Shelley Winters*. Sarah: *Ellen Greene*. Anita: *Lois Smith*. Robert: *Christopher Walken*. Connie: *Dori Brenner*. Bernstein: *Antonio Fargas*. Herb: *Lou Jacobi*. Pop: *Mike Kellin*. Herbert: *Michael Egan*. Herb's wife: *Helen Hanft*. Mrs.

Tupperman: *Rashel Novikoff*. Cop: *Joe Spinnell*. Doctor: *Rochelle Oliver*. Clyde: *Jeff Goldblum*.

See Volume 1 for additional reviews

Monthly Film Bulletin, February 1977 (p. 27)
Geoff Brown

". . . Mazursky . . . reduces the film's conviction by structuring his material erratically. Larry meanders, even more than Harry and Tonto, scattering the seeds of a plot here and there, but never in sufficient quantity for anything to grow. Mazursky also betrays a fatal fondness for extending scenes beyond their natural length, decorating their dying moments with irritating bits of business plainly designed to ingratiate . . . All of which is a great pity, for a much better film can be periodically glimpsed peeping through . . . Many of the unfamiliar players, too, show charm and skill (Lenny Baker, Ellen Greene and Dori Brenner), but Mazursky has managed throughout to stifle all the film's potential virtues."

© Monthly Film Bulletin, 1977.

The Times (London), 2/4/77 (p. 11)
David Robinson

". . . As with Mazursky's *Harry and Tonto*, English audiences are likely to find his characters a shade overcoloured and a degree or two too cloyingly lovable. But the stereotypes of the Village scenes are compensated by the scenes of Jewish family life—equally stereotypical, but done with a feeling and gusto and appalled affection that gives them their own life. The mother who arrives at all the most inopportune moments, bearing unwelcome gifts of bagels, strudel and boiled fowl, is Shelley Winters, an inveterate overdoer who can nevertheless always get away with it. Her permanently embarrassed husband is finely played by Mike Kellin. Mazursky does understand actors: Ellen Greene as the dully faithless girlfriend and Christopher Walken as the Village guru and Casanova are well cast; and Lenny Baker provides a finely detailed portrait of the lankly unprepossessing, timidly brash hero."

© The Times, 1977.

The Sunday Times (London), 2/6/77 (p. 39)
Alan Brien

". . . Paul Mazursky, who writes, directs, and produces, tells us that 'the biggest influence in my work remains my own life' and he is clearly determined not to sell out his younger self to amuse another generation. These newly graduated adults, conga-ing through the traffic from one coffee-bar to

another, conning each other with fantasy versions
of their past and future, are never quite having as
much fun as they pretend and often crash head-on
into tragic melodramas they cannot handle . . .

Lenny and Ellen are only briefly Romeo and Juliet,
soon enough more like Iago and Emilia. How will he
ever get to Hollywood with front teeth like a pair of
cardboard tombstones? I wonder at first. Can she
hold him looking like a kosher Minnie Mouse? . . ."

©The Sunday Times, 1977.

Alice (Tatum O'Neal) and Buck (Burt Reynolds) try to
escape a brawl in Peter Bogdanovich's **Nickelodeon**.

NICKELODEON

Director: *Peter Bogdanovich.* Screenplay:
W. D. Richter, Mr. Bogdanovich. Producers:
Irwin Winkler, Robert Chartoff. Photography:
Laszlo Kovacs. Editor: *William Carruth.* Distributor: *Columbia Pictures.* Running time 122
minutes. New York opening December 21,
1976, at the Columbia I and II Theatres. Classification: PG.

Leo Harrigan: *Ryan O'Neal.* Buck Greenway:
Burt Reynolds. Alice Forsyte: *Tatum O'Neal.*
H. H. Cobb: *Brian Keith.* Marty Reeves: *Stella
Stevens.* Franklin Frank: *John Ritter.* Kathleen
Cooke: *Jane Hitchcock.*

Newsweek, 12/27/76 (p. 56)
Jack Kroll

". . . There's no one making American movies
who's more intelligent than Peter Bogdanovich.
Something of an emotional puritan, he thinks his
way to his effects. You laugh a lot at *Nickelodeon*,
and then you notice you're laughing at creative
intelligence rather than at raw comic power. But
you laugh. There's a startling psychic healthiness
to *Nickelodeon*; Bogdanovich (who coauthored the
screenplay with W. D. Richter) really knows and
cares about goodness. He's a wizard with actors—
he actually gets Burt Reynolds to swap his smirking
macho camping for a quiet vulnerability and manly
yearning. But he should work with bigger performing energies—the biggest such energy in *Nickelodeon* is that of Tatum O'Neal. Bogdanovich seems
at a crossroads. He's turned the past into a spotless
workshop with locked doors. Knock, knock."

©Newsweek, Inc. 1976
reprinted by permission.

Women's Wear Daily, 12/22/76 (p. 16)
Howard Kissel

"Several of Peter Bogdanovich's films have been
constructed as acts of homage to directors he admires. In his latest, *Nickelodeon*, homage turns to
downright obsequiousness . . .

No one—not even people who saw *At Long Last
Love*—really wants Bogdanovich to engage in this
sort of self-abasement. All we really want is for him
to make as good a film as *The Last Picture Show*
rather than just another collection of scenes from
other people's films, which is pretty much what the
slapstick *Nickelodeon* is. With cardboard characters you can't really expect performances—even
Tatum O'Neal doesn't have much to do. As usual,
Laszlo Kovacs' photography steals the show."

©Women's Wear Daily, 1976.

New York Post, 12/22/76 (p. 16)
Frank Rich

". . . Amazing as it may sound, there are even
a few moments in *Nickelodeon* where you could
swear that Peter Bogdanovich had a heart.

continued on next page

continued from previous page

These moments, unfortunately, do not occur until the movie's final five or so minutes—and to get to them you must sit through a mirthless comic romance that never lives up to its considerable potential . . .

. . . Bogdanovich has never been able to put across anything more than a linear story; here he so overtaxes himself that *Nickelodeon* seems exhausted by the time the exposition has been laid out.

After a while, the director loses control of the screenplay entirely, and you begin to feel that major sections of the movie are taking place off-screen. The dramatic issues we care most about—the progress of the heroes' careers, the growth of the movie industry, the ups and downs of the love triangle—are all presented in unsatisfying fits and starts . . ."

Reprinted by Permission of New York Post.
©1976, New York Post Corporation.

Los Angeles Times, 12/23/76 (Pt. IV, p. 1)
Kevin Thomas

". . . *Nickelodeon* . . . is Bogdanovich's heartfelt and very knowledgeable evocation of the hectic formative years of the American film industry. It also is a romantic comedy-drama involving Ryan O'Neal, Burt Reynolds and exquisite newcomer Jane Hitchcock in an eternal triangle that becomes increasingly serious in its development. It is, however, more successful at the first than the second.

. . . it sets out to tell its story in the robust, broad-slapstick manner of the silent one-reelers. Then gradually it injects moments of greater realism in an attempt to emulate the evolution of the industry itself.

Stylistically, this is obviously a terrifically ambitious approach, and one that Bogdanovich has not been able to resolve fully . . .

Nickelodeon is full of stirring images, captured evocatively by cameraman Laszlo Kovacs . . .

Alas, if only *Nickelodeon* had found a way from the start to take its people as seriously as it does the cinema. Even so, O'Neal, Reynolds and the lovely Miss Hitchcock are consistently deft and ingratiating. Also very prominent and appealing are Stella Stevens . . . and Tatum O'Neal . . ."

©Los Angeles Times, 1976.

New Leader, 1/17/77 (p. 25)
Robert Asahina

". . . letting Bogdanovich fall flat on his face once more with *Nickelodeon* was a little like torturing a dumb animal. There ought to be a way to stop this blunderer from making films—something he clearly loves to do, his complete lack of talent notwithstanding . . .

Nickelodeon suffers most of all from an imitative fallacy: You never quite find out why a movie about the early days of slapstick should itself be a slapstick comedy. This meager conceit is insufficient to generate anything except blatant and utterly arbitrary gags—pie throwing, feet stuck in buckets, capricious pratfalls—that are far less amusing when performed by Burt Reynolds and Ryan O'Neal, the unfortunate stars of the movie, than by even the Three Stooges. The physical humor is so willfully engineered and so awkwardly executed that the effect is simply a coarse patronization of those old one- and two-reelers. The slightest familiarity with the early works of Hal Roach—not to mention D. W. Griffith, pretentiously quoted in *Nickelodeon*—reveals how little Bogdanovich understands his vastly superior predecessors . . ."

Reprinted with permission from
The New Leader, 1977.
©The American Labor Conference
on International Affairs, Inc.

Films in Review, January 1977 (p. 60)
Charles Phillips Reilly

". . . The film manages to present some of the artistic as well as economic difficulties of early movies. And there are some interesting scenes; the public's first awareness of 'stardom'; the difficulties faced in outdoor shooting; the premiere of *The Birth of a Nation*. But *Nickelodeon*'s script (W. D. Richter and Bogdanovich) fails to give its characters reality. The zany plot hinders rather than helps the development of interest in what is happening, and the characters are so empty one can understand why the director never made up his mind whether to opt totally for outrageous farce or sentimental melodrama. Early Hollywood deserved, and should have inspired, better than this."

©Films in Review, 1977.

Film Information, January 1977 (p. 2)
Robert E. A. Lee

"The movie *Nickelodeon* is harmless and almost pointless, funny and totally absurd. A creation of Peter Bogdanovich, critic turned filmmaker, it is an homage to the birth of the film industry . . .

. . . Bogdanovich chooses to use the old slapstick style of nickelodeon moviemaking for communicating with today's audiences. So every possible sight gag involving pratfalls and stunts with trains and cars and horses and trolleys and water and wind and fire is included. Many of these are genuinely funny but enough is enough; after a dozen pratfalls in as many minutes, the second dozen become a little stale.

Fortunately, Bogdanovich has the help of some skillful performers who cavort wackily and effectively throughout the ridiculous plot . . ."

©Film Information, 1977.

Saturday Review, 1/22/77 (p. 50)
Judith Crist

"Peter Bogdanovich is back in the fine form he
was developing and had perfected with *Paper
Moon* and *What's Up, Doc?* before his lapses with
Daisy Miller and *At Long Last Love*. With *Nickelodeon*, an affectionate and funny film about the pre-
World War I pioneering days of silent movies, he
captures both the facts and the fancies of movie
history in a charming 'slapstick drama.'

With a screenplay written with W. D. Richter,
Bogdanovich has concocted a tale about the men
and women who became involved with movies by
figurative and literal accident in the days when the
big producers had formed the Patents Company to
drive the independents out of business . . . There
are minor sags and some redundancies along the
way, but the film is warmed by Bogdanovich's love
for his medium and sparked by his nostalgic laughter."

©Judith Crist, 1977.

New York Magazine, 1/10/77 (p. 55)
John Simon

" . . . the crudest, stupidest, unfunniest farce of
this or any year, with two hours' worth of laughs
guaranteed to stick in the craw if they do not sink to
the pit of the stomach. *Nickelodeon* may well contain every gag—good, bad, or horrible—that ever
crawled, crashed, or sashayed onto the stage or
screen since Aristophanes or Melies, and slapped
together with minimal imagination or scruple. I can
foresee only two possible uses for the film. One is
as a catalog of no longer usable gags, gimmicks,
one-liners; if they are in this movie they are in so
advanced a stage of decomposition that they can't
even be buried without the gravediggers being is-
sued gas masks. The other is as a sanity test: Anyone who catches himself laughing at any of it at this
late date should seriously consider committing himself . . ."

©1977 by the NYM Corp. Reprinted with
the permission of NEW YORK Magazine.

The Times (London), 3/11/77 (p. 9)
David Robinson

" . . . Bogdanovich has chosen a particularly dramatic episode of history—the great Patents War . . .

It could have made a lively subject; but only intermittently does Bogdanovich seem to recall with a
start that this is the dramatic foundation of his comedy. More often the scenario saunters aimlessly
from incident to incident, following the picaresque
adventures of a movie outfit out West . . .

The film is best when Bogdanovich (originally a
historian and critic in his own right) remembers his
history . . .

More often, though, he is led astray by a misguided taste for slapstick, at which he is not very
skillful, so that you get the feeling only that an epidemic of some falling sickness has spread through
his unlucky cast. Given the chance, Ryan O'Neal
and Burt Reynolds and their partners, Jane Hitchcock and Stella Stevens, handle light comedy with
charm . . . Brian Keith is a prototypical buccaneer
impresario, and a lowering Tatum O'Neal is a child
prodigy scenarist from the mould of Anita Loos."

©The Times, 1977.

The Sunday Times (London), 3/6/77 (p. 37)
Alan Brien

" . . . Bogdanovich, former film critic and chroni-
cler of old Hollywood, now a young filmmaker with
too long a memory, ought to have been the ideal
director for an affectionate pastiche about the birth
of the silents . . .

. . . nobody works up much concern about anybody or anything. There is a running gag about
switched suitcases, signaled by a ponderous close-
up each time one of the trio picks the wrong bag,
which hardly generates a single laugh. With a perverse pedantic literalism which is almost beyond
belief, Bogdanovich misdirects his own script, de-
fusing his own squibs and getting kicked by his own
horseplay. Only Tatum O'Neal, a revived Jane
Withers, the scowling owl-eyed brat whose buzz-
saw tongue could have drawn blood from W. C.
Fields, emerges unsmothered from the desperate
chaos."

©The Sunday Times, 1977.

Film Information, February 1977 (p. 28)
Jonathan Rosenbaum

" . . . the dearth of fresh material in Bogdanovich's
repertoire inevitably incurs the law of diminishing
returns. Consequently, *Nickelodeon*—an obvious
labour of love which by rights should have been
Bogdanovich's *La Nuit Americaine*—lumbers
across the screen with a leaden gait that makes
even something like *The Sting* seem a triumph of
personal expression. The material in itself is scarcely in question: the final credits include a special ac-
knowledgement to Allan Dwan and Raoul Walsh . . .
Borrowing directly from his own *What's Up, Doc?*,
Bogdanovich moves his three principals about like
chess pieces—so that they improbably cross paths
and accidentally switch suitcases—overdirects slapstick in a manner that 'correctly' dots every 'i' and
crosses every 't' . . ."

©Film Information, 1977.

continued on next page

continued from previous page

Village Voice, 1/17/77 (p. 51)
Andrew Sarris

". . . By all present indications . . . *Nickelodeon*
does not seem likely to revive Bogdanovich's flag-
ging fortunes in Hollywood. The word was out on
this one long before it was released. As they say in
the theater, it was in trouble out of town. Indeed,
there were so many previews, so much recutting,
that a fall booking at the Radio City Music Hall was
lost. Too bad. The only commercial hope for *Nickelodeon* rests with the family trade inasmuch as children may find the frantic slapstick amusing. Unfortunately, adults may wonder why the pratfalls precede the establishing of characters. This error is so
obvious that one suspects a psychostylistic compul-
sion at work. Bogdanovich has certainly seen
enough old comedy classics to know that the biggest laughs require the most careful buildups . . ."

Reprinted by permission of The Village Voice.
Copyright © The Village Voice, Inc., 1977.

Like Frank Perry's *Rancho*, *92 in the Shade* centers on an odd assortment of off-centered characters, half-mad with heat and ennui, who turn to the
most bizarre acts as the only logical antidote to
boredom . . .
With all the logic and continuity of a dream,
McGuane hops from incident to incident in an almost hallucinative fashion . . .
The final clouded image of the two guides,
back-slapping and guffawing, brings the dream to
a peaceful close, gently reconciling the opposing
forces as the two of them sway gently in their skiff
on the placid water. McGuane may not be more
inspired as a director than he is as a novelist, but he
certainly is more laid back. Which helps *92 in the
Shade* drift all the more easily off the screen and
into the consciousness."

© Take One, 1975.

NINETY TWO IN THE SHADE

Director: *Thomas McGuane*. Screenplay:
Mr. McGuane, from his novel. Producer:
George Pappas. Photography: *Michael
Butler*. Editor: *Ed Rothkowitz*. Distributor:
United Artists. Running time 95 minutes.
Los Angeles opening August 22, 1975, at the
Bruin Theatre. Classification: R.

Players: *Peter Fonda, Burgess Meredith,
Warren Oates, Harry Dean Stanton, Margot
Kidder, Elizabeth Ashley, Louise Latham,
Sylvia Miles, William Hickey, and Joe Spinell*.

See Volume 1 for additional reviews

NO DEPOSIT, NO RETURN

Director: *Norman Tokar*. Screenplay: *Arthur
Alsberg, Don Nelson*. From a story by *Joe
McEveety*. Producer: *Ron Miller*. Photography:
Frank Phillips. Editor: *Cotton Warburton*.
Music: *Buddy Baker*. Production: *Walt Disney
Productions*. Distributor: *Buena Vista*. Running
time 112 minutes. Los Angeles opening Feb-
ruary, 1976, at several theatres. Classification:
G.

J. W. Osborne: *David Niven*. Duke: *Darren
McGavin*. Bert: *Don Knotts*. Sgt. Turner:
Herschel Bernardi. Carolyn: *Barbara Feldon*.
Tracy: *Kim Richards*. Jay: *Brad Savage*. Big
Joe: *Vic Tayback*.

See Volume 1 for additional reviews

Take One, 12/2/75 (p. 39)
Joseph P. Leydon

"Thomas McGuane has transferred his surrealistic novel *92 in the Shade* to the screen with remarkable ease and assurance for a novice director. It
may be more mood than movie, but McGuane's first
film as writer-director confirms the suspicions
raised by his screenplay for *Rancho Deluxe*--that
McGuane is the most easygoing absurdist pres-
ently at work in cinema.

The Times (London), 10/22/76 (p. 15)
Philip French

". . . every shot is held too long, every joke
repeated, and virtually every sequence extended to
twice its natural length. The kids, especially the
boy, are those whining, winning American infants
that are strictly for domestic consumption (preferably by W. C. Fields), and the millionaire—yet
another touching demonstration of the Disney An-
glophobia—is David Niven, who is given little to do,
and little guidance in how to do it. He spends most

of his time in an embarrassed neutral while switching gear from a grin to a frown.

Matching its content, *No Deposit, No Return* has
a bland, washed-out look, and once again one is
left wondering why there should be such an un-
bridgable gulf between the brilliant professionalism
and sometimes innovative genius of the Disney
Studio's animated films, and the dull artlessness
of the majority of their live-action pictures."

©The Times, 1976.

Films in Review, 4/76 (p. 243)
Harry Banta

"Imagine two runaway kids whose career mom is
off in Hong Kong; a rich, crusty grandpa who
despises them as much as they despise him . . . a
peregrinating skunk and kidnap threats (ransom
demands diminish when grandpa makes it evident
that he doesn't think the kids are worth a cent).
Here you have the latest Disney flick.

Director Norman Tokar has culled lively performances from the large cast. As the rebellious kids,
Brad Savage and Kim Richards are OK. In the role
of gramps, top-billed David Niven, smooth and
caustic as ever, has surprisingly little footage. Darren McGavin and Don Knotts make the reluctant
kidnappers an amusing pair."

© Films in Review, 1976.

New York Post, 7/6/76 (p. 24)
Archer Winsten

"*No Deposit, No Return* . . . is a Disney romp with
first-rate people like David Niven, Darren McGavin,
Herschel Bernardi and two good kids, Kim
Richards and Brad Savage, mired in the weighted
sentiment and slapstick comedy which is the mark
of that company.

That it strikes a grossly popular note there can be
no doubt. This has been proven too often in the
past.

That it offends a discriminating audience is
equally certain.

Therefore we need only note that this is not a cartoon, and not a nature study . . .

The film's happy ending, an outpouring of good
will and family relationships at last cemented, is
what has to be expected in a Disney view of the
world . . ."

Reprinted by Permission of New York Post.
©1976, New York Post Corporation.

Monthly Film Bulletin, 9/76 (p. 195)
David McGillivray

"The common problem of many of the Disney
studio's recent comedy-adventures has been their

scriptwriters' inability to develop a promising idea.
No Deposit, No Return (inspired by the Paul Getty
case?) gets off to an amusing start but is soon on
thin ice when one is expected to believe that anyone (particularly anyone in a Disney film) could
watch his grandchildren being abducted by two
strangers and then do nothing about it. Hereafter
the plot is cluttered up with a comic policeman, two
sets of crooks and the adventures of a pet skunk,
and by the time the child heroes have been locked
for no good reason in an airtight safe, the film's original concept ('the misadventures of two children
who fake their own kidnapping and hold themselves to ransom') has faded almost to
extinction . . ."

©Monthly Film Bulletin, 1976.

NORMAN . . . IS THAT YOU?

Director, Producer: *George Schlatter*.
Screenplay: *Ron Clark, Sam Bobrick, Mr.
Schlatter*. Based on the play by Mr. Clark and
Mr. Bobrick. Photography: *Gayne Rescher*.
Editor: *George Folsey*. Music: *William
Goldstein*. Distributor: *United Artists*. Running
time 91 minutes. New York opening Sep-
tember 29, 1976, at several theatres. Classifi-
cation: PG.

Ben: *Redd Foxx*. Beatrice: *Pearl Bailey*. Gar-
son: *Dennis Dugan*. Norman: *Michael Warren*.
Audrey: *Tamara Dobson*. Melody: *Vernee
Watson*.

Los Angeles Times, 9/29/76 (Pt. IV, p. 1)
Charles Champlin

"Having been up to our red-edged eyes in
movies made for television, we can now gaze in
wonder and mixed emotions at the arrival of the first
television made for the movies.

Norman . . . Is That You? began life as a play, but
it now looks like television, feels like television, was
cast from television (Redd Foxx), lit and shot like
television (on tape, mostly, rather than film) and
needs only a laugh track to come off like a slightly
gamier television sitcom . . .

It is not clear . . . whether the gay community or
the nongay community will find more to be exasperated about in *Norman*. Every straight community

continued on next page

253

continued from previous page

stereotype about gay life is trotted out to humorous effect, from the minicing nastiness to the hideous purple drapes, and while the movie makes a rather arch plea for tolerance, you detect the old business of having your cake and making fun of it, too . . ."

©Los Angeles Times, 1976.

New York Post, 9/30/76 (p. 26)
Archer Winsten

"*Norman . . . Is That You?*, having failed on Broadway six years ago, returns . . . as a movie, its Jewish parents deepened in color as played by Redd Foxx and Pearl Bailey, its Norman pleasantly and muscularly brown in the person of Michael Warren and its girlish homosexual Garson played by Dennis Dugan, a white.

Nothing is made of the color complications, which is a measure of continued movement in the realm of race in America, but the sex-sociology remains the same. Ben (Redd Foxx), the proprietor of a Tucson cleaning establishment, hastens to see his son in Los Angeles, having been upset when his wife Beatrice (Pearl Bailey) runs off with his brother and his automobile. But this is embarrassing because Norman has with him in his waterbed his permanent companion, Garson. Ben hasn't been told that his son is that way.

The rest of the picture deals extensively with Ben's efforts to turn Norman around sexually, hiring Audrey (Tamara Dobson), a handsome, six-foot prostitute for the purpose, and generally messing up everything he touches.

But Norman remains steadfast, and Garson does his best to give Ben a better view of the gay world.

The joke does seem to be pushed beyond its effective range . . ."

Reprinted by Permission of New York Post.
©1976, New York Post Corporation.

Women's Wear Daily, 9/24/76 (p. 8)
Christopher Sharp

"If a movie could be made from a thesaurus of cliches, it would probably turn out like *Norman . . . Is That You?* Director George Schlatter has used the film to celebrate some of the dumbest cliches in the . . . well, in the book.

The film is written by Ron Clark and Sam Bobrick, with Schlatter's help on the script. It is based on the play of the same name that was written by Bobrick and Clark. The story concerns a basically old-fashioned father who comes from Arizona to Los Angeles to finally discover that his son has a homosexual lover. The cliches run from the uninformed father telling his son that he too had once been a 'gay blade' to the old man finding

women's clothes in the closet and making comments about the size of his son's girlfriend . . ."

©Women's Wear Daily, 1976.

The Times (London), 1/21/77 (p. 13)
David Robinson

". . . Some of the best-intentioned people are inclined to get uptight about this picture, as they did about the original play by Ron Clark and Sam Bobrick on which it is (all too clearly) based, complaining that it is tasteless and flippant. As a contribution to social and human understanding, I am inclined to rate it rather higher than, say, the solemn *Saturday Night at the Baths*, or than *Guess Who's Coming to Dinner?*—a film of different themes but rather similar story approach.

For one thing it is very funny and relaxed, and doesn't bring into play automatic hostilities and defences and prejudices. For another, it's a lot subtler than is at first apparent, in the way it accepts and then questions stereotypes . . ."

©The Times, 1977.

The Sunday Times (London), 1/23/77 (p. 38)
Alan Brien

"The title of *Norman . . . Is That You? . . .* is unique in that it is also the punch line of the best joke in a joke-filled film about a father discovering that his son is a homosexual . . .

It's a static film, based on a Broadway play, with characters in the wings which director George Schlatter could have profitably developed, and a central situation and setting which never moves on or opens up. But this hardly matters. Almost every interchange is quotable, the wisecracks are whip-sharp, the observations precise and accurate, like Neil Simon at his best. Have we stumbled upon another master of dramatic campanology who can ring the changes on a single theme without exhausting it or us? . . ."

©The Sunday Times, 1977.

Monthly Film Bulletin, March 1977 (p. 48)
John Pym

"Constructed on the single premise that a sharp punch line justifies any scene, *Norman . . . Is that You?* breezes with apparent nonchalance into an only recently derestricted area of American farce. The overall failure of the movie, drawn from a play by Ron Clark and Sam Bobrick, can be partly blamed on George Schlatter's stage-bound direction; more serious, however, are the constraints placed on an energetic cast by a static plot which steadfastly fails to surprise . . . the action has to be tricked out with essentially superfluous episodes . . . but none compensates for the fundamental uncertainty underlying the whole enterprise . . ."

©Monthly Film Bulletin, 1977.

NOT A PRETTY PICTURE

Director, Screenplay, Producer: *Martha Coolidge*. Running time 80 minutes. New York opening April, 1976, at the New American Filmmakers series at the Whitney Museum. Classification: None.

Players: *Michele Manenti, Jim Carrington, Anne Mundstuck, John Fedinatz, Hal Studer, Amy Wright, Stephen Laurier, Martha Coolidge.*

See Volume 1 for additional reviews

Ms., 7/76 (p. 40)
Marjorie Rosen

" . . . Martha Coolidge's *Not a Pretty Picture* . . . utilizes both fictional recreation and documentary interviewing situations to retell the experience of the director's own rape at the age of 16. Coolidge weaves a complicated web, layering fact on feelings, intercutting drama and discussion. First her actors reenact the story of how she was forced into submission during a 'date rape' while still in high school. Then in the documentary segments--the director's probing and impromptu conversations with the leading lady, Michele Manenti, who not only plays Coolidge at 16 but was raped in school as well, and with actor Jim Carrington, who plays her rapist, Curly--the film attempts to localize the source of the victim's emotional paralysis and articulate how that incident irreversibly scarred her emotional life.

This is the first feature for Coolidge, who has won awards for her documentary shorts, *David: Off and On* (1973) and *Old-Fashioned Woman* (1974), and though the awkward dramatization and poor scripting reveal the struggles of a novice working with fiction for the first time, there's a real tenderness and earnestness and emotional desperation about *Not a Pretty Picture* . . . "

© Ms., 1976.

Village Voice, 4/26/76 (p. 149)
Molly Haskell

"*Not a Pretty Picture* deals with what Karen Durbin has called 'social rape,' that situation in which a high school or college date comes on with a girl . . . and keeps coming. That the boy is driven less by libido than by super ego--or by that masculine self-image that is reflected in the admiring eyes of his peers--becomes clear in the film, and in the candid discussions that take place among its participants . . .

The rationale rests on a knot of misunderstanding that it is taking years to unravel: that man's belief that somehow the woman really 'wants it,' and her corresponding conviction that somehow she 'asked for it.' Martha wonders if there isn't something masochistic about her even wanting to do the film, to relive the experience which warped her emotional life. The honesty and eloquence with which the young people confront the experience is the film's justification . . . "

Reprinted by permission of The Village Voice.
Copyright © The Village Voice, Inc., 1976.

Women's Wear Daily, 3/30/76
Howard Kissel

" . . . Coolidge's film is a half-fictional, half-documentary attempt to come to terms with her own rape when she was a boarding school student. The actress who plays Coolidge as a younger woman, Michele Manenti, has herself been raped. The film alternates between sensitively acted 'scenes' and either preparatory or post-mortem discussions, in which they try to understand the energies, the emotional undercurrents in their own experience and in the 'acting.'

The film is moving both as an examination of a painful subject and as a portrait of young artists honestly confronting their own attitudes and emotions. One of the most touching moments in the film comes when the director and the actress and the young actor (Jim Carrington) who plays the rapist are talking after the scene in which he forces the girl to have sex with him (we see only the emotional and physical bullying that precedes the act). All three are clearly disturbed by what has been 'acted out'--tears are running down Manenti's cheeks, smudging makeup that had been applied to indicate adolescent lack of skill.

Carrington, who has evidently known and worked with Manenti for some time, gently tweaks her nose, and, to break the unsettled mood, calls out, as if the three were on some huge Hollywood set, 'Makeup!' . . . "

© Women's Wear Daily, 1976.

OBSESSION

Director: *Brian De Palma*. Screenplay: *Paul Schrader*. Based on a story by Mr. De Palma and Mr. Schrader. Producers: *George Litto, Harry N. Blum*. Photography: *Vilmos Zsigmond*. Editor: *Paul Hirsch*. Music: *Bernard Herrmann*. Distributor: *Columbia Pictures*. Running time 98 minutes. New York opening August 1, 1976, at the Coronet Theatre. Classification: PG.

Michael Courtland: *Cliff Robertson*. Elizabeth Courtland: *Genevieve Bujold*. Sandra Portinari: *Genevieve Bujold*. Robert LaSalle: *John Lithgow*. Judy: *Sylvia (Kuumba) Williams*. Amy Courtland: *Wanda Blackman*. Third Kidnapper: *Patrick McNamara*. Inspector Brie: *Stanley J. Reyes*. Farber: *Nick Kreiger*. Dr. Ellman: *Stocker Fontelieu*. Ferguson: *Don Hood*. D'Annunzio: *Andrea Esterhazy*.

The Times (London), 9/24/76 (p. 13)
David Robinson

"Brian De Palma's *Obsession* is . . . a cinephile's film. The plot motivation, the characters, the understated virtuosity of the camerawork . . . the doomladen Bernard Herrmann score, are all homage to Alfred Hitchcock and (in particular) *Vertigo* . . .

As the plot thickens, with the hero drawn into a web of deceit which often takes on the appearance of supernatural happenings, the film sags. The Hitchcock touch does not outlast the first scenes; rather you realize just how inimitable is the master's ability to carry suspense from instant to instant, to give the insignificant characters a Dickensian vitality. De Palma is not helped, it is true, by having for his main actor Cliff Robertson, who seems never to have recovered from self-awe after playing the role of John F. Kennedy . . ."

©The Times, 1976.

Woman's Wear Daily, 7/30/76 (p. 9)
Howard Kissel

". . . *Obsession* works . . . because De Palma has directed the film so breathlessly that even the flagrant loopholes in the plot zip by quickly enough that one doesn't bother with them until the movie is over.

De Palma has matched Schrader's baroque sensibility with a strong sense of theatricality, of melodramatic expertise that gets the most out of each

moment. The overall effect is chilling in an old-fashioned way. One responds to the picture at the same time one senses in it serious flaws in logic and its manipulativeness—there must be a teenage girl in all of us.

The effectiveness of *Obsession* is heightened by Vilmos Zsigmond's lush photography and an ultra-romantic score by the late Bernard Herrmann. The casting is also intelligent—Cliff Robertson, a solid, low-keyed actor, makes the central character, who undergoes incredibly bizarre experiences, more credible than he has a right to. Genevieve Bujold gives a beautiful performance in the cryptic, vaguely mystical female role. John Lithgow is somewhat mannered as the villain, but he is giving the film what it needs, for *Obsession* is nothing if not an argument for mannerism."

©Women's Wear Daily, 1976.

New York Magazine, 8/16/76 (p. 60)
John Simon

". . . an unholy mess. Intended as an *hommage* to Hitchcock—especially to his murky and pretentious *Vertigo* (itself a kind of unwitting tribute to Clouzot's *Diabolique*)—*Obsession* attitudinizes in three directions: toward the Hitchcockian thriller, toward the old-fashioned tearjerker, and toward the sophisticated European film, with cultural references strewn like bread crumbs along the way of Hansel and Gretel . . .

Schrader and De Palma have loaded their penny dreadful with allusions high and low. There are overtones of *The Winter's Tale*, the Bluebeard story, *Rebecca*, and, of course, *Vertigo* . . .

Nothing could have saved the film, but the acting might at least have humanized it. Genevieve Bujold may be the only leading lady in Hollywood today who combines looks, talent, and intelligence without having any of the prevalent freakishness; but as Elizabeth she has very little to do, and as Sandra very little that makes sense . . ."

©1976 by the NYM Corp. Reprinted with
the permission of NEW YORK Magazine.

Saturday Review, 9/18/76 (p. 41)
Judith Crist

". . . Romantic both in content and in its lack of violence, *Obsession* is the kind of thriller that bears no detailing of its plot, let alone nit-picking logical appraisal. Suffice it that Cliff Robertson, as a man obsessed by guilt for the death of his wife in a kidnapping, and Genevieve Bujold as the wife and—oops—someone else, give their usual excellent performances. The score, by the late Bernard Herrmann, gives it all a Hitchcockian (and lush movie-palace) note. But Hitch, of course, wouldn't have let a weak performance (and I can't say by whom) weaken the suspense, nor would he have had one of those sit-down-and-let-me-explain conclusions, which also vitiated the effectiveness of De Palma's *Sisters*. But on its own, the film provides excellent diversion, and on his own, De Palma stands as a first-rate movie-maker."

©Judith Crist, 1976.

New York Post, 8/2/76 (p. 16)
Frank Rich

"Whatever you think of Brian De Palma's *Obsession*, you have to admire its creator's guts . . .

It's been a long time since a talented American director has produced a film as stylistically and emotionally vulnerable as this film is, and some audiences are bound to recoil from it in embarrassment—much as they might turn away from a stranger who stands weeping in the street. I can understand that, but I can't understand any moviegoer who doesn't at least try to take De Palma's plunge. Those who can accept *Obsession* on its own wildly idiosyncratic terms will find, as I did, that the movie takes you on a truly harrowing emotional jag; De Palma has made a perverse, moving, and bleakly funny romance, and in the end, his movie is neither a substitution for *Vertigo* nor even a true imitation of it . . .

. . . with the collaboration of cinematographer Vilmos Zsigmond (*McCabe and Mrs. Miller*), De Palma turns his New Orleans and Florence locations into a misty, drear-soaked netherworld that becomes the visual equivalent of the hero's passion . . ."

Reprinted by Permission of New York Post.
©1976, New York Post Corporation.

Village Voice, 8/30/76 (p. 87)
Andrew Sarris

". . . *Obsession* seeks to exploit the stunning stylistic effects in *Vertigo* without benefit of Hitchcock's careful development and comic diversions. The result is a critical essay on *Vertigo* rather than a film in its own right. But I hesitate to be the pro-Hitchcock heavy in this situation. For one thing, film history should not be used automatically as a club whenever one film is shown to be 'influenced' by another . . .

. . . What I would like to see once the first run of *Obsession* is completed is a double bill of both films. Then my readers could judge for themselves whether I'm correct in my judgment that *Vertigo* is one of Hitchcock's most hearteningly personal works, whereas *Obsession* is merely a mannered, cerebral exercise without any emotional underpinning or unconscious feeling of its own . . ."

Reprinted by permission of The Village Voice.
Copyright © The Village Voice, Inc., 1976.

Los Angeles Times, 9/1/76 (Pt. IV, p. 1)
Kevin Thomas

"*Obsession* . . . is writer Paul Schrader's and director Brian De Palma's heady homage to full-blown melodrama in all its unbridled romanticism. Certain to be too rich for everyone's taste, it should delight film specialists who will appreciate how lovingly Schrader, who authored *Taxi Driver*, and De Palma have adhered to the form's conventions to remind us how sheer romance has faded from our entertainments—and perhaps our lives as well . . .

Under De Palma's direction, Robertson, Miss Bujold and Lithgow are all highly persuasive in involving us in their fates. A sumptuous feast for both eyes and ears, *Obsession* has been lushly photographed by Vilmos Zsigmond and has been scored in the insistent '40s tradition by the late Bernard Herrmann . . . Perhaps more than any other single element in the film Herrmann's music contributes strongest to the creation of *Obsession*'s elegant but storm-tossed world of its own."

©Los Angeles Times, 1976.

Christian Science Monitor, 8/2/76 (p. 27)
David Sterritt

". . . Storywise, *Obsession* is that surest of sure bets, a rip-off of vintage Hitchcock—*Vertigo* to be exact. One or two of the best shots are cadged from the same source, which is one of the most resonant suspense films in history. Even the title has Hitchcockian overtones. There is also a dollop of Dante's *La Vita Nuova*.

Director De Palma makes the material his own, however, and comes up with the most thoughtful, tasteful, and all-around successful picture of his career . . .

A new De Palma emerges in *Obsession*— comfortable at last in the Hollywood mold, yet capable of shaping a scene and a story in ways that seem wholly personal . . .

But the main point of *Obsession* is thrills and chills, plenty of which are provided. Bonuses are Zsigmond's ravishing cinematography, and the pulsing score by the late Bernard Herrmann . . ."

Reprinted by permission from The Christian Science Monitor © 1976. The Christian Science Publishing Society. All rights reserved.

Newsweek, 8/9/76 (p. 69)
Janet Maslin

". . . De Palma, who has often expressed his admiration for the master, has none of Hitchcock's crispness or economy—or any of his moral authority: the guilt that consumed Jimmy Stewart in *Vertigo* is here glimpsed as nothing more urgent

continued on next page

continued from previous page

than a faraway look in Robertson's eye. Like Hitchcock, De Palma likes to set his characters at an emotional distance, yet he never turns that detachment into anything resembling Hitchcock's crucial sense of irony; *Obsession* merely seems cold. Oddly, De Palma also has a mile-wide streak of sentimentality that induces him to shoot the picture's upbeat ending in slow motion.

Some of the film's problems are built into Schrader's screenplay. Schrader is good at loading the late Robertson-Bujold romance with intriguingly perverse sexual overtones, but he backs off from following through on their implications . . .

Still, De Palma's flair for atmosphere—abetted by the masterful photography of Vilmos Zsigmond—is frequently arresting . . . And Robertson, Bujold and John Lithgow . . . perform so vividly that they imply a greater knowledge of what *Obsession* is up to than De Palma may have had himself . . ."

©Newsweek, Inc. 1976
reprinted by permission.

Film Information, 9/76 (p. 2)
Dave Pomeroy

"*Obsession* is a taut psychological suspense thriller—the kind of film you want to enjoy (if for nothing else than Cliff Robertson's riveting performance). The trouble is, once you start analyzing it, there are many plot incongruities . . .

The late Bernard Herrmann's music score is effective in building tension. And director Brian De Palma (*Greetings*, *Sisters*, *Phantom of the Paradise*) has placed *Obsession* well—except for the middle portion which dwells too long on Sandra becoming like Elizabeth—and has added some innovative camera pans. Robertson is the movie's chief asset, as he builds a credibly anguished portrait, while Miss Bujold is wooden in two roles which give her little to do. Primary fault is the screenplay of Paul Schrader . . ."

©Film Information, 1976.

Monthly Film Bulletin, October 1976 (p. 217)
Jonathan Rosenbaum

". . . De Palma's cool strategy—to reconstruct or 'restore' the mood and manner of Hitchcock's *Vertigo* some eighteen years after the fact without worrying too much about the reasons or impulses underlying them . . . Apart from its obvious pastiche elements, *Obsession* is striking mainly for what it manages to get away with on its own rather narrow terms . . . if the current film seems to differ most sharply from its source in its self-conscious awareness of its own deliberations (one does not feel that De Palma, like Hitchcock, is ever working close to

his unconscious), it remains seductive chiefly thanks to Herrmann's rich and affecting score. It is a fitting tribute to the composer that in his last film score to be released—drawing heavily on former work with Hitchcock—his music guides, inflects and shapes the narrative's action more decisively than the mise en scene, the acting, or even the script . . ."

©Monthly Film Bulletin, 1976.

Films in Review, October 1976 (p. 504)
Jane Morgan

"In *Obsession*, allusions are piled on each other as if quantity might add up to quality. There are echoes from Dante through D'Annunzio to Hitchcock (ads call it an 'hommage' to Hitchcock) . . .

. . . We are evidently expected to make connections with *Vertigo* (the look-alike of an apparently dead woman), *Psycho* (the child's resurrection of the dead mother), etc: *Obsession* is directed by Brian De Palma without intentional humor, but when I saw it there was laughter in the audience. Bernard Herrmann's music and Vilmos Zsigmond's photography are appropriately romantic. The actors perform well. The fault is not in the stars but in the screenplay, written by Paul Schrader from a story by himself and De Palma."

©Films in Review, 1976.

ODE TO BILLY JOE

Director: *Max Baer*. Screenplay: *Herman Raucher*. Producers: *Mr. Baer, Roger Camras*. Photography: *Michael Hugo*. Editor: *Frank E. Morriss*. Music: *Michel Legrand*. Based on the song and sung by Bobbie Gentry. Distributor: *Warner Bros*. Running time 108 minutes. Los Angeles opening June 30, 1976, at several theatres. Classification: PG.

Players: *Robby Benson, Glynnis O'Connor, Joan Hotchkis, Sandy McPeak, James Best, Terence Goodman, Becky Bowen, Simpson Hemphill, Ed Shelnut, Eddie Tair, William Hallberg, Frannye Capelle, Rebecca Jernigan, Ann Martin, Will Long, John Roper, Pat Purcell, Jim Westerfield, Jack Capelle, Al Scott.*

Los Angeles Times, 6/29/76 (Pt. IV, p. 1)
Kevin Thomas

"Nine years after the release of Bobbie Gentry's haunting ballad, *Ode to Billy Joe*, we're at last finding out what was thrown off the Tallahatchie Bridge and why Billy Joe McAllister jumped off it—in Max Baer's remarkably sensitive and powerful version . . .

Ode to Billy Joe . . . is . . . a timeless, nearly universal tale of young love in which a boy and a girl are torn between their natural inclinations and the dictates of the society in which they live . . .

. . . it is Baer's total commitment to his people and deep feeling for them that makes *Ode to Billy Joe* work. True, this is strong material—so strong it can sustain lots of unduly poeticized and literary Herman Raucher dialogue that is further mushily underlined by an overdose of Michel Legrand romanticism on the soundtrack . . .

Above all else, *Ode to Billy Joe*'s key accomplishment is in taking the tragic view instead of indulging in an easy or patronizing passing of judgment. Bobbie Gentry has described her song as a study in innocent cruelty. How much of the movie is actually autobiographical, she apparently isn't saying. No matter, for this film has its own ring of truth . . . "

© Los Angeles Times, 1976.

Newsweek, 6/21/76 (p. 77)
Janet Maslin

" . . . *Ode to Billy Joe*'s smug condemnation of backwoods conservatism is even more objectionable than the brand of puritanism that drives Billy to suicide; thus the attractiveness of its two central performances represents a small triumph. Robby Benson does as well as anyone could with Billy Joe's literally overnight transition from callowness to debasement, but it is Glynnis O'Connor who most effectively propels the picture . . . O'Connor, even when struggling with the weariest of Raucher's cornpone ('You are no gentleman, suh!'), possesses the same strain of demure singlemindedness that made the song so enticing to begin with.

Still, neither she nor Benson can do much to more than upstage their vehicle's myriad contradictions. The picture opens with a title explaining that it was filmed on location in Mississippi, 'where this story actually took place.' It closes with a disclaimer that all persons and incidents depicted are fictitious. The intervening moments seldom make any more sense than that."

© Newsweek, Inc. 1976
reprinted by permission.

Women's Wear Daily, 8/19/76 (p. 9)
Howard Kissel

". . . In the song the reason Billy Joe threw himself off the Tallahatchie Bridge is never explained. Screenwriter Herman Raucher has come up with an explanation that is obviously supposed to surprise us—Billy Joe kills himself because he made love to a man . . .

The film spends so much time preparing us (or, more accurately, not preparing us) for this Big Surprise that it seems almost like a hoax. We have a complete picture of the family of Billy Joe's girlfriend, but we don't see his father until almost the end. We see Billy Joe only from her point of view. At the end we feel as surprised as she does, but we also feel as if the filmmakers told us the wrong story—Billy Joe is as much a mystery when the picture is over as he was at the beginning. In the song his death was a puzzle—here it seems a contrivance.

Billy Joe is well photographed and decently acted, particularly in the final scene where Billy Joe's girlfriend meets his lover. But the whole idea is too calculated to be genuinely moving."

©Women's Wear Daily, 1976.

Monthly Film Bulletin, 8/76 (p. 170)
Jonathan Rosenbaum

". . . after acknowledging the shaky elements in Robby Benson's performance and Max Baer's first job of direction, the red herrings in Herman Raucher's script and the mushy embarrassment of the Michel Legrand score, one is forced to recognize that *Ode to Billy Joe* actually succeeds in doing something rather extraordinary. Not merely does the film 'fill in the blanks' of the song while contriving to leave its power intact; it also uses the initial stimulus—audible only during the opening and final credits—to create a remarkably persuasive portrayal of a backwoods Mississippi community in the early Fifties. The script bristles with flavoursome details and lines . . . But the real triumphs of the film are the performances of Joan Hotchkis and James Best; the scenes of each with the heroine are so beautifully observed and finely developed that they bypass anything to be found in Renoir's *The Southerner*, for instance . . . "

©Monthly Film Bulletin, 1976.

New Leader, 9/13/76 (p. 23)
Robert Asahina

". . . on its own sentimental terms, the film works. The Tallahatchie Bridge is no more unlikely a locale for a contemporary *Romeo and Juliet* than is a laundromat in Cambridge, Massachusetts; sup-

continued on next page

continued from previous page

posedly sophisticated filmgoers whose tears were jerked by the mechanical contrivances of the Harvard-Radcliffe *Love Story* have no right to be condescending toward this backwoods romance. O'Connor is quite winsomely virginal, even if she has made a career out of playing precisely the same innocent teenager (most recently, in *Baby Blue Marine*). Benson is much less good, but Sandy McPeak and Joan Hotchkis embody Mr. and Mrs. Hartley with an affecting warmth that rises above the banalities of the script.

The movie owes its success in no small part to the director and producer, Max Baer . . ."

Reprinted with permission from
The New Leader, 1976.
© The American Labor Conference
on International Affairs, Inc.

Film Information, July/August 1976 (p. 1)
Frederic A. Brussat

". . . Set in the Delta country of Mississippi, this movie is an affecting tale of young love, old morality and a senseless suicide. *Ode to Billy Joe* . . . suffers from director Max Baer's choppy pacing of its flowing story line. The saccharine music by Michel Legrand is a bit too much, and the dialogue at times comes across as stilted . . .

. . . Although it doesn't succeed as an aesthetically pleasing work of art, the film is stoutly human. And it has something relevant to say about the clash between puritanical religion and a holistic understanding of sexuality.

During the closing credits I wondered whether most Christian parishes would have anything helpful to say to Billy Joe McAllister about his so-called sin against nature and God. And could we appreciate Bobbie's graceful deed of reconciliation? *Ode to Billy Joe* proves once again that we have many bridges to cross in our attempts to take seriously the connections between faith and flesh."

© Film Information, 1976.

New York Post, 8/19/76 (p. 19)
Frank Rich

"*Ode to Billy Joe*, the new Technicolor romance based on Bobbie Gentry's hit 1967 pop song, is a perfectly silly little movie, but it's almost impossible to hate. While I went expecting the worst—mainly because I found Gentry's ode to be tedious in the first place—in the end the film almost won me over on its own, junky terms . . .

Up until its finale the movie is a mindlessly absorbing tale about two kids who must deal with one of the most enduring problems of adolescence: At what moment is it right and proper for a high school

couple to go all the way? The film pursues this question with a philosophical ardor that borders on the Aristotelian, and, by the time the answer is revealed, even a post-adolescent viewer can become nostalgic for the days when to do it or not was the only matter in life worth brooding about . . ."

Reprinted by Permission of New York Post.
©1976, New York Post Corporation.

New York Magazine, 9/6/76 (p. 72)
John Simon

". . . Only someone like Baer, who carries a $2-million indemnity policy (as he told *People* magazine) so he can punch out 'at least eight SOBs . . . who have it coming,' and whose next movie will be a bawdy Women's Army Corps comedy entitled *WAC-Off*, could have made a film so redolent with imbecile sentimentality in which young lovers moon or fumble in picture-postcard shot after shot, and sometimes, thanks to slow dissolves, in what feels like two shots simultaneously. There is also lots of wonderful rustic atmosphere and rural humor thanks to assorted yahoos, Yazoo City whores, sweetly understanding parents, a dog named Dog, a comic minister, and quaint folkways such as people copulating with their clothes on, either because that's the way it is done in the Deep South or because that's the way one gets a PG rating . . ."

© 1976 by the NYM Corp. Reprinted with
the permission of NEW YORK Magazine.

Christian Science Monitor, 8/23/76 (p. 23)
David Sterritt

". . . *Ode to Billy Joe* is a Warner Bros. movie directed by Max Baer of *Beverly Hillbillies* fame. Herman (*Summer of '42*) Raucher wrote the screenplay, again betraying his weakness for adolescent vulgarity. Naturally it focuses on the main events of the song, filling in details where the singer only gave clues. It also adds touches, pleasant and unpleasant— such as what sordid secret made Billy Joe run away from home after the local music festival and drinking orgy?

On-screen *Ode to Billy Joe* is down-home soap opera, no more. But the story flows in a mildly interesting way, despite some distasteful interludes: Glynnis O'Connor gives a wonderful fresh-faced portrayal of the heroine Bobbie Lee; and Robby Benson—good in *Lucky Lady*—is quirkily winning as the lead who longs for her. Joan Hotchkis heads a solid supporting cast . . ."

Reprinted by permission from The Christian
Science Monitor © 1976.
The Christian Science Publishing Society.
All rights reserved.

OFF THE WALL

Director, Screenplay: *Rick King*. Producer, Editor: *James Gregory*. Photography: *Chris Beaver, Jon Else, Judy Irving*. Production: *Oz Associates*. Distributor: *Oz Releasing Company*. Running time 83 minutes. New York opening March 29, 1977, at the Whitney Museum of American Art. Classification: None.

John Little: *Harvey Waldman*. Dan: *Gary Schnell*. Rob: *John French*. Jane: *Katy Roberts*. Betsy: *Judy Fell*. Lennie Howe: *Pat Crowley*.

New York Post, 3/30/77 (p. 50)
Archer Winsten

"*Off the Wall* . . . handicaps itself with a character of questionable charm and concentrates on his notably helter-skelter career. Exactly why he should be the subject of a TV documentary being shot in May 1976 for San Francisco's KSQL is never clear.

He's 25, native of the Bronx 10 years in California, jobless, and given to fits of anger. Asked if he loved the woman he was living with, he admits that he failed to say so. She kicked him out.

He answers the question as to having made love with a man, "Yes," but rather vaguely, not with enthusiasm . . .

For no very obvious reason, he suddenly robs a bank . . .

Director-writer Rick King . . . has a good grasp of a drifter's psychology. It would have been nice if he had chosen a more interesting subject this time, and a more enticing person, for there isn't much relief from this anti-hero."

Reprinted by Permission of New York Post.
© 1977, New York Post Corporation.

OLD DRACULA

Director: *Clive Donner*. Screenplay: *Jeremy Lloyd*. Producer: *Jack Wiener*. Photography: *Anthony Richmond*. Distributor: *American International Pictures*. Running time 89 minutes. New York opening January, 1976, at several theatres. Classification: PG.

Count Dracula: *David Niven*. Countess Vampira: *Teresa Graves*. Maltravers: *Peter Bayliss*. Angela: *Jennie Linden*. Marc: *Nicky Henson*.

See Volume 1 for additional reviews

Films in Review, 4/76 (p. 243)
Harry Banta

"After *Young Frankenstein* it was inevitable. Off-beat casting has David Niven playing Count Vladimir the Impaler, resuscitating his beloved Vampire (Teresa Graves), after a 'sleep' of some fifty years. The blood transfusion that activates her body develops a fluke along the way and she turns from white to black. For several reels Vladimir tries to discover which blood from which luscious call girl he had been experimenting with will turn Vampire white once more. His efforts backfire.

Clive Donner's direction is serviceable but Jeremy Lloyd's sophisticated script elicits only occasional chuckles instead of belly laughs . . . Though the wit is labored, this American International release has fine color photography and elaborate sets."

© Films in Review, 1976.

OLD GUN, THE
(LE VIEUX FUSIL)

Director: *Robert Enrico*. Screenplay (French with English subtitles): *Pascal Jardin, Claude Veillot, Mr. Enrico*. Photography: *Etienne Becker*. Music: *Francois de Roubaix*. Production: *Carmen F. Zollo*. Distributor: *Surrogate Releasing Company*. Running time 104 minutes. New York opening June 29, 1976, at the Coronet Theatre. Classification: None. Origin: France.

Julien: *Philippe Noiret*. Clara: *Romy Schneider*. Francois: *Jean Bouise*. Mere de Julien: *Madeline Ozeray*.

New York Post, 6/30/76 (p. 44)
Archer Winsten

"*The Old Gun* . . . starts by establishing a firm and loving relationship among Julien (Philippe Noiret), the surgeon, his wife Clara (Romy Schneider) and their child.

It's 1944 in southern France. The Americans have landed in Normandy, and the retreating Germans

continued on next page

continued from previous page

are behaving harshly and so are the Vichy French. So Julien sends his wife and child out of the city for greater safety, since he has been threatened for his suspected treatment of partisans in the hospital.

What happens next is dreadful irony, a tragedy leading to the doctor's turning to an ultimate vengeance.

The picture's motivation is sound enough, reaching a high level of wish-fancy, but the events strain the bounds of credibility, though they are staged with reason and logic.

Noiret's acting, as always, possesses the advantage of the massive ease his style and size suggest. The situation calls for an extreme of emotion, and he certainly does demonstrate it.

Romy Schneider, functioning brilliantly both in the present and in numerous flashbacks, makes her love deeply felt.

Director Robert Enrico handles the violent action with the precision first noted in his early success, *Incident at Owl Creek*, which won a short film Oscar in 1964 . . .''

Reprinted by Permission of New York Post.
© 1976, New York Post Corporation.

formation into a ruthless, single-minded killer is no mean feat . . .''

©Newsweek, Inc. 1976
reprinted by permission.

New York Magazine, 7/19/76 (p. 85)
John Simon

''. . . Its appeal is not only to brutality, but also to chauvinism—one justly aroused Frenchman being the equal of any number of superiorly armed krauts—and its obviousness remains virtually unalleviated . . .

. . . This movie . . . merely reawakens the old patriotic lies, stirs up the ancient, bloody bitterness leading to no understanding, no peace.

The film won the Cesar, the French equivalent of the Oscar, which only shows that, in any language, Oscar spells nonsense. Similar awards went to Philippe Noiret, for his portrayal of the hero, and Francois de Roubaix, for his score. Noiret is one of the finest comic and character actors in movies today; he does everything possible to infuse a dram of humanity into the proceedings, but all to little avail . . .''

©1976 by the NYM Corp. Reprinted with
the permission of NEW YORK Magazine.

Newsweek, 7/19/76 (p. 77)
Janet Maslin

''The year is 1944, the locale is provincial France, and the occupying Nazi forces, panicked by the Allies' advances after Normandy, are indulging in random brutality. Julien, a kindly, lumbering doctor (Philippe Noiret), packs his adored second wife and child off to the safety of the family chateau. As irony would have it, the chateau is located in the path of an especially nervous German contingent. When the doctor arrives for his first visit, he discovers that the Germans have slaughtered his family and moved, machine guns and all, into the chateau.

The Old Gun, which was voted last year's best French film by the French Academy of Cinema Arts and Techniques, is an unusually sympathetic account of the doctor's revenge. That process eventually matches the Nazis' own penchant for sheer viciousness . . . but this is not a film about blood lust. Rather, it is a backhanded paean to mature love . . .

. . . director Robert Enrico demonstrates a rare gift for exploring rich, mutually rewarding marriages between levelheaded adults. Noiret's affectionate memories of his young wife (Romy Schneider at her most radiant) become as seducive for the viewer as they are for the bereaved medic.

Enrico cuts each flashback tantalizingly short, returning to the present so abruptly that Noiret's mounting frustration becomes agonizingly palpable. Explicating this quiet, gentle character's trans-

Los Angeles Times, 9/24/76 (Pt. IV, p. 15)
Kevin Thomas

''. . . quite possibly the grisliest contemporary film yet with any pretensions to seriousness . . .

. . . Noiret . . . finds that the Nazis have slaughtered everybody in the tiny village . . . His wife is a charred corpse, his daughter has been shot to death.

In thoroughly horrifying flashbacks we see Miss Schneider gang-raped and then incinerated before our eyes with a flamethrower. So now it's *Death Wish* time, with Noiret reaching for his antique but highly servicable hunting rifle and wiping out the entire platoon of Nazis, who have lingered on in the village after the massacre.

Like *The Omen*, *The Old Gun* . . . is technically superb and boasts the stunning performances by Noiret and Miss Schneider that are typical of them. It is likewise outrageously manipulative, underlying Noiret's agony by his flashbacked memories of the radiant Miss Schneider . . .

. . . when you get right down to it *The Old Gun* is really nothing but a classy (and actually quite obvious) exploitation picture that suggests the vigilante genre has now gone international.''

©Los Angeles Times, 1976.

OMEN, THE

Director: *Richard Donner*. Screenplay: *David Seltzer*. Producer: *Harvey Bernhard*. Photography: *Gil Taylor*. Music: *Jerry Goldsmith*. Distributor: *Twentieth Century-Fox*. Running time 111 minutes. New York opening June 25, 1976, at several theatres. Classification: R.

Robert Thorn: *Gregory Peck*. Katherine Thorn: *Lee Remick*. Jennings: *David Warner*. Mrs. Baylock: *Billie Whitelaw*. Damien: *Harvey Stephens*. Father Brennan: *Patrick Troughton*. Father Spiletto: *Martin Benson*.

Film Information, 6/76 (p. 1)
Frederic A. Brussat

" . . . *The Omen* is a spine tingling thriller about the Antichrist. Some of the mysterious references of Revelation 13 are dealt with in a modern story that sets the mind buzzing with images of the demonic. It explores the possible connections between evil and the animal world, flushes out dread about the vulnerability of political leaders to Satanic purposes, and brings to the surface our often unspoken fright about war, devastation, and anarchy as the shape of the future. *The Omen* compels our attention with its rare blend of realism and supernaturalism . . .

Director Richard Donner, in superb command of this material, leads us through the labyrinthian story line, scaring and surprising us along the way. Gregory Peck does heroic battle with these forces of evil and we identify with him throughout. *The Omen* does not aim to convert anyone to a belief in the Antichrist; but by the end of the film, even the most skeptical may feel chilled and shaken at the imagining of such a supernatural embodiment of evil . . ."

© Film Information, 1976.

New York Post, 6/26/76 (p. 15)
Frank Rich

"*The Omen* . . . is a very cagey, though far from air-tight, horror movie that attempts to exorcise yet one more devil for fun and profit.

How much you enjoy the film depends, to a great extent, on how seriously you take the Book of Revelations, with its dire prophecy of Armageddon, and all the rest of that ecclesiastical paraphernalia that has lately been the stock-in-trade of gory religious pictures.

If all that Biblical stuff really turns you on--no matter how much interpretive license is taken by filmmakers who exploit it--you'll probably be able

to forgive *The Omen* its narrative trespasses and be carried away by its surefire scare tactics and classy production values. But if, like me, your blood doesn't boil at the mere prospect of the Anti-Christ and you are just looking for a plain old trashy suspense movie, you may find yourself constantly distracted by the holes that permeate *The Omen*'s plot . . .

. . . Peck is a more prepossessing diplomat than any appointed by recent Washington administrations, and Miss Remick continues to be about the loveliest woman on earth. Miss Whitelaw, a fine British character actress, has an easy time with a role not unlike that played by Lotte Lenya in *From Russia, With Love*, and David Warner, too, is absurdly overqualified for the role of a photojournalist who tries to solve *The Omen*'s mystery much as David Hemmings attempted to solve that of *Blow Up* . . ."

Reprinted by Permission of New York Post.
© 1976, New York Post Corporation.

Los Angeles Times, 6/25/76 (Pt. IV, p. 1)
Kevin Thomas

"There's no getting around it. No matter how much you may dislike *The Omen* . . . there's just no denying that it is an absolutely riveting, thoroughly scary experience, a triumph of sleek film craftsmanship that will inevitably but not necessarily unfavorably be compared to *The Exorcist* . . .

Inspired by the foretelling of the coming of Armageddon in the book of Revelations, *The Omen*, which was cleverly written by David Seltzer and directed smashingly well by Richard Donner, makes a persuasive case that the time is ripe for the birth of the Anti-Christ in the form of a human who will be mistaken for a savior by mankind.

Why then is *The Omen* so off-putting? Simply because it is so relentlessly, graphically and gratuitously grisly in its depiction of the hideous ways in which various people meet their ends . . . *The Omen* works hard to capture the imagination, and then leaves nothing to it . . ."

© Los Angeles Times, 1976.

The Sunday Times (London), 9/19/76 (p. 35)
Harold Hobson

" . . . One of the great merits of *The Omen* . . . is that it has the courage of its own stupendous follies.

Its hero is an American ambassador to the Court of St. James who has an unparalleled thickness of head. This moron (Gregory Peck) allows another baby to be substituted for his own in a convent hospital in Rome, but says nothing about it to his wife, who thinks the child is hers . . .

continued on next page

263

continued from previous page

. . . the Ambassador blunders on, always silent, incidently getting a friendly photographer (David Warner) beheaded after being savaged by dogs in a cemetery. He eventually decides that he must murder the child, and we see him sticking a knife into him.

The last shot of the film is particularly interesting. Its rosy smile will delight child-lovers. When modern science is accused of having killed our belief in God, it can retort that it has at least restored our faith in the Devil. *The Omen* is a ludicrous film, but wonderfully entertaining, and it nearly frightened me out of my life."

©The Sunday Times, 1976.

The Times (London), 9/17/76 (p. 10)
David Robinson

"As a story of satanism that is a cut above the rest of the current cycle, *The Omen*, be warned, bids fair to be a successor to *The Exorcist* and *Jaws* as an audience lure. It is a cut above the rest in that it has an ingenious premise, a teasingly labyrinthine development, a neat sting in its tail, and enough confidence in its own absurdities to carry them off . . .

The film charges cheerfully on through its improbabilities, thanks to a fast-moving script and determined, professional direction. The director, Richard Donner, has clearly come a long way since 1970 when he made an awful film called *Twinky*. The film also boasts some extraordinarily good special effects work, applied to Lee Remick's incor-

rigible penchant for falling from great heights, and to the whirlwind storm in Bishop's Wood which leads to the death of the little priest.

It is a gripping, genuinely frightening piece of nonsense . . ."

©The Times, 1976.

Saturday Review, 7/24/76 (p. 43)
Judith Crist

"Contrivance is self-evident in *The Omen*, wherein Scripture is quoted endlessly to warn us that the Antichrist is upon us. The original screenplay, by David Seltzer, offers us Gregory Peck as a multimillionaire ambassador to the Court of St. James who permitted the instant substitution of an orphaned infant for his stillborn son in Rome and five years later finds some pretty dreadful stuff going on in his London home . . . *The Exorcist* or even *Rosemary's Baby* this isn't, since it demands a total suspension of disbelief from all but convinced satanists. Richard Donner, a television director making his feature-film debut, conducts the incredible doings with a straight face, and the actors respond in kind. The resultant idiocy offers more laughs than the average comedy."

©Judith Crist, 1976.

New York Magazine, 7/12/76 (p. 75)
John Simon

". . . *The Omen* is certainly all dog from snout to

Lee Remick and Gregory Peck (center), as an ambassador and his wife, happily watch their son (Harvey Stephens) celebrate his birthday. It is not long before the terror begins in **The Omen**, a thriller about the Antichrist.

tail. It was directed by Richard Donner, who comes from television serials, which may account for the film's being made up of isomorphic segments, each with its machine-tooled climax and archly suspenseful little hint about next week's installment, supposed to keep us on tenterhooks of delicious anticipation . . .

The biggest laughs . . . come from a supposedly biblical prophecy translated into good American doggerel that serves as the movie's spiritual core; it predicts the coming of the Antichrist when, among other things, 'the Holy Roman Empire rises,' which the film's Bible exegetes interpret as the rise of the European Common Market! . . .''

©1976 by the NYM Corp. Reprinted with the permission of NEW YORK Magazine.

Christian Science Monitor, 8/4/76 (p. 22)
David Sterritt

'' . . . *The Omen* is a slick, commercial, humorless, paranoiac, obsessively frightening thriller. Scariest thing I've seen in ages.

Some of the shock effects are graphically gruesome. The story piles one harsh climax on another. But there is a plus side here: In these uncertain times, rarely does a movie draw so firm a line between good and evil, and align all the attractive characters firmly on the side of good (represented by a rather superstitious concept of Christianity). There is no dubiousness about this battle, or about who we are supposed to root for . . .

Original, it's not. Director Richard Donner has a way with spooky images, and David Seltzer's script is fairly straightforward, except for some howlingly silly lines and several huge holes in the logic of it all.''

Reprinted by permission from The Christian Science Monitor © 1976. The Christian Science Publishing Society. All rights reserved.

Newsweek, 7/12/76 (p. 70)
Jack Kroll

'' . . . *The Omen* is a dumb and largely dull movie, despite Twentieth Century-Fox's hope that it will capture the sunstruck summer audience as *Jaws* did last year. No true connoisseur of kitsch will confuse the work of writer David Seltzer and director Richard Donner with the masterpiece of psychic manipulation contrived by William Peter Blatty and William Friedkin in *The Exorcist*, not to mention what the diabolical Roman Polanski made out of Ira Levin's *Rosemary's Baby*. Savants of stunts, however, will admire several sensational specimens in this movie—Lee Remick's crunching fall from a high landing, the decapitation of a character by a runaway truck, the gracefully grisly suicide-by-hanging of a young woman . . .''

©Newsweek, Inc. 1976 reprinted by permission.

Monthly Film Bulletin, 8/76 (p. 170)
Richard Combs

''A matter-of-fact exercise in Satanic blood and thunder, both less grandiloquent and less pretentiously put together than *The Exorcist* . . . In fact, the narrative is so straightforward, and so mundanely concerned with developing ever more ingenious ways at a rapidly increasing clip, of disposing of its starry cast, that the spiritual torment is skipped . . . Rather like ghostly visitations themselves, the motifs flicker through the film, but are edged out by the plot's prosaic drive towards its banal bicentennial coup, as the devil finally lands himself in the White House.''

©Monthly Film Bulletin, 1976.

Films in Review, August/September 1976 (p. 440)
Dorothy Dean

'' . . . While the film's theological leverage is precarious (e.g., the formation of the European Economic Community is taken as fulfilling prophecy of the rebirth of the Holy Roman Empire), the plot generally unfolds convincingly for purposes of coherent entertainment. The photographic effects are spectacular, to say the least—an onslaught of maddened baboons resident in a peaceful English countryside wild-life preserve is enough to frighten one away from zoos forever; a sudden fatal thunderstorm in a London park is equally sinister; vicious snarling Cerberian mastiffs abound. Director Richard Donner (of TV background) has a decided touch for the creepy, as do his entire cast, especially Billie Whitelaw as the nanny in mephistophelean collusion with her ward. David Warner (who once played *Morgan*) and Patrick Troughton are also very good as well-meaning but nonetheless doomed photographer and priest, respectively, who attempt to enlighten the skeptical Ambassador . . .''

©Films in Review, 1976.

Cineaste, Winter 1977 (p. 46)
Duncan Leigh Cooper

'' . . . Despite its improbable story line and abundance of gratuitous violence, *The Omen* does succeed in its attempt to frighten, terrorize, and just plain scare the pants off most of the audience. Impressive performances by Gregory Peck as the perplexed Mr. Thorn, Lee Remick as his terrified spouse Kathy, Patrick Troughton as the doomed cleric Father Brennan, and Billie Whitelaw as Damien's mysterious new governess, Mrs. Baylock, plus a chilling mock-religious score by Jerry Goldsmith and the skillful direction of Richard Donner, all contribute to the suspension of disbelief required to draw the audience into the film's web of terror. Nor can *The Omen* be faulted on its special effects . . .''

©Cineaste, 1977.

ONE FLEW OVER THE CUCKOO'S NEST

Director: *Milos Forman*. Screenplay: *Lawrence Hauben, Bo Goldman*. Based on the novel by Ken Kesey. Producers: *Saul Zaentz, Michael Douglas*. Photography: *Haskell Wexler*. Additional Photography: *Bill Butler, William Fraker*. Editors: *Richard Chew, Lynzee Kingman, Sheldon Kahn*. Music: *Jack Nitzsche*. Production: *Fantasy Films*. Distributor: *United Artists*. Running time 129 minutes. New York opening November 19, 1975, at the Sutton and Paramount Theatres. Classification: R.

Randle Patrick McMurphy: *Jack Nicholson*. Nurse Ratched: *Louise Fletcher*. Harding: *William Redfield*. Chief Bromden: *Will Sampson*. Billy Bibbit: *Brad Dourif*. Candy: *Marya Small*. Scanlon: *Delos V. Smith, Jr.* Nurse Pilbow: *Mimi Sarkisian*. Dr. Spivey: *Dean R. Brooks*. Turkle: *Scatman Crothers*. Martini: *Danny De Vito*. Sefelt: *William Duell*. Cheswick: *Sydney Lassick*. Taber: *Christopher Lloyd*. Rose: *Louise Moritz*.

See Volume 1 for additional reviews

Sight and Sound, Spring 1976 (p. 120)
Richard Combs

" . . . What Forman achieves with most consistency in *One Flew Over the Cuckoo's Nest* . . . are the group portraits--the scenes of inmates embarking on some joint enterprise of liberating madness, such as their ecstatic display before the blank television screen as McMurphy leads them in an animated re-creation of the World Series baseball game that Ratched's working schedule has forbidden them to watch. The precariousness of such moments is given particular edge by the way Forman usually cuts from them--like a dousing of cold water--to the doctors' solemn post-mortems. What remains unsolved, however, is the problem of translating the heightened style and imagery of Kesey's anti-Establishment diatribe into the gentle rhetoric of Forman's social comedy, which seems to be continually drawing the disputants together as if nothing more had to be settled than a domestic disagreement."

© Sight and Sound, 1976.

Cineaste, Fall 1976 (p. 43)
Ruth McCormick
" . . . Basically . . . *One Flew Over the Cuckoo's Nest* is not a political film, but an 'inspirational' one. What politics it has are as outdated as the Beat

and early hippie movements. That the film could be made now, and be so loved and accepted by so many people, ultra-conservatives as well as revolutionaries, lies in the fact that while it is warm and moving, it tells us nothing new . . .

In the end, when Bromden breaks away, there is scarcely a dry eye in the house, but this is more a tribute to Forman's directorial talents and an admission of most people's desires to break away themselves, than a political statement. The film appeals to our emotions, not to critical thought, and the ending becomes a catharsis that leaves us breathless for a while, but in the same vacuum that the 60s 'youth' movement did, with no real alternatives outside of our own heads.''

©Cineaste, 1976.

OUTLAW JOSEY WALES, THE

Director: *Clint Eastwood*. Screenplay: *Phil Kaufman, Sonia Chernus*. Based on the novel GONE TO TEXAS by Forrest Carter. Producer: *Robert Daley*. Photography: *Bruce Surtees*. Editor: *Ferris Webster*. Production: *Malpaso Company*. Distributor: *Warner Bros*. Running time 137 minutes. New York opening August 4, 1976, at several theatres. Classification: PG.

Josey Wales: *Clint Eastwood*. Lone Watie: *Chief Dan George*. Terrill: *Bill McKinney*. Laura Lee: *Sondra Locke*. Fletcher: *John Vernon*. Grandma Sarah: *Paula Trueman*. Jamie: *Sam Bottoms*.

Los Angeles Times, 7/14/76 (Pt. IV, p. 9)
Kevin Thomas

" . . . the fifth and most ambitious film Eastwood has directed himself. Inescapably (but not lingeringly) bloody and violent, this handsome Warner's presentation nonetheless develops masterfully into a full-scale saga of great impact . . .

In *The Outlaw Josey Wales* Eastwood is essentially playing the invincible, monosyllabic gunfighter he creates in Sergio Leone's Italian Westerns . . . But here he becomes the full-dimension hero of an epic, imaginatively and eloquently devised by writers Phil Kaufman and Sonia Chernus from Forrest Carter's *Gone to Texas*. In Josey Wales' destiny it is possible to perceive that of all men.

Eastwood's direction is assured and highly evocative through the film's various shifts of mood.

His own performance and everyone else's are fully satisfying . . ."

©Los Angeles Times, 1976.

The Times (London), 8/6/76 (p. 7)
David Robinson

"As an actor, without the dynamic framing provided by Don Siegel or a spaghetti Western, Clint Eastwood is inclined to be sympathetic but rather monotonous. The quality seems generally to be imparted to his films as director. *The Outlaw Josey Wales*, set in the aftermath of the Civil War, with renegades marauding the countryside, is a familiar tale of revenge, with Eastwood as hero, monumental, intractable, indestructible.

Too long for its own strength . . . the film livens up considerably when Eastwood is joined on the trail by Chief Dan George who wistfully mourns the old lore and skills he has forgotten since being 'civilized' by the white man . . ."

©The Times, 1976.

The Sunday Times (London), 8/8/76 (p. 30)
Dilys Powell

". . . It is the reverse of the Westerns we have come to expect from John Wayne, usually seen as the upholder of law and order. Nevertheless Josey Wales, too, is a moral figure. The film is in a way old-fashioned. Its hero is infallible; repeatedly he escapes what looks like certain capture. But he is also the defender of the weak . . .

In fact it is a thoroughly likeable Western. I even thought we were going to get through without any mishandling of the horses—until, nearly at the end, there was a ferocious fall. Or was the victim a model? I certainly hope so; for the rest of the riders very properly took the falls themselves. The script is witty as well as humane (the comments given to Chief Dan George are as lively as his performance). The landscape looks magnificent in Bruce Surtees' camera work . . ."

©The Sunday Times, 1976.

Monthly Film Bulletin, 8/76 (p. 171)
Tom Milne

". . . *The Outlaw Josey Wales* is fairly predictable and even a trifle perilous: a sort of latter-day *Miracle in Milan*, with the victims of man's inhumanity to man at last finding their little home on the West. What is remarkable about the film, however, is the skill with which Eastwood gives this theme a resonantly full orchestration while at the same time silencing any propensities to pretension or sentimentality lurking in the script. A brooding apocalyptic prologue, rather reminiscent of *The Beguiled* in its lush

romantic style (both films were shot by the superb Bruce Surtees), shows Josey Wales metamorphosed from peaceful farmer to Byronic hero . . ."

©Monthly Film Bulletin, 1976.

Christian Science Monitor, 7/26/76 (p. 22)
David Sterritt

"*The Outlaw Josey Wales* is one part very ordinary and one part very peculiar. Though it is one of the dullest movies Clint Eastwood has directed himself in, its plot provides more unexpected twists and turns than any other recent western . . .

The way is littered with violent and distasteful episodes that make one gasp anew at the unpredictability of which films get a PG rating . . .

But there are quiet niceties in *Josey Wales* as well. Some clever camera work in the first half; for example, and many lovely images from cinematographer Bruce Surtees. The supporting cast is excellent, too. The talented Paula Trueman stands out vividly as a senior citizen of the frontier, battling her way through blood and thunder toward the oasis in which she really believes . . . Chief Dan George is gently affecting as an old brave who has never quite mastered the art of sneaking up on people. Sondra Locke deftly understates as an introspective young girl . . ."

Reprinted by permission from The Christian Science Monitor © 1976. The Christian Science Publishing Society. All rights reserved.

New York Post, 8/5/76 (p. 21)
Archer Winsten

"Clint Eastwood returns to his basic success principles in *The Outlaw Josey Wales* . . . He's the grim all-purpose killer, and with good reasons established at the very beginning. It's the Kansas-Missouri location just after the Civil War when marauding bands of soldiers were active on both sides. One such band murders the family of Josey Wales (Clint Eastwood), and the rest of the picture is his vengeance and the attempts of the soldiers, bounty hunters and gunmen to collect the rewards for his death . . .

. . . Clint has never been more impressibly invulnerable. As director he has known how to give himself the best of it without seeming to slight his friends, enemies and supporting cast . . ."

Reprinted by Permission of New York Post. © 1976, New York Post Corporation.

Film Information, 9/76 (p. 5)
William C. Winslow

"*The Outlaw Josey Wales*, directed by the starring Clint Eastwood, will delight fans of the vengeance-violence genre. There's plenty of action.

continued on next page

continued from previous page

Spectacular close-up gunfights, riders shot out from under their mounts, barroom shootouts, hot pursuits. It's all there. The plot is standard Western. Clint Eastwood gives another of his usual low-key portrayals. And the western scenery is absolutely gorgeous . . .

. . . I stopped counting the killings at 25, including a mass slaughter by machine gun. Probably, the producers decided they had historical license to commit mayhem as the story takes place just after the Civil War and is about 'lawless men in a lawless land' . . .''

©Film Information, 1976.

Sight and Sound, Autumn 1976 (p. 256)
Richard Combs

"Since Clint Eastwood assumed the hats of both actor and director, his films, not surprisingly, have been busily redefining the myth of the Man With No Name. What is surprising is how irreverent the process has become, admitting that every macho trait has its comic inverse. The hard-boiled loner and wandering man of mystery is also something of a social freak; the gunfighter whose whole existence is concentrated in his superhuman expertise can appear oddly unformed and unprepared in other contexts. *High Plains Drifter* provided the most ironic explanation, interpreting the riddle of the inscrutable Eastwood persona as a supernatural phenomenon; *The Outlaw Josey Wales* . . . treats it rather as a communal crossword, on which a number of characters, assorted pilgrims inadvertently acquired by Josey while in pursuit of his revenge, set their own impressions.

A rambling, picaresque tale . . .''

©Sight and Sound, 1976.

PAPER TIGER

Director: *Ken Annakin*. Screenplay: *Jack Davies*. Producer: *Euan Lloyd*. Photography: *John Cabrera*. Editor: *Alan Pattillo*. Music: *Roy Budd*. Production: *MacLean & Company*. Distributor: *Joseph E. Levine*. Running time 99 minutes. New York opening September 16, 1976, at Radio City Music Hall. Classification: PG. Origin: Great Britain, 1974.

Walter Bradbury: *David Niven*. Kagoyama: *Toshiro Mifune*. Koichi: *Ando*. Gunther Muller:

Hardy Kruger. Foreign Secretary: *Ivan Desny*. Talah: *Irene Tsu*. Sergeant Forster: *Ronald Fraser*.

New York Post, 9/17/76 (p. 20)
Archer Winsten

"*Paper Tiger* . . . is a kidnap melodrama which scores surprisingly well because it has such excellent actors as David Niven and Toshiro Mifune impersonating, respectively, an English pedagogue and phony hero, and Kagoyama, Japanese ambassador to the Malaysian country of Kulagong (fictional); also because the Ambassador's son, Koichi, is beautifully played by a boy named Ando; also because director Ken Annakin has utilized Malaysian color to the full while showing people of the foreground and background most effectively.

What emerges is a semi-routine kidnapping of the 1970s, the kidnapping of an innocent victim to be used to free revolutionary prisoners with the threat of killing the hostage . . .''

Reprinted by Permission of New York Post.
©1976, New York Post Corporation.

The Times (London), 5/2/75
David Robinson

"*Paper Tiger*, directed by Ken Annakin, is modest, cheerful and predictable entertainment, with David Niven as a pathological mythomane who becomes tutor to the son of a far-flung Japanese ambassador, and finds himself obliged to live up to his fantasies, when he and the child are kidnapped by political terrorists.

Heavy handling of the drama makes it a bit difficult to distinguish how much of the action is real and how much is in the imaginations of the child and the man. The child Ando is winning: David Niven snuggles happily into his character; but it is sad to see the great Toshiro Mifune humiliated to such a tame supporting role . . .''

©The Times, 1975.

Monthly Film Bulletin, 4/75 (p. 85)
Clyde Jeavons

". . . In light of his performance as Terence Rattigan's bogus major in *Separate Tables*, David Niven's appearance as a human vestige of the defunct British Empire with a Billy Liar complex might have proved a rewarding conceit, had Ken Annakin's tiresome film not been too busy hedging its bets with catchpenny production devices to extend its characters beyond first premises . . . Annakin cannot decide, moreover, whether to play the whole thing seriously or to wring it for a few laughs; his revolutionaries, for example, make solemn speeches about freedom and oppression, yet their behaviour at times suggests that the film could just as easily have been called *Carry On Comrade*. Niven and Toshiro Mifune do well to keep their professional dignity intact throughout these muddled proceedings . . ."

©Monthly Film Bulletin, 1975.

Christian Science Monitor, 10/7/76 (p. 22)
David Sterritt

"Back in family-film territory, or somewhere near there, we have a new international hodge-podge called *Paper Tiger*. David Niven, Toshiro Mifune and Hardy Kruger—what have you wrought? . . .

Ken Annakin directed with an uneasy sense of fun, except in the terrorist scenes, which have an uneasy sense of sadness. I suspect the makers had in mind a general-audience movie for grown-ups and all but the younger children, a rousing entertainment with a message. Unfortunately, the finished product is too slipshod to serve as art, too indecisive to convince us of its message, and too nervous to entertain us effectively . . ."

Reprinted by permission from The Christian
Science Monitor ©1976.
The Christian Science Publishing Society.
All rights reserved.

PART 2 SOUNDER

Director: *William Grahams*. Screenplay: *Lonne Elder III*. Based on the novel by William H. Armstrong. Producer: *Robert B. Radnitz*. Photography: *Urs B. Furrer*. Music: *Taj Mahal*. Distributor: *Gamma III*. Running time 92 minutes. New York opening October 13, 1976, at several theatres. Classification: G.

Nathan Lee Morgan: *Harold Sylvester*. Rebecca Lee Morgan: *Ebony Wright*. Ike Phillips: *Taj Mahal*. Camille Johnson: *Annazette Chase*. David Lee Morgan: *Darryl Young*.

Film Information, November 1976 (p. 4)
William C. Winslow

". . . In a clean, simple story line, Lonne Elder III tells of the struggles of a poor black community of sharecroppers to build a school . . .

There is a richness in the presentation of tightly-knit family life (the Morgan family is portrayed by

Harold Sylvester and Ebony Wright as the parents, and Darryl Young, Erica Young, and Ronald Bolden as the children), showing the sacrifice of parents in money and labor for their next generation, and in the basic humanity of a community united in a common cause . . .

A beautiful, flowing, happy, sad and haunting film this . . .

Part 2 Sounder follows in the tradition of *Sounder*. It teaches us about the dignity of people . . ."

©Film Information, 1976.

Newsweek, 11/8/76 (p. 107)
Janet Maslin

"The sequel to *Sounder* picks up where the original was smart enough to leave·off . . . The year is still 1933 and the setting is still rural Louisiana, but this time the only real action is at the joyful community get-togethers, where everybody eats and rassles while Taj Mahal, still the neighborhood's resident entertainer, plays the guitar.

Trying hard to stir up enough trouble for a plot, screenwriter Lonne Elder III reacquaints the school-teacher, Miss Camille (played in this version by Annazette Chase), with the Morgans' young son, David Lee (Darryl Young, filling in for Kevin Hooks). He, as before, desperately wants an education, but he won't get one unless Camille turns down an offer to move North to teach in Cleveland . . .

The movie lasts an hour and a half, most of which is devoted to arrangements about buying lumber, a rainstorm that delays construction a few days, and Nathan's talks with Miss Camille about her obligations to the community in which she was born. Miss Camille is a real looker, but Nathan never flirts with her, because this isn't that kind of movie. No wonder the dog spends so much time napping."

©Newsweek, Inc. 1976
reprinted by permission.

Christian Science Monitor, 11/1/76 (p. 22)
David Sterritt

"*Part 2 Sounder*, the latest picture from family-fare specialist Robert B. Radnitz, is a spare and gentle drama about good people trying to do a good thing.

In its simplicity and earnest motives it remains true to the original *Sounder*— which amazed even its director, Martin Ritt, by zooming to success despite a total avoidance of sex, violence, trendiness and other titillations. Yet *Part 2* is perhaps too uncompromising for its own good: It refuses to meet halfway with current forms, fashions, or foibles. Its means are basic and its key is low. It requires you to open your heart to its people and

continued on next page

continued from previous page

events. If you do so, you will be warmly touched. If you don't, *Part 2 Sounder* might pass you right by . . ."

Reprinted by permission from The Christian
Science Monitor © 1976.
The Christian Science Publishing Society.
All rights reserved.

PEOPLE OF THE WIND

Documentary. Director: *Anthony Howarth.* Screenplay: *David Koff.* Producers: *Mr. Howarth, Mr. Koff.* Executive Producer: *Elizabeth E. Rogers.* Photography: *Mike Dodds.* Editor: *Carolyn Hicks.* Music: *G. T. Moore, Shusha.* Featuring the voice of James Mason. Distributor: *Carolyn Films.* Running time 127 minutes. New York opening October 29, 1976, at the D.W. Griffith Theatre. Classification: None.

Note: There is no cast in this film.

Christian Science Monitor, 11/10/76 (p. 20)
David Sterritt

"Jafar Qoli, who looks a lot like Charlie Chaplin, is kalantar—chief—of the Babadi, who are a subtribe of the Bakhtiaris of southern Iran. Twice each year, he and his people undertake a migration that lasts around eight weeks and covers some 200 miles. They travel on foot over mountains and through rivers, in rain and wind and snow. In a good year all the people and most of the animals survive.

If such a journey sounds formidable, imagine going along as a guest and filming the affair from start to finish . . .

Actor James Mason keeps up a running commentary on the soundtrack, presumably taken from the actual words of Jafar Qoli. Mason's voice sounds incongruous at first, but one gets used to it; a worse problem is the crass pop music that keeps recurring. The photography, by Mike Dodds, is sweeping and at times stunning . . .

. . . it is an admirable but rather stodgy achievement."

Reprinted by permission from The Christian
Science Monitor © 1976.
The Christian Science Publishing Society.
All rights reserved.

Los Angeles Times, 12/25/76 (Pt. IV, p. 10)
Linda Gross

"The Bakhtiari tribes of Southern Iran are moun-

tain nomads whose life-style has remained unchanged for more than 2,000 years. Twice a year they travel 200 miles across the Zargos mountains from summer to winter pastures. If they didn't migrate, their animals would die of starvation or cold and the Bakhtiari could not survive.

People of the Wind . . . is a sprawling, stunning saga of survival that recounts the adventures and hardships of their migration.

British filmmaker Anthony Howarth, with a small movie crew, 23 mules and two tons of camera equipment, accompanied Chief Jafar Qoli of the Babadi, one of the Bakhtiari subtribes, and his tribesmen on their spring migration through icy rivers, deserts and narrow mountain passes . . .

The film captures the life of the Babadi . . .

The film has been magnificently photographed by Mike Dodds with stirring music by G. T. Moore, and Shusha sings the lovely songs. It is keen adventure—a vast and visually elegant depiction of life in the bygone tradition of Kipling."

©Los Angeles Times, 1976.

PIECE OF PLEASURE, A (UNE PARTIE DE PLAISIR)

Director: *Claude Chabrol.* Screenplay: *Paul Gégauff.* Producer: *Andre Genoves.* Photography: *Jean Rabier.* Production: *Les Films De La Boetie-Sunchild Productions* (Paris) and *Gerico Films* (Rome). Distributor: *Joseph Green Pictures.* Running time 100 minutes. New York opening May, 1976, at the Juliet 1 Theatre. Classification: R. Origin: France.

Philippe: *Paul Gégauff.* Esther: *Danielle Gégauff.* Sylvia: *Paula Moore.* Katkof: *Michel Valette.* Michel: *Pierre Santini.*

New York Times, 5/21/76 (p. C7)
Vincent Canby

" . . . *Une Partie de Plaisir* is not a melodrama . . . It's almost a comedy, and it's intensely bitter and cruel. The film focuses mostly on the demonically egocentric Philippe, but it's Esther who emerges as the more interesting character. In the course of the film it's Esther who grows up and away from Philippe, even though torn by her old dependence on him to the point where she actively participates in his humiliation of her.

Not since *Les Biches* has Mr. Chabrol so wittily (and mercilessly) examined the wars that are fought in life's living rooms and bedrooms, in kitchens and over dining room tables with friends as neutral, sometimes appalled observers. It's a fascinating film and a very harrowing one.

Mr. Gégauff, who has written many of Chabrol's screenplays, including those for *Les Biches* and this film, is supremely self-confident and alienating as Philippe . . .

Miss Gégauff . . . is a stunning actress with large gray-green eyes, almost like a cat's, and a beauty that has as much to do with manners and expressions as with nose and jaw lines. That she remains for us someone almost as mysterious as she becomes to her husband––who never has the slightest understanding why she finally leaves him––prevents the film from turning into a predictable treatise on open marriage . . ."

© New York Times, 1976.

Los Angeles Times, 6/2/76 (Pt. IV, p. 1)
Kevin Thomas

"With Claude Chabrol's *A Piece of Pleasure* . . . his usual scenarist Paul Gégauff steps in front of the camera along with his ex-wife Danielle in an apparently largely autobiographical account of the break-up of their marriage.

This engrossing, wonderfully elegant film, however, is remarkable not only as Gégauff's utterly unsparing act of self-revelation but also as a fresh, far-ranging expression of Chabrol's recurrent themes and preoccupations . . .

Gégauff's superbly crafted script, in which every word of its beautifully wrought, reflective dialogue is made to count, provides a richly detailed blueprint for Chabrol and allows him to build tension just as adroitly as ever, but refreshingly outside his familiar thriller format.

Admirably trim in age, Gégauff proves to be every bit as able an actor as he is a screenwriter, portraying a polished man of confident charm and tenderness who turns into a beast before our eyes. An ideal counterpart, Danielle Gégauff, pretty, self-effacing and docile, shows us a woman gathering the courage to liberate herself . . ."

© Los Angeles Times, 1976.

Village Voice, 6/7/76 (p. 107)
Andrew Sarris

"Claude Chabrol's *Une Partie de Plaisir* (*A Piece of Pleasure*) has slipped into distribution without any undue fanfare. Nonetheless, this marvelous saga of marital tragedy is not to be missed under any circumstances. The film is in every sense a collaboration between Chabrol and his scriptwriter-lead actor, Paul Gégauff, who, in turn,

has worked out with his wife Danielle certain of their own marital problems and fantasies . . .

The trenchant irony of Chabrol's style undercuts Gégauff's egomania even as it underlines it. Gégauff himself seems fully aware of his own absurdity. Nonetheless, the unwary viewer may choose to identify the character's attitude with the film's, and thus make the alienating effect virtually unbearable. My own reading of the film is quite the contrary, in that the magnificence of Danielle Gégauff's incarnation of the awakened woman shifts not only sympathy but also stature from the male to the female. In this respect, Chabrol knows whereof he speaks when he describes himself as the screen's foremost feminist . . ."

Reprinted by permission of The Village Voice.
Copyright © The Village Voice, Inc., 1976.

New York Magazine, 6/7/76 (p. 74)
John Simon

" . . . The story of what happens to the quasi-marriage of a male chauvinist when, at the gander's prompting, the goose helps herself to some sauciness, is partly trivial, partly unbelievable. The people are too bad, too good, or too stupid to be true, and neither plot nor dialogue comes to the rescue. Granted, there are good-looking faces, elegant clothes and furniture, and catchy land and townscapes, photographed by Jean Rabier with his usual imitation-Marie Laurencin palette, but none of that is enough, not even a very winning performance by Mme. Gégauff.

What this contrived and banal film elicits, though, is a sense of regret. Chabrol is truly a master of technique: watch closely how he moves his camera about, how he intercuts an extreme closeup of a detail with a sequence in medium long shot, or how he dazzlingly switches camera angles in midstream . . ."

© 1976 by the NYM Corp. Reprinted with the permission of NEW YORK Magazine.

Newsweek, 6/14/76 (p. 90)
Jack Kroll

" . . . The husband in this film, marvelously played by Paul Gégauff, is perhaps the most authentic and fascinating male chauvinist ever to make a woman cry on screen. His victim is played by Danielle Gégauff, who is his real-life wife, and her performance is also a marvel as the young woman who is a kind of cleverly updated version of Ibsen's Nora. Unlike Ferreri with his schoolboy shock tactics, Chabrol knows that real horror comes out of the simplest realities. This director, who increasingly reminds me of Simenon in his examination of the apocalypses of the ordinary, has

continued on next page

continued from previous page

made an absorbing and powerful film about modern men and women."

© Newsweek, Inc. 1976
reprinted by permission.

New York Post, 5/20/76 (p. 21)
Archer Winsten

" . . . It is one of the most impressive of Claude Chabrol's 28 films poured out in a busy 18-year career as director and co-founder of the French New Wave.

The secret of its unusual penetration seems to be the fact that its stars, Paul Gégauff and wife, Danielle, work from their own marital experience. Gégauff wrote the screenplay, based on a marital experiment in the stimulus of mutual infidelity frankly discussed between husband and wife.

It ends badly, the experiment, that is, as such Bohemian procedures often have in the past 50 years. But it is the truth of the step-by-step deterioration of the relationship, the detailing of emotional outbursts and silences, the changes of attitude and the surprises that make this picture so utterly recognizable in all its aspects . . .

The principals, Gégauff & Gégauff, are letter-perfect in themselves. The supporting cast is quietly effective in the background or in bed . . . "

Reprinted by Permission of New York Post..
© 1976,New York Post Corporation.

Film Information, 5/76 (p. 4)
Frederic A. Brussat

" . . . Chabrol calls this creation 'a portrait of a fascist in love.' Philippe (Paul Gégauff) and Esther (Danielle Gégauff) live together out of wedlock with their young daughter. They have a country house and a small walnut grove. He is the ultimate male chauvinist--forcing Esther to serve him mentally, physically and, in an odd way, spiritually. A crisis in this master-slave relationship ensues when he, admitting that he has already done so, suggests she take a lover. Philippe is sexually excited by the idea of their having affairs with others while still remaining attached to each other.

The scheme backfires when Esther falls in love with Habib, a quiet sensitive man whose travels to the Far East have given him a nonaggressive slant on life. Philippe senses he is losing control over Esther, especially when they move to an apartment in Paris and she takes a job. After he hits and humiliates her one evening, she leaves him. Philippe eventually marries a young woman but is not able to find happiness.

A Piece of Pleasure is a bit too pat in its portrayal of the unfulfilling relationship between the aggressive, forceful male and the passive, docile female.

Nonetheless, the film has a richness of behavioral nuance and detail characteristic of all Chabrol's work. *A Piece of Pleasure* is an interesting, albeit minor, work in Chabrol's continuing exploration of sexual politics."

© Film Information, 1976.

Commentary, October 1976 (p. 78)
William S. Pechter

". . . seems to me one of the good Chabrols, shot with some forcefulness and played with a violent edge: another study of the bourgeoisie, but bound up this time with a jumble of feelings on the changing relationships between the sexes. The story is neatly ironic: a man urges his (common-law) wife to intellectual 'growth' by her taking lovers as he has, but finds himself not quite so free as he thought of 'outmoded' jealousies when she does. Moreover, what she grows into isn't Baudelaire but Kahlil Gibran, until, in the end, she 'outgrows' her husband as well; Pygmalion succeeds all right, but this Galatea isn't quite what he had in mind.

Up to this point, the film's elements are shrewdly managed . . . The trouble is that, like the rest of us, Gegauff and Chabrol don't know where our current upheavals in the relations between the sexes are taking us, and so the film concludes with a reversion to what Chabrol and Gegauff . . . know best—the movies—with a tacked-on, brutal act of murder . . . "

©Commentary, 1976.

PINK PANTHER STRIKES AGAIN, THE

Director, Producer: *Blake Edwards.* Screenplay: *Frank Waldman, Mr. Edwards.* Photography: *Harry Waxman.* Editor: *Alan Jones.* Music: *Henry Mancini.* Animation and Titles: *Richard Williams.* Distributor: *United Artists.* Running time 103 minutes. New York opening December 15, 1976, at several theatres. Classification: PG.

Inspector Clouseau: *Peter Sellers.* Dreyfus: *Herbert Lom.* Alec Drummond: *Colin Blakely.* Quinlan: *Leonard Rossiter.* Olga: *Lesley-Anne Down.* Cato: *Burt Kwouk.* Francois: *Andre Maranne.* Deputy Commissioner: *Marne Maitland.* Dr. Fassbender: *Richard Vernon.* Jarvis: *Michael Robbins.* Margo Fassbender: *Briony McRoberts.* President: *Dick Crockett.* Secretary of State: *Byron Kane.*

Women's Wear Daily, 12/15/76 (p. 22)
Howard Kissel

"Even more than in earlier films, Peter Sellers in *The Pink Panther Strikes Again* moves across the screen like a cartoon figure, eyes darting furtively about, his not very imposing, trenchcoated body narrowly missing and sometimes inadvertently causing catastrophes on all sides. Cartoons are filled with improbable absurd violence, as if the whole universe is taking revenge on some hapless character—what makes them fun is that the hapless character, almost obviously, emerges victorious.

Panther is full of preposterous delights—Sellers trying on a Quasimodo suit with an inflatable hump, which floats him out the window just in time to avoid the explosion of a building, Sellers avoiding being shot by assassins in adjoining toilet stalls by reaching down to retrieve an escaping roll of toilet paper . . ."

©Women's Wear Daily, 1976.

New York Post, 12/16/76 (p. 41)
Frank Rich

". . . While this movie . . . is wildly uneven—it begins gloriously and later trails off into unnecessary plot complications—Clouseau fans will be able to forgive the pokey stretches and cherish the high-points. Non-fans, it goes without saying, would be wise to stay away.

Whichever category you fall into, however, you'd probably agree that the latest Clouseau outing is a significant improvement over *The Return of the Pink Panther*, its immediate predecessor. Though *Return* had a few choice moments, much of it was soggy and sleep inducing. *The Pink Panther Strikes Again*, in joyous contrast, has a few sequences that can hold their own with the best of the early *Panther* films, and even its lesser material is energetic, if less than hilarious . . ."

Reprinted by Permission of New York Post.
© 1976, New York Post Corporation.

Newsweek, 12/27/76 (p. 57)
Janet Maslin

". . . The current installment is a bit funnier than its predecessor, but the success of the *Panther* series has never depended solely on laughs. Blake Edwards' slick, seamless direction makes even the flimsiest routines seem stylish; in addition to its comic virtues, this is one of the best-looking movies of its kind in recent memory . . .

As usual with *Panther* films, a highlight is the opening animated credit sequence, prepared by the Richard Williams Studio. This time it sends up other movies. As the caricatured Clouseau sits in a theater, his Panther nemesis appears on the screen as Gene Kelly (in *Singin' in the Rain*), King Kong and, in the movie's most affectionate gibe, Edwards' wife, Julie Andrews, singing atop an Alp . . ."

©Newsweek, Inc. 1976
reprinted by permission.

The Sunday Times (London), 12/19/76 (p. 27)
Alan Brien

". . . The latest Pink Panther installment is often genuinely funny so long as Sellers is restricted to deploying his repertoire of strangulated mannerisms in the cardboard world of the Agatha Christie puzzle. But its writers, Frank Waldman and director Edwards, fall into the familiar trap of supposing what is funny once must be hilarious repeated again and again. Not only is Sellers' Inspector Clouseau the usual mobile disaster-area, but his perennial rival and former boss, Herbert Lom, has gone staggering round the bend, out to rule the world like Dr. No, matching half-wits against a lumbering, stumbling President Ford. Some routines, like Sellers falling into the moat of Lom's castle, continue long after we have tired of them.

Still it's worth hanging on for the archetypal Sellers solo where, invited to bed by his lovely stranger (the delectable Lesley-Anne Down) he throws off his jacket like a matador of the boudoir only to find he cannot remove his tie and trousers."

©The Sunday Times, 1976.

Village Voice, 12/27/76 (p. 45)
Andrew Sarris

"Blake Edwards' *The Pink Panther Strikes Again* is about the only holiday attraction that has exceeded expectations. Critics and audiences have been so enthusiastic, one would think that this fourth installment of Peter Sellers' Inspector Clouseau was a brand-new edition.

For the past decade and a half I have argued that Peter Sellers is the funniest comedian in the movies. Back in the mid-'60s I had to contend with the French Cahierist fancy for Jerry Lewis. Nowadays Mel Brooks and Woody Allen are the fashionable funnymen. But Sellers just keeps rolling along as the most proficient comic technician of them all, particularly when he teams up with Blake Edwards and Inspector Clouseau in the Pink Panther series . . ."

Reprinted by permission of The Village Voice.
Copyright ©The Village Voice, Inc., 1976.

Christian Science Monitor, 12/27/76 (p. 18)
David Sterritt

". . . *Strikes Again* is funny only intermittently.

continued on next page

continued from previous page

Edwards' affection for old gags is not always contagious, and too many bits seem borrowed from previous Clouseau epics or earlier sources. Sometimes bright parody seems around the corner, as in a kung-fu sequence and a White House episode peopled by Ford administration lookalikes; the filmmakers choose to whet rather than satisfy the appetite, however.

Worse yet, Edwards' visual sense seems flatter than usual, and his editing rhythms—crucial in comedy—are sometimes choppy. Perhaps last-minute cutting is partly to blame . . .

Still, before I sound too much like the Scrooge of this pink Christmas season, let me hasten to add that the Panther crew provides some merry ᵢnoments despite all this. Sellers' dead pan and extraterrestrial accent . . . are as hilarious as ever, and Herbert Lom has a high old time as the insane Dreyfus playing a pipe organ a la Lon Chaney and plotting to conquer the universe. Nice bits also come from Colin Blakely, Burt Kwouk, and Lesley-Anne Down . . .''

Reprinted by permission from The Christian Science Monitor © 1976. The Christian Science Publishing Society. All rights reserved.

Monthly Film Bulletin, February 1977 (p. 29)
Richard Combs

"Against all odds, *The Pink Panther Strikes Again* largely manages to reinvent the Clouseau formula— from behavioural freak to comic-strip grotesque—and its movie-quipping, history-of-slapstick style more closely reprises *The Great Race* than any of the other Clouseau sagas . . . All the scenes of fumbling and bumbling, and Clouseau-oriented chaos . . . now look like deliriously abstract spasms that coolly apply the physical mangling of a "Road Runner" cartoon to the psychological comedy of embarrassment . . . overkill testifies to the bizarre mechanisms of all Edwards' comedies—a universe of relentless mathematical absurdities— and, in the present case, perhaps to a desire to have done with Clouseau by constructing a series of pratfalls to top them all."

© Monthly Film Bulletin, 1977.

Film Information, January 1977 (p. 3)
Bea Rothenbeuchner

". . . Clouseau, in charge of the worldwide search for the escaped mad killer, proceeds with his detective work, blithely unaware of the menace that strikes time and again—and always just misses him, whether he is in a gay bar in London, a Dracula-like castle in Bavaria, or his own Paris apartment which is blown up as he floats out the window in a helium inflated Quasimodo costume. Sellers masquerading in his Quasimodo costume is utterly ridiculous and, fortunately, no explanation is offered as to *why* he wears it.

If slapstick pleases you and you don't mind people falling (often into water), tripping, or doing foolish things . . . you may find that this British-made concoction is your cup of tea . . .''

© Film Information, 1977.

Saturday Review, 1/22/77 (p. 50)
Judith Crist

"With *The Pink Panther Strikes Again* there is a nagging consciousness that one is laughing one's fool head off—from time to time—over the most blatantly obvious contrivances and setups that Blake Edwards has yet devised for his Inspector Clouseau. But laugh one does—and a good feeling it is . . .

. . . Suffice it to say that along the convoluted way of the tale not a sight gag, double entendre, slip, slide, crash, or bang is overlooked, with boggling flights of comedic fancy involving a Quasimodo disguise kit with an inflatable hunch and encounters with a suit of armor, laughing gas, a castle moat, a drag queen, and a huge assortment of other odd characters, chief among them recent inhabitants of the Oval Office.

By now Sellers' unique French accent is a bit strained, and Edwards inventions are a bit familiar. But star and director are still the masters of their art and will make you laugh in spite of yourself . . .''

© Judith Crist, 1977.

New York Magazine, 1/17/77 (p. 55)
John Simon

"*The Pink Panther Strikes Again* is, at least for its first half, quite good knockabout farce. Distinctly superior to its predecessor, *The Return of the Pink Panther*, it features also some jolly movie parodies and mild political satire along with good-natured and often amusing slapstick, old hat though it be. Peter Sellers, once again Inspector Clouseau, is beginning to look moderately venerable, which enhances the comic incongruity; Herbert Lom supplies him with a condignly maniacal antagonist who goes bananas with brio. The supporting cast is . . . good enough for this type of enterprise . . . Michael Robbins, as a gentleman's gentleman who hankers to be a lady, is better than that, while Dick Crockett provides a well-aimed and well-merited parting kick at a certain president's behind. Lesley-Anne Down, though pretty, is not very Russian, but Omar Sharif, in an uncredited cameo, is as Egyptian as a scarab from a pharaoh's tomb.''

© 1977 by the NYM Corp. Reprinted with the permission of NEW YORK Magazine.

Films in Review, March 1977 (p. 188)
Rob Edelman

"Peter Sellers appears for the fourth time in 12 years as bumbling French detective Jacques Clouseau in *The Pink Panther Strikes Again*. This flatfoot is no Sherlock Holmes: he is a walking disaster who cannot open a refrigerator door, exercise in a gymnasium, or point a finger at someone without causing chaos. This time around, his nemesis is a farcically insane former chief inspector (Herbert Lom) driven so presumably by Clouseau; Lom wants to do away with the detective.

The film is no more than a series of sight gags; although Clouseau's pratfalls are about as original as is the character itself, many are hysterically funny. Sellers, who speaks as if his lips are partially glued together, has Clouseau's comic mannerisms down pat . . ."

©Films in Review, 1977.

PINK TELEPHONE, THE

Director: *Edouard Molinaro.* Screenplay: *Francis Veber.* Producer: *Alain Poire.* Editor: *Gerard Hameline.* Music: *Vladimir Cosma.* Distributor: *S. J. International Pictures.* Running time 95 minutes. New York opening December 23, 1976, at the Fine Arts Theatre. Classification: R. Origin: France.

Benoit Castenjac: *Pierre Mondy.* Mrs. Castenjac: *Francoise Prevost.* Christine: *Mireille Darc.* American Company President: *Michel Lonsdale.* Public Relations Director: *Daniel Ceccaldi.*

New York Post, 12/24/76 (p. 9)
Archer Winsten

"*The Pink Telephone* . . . is a French inspection of unhallowed business practices of the modern world.

An American corporation, in the persona of its president (Michel Lonsdale) and its PR man (Daniel Ceccaldi) are taking control of a small French manufacturing concern owned by peppery Benoit Castenjac (Pierre Mondy). In order to soothe their victim they hire a handsome call girl, Christine (Mireille Darc) to make him feel happy while in Paris . . .

As a comment on the use of sex in selling or a form of bribery, the picture is too obvious on the surface and not wholly credible in its contrasts of French innocence and American corruption. Still and all, it does hammer home a point, using some attractive performers in the course of a comedy trying to work with sociological and labor material. Director Edouard Molinaro has handled his material without inspiration but very professionally . . ."

Rreprinted by Permission of New York Post.
©1976, New York Post Corporation.

PIPE DREAMS

Director, Screenplay, Producer: *Stephen F. Verona.* Executive Producer: *Barry L. Hankerson.* Music: *Dominic Frontiere.* Soundtrack Songs: *Gladys Knight and the Pips.* Photography: *Sven Walnum.* Editor: *Robert L. Estrin.* Distributor: *Avco Embassy Pictures.* Running time 89 minutes. New York opening December 23, 1976, at several theatres. Classification: PG.

Maria Wilson: *Gladys Knight.* Rob Wilson: *Barry L. Hankerson.* The Duke: *Bruce French.* Loretta: *Sherry Bain.* Mike Thompson: *Wayne Tippit.*

Los Angeles Times, 12/2/76 (Pt. IV, p. 27)
Charles Edison, Jr.

"Sooner or later someone had to break cinematic ground on the Alaskan pipeline issue. So it is we now receive *Pipe Dreams*, an amateurish, home movie-style romance/melodrama starring Gladys Knight and husband/executive producer Barry Hankerson. The film is as bleak as its Arctic locale.

Not that it isn't charming for a loving couple to engage in a public expression of their real-life devotion. The few poignant moments in what is sadly misbilled as the most romantic film of the year arise from their obvious mutual affection.

But what a sorry vehicle. The story progresses with all the finesse and grandeur of a Dick and Jane reader. The dialogue is lifted from Saturday morning cartoons and the talent looks to have been pooled from a beginning actors' workshop . . ."

©Los Angeles Times, 1976.

New York Post, 12/24/76 (p. 10)
Archer Winsten

"*Pipe Dreams* . . . is rare in its Alaskan pipe-

continued on next page

275

continued from previous page

line location, and unique in choice of characters for such a spot. You get Gladys Knight, the black singer, playing Marie Wilson, not a singer but rather a deserted wife from Altanta, Georgia. She has pursued her husband to Valdez, Alaska . . . she becomes a 'mixologist' (bartender) . . .

The plot goes in for villainy and nobility, bad girls (whores) with good hearts and tangled male-female relationships. Mainly it has to do with Marie's efforts to win back her husband from his temporary girl, and her resistance to all bad influences, including marijuana, liquor, and willing men with lots of money.

Neither plot nor performances deserve praise beyond the ordinary . . .

Director-writer-producer Stephen Verona had priceless backgrounds in the Alaskan terrain but proved indulgent with himself as writer and director . . ."

Reprinted by Permission of New York Post.
© 1976, New York Post Corporation.

POM POM GIRLS, THE

Director, Screenplay, Producer: *Joseph Ruben*. From a story by Robert Rosenthal and Mr. Ruben. Photography: *Stephen M. Katz*. Editor: *George Bowers*. Music: *Michael Lloyd*. Distributor: *Crown International Pictures*. Running time 90 minutes. Los Angeles opening September 1976 at several theatres. Classification: R.

Players: *Robert Carradine, Jennifer Ashley, Michael Mullins, Lisa Reeves, Bill Adler, James Gammon, Susan Player, Rainbeaux Smith, Diane Lee Hart, Lou Pant, John Lawrence.*

Los Angeles Times, 9/10/76 (Pt. IV, p. 16)
Kevin Thomas

". . . talented young writer-producer-director Joseph Ruben, in projecting this postadolescent fantasy, observes the rules. His young people raise hell, but they aren't vicious, cruel or destructive. Even though vehemently anti-intellectual they're a pretty likeable bunch, possessing some dimension and, most important, vulnerability. As a result—and because it has an abundant sense of humor—*The Pom Pom Girls* succeeds as an evocation of the

kind of freedom that youth symbolizes but practically no one, today or in the past, ever really gets to enjoy.

There's practically no plot. It is the beginning of a new school year, with the big game with a hated rival looming and the boys and girls pursuing each other. Campus clown and rebel leader Robert Carradine wins nice girl Jennifer Ashley after some misunderstandings; the school's moody Lothario, Michael Mullins, after overcoming some image problems, succeeds with golden girl Lisa Reeves. These young people are all capable and effective, but the film's standout is Bill Adler as Mullins' amusingly lummoxlike rival for Miss Reeves."

©Los Angeles Times, 1976.

PREMONITION, THE

Director, Producer: *Robert Allen Schnitzer*. Screenplay: *Arthur Mahon, Mr. Schnitzer*. Distributor: *Avco Embassy Pictures*. Running time 94 minutes. New York opening May 19, 1976, at several theatres. Classification: PG.

Players: *Ellen Barber, Richard Lynch, Edward Bell, Chiitra Neogy, Danielle Brisebois, Sharon Farrell, Rosemary Mcnamara, Jeff Corey, Thomas Williams, Margaret Graham.*

New York Post, 5/20/76 (p. 21)
Archer Winsten

" . . . The movie medium, properly handled, can put on quite a show of sudden, terrifying apparitions, and that is what happens here.

Robert Allen Schnitzer, producer, director and co-author, hates having his picture shown as a suspense-and-horror feature. He wants it to be taken seriously, and he lavishes considerable skill and care on such items as casting, dialogues and vague menace.

What neither he nor all the powers that he can accomplish is the avoidance of sense of management. These thought transferences occur with startling regularity and purpose, coinciding rather remarkably with exigencies of the plot . . .

Actually the thing is done so well that if you're at all susceptible to that sort of fantasy it can stand up as something both possible and terrifying . . .

A pat ending makes it difficult to accompany Mr. Schnitzer the whole way, but it must be admitted he has made a good try, very greatly assisted by the performances of Ellen Barber, Sharon Farrell,

Richard Lynch and, of course, that veteran all purpose actor, Jeff Corey, here thinking hard as a detective."

Reprinted by Permission of New York Post.
© 1976,New York Post Corporation.

PROVIDENCE

Director: *Alain Resnais.* Screenplay: *David Mercer.* Producers: *Yves Gasser, Klaus Hellwig.* Photography: *Ricardo Aronovich.* Editor: *Albert Jurgenson.* Music: *Miklos Rozsa.* Production: *Action Films.* Distributor: *Cinema 5 Films.* Running time 104 minutes. New York opening January 25, 1977, at Cinema 3. Classification: R.

Sonia Langham: *Ellen Burstyn.* Claud Langham: *Dirk Bogarde.* Clive Langham: *John Gielgud.* Kevin Woodford: *David Warner.* Helen Wiener/Molly Langham: *Elaine Stritch.* Dave Woodford: *Denis Lawson.* Dr. Mark Eddington: *Cyril Luckham.* Miss Boon: *Kathryn Leigh-Scott.* Mr. Jenner: *Milo Sperber.* Karen: *Anna Wing.* Nils: *Peter Arne.*

Village Voice, 2/7/77 (p. 45)
Molly Haskell

". . . The film is stunning to look at, an elegant marmoreal maze, all silver and ebony, cold and shiny as a king's mausoleum. But once the film has yielded the solution to its Oedipal theme, it becomes less interesting. Mercer the absurdist playwright (he also wrote the screenplay for *Morgan!*) believes, with Resnais, that traditional narrative is impossible since history is not fixed; truth is not what happened but what is thought to have happened as it determines the fluid present. But unlike Resnais' previous films, with their multiple points of view, *Providence* has only one version of events, and that version, which relies heavily on the shock effect of incongruous images, never has to explain itself or be held to account.

Gielgud proves again, if it needs proving, that he is the greatest living actor in the English language . . ."

Reprinted by permission of The Village Voice.
Copyright © The Village Voice, Inc., 1977.

Christian Science Monitor, 2/7/77 (p. 26)
David Sterritt

". . . Those who enjoyed the gripping perplexities of earlier Resnais triumphs—*Hiroshima Mon Amour*,

Last Year at Marienbad, Muriel—will relish this first English-language effort of the famed French filmmaker, who returns to the enormous visual complexity that has seemed dormant in his more recent work. Fans of Dirk Bogarde, David Warner, and John Gielgud will also have much to admire among the all-star cast, though Ellen Burstyn doesn't quite bring off the early contradictions of her role.

Providence is not for the squeamish or the squirmish. Nor does it find the visual consistency it needs to unify its moods and meanings, despite the precision of Resnais' direction, which ranges from a *Citizen Kane* type of pastiche to pure art-film individualism . . ."

Reprinted by permission from The Christian
Science Monitor © 1977.
The Christian Science Publishing Society.
All rights reserved.

New York Post, 1/26/77 (p. 42)
Frank Rich

". . . *Providence*, I'm sorry to report, is one of Resnais' failures—it's right up there with the glittery, overfurnished and fundamentally empty *Last Year at Marienbad*. Though the film is pretty (in its cool metallic way), and though it has a potentially exciting Anglo-American cast (Dirk Bogarde, Ellen Burstyn, John Gielgud, David Warner), it's thin and malconceived stuff. Resnais' style doesn't serve so much to elucidate this movie's meaning as to obfuscate that meaning—as if he capriciously wants to delay our discovery of the mediocrity that lies at the project's heart . . .

. . . Gielgud has a marvelous time as the decrepit, thundering novelist, and Bogarde, whose character undergoes a 100 percent reversal in the film's denouement, reminds us again of his magnificent range . . ."

Reprinted by Permission of New York Post.
© 1977, New York Post Corporation.

Women's Wear Daily, 1/24/77 (p. 7)
Howard Kissel

". . . What is fascinating about the way the film builds is that by presenting the characters as the figments of an author's obsessed imagination, Resnais moves us beyond the point where we can discuss them in conventional Freudian terminology. Someone asks one of his characters, for example, 'How do you do?' He says: 'Not very well. Something must have gone wrong at an early stage. It could be childhood—but I don't want to spend my life attributing it to that.' In the line is a realisation that it is possible to use classical Freudianism as an excuse—Freud can let one view one's life as rigidly determined by incidents in the first few years, which can be used as an explanation for everything that happens afterward. Resnais wants to move beyond this sort of clinical 'amnesty.' In some ways his arguments are mitigated by the fact that his novelist

continued on next page

continued from previous page

has so distorted an imagination. Moreover, the dialog the writer imagines for his characters is often rigid and foppish, which adds to the ironies of the overall conception, but makes Resnais' questions about how we should regard character motivations and fictional use of moral themes less serious . . ."

©Women's Wear Daily, 1977.

Nation, 2/12/77 (p. 188)
Robert Hatch

"*Providence*, Alain Resnais' first movie in English, strikes me as a work very much at the mercy of the viewer's mood of the moment. It takes place largely in the mind of Clive Langham (John Gielgud), a writer who presumes to feel himself cheated of the mantle of, say, Somerset Maugham, and who is panicked into a style of aphoristic savagery by this less than Olympian hubris. A septuagenarian steeped in expensive alcohol and mortally afflicted with rectal cancer . . . he passes a pain-ridden, increasingly sodden night trying to compose in his mind yet another 'social comedy'—this one to be peopled by the members of his family, as he sees them.

Not surprisingly, given the self-pity and rancor that possesses this unseemly old man, he perceives them in the worst possible light, projecting their foibles, follies and deficiencies of personality to extremes that produce manikins of singular implausibility . . .

. . . I went to the picture on an idle Sunday afternoon, of a mind to be entertained, and it entertained me.

That happened, I think, partly because of the behavior of the enthralled characters and partly because of the zany travelogue progress of the plot, which I took to be a sardonic comment on the deluxe tourism of the more cynical French films for export . . ."

©The Nation, 1977.

New York Magazine, 1/31/77 (p. 70)
John Simon

". . . Alas, *Providence*, Resnais' first English-language film, with a script by the playwright-scenarist David Mercer (best known here for *Morgan!*), strikes me as his first unmitigated disaster. There is not even the cinematography of Jean Boffety or the beauty of Olga Georges-Picot that palliated the absurdities of *Je t'aime, je t'aime* . . .

. . . Matters are not helped . . . by the first four fifths of *Providence* being something like Noel Coward rewritten by Harold Pinter, and the last fifth like David Storey rewritten by Arnold Wesker.

You may have gathered that the worst thing

about the script is its tone, situated at the intersection of drawing-room comedy with existential undertones, social satire with ominously metaphysical overtones, and high camp . . ."

©1977 by the NYM Corp. Reprinted with the permission of NEW YORK Magazine.

Commonweal, 3/18/77 (p. 182)
Colin L. Westerbeck, Jr.

". . . Since this film is a character study rather than a philosophical inquiry of Resnais' own, it has to remain true to Clive's mental state. And that state is, though facile and often amusing, also unstable to say the least. The sort of aesthetic ordering which disclosed meaning within the confusion and made past Resnais films great is here inappropriate. Here the point is for the free flow of associations to be truly free and rambling. Here it is not only the reality that is interior, but the view of reality as well. Consequently, much of the imagery in the film seems at last to be purely gestural rather than thematic.

Men turn into werewolves, a cadaver is dissected, white wine is drunk almost continuously—but none of these things ever really acquires any meaning. Like everything else in the film, as they are part of the personality of one character, they are essentially histrionic rather than symbolic in nature . . ."

©Commonweal, 1977.

Newsweek, 2/28/77 (p. 72)
Jack Kroll

". . . You will seldom see a more dazzling film than *Providence*, or a more exasperating one.

Resnais' theme is always uncertainty, evanescence, the mysterious nature of the information supplied by human consciousness. This is a great theme, but Resnais does not voyage daringly into this mystery—he wallows in it . . .

All this might have been gripping, but Resnais' style is so glitteringly self-absorbed that it caresses itself to death. David Mercer's script seems to have intimations of solidity, with all sorts of psychological and political hints that are left to fade away like wisps of incense. Two very gifted actresses—Burstyn and Stritch—are lost in Resnais' no-man's land, but Bogarde and Gielgud make the French director's first English-language film worth seeing—and hearing. Gielgud is simply sensational . . ."

© Newsweek, Inc. 1977 reprinted by permission.

Saturday Review, 3/5/77 (p. 42)
Judith Crist

". . . It is Resnais' vision that holds the attention: the suggestion and shadow of the environment, the lurking terrors of the night, the quicksilver changes of character from flesh and blood to puppetry, the foisting of the narrator's suspicions and self-hatreds upon others. And it is Gielgud's civilized tone, the self-mockery leavening the bitterness, that enthralls and delights the ear, complemented by Bogarde's icy righteousness as the son, and his refusal to yield to emotional pulls.

Beyond these two, the casting is unfortunate, simply because Mercer's dialogue is so overstylized that it is ultimately nothing more than mechanized banality, beyond redemption . . .

The dialogue becomes obvious, tedious, and intolerable in its stilted wordplay . . . But as Gielgud says early on: 'If one has led a fatuous life one must have fatuous nightmares.' As for Resnais—even a fatuous screenplay can become intermittently interesting in his hands."

©Judith Crist, 1977.

Take One, March 1977 (p. 8)
James Monaco

". . . What really holds our interest throughout most of it . . . is not the drama but the play. Clive's nightmare is an actor's dream. As Claud, Dirk Bogarde plays with virtuoso broad panache. He is slimily thin, outrageously effete, wonderfully nasty. He displays an entire catalogue of impetuously nasty moves and looks. David Warner's Kevin is as dumb and mushy as Bogarde's Claud is sinewy and sharp. Warner, his massive, craggy, pocked face looming like a parody of Mount Rushmore, has never hulked better. The two of them are obviously enjoying their music-hall melodrama enormously.

If Resnais and Mercer had stopped there, however, the result would have been simply camp. The key to the conception lies elsewhere. Resnais has purposefully cast two quintessentially American actresses in the major women's roles. Ellen Burstyn and Elaine Stritch are utterly, thoroughly, magnificently wrong for the roles . . . Providence is Alain Resnais' first comedy.

But the irony of the interplay of the fictions Clive invents can go only so far . . ."

©Take One, 1977.

Film Information, March 1977 (p. 2)
Robert E. A. Lee

". . . A film of feelings to absorb rather than ideas to understand, Providence is a difficult, brooding, and troubled film with touches of brilliance. Although it deals with agonizing questions of death, its title is not particularly appropriate. It is in its questions of life and its meaning that Providence reveals a rather pathetic emptiness . . .

Even though heavy with metaphysical and philosophical elements, the movie Providence is never boring. Director Resnais spreads a broad cinema canvas of surrealistic dimensions. He appears to see film art as an opportunity for the artist to represent himself abstractly rather than to communicate with an audience in simple words and pictures. The result may be a film to study rather than one to see quickly as passing entertainment . . ."

©Film Information, 1977.

Films in Review, March 1977 (p. 186)
Jane Morgan

"*Providence* is a portrait of the artist as an old man, who lives—or, rather, is 'still dying'—in a mansion on an estate called 'Providence.' Director Alain Resnais has always been concerned with ambiguities, the permanent impermanence of time, the simultaneity or juxtaposition of disparate events, the thin line between the conscious and the unconscious. *Providence* has two sides. One is pictured at night, the other in sunlight. One is a nightmare, cold and dark; the other a daydream, warm and bright . . .

In this psychological study of the bourgeois artist, Resnais has found a subject close enough to his own political vacillations between left and center and to his own personal intellectual pursuits to make his imagist method work without spinning out of control. It is his first English-speaking film, in deference to the very British screenplay by David Mercer. John Gielgud is brilliant. Bogarde and Burstyn spectacular."

©Films in Review, 1977.

PSYCHIC KILLER

Director: *Raymond Danton*. Screenplay: *Greydon Clark, Mike Angel, Mr. Danton.* Producer: *Mardi Rustam*. Distributor: *Avco Embassy*. Running time 90 minutes. New York opening February, 1976, at the Criterion and 86th Street East Theatres. Classification: PG.

Players: *Jim Hutton, Paul Burke, Della Reese, Mary Wilcox, Rod Cameron, Aldo Ray, Julie Adams, Whit Bissell, Nehemiah Persoff, Judith Brown, Neville Brand, Joe Della Sorte.*

See Volume 1 for additional reviews

Los Angeles Times, 5/5/76 (Pt. IV, p. 17)
Linda Gross

"*Psychic Killer* . . . is about a psychotic man (Jim

continued on next page

continued from previous page

Hutton) who uses psychic energy to perform a series of 'out of body' murders.

The film boasts an excellent repertory of performances by veteran character actors, excruciatingly scary sequences and a kinky, macabre sense of humor. Unfortunately, *Psychic Killer* loses a lot by using graphic gruesomeness and simplistic Freudian and parapsychological cliches . . .

The script by Greydon Clark, Mike Angel and Raymond Danton oscillates between effective plotting, weird wit and off-key bad taste. Jim Hutton is very impressive and reasonable––most of the time. Miss Adams, Burke, Aldo Ray and Persoff are all sympathetic and credible. Della Reese has an amusing cameo as a lady shopper.

William Kraft's music is effectively frightening. Director Danton successfully builds up suspense but loses control when confronted with madness . . ."

© Los Angeles Times, 1976.

PUMPING IRON

Documentary. Directors, Producers: *George Butler, Robert Fiore.* Based on the book by Charles Gaines and Mr. Butler. Photography: *Mr. Fiore.* Editors: *Larry Silk, Geof Bartz.* Distributor: *Cinema 5 Films.* Running time 85 minutes. New York opening January 18, 1977, at the Plaza Theatre. Classification: PG.

Note: There is no cast in this film.

Women's Wear Daily, 1/12/77 (p. 44)
Howard Kissel

"Probably the best way to regard *Pumping Iron* is as a tract designed to awaken the average moviegoer to the beauties of bodybuilding. That the film succeeds is due largely to the personal charm of its focal point, Arnold Schwarzenegger, who, unlike some other subjects, developed his body in addition to, rather than instead of, his mind and personality.

In some ways it is hard to think of bodybuilding as a sport since, as Schwarzenegger himself points out, it is an art comparable to sculpture, but done from within rather than merely adding clay from without. Though the heart of bodybuilding is a man working on himself there are competitions, and George Butler's film does a remarkable job of letting us in on the mentality at work here . . . The film is moving because it manages to capture so much

of this psychic rivalry, which becomes even more poignant when you realize one part of the body some of these men don't worry about developing is the brain . . ."

©Women's Wear Daily, 1977.

New York Post, 1/19/77 (p. 46)
Frank Rich

". . . We meet some of the outstanding bodybuilders of our time, and we get a taste of their exotic subculture—but beyond that, *Pumping Iron* is curiously reticent about its characters.

The more intriguing issues raised by bodybuilding—issues involving sexuality, narcissism, and the human drive for power—are glossed over in order to provide the audience with an upbeat show. Instead of an exciting movie full of human insights, we get a trivial, if entertaining exercise in esoterica . . .

Schwarzenegger is really special: He has the princely spirit we associate with all athletic legends—he's a newfangled Muhammad Ali—and his easygoing air of complete and utter self-assurance lights up *Pumping Iron* . . ."

Reprinted by Permission of New York Post.
© 1977, New York Post Corporation.

Village Voice, 1/31/77 (p. 39)
Andrew Sarris

". . . As far as propagating muscle building is concerned, the full-bodied assault of *Pumping Iron* is infinitely preferable to the coy evasions of Bob Rafelson's *Stay Hungry*, which made muscle builders seem completely freakish. George Butler, Charles Gaines, Robert Fiore, and Jerome Gary, in their various writing, directing and producing functions, have humanized their muscle men, though at times with dubiously cute contrivances. They have also come up with a pair of lovable losers in Mike Katz and Louis Ferrigno (a real-life Rocky to the nth degree). We are a long way from the strained mockery of *Muscle Beach*.

By contrast, *Pumping Iron* functions as partisan propaganda for the ethos and aesthetics of weight lifting . . .

Arnold Schwarzenegger is something else again as a kind of canny Superman. Arnold S. seems to have traveled the necessary ironic distance between what he is and what he does, which is more than one can say for his seemingly vulnerable colleagues . . ."

Reprinted by permission of The Village Voice.
Copyright © The Village Voice, Inc., 1977.

Christian Science Monitor, 1/28/77 (p. 18)
David Sterritt

". . . Though the romance of working out still

largely escapes me, I found *Pumping Iron* a frequently intelligent and witty look at some people, places, and attitudes the average 97-pound weakling doesn't run across every day.

The documentary's central character is champion bodybuilder Arnold Schwarzenegger, who won the sport's top prize, the Mr. Olympia title, six years running before retiring and going Hollywood in *Stay Hungry* and now *Pumping Iron*. He is a bright, articulate and cheery fellow, not your usual movie-star type but fun to watch and listen to . . .

. . . Though it did not convert me to a fan or participant, directors George Butler and Robert Fiore are to be commended for their careful handling of an unusual subject . . ."

Reprinted by permission from The Christian Science Monitor © 1977. The Christian Science Publishing Society. All rights reserved.

New York Magazine, 1/24/77 (p. 85)
John Simon

". . . about musclemen—body-builders, to give them their preferred, more architectural, title—and to a much lesser extent, their families, trainers, fans. It is a film that cannot help having a certain freak-show appeal: Monumental exaggeration—whether in architecture, conversation, musculature, or anything else—casts an unwholesome spell. These bodies, supposedly recreating the marvels of Greek sculpture in living flesh, are actually rococo excrescences, grotesque hyperboles, delusions of fleshy grandeur . . .

And yet the film has its riveting passages, as when we see the screen well-nigh explode with the superhuman, or superbovine, exertions of these body-builders, or when Arnold Schwarzenegger, the champion of champions, gives out with mischievous bits of witty cynicism . . ."

© 1977 by the NYM Corp. Reprinted with the permission of NEW YORK Magazine.

Newsweek, 1/24/77 (p. 61)
Jack Kroll

". . . It's a surprising piece of work with an easy rhythm, an ingratiating air of humane seriousness, the right touches of irony, a sense of character that goes beyond 'sports' films and a good deal of suspense.

The suspense has to do with who's going to win the two major body-building competitions (in 1975) for the all-embracing titles of Mr. Universe and Mr. Olympia. Austrian-born Schwarzenegger is the Muhammad Ali of body-building who's won most of the major titles for the last decade or so. At 29 he's turned himself into a Michelangelesque masterpiece of self-sculpture, and everybody else is trying to knock this living statue off its pedestal. The movie deftly sketches in the competitors as they drive

themselves through the pain thresholds of 'pumping iron'—the variegated weight lifting that pushes the human musculature to its ultimate development . . ."

© Newsweek, Inc. 1977 reprinted by permission.

Film Information, March 1977 (p. 3)
Frederic A. Brussat

"Watch their muscles develop. 'When you have driven your body past the barrier . . . and then you relax, all the blood comes rushing, pounding back into your muscles. You feel like you're swelling up, like your skin is about to explode. That's the pump,' says Arnold Schwarzenegger, the Austrian-born world body-building champ for the last six years in a row. This documentary features some of the philosophy, exercises, competition, and subculture of the ninth-largest spectator sport in America . . .

Pumping Iron contains some visually poetic segments and is an informative meditation on the sport as an odd mixture of pain and narcissistic pleasure. Schwarzenegger, who was seen in Bob Rafelson's film *Stay Hungry*, recently retired from body-building. He is sure to have a career in the movies."

© Film Information, 1977.

RAGGEDY ANN & ANDY

Director: *Richard Williams*. Screenplay: *Patricia Thackray, Max Wilk*. Based on the stories by Johnny Gruelle. Producer: *Richard Horner*. Photography: *Al Rezak Inc.* Editors: *Harry Chang, Lee Kent, Kenneth McIlwain, Maxwell Seligman*. Production: *Lester Osterman Productions*. Distributor: *Twentieth Century-Fox*. Running time 84 minutes. New York opening April 1, 1977, at several theatres. Classification: G.

Marcella: *Claire Williams*. Voices: *Mason Adams, Mark Baker, Marty Brill, Didi Conn, Paul Dooley, Niki Flacks, Hetty Galen, Margery Gray, Sheldon Harnick, George S. Irving, Ardyth Kaiser, Joe Silver, Arnold Stang, Fred Struthman, Lynne Stuart, Alan Sues, Allen Swift*.

Women's Wear Daily, 4/1/77 (p. 52)
Howard Kissel

"As personalities, Raggedy Ann and Andy have

continued on next page

281

continued from previous page

never been as forceful, or dynamic as, say, Bugs Bunny, their contemporary Peter Rabbit, or, of course, Mickey Mouse. For many years, in fact, there was an ingrained prejudice that maintained there was something inherently sluggish, even limp-wristed in the psychological makeup of all rag dolls. I had hoped Richard Williams' animated version of *Raggedy Ann & Andy* would refute this kind of thinking, but, alas, it doesn't.

The film, though it has some delightful animated sequences, some nice characterizations and a good song . . . is a disappointment, largely because its story is so diffuse. The visuals are sophisticated, but there is no drama behind them . . ."

©Women's Wear Daily, 1977.

New York Post, 4/2/77 (p. 33)
Archer Winsten

". . . *Raggedy Ann & Andy* comes up with odd creatures, pie-throwing slapstick heightened to machine reproduction, songs galore, and noise that passes for fun. One of the leading types, a midget king who can grow large only when laughing violently, is made to expand enormously.

Is this truly funny?

Might a child find it explosive?

I don't really know. All I can testify is that seeing the picture with an audience of sullen adults, I heard no single titter, nor was I tempted to guffaw myself. Technically the picture is a labor of immense skill and dedication. They've worked their fingers to the bone, you might say, but I have the feeling that what you experience is more perspiration than inspiration. And yet, it's such an imaginative piece visually you wonder why it isn't more enjoyable."

Reprinted by Permission of New York Post.
©1977, New York Post Corporation.

RAPE KILLER, THE

Director: *Dacosta Carayan*. Screenplay: *Telly Livadas*. Producer: *Joseph Brenner*. Editor: *Jimmy Russo*. Music: *Yani Spannos*. Distributor: *Mutual*. Running time 80 minutes. Los Angeles opening November 1976 at several theatres. Classification: R. Origin: Italy.

Players: *Leslie Bowman, Anthony Carr, Angela Clianto, Larry Daniels, Terry Livadas, Dorothy Moore.*

Los Angeles Times, 11/19/76 (Pt. IV, p. 30)
Linda Gross

"*The Rape Killer* . . . is a muddled Italian sickie about a psychopath who strangles women after he rapes them . . .

. . . scriptwriter Telly Livadas is so busy flashing anguished, undressed women, dying slowly, that he intermittently forgets to dwell on the diminished plot. The dubbing is terrible but some of the dialogue—'Death is a beautiful, dreamless sleep'—would probably be better left not translated.

Jimmy Russo's editing appears garbled and Yani Spannos' music is obscenely literal: 'I Want It Now' —as the women get slaughtered. Dorothy Moore is frailly attractive as the deceived wife. The movie has been limply directed by Dacosta Carayan. Sadistic trash for masochistic gluttons for gore."

©Los Angeles Times, 1976.

RAPE OF INNOCENCE

Director: *Yves Boisset*. Screenplay (French with English subtitles): *Jean-Pierre Bastid, Michel Martins*, adapted by Jean Curtelin and Mr. Boisset. Producers: *Catherine Winter, Gisele Rebillon*. Photography: *Jacques Loiseleux*. Music: *Vladimir Cosma*. Production: *Sofracima*. Distributor: *New Line Cinema*. Running time 95 minutes. New York opening July 28, 1976, at the Fine Arts Theatre. Classification: None. Origin: France.

Georges Lajoie: *Jean Carmet*. Colin: *Pierre Tornade*. Boular: *Jean Bouise* Schumacher: *Michel Peyrelon*. Ginette Lajoie: *Ginette Garcin*. Mme. Colin: *Pascale Roberts*. Leo Tartaffione: *Jean-Pierre Marielle*. Loulou: *Robert Castel*. Vigerelli: *Pino Caruso*. Brigitte Colin: *Isabelle Huppert*.

New York Post, 7/29/76 (p. 16)
Archer Winsten

"*Rape of Innocence* . . . is a French film of exceptional restraint and power . . .

The film comes to its climax and unifying theme when Georges happens upon his son's girl friend, Brigitte . . . when she's taking a nude sunbath in the tall grass. The older man makes a pass, attempts to rape her, and accidentally kills her.

Inevitably the blame is shifted to nearby Arab workmen, which permits director Yves Boisset and his scriptwriters . . . to train a pitiless and revealing light upon the good French patriots in the camp, the procedure of the police and the interventions of those who take the long view of national policy . . .

Performances are all of a piece, French and alive with their characters. The Italians and the Arabs are sufficiently different to stand out . . ."

Reprinted by Permission of New York Post.
©1976, New York Post Corporation.

RATTLERS

Director, Producer: *John McCauley*. Screenplay: *Jerry Golding*. Photography: *Richard Gibb, Irv Goodnoff*. Editor: *Sandy Glieberman*. Snake Trainer: *Ray Folsum*. Production: *Harry Novak*. Distributor: *Boxoffice International*. Running time 82 minutes. Los Angeles opening September 1976 at several theaters. Classification: PG.

Players: *Sam Chew, Elisabeth Chauvet, Dan Priest, Ron Gold, Tony Ballen, Richard Lockmiller, Jo Jordan, Al Dunlap*.

Los Angeles Times, 9/23/76 (Pt. IV, p. 23)
Kevin Thomas

". . . A pair of little boys wander from their families' Mojave Desert campsite and are later found dead at the bottom of a rocky cliff, clearly the victims of not just one snake but a virtual regiment . . .

To their credit producer-director John McCauley and writer Jerry Golding, who are reportedly making their feature debuts, avoid completely the lurid grisliness that characterizes the animal horror genre. If anything, *Rattlers* is a little too low-key for its own good. However, McCauley and Golding wisely go for naturalness both in performances and dialogue. In this film they demonstrate that they know how to establish a plausible premise; next time out they should concentrate on picking up pace and building suspense in a more taut fashion . . ."

©Los Angeles Times, 1976.

RETURN OF A MAN CALLED HORSE, THE

Director: *Irvin Kershner*. Screenplay: *Jack*

Dewitt. Based on a character from A MAN CALLED HORSE by Dorothy M. Johnson. Producer: *Terry Morse, Jr*. Photography: *Owen Roizman*. Editor: *Michael Kahn*. Music: *Laurence Rosenthal*. Distributor: *United Artists*. Running time 125 minutes. New York opening July 1976 at the Ziegfeld Theatre. Classification: PG.

John Morgan: *Richard Harris*. Elk Woman: *Gale Sondergaard*. Zenas Morrow: *Geoffrey Lewis*. Tom Gryce: *Bill Lucking*. Running Bull: *Jorge Luke*. Chemin d'Fer: *Claudio Brook*. Raven: *Enrique Lucero*. Blacksmith: *Jorge Russek*. Moonstar: *Ana De Sade*. Standing Bear: *Pedro Damien*. Thin Dog: *Humberto Lopez-Pineda*. Grey Thorn: *Patricia Reyes*. Lame Wolf: *Regino Herrera*. Owl: *Rigoberto Rico*. Red Cloud: *Alberto Mariscal*.

John Morgan (Richard Harris), right, talks with Raven (Enrique Lucero) in **The Return of a Man Called Horse**.

Women's Wear Daily, 7/29/76 (p. 9)
Howard Kissel

". . . Horse (well played by Richard Harris) leads the down-trodden tribe that adopted him to victory over cynical, hostile fellow Indians and over the crude, commercial-minded Americans who have instigated their misfortunes. The ending is happy, even though we know it is only temporarily so—in a few decades the crude commercial-minded Americans will have regained the upper hand.

Much of *Return* is clumsy, conventional and crudely melodramatic. Moreover its focal point— the harrowing ritual—is a reprise of the 'hit number' of the earlier film, somewhat less horrible, but a repeat of an earlier success nevertheless. Still

continued on next page

continued from previous page

Return is an encouraging film, because it points to new directions for the Western, new ways of building myths, a welcome sign now that the anti-myth is itself becoming a cliche."

©Women's Wear Daily, 1976.

Saturday Review, 9/18/76 (p. 42)
Judith Crist

"For those who care to touch the bestial, there's *The Return of a Man Called Horse*, a sequel to the 1970 Richard Harris vehicle equally guaranteed to please sadists and those who share the creator's fixation with pectoral torture. This time, the silliness is scripted up, once again, by Jack DeWitt and brought to tedious exposition by Irvin Kershner . . . Harris, that early-nineteenth-century English milord adopted by Sioux, returns from his stately home seemingly to teach psychedelia and superstition to his foster tribe. The emphasis is on braves' being strung up by their breasts. All the Indians except Gale Sondergaard get to talk subtitled Sioux (she talks bodega-type English), and Kershner maintains a tidy balance between nausea and boredom for the viewer."

©Judith Crist, 1976.

New York Magazine, 8/23/76 (p. 61)
John Simon

"Quality in a sequel is rarer than a pearl in an oyster—almost as rare as a pearl in a clam. In this case, however, the original was bad enough to look like a clear case of no deposit, no return. But, I guess, we had to have further views of Richard Harris' pectoral muscles being shredded in a purification ritual. Irvin Kershner provides some nice directorial touches, though he is no good at battle scenes, and Owen Roizman's cinematography is wonderfully various and evocative. Laurence Rosenthal's score is a lot of noisy swagger, and there are a few unintentional laughs . . . in Yellowhand Sioux, 'horse' is . . . *hunkawanka*; yet complex English sentences in the subtitles are dispatched with a few curt syllables by the on-screen Indians."

©1976 by the NYM Corp. Reprinted with the permission of NEW YORK Magazine.

Christian Science Monitor, 8/4/76 (p. 22)
David Sterritt

" . . . Director Irvin Kershner cares about Indians and gives much of *The Return* an urgent rhythm

and deep-set dignity. Even in the exploitable sun-vow sequence he often cuts away from physical detail to evoke instead a sense of tribal mystery . . .

The film's emphasis on mysticism becomes so involving the violent heroics of the climax seem all the more disappointing by contrast. Once the Yellowhands are 'reborn' they embark on a quest for their old lands and sacred burial ground. This translates into movie terms as a rip-roaring shoot-out with the bad guys. Here Kershner has nothing new to offer. We have seen this ponderous kill-fest hundreds of times before.

Harris' portrayal of Morgan-Horse is mild and modulated. Veteran actress Gale Sondergaard has poise and conviction . . ."

Reprinted by permission from The Christian Science Monitor © 1976. The Christian Science Publishing Society. All rights reserved.

The Sunday Times (London), 10/31/76 (p. 35)
Alan Brien

" . . . Once again he offers himself as sacrificial victim, tied to a pole by pinions cut into the flesh above his nipples—a bizarre, bloody exhibition which was the most notorious, and least appreciated feature of the early film. Whatever the anthropological intentions, the effect is noticeably condescending. The white colonial master from across the ocean not only survives all these endurance tests, but then sets about teaching the tribe the use of their own weapons and the tactic of guerrilla warfare.

Irvin Kershner's camera moves as ponderously as a dinosaur's head from side to side, up and down, while syrupy music flows over the 90mm cricket-pitch screen like treacle over suet pud. The Indians are mainly swarthy Latins plus Gale Sondergaard as the Elk Woman. Richard Harris' stony Mount Rushmore head has few more expressions than a cannonball. At two hours and five minutes, *The Return of a Man Called Horse* is an epic grounded by elephantiasis."

© The Sunday Times, 1976.

The Times (London), 10/29/76 (p. 11)
David Robinson

" . . . So he returns, only to find his tribe decimated by white rotters and Indian renegades. The survivors still relish their sadistic custom of hanging braves up by cords stitched through their pectoral muscles. In *A Man Called Horse* only Harris suffered the treatment. In *Return of a Man Called Horse* the whole male part of the tribe indulges, strung up on a sort of merry-go-round. The consequent spiritual uplift heartens them to repel their enemies.

Surprisingly, Irvin Kershner succeeds in giving

this slight nonsense moments of panache, with good looking visuals and a couple of stirring set-pieces. The film could be forgiven much, too, for having the admirable Gale Sondergaard in the role of a walnut-wrinkled old Indian wise woman . . ."

©The Times, 1976.

Monthly Film Bulletin, November 1976 (p. 234)
Clyde Jeavons

"Sequels are often superfluous, but few can be as pointless or as self-indulgent as this lengthy reprise of Richard Harris' pectoral work-out (first observed in *A Man Called Horse*), which must make him the leading contender for Marlon Brando's crown as Hollywood's most obsessive masochist. As a study of authentic tribal behaviour among North American Indians, Irvin Keshner's film is even less convincing and more condescending than its precursor, while John Morgan's motivation in going native seems rooted not so much in a mystical empathy with the Yellowhands as in a profound boredom with fox-hunting. In any event, the film's anthropological pretensions are at length abandoned . . ."

©Monthly Film Bulletin, 1976.

RETURN OF THE TALL BLOND MAN WITH ONE BLACK SHOE, THE (LE RETOUR DU GRAND BLOND)

Director: *Yves Robert*. Screenplay (French with English subtitles): *Francis Veber, Mr. Robert*. Producer: *Alain Poire, Mr. Robert*. Photography: *Rene Mathelin*. Music: *Vladimir Cosma*. Production: *Gaumont International-Productions de la Gueville*. Distributor: *Group IV/Lanir*. Running time 87 minutes. Los Angeles opening December 31, 1975, at the Los Feliz Theatre. Classification: None. Origin: France.

Players: *Pierre Richard, Mireille Darc, Jean Rochefort, Jean Carmet, Michel Duchaussoy, Paul Le Person, Colette Castel, Jean Bouise, Herve Sand, Henri Guybert*.

See Volume 1 for additional reviews

New York Post, 7/24/76 (p. 15)
Archer Winsten

". . . farce and slapstick of the broadest kind, ren-

dered palatable to students of the French language (with subtitles added), and pleasing to slapstick lovers because they react automatically. Richard himself, displaying some comedic kinship with that idol of French critics, Jerry Lewis, and maybe a soupcon of Danny Kaye, continues the portrayal he established in the earlier picture . . .

. . . a pleasant surprise to experience more entertainment in the sequel than in its original. This is doubtless because there is less effort to be funny and more attention to the semi-serious conflicts within these two government agencies at war with each other and using Pierre Richard as their mutual weapon. This turns out to be an idea with good possibilities, all of which are exploited by some of France's best deadpan farceurs, including Jean Rochefort, Michel Duchaussoy and Jean Carmet . . ."

Reprinted by Permission of New York Post.
©1976, New York Post Corporation.

Monthly Film Bulletin, 9/76 (p. 198)
Sue Scott-Moncreiff

"A sequel to *Follow That Guy with the One Black Shoe*, *The Return of the Tall Blond* begins with a recap of past events, although the film is in no way a pale imitation of the earlier hit and succeeds well enough on its own terms. The humor is essentially visual (verbal wit was perhaps lost in the dubbing), but Yves Robert's subtle direction avoids any slapstick treatment of the absurd situations in which the Tall Blond finds himself . . . The idea is introduced that those protecting and upholding the law are social misfits who can only relate to people as dossiers, but the film never loses its light-hearted humor, and the flying bullets are either blanks or fail to find their targets . . ."

©Monthly Film Bulletin, 1976.

RIDE A WILD PONY

Director: *Don Chaffney*. Screenplay: *Rosemary Anne Sisson*. Based on James Aldridge's novel, *A Sporting Proposition*. Producer: *Jerome Courtland*. Photography: *Jack Cardiff*. Editor: *Mike Campbell*. Music: *John Addison*. Production: *Walt Disney*. Distributor: *Buena Vista*. Running time 90 minutes. Los Angeles opening December 25, 1975, at the Fine Arts Theatre. Classification: G.

continued on next page

continued from previous page

Players: *Michael Craig, John Meillon, Robert Bettles, Eva Griffith, Graham Rouse, Alfred Bell, John Meillon Jr., Roy Haddrick, Peter Gwynne, Melissa Jaffer, Lorraine Bayly, Wendy Playfair.*

See Volume 1 for additional reviews

Monthly Film Bulletin, December 1976 (p. 255)
Geoff Brown

". . . Children should find the results irresistible, if a little protracted toward the end (as in so many films, the dramatic tension sags perceptibly once the characters get into a courtroom); parents in tow should be equally contented, especially as the script cunningly deflects a good deal of sympathy away from the crippled heroine by making her spoilt and petulant. Other bonuses include Jack Cardiff's crystal-clear photography and the natural acting: John Meillon (the mayor from *The Cars That Ate Paris*) stands out particularly as the lawyer defending the bush boy's rights with nonchalant impishness. Only Don Chaffney's direction spoils the film's pleasures, for he uses the kind of mannered camera set-ups and distorted close-ups best left to lurid and unreal exercises like his Tyburn horror *Persecution*."

© Monthly Film Bulletin, 1976.

Films in Review, 4/76 (p. 242)
Tatiana Balkoff Lipscomb

"The label, 'A Disney Production' on a screenplay tells most movie-goers the type of picture they are going to see. They can usually look forward to location shots such as they are offered here, with a taste of the outback and ranching in Australia. (This picture was filmed in Victoria and New South Wales.)

They can also look forward to the handling of a human situation with sentiment, and to a sunshine-structured resolution of the hero's problems. In *Ride a Wild Pony* it is a fairly difficult-to-resolve conflict between two sub-teen-aged children—a poor 'outback homesteader's' boy and a spoiled crippled-by-polio rich girl. Both children claim to be the owner of a fine Welsh pony who makes a willful, spunky hero.

The young protagonists, Robert Bettles and Eva Griffith, are believable: The featured adult cast is made up mainly of Australians, which lends the story an authentic flavor. It is particularly refreshing to have adults presented generally as a fair-minded, decent lot, despite misunderstandings. *Ride a Wild Pony* is a satisfactorily touching morsel for the unjaded appetite . . ."

© Films in Review, 1976.

New York Post, 7/17/76 (p. 17)
Archer Winsten

"*Ride a Wild Pony* . . . is a pleasant amalgam of Disney sentiment and Australian realism, both in a setting of boy-girl conflict over ownership of an Australian-Welsh bush pony . . .

What with a sturdy performance by young Bettles who rides the pony like an Indian, bareback and in a fast gallop, and who fights his elders without hesitation, and a generally proper Australian setting and cast, the picture balances its obvious melodrama and touching sentiment with a rough honesty of dialogue and people . . .

. . . it turns out to be a family picture of more than ordinary appeal, plus the far-flung element of a trip to the Australian hinterland.

Director Don Chaffney has done nothing to counteract the screenplay of Rosemary Anne Sisson . . . The story holds you and the movie takes you into the very midst of it."

Reprinted by Permission of New York Post.
© 1976, New York Post Corporation.

Christian Science Monitor, 7/28/76 (p. 22)
David Sterritt

". . . The Disney people show unwonted thoughtfulness in portraying the boy's poverty as a disability comparable to the girl's physical one. Moreover, the movie's emphasis is on childlike strength and resilience going a long way toward overcoming both kinds of disadvantage. The result is optimistic, and optimism is especially welcome in today's movie world. Unfortunately, the result is also cloying in too many spots—an old Disney sin coming to roost for the umpteenth time.

The child actors are only adequate this time around . . . Most of the adults are relegated to small and quiet roles, but the faces of the small-town characters have been carefully chosen, and look as rough-hewn as their New South Wales surroundings."

Reprinted by permission from The Christian
Science Monitor © 1976.
The Christian Science Publishing Society.
All rights reserved.

RISING TARGET

Documentary. Director, Producer: *Barbara Frank*. Photography: *James Joanides, Robert Eberlein, Ell Hollander, Joan Churchill, Eric Saarinen*. Editor: *Jean-Claude Lubtchansky*. Distributor: *Joshua Films*. Running time 80 minutes. New York opening September 16,

1976, at the second International Festival of Women's Films, at the Cinema Studio. Classification: None.

Village Voice, 9/20/76 (p. 91)
Molly Haskell

"*Rising Target*, a documentary and the only new feature-length film by an American woman, consists of loosely strung together footage of the Bobby Kennedy California primary, beginning on the campaign train and leading up to the murder (which we don't see) and its aftermath. It is Bobby Kennedy as seen from the point of view of an outsider . . . and a rather short outsider at that: we always seem to be looking up into a blaze of cameras and the backs of heads, with celebrities darting in and out of view. As such, we see the candidate from the physical vantage point of his constituency—the old ladies, the blacks, the young people—but without the intensity that seeing him through the eyes of anyone of them would have supplied, without the dramatic shaping of media coverage, and without the reflective long view that one might expect in a film made so long after the event."

Reprinted by permission of The Village Voice.
Copyright © The Village Voice, Inc., 1976.

RITZ, THE

Director: *Richard Lester*. Screenplay: *Terrence McNally*. Based on the play by Mr. McNally. Producer: *Denis O'Dell*. Photography: *Paul Wilson*. Music: *Ken Thorne*. Distributor: *Warner Bros*. Running time 91 minutes. New York opening August 12, 1976, at the Cinema 1 Theatre. Classification: R.

Gaetano Procio: *Jack Weston*. Googie Gomez: *Rita Moreno*. Carmine Vespucci: *Jerry Stiller*. Vivian Procio: *Kaye Ballard*. Chris: *F. Murray Abraham*. Claude: *Paul B. Price*. Michael Brick: *Treat Williams*.

Saturday Review, 9/4/76 (p. 55)
Judith Crist

". . . McNally's near-nonsensical but ultra-savvy comedy focuses on the very gay, super-art deco Ritz bathhouse, in New York, wherein a fat garbageman from Cleveland is hiding out from his Mafia brother-in-law, who's out to get him; the

brother-in-law is on the prowl; and Googie Gomez, the ultimate ambitious no-talent entertainer, is entertaining . . .

Lester, in a stylish return to his early days of Beatlemania, keeps the fun as frenzied and judiciously timed as its tightrope walk across the boundaries of taste demands. Best of all, the three delights of the Broadway production—Rita Moreno, whose Tony-award-winning Googie is a classic comedy creation; Jack Weston, whose ungay garbageman is a joy; and Jerry Stiller as the Mafia-oriented brother-in-law—are on hand, augmented by Kaye Ballard as the garbageman's wife and by a fine supporting cast . . . *The Ritz* is about as sophisticated as good old-fashioned lowbrow comedy can get."

©Judith Crist, 1976.

Women's Wear Daily, 8/10/76 (p. 9)
Howard Kissel

". . . Terrence McNally's *The Ritz*, which worked so beautifully as a theater piece, suffers in its screen translation because we're brought a little too close to things that worked on stage because we could keep our distance. The best thing about the film is that it preserves the performances by Rita Moreno, as the Puerto Rican entertainer hoping she will be 'discovered' in her appearance at a place resembling the Continental Baths, and Jack Weston, as a Cleveland businessman trying to escape his wife's vengeful family by taking refuge in the baths. Moreno does an outrageous caricature of a bewildered but grasping no-talent, and Weston is wonderful as an image of overweight innocence. F. Murray Abraham also repeats his fine performance . . ."

©Women's Wear Daily, 1976.

New York Magazine, 8/30/76 (p. 50)
John Simon

"Why is *The Ritz*, Terrence McNally's film adaptation of his own stage farce, even less funny and effective than the play? Jack Weston, Rita Moreno, Jerry Stiller, and F. Murray Abraham recreate their stage roles, the newcomers are not inferior to their Broadway predecessors, and Richard Lester is a competent farce director, whether he is directing farce or anything else. Yet the movie falls, unfarcically, flat.

One reason for this has been generally recognized: Stage performances merely transposed, rather than translated, to the screen become too broad, brash, big for the film medium, which, quite literally, magnifies gestures and expressions. But a less noted reason may be even more important: A screen adaptation falls, precisely, *flat* . . . Take

continued on next page

continued from previous page

away the spatial antics of farce, its solid geometry, and you're left with a flimsy contrivance . . ."

© 1976 by the NYM Corp. Reprinted with
the permission of NEW YORK Magazine.

Newsweek, 8/30/76 (p. 74)
Jack Kroll

"Onstage Terrence McNally's *The Ritz* worked—up to a point. On-screen, it is a disaster. Why? Well, this farce about a fat, baldish, middle-aged guy hiding out from the Mafia in a homosexual baths-hotel-nightclub depended to a great extent on its setting. In the multileveled rabbit warren, with its slamming doors and crisscrossing staircases, you could pretend you were watching a Feydeau farce as the towel-draped gays play human pinball in their lustful chase after each other and the poor slob of a straight who didn't realize where he was. On-screen, despite the fact that the screenplay is credited to the playwright, *The Ritz* loses this containing vessel that gave an explosive quality to its endless burlesque-type gags about sexual inversion, organised crime, showbiz and other pressing concerns of homo sapiens . . ."

© Newsweek, Inc. 1976
reprinted by permission.

New York Post, 8/13/76 (p. 16)
Frank Rich

"An unfunny thing has happened to *The Ritz* on its way from the Broadway stage to the movie screen—the life has been kicked out of it. While the movie . . . preserves most of the text and original cast of Terrence McNally's hit play, the film has lost about three quarters of the show's laughs and all of its frothy tone. What was light and funny and benignly naughty on stage comes out abrasive, flat and nasty on film.

What, you may ask, has gone wrong? Well, if there must be a culprit, sheer process of elimination indicates that the culprit is Richard Lester, the film's director and the only significant creative personality to join *The Ritz*'s Broadway staff for the movie version . . ."

Reprinted by Permission of New York Post.
© 1976, New York Post Corporation.

Village Voice, 8/23/76 (p. 117)
Andrew Sarris

". . . rumor has it that Richard Lester never saw *The Ritz* performed, which may explain why so little of the rhythm and raunchiness of the stage production was preserved. Theatre people still froth at the mouth when Lester's direction of *A Funny Thing Happened on the Way to the Forum* is mentioned. I am not sure that I can defend his direction in either instance, but at least I think I can understand the emotional roots of his style. The close-ups of fat, unappealing characters (played by Jack Weston, Jerry Stiller and Kaye Ballard) create a mood of hopeless frustration in the midst of the sexual revolution. Weston, a strange meld of William Bendix (urban obstinacy) and Jack Haley (sexual panic), virtually runs the gamut of fearful role-playing to that curious triumphant moment of discovering his true self in drag. The big trouble with *The Ritz* is that it is neither a fully articulated Lester film nor a faithfully adapted McNally play. But there is enough of Lester's feeling and McNally's flair to make it a worthwhile entertainment."

Reprinted by permission of The Village Voice.
Copyright © The Village Voice, Inc., 1976.

Film Information, 9/76 (p. 6)
Unsigned

"In Richard Lester's new movie, based on the hit Broadway comedy by Terrence McNally, the farcical elements of the stage play become overblown and exaggerated. Jack Weston escapes the murderous clutches of his Mafioso brother-in-law by hiding out in a gay bathhouse in New York City. Populated by such diverse types as Googie Gomez (Rita Moreno), a would-be singer trying to make it into the big time, F. Murray Abraham as an eager-but-often-rejected playmate, and an amateur detective hired by Stiller who talks in a falsetto, the establishment begins to make Weston more nervous than Stiller did. When his wife (Kaye Ballard) and Stiller arrive, the already-frantic happenings become even more slapstick. Lester allows his actors to run wild, always going for the easy joke at the expense of subtlety. He substitutes burlesque stage mannerisms for his usual frenetic camera and quick cutting . . ."

©Film Information, 1976.

Monthly Film Bulletin, December 1976 (p. 256)
John Pym

". . . *The Ritz* is above all redolent with waspish self-parody. Instead of developing this or playing off its incidental details, Lester for the most part keeps his camera on and tells the story through Jack Weston's ingenuous Procio, whose essentially straight attitude to the goings-on in the bathhouse eventually rubs off on the viewer who is treated not as a confidential accomplice, but rather, like Procio himself, a faintly embarrassed outsider. Lester's heavy hand cannot, however, completely dispel the gutsy exuberance of McNally's script. Rita Moreno, in particular, is a consistent gum-chewing pleasure, whether struggling with the American language . . . or, best of all, losing a shoe during a brilliantly awful rendition of 'Everytin's Comin' Op Rossses.' ''

©Monthly Film Bulletin, 1976.

Los Angeles Times, 10/6/76 (Pt. IV, p. 1)
Charles Champlin

'' . . . By some miracle of common sense, the original cast of Terrence McNally's *The Ritz* was hired, with two exceptions in lesser roles, for the movie version that Richard Lester has directed.

Accordingly, the strength and chief attraction of *The Ritz* is that it centers on two of the most flamboyantly entertaining and skillful comedy performances of the year, with another two or three supporting roles of nearly equal zest and brilliance.

Jack Weston is a bumbling Brooklyn goon trying to find refuge from a murder-minded brother-in-law in a homosexual bathhouse in Manhattan. Rita Moreno is an off-key but fanatically determined Puerto Rican singer and dancer hoping to be discovered in the bathhouse night club, just as Bette Midler was at the real-life Continental Baths . . .

McNally's farce is brilliantly plotted, achieving confrontations of crazy but logical complication. The stage set was three levels with dozens of doors. The movie has some (few) slow patches, when the close-up defeats the lovely sense of simultaneity a staged farce has. But the funniest moments are deliriously funny, and those star turns are caviar . . .''

©Los Angeles Times, 1976.

The Sunday Times (London), 12/19/76 (p. 27)
Alan Brien

'' . . . As well as the aggrieved hippo of Weston, who is a delight throughout, and Rita Moreno, a kind of Carmen Miranda in female form, at once agreeably lewd and ludicrous, there is a riotous selection of assorted torsos embodying every kind of homo swinger, all weirdly, and rather innocently deployed, at least on camera. About two-thirds of the way through, like all action directors, Richard Lester hits that critical point in his bathhouse follies where he must decide whether to wind up or wind down the merry-go-round. Perhaps the pace had never been really fast enough. Nevertheless, *The Ritz*, a British film based on a Broadway original, keeps on whirling.''

©The Sunday Times, 1976.

The Times (London), 12/17/76 (p. 15)
David Robinson

'' . . . Terrence McNally's script provides a few good jokes along the line, and Richard Lester occasionally retrieves them, though he does not al-

ways avoid a rather cheaply condescending send-up of homosexuals (for which campers-up like F. Murray Abraham must take much of the blame).

There is the consolation of some nicely styled comic performances. Jack Weston goes through the gamut of misery and bewilderment, trying vainly, the while, to hide himself within a disintegrating raven-hued wig. Paul B. Price is funny as the good-naturedly obsessed little man who will cheerfully hatchet his way through any door to get at a fat man; Treat Williams, the falsetto detective, has a very promising line in poker-face comedy; and Bessie Love has a nice walk-on role as the baths' White Rabbit lady accountant . . .''

©The Times, 1976.

RIVER NIGER, THE

Director: *Krishna Shah*. Screenplay: *Joseph A. Walker*. Based on the play by Mr. Walker. Producers: *Sidney Beckerman, Ike Jones*. Photography: *Michael Margules*. Editor: *Irving Lerner*. Music: *War*. Distributor: *Cine Artists Pictures*. Running time 105 minutes. New York opening April 14, 1976, at several theatres. Classification: R.

Mattie Williams: *Cicely Tyson*. Johnny Williams: *James Earl Jones*. Dr. Dudley Stanton: *Lou Gossett*. Jeff Williams: *Glynn Turman*. Big Moe Hayes: *Roger E. Mosley*. Ann Vanderguild: *Jonelle Allen*. Grandma Brown: *Hilda Haynes*. Chips: *Theodore Wilson*. Skeeter: *Charles Weldon*. Al: *Ralph Wilcox*. Gail: *Shirley Jo Finney*. Police Lieutenant: *Ed Crick*. Policeman: *Tony Burton*.

Films in Review, 4/76 (p. 241)
Charles Phillips Reilly

'' . . . Krishna Shah's direction lags at times, particularly in handling the lesser characters in Joseph Walker's screenplay of his Tony Award winning play. This results in most of the acting being only adequate . . .

The movie, however, is uplifted by the magnificent performances of Jones and Tyson. Mr. Jones has the physique and manner to suit his role of African chieftain and patriarch and is utterly believable as the creator of the poem 'I Am the River Niger,' a paean to the Black race. Miss Tyson con-

continued on next page

continued from previous page

tinues to be an actress transcending race here as the Black woman to whom suffering comes as a grace from God: her final expletive on which the film ends is the expression of her despair in her determination to see the wishes of 'her man' honored. *The River Niger* is tough on the young Black: Jeff doesn't hesitate to use muscle on his 'friends' who include a hood, a dope fiend, a pervert. Only Johnny and Mattie's sacrifice give their lives meaning. Cicely Tyson and James Earl Jones, we salute you."

© Films in Review, 1976.

New York Post, 4/15/76 (p. 18)
Frank Rich

"*The River Niger* . . . has intentions that are almost unique in our movies right now, for it attempts to deal seriously with the lives of black people in contemporary urban America. Sadly enough, the execution of those intentions is another story; *The River Niger* is simply flooded with incompetence, and it has the sure potential to bore moviegoers of all races out of their skulls . . .

. . . Krishna Shah, the East Indian director responsible for the film, has put together an almost oblique collage of unfocused family anecdotes, misplaced reaction shots, unmotivated comings and goings, and gimmicky freeze frames . . .

. . . While the cast tries hard to fill in the gaps, the fractionalized editing style of the film often makes you feel that the actors performed their roles in relay rather than in concert . . ."

Reprinted by Permission of New York Post.
© 1976, New York Post Corporation.

Los Angeles Times, 4/7/76 (Pt. IV, p. 22)
Kevin Thomas

"Joseph A. Walker's award-winning play, *The River Niger*, which Walker himself has adapted for the screen . . . has the ingredients for a powerful stage drama, but its intense, fullblown theatricality is so at odds with the ultra-realistic manner in which it has been filmed that credibility is at best intermittent. However, Walker has provided a large, fine cast some glorious moments under Krishna Shah's impassioned direction . . .

Performances are indeed vivid, with Jones most commanding (though not very sympathetic) and Cicely Tyson likewise as his devoted, cancerstricken wife. Lou Gossett is their loyal physician friend, and Shirley Jo Finney is especially impressive as Mosley's loving girlfriend.

The River Niger is best when it concentrates on Turman and his aspirations, worst in its selfindulgent hatred of whites . . ."

© Los Angeles Times, 1976.

New York Magazine, 4/26/76 (p. 72)
John Simon

"*The River Niger* is, I am sorry to say, another incendiary, white-hating movie. The script is by Joseph A. Walker, from his own prizewinning play of 1972 . . .

Now, I myself was somewhat taken in by the play version of *Niger*. But the film is an oversimplification of it, and, though the performances are good, lacks the ensemble playing that Douglas Turner Ward and the Negro Ensemble Company were able to impose on it . . .

The acting is mostly accomplished, though differences in acting styles militate against that tightknit atmosphere the stage cast was able to convey. James Earl Jones, although perhaps a bit too young for the part, is a splendid Johnny, managing to unify the character's disparate components into believable and touching humanity. As Mattie, Cicely Tyson is also very good. . . ."

© 1976 by the NYM Corp. Reprinted with the permission of NEW YORK Magazine.

Film Information, 4/76 (p. 3)
Frederic A. Brussat

"Joseph A. Walker's award-winning 1972 play is rich in both theme and characterization. It is at once a touching family drama, an exploration of the meaning of black identity, and a moving parable about the nature of love. Although the language is gritty, and the story line at times untidy, *The River Niger* possesses a blazing intensity . . .

The performances in this film version of *The River Niger* are superlative. First and foremost, there is the passionate and convincing depiction of Johnny by James Earl Jones. Cicely Tyson brings to the role of Mattie an understated yet persuasive power. Lou Gossett is excellent as Dr. Stanton. Glynn Turman's portrayal of Jeff sizzles with an urgency and a beauty all its own. Good in support are Roger E. Mosley as the gang leader, Jonelle Allen as Ann, and Hilda Haynes as Grandma. These sharply realized characterizations are further enhanced by the tight direction of Krishna Shah and the music of War."

© Film Information, 1976

ROBIN AND MARIAN

Director: *Richard Lester.* Screenplay: *James Goldman.* Producer: *Denis O'Dell.* Photography: *David Watkin.* Editor: *John Victor Smith.* Music: *John Barry.* Production: *Ray*

Stark-Richard Shepherd. Distributor: *Columbia Pictures*. Running time 112 minutes. New York opening March 11, 1976, at the Radio City Music Hall. Classification: PG.

Robin Hood: *Sean Connery*. Maid Marian: *Audrey Hepburn*. Sheriff of Nottingham: *Robert Shaw*. King Richard: *Richard Harris*. Little John: *Nicol Williamson*. Will Scarlett: *Denholm Elliott*. Sir Ranulf: *Kenneth Haigh*. Friar Tuck: *Ronnie Barker*. King John: *Ian Holm*.

See Volume 1 for additional reviews

The Times (London), 5/28/76 (p. 11)
Philip French

"Richard Lester's *Robin and Marian*, a picture about being middle-aged in the Middle Ages, and a forceful demonstration of the old saying that you can't go home again, especially if your home was built of twigs in Sherwood Forest and you've spent 20 fruitless years slaughtering Saracens in the Holy Land . . .
Robin and Marian is an elegiac tragi-comedy, sensitively performed, well photographed and all very modest. Unlike some other Lester pictures, the jokes arise naturally from the dramatic situations and are rarely ends in themselves, while the grimness of medieval life is a part of the dramatic fabric, not a matter for special comment. Yet ultimately there is a sense of strain about this work, a contemporary self-consciousness that distances us from the action in a non-Brechtian way--which is to say that we are neither powerfully caught up in the events or placed in an intelligently critical position in relation to them . . . "

© The Times, 1976.

The Sunday Times (London), 5/30/76 (p. 37)
Alan Brien

"James Goldman's script is replete with good ideas. The crusades are over, the pillaging and the slaughter and the false heroics, with Richard Harris's Richard the Lionheart exposed as a psychopathic poseur. Robin Hood (Sean Connery) and Little John (Nicol Williamson) return home after 20 years, like ageing gunfighters coming back to a tamed West, half lying legend, half exploded myth.
Both in dialogue and direction, the ironic humor of the situation is given full play . . .
So far, so good. But Messrs. Goldman and Lester tend to overdo their self-conscious sophistication, with the laughter up their sleeves growing more and more hollow. The backgrounds and emotions are

realistic--'You never wrote,' complains Audrey Hepburn's Abbess Marion; 'I don't know how,' explains the old Robin. But the action thereby grows increasingly less spectacular and epic . . . "

© The Sunday Times, 1976.

Monthly Film Bulletin, 5/76 (p. 105)
Geoff Brown

" . . . the film is quasi-serious, its thematic concerns signposted with ominous lack of subtlety by the opening images of apples--first golden and then withered. As James Goldman's glibly phrased script repeatedly points out, even legendary characters begin to grow old and change . . . One has no complaints about the performances: Connery has become peculiarly adept at playing rugged, restless period adventurers (and the liability of his Scots accent is ingeniously reduced by making all the other outlaws sport one); Audrey Hepburn's screen comeback is refreshingly dignified, and Nicol Williamson makes a particularly fine (and surprisingly restrained) Little John, dotingly fond of his master. But acting can only partially redeem the weaknesses of a script burdened with sagging dramatic tension and fuzzy characterisations-- especially as the director himself proves insufficient support."

© Monthly Film Bulletin, 1976.

Saturday Review, 4/17/76 (p. 44)
Judith Crist

" . . . Well, settle down to a story as satisfying as any that came before, and far, far richer in nuance, detail, and pertinence, thanks to two masters of the genre--screenwriter James Goldman (*The Lion in Winter*) and director Richard Lester (*The Three Musketeers* and *The Four Musketeers*) . . .
These are lions in autumn. Sean Connery's Robin, not glibly articulate, aware of waste and suffering, but slow to settle for the glory day that makes a life; Nicol Williamson's Little John, not blind to realities but merely without choice in his loyalty; Richard Harris's Richard, cruel and curt and crafty; Robert Shaw's sheriff, shrewd, patient, cognizant of his foeman's worth. And Audrey Hepburn's Marian--as lovely as ever with the seasoning of years, her eyes a testament to passion preserved, soft enough to dream of life in Sherwood (but now thinking of a two-room bower, of a bed with blankets, something on the floor, a chest for clothing), and hard enough to give a legend eternal life.
This is, in fact, what this immaculate production accomplishes, with subtle underlining from John

continued on next page

continued from previous page

Barry's score. And it is a legend in itself, of heroes who grow old in flesh but not in spirit, who can still have a glory day . . . ''

© Judith Crist, 1976.

Films in Review, 4/76 (p. 241)
Charles Phillips Reilly

"Even a hero like Robin Hood (Sean Connery) and a heroine like Maid Marian (Audrey Hepburn) find it difficult to face their own mortality in this film of romantic decay written by James Goldman and directed by Richard Lester.

Disillusioned with the Crusades and the dissolute death of Richard the Lionhearted (Richard Harris), Robin returns after a 20-year absence with Little John (Nicol Williamson) to a Sherwood Forest which is the same yet different . . .

Scenarist Goldman has introduced elements of Tristan and Isolde into the adventures of the one-time young and handsome Robin Hood, even to a fatal cup administered by Marian to the wounded hero. Unfortunately she has no liebestod to sing, but only an apostrophe to love which Miss Hepburn affectedly recites.

Director Lester pulls no punches. His first shot, of three almost green apples which quickly become speckled and rotten, tells us he's dealing unmercifully with the two greatest taboos of our culture: old age and death. His film partially succeeds through a sometimes witty, sometimes boring script but mainly through a fine performance by Connery who is convincing as the grey-bearded, balding Robin, seeking just one more gaudy day and finding it.''

© Films in Review, 1976.

Film Information, 4/76 (p. 3)
Eugene A. Schneider

" . . . No one who knows Richard Lester's work (*A Hard Day's Night*, *The Knack*, *Petulia*, *The Three Musketeers*, part I and part II, to mention only a few of his films) would expect him to deal in traditional style with Robin Hood, the revered 12th century model of courage and generosity who robbed the rich to give to the poor. And purists who object to meddling with legends may find *Robin and Marian* a confused melange of ideas and gags.

As Robin, Sean Connery is splendid. He continues to shake his James Bond image, which he had already begun to do successfully in *The Wind and the Lion* and *The Man Who Would Be King*. Ms. Hepburn, who has not appeared in a film since *Wait Until Dark* (1967), shows that she has not lost her ability to command the audience's rapt attention. The two performers are consistently convincing

and it is to their credit that they manage to sustain the film's appealing love story in the midst of some Lesterian excesses . . . ''

© Film Information, 1976.

ROCKY

Director: *John G. Avildsen.* Screenplay: *Sylvester Stallone.* Producers: *Irwin Winkler, Robert Chartoff.* Photography: *James Crabe.* Editor: *Richard Halsey.* Music: *Bill Conti.*
TV Commentator: *Diana Lewis*
Distributor: *United Artists.* Running time 121 minutes. New York opening November 21, 1976, at the Cinema II Theatre. Classification: PG.

Rocky: *Sylvester Stallone.* Adrian: *Talia Shire.* Paulie: *Burt Young.* Apollo: *Carl Weathers.* Mickey: *Burgess Meredith.* Jergens: *Thayer David.* Gazzo: *Joe Spinell.* Mike: *Jimmy Gambina.*

Films in Review, January 1977 (p. 56)
Marcia Magill

"In a year notably lacklustre in fine American films, along comes United Artists' winner, *Rocky.* A joyous evocation of man's indomitable spirit, it stars sometime boxer-actor Sylvester Stallone, who also penned the outstanding screenplay (in three days, we are told). At the same time he wisely refused to let others suggested for the lead (James Caan, Burt Reynolds) have the starring role. In its honesty, unpretentiousness, and stark social realism, it will remind many of an updated *Marty* . . .

Under John G. Avildsen's sure direction, and James Crabe's breathtaking photography, Rocky does more than go the distance. He reaffirms our faith that good scripts can be written and good films can be made. And, despite overwhelming odds, Cinderella can still go to the ball. *Rocky* is a knockout.''

© Films in Review, 1977

New York Times, 11/22/76 (p. C19)
Vincent Canby

" . . . Rocky is a young man who, by day, is a small-time Mafia collector, the sort of fellow who shows his heart of gold by hesitating to break a client's thumbs, and at night pursues a third-rate boxing career in fleabag sporting arenas.

Under the none too decisive direction of John G. Avildsen (*Joe, Save the Tiger*), Mr. Stallone is all over *Rocky* to such an extent it begins to look like a vanity production . . . It's as if Mr. Stallone had studied the careers of Martin Scorsese and Francis Ford Coppola and then set out to copy the wrong things.

The screenplay of *Rocky* is purest Hollywood make-believe of the 1930s, but there would be nothing wrong with that, had the film been executed with any verve . . .

The person who comes off best is Miss Shire, Mr. Coppola's sister who made brief, effective appearances in the two *Godfather* films. She's a real actress, genuinely touching and funny as an incipient spinster who comes late to sexual life. She's so good, in fact, that she almost gives weight to Mr. Stallone's performance, which is the large hole in the center of the film . . . "

© 1976 by the New York Times Company.
Reprinted by permission.

New York Magazine, 11/29/76 (p. 70)
John Simon

". . . Even the smallest roles are well taken, and above all of them floats, securely and gracefully, Sylvester Stallone as Rocky. With the sharply etched yet always a bit sleepy face of a Roman patrician misplaced in a Philadelphia gutter, his eyelids almost always at half-mast, his voice see-sawing between hopeful entreaty and ironic resignation, Stallone weaves through the film with a kind of indolent swagger. One restrains one's physical strength, he seems to be saying with gentle self-mockery; one comes to terms with life by keeping up a steady, bantering patter. But when the right woman or the goddess Fortune beckons, one deploys one's every decent resource to win. Rocky is the most likable and unaggressive of punks, and, certainly, an original. Stallone has imagined him with intense, bristling love, and plays him with relaxed affection . . . "

© 1976 by the NYM Corp. Reprinted with
the permission of NEW YORK Magazine.

Village Voice, 11/22/76 (p. 61)
Andrew Sarris

"The American Dream has resurfaced in Ethnic Drag. This bicentennial bonbon from Philadelphia, of all places, owes much of its snap and sting to its lead actor-scenarist, Sylvester Stallone, who has written and played the character of Rocky Balboa, the 'Italian Stallion,' as if to make up for many past injustices. Thus, Stallone can be considered, in old Cahiers parlance, to be the auteur of *Rocky*, whereas director John Avildsen is merely the meteur-en-scene . . .

. . . Whereas Stallone's script sets out to be romantic and heroic, Avildsen's direction strains to be realistic and satiric. Fortunately, Avildsen is ulti-

mately overcome by the sheer good spirits of the enterprise, much as he was in *W. W. and the Dixie Dancekings*, which is why, despite all the blood and gore in the climactic fight scenes, *Rocky* ends as a joyous 'up' experience . . . "

Reprinted by permission of The Village Voice.
Copyright © The Village Voice, Inc., 1976.

Saturday Review, 11/27/76 (p. 40)
Judith Crist

"The pop-culture present is exploited to excellent effect in *Rocky*, a delightful human comedy that will undoubtedly wind up as the sleeper of this movie year. Very much a latter-day *Marty* in its romantic story of two 'losers,' it is a strong, unsentimental, and deeply stirring affirmation of human aspiration, of strength of character, and of simple decency . . .

Stallone, whom you may recall as the big, dumb marriage patsy in *The Lords of Flatbush*, portrays, in the title role, a blue-collar Philadelphia slugger, a boxer who's all heart and no steam, a neighborhood loan shark's enforcer with more compassion than muscle, a man very much aware of his own limitations and of the possibilities of others . . .

The characters are as penetrating as the Philadelphia street atmosphere, with Talia Shire, hitherto *The Godfather* sister, radiant in her flowering under the warmth of respectful love, a fitting complement to the emerging dignity of Stallone as a self-described 'nobody' becoming an individual in his own eyes . . . Packed with moments of comedy, perception, and sensitivity, *Rocky* is a sincere, rousing little film that raises the spirits and gladdens the heart."

© Judith Crist, 1976.

Newsweek, 11/29/76 (p. 113)
Janet Maslin

". . . This is one of the few recent movies (*One Flew Over the Cuckoo's Nest* was another) to approach its subject with such black-and-white moral certitude that viewers know exactly which side they're on and don't mind at all the blatant way in which they've been manipulated. Crisply directed by John Avildsen, *Rocky* so skillfully slaps a modern, street-wise veneer onto one of the half-dozen oldest stories in the world that it can freely traffic in sentimentality while seeming to hang tough . . .

Throughout, Stallone is funny, immensely likable, and so consistently monolithic that his acting ability is difficult to assess: at times he seems to be giving not so much a full performance as a brilliant monologue. By the time the heavyweight bout takes place, *Rocky* has become completely engaging . . . "

© Newsweek, Inc. 1976
reprinted by permission.

continued on next page

continued from previous page

Rocky (Sylevster Stallone) is interviewed for TV by Diana Lewis as he trains for the championship in a meat-packing plant in **Rocky**, Academy Award winner for Best Picture of the Year. Stallone also wrote the screenplay for the film.

Christian Science Monitor, 11/22/76 (p. 27)
David Sterritt

". . . *Rocky* is a deeply humane look at human nature, a compassionate travelogue through byways of the human condition that many would prefer to ignore. It is also the toughest, most tender, most gripping American movie of the year . . .

Mr. Stallone's Rocky is as near-perfect a performance as I've seen in years. It is no easy part, this jocular oaf with hard hands, a soft heart, and a love of words matched only by his lack of anything much to say. Stallone hits scarcely a false note, and deserves every accolade.

Similar praise goes to Burt Young, who devastatingly plays Paulie, an inarticulate misfit with a last-ditch resistance that anyone could envy. Joe Spinell also stands out as the hoodlum Gazzo. Talia Shire starts too deliberately mousy as Rocky's girlfriend, but comes movingly to life as her character unfolds . . ."

Reprinted by permission from The Christian
Science Monitor © 1976.
The Christian Science Publishing Society.
All rights reserved.

New York Post, 11/22/76 (p. 18)
Frank Rich

"*Rocky* . . . is a Horatio Alger story about a strug-

gling prizefighter, and it believes in values that most movies don't believe in anymore. It believes in the American dream. It believes in the essential goodness of people and in the almighty power of human will. It even believes in happy endings.

Which is to say that *Rocky* is almost 100 percent schmaltz—and yet it's honest schmaltz, not cynical schmaltz, and that makes all the difference in the world . . .

Rocky is most enjoyable, however, if you don't examine the story too closely—for even by the standards of fairy tales, it strains logic . . .

. . . Stallone has given himself a great role, and his acting is well up to his script's demands . . .

The movie's direction, I'm sorry to say, could be much better. John Avildsen—whose *Joe* and *Save the Tiger* are among the more smarmy movies in recent years—has an instinct for making serious emotions look tawdry . . ."

Reprinted by Permission of New York Post.
© 1976, New York Post Corporation.

New Leader, 11/22/76 (p. 28)
Robert Asahina

"What ultimately enables the movie in its best moments to transcend all the cliches and avoid lapsing into a lame parable about reverse discrimination . . . is its strong and authentic expression of artistic personality . . . Following writers like Mailer, he sees the ring as an arena for the dramatic unfolding of the self's possibilities; the artist's own struggle for identity finds its perfect 'objective correlative' in the figure of the boxer, who submits himself to the most naked and brutal test possible in a civilized society. The script is so sincerely conceived by writer Stallone and the hero is given such animation by actor Stallone that Rocky ceases to be simply a stock character and becomes the artistic embodiment of his creator's persona.

Although this cannot obscure the film's lapses, it infuses *Rocky* with a naive spirit that is particularly refreshing in our age of jaded, self-conscious cinema . . ."

Reprinted with permission from
The New Leader, 1976.
© The American Labor Conference
on International Affairs, Inc.

Film Information, December 1976 (p. 2)
Bea Rothenbeuchner

"*Rocky* opens with a pan shot from a wall mosaic of a Christ-like head down to an arena where boxers are pummeling each other. Although Rocky belongs in this tough, sweaty world, he is not the hero one expects. He is gentle, loves birds, animals, and a plain girl too introverted to go out with him—but when at long last she does, the change in her is for the better. Rocky cares about people. And Rocky prays; before his big fight we see him kneeling in front of a washstand in the men's room.

An unlikely story for the violent 1970s . . . but Stallone's screenplay has heart and humor and a believable hero. Stallone is right as Rocky. And John G. Avildsen, known for his ability to create low-budget successes (*Joe*, *Save the Tiger*, *W. W. and the Dixie Dancekings*) was the right choice for director. He gives the film a strong feeling of authenticity, playing up the gritty urban environment while bringing out the humanity of the characters . . ."

© Film Information, 1976.

SAILOR WHO FELL FROM GRACE WITH THE SEA, THE

Director, Screenplay: *Lewis John Carlino*. Based on the novel by Yukio Mishima. Producer: *Martin Poll*. Photography: *Douglas Slocombe*. Editor: *Anthony Gibbs*. Music: *John Mandel*. Distributor: *Avco Embassy Pictures*. Running time 105 minutes. New York opening April 11, 1976, at the Coronet Theatre. Classification: R.

Anne Osborne: *Sarah Miles*. Jim Cameron: *Kris Kristofferson*. Jonathan Osborne: *Jonathan Kahn*. Mrs. Palmer: *Margo Cunningham*. Chief: *Earl Rhodes*.

Newsweek, 4/19/76 (p. 95)
Katrine Ames

"*The Sailor Who Fell From Grace With the Sea* drowned while making the crossing from the printed page to celluloid . . . Writer-director Lewis John Carlino preserves much of the plot (though he moves it from Japan to England), but corrupts the tale by reducing it to a muddled simplicity.

Sarah Miles rather desperately plays Anne, a widow who lives with her precocious son, Jonathan (a role undertaken with an odd mixture of impassivity and discomfort by Jonathan Kahn). Into their quiet, ordered life comes a rugged American ship's officer, Jim (self-consciously portrayed by Kris Kristofferson), who quickly becomes Anne's bedfellow and a hero to Jonathan. Jim decides to stay on land––a course that meets with disapproval from Jonathan and his pals, who have formed a secret society to uphold what they deem the 'perfect order' of the world, no matter what the cost. As cats belong in the jungle, the boys reason, so does a sailor belong on the sea. Their scheme to return Jim to his rightful place and thus to the sea's graces, so chilling and tense in the book, is now merely grotesque. The movie pounds the audience with repetition and heavy-handed symbolism. It is only slightly redeemed in the taut performance of Earl Rhodes, who plays the leader of Jonathan's group as a brilliant, icy despot."

© Newsweek, Inc. 1976
reprinted by permission.

Women's Wear Daily, 4/12/76 (p. 13)
Christopher Sharp

"One would think that a movie combining the acting of Sarah Miles and a story by Yukio Mishima might be at best an excellent film, or at the very least an average one. So it comes as a surprise that director and screenwriter Lewis John Carlino could so abuse his rich raw materials and give us a show as unpleasant as it is empty.

The Sailor Who Fell From Grace With the Sea brings Kris Kristofferson and Miles together in a way that is best put by Carlino's dialog. Before a critical transition she says, 'I've never had a sailor.' He says, 'I've never had a lady.' This is one of the better exchanges in the show . . .

The best thing that can be said about the film is that Carlino juxtaposes the boring and the nauseating scenes with a certain equanimity."

© Women's Wear Daily, 1976.

continued on next page

continued from previous page

New York Magazine, 4/26/76 (p. 72)
John Simon

"*The Sailor Who Fell From Grace With the Sea*, Lewis John Carlino's film based on Yukio Mishima's novella, is very pretty to look at and makes absolutely no sense. It concerns a small gang of boys in their early teens who kill a sailor about to marry the widowed mother of one of them--kill him because they feel he has betrayed the perfect order of things by abandoning the perilous, glorious sea for land-locked, bourgeois safety . . .

There are some compensations. Besides the already mentioned scenic beauties, there is also the extraordinary sensual appeal and splendid performance of Sarah Miles, than whom no one has ever better conveyed naked sexual longing. Her masturbation scene, for example, is deeply erotic, without becoming in the least bit tasteless . . .

Kris Kristofferson, who has lost so much weight that he seems to be rattling around in his own clothes, plays the sailor without any expression, any suggestion of inner life . . ."

© 1976 by the NYM Corp. Reprinted with the permission of NEW YORK Magazine

Christian Science Monitor, 5/5/76 (p. 22)
David Sterritt

"*The Sailor Who Fell From Grace With the Sea* is the most lyrical title so far this year. The look of this new movie is lyrical, too, but the story underneath is not so benign . . .

. . . Lewis John Carlino's movie version . . . follows Mishima quite literally despite the Westernization of the setting. The result has its own poisonous power, though it lacks Mishima's sinewy rawness, and seems too flabby and gratuitous to function as a cautionary fable.

The people in *Sailor* are generally effective, from Kris Kristofferson as the bland hero to the strong actress who plays the housemaid, with a face that evokes one of those statues on Easter Island. But as the story draws to its understatedly grim conclusion, you may find yourself wondering why you took this trip after all. The movie, for all its dazzling pictures of sea and shore, offers little in the way of an answer."

Reprinted by permission from the Christian Science Monitor © 1976.
The Christian Science Publishing Society.
All rights reserved.

Saturday Review, 5/15/76 (p. 52)
Judith Crist

" . . . What Carlino, as author as well as director, has done is take the 'polished pebble' of Mishima's exquisitely internal and understated story and embed it in sludge, literalizing and thereby exploiting all that was merely suggested, turning what was an exploration of the obsessed psyche and the 'objective' heart into a pretentious little horror story . . .

Sarah Miles, the embodiment of erotic femininity . . . is lovely as the widow, and her seemingly endless couplings with Kris Kristofferson--Kansas-born solid, and prosaic to match, as the sailor--are, initially at least, lyrical and sensual. Jonathan Kahn, as the troubled and jealous son, and Earl Rhodes, as his obviously psychotic chief, are as thoroughly abominable as their roles require. But neither good performance nor exquisite scenery (all was filmed on location) can hide the ugliness at the core."

© Judith Crist, 1976.

New York Post, 4/12/76 (p. 38)
Frank Rich

" . . . Carlino makes his directorial debut with this film, and while he's had the good sense to trust Douglas Slocombe with the cinematography (Slocombe makes Dartmouth look like the most ravishing vacation spot in the world) his cinematic intelligence ends there. Carlino has assembled the movie almost entirely with dissolves--a device that, when used with this vengeance, can make a film look like mush--and he's loaded the picture with arty images (i.e. a stuffed iguana) that don't come off.

He has even been unable to make the Miles-Kristofferson sex scenes erotic--despite the fact that he seems to have taken painstaking efforts to duplicate the mood of the supercharged lovemaking Nicolas Roeg devised for Julie Christie and Donald Sutherland in *Don't Look Now*.

Carlino hasn't done well by his actors, either. Kristofferson . . . has never been so blank or enervated as he is here. Miss Miles is overheated and drippy . . ."

Reprinted by Permission of New York Post.
© 1976, New York Post Corporation.

Film Information, 5/76 (p. 4)
Robert E. A. Lee

"When beauty and horror are mixed, good drama can sometimes result. When tenderness and violence are juxtaposed, emotional tension increases. This happens in *The Sailor Who Fell From Grace With the Sea* . . .

Both Sarah Miles and Kris Kristofferson project an internal as well as an external attractiveness that makes them seem almost ideal as the romantic couple. Miss Miles is the essence of loneliness as the sensually starved widow. Kristofferson exudes a kind of soft and gentle masculinity. He proposes.

She accepts. But her son does not. And so the perfect love story is flawed by an outside force of diabolical dimensions. It causes a problem in drama when the characters are acted upon or manipulated through influences beyond their own control. They become merely victims of fate. We can say 'poor sailor' or 'poor widow,' but we are detached because we cannot identify with their struggle . . ."

© Film Information, 1976.

Monthly Film Bulletin, 8/76 (p. 172)
Tony Rayns

". . . the novel has a central kernel of interest (entirely consistent with Mishima's better work) in its sketch of a kind of unvoiced conspiracy: the defeated self-awareness of the adult characters unwittingly connives with the berserk idealism of the boys to lead to a grim but understated resolution whose poetic logic is flawless. This theme, isolated as it is in a virtually eventless psychological narrative, presents obvious difficulties for a film adaptation; it is symptomatic of Lewis John Carlino's dismal failure that it hardly even emerges as a theme in the present film, being eclipsed by more crucial problems at the levels of plotting, acting and basic conception . . ."

©Monthly Film Bulletin, 1976.

Los Angeles Times, 5/18/76 (Pt. IV, p. 7)
Charles Champlin

" . . . *Sailor* is told with portentous solemnity as if every lichened crevice were fraught with meaning. It is an extremely artificial parable recited with unwavering humorlessness, and it becomes a very odd exercise, reverential and bordering on the ridiculous.

According to producer Martin Poll, who also did *The Lion in Winter*, Mishima refused to have the story filmed with a Japanese setting. But the sea-change to the West of England is unhelpful, despite the respectful care of Carlino's adaptation . . .

Sailor is exquisitely pretty, photographed at Dartmouth on the English Channel by the masterful Douglas Slocombe, who helps you taste the salt air and feel that the sea really does have a majesty from whose grace a man could fall. The editing by Anthony Gibbs has the fine joinery of a Chippendale piece.

The only real performance is by Sarah Miles, and she has a warmth and vulnerability that is quite a change from the strident, neurotic bitterness of many of her earlier roles. The Kristofferson part is hardly a part at all. He is a bearded symbol, a bit unnatural and uncomfortable at being so far from himself . . ."

© Los Angeles Times, 1976.

Village Voice, 6/28/76 (p. 136)
Andrew Sarris

"Writer-director Lewis John Carlino and cinematographer Douglas Slocombe have collaborated on some beautiful landscapes, against which an unconvincing scenario is enacted. The transposition of the late Yukio Mishima's pitiless fable of purity and horror from Yokohama to Dartmouth makes little sociological sense. Hence, the four little boys who first dismember a cat, and then, ultimately, a sailor, for their having lapsed from functional grace, sound like pretentious little twits in English, whereas, in Japanese, who can tell. So much for the foreground of the film. In the background are Sarah Miles, as the mother of one of the twits, and Kris Kristofferson, as the sailor who falls from grace with the sea by falling into bed with the widowed mother. Even critics who couldn't stomach the four twits have given good notices to Miss Miles and Mr. Kristofferson both in and out of the sack. I disagree. It is not that the two players lack the requisite sensuality for their roles, but rather that they are dramatically and psychologically disconnected from any kind of social power source . . ."

Reprinted by permission of The Village Voice.
Copyright © The Village Voice, Inc., 1976.

ST. IVES

Director: *J. Lee Thompson*. Screenplay: *Barry Beckerman*. Based on the novel THE PROCANE CHRONICLE by "Oliver Bleeck" (Ross Thomas). Producers: *Pancho Kohner, Stanley Canter*. Photography: *Lucien Ballard*. Editor: *Michael Anderson*. Music: *Lalo Schifrin*. Distributor: *Warner Bros*. Running time 94 minutes. Los Angeles opening August 25, 1976, at several theatres. Classification: PG.

Players: *Charles Bronson, John Houseman, Jacqueline Bisset, Maximilian Schell, Harry Guardino, Dana Elcar, Harris Yulin, Michael Lerner, Dick O'Neill, Elisha Cook, Val Bisoglio, Burr De Benning, Daniel J. Travanti.*

New York Magazine, 9/6/76 (p. 76)
John Simon

"*St. Ives* is supposed to be a sophisticated specimen of the mystery genre, in which a crime

continued on next page

continued from previous page

columnist turned would-be novelist is enmeshed in a sinister tissue of plots and counterplots involving eccentric millionaires, murderous lovelies, missing documents of an incriminating nature . . .

Yet the writing is surpassed in platitudinousness by the directing of J. Lee Thompson, with shot after shot coming from the point of view of an unseen or barely glimpsed figure spying on, or shooting at, the protagonist. There is also much crosscutting of the sort where the only events you care less about than those cut from are the ones cut to. The director permits himself even what may be the hoariest cliche of all: cutting from a woman getting into bed with a man to a shot of exploding fireworks. In the end, you just sit there in a theater festooned with disbelief, and every line spoken and plot turn taken inspires mad giggles . . ."

©1976 by the NYM Corp. Reprinted with the permission of NEW YORK Magazine.

Monthly Film Bulletin, 8/76 (p. 175)
John Pym

"*St. Ives* begins with promising vigor . . . The intriguing possibilities . . . quickly vanish, however, as the listless principals resign themselves to the plot's vacuous predictability, Bronson with his characteristic dogged passivity and Houseman, complete with startling orange hair, by the sententious stress he appears to place on every first syllable. J. Lee Thompson's strained effort to vitalize the unprepossessing story often overwhelms the material: titles breathlessly flash the exact time of day; familiar high-angle shots signal the menacing approach of a man watching Ray; and during the climactic heist at the drive-in theatre, the same clip from an interminable Western stampede appears again and again, and ultimately compels all attention . . ."

©Monthly Film Bulletin, 1976.

Los Angeles Times, 8/25/76 (Pt. IV, p. 16)
Charles Champlin

". . . the direction by J. Lee Thompson is so paralytically calm that it is as if he had recorded the first reading only. Lucien Ballard's pictures of rich L.A., poor L.A. are handsomely atmospheric and Lalo Schifrin has contributed a hardworking musical score.

It is just that although Bronson is here cast as a public lip, you might say, instead of a private eye, *St. Ives* is the kind of ricky-dick fare television spins out by the hours every week, not any better but not worse.

The violence is restrained, which is nice, and the production . . . is solid and decorative. Bronson continues to be a strong and attractive figure, even

when he has as little to do as stroll through this charade."

©Los Angeles Times, 1976.

New York Post, 9/2/76 (p. 19)
Archer Winsten

". . . It's a bit repetitious, but the circumstances do vary. Bronson stalls about in that walk of his which is unique, narrowly escaping death on numerous occasions, and always going back for more. That's one thing you have to accept in crime thriller heroes. They know the author isn't going to kill them no matter what the odds or how many guns are aimed at their heart. It would be the end of the story ahead of time . . .

The action takes less than a week, but it's intense. Bronson handles his frequent emergencies without losing his cool.

J. Lee Thompson directed the Barry Beckerman script, with what seems to be an absolutely straight face. When it's all over you may still be wondering how they did it, which does make the mystification as complete as the deaths are final."

Reprinted by Permission of New York Post.
©1976, New York Post Corporation.

SALUT L'ARTISTE

Director: *Yves Robert.* Screenplay (French with English subtitles): *Jean-Loup Dabadie, Mr. Robert.* Executive Producers: *Alain Poire, Mr. Robert.* Photography: *Jean Penzer.* Music: *Vladimir Cosma.* Production: *Gaumont International.* Distributor: *Excel Film Group.* Running time 96 minutes. New York opening February 22, 1976, at the Baronet Theatre. Classification: None. Origin: France.

Nicholas: *Marcello Mastroianni.* Peggy: *Francoise Fabian.* Clement: *Jean Rochefort.* Elizabeth: *Carla Gravina.* Zeller: *Xavier Gelin.*

See Volume 1 for additional reviews

Los Angeles Times, 11/17/76 (Pt. IV, p. 1)
Charles Champlin

". . . *Salut L'Artiste (Hail, Artist)*, coauthored and

directed by Yves Robert, who did *The Tall Blond Man With One Black Shoe*, is an inviting and un-assuming romantic comedy starring Marcello Mastroianni as a middle-class actor living and working in Paris . . .

Like most good comedies, *Salut L'Artiste* carries a strong savor of reality and overtones of melancholy. Its jokes are jokes, all right, and we laugh a lot, but they are only slight extensions of the possible. They stop well short of the absurd.

It is the best role Mastroianni has had in some time, and he is an amusing and still affecting mean, sensual man, a far from tragic figure though one for whom the interior vita is not really dolce . . .''

©Los Angeles Times, 1976.

New Leader, 4/12/76 (p. 25)
Robert Asahina

" . . . The whole of *Salut L'Artiste* is thus less than the sum of its parts. The structure is simply too shaky to sustain either its length or its feeble gestures at significance. Still, if Robert cannot be credited for conception or execution, he cannot be faulted for the direction of his players. All perform exceptionally well. And Mastroianni, who has matured as an actor as he has gracefully grown older, nearly ceases the artless and distracting mugging (the curse of the Italian male star) that characterized many of his earlier performances. Indeed, the uniformly inspired acting manages to overcome the failures of the movie and powerfully evoke its major theme--the joy of role playing.''

Reprinted with permission from
The New Leader, 1976.
© The American Labor Conference
on International Affairs, Inc.

Film Information, 4/76 (p. 4)
David Bartholemew

" . . . Director Yves Robert has given an admirably light touch to the film. He emphasizes the opening day as an apt image of Mastroianni's life. So busy but running in place, the artist is less concerned with art than with working. Unconsciously, he has incorporated play-acting into his emotional life--giving a subtler meaning to the title. The women in his life realize this fact before he does ('You have an act for everyone--all bad,' says Fabian). Mastroianni brings off the role very nicely, and his comic talents are adroit, especially when playing against the suave type of screen lover he built his own career on.

Rochefort lends strong support as the friend who opts out of the busy struggle for an ad exec job. Gravina and Fabian are fine also, and the script allows them the respect and individuality missing from so many American movies today . . .''

© Film Information, 1976.

Nation, 3/13/76 (p. 317)
Robert Hatch

" . . . Mastroianni's limitation as an actor, I think, is that when he is not given material strong enough to engage fully his intelligence and sensibilities, he coasts through a film on his technical equipment, confident that the spectacle of Mastroianni doing his thing will satisfy the public. And since his bag of tricks is as well-stocked as that of any in the profession, he gets too many assignments that encourage him to play to the box office. It is a malady latent in many 'accomplished' actors, but I think it is fair to say that with Mastroianni you are too often given a performance rather than a characterization.

Salut L'Artiste almost caricatures the point. Not only is it a bit of paper pathos, tricked out with sprigs of irony, but it casts Mastroianni as a not quite successful actor who earns a frantic living by scampering about Paris from early morning to late at night, playing a movie extra here, doing a stage bit there, fitting a night-club comedy magic act into a spare hour, dubbing an animated cartoon in a funny voice at odd moments and trying by telephone calls and flying visits to keep his family and his mistress in states short of open rebellion. It is, as you can see, a part calling for heavy reliance on the bag of tricks . . .

About half way through the film, I decided that Mastroianni was sufficiently warmed up and ought to get started. Unfortunately, the 'laugh, clown, laugh' script gave him nothing to get started with, and he was still doing his exercises when the show ended.''

© The Nation, 1976.

SANDSTONE

Directors, Producers: *Jonathan Dana, Bunny Peters Dana*. Photography: *Patrick Darrin*, Editors: *Mr. Darrin. Mr. Dana, Ms. Dana*. Music: *Dennis Dragon*. Distributor: *Don Henderson Film*. Running time 80 minutes. Los Angeles opening May 5, 1976, at several theatres. Classification: X.

Los Angeles Times, 5/3/76 (Pt. IV, p. 16)
Linda Gross

" . . . *Sandstone* is a low-keyed and intelligent X-rated documentary about communal living and open marriage. The film was shot in seven weeks

continued on next page

continued from previous page

by a husband and wife team of documentary film-makers, Jonathan and Bunny Dana, who spent 18 months participating in the Sandstone experience.

What emerges is a portrait of a liberated life-style as well as an earnest investigation of the attitudes of the many different types of people who either regularly visit or live at Sandstone. Residents, who are neither self-conscious nor particularly photogenic, are filmed in the nude--working, cooking, balancing budgets, planning meals and dissecting the sexual and personality hangups of other group members . . .

Filmmakers Jonathan and Bunny Dana have comprehensively and sympathetically conveyed the ambience of *Sandstone*. The documentary, like the retreat, offers no real answers--only permission to experiment and an opportunity for openness."

© Los Angeles Times, 1976.

New York Post, 3/5/77 (p. 19)
Archer Winsten

". . . The point is made in conclusion that group marriage has something serious to be said in favor of it. Monogamy, conventional fidelity and hetero-limitations are things of the past. New horizons are being approached with a sense of freedom from restraint.

They seem to have a strong sense of happiness in what they're achieving, but 'for sure, can't say where we'll be five years from now.'

The Danas, Jonathan and Bunny, previously known for two documentaries, *Darkness, Darkness* (heroin addiction) and *Glass Houses* (amphetamine and barbiturate abuse in America), have succeeded rather remarkably in avoiding porn elements in what is essentially the story of sexual release among the inhibited."

Reprinted by Permission of New York Post.
© 1977, New York Post Corporation.

SATURDAY NIGHT AT THE BATHS

Director: *David Buckley*. Screenplay: *Franklin Khedouri and Mr. Buckley*. Photography: *Raif Bode*. Editors: *Jackie Raynai and Suzanne Fenn*. Production: *Mr. Buckley and Steve Ostrow*. Running time 102 minutes. New York opening June, 1975, at the RKO 59th Street Twin I Theatre. Classification: R.

Michael: *Robert Aberdeen*. Tracy: *Ellen Sheppard*. Scotti: *Don Scotti*.

See Volume 1 for additional reviews

Monthly Film Bulletin, 8/76 (p. 173)
Colin Pahlow

"If *Saturday Night at the Baths* concerned only heterosexuals, it would probably be quickly dismissed as a padded, saccharine, but nicely performed story of an illicit love in bloom. However, as it ostensibly involves the trendy question of bisexuality, its strengths or failings as a film will probably be overshadowed by its attraction as a sexual forum. In fact, its overly fussy script does little to elucidate the motivations of either the characters or the filmmakers, while David Buckley's first job of direction is ultimately too relaxed to lead the subject anywhere interesting, and consistently prevents its three leads from emerging as anything other than crude symbols . . ."

©Monthly Film Bulletin, 1976.

The Times (London), 6/25/76 (p. 11)
David Robinson

" . . . *Saturday Night at the Baths* . . . questions the concept of 'normality' in sexual relationships.

The leading character is a fresh-faced, uptight young man whose mistress is keenly aware of the immaturity of his playful sexual relationship with her. He takes a job as piano player in the Continental Baths; and is at first nervous, patronizing and scornful of the homosexual clientele of the place. A growing friendship with one of the staff of the place, however, leads him to discover the possibility of more complex emotional relationships than his inborn habits and prejudices have previously allowed him to acknowledge.

The tractarian quality in the film is perhaps over-emphasized by the awkwardness of much of the playing; but under the stiff dialogue there is a degree of subtlety and perception in the relationship of the hero, his mistress and the young man who will become his--perhaps their--lover. The sexual scenes are handled with a skillful appreciation both of the erotic and romantic aspects."

© The Times, 1976.

SCENT OF A WOMAN (PROFUMO DI DONNA)

Director: *Dino Risi*. Screenplay: *Ruggero*

Maccari, Mr. Risi. Based on a novel by *Giovanni Arpino.* Photography: *Claudio Cirillo.* Editor: *Alberto Gallitti.* Music: *Armando Trovaioli.* Distributor: *Twentieth Century-Fox.* Running time 104 minutes. New York opening January, 1976, at the Paris Theatre. Classification: R. Origin: Italy.

Blind Captain: *Vittorio Gassman.* Ciccio: *Alessandro Momo.* Sara: *Agostina Belli.*

See Volume 1 for additional reviews

Christian Science Monitor, 5/7/76 (p. 25)
David Sterritt

"*Scent of a Woman*--nominated for a best-foreign-language-film Oscar--features Vittorio Gassman in a tour-de-force performance as a blind soldier of fortune leching his way through various Italian cities with the help of a bewildered youth who signed on for the trip without knowing what he was in for.

Gassman's work is astonishingly energetic and convincing. But all this splendid acting is at the service of a lumpy and, at the end, confused plot that is neither involving nor especially likeable. Dino Risi directed, allowing Gassman all the elbow room he needs but failing to pull the movie's loose ends together. The climactic tragedy seems pointless rather than moving, and the conclusion offers few clues as to what the whole project is trying to do . . ."

Reprinted by permission from The Christian
Science Monitor © 1976.
The Christian Science Publishing Society.
All rights reserved.

SCORCHY

Director, Screenplay, Producer: *Hikmet Avedis.* Photography: *Laszlo Pal.* Editor: *Michael Luciano.* Distributor: *American International Pictures.* Running time 99 minutes. New York opening October 8, 1976, at several theatres. Classification: R.

Jackie Parker: *Connie Stevens.* Philip Bianco: *Cesare Danova.* Claudia Bianco: *Marlene Schmidt.* Carl Henrich: *William Smith.* Chief O'Brien: *Norman Burton.* Nicky: *John David Chandler.* Mary Davis: *Joyce Jameson.* Alan: *Greg Evigan.* Steve: *Nick Dimitri.*

New York Post, 10/9/76 (p. 21)
Archer Winsten

". . . another tough melodrama about a bold girl undercover agent who's hot on the trail of a million dollar heroin import.

A suave Italian antique dealer, Philip Bianco (Cesare Danova) and his sister Claudia (Marlene Schmidt) are waiting at this end in Seattle. Jackie Parker (Connie Stevens), the girl agent, starts following Carl Henrich (William Smith), the heroin-carrying priest, in Rome.

The action explodes in Seattle, which is thoroughly covered in cars, motorboats, a helicopter, one motorcycle and a panel truck as everyone chases, steals and murders for the heroin.

Outstanding sights are Seattle itself, the bulging biceps of mean William Smith, and the breasts of Connie Stevens . . ."

Reprinted by Permission of New York Post.
© 1976, New York Post Corporation.

SENTINEL, THE

Director: *Michael Winner.* Screenplay, Producers: *Jeffrey Konvitz, Mr. Winner.* Based on the novel by Mr. Konvitz. Photography: *Dick Kratina.* Music: *Gil Melle.* Special Effects: *Albert Whitlock.* Distributor: *Universal Pictures.* Running time 105 minutes. New York opening February 11, 1977, at several theatres. Classification: R.

Players: *Martin Balsam, John Carradine, Jose Ferrer, Ava Gardner, Arthur Kennedy, Burgess Meredith, Sylvia Miles, Jerry Orbach, Deborah Raffin, Cristina Raines, Chris Sarandon, Eli Wallach.*

Los Angeles Times, 2/11/77 (Pt. IV, p. 23)
Kevin Thomas

". . . Whether intended or not, *The Sentinel* seems above all a parody of every chiller dealing with the supernatural from *Rosemary's Baby* through *The Exorcist* to *The Omen.* Indeed, the material is so derivative and therefore essentially unconvincing that it's hard to imagine how else it could have been played by director Michael Winner, who wrote and produced with Jeffrey Konvitz, author of the novel upon which the film is based. Anyway, Winner's approach allows for lots of

continued on next page

continued from previous page

amusing and showy tongue-in-cheek cameos by numerous veterans, but it's at the expense of seeming to be unduly callous to the increasingly harrowing plight of its heroine, whose terror is depicted with sincerity and conviction by Miss Raines . . ."

©Los Angeles Times, 1977.

Monthly Film Bulletin, March 1977 (p. 52)
Richard Combs

". . . moral or ironic points are hard to discern in the eye-wrenching flux of a Michael Winner movie, which drifts and zooms across its polished people and places in a continual caressing motion, as crudely excitatory as any sex movies when the climaxes are approaching. What slows this lushly photographed number down is its incorporation of the *Orient Express* all-star tour, with familiar faces . . . popping up to make weighty work of inconsequential bits of plot. When it comes to delivering the emotional goods, however, Mr. Winner is no laggard, and as the gates of hell are finally opened to let loose a handsomely decorated collection of ghouls (even if the special effects can occasionally seen to be done), he establishes, if not the imaginative right to the Miltonian verse on hell that is so freely bandied about in the film, at least his ability to milk a trend for all it's worth."

©Monthly Film Bulletin, 1977.

Film Information, March 1977 (p. 3)
Dave Pomeroy

"Among the most important of any Hollywoodian Ten Commandments is surely: Thou shalt follow a commercial success with multitudinous copies. Just so has *The Exorcist* spawned its imitations, of which *The Sentinel* is the latest. It appeals to a regnant supernaturalism in popular Christian thought that ends up reaching for cheap thrills . . .

Most distressing is the film's superficial and offensive portrayal of the Roman Catholic Church's understanding of sin and Hell—epitomized by a priest's caricatured and supercilious, 'You must have faith, my child,' to Allison.

A gaggle of stars have been recruited for 'bits' . . . with only Arthur Kennedy, as the priest, and Burgess Meredith, as the neighbor-cum-demon, breathing any life into their roles . . ."

©Film Information, 1977.

New York Magazine, 2/28/77 (p. 55)
John Simon

"*The Sentinel*, where Michael Winner's talent for making unspeakably vulgar movies peaks, is meant to be in the supernatural horror genre a la *Rosemary's Baby*, *The Exorcist*, etc. But this script by Jeffrey Konvitz, from his own best seller, is not

good enough to pass for trash; its stupidity can best be conveyed by a perfectly serious reference in it to Milton as 'the English religious writer.' Or take the conceit that the entrance to hell, which is on the ground floor of a Brooklyn brownstone, must be guarded by someone sitting on the fifth floor, who looks the other way and is, furthermore, blind. Everything is dreadful here . . ."

©1977 by the NYM Corp. Reprinted with the permission of NEW YORK Magazine.

New York Post, 2/12/77 (p. 40)
Archer Winsten

"*The Sentinel* . . . is a morality picture with a heavy emphasis on the mystic, the horrible, the misshapen and the spouting properties of blood . . .

Jeffrey Konvitz, author of the novel, cowriter of the screenplay with director Michael Winner, and coproducer with Winner, must deserve most of the credit and discredit. A cast of 12 known stars, including Martin Balsam, John Carradine, Jose Ferrer, Deborah Raffin, Eli Wallach and Jerry Ohrbach . . . keeps the picture professional.

It does seem, though, that this picture's attack on sin seems to wallow in it rather than purify itself. The total becomes both ludicrous and offensive to a well-armed skeptic like this one."

Reprinted by Permission of New York Post.
©1977, New York Post Corporation.

Newsweek, 2/28/77 (p. 72)
Janet Maslin

"A man with a face that looks like chicken giblets, a naked whore with a mouse on her thigh, a cat devouring a canary and Sylvia Miles in a tight leotard —these are some of the highlights of *The Sentinel*, a perfect movie for anyone who likes to slow down to get a good look at traffic accidents. With the aid of makeup . . . director Michael Winner has assembled a not-very-scary creep-show, borrowing freely from other recent movies of the Catholic bugaboo school. But in this particular battle between good and evil, no one seems to be on either side, not even the obligatory worried priests. This movie isn't concerned with who wins; it's only interested in close-ups of the carnage . . ."

©Newsweek, Inc. 1977
reprinted by permission.

Christian Science Monitor, 3/2/77 (p. 22)
David Sterritt

". . . It seems that a kind of supernatural security guard must stand over this creepy gate to make sure it stays latched, and the latest hireling has been falling asleep on the job. So some priests pick a young fashion model for the assignment—who knows why?—and she finds herself the center of many dark doings before the script lets her in on what's going on.

This nonsense marks the lowest ebb yet in the *Rosemary's Baby* sweepstakes. Director Michael Winner squirts gore across the screen and turns the climax into a degrading sideshow featuring physically handicapped people. He also elicits an anthology of bad acting from a big-name cast . . . Only Burgess Meredith and Eli Wallach come across like the pros they are. Oh yes—and the screenplay also seems to believe that John Milton wrote his English poems in Latin. That's going too far!''

Reprinted by permission from The Christian Science Monitor © 1977. The Christian Science Publishing Society. All rights reserved.

SERAIL

Director: *Eduardo de Gregorio.* Screenplay (French with English subtitles): *Michael Graham, Mr. de Gregorio.* Producers: *Hubert Niogret, Hugo Santiago, Jacques Zajdermann.* Photography: *Ricardo Aronovich.* Editor: *Alberto Yaccelini.* Music: *Michel Portal.* Distributor: *Caribou Films.* Running time 90 minutes. Los Angeles opening November 24, 1976, at the Westmoreland Theatre. Classification: R. Origin: France.

Celeste: *Leslie Caron.* Ariane: *Bulle Ogier.* Agathe: *Marie-France Pisier.* Eric: *Corin Redgrave.*

Los Angeles Times, 11/24/76 (Pt. IV, p. 5)
Charles Champlin

''. . . Eduardo de Gregorio's Serail (Seraglio), a French film with dialogue partly in English and partly in French with subtitles, is a stylish, atmospheric and well-acted whahappened? which leaves you leaning toward exasperation only because its swift and cryptic finale seems arbitrary and contrived.

It is a little as if the director (who coauthored the script with Michael Graham) had flipped a franc between a chilly but logical denouement and another, ghostly and mysterious. The coin landed occult side up.

If I can refer to a movie I didn't see but feel as if I did, *Serail* might be called an unburnt offering whose principal feature is a vast, shuttered, decaying mansion in the French countryside . . .''

©Los Angeles Times. 1976.

Christian Science Monitor, 10/22/76 (p. 27)
David Sterritt

''. . . Director Eduardo de Gregorio loves this sort of mystification. Though *Serail* is his directorial debut, he has scripted *The Spider's Stratagem* for Bernardo Bertolucci, as well as such Jacques Rivette pictures as the magical *Celine and Julie Go Boating* and the mythical *Duelle* (which shows many parallels with *Serail*). It is unfortunate his style as a director is too detached to elicit much warmth from the characters, who remain more diverting than involving. *Serail* is excessively cool and self-conscious, an exercise rather than a commitment.

It gains from the presence of its three very gifted actresses, however, and it will please many viewers with its restraint in nearly always looking the other way on the few occasions when the action threatens to become openly distasteful.''

Reprinted by permission from The Christian Science Monitor © 1976. The Christian Science Publishing Society. All rights reserved.

New York Magazine, 1/17/77 (p. 56)
John Simon

''*Serail* is pretentious trash of the most deplorable sort about a haunted house that consumes its tenants with the help of some mysterious women. Written and directed by Eduardo de Gregorio, the scenarist for the atrocities of Jacques Rivette and the highfalutin obscurantism of Bertolucci's *Spider's Stratagem*. Besides being a modish ghost story, it is also part paean to oral sexuality (perfectly all right in its place, but why here?), part feeble in-jokes, such as calling the hero, an English novelist, by the unlikely name of Eric Sange. Why? Because of the well-known producing company, Films du Losange, owned by Barbet Schroeder, the boyfriend of Bulle Ogier, one of the actresses in *Serail*. Nothing here makes much sense, nor does the film play fair with us, freely trampling across the thin line separating legitimate ambiguity from willful obfuscation . . .''

©1977 by the NYM Corp. Reprinted with the permission of NEW YORK Magazine.

SEVEN BEAUTIES

Director: *Lina Wertmuller.* Screenplay (Italian with English subtitles): *Ms. Wertmuller.* Photography: *Tonino Delli Colli.* Editor: *Franco Fracatelli.* Music: *Enzo Iannacci.* Distributor:

continued on next page

continued from previous page

Cinema V. Running time 116 minutes. New York opening January, 1976, at the Cinema II Theatre. Classification: None. Origin: Italy.

Pasqualino Frafuso: *Giancarlo Giannini.* Pedro: *Fernando Rey.* Commandant: *Shirley Stoler.* Concettina: *Elena Flore.* Don Raffaele: *Enzo Vitale.* Totonno: *Mario Conti.* Francesco: *Piero Di Orio.* Mother: *Ermelinad De Felice.* Carolina: *Francesca Marciano.* Lawyer: *Lucio Amelio.* Socialist: *Roberto Herlitzka.* Doctor: *Doriglia Palmi.*

See Volume 1 for additional reviews

Commentary, 5/76 (p. 75)
William S. Pechter

" . . . like her earlier films (though raised here to a higher power), it's an exercise . . . in the art of saying all things to all men: of throwing everything into one cramped melange, in hopes that somehow it will all work out. That it does work, one can have no doubts: Miss Wertmuller is currently the hottest foreign-language film director in New York, object of extravagant encomia from virtually every movie critic to be found there (with the honorable exceptions of Molly Haskell, Pauline Kael and Ellen Willis). This time Miss Wertmuller's travelling circus sets up at the Nazi death camps, to perform a gaudy, sensation-mongering freak show featuring garbled 'profundities' on such themes as the human condition and what-price-survival . . .
. . . What *Seven Beauties* is, in fact, is a centrifuge of screeching effects in the center of which stands the saucer-eyed Giannini, doing his reprise of his *Seduction of Mimi* reprise of Marcello Mastroianni's strutting, greasy-haired Lothario. What does it matter what *Seven Beauties* 'stands for'--what does anything matter in the face of a work so coarsely unfeeling? . . . "
© Commentary, 1976.

Monthly Film Bulletin, December 1976 (p. 254)
Tom Milne

" . . . elephantine irony, drawing parallels between Italy's conception of personal honour and Nazi Germany's conception of national pride, is the main weapon of a film which rarely rises above a tone of naughty schoolgirl irreverence. Coasting along on the facile cynicism of the opening sequence . . . Lina

Wertmuller simply works up a series of analogies that are most telling when least grotesque . . . More often . . . the cross-fertilising elements of farce and horror in each scene are so crudely handled that the desired synthesis into one huge, horrific farce never quite takes place. *Seven Beauties* is a treasure trove for hunters of significant allusions . . . "
©Monthly Film Bulletin, 1976.

SEVEN-PER-CENT SOLUTION, THE

Director, Producer: *Herbert Ross.* Screenplay: *Nicholas Meyer.* Based on the novel by Mr. Meyer. Photography: *Oswald Morris.* Editor: *Chris Barnes.* Music: *John Addison.* Distributor: *Universal Pictures.* Running time 113 minutes. New York opening October 24, 1976, at the Plaza Theatre. Classification: PG.

Sherlock Holmes: *Nicol Williamson.* Sigmund Freud: *Alan Arkin.* Dr. Watson: *Robert Duvall.* Lola Devereaux: *Vanessa Redgrave.* Professor Moriarty: *Laurence Olivier.* Lowenstein: *Joel Grey.* Mary Watson: *Samantha Eggar.* Baron von Leinsdorf: *Jeremy Kemp.* Mycroft Holmes: *Charles Gray.* Mrs. Freud: *Georgia Brown.* Madame: *Regine.* Freda: *Anna Quayle.* Mrs. Holmes: *Jill Townsend.* Berger: *John Bird.* Mrs. Hudson: *Alison Leggatt.* Marker: *Frederick Jaeger.*

Saturday Review, 10/30/76 (p. 53)
Judith Crist

" . . . brought to the screen by producer-director Herbert Ross not only with noteworthy elegance and taste but also with a new climactic plot provided by Meyer's screenplay, which supplies a crisper story line and further diversion for those familiar with the best seller. And perhaps above all, an excellent cast brings this romantic adventure to life with its literary tongue-in-cheek nuances intact and its cinematic possibilities exploited to the full. . .
The cast is as urbane as the directorial tone. Nicol Williamson and Robert Duvall bring a refreshing vigor and muscularity to the Holmes-Watson screen tradition, with an interesting new emphasis on the egalitarian friendship between them. But there is small doubt that Alan Arkin as an energetic and activist Freud practically steals the show . . . "
©Judith Crist, 1976.

Christian Science Monitor, 10/18/76 (p. 27)
David Sterritt

". . . Though Meyer's script gets verbose at
times, a sturdy cast makes most of it seem fun.
Nicol Williamson's Holmes is as high-strung as he is
brilliant, making us wonder about his emotional
health even as we applaud his single-minded determination to find the bad guys out . . .

Alan Arkin's Freud is too restrained; still, he provides a relief from the overplaying that has marred
much of Arkin's work, and lends extra charm to the
doctor's amusingly ironic childish gestures. Robert
Duvall turns from his sinister *Godfather*-isms to give
us a rousingly fussy Watson, and Vanessa Redgrave is admirably cast as the beautiful victim. Sir
Laurence Olivier splendidly plays an unjustly maligned (that's right) Moriarty . . .

Herbert Ross' direction is, if anything, too meticulous. Careful and colorful, it well illustrates the
ballet-trained filmmaker's concern with the serious
subtexts of his plots . . ."

Reprinted by permission from The Christian
Science Monitor © 1976.
The Christian Science Publishing Society.
All rights reserved.

New York Post, 10/25/76 (p. 12)
Frank Rich

"*The Seven-Per-Cent Solution* . . . is supposed to
be a witty, suspenseful comic romp about what
might have happened if Sherlock Holmes and Sigmund Freud had met each other and then banded
together to solve a juicy mystery. Or at least I think
that's what it's supposed to be. This movie is so
dull and colorless that it might just as well be about
two anonymous Victorian-era lawyers who get together to probate a will . . .

Bad as the screenwriter's work is, though, one
can't say that Herbert Ross, the director, has done
anything to help the script along; indeed most of the
direction is downright embarrassing. In a sequence
where Holmes is suffering his drug-withdrawal
agonies, Ross gives us distorted images, hand-held
camera jaggedness, and dumb nightmare visions of
rattlesnakes and worms; we don't believe the detective is so much sweating off cocaine as taking a
'house of horrors' ride at a tacky amusement
park . . ."

Reprinted by Permission of New York Post.
© 1976, New York Post Corporation.

Women's Wear Daily, 10/18/76 (p. 14)
Mort Sheinman

". . . Such a venture—this mixing of fact and fiction—could easily have been a disaster. It is not,
and the credit for that belongs to screenwriter
Meyer, who has concocted a sophisticated script;
director Herbert Ross, who had fun with his subject
without condescending to it, and a perfectly splendid cast . . .

Although Nicol Williamson plays Holmes with
much of the priggishness Basil Rathbone brought to
the part, his Holmes is not an infallible man. He can
be impatient and angry and—yes—even frightened,
a man who fears for his sanity. Dr. Watson, portrayed by Nigel Bruce for years as a rather dodder-
ing, well-meaning, generally ineffectual chap, is
here interpreted by Robert Duvall in a much more
interesting way—as a younger, more vigorous fellow with a pretty wife, a man capable of great empathy as he sees Holmes' suffering. Alan Arkin
again displays his remarkable range, giving us a
'Freud who is humble and good-humored, patient
and probing. Holmes, Watson, Freud—all are three-
dimensional figures . . ."

© Women's Wear Daily, 1976.

Monthly Film Bulletin, February 1977 (p. 31)
Geoff Brown

"For a short time *The Seven-Per-Cent Solution*
promises to be a pleasingly sophisticated, bookish
jest . . . But as the story unravels, disillusion rapidly
sets in: Nicholas Meyer has brought together
Holmes and Freud only to draw superficially on
their respective legends, showing none of the ingenuity and sympathy Wilder and Diamond lavished
on *The Private Life of Sherlock Holmes* . . . In between their startlingly routine adventures, Holmes
indulges in a few bouts of deductive reasoning and
Freud follows suit with some psychoanalysis; the
meeting of minds lamely fizzles out with the trite
revelations of Holmes' childhood traumas . . ."

© Monthly Film Bulletin, 1977.

Los Angeles Times, 11/12/76 (Pt. IV, p. 1)
Charles Champlin

". . . It is a particularly handsome period piece,
beautifully staged and acted and most genuinely
charming. The hard and elusive trick in an exercise
of calculated nostalgia like this is to find and hold to
precisely the right tone, somewhere between low
imitation and high burlesque, making the story interesting on its own terms, affectionate if not quite
reverential and somehow startling but credible in
the context of what Doyle has already told us.

Despite the evident care, cost, enthusiasm and
respect that went into the Billy Wilder Sherlock
Holmes, for example, the magic never worked. But
it works extremely well in *The Seven-Per-Cent
Solution*. There is, of all unexpected things, a sincerity about the story, a welcome freedom from the
ain't-we-clever winking at the audience. If there is a
problem, in fact, it is that a key sequence is too
long and too sincere . . ."

© Los Angeles Times, 1976.

continued on next page

continued from previous page

New York Magazine, 11/8/76 (p. 79)
John Simon

". . . Nicholas Meyer, in his novel as now in his screenplay, falls short of his conception: In this scheduled wedding of intuition and rationality, bride and bridegroom are left waiting at separate altars. Neither the analysis nor the crime detection rises above the commonplace . . .

The light of the stellar cast is overcast by mis-casting. Nicol Williamson suggests, as usual, a self-indulgent sensualist and social upstart rather than the ascetic, upper-class Holmes; his querulous, high-pitched nasal twang is more suited to the rail-ings of a Thersites than to the voice of reason, even if temporarily perturbed. Robert Duvall makes Wat-son even more elementary than need be . . . Alan Arkin turns Freud into a refugee from the movie *Hester Street* . . ."

©1976 by the NYM Corp. Reprinted with
the permission of NEW YORK Magazine.

Newsweek, 11/1/76 (p. 83A)
Janet Maslin

". . . Director Herbert Ross just lets things slide along. Ross has assembled a brilliantly heterogene-ous cast—including Vanessa Redgrave as a kid-napped courtesan, Joel Grey as a petty crook and Laurence Olivier as a surprisingly meek, enfeebled Moriarty—and scouted some sumptuous Viennese locales, but not even these assets are much help. When the drug-crazed Holmes (Nicol Williamson) is lured to Vienna by loyal Watson (Robert Duvall) so that the famous new specialist can undertake his cure, the film promises to take an amusing turn. But Alan Arkin's droll, understated Freud is soon over-whelmed by scenes of Holmes experiencing with-drawal seizures (most of his nightmares feature ser-pents) that inject a jarringly gruesome note into this otherwise trivial fable . . ."

©Newsweek, Inc. 1976
reprinted by permission.

Nation, 11/13/76 (p. 508)
Robert Hatch

". . . Williamson and Duvall are precisely 'right' in their celebrated roles, with the proviso that William-son's Holmes is significantly more neurotic than Conan Doyle's—as indeed he must be in a scheme that embraces the nascent ideas of Sigmund Freud. Of the three, however, Arkin's characterization is the most absorbing and most entertaining—for the paradoxical reason that the real young man he plays is far less well known to the public than are the two storybook figures portrayed by his col-leagues. He has more freedom, thus, to imagine

how readily a man of Freud's training and interests might grasp and apply Holmes' deductive methods . . .

Finally, the spectacle of Holmes and Freud riding full tilt at each other on the backs of their respective 'methods' is as witty a bit of parody as one might hope to encounter in a work of 'mere' entertain-ment. *The Seven-Per-Cent Solution* is sophisticated tomfoolery, a commodity always in short supply."

©The Nation, 1976.

Film Information, November 1976 (p. 5)
David A. Tillyer

". . . You don't have to believe this patchwork fantasy to love it. And you will. It is an artful mix of psychoanalytic theory and tweedy fiction that is bizarre, fun and funny . . .

SPS has something for everyone. There is a de-tective mystery, with clues left everywhere, and plenty of swashbuckling action (including a riotous chase in and on top of a fast-moving train) and a masterful blend of Anglo/American humor.

The location cinematography in London and Vienna has a daguerreotype aura, and the musty characters are phenomenally realistic. The fine En-glish actor Nicol Williamson is as convincing suffer-ing withdrawal symptoms as he is doing his usual detection work. Dr. Watson is more forceful than we have seen him before, and Mr. Duvall makes this switch believable. Alan Arkin is perhaps a little more dashing than we expect the Austrian doctor to be, but it is fun to see someone outshine a tradi-tional hero like Holmes once in a while . . ."

©Film Information, 1976.

Village Voice, 11/8/76 (p. 53)
Andrew Sarris

". . . I very much wanted to like this movie, but I couldn't. Apparently some people do. Why? They obviously attended a different screening. When I saw it everyone was yawning and checking the time . . .

As it turned out, Nicol Williamson is much too heavy for any light entertainment. His raging tem-perament is too violent even for *Uncle Vanya*, much less for the supposedly cerebral Sherlock Holmes. I never thought it was a particularly good idea to probe Holmes' unconscious, but the very last thing I want is to probe Williamson's unconscious . . .

By contrast, Alan Arkin's Freud settles into the somnolence of semireverence and his nice-guy/ nice goy relationship with Holmes. We get neither the crazy absurdism of which Arkin is capable nor any of the disturbing overtones of Freud's person-ality. It is almost as if Holmes were Freud and Freud were Holmes. Another problem is the childish derring-do and conventionality of the plot . . ."

Reprinted by permission of The Village Voice.
Copyright ©The Village Voice, Inc., 1976.

Films in Review, November 1976 (p. 567)
Charles Phillips Reilly

"If style were the sole criterion for the excellence of a picture, this one would be tops. Producer-director Herbert Ross has given it loving care . . . but he is stuck with Nicholas Meyer's script (based on Meyer's best-selling book), and his own direction . . .

Satire and irony demand ensemble acting at which this cast is first-rate, but the direction fails to meet the demand. Nevertheless, there are moments worthy of your interest: Mycroft ordering a cab; the verbal duels between Holmes and Freud; a court tennis game between the Baron and Freud; and a railroad chase."

©Films in Review, 1976.

17 AND ANXIOUS

Director: *Zbynek Brynych*. Screenplay: *Alexander Fuhrmann*. Producer: *Martin Friedman*. Photography: *Joseph Vanis*. Editor: *Li Bonk*. Music: *Peter Thomas*. Distributor: *Cinema National*. Running time 85 minutes. Los Angeles opening December 1976 at several theatres. Classification: R. Origin: West Germany.

Players: *Armond August, Edward Dux, Anne K. Kuster,* Siegfried Rauch, Nadja Tiller, Karl M. *Vogler, Hanna Welder.*

Los Angeles Times, 12/11/76 (Pt. II, p. 6)
Linda Gross

"*17 and Anxious* . . . is a soporific soft-core trash about a pretty, young girl (Anne M. Kuster) who withdraws into fantasy because of the restrictive life-style imposed upon her by her self-absorbed parents (Nadja Tiller and Karl M. Vogler).

This badly dubbed German-made movie attempts to dramatize a schoolgirl's psyche when she escapes into sexual reveries while at school or at home. But from the beginning, the girl is only a pretext for a free-floating photographic essay on youth and mores in a German metropolis accompanied by lots of loud rock music by Peter Thomas and innumerable renderings of 'Oh Happy Day' by the Edwin Hawkins Singers . . ."

©Los Angeles Times, 1976.

SEX MACHINE, THE

Director, Screenplay: *Pasquale Festa Campanile*. Producer: *Silvio Clementelli.* Photography: *Franco Di Giacomo*. Editor: *Sergio Montanari*. Music: *Fred Bongusto*. Distributor: *Seymour Borde & Associates*. Running time 80 minutes. Los Angeles opening January 1977 at several theatres. Classification: R.

Players: *Agostina Belli, Christian De Sica, Luigi Proietti.*

Los Angeles Times, 1/25/77 (Pt. IV, p. 9)
Linda Gross

"*The Sex Machine* . . . is a crudely entertaining, erotic and farfetched fantasy with political overtones that proposes a unique way to deal with the energy crisis.

The movie takes place in the 21st century when the world's supply of natural fuel has been depleted and electrical power has been eliminated . . .

Enter the enterprising professor of science, Luigi Proietti, who is steeped in the theories of Wilhelm Reich and convinced that a correlation exists between sexual and universal energy. Proietti plans to transfer energy created by two people making love into electricity . . .

. . . Working with a contrived but clever premise, Campanile tries too hard to straddle the fence between soft-core science-fiction and ideas about guilt, hypocrisy and the exploitation of sexual attraction.

As a director, Campanile stylishly handles sex scenes, slapstick and satire. He also imaginatively conveys a cheerful and chilling *Brave New World* . . ."

©Los Angeles Times, 1977.

SHADOW OF THE HAWK

Director: *George McCowan*. Screenplay: *Norman Thaddeus Vane, Herbert J. Wright*. Based on a story by Peter Jensen. Producer: *John Kemeny*. Photography: *John Holbrook, Reginald Morris*. Editor: *O. Nicholas Brown*. Music: *Robert McMullin*. Production: *International Cinemedia Center/Rising Road*, with the participation of the *Canadian Film Development Corporation* and the *Odeon Theaters* (Canada). Distributor: *Columbia Pictures*.

continued on next page

continued from previous page

Running time 92 minutes. Los Angeles opening August 1976 at several theatres. Classification: PG.

Players: *Jan-Michael Vincent, Marilyn Hassett, Chief Dan George, Pia Shandel, Marianne Jones, Jacques Hubert, Cindi Griffith, Anna Hagen, Murray Lowry.*

Los Angeles Times, 8/18/76 (Pt. IV, p. 13)
Kevin Thomas

". . . Since the Indian-style supernatural served up here in the Canadian-made *Shadow of the Hawk* . . . has been played absolutely straight, the result is an unduly solemn and tedious business that is lots more likely to put you to sleep than into a trance. Of course, Indian beliefs and rituals should be regarded with respect, but *Shadow of the Hawk* is so relentlessly serious and unfunny that, if anything, it becomes occasionally funny by default, thanks to flat dialogue and unstylish, unimaginative direction . . .

The film's simple-minded script pretty much muzzles the usually dynamic Vincent and offers virtually nothing to pretty Marilyn Hassett . . . An irrepressible scene-stealer with a lot of ham in him, the chief easily dominates. However, outside of some nice British Columbia scenery, *Shadow of the Hawk* doesn't have much going for it."

©Los Angeles Times, 1976.

New York Post, 10/7/76 (p. 28)
Archer Winsten

"Jan-Michael Vincent, who has won himself a deserved popularity with pictures like *Buster and Billie* and *Baby Blue Marine*, is not going to continue his rise if he can't choose better starring vehicles than *Shadow of the Hawk* . . .

It's an extended tussle with apparitions out of Indian mythology of the northwest.

Chief Dan George comes in to make it sound remotely authentic, and Marilyn Hassett accompanied Vincent into the backwoods for romantic interest under the guise of journalism.

They've chosen one of the most spectacular cities of North America, Vancouver, B.C., for background, and then traveled into nearby mountains for their adventures with wraiths, a bear, high winds on a suspension footbridge, unexpected failure of auto brakes on a steep road, loss of steering control on another danger spot, etc. etc. But it all amounts to

minimal rewards for the spectator, either in natural beauty or the excitement of the supernatural . . ."

Reprinted by Permission of New York Post
©1976, New York Post Corporation

SHAGGY D.A., THE

Director: *Robert Stevenson.* Screenplay: *Don Tait.* Based on THE HOUND OF FLORENCE by Felix Salten. Producer: *Bill Anderson.* Photography: *Frank Phillips.* Editors: *Bob Bring, Norman Palmer.* Music: *Buddy Baker.* Distributor: *Buena Vista.* Running time 91 minutes. New York opening December 25, 1976, at several theatres. Classification: G.

Wilby Daniels: *Dean Jones.* Betty Daniels: *Suzanne Pleshette.* John Slade: *Keenan Wynn.* Brian Daniels: *Shane Sinutko.* Tim: *Tim Conway.* Katrinka Muggelberg: *Jo Anne Worley.* Admiral Brenner: *John Myhers.* Eddie Roschak: *Vic Tayback.* Professor Whatley: *Hans Conried.* Bartender: *Pat McCormick.*

Film Information, January 1977 (p. 3)
Paul Coleman

". . . a level aimed solidly at general audiences at holiday time.

This is the cinema of frustration, so there's little surprise when each scene inevitably brings out the woolly mane on Jones' face and hands. A side plot with Tim Conway as an ice cream vendor and Jo Anne Worley as queen of the roller derby provides additional physical gagery. The pallid plotting, however, gives little chance for the talented people at work here (including Suzanne Pleshette as Jones' patiently unruffled wife) to be anything but perfunctory.

One exception is Jones' performance of the title song over the opening credits in which he provides punch and zing in the style of a campaign speech. So get to the theatre on time."

©Film Information, 1977

New York Post, 12/27/76 (p. 44)
Archer Winsten

"*The Shaggy D.A.* . . . is that standard Disney product, slapstick fantasy, which has proved too popular to be lambasted as thoroughly as I would like. It's a sequel to *The Shaggy Dog*, a hit of 1959, in which a teenager turned into a dog whenever the inscription on a scarab ring was read.

Now the lad is a grown-up . . . and he is about to run for District Attorney because the current incumbent . . . is so corrupt . . .

Before the election takes place a feverish plot must be surmounted . . .

There may be, there must be, someone, perhaps millions, who find this kind of hocus-pocus sidesplitting. For me, having been subjected to this brand of tripe for too many years, I find it hard to keep a civil typewriter in lap or stay awake. In short, *The Shaggy D.A.* bored me silly, and I suspect it could do the same for you."

Reprinted by Permission of New York Post.
© 1976, New York Post Corporation.

Los Angeles Times, 12/20/76 (Pt. IV, p. 16)
Charles Champlin

"Watching *The Shaggy D.A.* . . . . you get the feeling that time has stood still at Disney if nowhere else in the film world.

It is not an unpleasant feeling at all. There is something quite reassuring in the possibility that a man can be changed into a great hairy white sheep dog, and back again, at the recitation of a Latin motto inscribed in an ancient scarab ring said to have been used by the Borgias when poisoning their enemies lost its tang . . .

There are times when Disney comes close to satirizing itself, but the things are done with a kind of light-hearted sincerity which is nice and which saves the day. *The Shaggy D.A.* is in its formulated way expert and competent fun, populated as always with attractive people and free of sex, violence, issues or overtones.

The players by now constitute a new Disney stock company of skilled and engaging light comic actors, never stretched very far but pleasant to watch . . .

The Shaggy D.A. is right off the assembly line, but it is still the most competent line of its kind."

© Los Angeles Times, 1976.

SHOOT

Director: *Harvey Hart*. Screenplay, Executive Producer: *Dick Berg*. Based on the novel by Douglas Fairbairn. Producer: *Harve Sherman*. Photography: *Zale Magder*. Editors: *Ron Wisman, Peter Shatalow*. Music: *Doug Riley*. Distributor: *Avco Embassy Pictures*. Running time

94 minutes. Los Angeles opening November 1976 at several theatres. Classification: R.

Rex: *Cliff Robertson*. Lou: *Ernest Borgnine*. Zeke: *Henry Silva*. Pete: *James Blendick*. Bob: *Larry Reynolds*. Jim: *Les Carlson*. Paula: *Helen Shaver*. Ellen: *Gloria Carlin Chetwynd*. Mrs. Graham: *Kate Reid*.

Film Information, July/August 1976 (p. 5)
Eugene A. Schneider

"*Shoot* is a gun picture catering to those who like to see people maimed and killed. The plot is minimal. Five bored, vulgar, unhappily married men go to a hunting lodge for a weekend. They tramp through the woods for hours and can't find any target until they spot some hunters across the valley. Shots are exchanged leaving one of the 'other hunters' dead.

Both groups decide to return the following weekend to settle the issue. Since they all have large private collections of illegal automatic weapons and are members of gun clubs and the local army reserve, the all-out confrontation leaves everybody dead but one.

Aside from a fine performance by Cliff Robertson as a man who mobilizes his 'army' with chilling military discipline, this made-in-Canada film has little to recommend it. We never really know what motivates these men—what frustrations in their lives could lead them to the film's unrealistic climax . . ."

© Film Information, 1976

New York Post, 1/20/77 (p. 43)
Archer Winsten

"*Shoot* . . . is a picture that can be taken at two levels. First, it is a straight account of five weekend hunters, gun-lovers, who quit their homes and wives as fast as they can for the outdoor camaraderie and dirty jokes of their long-time pals . . .

The conclusion . . . represents the other response, that of strong anti-gun propaganda.

The performances, dialogues and settings are quite good. The basic premise, however, is so far-fetched that one has trouble taking it seriously. As often happens when the executive producer is also the screenplay author, Dick Berg, a certain degree of indulgence is found in the continuity."

Reprinted by Permission of New York Post.
© 1977, New York Post Corporation.

continued on next page

continued from previous page

Los Angeles Times, 11/3/76 (Pt. IV, p. 11)
Kevin Thomas

". . . Deftly adapted by the film's executive producer Dick Berg from the novel by Douglas Fairbairn and directed by Harvey Hart with apt terseness and precision, *Shoot* lays bare the juvenile macho-obsessed psyche as suspense relentlessly builds and builds. That *Shoot*'s plea for gun control remains implicit allows it to raise the near-universal question of how will man ever learn to curb his propensity for violence and love of killing—especially as the times seem to grow ever more paranoid.

The crucial figure is Robertson, who delineates with steely authority a latent maniac, a handsome, dominating, even cruel man sexually attractive to women but who would clearly rather make war than love. (Without pushing it too far, *Shoot* touches upon the relationship between sex and violence) . . ."

©Los Angeles Times, 1976.

SHOOTIST, THE

Director: *Don Siegel*. Screenplay: *Miles Hood Swarthout, Scott Hale*. Based on a novel by Glendon Swarthout. Producers: *M. J. Frankovich, William Self*. Photography: *Bruce Surtees*. Editor: *Robert Boyle*. Music: *Elmer Bernstein*. Distributor: *Paramount Pictures*. Running time 100 minutes. New York opening August 11, 1976, at the Loews Astor Plaza. Classification: PG.

J. B. Books: *John Wayne*. Bond Rogers: *Lauren Bacall*. Gillom Rogers: *Ron Howard*. Dr. Hostetler: *James Stewart*. Sweeney: *Richard Boone*. Pulford: *Hugh O'Brian*. Cobb: *Bill McKinney*. The Undertaker: *John Carradine*.

Saturday Review, 8/21/76 (p. 45)
Judith Crist

". . . Siegel has come up with a turn-of-the-century (both in set and in quality) western concocted by Miles Hood Swarthout and Scott Hale from a novel by Glendon Swarthout, Miles' dad.

John Wayne, tall and mountainous in the saddle, shoots down a highwayman for openers and rides into Carson City, Nev. . . . where he learns from James Stewart, who saved his life after a shootout fifteen years ago, that he has 'a cancer—advanced' and not long to live. He is directed to a widow's boardinghouse, where Lauren Bacall gives him a room, with reluctance, at the sight of his shooting irons . . .

Where legends—about directorial skills or gunfighters—die is in the confrontation with fact, in the credibility factor, and in the empathy generated by the protagonist. The tyro scenarists are never quite sure if they are writing about a killer or a cancer-ridden man, about the ironies of how a murderer faces death or about the truism of living and dying by the gun. One suspects something as trite as the last . . . but in the bloody finale, the pointlessness of Siegel's film is the dominant factor. Wayne, mustachioed and chin-whiskered, is more behemoth than human, Bacall, maturely handsome, never finds coincidence between her sophisticated glance and the idiot dialogue assigned her . . ."

©Judith Crist, 1976.

Sight and Sound, Autumn 1976 (p. 257)
Geoff Brown

". . . Whether designed as a swan-song or not, *The Shootist* is an exceedingly strange affair, both for Wayne and its director Don Siegel. The themes it touches on are now commonplace. There is the aging gunman neatly reaching the end of his life early in the new century, where his ethical code no longer operates; round him gather journalists, local politicians and ancient floozies, eager to capitalize on his demise and turn him into a money-spinning property. Far less commonplace is the stylistic method adopted by Siegel and his screenwriters (working from a novel by Glendon Swarthout). Every element—structure, characterisation, dramatic incident, the soundtrack music—is pared down to a degree surprising for an American Western. The intimate qualities suggest instead Japanese cinema . . .

Certainly it's bracing to find a Hollywood movie pursuing its chosen theme and style with such resolution, but one can't help wondering whether things haven't been stripped too bare for comfort . . ."

©Sight and Sound, 1976.

New York Magazine, 8/23/76 (p. 60)
John Simon

"*The Shootist* is one of those relatively few movies whose badness makes one feel genuinely sad. It is the sort of picture that, had it been made in almost any other country—i.e., any country that can see itself and its people straight rather than through a veil of myth and legend—could have emerged human and moving. Instead, it is superficial, cliche-ridden, and torn apart by conflicting aims of abiding by and debunking or transcending its genre.

On the right track are the direction and most of the casting; wrong are the screenplay and, to a lesser extent, the production values. Don Siegel is one of the very few remaining, tenaciously perdurable, intelligently workmanlike directors of genre pictures . . . and his technique, without being extraordinary, is in every way adequate to his modest yet not undemanding material. But that is where the problem lies: a novel by a run-of-the-mill author like Glendon Swarthout . . . adapted to the screen by his son Miles Hood Swarthout and the actor and dialogue coach Scott Hale, is hardly the material with which to transcend genre . . .

Something, however, is left. John Wayne gives a surprisingly effective performance as Books, a role somewhat more demanding than Rooster Cogburn in *True Grit* . . ."

©1976 by the NYM Corp. Reprinted with the permission of NEW YORK Magazine.

Christian Science Monitor, 8/25/76 (p. 22)
David Sterritt

"*The Shootist* sets out to be the ultimate John Wayne movie—an epic that will sum up the star's career, epitomize the western format, and make a kind of epitaph for bygone cinematic virtues.

Though this film shares some of these virtues—directness, ruggedness, simplicity—it never musters the visual eloquence of the John Ford and Howard Hawks classics that it profusely admires. *The Shootist* is both a noble experiment and a fairly conventional afternoon at the movies . . .

Siegel's finest inspiration in *The Shootist*, and his most endearing gesture, has been to celebrate the western tradition by using a passel of actors whose faces and names symbolize the movie heritage. Thus James Stewart plays the country doctor, with John Carradine his opposite as a slithery undertaker. Lauren Bacall plays the widow who reluctantly befriends Books; she is pestered by Richard Boone's hard-faced villain . . ."

Reprinted by permission from The Christian Science Monitor © 1976. The Christian Science Publishing Society. All rights reserved.

New York Post, 8/12/76 (p. 18)
Frank Rich

". . . The principal virtue of *The Shootist*, the new and frequently overwrought Don Siegel film . . . is that it allows Wayne's distinctive star qualities to emerge in all their splendor. Watching this film is like taking a tour (albeit a very slow tour) of a Hollywood legend: as J.B. Books, a famous Western

'shootist' (i.e., gunslinger) who's dying of cancer, Wayne is, by turns, heroic, sardonic, chivalrous, mean, romantic, tough, frightened, fatherly and ever so tentatively sentimental . . .

Don Siegel (*The Invasion of the Body Snatchers*, *Charlie Varrick*) can be a fine director, but here he's trapped by his faithfulness to his material: He presents *The Shootist* in a stately, somber and distancing manner that is all too elegantly reverential . . ."

Reprinted by Permission of New York Post. ©1976, New York Post Corporation.

Women's Wear Daily, 7/26/76 (p. 13)
Howard Kissel

". . . There is something about making a hardened gunslinger an object of pathos—it is a more original way of depicting the death of the West than most recent efforts, which have settled for easy satire. *The Shootist*, however, doesn't really work because it never really gives us characters, only cliches. As a result, the final shootout has no emotional impact though it is effectively staged, and the death of the hero doesn't really produce the expected tears because you can't mourn someone you don't know very well . . .

John Wayne plays the cancer-ridden cowboy with his usual mannerisms and a very stiff upper lip. James Stewart is fine as the doctor who makes the tragic diagnosis, and Lauren Bacall is strong as the wise landlady . . .

The film is beautifully designed and photographed, capturing the innocent warmth of a turn-of-the-century American town. So much care went into the physical production it's a shame the human drama comes off so scant."

©Women's Wear Daily, 1976.

Films in Review, October 1976 (p. 504)
Hugh James

". . . The stars give fine performances with Wayne at his very best. A supporting cast of Richard Boone, Hugh O'Brian, Harry Morgan, John Carradine, and Sheree North help the direction of Don Siegel who never forgets that this film is a vehicle for a superstar. Bruce Surtees' photography is adequate.

The Shootist addresses itself to more than just the ambience of the West. Cancer is not the usual way film stars die: its frank acceptance here may be attributable in good part not only to Wayne, but to the writers Miles Hood Swarthout and his father Glendon Swarthout, as well as Scott Hale. A provocative film."

©Films in Review, 1976.

continued on next page

continued from previous page

Monthly Film Bulletin, October 1976 (p. 219)
Richard Combs

"*The Shootist* is a curiosity: a chamber Western
which first anchors its hero indoors with a bottle
of laudanum and the prospect of waiting out the
brief but painful last span of his life, and then sets
him about with human vultures—a blow-hard marshal delighted to have a legend expiring in his
parish, an opportunistic newspaperman, a money-
grubbing ex-love, a cadaverous undertaker—like
persecuting cameos in a bad dream. In the event,
this promisingly existential premise is never really
developed; the mood of psychological reckoning
which it suggests is kept at bay by the gruff
pragmatism of the script . . . Its stiffness in this
respect is compounded by the clutter of mythology
in the opening scenes, which self-consciously intermingle the John Wayne legend with Books' own.
The character's gunfighting career is summed up
in a black-and-white montage of clips from old
Wayne movies . . ."

©Monthly Film Bulletin, 1976.

Film Information, 9/76 (p. 2)
Paul Coleman

". . . John Wayne's acting ability is becoming
less a subject of controversy than an object of as-
tonishment. *The Shootist* gives him his finest opportunity to define a character since *True Grit*. Salty
wisecracks and feisty confrontations have always
been his strong suit, and this script provides him
with repeated upper hands. Yet the chilly awkwardness of disability is clearly uncomfortable for
him. When he slips in the bathtub or fumbles a shot,
the camera discreetly glances just aside, carefully
avoiding the disability which claims central attention in the script.
Surprises are in store from the rest of the cast.
Lauren Bacall rises to the occasion of playing a reticent, somewhat demure widow with fine restraint.
Ron Howard as her impressionable son develops
remarkable breadth in a character drawn to
Wayne's heroics . . ."

©Film Information, 1976.

Newsweek, 8/16/76 (p. 68)
Janet Maslin

". . . Siegel directs most of the film with an eloquent restraint, culminating in a heartbreaking final
exchange between Wayne and Bacall. The widow,
who is surprised to find herself growing deeply
found of this roughneck, is well aware of his plans
to hasten the inevitable, but she also knows that

Books could never abide a tearful farewell. So on
the eighth morning, she sees him off with a smile.
Her grief is evident, but only tacitly so: she is already dressed in mourning . . .
. . . *The Shootist* never jeopardizes its hard-
boiled integrity by making apologies for either
Books or Wayne; it unabashedly advocates the
manly art of self-defense, the occasional necessity
for vigilante justice and a number of other
things . . .
Wayne's proud, quietly anguished performance,
one of his very best and certainly his most
moving, has a richness that seems born of
self-knowledge . . ."

©Newsweek, Inc. 1976
reprinted by permission.

The Sunday Times (London), 10/10/76 (p. 35)
Alan Brien

". . . Though the settings, especially the saloon,
are heavy with memories of old movies, and the
climax explosive with ketchup, *The Shootist* does
not hold together. Wayne is said, mainly by Wayne,
to be the last of a noble breed, never to be threatened, manipulated or touched. As they do unto
him, so he does unto others. But he sticks his gun
into the mouth of a pushy reporter (perhaps meant
to symbolize all film critics?) and kicks his behind.
He produces no justification for endangering the
lives of the three men he challenges. The domestic
scenes between Wayne and Bacall are mawkish
and endless.
And Wayne himself, face expressive as an old
saddle, enlivened by a pair of moist blue eyes,
is not equipped for emotional complexities. Between sickroom and barroom, it is a long two hours
and 20 minutes with nothing to do except praise
the laudanum and pass the ammunition."

©The Sunday Times, 1976.

The Times (London), 10/8/76 (p. 8)
Richard Combs

". . . *The Shootist* is the Compleat John Wayne
reader. Before the credits, the career of aging gunfighter J.B. Books is summarized with a few clips
from old Wayne movies; and the protagonist's
painful burden soon proves to be an incurable
cancer, diagnosed by fellow-Olympian James
Stewart. Slyly, however, the film proves to be not
so much indulging as measuring these myths. And
although it contains not a scene or a character not
hallowed by movie tradition, *The Shootist* is probably the most original American Western in many
years.
Its peculiarity could be due to many things.
Director Don Siegel is known more for terse urban
thrillers, and he deals with the Western setting with
a parsimony bordering on the elliptical; as Books,

Wayne gives an impressively contained performance, hinting at reserves of character not touched on by the script; and the whole is such a self-conscious theatrical artifice—other characters come and go in brief cameo turns—that it acquires the dry, self-reflecting quality of incontrovertible myth . . ."

©The Times, 1976.

SHOUT AT THE DEVIL

Director: *Peter H. Hunt*. Screenplay: *Stanley Price, Alistair Reid, Wilbur Smith*. Based on the novel by Mr. Smith. Producer: *Michael Klinger*. Photography: *Michael Reed*. Editor: *Michael Duthie*. Music: *Maurice Jarre*. Distributor: *American International Pictures*. Running time 128 minutes. Los Angeles opening November 1976 at several theatres. Classification: PG

Flynn: *Lee Marvin*. Sebastian: *Roger Moore*. Rosa: *Barbara Parkins*. Fleischer: *Rene Kolldehof*. Mohammed: *Ian Holm*. Von Kleine: *Karl M. Vogler*. Kyller: *Horst Janson*. Braun: *Gernot Endemann*.

The Sunday Times (London), 4/18/76 (p. 37)
Dilys Powell

" . . . Based on the novel by Wilbur Smith, the script owes a small debt to history; during the First World War a damaged German battleship did indeed take shelter on an African river. And that was enough to set Mr. Wilbur Smith, Mr. Klinger, Mr. Hunt and a multiracial cast including a faithful dumb African servant (Ian Holm) off on a Boy's Own action-fantasy. There are skirmishes, hangings, shootings and a crocodile. There is shipwreck. There is an air crash. I have to admit that there is a bit of marriage, too, but the girl (Barbara Parkins) is a brick, heroic under threat of death and as ready as anyone to plug a German prisoner. Mr. Marvin himself is given to letting other people get the dirty end of the stick, but he turns out a brick, too, in the end, staying behind in a dangerous spot with a machine-gun, prepared to mow down everybody in sight.

The only character who isn't a brick is the German Commissioner . . ."

©The Sunday Times, 1976.

New York Post, 11/26/76 (p. 30)
Archer Winsten

" . . . No matter how much money and time director Peter Hunt and producer Michael Klinger expend on the physical aspects—and it does seem they've set up some spectacular fires, explosions, and huge wheels rolling down a hill—the whole thing keeps boiling down to the romantic and melodramatic residue, which seems pure fiction despite all the foundation of fact . . .

Throughout Lee Marvin swaggers, when he isn't staggering, Barbara Parkins suffers the death of her infant with natural female fury, and Roger Moore retains his dignity no matter how much blood (catsup) they pour on his face.

The picture emerges as a lively fiction, not good enough to be taken seriously but not so bad at any point that you can't accept the action as the standard offering of movie excitement . . ."

Reprinted by Permission of New York Post.
©1976, New York Post Corporation.

Los Angeles Times, 11/5/76 (Pt. IV, p. 16)
Kevin Thomas

" . . . In *Shout at the Devil* there's much familiar derring-do and lots of gorgeous scenery. But it's a very dated, very meandering tale (that was originally 21 minutes longer than its current 128 minutes) that director Peter Hunt and his writers have to tell. Africa and its resources are treated as prizes for white men to fight over without any regard for its native people. Of course, that was largely the way it was (and in some places is still struggling to be), but *Shout at the Devil* unfortunately finds no evil or irony in depicting scores of black people who are all either servants, lackeys or victims of the white man. After all, it's one thing to make a movie set in 1913 and another to make one that in its level of awareness could just as easily have been made back then . . ."

©Los Angeles Times, 1976.

SILENT MOVIE

Director: *Mel Brooks*. Screenplay: *Ron Clark, Rudy DeLuca, Barry Levinson, Mr. Brooks*. Based on a story by Mr. Brooks. Producer: *Michael Hertzberg*. Photography: *Paul Lohmann*. Editors: *John C. Howard, Stanford C. Allen*. Music: *John Morris*. Distributor:

continued on next page

continued from previous page

Twentieth Century-Fox. Running time 88 minutes. New York opening June 30, 1976, at the Cinema 1 and Cinema 2 Theatres. Classification: PG.

Mel Funn: *Mel Brooks*. Marty Eggs: *Marty Feldman*. Dom Bell: *Dom DeLuise*. Vilma Kaplan: *Bernadette Peters*. Studio Chief: *Sid Caesar*. Engulf: *Harold Gould*. Devour: *Ron Carey*. Pregnant Lady: *Carol Arthur*. News Vendor: *Lima Dunn*. Maitre D': *Fritz Field*. Studio Gate Guard: *Chuck McCann*. Studio Chief's Secretary: *Yvonne Wilder*. Intensive Care Nurse: *Valerie Curtin*. Acupuncture Man: *Arnold Soboloff*. Hotel Bellhop: *Patrick Campbell*. Man in Tailor Shop: *Harry Ritz*. Blind Man: *Charlie Callas*. Fly-in-Soup Man: *Henny Youngman*. British Officer: *Eddie Ryder*.

Women's Wear Daily, 6/30/76 (p. 12)
Howard Kissel

" . . . *Silent Movie* is Brooks' most consistently funny film.
It is indeed a silent movie. Set in 'Hollywood, the film capital of Greater Los Angeles,' it concerns the once-great director Mel Funn, who, after years on the bottle, wants to make a silent movie. He persuades the Current Studio Chief (Sid Caesar) that this may be the picture that will save the studio from being taken over by the menacing conglomerate, Engulf and Devour. Funn persuades some of the biggest stars in Hollywood to appear in the film and wards off the advances of Ms. Vilma Kaplan (Bernadette Peters), aptly described as 'A Bundle of Lust,' who was sent by Engulf and Devour to prevent *Silent Movie* from being made.
Among the achievements in *Silent Movie* is that Brooks has made a film that critics can barely describe without spoiling the fun––and what Hollywood executive has not dreamed of finding a way to create Silent Critics? Brooks, like Mel Funn, whom he plays, has persuaded some of the biggest stars in Hollywood to appear in the picture. None of the big stars in cameo roles is identified in any of the publicity and one would be a churl to spoil the surprise . . . "

© Women's Wear Daily, 1976.

New York Post, 7/1/76 (p. 24)
Frank Rich

"Mel Brooks' new film, *Silent Movie*, is exactly what its title says it is––and that's just how it had to be. This film . . . is, quite simply, too funny for words: the roar of laughter it produces is so steady that even if there were any spoken dialogue, you wouldn't be able to hear it above the audience's din.
Silent Movie isn't just funny, either––it has charm and warmth . . .
Like the last two Brooks movies, *Silent Movie*'s subject is old movies, but this time Brooks has not restricted his line of comic attack to a single genre. *Silent Movie* does, of course, uphold the traditions of classic silent film comedy, but it also has fun with old-time musicals, gangster pictures, alcohol-sotted melodramas, show-biz sagas and even low-budget foreign coproductions.
More juicy still, *Silent Movie* takes after the industry itself: set in contemporary Hollywood, 'the film capital of Greater Los Angeles,' *Silent Movie* offers us a pantheon of crazy show-business types such as have not been since Kaufman and Hart satirized the movie business in *Once in a Lifetime* . . .
It's the first time that Brooks has clearly demonstrated that he has a directorial personality as well as comic one––and, golden as the silent of *Silent Movie* is, the film inevitably leaves you joyously hungry to see what this new, mature Mel Brooks will do once he goes back to making talkies."

Reprinted by Permission of New York Post.
© 1976, New York Post Corporation.

The Times (London), 1/21/77 (p. 13)
David Robinson

" . . . Brooks is undoubtedly a prolific comic inventor. The dominant motivation of his humour is literal and realistic reexamination of convention and cliche. How, for instance, if you take a figure of speech quite literally? 'The boys'll flip . . .,' he says, and next thing you see them actually flipping, on the pavement. What if the wedding cake on which an Astaire-Rogers couple dance is *real*, covered with a slush of real icing? Or what if the delivery men who hurl bundles of newspapers off their vans *always* succeed in hitting the news vendor? (The last produces one of the film's nicest running gags.) Yet, however funny in its parts, without the resolve of the classic comedians to shape the gags into a total and determined structure Brooks' large gifts tend to be diffused and defused long before the end."

© The Times, 1977.

The Sunday Times (London), 1/23/77 (p. 38)
Alan Brien

" . . . Mel Brooks does not impress us as someone who can keep his mouth shut. His cocky, clever, mobile face of the New York Jewish jester is about as far from the stony petrification of a Buster Keaton as can be imagined. Still, with some help from camera syncopation, he proves a winning, wayward hero. And several purely pictorial gags do work extremely well—as when the cardiac monitor by the Current Studio Chief's bed is adjusted by his visitors to operate as an electronic tennis game.

With three writers (Ron Clark, Rudy DeLuca, Barry Levinson) as well as Brooks, the script is endlessly prodigal in its gags, some running, a few limping, one or two dead on arrival, others exploding gloriously in your hands, so if you miss one, there's always another behind. *Silent Movie* doesn't fulfill Mel Brooks' hope of creating a pure cinema of images with only body language but is a worthy pardner to *Blazing Saddles*."

© The Sunday Times, 1977.

Monthly Film Bulletin, December 1976 (p. 256)
Geoff Brown

". . . as with all Brooks movies, gags and performers are recklessly piled on top of each other and the motivating idea is submerged, resulting in a crazy tangle of variable comic routines. A clutch of Hollywood stars appear in separate sequences to fairly disastrous effect, guying their own images with heavy self-consciousness (though one relishes the sight of Mrs. Mel Brooks dancing a crazy tango with her husband). The film is further harmed by having a triumvirate cutting the capers rather than Brooks alone: all the neatest jokes are centred round Brooks himself (imagining himself dancing with his lovely spy on top of a none too sturdy wedding cake) or appear as throwaway details (the patrician graffiti in the washroom at Engulf and Devour), while Marty Feldman and Dom DeLuise only provide unfunny mugging . . ."

© Monthly Film Bulletin, 1976.

Newsweek, 7/12/76 (p. 69)
Jack Kroll

". . . The gags as usual vary in quality from gold to zinc, but what makes *Silent Movie* more than a string of gags is the comic sensibility of Brooks. Believe it or not, the master of bad taste becomes almost endearing in this film—as when he pays homage to the good old bump and grind with a pelvic paroxysm by the pneumatic Bernadette Peters. The film's foremost quality is a genuine sweetness of tone . . . Brooks knows that the quality common to the old silent comedies was this rippling rhythm of sweet, silly humanity, and he captures it to a remarkable degree without any camp or condescension.

The sharp, clear comic behavior of the actors (this is Brooks' finest performance), the cleverly interspersed titles (just enough of them) and John Morris' remarkably effective music make a lovely and amusing texture . . ."

© Newsweek, Inc. 1976
reprinted by permission.

Dom Bell (played by Dom DeLuise) hotrods in a wheelchair in **Silent Movie**, a comedy Mel Brooks directed.

Christian Science Monitor, 7/19/76 (p. 22)
David Sterritt

". . . As usual in a Brooks opus, there are moments of childish vulgarity. But Brooks' worst failing—a reliance on shouting and verbal repetition to boost weak ideas—is absent from *Silent Movie* because of the nature of the beast. In a way, wordlessness is the best discipline Brooks could have imposed on himself. He still shouts visually, carrying jokes on too long and punctuating even the most obvious gags. *Silent Movie* is the most restrained Brooks farce so far, however, and could point to a welcome mellowing in his manner; even the character played by Brooks is less abrasive than usual.

Brooks doesn't hesitate to sabotage our movie expectations. He shot *Young Frankenstein* in unheard-of black-and-white. Now he returns to color but leaves out the voice track. Risky business, and not all the risks work . . ."

Reprinted by permission from The Christian
Science Monitor © 1976.
The Christian Science Publishing Society.
All rights reserved.

continued on next page

continued from previous page

Saturday Review, 8/7/76 (p. 44)
Judith Crist

". . . one can readily see that Brooks has concocted a talkie with a gimmick. The gimmickry here involves parodies of silent-movie jokes and simplistic plotting. The absence of realistic sound and speech is complete with the exception of one word—spoken, of course, by the mime Marcel Marceau. Above all, it's an oral comedy, with its verbal humor obvious in signs, names, and title cards . . .

Brooks, Feldman, and DeLuise become a cross between the Three Stooges and the Ritz Brothers, with Feldman parodying lechery, DeLuise branching out for gluttony, and Brooks portraying the romantic hero. High points include a fantasy wedding-cake bride-and-groom dance with Peters and a solo bit involving the fatal bottle of whiskey. The three outdo themselves in a nightclub tango routine with Bancroft, who shares with us what seems to be the time of her life in some superb mugging; in a shower with Reynolds, who is engagingly self-satiric; in a bedside visit with Caesar, whose heart attack opens the way to some deliciously sadistic hospital gags (topped by an electronic Ping-Pong match on a heart monitor); and in a mad wheelchair race with Newman . . ."

©Judith Crist, 1976.

Commonweal, 7/30/76 (p. 500)
Colin L. Westerbeck, Jr.

"Brooks' *Silent Movie* could easily have been . . . mechanical in its execution, for it . . . reworks the same situation four or five times. The situation is that a has-been director named Funn (Brooks himself) is trying to make a comeback by lining up a lot of stars to act in a silent movie. What keeps Brooks' treatment from becoming repetitious is that he works the opposite way from Simon . . . Brooks obviously begins with the end result of the gag, some funny visual that has occurred to him, and just makes the plot lead up to it somehow. One such gag Brooks includes, for example, is the sight of a stilt-man in a raincoat run over by a steamroller whose driver thinks he has squished a giant. To work up to this gag, Brooks simply has Funn approach Burt Reynolds for the film by standing on the shoulders of two assistants (Dom DeLuise and Marty Feldman) inside such a raincoat. The steamroller is passing in the street as Reynolds loses patience and tackles this triple-decker, etc.

The fact is that the very irrelevance of this whole routine to the plot makes it all the funnier . . . Brooks . . . understands, like Chaplin, when you put such physically improbable gags before the camera, it will be in little, accidental details of the execution that the gags will become truly hilarious . . ."

©Commonweal, 1976.

New York Magazine, 7/19/76 (p. 84)
John Simon

". . . *Silent Movie* has some quite funny sight gags, though the invention wears progressively thinner; it also has exaggerated sound effects that have good and bad moments; it has, further, a puckish score by John Morris that sometimes merely puckers; and there are some amusing intertitles . . .

The scenario is basically no sillier than those of the old silent comedies, but the innocence is gone. Some gags are too elucubrated and esoteric; others are takeoffs on the old ones, and seem to kid something that depended on its deadpan dedication. Brooks is not an eloquent mime; Feldman is nearer the mark, but gets less good material; DeLuise, whose comic persona is that of a swish baby, is simply distasteful. Among the guest stars, the ones who kid themselves the most wholeheartedly—Burt Reynolds and Anne Bancroft—come off well; the others are left stranded with nothing to play. Sid Caesar and Miss Peters work hard to little effect, and a growing desperation churns its way through the movie . . ."

©1976 by the NYM Corp. Reprinted with the permission of NEW YORK Magazine.

Village Voice, 7/19/76 (p. 103)
Molly Haskell

". . . Mel Brooks' latest is not up to the wackiest belly laughs of *Young Frankenstein*, *Blazing Saddles* or *The Producers*, but it is a smile riot in keeping with the noiseless m.o. that is its claim to fame. (It is actually one of the least silent movies ever made, with John Morris' breezily explicit score nailing down the gags, and allowing the subtitles to go their own boisterous way.) . . .

Some of the best moments are in the 'love interest' scenes with Bernadette Peters, who herself is able to evoke both the absurdity and the total conviction of the femme fatale. The loveliest thing about *Silent Movie*, in imposing new faces on old routines, is its appreciation of the lunacy of the current movie business and its stars who are not as far from pioneering prima donnas as they like to think."

Reprinted by permission of The Village Voice.
Copyright © The Village Voice, Inc., 1976.

Films in Review, August/September 1976 (p. 441)
Hugh Bernard

"When it comes to sight gags there's no one better in movies today than director-actor Mel Brooks who stars in *Silent Movie* as a has-been movie director who sells producer Sid Caesar on backing Brooks' brilliant new idea—a silent movie. Both need a hit as Engulf and Devour, the conglomerate, is about to take over the studio. With Dom DeLuise, Marty Feldman and Bernadette Peters helping Mel, he completes his movie, but not before signing up Burt Reynolds, Liza Minnelli, Anne Bancroft, James Caan and Paul Newman, each of whom has about 5 to 10 unbilled minutes of very funny screen time.

Laughter has no age limit, but a couple of moments in the film will make some parents unhappy about seeing it . . ."

©Films in Review, 1976.

Film Information, 9/76 (p. 4)
Robert F. Moss

". . . The humor, which ranges from buffoonish to satirical to risque, is not unlike the material Brooks used to write for Sid Caesar (who appears in the film). If it lacks the occasional manic inspiration of *Young Frankenstein*, it's also free of the extreme vulgarity of *Blazing Saddles*.

The film is hampered by casting errors, the worst of which is Brooks himself, who has followed Woody Allen's bad example of grabbing the leading role in the film, despite minimal acting talents. Similarly, Brooks might have spared us Marty Feldman, working his bug-eyed stare to death, and Dom DeLuise as a fat man who (surprise) loves to eat. On the other hand, Sid Caesar is effective as a hypertense producer, and Bernadette Peters is irresistible as the pouty-mouthed vamp . . ."

©Film Information, 1976.

New Leader, 8/2/76 (p. 23)
Robert Asahina

". . . *Silent Movie* simply isn't very funny. Brooks' rabid partisans will no doubt dispute this, having convinced themselves of the director's comic 'genius.' . . .

Like all of Brooks' work (with the possible exception of *Young Frankenstein*), this one is guilty of obviousness. That is not to say that the humor is excessively broad—though it happens to be—but rather that it is at the level of a dull five-year-old. For instance, after Funn finally convinces the head of Big Picture Studios (Sid Caesar) to produce his silent movie, the title reads: 'Wait'll I tell the guys—they'll flip.' Sure enough, in the next scene they do just that: Dom Bell (Dom DeLuise) flips Marty Egg (Marty Feldman) in a back handspring. In another sequence Funn carefully mouths, 'You stupid son-of-a-bitch'; the title says, 'You bad boy.'

This kind of blatant gag can only succeed when contrasted to more subtle humor. But Brooks provides no shadings; he never misses a chance to stick his finger in your eye—twice in a row, if possible . . ."

Reprinted with permission from
The New Leader, 1976.
©The American Labor Conference
on International Affairs, Inc.

SILVER STREAK

Director: *Arthur Hiller*. Screenplay: *Colin Higgins*. Producers: *Edward K. Milkis, Thomas L. Miller*. Photography: *David M. Walsh*. Editor: *David Bretherton*. Music: *Henry Mancini*. Distributor: *Twentieth Century-Fox*. Running time 104 minutes. New York opening December 8, 1976, at the National and Loews Tower East Theatres. Classification: PG.

George Caldwell: *Gene Wilder*. Hilly Burns: *Jill Clayburgh*. Grover Muldoon: *Richard Pryor*. Roger Devereau: *Patrick McGoohan*. Sweet: *Ned Beatty*. Sheriff Chauncey: *Clifton James*. Mr. Whiney: *Ray Walston*. Johnson: *Stefan Gierasch*. Chief: *Len Birman*. Plain Jane: *Valerie Curtin*. Reace (Goldtooth): *Richard Kiel*. Rita Babtree: *Lucille Benson*. Ralston: *Scatman Crothers*.

Christian Science Monitor, 12/27/76 (p. 18)
David Sterritt

". . . Gene Wilder stars as a quiet and bookish man heading out on a quiet and bookish train trip to Chicago. He makes the mistake of having a liaison with a pretty lady, sees a corpse being flung past his window, and ends up involved with a murder plot, an archvillain, and a bunch of letters by Rembrandt. The climax is vintage chase—movie stuff with a *King Kong*-type denouement wherein a locomotive does in a railroad station . . .

Arthur Hiller's directing can't decide whether to emphasize romance, comedy, or thrills, so it's often hard for us to decide whether to sigh, laugh, or get worried. Probably we're supposed to do all three at once, but this would take a finer meshing of talents than *Silver Streak* provides. Unless you have a secret hostility toward railroad stations, you're likely to be disappointed."

Reprinted by permission from The Christian
Science Monitor ©1976.
The Christian Science Publishing Society.
All rights reserved.

New York Post, 12/9/76 (p. 23)
Frank Rich

". . . Despite its $5-million cost, this movie looks as tacky as it's written, and its comic bits never mesh with its allegedly suspenseful action. Hiller's only real directorial achievement is an elaborate train-crash climax; otherwise he seems to have devoted most of his energy to plugging Henry Mancini's dippy musical theme . . ."

continued on next page

continued from previous page

Except for Pryor, the movie's actors are sorely misused. Wilder is spectacularly miscast as a Cary Grant-styled romantic lead; while he's funny in his few zany moments—he does a hilarious jig of despair after he fails to jump aboard a moving train—mainly he's just plain drab. Miss Clayburgh . . . doesn't have a role to play, but she is appealing and idiosyncratically attractive . . .

Pryor is spared the fate of his co-stars for the simple reason that his role, which seems an afterthought in Higgins' script, has nothing to do with the movie's plot; he's free to do his own ingratiating shtick without having to give a damn about the nonsense transpiring around him . . ."

Reprinted by Permission of New York Post,
©1976, New York Post Corporation.

Women's Wear Daily, 12/7/76 (p. 16)
Howard Kissel

"*Silver Streak*, a film about intrigue on a train, is supposed to combine comedy and suspense in the way Hitchcock did in films like *North by Northwest* or *The Lady Vanishes*. What is interesting about the film, which is largely built out of cliches from other films, is that its hero is patterned after not Cary Grant or some other light romantic lead, but Woody Allen.

Who would have thought that a likable Jewish quasi-highbrow shlep could be the hero of a detective story? Allen paved the way, and, in *Silver Streak*, Gene Wilder brings his own charm to the role. Jill Clayburgh is much more successful and appealing as the romantic lead here than she was in Gable and Lombard . . .

Though Clayburgh is ostensibly the romantic lead, the film only comes alive when Richard Pryor enters . . . One suspects Pryor wrote his own material because his scenes are more outrageous, more inventive than the rest of the film . . ."

©Women's Wear Daily, 1976.

Newsweek, 12/13/76 (p. 106A)
Janet Maslin

"*Silver Streak* stars funnymen Gene Wilder and Richard Pryor, but it isn't a comedy—it's a sluggish adventure movie about an L.A.-to-Chicago train trip that wastes two considerable talents . . .

Arthur Hiller paces the action so slowly that *Love Story*, which he also directed, looks like slapstick by comparison. When Richard Pryor finally puts in an appearance well over an hour into the story, his frantic timing and good-natured vulgarity are welcome . . .

Pryor isn't around long enough to wear out his welcome, since twenty minutes after he shows

up the movie abruptly culminates in a bloody shootout, an expensive chase sequence and some unexpectedly elaborate train-crash special effects. Wilder isn't so lucky. He manages to bring a comic composure to even the tightest squeezes, and he shows that he has the makings of a romantic leading man. But his love scenes are enough to curdle milk . . ."

©Newsweek, Inc. 1976
reprinted by permission.

Village Voice, 12/20/76 (p. 80)
Molly Haskell

". . . careens wildly from one genre to another without satisfying the demands of any. It stars Gene Wilder as an editor of 'how-to' books (specializing in horticulture), Jill Clayburgh as a secretary (specializing in 'phone'), Ned Beatty as a federal agent convincingly disguised as a back-slapping, skirt-chasing vitamin salesman, Patrick McGoohan as a class-act villain, and Richard Pryor as a car thief on the lam and the single best reason for seeing the movie. What begins as a less-than-sparkling boy-girl romance lurches into an unfunny bumbling-hero-on-the-lam comedy, slides into a buddy-buddy film (when Wilder, who has witnessed the murder of Clayburgh's art-historian boss, makes an unscheduled departure from the train and encounters Pryor in the back seat of a police car), crashes into a mock-disaster film in the Chicago train station, where it comes full circle to the (possibly still virginal) boy and girl romance! . . ."

Reprinted by permission of The Village Voice.
Copyright ©The Village Voice, Inc., 1976.

Saturday Review, 1/22/77 (p. 49)
Judith Crist

"Gene Wilder and Richard Pryor are very likable performers under any circumstances; in *Silver Streak* they are done in by inept direction. In this case it is Arthur Hiller who is slogging along one beat behind the action of the Colin Higgins screenplay . . .

Wilder does relatively well in his first foray into a straight romantic role, although he is at his best when his comic persona emerges in near hysterical ineptitudes. Clayburgh is restricted by a script that gives her a peculiarly passive role. Ned Beatty, this time a federal agent disguised as a lecherous traveling man; Clifton James, again as a singularly dumb red-neck sheriff; Patrick McGoohan, as one of the suavest villains since George Sanders was in flower; and Pryor, supercool and ultra-savvy, all provide bright spots. Throughout, however, there is a nagging consciousness that things should be funnier than they are."

©Judith Crist, 1977.

Los Angeles Times, 12/9/76 (Pt. IV, p. 1)
Kevin Thomas

"*Silver Streak* . . . takes a bit too long in arriving to its quite literally smash finish, but the getting there is pleasant and fairly amusing . . .

Movies and mystery novels have long made train journeys synonymous with adventure and romance. But when a film's hero is Gene Wilder you can be pretty sure that there's going to be comedy as well.

Wilder is the proprietor of a small publishing firm who boards the Chicago-bound Silver Streak in Los Angeles and encounters an especially sultry and inviting Jill Clayburgh, secretary to a noted art historian.

By chance—or is it?—Wilder and Miss Clayburgh have adjoining compartments with a connecting door with a notably unreliable latch. Romance ensues—but what's the corpse of Miss Clayburgh's employer doing dangling outside her window?

That is just the beginning of the ever-multiplying mayhem in store for Wilder . . .

. . . *Silver Streak* is by no means an *Orient Express*, but still it's a pretty diverting trip."

©Los Angeles Times, 1976.

Film Information, January 1977 (p. 2)
David Bartholemew

"*Silver Streak* is an amiable, well-cast comedy adventure with Gene Wilder, Richard Pryor and Jill Clayburgh about an L.A.-to-Chicago train trip. Director Arthur Hiller seems to have taken as his model the kind of stylish fun (*Charade*, *Arabesque*) Stanley Donen used to have with Hitchcockian stories, but the film, written by Colin Higgins, is uneven and unstylish and is not so much derailed as occasionally lured into uninteresting sidings. In the last reel the villains turn rough, the bloodshed mounts up, and *Silver Streak* quickly turns into a disaster movie (somewhat in the manner of *Lucky Lady*, Fox's Christmas film last year) as an empty runaway train plows through the Chicago station, a poor alternative to an ending that is as extraneous to what has gone before it as it is technically proficient . . ."

©Film Information, 1977.

Films in Review, January 1977 (p. 59)
Rob Edelman

"*Silver Streak* has something for everybody—romance, mystery, comedy, jive-talking Richard Pryor, and a locomotive speeding out of control towards a crowded passenger terminal . . .

. . . *Silver Streak* is also hilarious comedy, particularly when Wilder, in order to evade the police, does himself up in blackface. The film unfortunately attempts to be several different movies at once, but

under the smooth, professional direction of Arthur Hiller, we forgive (or forget) that fact as we sit back and enjoy ourselves.

While all the performers are fine, Pryor runs away with the film as a resourceful thief who comes to Wilder's aid. *Silver Streak* is a diverting example of Hollywood escapism."

©Films in Review, 1977.

New York Magazine, 1/17/77 (p. 56)
John Simon

". . . as it tries to stretch out a gray dot of an idea into an extended silver streak, the film huffs and puffs and wheezes like a worn-out locomotive.

David M. Walsh's cinematography has its impressive, boldly antirealistic moments, and Jill Clayburgh, once again unworthily cast, once again keeps her head above ditchwater (the actress, as Colin Higgins might wittily have put it, gives great head-above-ditchwater). The special effects people do fairly well by a runaway train destroying an unwary railroad station, but Henry Mancini may be the only film composer who would accompany a lost man's hapless trekking through the desert with ballroom music—not even funny enough to work as a joke. Gene Wilder is miscast in a young-Jimmy Stewart role, and Patrick McGoohan, even as a villain, is loathsome above the line of duty. Richard Pryor has the best part, and he and Wilder have a few chuckle-begetting moments; but what can anyone do with a scenarist who'll write, 'Always be nasty to nasturtiums'?"

©1977 by the NYM Corp. Reprinted with the permission of NEW YORK Magazine.

The Times (London), 4/1/77 (p. 17)
David Robinson

"You cannot go far wrong with a film about trains, and *Silver Streak* gets off to a flying start with a Disappearing Professor, to recall Hitchcock's Vanishing Lady. The leading character however is the Silver Streak itself, slicing its way across the continent from Los Angeles to Chicago, with a suitably colourful passenger list . . .

The story, by Colin Higgins, dashes brightly along, introducing on its way a fine range of eccentrics, including Patrick McGoohan's smooth and lethal villain and a fine comedian, Richard Pryor, as an amiable thief who tags along with George and has a talent for disaster-prone notions like using boot polish to disguise himself as a black hippie. The major distinction of the film, though, is the director Arthur Hiller's ability to juggle both the comedy and the adventure spectacle. Offering a noisily destructive car chase and full-scale disaster movie climax, with the Silver Streak carving its way through Chicago's Union Station, the film carries the heavy stuff commendably lightly."

©The Times, 1977.

SKY RIDERS

Director: *Douglas Hickox.* Screenplay: *Jack Dewitt, Stanley Mann, Garry Michael White.* Based on a story by *Hall T. Sprague, Bill McGaw.* Executive Producer: *Sandy Howard.* Producer: *Terry Morse Jr.* Photography: *Qusama Rawi.* Editor: *Malcolm Cooke.* Aerial Cameramen: *Greg MacGillivray, Jim Freeman.* Distributor: *Twentieth Century-Fox.* Running time 90 minutes. New York opening March 26, 1976, at the RKO 86th Street Twin II Theatre. Classification: PG.

McCabe: *James Coburn.* Ellen: *Susannah York.* Bracken: *Robert Culp.* Nikolidis: *Charles Aznavour.* No. 1: *Werner Pochath.* No. 6: *Zouzou* Wasserman: *Kenneth Griffith.*

See Volume 1 for additional reviews

The Times (London), 5/28/76 (p. 11)
Philip French

"*Sky Riders* is a mindless international thriller that begins like Chabrol's *Nada* with the ferocious kidnapping of a rich American industrialist's wife (Susannah York) and children by a left-wing terrorist group disguised in ice hockey masks, and ends like *Where Eagles Dare* with a blazing assault on an inaccessible mountain-top monastery where the gang is holding its victims. The change in direction between this apparently serious opening and the lightheartedly violent ending is partly achieved by casting James Coburn as the professional smuggler who casually recruits a team of itinerant American hang-glider experts to attack the monastery at night . . . Despite being unduly protracted, the final sequence is fairly spectacular as the hang-gliders float through the air between towering rock formations while snipers take pot shots at them."

© The Times, 1976.

The Sunday Times (London), 5/30/76 (p. 37)
Alan Brien

"What a lot of trouble families of the rich cause these days on and off the screen, by presenting such tempting targets for kidnappers out to redistribute the world's wealth in their own direction. I couldn't help wondering what the husband here, an American businessman in Greece, had contributed to humanity to be able to cough up 25 million dollars worth of military hardware, including a Phantom Jet with Sidewinder missiles and three anti-aircraft guns, to the 'World Activist Revolutionary Army' which snatched his wife and daughter.

Not to mention the cost in human life to his servants, the Greek Army and police, a team of aerial acrobats, and the ranks of the WARA . . .

There are some exhilarating sequences of hang-gliding, the bat-winged camera riding the air currents through fearsome canyons. But the rest of the film is notably pedestrian, and rather thickankled at that."

© The Sunday Times, 1976.

Monthly Film Bulletin, 5/76 (p. 107)
Richard Combs

"A startlingly brash opportunistic venture, combining some lyrical hang-gliding interludes with the no-nonsense, leftist-squelching fervour of the plot. Except when he succumbs to the itch to sightsee that seemed to have bitten him badly in *Brannigan*, Douglas Hickox somehow strings it all together in a far livelier fashion than it deserves. He ploughs through the absurdities of every scene in a forcefully crisp, brightly-lit style, and over characters of best Boy's Own cardboard sprinkles just a little tetchy instability. But the machinations of the committee of scriptwriters are alarmingly crude . . . and the primitive, computerised dialogue steadily crushes all sense and sensibility out of the film . . . In even more confident helpings than its own wind-up action climaxes, *Sky Riders* dishes out a political message that might be summed up as sneeringly smug advertising for its own lush production values."

© Monthly Film Bulletin, 1976.

Films in Review, 5/76 (p. 315)
William Bernard

"If you love action-adventure films, *Sky Riders* is for you. The wife (Susannah York) and the children of an American millionaire (Robert Culp), living in Greece, are kidnapped by terrorists demanding $5,000,000 in ransom to foster world revolution. James Coburn plays Miss York's ex-lover, also the father of her son. Coburn is an adventurer who wants quick action, dissatisfied with Police Chief Nikolidis' (Charles Aznavour) slow handling of the case. Once Coburn learns that the kidnappers are using an almost inaccessible, abandoned mountain-top monastery as a hide-out, he hires a group of hang gliders (girls as well as men) for his rescue plans. *Sky Riders* then takes wing away from its improbable plot.

Director Douglas Hickox has beautifully handled the gliding sequences, with the help of cinematographer Qusama Rawi . . ."

© Films in Review, 1976.

Los Angeles Times, 4/21/76 (Pt. IV, p. 10)
Kevin Thomas

" . . . For the most part, *Sky Riders*, written by various hands and directed zestfully by Douglas Hickox, moves too fast to allow you to ponder its credibility, something that could perhaps be fatal to the film.

As it is, the hang-gliding sequences (photographed dazzlingly by Greg MacGillivray and Jim Freeman) are so breathtaking and beautiful--they cost one fatality and a dozen injuries to stage--that seeing is believing.

There's not much time for characterizations, but *Sky Riders* first-rate cast supplies all the needed dimensions. Coburn is especially effective, combining warmth with a wry knowingness that gives his character--and thereby the film--some edge. (Even so, we'd like to know at least a little more about him.)

Sky Riders has been most handsomely produced (by Sandy Howard), and along with its superb camerawork, boasts an aptly full-bodied score by Lalo Schifrin that enhances the film's suspense and action."

© Los Angeles Times, 1976.

SLAP, THE (LA GIFLE)

Director: *Claude Pinoteau*. Screenplay: *Mr. Pinoteau, Jean-Loup Dabadie*. Executive Producer: *Alain Poire*. Photographer: *Jean Collomb*. Distributor: *Silver Screen Productions*. Running time 104 minutes. New York opening January, 1976, at the 68th Street Playhouse. Classification: None. Origin: France.

Jean: *Lino Ventura*. Isabelle: *Isabelle Adjani*. Helene: *Ann Girardot*. Marc: *Francis Perrin* Remy: *Jacques Spiesser*.

See Volume 1 for additional reviews

Christian Science Monitor, 5/7/76 (p. 25)
David Sterritt

" . . . The heroine of *The Slap* is played by young and lovely Isabelle Adjani, currently an international favorite: e.g., the title role in Francois Truffaut's unique *Story of Adele H*. But in *The Slap* Miss Ad-

jani plays no exotic, be-dazzled romantic.

Rather, her character is an ordinary 18-year-old who tries to make her latest romance work, feuding with daddy, and eventually runs away from home and hearth in search of a freer life with mom and mom's new man. What she really needs, of course, is to grow up--a common enough movie theme, treated here with polish but no new insight.

Lino Ventura and Annie Girardot give firm portrayals as the put-upon mom and pop, and there are some amusingly clumsy moments . . . with the heroine's silly boyfriend . . . But Claude Pinoteau's direction is slow and most staid, provoking more yawns than gasps or giggles."

Reprinted by permission from The Christian
Science Monitor © 1976.
The Christian Science Publishing Society.
All rights reserved.

SLAP SHOT

Director: *George Roy Hill*. Screenplay: *Nancy Dowd*. Producers: *Robert J. Wunsch, Stephen Friedman*. Photography: *Victor Kemper*. Editor: *Dede Allen*. Music: *Elmer Bernstein*. Production: *Pan Arts*. Distributor: *Universal Pictures*. Running time 122 minutes. New York opening February 25, 1977, at several theatres. Classification: R.

Reggie Dunlop: *Paul Newman*. Ned Braden: *Michael Ontkean*. Lily Braden: *Lindsay Crouse*. Francine Dunlop: *Jennifer Warren*. Suzanne: *Melinda Dillon*. Joe McGrath: *Strother Martin*. Dave "Killer" Carlson: *Jerry Houser*. Denis Le Mieux: *Yvon Barrette*. Steve Hansen: *Steve Carlson*. Jeff Hansen: *Jeff Carlson*. Jack Hansen: *Dave Hanson*. Jim Carr: *Andrew Duncan*. Dickie Dunn: *Emmett Walsh*. Jim Ahern: *Stephen Mendillo*. Johnny Upton: *Allan Nicholls*. Helen Upton: *Swoosie Kurtz*. Drouin: *Yvon Ponton*. Wanchuk: *Brad Sullivan*. Anita McCambridge: *Kathryn Walker*. Tim McCracken: *Paul D'Amato*. Charlebois: *Guido Tenesi*. Brophy: *John Gorfton*. LeBrun: *Ronald L. Docken*. Charlie: *Matthew Cowles*.

Village Voice, 3/14/77 (p. 41)
Andrew Sarris

"First, the good news: *Slap Shot* is the funniest hockey movie since Walt Disney's *Hockey Homicide* with Goofy at his meanest and most murder-

continued on next page

continued from previous page .

ous. For a change, the female leads (Jennifer Warren, Lindsay Crouse) are given parts with zing and feeling, and men hunger after them. A marvelous trio of moronic zanies (Jeff Carlson, Steve Carlson, David Hanson) come on like the Marx Brothers, though mostly Chico, and the production zips along with unflagging pace. So far, so good. Why then do I remain uneasy enough to keep all my critical options open? Perhaps I find something fundamentally hypocritical in the way director George Roy Hill and scenarist Nancy Dowd poke fun at hockey macho in a movie that is itself raunchy and violent, which is to say that Hill and Dowd are not above taking a few cheap shots of their own . . .''

Reprinted by permission of The Village Voice.
Copyright © The Village Voice, Inc., 1977.

New York Post, 2/26/77 (p. 28)
Frank Rich

''. . . *Slap Shot* . . . is a celebration of locker-room humor in all its raunchy glory—and it is no-holds-barred funny.

Whether you'll find this film as amusing as I did is something of an open question. *Slap Shot* is the dirtiest-mouthed major studio movie I've ever seen —and those moviegoers who still recoil from four-letter words should be warned. For anyone else, though, the freewheeling scatological language of *Slap Shot* will be a real treat . . .

The film's director, George Roy Hill (*Butch Cassidy*, *The Sting*), is presumably responsible for the generally high level of acting, and he has given the movie an exuberant spirit as well . . .

I only wish that this director hadn't settled for Paul Newman as his star. While Newman provides another one of his ingratiating *Cool Hand Luke*-style performances, he's never convincing as a low-rent jock . . .''

Reprinted by Permission of New York Post.
©1977, New York Post Corporation.

Christian Science Monitor, 3/16/77 (p. 30)
David Sterritt

''. . . in the midst of all the tumbling about you'll find some funny gags, insightful portrayals, and one of Newman's most thoughtful performances ever. His character is a rake and a heel. He is unwilling and unable to hold his marriage together, abusive to friends and enemies alike, eager to move in on a teammate's wife if it means putting fire into the next game. Newman gives him perhaps too much raffish charm, but lets us peek at the vulnerability beneath the bravado . . .

Points go also to Lindsay Crouse as a miserable hockey wife, Michael Ontkean as the sensitive grad, Melinda Dillon as a promiscuous friend—in one of

the frank scenes that indicate a deep sexual insecurity among many of the characters—Jennifer Warren, Allan Nicholls, Strother Martin, Yvon Barrette, and the rest of the slightly crazy hockey jocks who swirl about the ice and film. Their abilities help save *Slap Shot* from its own indulgences in the roughness that has lately coarsened both sports and entertainment.''

Reprinted by permission from The Christian
Science Monitor © 1977.
The Christian Science Publishing Society.
All rights reserved.

Los Angeles Times, 2/25/77 (Pt. IV, p. 1)
Kevin Thomas

''. . . Written by Nancy Dowd, an alumna of Smith College and UCLA's motion picture division, *Slap Shot* has the ingredients of a movie that could be both a lively entertainment and a comment upon the public's blood lust for violence in sports. Instead, *Slap Shot* uses its mill-town milieu and its third-rate athletics to justify the foulest dialogue yet heard in a mainstream commercial movie, a nude sequence that if not unwarranted plays exploitatively, and dosages of violence (mixed with mealy-mouthed protestations that violence is awful) that make the movie into the objects of its own hypocritical scorns. The pot satirizes the kettle, and Sadie Thompson complains of the low moral tone in the Tropics . . .

It is dismaying to see Newman, an actor of intelligence and sensitivity as well as charm, trapped in that aw-shucks charm, leavened here in a gaseous way with the vilest of the script's language. You wonder if he winced, or if he spoke out of some felt contempt for what the movies had for the moment come to . . .''

©Los Angeles Times, 1977.

Saturday Review, 4/2/77 (p. 41)
Judith Crist

''. . . George Roy Hill's comedy about a third-rate minor-league ice-hockey team on the verge of extinction. Reminiscent of *Paperback Hero*, a 1975 Canadian film that approached the subject seriously, what plot there is stems from the player-coach's attempt to inspire a last-ditch reversal of the team's losing streak and to reconcile, amid his womanizing, with his wife. What point there is, beyond the depiction of seedy hockey pros and their fans as foul-mouthed, bloodlusting semiliterates, eludes me . . .

Paul Newman, his face scarred and his teeth given a denture look, brings his usual charm to the player-coach role, but even he seems out of tune with the gutter talk. Jennifer Warren, so interesting a personality in *Night Moves*, manages to make no mark on the feelings in the role of his alienated wife . . . But all play second fiddle to the predominant notion that bare behinds and four-letter words make for high comedy.''

©Judith Crist, 1977.

New York Magazine, 3/7/77 (p. 78)
John Simon

". . . The real problem here is that the film has no point of view nor even consistency of style. It fluctuates between realism and absurdism, cynical casualness and manic exaggeration, moral indignation and total indifference. The trouble with this is that the lurking seriousness undercuts the free-wheeling humor, and the almost surreal stylization mitigates against the ethical values that seem, at times, to be promulgated. In fact, something is apparently being said about sports, sex, and violence here, but it is said so self-contradictorily, in so irresponsibly effect-hunting a way that the result makes you feel queasy. Yet, bit by bit, the film is often quite funny, well acted on the whole, and very tidily directed. There is even some extremely good hockey action photography that, in the end, goes for nothing . . ."

© 1977 by the NYM Corp. Reprinted with the permission of NEW YORK Magazine.

SLIPPER AND THE ROSE: THE STORY OF CINDERELLA, THE

Director: *Bryan Forbes.* Screenplay: *Robert B. Sherman, Richard M. Sherman, Mr. Forbes.* Producer: *Stuart Lyons.* Music and Lyrics: *Messrs. Sherman.* Photography: *Tony Imi.* Editor: *Timothy Gee.* Production: *Paradine Co-Productions Ltd.* Distributor: *Universal Pictures.* Running time 128 minutes. New York opening November 4, 1976, at Radio City Music Hall. Classification: G. Origin: England.

Prince: *Richard Chamberlain.* Cinderella: *Gemma Craven.* Fairy Godmother: *Annette Crosbie.* Dowager Queen: *Edith Evans.* John: *Christopher Gable.* King: *Michael Hordern.* Stepmother: *Margaret Lockwood.* Lord Chamberlain: *Kenneth More.* Montague: *Julian Orchard.* Queen: *Lally Bowers.* Palatine: *Sherrie Hewson.* Isobella: *Rosalind Ayres.*

The Times (London), 3/26/76
David Robinson

". . . *The Slipper and the Rose* is altogether a bold innovation in contemporary cinema, as a film which sets out only to please, charm, seduce and entertain, without any ulterior object of impressing by cleverness or thrilling with the sort of stimulation of sluggish sensations that has become the stuff of most English-language cinema. The intentions alone are appealing; and the film to a great extent achieves them.

The book is bright and funny and has the right pantomime quality of comic anachronism and contemporary reference. The alterations to the story are variations, not departures. The music and musical numbers are recognizably from the same stable as *Mary Poppins* and *Chitty Chitty Bang Bang* . . ."

©The Times, 1976.

New York Magazine, 11/15/76 (p. 117)
John Simon

". . . Bryan Forbes' *The Slipper and the Rose: The Story of Cinderella* very nearly succeeds on all counts despite a title that sounds more like a doctoral dissertation than gossamer and stardust . . .

The script Forbes devised with some help from his composers—for this is a musical—is both a reasonably faithful retelling of the story and a mild elaboration and modernization of it . . . If the disparate components fail to coalesce, they can be savored bit by bit.

There is, first of all, a feast of performances. Forbes, himself a former actor, chooses often unexpected but always apt interpreters, and gets them to believe in and flush out whatever may be thin and precarious. As the King, Michael Hordern, surely the cinema's most scrumptious fussbudget, grouses, blusters, and dithers away to frantic perfection, regardless of whether he has funny, unfunny, or no lines at all . . ."

© 1976 by the NYM Corp. Reprinted with the permission of NEW YORK Magazine.

Los Angeles Times, 3/25/77 (p. 16)
Charles Champlin

". . . The virtues of the movie, not necessarily in this order, are that it is richly produced, pleasantly witty, and graced by some colorful and engaging performances. It should earn some grown-up gratitude because it demonstrates that family fare does not have to be childish.

Forbes and the Shermans have, in fact, created a movie which in content and tone is well within the interest of very young viewers. At the same time, without sneering at the material or compromising its fairy-tale straightforwardness, *The Slipper and the Rose* embroiders the story with a lightly joshing look at court shenanigans and the ways of royalty which gives the grown-ups their own distinct amusements . . .

Tone and texture are the hardest tricks in an un-

continued on next page

continued from previous page

dertaking like *Slipper and the Rose*, and while the texture is feathery soft, it is not so sugary as to cause skin eruptions.

A brisker pace and even slightly more verve would have made a disproportionately positive difference in the film. A little languidity goes a long way. Still and all, the movie is handsome, intelligent, and expansive and, given the continuing shortage of family outings, welcome . . ."

©Los Angeles Times, 1977.

New York Post, 11/5/76 (p. 26)
Frank Rich

". . . Against all odds, the creators of this movie have managed to mangle the Cinderella story almost beyond recognition—and they haven't even performed their demolition job with any particular zest . . .

. . . They've draped the original fairy tale with so many superfluous songs, irrelevant characters and jokes that you can barely find the romantic thread that's supposed to stitch the junk together.

The script is littered with mild, half-hearted wisecracks that witlessly parody fairy tale conventions—and the authors add almost a half-hour of plot to the original story by contriving some unconvincing class conflict between Cinderella and the royal family of her beloved prince . . ."

Reprinted by Permission of New York Post.
© 1976, New York Post Corporation.

Film Information, December 1976 (p. 3)
Dave Pomeroy

"*The Slipper and the Rose: The Story of Cinderella* is an entertaining, if unspectacular, addition to the genre of family films. Comparisons will inevitably be made with the Disney version of some years back, and where *Slipper* comes off worst is in the songs (hearing the tepid 'Suddenly It Happens' leaves one longing for the bounce of 'Bibbidy Bobbidy-Boo'). Robert B. and Richard M. Sherman have hardly composed and written with the same elan as they did for *Mary Poppins* and *Chitty Chitty Bang Bang*.

But director/writer Bryan Forbes and coauthors the Shermans have made some interesting emendations to the familiar story . . ."

©Film Information, 1976.

The Sunday Times (London), 3/28/76
Dilys Powell

". . . the film opens with the dash which you don't often encounter in British cinema. It is confident. It expects to be enjoyed. And it works. I

don't, I take it, have to tell anybody what it is about. The expected figures are all there. The Prince (Richard Chamberlain, modest, agreeable, gracefully acrobatic when acrobatics are required); Cinderella (Gemma Craven, appealing in her first film); the usual assortment of stepmother, Fairy Godmother and other relations—everybody does his or her singing and does it well enough to put us all at our ease; and if the songs by Richard Sherman and Robert B. Sherman aren't quite Rodgers and Hammerstein, they will do to be going on with.

Just to finish with my slight, my very slight discomforts, let me say that I don't find the choreography exciting . . ."

©The Sunday Times, 1976.

Films in Review, December 1976 (p. 633)
William K. Everson

". . . it is full of those British characteristics which lost us the Empire: good intentions and good taste outweighed by an overall dullness and lack of imagination. Above all, the film lacks *magic*. Any single reel of Herbert Brenon's silent *A Kiss for Cinderella* contained more genuine fairy-tale enchantment than all of these two ponderous hours . . . Apart from some pleasant outdoor locations, the plus factors are almost solely limited to the cast, with some excellent performances from British veterans ranging from Kenneth More and Margaret Lockwood (still looking much too attractive to be cast as the evil stepmother) to Edith Evans and Valentine Dyall . . ."

©Films in Review, 1976.

Newsweek, 11/29/76 (p. 113)
Janet Maslin

". . . Directed by Bryan Forbes, this is one so-called children's movie that is moderately witty and mercifully short of treacle.

As the heroine, Gemma Craven has the requisite freshness of beauty and tininess of feet. As the Prince, Richard Chamberlain occasionally lapses into mannerisms better suited to the Prince of Denmark. But, in general, he treats the project as harmless good fun, and old 'Dr. Kildare' fans will be glad to be reminded that he sings nicely, too. The movie also features a superb English supporting cast (Dame Edith Evans in her last performance as a dotty old Dowager Queen, Michael Hordern as the fumbling King and Annette Crosbie as the beleaguered Fairy Godmother), a tolerably tuneful score by Richard and Robert Sherman and an especially winning performance by 'Fred' as the Fairy Godmother's helpful dog."

©Newsweek, Inc. 1976
reprinted by permission.

Christian Science Monitor, 12/6/76 (p. 50)
David Sterritt

". . . *The Slipper and the Rose* is all frilly dresses
and silly old men and dull songs. Somewhere along
the way Cinderella forgives her wicked step-rela-
tives, as in Perrault, and I haven't seen a less convincing heart-warmer all year. The screenwriters
have reshuffled the ending in a try at surprise; the
result merely stretches the movie well beyond
two slow hours.
    On the plus side, Bryan Forbes' direction is noth-
ing if not picturesque. Richard Chamberlain makes
a convincing Prince, and Gemma Craven is
okay as the long-suffering Cinderella. Good performances also come from Michael Hordern as
the King, the late Dame Edith Evans (briefly) as
a wacky dowager, and Kenneth More . . ."

Reprinted by permission from The Christian
Science Monitor © 1976.
The Christian Science Publishing Society.
All rights reserved.

Saturday Review, 12/11/76 (p. 78)
Judith Crist

    "The quality of fairy tales is sustained with charm,
taste, and that soupcon of sophistication that the
British customarily provide for such entertainments
in *The Slipper and the Rose: The Story of Cinderella*. Directed by Bryan Forbes, who wrote the
screenplay with Robert B. and Richard M. Sherman,
this wonderfully lush, lilting, and lavish musical
is all that children of all ages, including mine, would
ask from a refurbished fairy tale, with some neat
twists of plot and personality to refresh the legend
and some imaginative and divertingly witty variations added. Freed from Disney strictures, the
brothers Sherman have let loose with jolly and
sweet tunes and some Gilbert & Sullivanish lyrics.
Richard Chamberlain emerges as the ultimate singing charming prince, with Gemma Craven a lovely
Cinderella . . ."

© Judith Crist, 1976.

SMALL CHANGE (L'ARGENT DE POCHE)

Director: *Francois Truffaut*. Screenplay
(French with English subtitles): *Suzanne
Schiffman, Mr. Truffaut*. Photography:
Pierre William Glenn. Editors: *Yann Dedet,
Martine Barraque, Jean Gargonne, Stephanie
Granel, Muriel Zeleny*. Music: *Maurice*

Jaubert. Production: *Les Films du Carrosse;
Les Productions Artistes Associes*. Distributor: *New World Pictures*. Running time
104 minutes. New York opening October 1,
1976, at the New York Film Festival, Lincoln
Center. Classification: PG. Origin: France.

Patrick: *Geory Desmouceaux*. Julien: *Philippe
Goldman*. Mathieu Deluca: *Claudio Deluca*.
Franck Deluca: *Franck Deluca*. Richard Gol-
fier: *Richard Golfier*. Laurent Riffle: *Laurent
Devlaeminck*. Bruno Rouillard: *Bruno Staab*.
Oscar: *Sebastien Marc*. Sylvie: *Sylvie Grezel*.
Martine: *Pascale Bruchon*. Corinne: *Corinne
Boucart*. Patricia: *Eva Truffaut*. Jean-Francois
Richet: *Jean-Francois Stevenin*. Chantal Petit:
Chantal Mercier. Monsieur Riffle: *Francis De-
vlaeminck*. Nadine Riffle: *Tania Torrens*. Lydie
Richet: *Virginie Thevenet*. Madeleine Doinel:
Laura Truffaut.

New York Times, 10/1/76 (p. C 11)
Vincent Canby

    ". . . *Small Change* is an original, a major work in
minor keys. It's a labor of love that ignores precedent with splendid verve and a film with so many
associations to other Truffaut films that watching it
is like meeting a previously unknown relative,
someone both familiar and utterly new and
surprising . . .
    The film, photographed in Thiers in South Centra
France, is a series of interlocking vignettes about
the world as seen by children from 2 weeks of age
to approximately 14 . . .
    Most prominent are Julien Leclou and Patrick
Desmouceaux, both 12½, who are immediately
identifiable to any student of Truffaut films as two
aspects of Antoine Doinel. Julien, dark-eyed, truc-
ulently self-reliant, is the delinquent, and experi-
enced thief, a scavenging wild child in the midst of
bourgeois plenty. Patrick is fair-haired, shy, a companion to his paralyzed father and hopelessly in
love with the beautician-mother of a school
friend . . .
    The children are incomparably funny and affect-
ing. The adult actors, including Jean-Francois
Stevenin and Chantal Mercier, who play teachers,
are equally good, I suspect, because the children,
not being savvy stage monsters, are performers to
whom they can respond.
    Small Change is Mr. Truffaut's 15th feature and
one of the most personal, idiosyncratic films in a
body of work that now matches the work of any director active today . . ."

© 1976 by the New York Times Company.
Reprinted by permission.

continued on next page

continued from previous page

Women's Wear Daily, 10/1/76 (p. 80)
Howard Kissel

". . . the underlying assumption in *Small Change* is that adults and children occupy quite separate realms—the remarkable thing about the film is that you don't doubt for a minute that the ways of perceiving things are those of children, not those of adults trying to recapture or idealize the vision of childhood.

Though Truffaut and Suzanne Schiffman created a scenario structuring the film around the events that take place in a school year from summer to summer, through some of the incidents . . . were based on newspaper clippings, the dialog, the movements, come from the children themselves, most of whom were recruited in the small town of Thiers, where the film was made. When adults are asked to improvise scenes from their lives, the results are often reflective and more intense than they would be in reality. When children are asked to improvise—or at least when Truffaut asked them— the results seem just as fresh as if the incidents were happening the first time. The awkwardness, the pleasures, of childhood are conveyed so completely, so honestly, so unself-consciously that one comes away convinced that childhood, whatever pain one remembers from one's own, is indeed a period of grace. *Small Change* is so enchanting it may even make children fashionable again."

©Women's Wear Daily, 1976.

Christian Science Monitor, 10/4/76 (p. 19)
David Sterritt

"The much-awaited *Small Change*, latest exploration of childhood from France's Francois Truffaut, is a romance, a satire, a farce, a lament, and a lecture.

If it seems a minor work from such stature, it is no less fetching for all that. Go with your heart open, your expectations child-sized. And you'll enjoy . . .

From about a dozen children and adults, including two Truffauts named Eva and Laura, the director has elicited likeable performances. The screenplay comes from Truffaut and Suzanne Schiffman. The rating is PG . . . an apparent compromise since most of the material is of G quality but the occasional rough-speaking subtitles use, once, a word that formerly required an R.

The deep poignancy of Truffaut's feature debut, *The 400 Blows*, is missing from this later look at youth. But the unconvincing nostalgia of *Les Mistons* is gone, too. *Small Change* is a pleasant diversion, more celebration than cerebration. One has every reason to expect that Truffaut will return to more pungent visions in the future."

Reprinted by permission from The Christian Science Monitor © 1976. The Christian Science Publishing Society. All rights reserved.

New York Post, 10/1/76 (p. 23)
Frank Rich

". . . *Small Change* is a comedy—resplendent with sunlight and bright spring colors—about a dozen or so children (ranging in age from roughly two weeks to 12 years) who live in the medium-size French town of Thiers. The movie is set over a period of several weeks, climaxing with the recess of school for summer vacation, and it consists of a collection of interconnected anecdotes that describe the daily existence of its young protagonists: We watch the children suffer through school, play, joke, shoplift, go to movies, and in general, try to cope with the often pleasant but sometimes confounding adults around them.

There are few big dramatic events and no plot as such: Truffaut spins a quiet, poetic reality out of the ordinary stuff of life, until finally he arrives at a complex and highly personal vision of humanity—a vision that speaks equally to young and old alike.

The key to *Small Change*'s cross-generational appeal is that Truffaut, almost uniquely among contemporary directors (or contemporary adults, for that matter), respects children as real people . . .

. . . surely there are few more rewarding pleasures in film than to sit before this director's movies and hear and see all that he has to teach us about life."

Reprinted by Permission of New York Post. ©1976, New York Post Corporation.

Los Angeles Times, 12/22/76 (Pt. IV, p. 16)
Charles Champlin

". . . *Small Change* is affecting over a wide range of the young experience, from the small naughtinesses to the large confrontations with the real problems of grown-ups.

It is, if you will, a small and major film, stunningly brought off. The natural light photography (that's the feeling of it) is by the excellent Pierre William Glenn. Truffaut wrote the script with his frequent collaborator Suzanne Schiffman. There is a pleasant score by Maurice Jaubert and a marvelously apt song ('Children Are Bored on Sunday') written and sung by Charles Trenet.

Subtitles are usually a source of complaint, but not this time . . ."

©Los Angeles Times, 1976.

Film Information, November 1976 (p. 1)
Peter P. Shillaci

"*Small Change* is the latest tribute to childhood by French director Francois Truffaut. The 'small change' of the title are the children themselves, anything but inconsequential, since their transparent, innocent faces dominate this happy fantasy of the child's world . . .

Truffaut's unhappy childhood is well-known, directly from his autobiographic Doinel trilogy in which he traces his past through actor Jean-Pierre Leaud's development from street urchin to young manhood (*Stolen Kisses*) and a problematic marriage (*Bed and Board*). Later, in *The Wild Child*, Truffaut captured the tragic innocence of a youngster unable to adjust to an accelerated course in 'civilization.' With Julien Leclou, the problem addressed is that of the 'battered child,' a boy physically abused by drunken mother and grandmother.

These and other threads of narrative are woven into the fabric of *Small Change*, a film so dominated by children that its adults seem to hover on the periphery . . ."

©Film Information, 1976.

Films in Review, December 1976 (p. 634)
Marsha McCreadie

"In the enchanted and benevolent world of Francois Truffaut's *Small Change*, not even a baby falling from a balcony meets a dire fate. 'Kids are in a state of grace,' explains one of the adults. Truffaut's direction of children—in this film none are professional actors—is uncanny . . .

Mostly we see the pranks and ploys of childhood: and the implication is that, as adults, we lose both the spontaneity and composure of childhood. The upbeat quality of the film comes, too, from the cheery primary colors in which it was shot (the cinematography is by Pierre-William Glenn; the screenplay by Truffaut and Suzanne Schiffman).

Small Change (the actual translation is *Pocket Money* but that title was used for a '72 Paul Newman movie) is a beautiful bubble, but not for those uninterested in kids."

©Films in Review, 1976.

Saturday Review, 10/30/76 (p. 53)
Judith Crist

"There is nothing posh and everything pleasing about Francois Truffaut's *Small Change* (*L'Argent de poche*), a completely winning portrait of children in a variety of shapes, forms, and dispositions. It is a sunlit film, a burble of laughter and a wistful sigh perpetually edging into its episodic exploration of youngsters in and out of school and home, with adults intruding occasionally but serving largely as background. In the catalytic person of a 'welfare' child, it will, of course, bring the French artist's first film, *The 400 Blows*, to mind; but if its 'message' is the ringing defense of the rights of children delivered by a teacher, the film is stating what was inherent in that first small masterpiece. However, the seventeen years between have enabled Truffaut to see the experiences of the young

in far more optimistic terms—and with a new appreciation of their resiliency . . ."

©Judith Crist. 1976.

New York Magazine, 10/18/76 (p. 80)
John Simon

"Francois Truffaut's fifteenth feature, *Small Change* . . . is small potatoes, and this not because most of the performers are small fry—kids from two to fourteen, disporting themselves in the small town of Thiers in central France. Rather, it is a matter of nothing happening in the movie despite its continuous busyness . . .

Small Change is a totally unstructured agglomeration of episodes, some charming, some ordinary, some tired and rather tiresome. It all leads up to nothing more than a lengthy tirade or homily by a sympathetic teacher who lectures his pupils about the need for parental comprehension and love. The lecture is as unimpeachable as it is platitudinous . . ."

©1976 by the NYM Corp. Reprinted with the permission of NEW YORK Magazine.

Take One, October 1976 (p. 38)
Will Aitken

". . . Francois Truffaut manages to give us two hundred children for two hours in his new *L'Argent de poche*—certainly a glut for any but the most ardent pedophiles . . .

Somewhere . . . *L'Argent de poche* runs aground on the shores of Icky-poohland. We are dragged through every possible obligatory scene of childhood—awkward adolescents necking at the movies, a bashful lad's infatuation with an older woman, the delinquent's essays at petty thievery, a delightful gamin wreaking havoc on his mum's groceries . . .

Visually, *L'Argent de poche* is a strikingly pretty film, Thiers and the children equally photogenic. There are, in fact, no ugly children among the 200—no one sports glasses or braces or cheeksful of acne. One positively longs for an evil-smelling nose-picking noxious little brat, for a real kid complete with the monstrous complexities of childhood . . ."

©Take One, 1976.

SMALL TOWN IN TEXAS, A

Director: *Jack Starrett*. Screenplay: *William Norton*. Producer: *Joe Solomon*. Photography:

continued on next page

continued from previous page

Bob Jessup. Music: *Charles Bernstein*. Distributor: *American International Pictures*. Running time 95 minutes. New York opening July 9, 1976, at several theatres. Classification: PG.

Poke: *Timothy Bottoms*. Mary Lee: *Susan Buck.* Duke: *Bo Hopkins.* Boogie: *Art Hindle*. Lenny: *John Karlen*. C.J. Crane: *Morgan Woodward*. Cleotus: *Hank Rolike*. Bull Parker: *Buck Flower*. Junior: *Clay Tanner*.

Los Angeles Times, 7/21/76 (Pt. IV, p. 15)
Kevin Thomas

''. . . Starrett gives the film more than it deserves, makes us care about his people, but nonetheless it winds up just another piece of grisly trash . . .

It is no less dismaying to note that the film was written by another talented craftsman, William Norton. We'd like to get to know better Miss George (for once cast sympathetically), Bottoms and Bottoms' appealing friends . . . but in this formula production mayhem comes far before character development or exploration of relationships. There's the feeling that Bottoms was a high school hero and Miss George the most popular girl in the class, but no time's been given to make a point about this.

Before the bone-crushing and the shootouts completely take over, the cast . . . registers effectively. Like so many other movies these days, *A Small Town in Texas* wastes its not inconsiderable talents in a deplorably brutal way (that unaccountably has been accorded only a PG rating).''

©Los Angeles Times, 1976.

Film Information, 9/76 (p. 4)
Paul Coleman

''. . . The film . . . is pulled between two poles—action and reflection—and it increasingly becomes two different movies that seem to have been edited arbitrarily together.

The three main players provide convincing nuances in their characterizations. In recent years, a number of critics have become champions of Susan George's ability to suggest a barely suppressed hysteria in her every action. *A Small Town in Texas* provides her with plenty of opportunity to simmer. Bottoms, who has been too long absent from the screen as he awaited a proper vehicle, may not have chosen wisely here, but he acquits himself with remarkable skill and patience, even in the brutally violent confrontations which the plot must deliver.''

©Film Information, 1976.

Films in Review, October 1976 (p. 507)
Tatiana Balkoff Lipscomb

''*A Small Town in Texas* has the makings of a really good movie. Sensitive casting: Timothy Bottoms, Susan George, Bo Hopkins look 'right' and give *believable*, unexaggerated performances. The supporting cast, Art Hindle, John Karlen, Morgan Woodward, Hank Rolike, Buck Flower, Clay Tanner—all deserve to be mentioned.

The stark atmosphere evinced by Bob Jessup's careful photography, e.g. the stunt motorbike chase—rivet the viewer's attention, and the low-key, underlying menace theme hones and advances the story.

Then, all at once Jack Starrett's fine paced direction explodes into *overblown* police-car chase mayhem . . .''

©Films in Review, 1976.

Monthly Film Bulletin, November 1976 (p. 236)
Verina Glaessner

''If the whole of Texas was revealed as part of a vast conspiracy in Jack Starrett's last film, *Race With the Devil*, he has at least narrowed the odds a bit in *A Small Town in Texas*, and the benign Poke finds ample support in his flight from the long and lethal arm of the silent majority. The rather random overkill of the previous film is here replaced by the disciplines imposed by the small town drama, though Starrett's heart evidently remains with the road movie: Poke has no sooner arrived home than he is back on the road, and the spectacular demolition derbies that occur with increasing frequency at least inject an excitement that Starrett's punchy directorial style is not able to elicit from the central conflict of character . . .''

©Monthly Film Bulletin, 1976.

New York Post, 7/10/76 (p. 15)
Archer Winsten

''*A Small Town in Texas* . . . addresses itself to the corruption of a sheriff and the destruction of so many cop cars with their flashing lights that you begin to wonder if Texas has any left . . .

Cars roll over, crash into each other, burst into flames, sink in water and/or fly off cliffs. The police force is decimated, and a good thing too, for they are pursuing a high-spirited Texas innocent.

Let us immediately concede that Timothy Bottoms is a charmer, Susan George full of likeable pathos, and Bo Hopkins every inch a villain worth hissing. And just in case you'd like another villain, they have one in reserve, C.J. Crane . . . the man who supplied the money for the political killing. The plot lets him off scotfree, perhaps because they didn't have any more cars to destroy . . .''

Reprinted by Permission of New York Post.
©1976, New York Post Corporation.

SMILE ORANGE

Director, Screenplay: *Trevor Rhone.*
Producers: *Milton L. Verley, Eddie Knight.*
Photography: *Davie McDonald.* Running time
93 minutes. New York opening May 19, 1976,
at the Festival and New Yorker Theatres. Classification: None. Origin: Jamaica.

Ringo: *Carl Bradshaw.* Busboy: *Glen
Morrison.* Ass't. Manager: *Vaughn Croskill.*
Joe: *Stanley Irons.*

New York Post, 5/20/76 (p. 20)
Archer Winsten

"*Smile Orange* . . . has the considerable virtues
of original work by totally fresh talents in Jamaica.
But it would be a mistake to urge it upon the general
public as entertainment that is completely satisfactory in its satirical view of tourists from the USA and
native hotel workers who serve them in several
ways.
Trevor D. Rhone, writer and director, has found in
Carl Bradshaw an ideal Lothario-waiter-con-man
Ringo, who cannot only practise what he preaches
('If you're black and can't play a part, you'll starve to
death') but maintain humor and fast footwork in the
midst of demanding guests, a pursuing wife and
her two strong brothers, and an assistant manager
(Vaughn Croskill) who is also leaning on him . . .
What does emerge is something of native
character and humor, making an entertainment that
is pleasant enough if you don't try to push it beyond
its proper sphere as lively Jamaican, semi-primitive
cinema."

Reprinted by Permission of New York Post.
© 1976, New York Post Corporation.

SOLARIS

Director: *Andrei Tarkovsky.* Screenplay (Russian with English subtitles): *Friedrich Gorenchtein, Mr. Tarkovsky.* Based on the novel by
Stanislaw Lem. Photography: *Vadim Youssov.*
Music: *Eduard Artemiev.* Production: *Mosfilm.*
Distributor: *Magna Distribution Corporation.*
Running time 132 minutes. New York opening
October 6, 1976, at the Ziegfeld Theatre.
Classification: None. Origin: U.S.S.R.

Players: *Donatis Banionis, Natalya Bondarchuk, Yuri Jarvet, Nikolai Grinko, Vladislav
Dvorzhetski.*

Los Angeles Times, 8/13/76 (Pt. IV, p. 22)
Kevin Thomas

". . . Fiercely demanding and not always clear
despite literate English subtitles, *Solaris* should be
seen several times to be fully comprehended and
appreciated. It is a dazzlingly imaginative work of
the highest order with awesome production values
and special effects that bear comparison to those
of *2001*.
In essence, it is the odyssey of a Soviet scientist
(Donatis Banionis), a trained psychologist, who
travels to a space station hovering over the remote
planet Solaris . . .
What ensues allows writer-director Andrei Tarkovsky to contemplate the meaning of life itself
through the interplay of science, philosophy and
emotion in a quest to determine the relative importance of each. *Solaris* is finally an unabashedly
romantic work in which the primacy of love is
asserted—but, as Jarvet says, 'To preserve the
truth we need mysteries.' "

©Los Angeles Times, 1976.

Film Information, November 1976 (p. 6)
Paul Coleman

". . . This production has virtually no similarities
to the mechanized future of *Logan's Run* and *The
Man Who Fell to Earth*. The drama is internal and
introspective, as it provides Kelvin—and through
him the audience—the task of groping for spiritual substance.
Although the print now in release here has been
cut from four hours to the current two hours and
twelve minutes, the pacing is slow and the narrative
halting. Awkward subtitles hardly help. Director
Tarkovsky lingers over many lovely images, but
often magnifies their significance into absurdity.
The solemn becomes pretentious and the lighthearted silly. But it does indicate a faith in the philosophical aspects of science fiction that still haunts
our memories from *Metropolis, The Day the Earth
Stood Still*, and *Forbidden Planet*."

©Film Information, 1976.

Newsweek, 10/25/76 (p. 107)
Jack Kroll

". . . *Solaris* achieves a real poetry of terror in
its insistence that the ultimate space trip for man
is a rendezvous with his own nature. Each of the
scientists is accompanied by a 'guest'—an incarna-

continued on next page

continued from previous page

tion of the guilts and fears of their past lives, and it doesn't seem farfetched to see the film as related to the spirit of Solzhenitsyn, an allegory about the excessive pride of a society that has mistakenly tried to marshal the complex forces of human life along strictly materialistic lines. The space station is filled with objects from the humanist past of Europe: the scientists read *Don Quixote*, and in one lovely image Chris and Hari float weightlessly together in a room full of Brueghels.

. . . Mysteriously, the U.S. version of *Solaris* has been cut from a reported four hours to two hours and twelve minutes. This results in some discontinuities, but not enough to impair an extraordinary film of great sensitivity and lyrical power. Tarkovsky has a touch of genius . . ."

©Newsweek, Inc. 1976
reprinted by permission.

Christian Science Monitor, 11/3/76 (p. 31)
David Sterritt

". . . *Solaris* remains a towering movie, one of the most thoughtful sci-fi epics ever and one of the few worthy successors to Stanley Kubrick's *2001: A Space Odyssey*. Its pace is slow and painstaking—an unimpressed colleague warned me it was 'like watching moss grow on a tree'—yet its impression is one of contemplation and concentration rather than self-indulgent lingering.

The performances by Donatis Banionis, Natalya Bondarchuk, and small supporting cast are generally insightful, and the few fantastic visual effects are handled with welcome restraint. The ending is very different from the conclusion of Lem's novel, but is equally provocative, more striking to the eye, and fully charged with Lem's awe of 'the time of cruel miracles' that pervades both book and film.

Solaris is an exceptionally challenging work of art and a quietly exhilarating experience. Seek it out if you enjoy having your mind opened, rather than diverted or assaulted, at the movies."

Reprinted by permission from The Christian
Science Monitor ©1976.
The Christian Science Publishing Society.
All rights reserved.

New York Post, 10/7/76 (p. 28)
Archer Winsten

". . . It is remarkable that, with so many unanswered questions and events that stagger one's imagination, the picture does achieve a degree of human relevance. Without going beyond the farthest reaches of possibility the picture establishes its people firmly, largely as Russians despite their names, and then they take logical steps to situations and events entirely foreign to this world of ours.

I would assume, therefore, that it will appeal to a larger audience than is normally open to Russian science fiction. It does stretch your mind and imagination, and if you are willing to make the effort to stay with it, there is a considerable reward both in splendid production values and excellent human performers."

Reprinted by Permission of New York Post.
©1976, New York Post Corporation.

Women's Wear Daily, 10/6/76 (p. 50)
Christopher Sharp

". . . What makes the film work is director Andrei Tarkovsky's delicate tickling of our private mystical fantasies without preempting them with his private mysticism. The ending is open to at least two interpretations—either what is happening is coming from within or without the main character. In this case the movie charms interpretations from the audience, just as successful minimalist art can suggest the ideas best suited for each individual viewer. The viewer's participation in completing the ideas suggested by *Solaris* brings us closer to the film.

At least one thing about *Solaris* is clear: The movie celebrates the inner self, which is something that is quite fashionable to do these days.

Vadim Youssov's photography is a magical tapestry. Youssov has an instinct for choosing the appropriate color and style of film for each kind of scene . . .

Solaris has that combination of ingredients that can keep one's attention on the screen even when it's not exactly clear what is happening on the screen. It is a significant experience."

©Women's Wear Daily, 1976.

New York Magazine, 10/25/76 (p. 92)
John Simon

"*Solaris*, a Russian sci-fi film by Andrei Tarkovsky, is . . . cut to about half its original length. Based on a novel by the modish Pole Stanislaw Lem, the film is inscrutable, preposterous, and rather dull. Sci-fi needs, as a bare minimum, good special effects and a big budget, neither of them forthcoming here. The film abounds in existential and metaphysical anguish and esoteric pseudo-science, both of them impenetrable and uncompelling. Eduard Artemyev's score is the usual Russian movie bluster; Vadim Youssov's highly touted cinematography is routine stuff; Tarkovsky's direction is plodding; and the subtitles are practically nonexistent. The acting is generally unimpressive . . ."

©1976 by the NYM Corp. Reprinted with
the permission of NEW YORK Magazine.

SONG REMAINS THE SAME, THE

Directors: *Peter Clifton, Joe Massot.* Photography: *Ernie Day.* Editor: *Mr. Clifton.* Sound: *Jimmy Page.* Distributor: *Warner Brothers.* Running time 136 minutes. New York opening October 20, 1976, at the Cinema I Theatre. Classification: PG.

Players: *John Bonham, John Paul Jones, Jimmy Page, Robert Plant, and Peter Grant.*

Christian Science Monitor, 11/3/76 (p. 31)
David Sterritt

". . . the latest in the thin but continuing stream of rock-concert movies. This one stars the Zep, and is somewhat more ambitious than such recent competitors as *Yessongs* and *Ladies and Gentleman . . . the Rolling Stones.* It fills out its intimidating 136 minutes with dream sequences, staged fantasies, and dull documentary footage, in addition to the usual adoring views of the interior of the wailing vocalist's mouth.
Some of the fantasies show vague lapses of taste, enough to earn the film a PG (parental guidance) rating. But most of the going is harmless enough to the mind and eyes—though your eardrums may suffer."

Reprinted by permission from The Christian Science Monitor © 1976. The Christian Science Publishing Society. All rights reserved.

New York Post, 10/21/76 (p. 24)
Archer Winsten

". . . Vocalist Robert Plant, he of the blond frizzled hair, hip-slung pants and bare breast, gives his all most of the time. So does John Bonham, the black-bearded drummer, and Jimmy Page on lead guitar comes in for his own spectaculara. Let us not forget John Paul Jones on keyboards and bass who does less with his body but contributes mightily to the sound crescendoes . . .
Obviously there is a ready-made audience for this film reproduction of the Led Zeppelin Madison Square Garden concert, plus photographic asides of a personal, travelogue and cinematic nature that are not devoid of beauty and interest. Unfortunately, the total effect ends up as a kind of torture chamber in which small rodents might die and people, not inured to Led Zeppelin, wonder if they can stand it without permanent damage to their eardrums."

Reprinted by Permission of New York Post. © 1976, New York Post Corporation.

SONS OF SASSOUN

Director, Screenplay: *Sarky Mouradian.* Producer: *Paul Z. Akian.* Photography: *Gregory Sandor.* Editor: *S. K. Mordar.* Music: *Paul Francis Webster.* Distributor: *Hye Arts International, Inc.* Running time 102 minutes. Los Angeles opening April 14, 1976, at the Los Feliz Theatre. Classification: PG.

Players: *Manuel, Lana Wood, Peter Lorre, Jr., Victor Izay, Maurice Sherbanee, John Valian, Sheri Jo Vitolo, Buck Kartalian, Mark Tombazian.*

Los Angeles Times, 4/14/76 (Pt. IV, p. 18)
Linda Gross

". . . Sarky Mouradian's screenplay is disjointed. Sudden outbursts of violence, song and patriotism are basted rather than sewn into the story. As the director, Mouradian alternates haphazardly between camp, light opera and serious drama. Paul Francis Webster's music is exhilarating but sometimes inappropriate. The film has been beautifully photographed in California (of all places) by Gregory Sandor.
Manuel is bombastic as the bandit. Miss Wood acts like Karen Valentine, Peter Lorre, Jr., emerges as a sympathetic Turkish officer, less bloodthirsty than his compatriots.
Sons of Sassoun is an energetic diversion but its ethnic flavor is cloying and superficial, unlike full-bodied Saroyan authenticity."

© Los Angeles Times, 1976.

SPARKLE

Director: *Sam O'Steen.* Screenplay: *Joel Schumacher.* Based on a story by Mr. Schumacher, Howard Rosenman. Producer: *Mr. Rosenman.* Photography: *Bruce Surtees.* Editor: *Gordon Scott.* Music: *Curtis Mayfield.* Distributor: *Warner Brothers.* Running time 99 minutes. New York opening April 7, 1976, at several theatres. Classification: PG.

Stix: *Philip M. Thomas.* Sparkle: *Irene Cara.* Sister: *Lonette McKee.* Dolores: *Dwan Smith.* Mary Alice: *Effie.*

continued on next page

continued from previous page

Films in Review, 5/76 (p. 315)
Michael Buckley

"The success story of a ghetto girl who makes good. Cliches abound in Joel Schumacher's bubble-gum screenplay, which encompasses romance, the drug scene, the record world, prison, the Mafia, and a happy ending at Carnegie Hall. Set in Harlem in '58, it seems a potpourri of past picture plots (*Lady Sings the Blues*, *Imitation of Life*, *There's No Business Like Show Business*, et al.). Sam O'Steen directed.

The film features several fine performances. Third-billed Lonette McKee (who was Vonette McGee when she had the female lead in *Shaft in Africa*) is impressive as the title character's sister, whose promising career is fatally wrecked by drugs. In the title role Irene Cara is very appealing . . . "

© Films in Review, 1976.

Film Information, 4/76 (p. 6)
Unsigned

"This black film deals with the '50's rise of a female singing group who remind us an awful lot of the Supremes. Irene Cara (*Aaron Loves Angela*) plays Sparkle. She is surrounded by kids growing up bad, good (like herself) and somewhere in between. Sister, the lead singer, nicely played by Lonette McKee, succumbs to drugs and a vicious, low-echelon hood, but Sparkle replaces her and becomes a star . . .

In the middle of this visually oblique movie, director Sam O'Steen (a former film editor and a good one) loses himself in a sea of unlikely suds and thunderstormy movie memories, and he largely fails to inject the characters with even the melodramatic potential Joel Schumacher's screenplay provides."

©Film Information, 1976.

New York Post, 4/8/76 (p. 24)
Archer Winsten

" . . . The performances range from competently documented cliches of the race condition to personally appealing portraits that are also fairly familiar. Irene Cara, the girl who rises, looks very sweet when she's young and hopeful. As a success, her brilliant make-up reduces her to that ordinary face that looks alike no matter whose head it's painted on . . .

Some songs used in demonstration of the talent of the girls are acceptable as standard items. The dark dives of the nightclubs are reasonably convincing as directed by Sam O'Steen. Still, there's nothing in the picture that doesn't sound an echo of some other race picture, which is to say that in plot, dialogue, and characterizations *Sparkle* is strictly the scene as seen before, good enough, but less than memorable."

Reprinted by Permission of New York Post.
© 1976, New York Post Corporation.

Los Angeles Times, 5/21/76 (Pt. IV, p. 18)
Kevin Thomas

"It's astounding how an infusion of soul, expressed with an abundance of talent through superbly modulated direction, can transmute the old backstage saga of success and heartbreak into a genuinely rich emotional experience.

This is precisely what *Sparkle* . . . accomplishes so superlatively . . .

. . . Joel Schumacher's script, based on a story written in collaboration with the film's producer, Howard Rosenman, pulls out all the stops––but with insight and passion, which allows the film's truly splendid cast to dazzle under the very carefully nuanced and controlled direction of O'Steen, long one of the most distinguished of film editors here in a most impressive theatrical film debut . . .

Everyone involved is terrific, but Miss McKee is downright haunting, running the gamut credibly from Diana Ross to Billie Holliday. *Sparkle* has a rich atmospheric look to it, thanks to Bruce Surtees' lensing, and above all, boasts half a dozen knockout songs by Curtis Mayfield. *Sparkle,* a real gem, glows from start to finish."

© Los Angeles Times, 1976.

SPASMO

Director: *Umberto Lenzi.* Producer: *Ugo Tucci.* Distributor: *Libra Films.* Running time 96 minutes. New York opening June, 1976, at the Quad Theatre. Classification: None. Origin: Italy.

Players: *Suzy Kendall, Robert Hoffman, Monica Monet, Ivan Rassimov, Guido Alberti.*

New York Post, 6/24/76 (p. 23)
Archer Winsten

"*Spasmo* . . . takes the easy way to suspense and mystification: waxwork figures brutally stabbed or hanged or bloodied, a masked sadist at work, creaking doors, no lights, a dead dog obviously killed, and unidentified murderers showing up very suddenly.

Christian (Robert Hoffman), scion of a rich family, and Barbara (Suzy Kendall) find themselves very much in the midst of all this. They're always on the verge of making love, but violent happenings always intervene.

Is someone trying to kill Christian? Are they trying to kill or make off with Barbara?

After a while you are apt to settle back, secure in the knowledge that eventually, at the very end, you will get the explanation . . .

. . . this is a chiller thriller made in fine Italian surroundings . . . and thrown to the public with appropriately minimal hosannahs."

Reprinted by Permission of New York Post.
© 1976, New York Post Corporation.

SPECIAL DELIVERY

Director: *Paul Wendkos.* Screenplay: *Don Gazzaniga.* Producer: *Dick Berg.* Photography: *Harry Stradling, Jr.* Editor: *Houseley Stevenson.* Music: *Lalo Schifrin.* Production: *BCP.* Distributor: *American International Pictures.* Running time 99 minutes. Los Angeles opening January 1977 at several theatres. Classification: PG.

Players: *Maria Adams, Phillip R. Allen, Tom Atkins, Timothy Blake, Sorrell Booke, Corinne Cole, Alex Colon, Joe di Reda, Lawrie Driscoll, Jeff Goldblum, Gerrit Graham, Michael C. Gwynne, Robert Ito, Lynette Mettey, Richard Drout Miller, Ed Peck, John Quade, Mel Scott, Cybill Shepherd, Bo Svenson, Vic Tayback, Edward Winter.*

Los Angeles Times, 1/22/77 (Pt. IV, p. 22)
Kevin Thomas

". . . In the film's excitingly staged opening sequence four Vietnam vets, demoralized by various disabilities and difficulties in finding jobs, led by Bo Svenson, knock over a large, old downtown bank. Unfortunately, a guard manages to sound an alarm, and only Svenson gets away.

While on the run he jams a briefcase stuffed with cash into a street-corner mailbox in a seedy part of town . . .

Much of *Special Delivery* takes place on an old street set—it looks like Paramount's. This setting,

along with Harry Stradling, Jr.'s, low-angle, shadowy camerawork and Lalo Schifrin's moody score, contributes much to the picture's *film noir* aura. More important, the film actually has an old-fashioned sense of morality, which is capped by its witty, classic fadeout sequence. Throughout, *Special Delivery* is highly expressive and strong on sinister atmosphere . . ."

©Los Angeles Times, 1977.

Monthly Film Bulletin, August 1976 (p. 174)
Tom Milne

"*Special Delivery* is an uneasy mixture of good and bad, but at least it is less sententious than *Breaking Point* . . . Quite ingeniously conceived and very sleekly staged, with the robbers posing as toy salesmen producing sample toy weapons in the hope of extracting a bank loan, then making their escape over the rooftops by using commando skills, the opening sequence would have been perfectly acceptable but for the nagging memory flashes which elaborate, awkwardly and unnecessarily, the Vietnam background . . . Less awkwardly but still somewhat ponderously, there follows a series of expository scenes . . . Once these elaborate preparations are over and night falls on the sleazy little square, Wendkos suddenly assumes control and turns the film into a riveting chamber drama . . ."

©Monthly Film Bulletin, 1976.

SPECIAL SECTION (SECTION SPECIALE)

Director: *Costa-Gavras.* Screenplay: *Jorge Semprun, Mr. Gavras.* Producers: *Jacques Perrin, Giorgio Silvagni.* Photography: *Andreas Winding.* Editor: *Francoise Bonnot.* Music: *Eric Demarsan.* Production: *Reggane Films-Artistes Associes; Goriz Films; Janus Films.* Distributor: *Universal Pictures.* Running time 110 minutes. New York opening December 7, 1975, at the Beekman Theatre. Classification: PG. Origin: France.

Minister of Justice: *Louis Seigner.* Minister of the Interior: *Michel Lonsdale.* Admiral: *Ivo Garrani.* Deputy General: *Francois Maistre.* Attorney General: *Pierre Dux.* State Prosecutor: *Jacques Francois.* President of the Special Section: *Claude Peiplu.* Counsellor Linais: *Jean Bouise.* President Cournet:

continued on next page

continued from previous page

Michel Galabru. Major Beumelburg: *Heinz Bennent.* Brechet: *Guy Retore.* Bastard: *Yves Robert.* Trzebrucki: *Jacques Rispal.* Samplaix: *Bruno Cremer.* Lawyer Lafarge: *Jacques Perrin.*

See Volume 1 for additional reviews

The Times (London), 3/18/77 (p. 10)
David Robinson

"*Section Speciale* is the most recent collaboration of Costa-Gavras and the writer Jorge Semprun. This time they take a nightmare from recent French history—the special sections that were set up in the French appeals courts, by ordinance of August 1941, to deal with infractions concerning Communist or anarchist activity.

The incident that the film traces was actual. The Resistance assassinated a German officer cadet at the Barbes metro. The nervous Vichy Government was readily persuaded by the ruthless Minister of the Interior that the French must forestall German reprisal by themselves taking and killing a suitable number of hostages. To provide the victims, the hastily formed Court of the Special Section retried six Communists who had already been sentenced, making a new law retroactive for the purpose. Despite growing embarrassments at this travesty of all judicial practices, three of the men were convicted .and shot the next day.

Costa-Gavras and Semprun have for once failed in their usual method of extracting both drama and political philosophy out of a reconstructed incident in history. As drama, *Section Speciale* is vitiated by the predictable stock characters. At the level of political debate, the film fails ever really to come to grips with the crucial questions involved . . ."

©The Times, 1977.

The Sunday Times (London), 3/20/77 (p. 38)
Alan Brien

"About Costa-Gavras' *Section Speciale* . . . let me quickly say that if you are at all interested in films about politics—that is about the moral choices facing us when dealing with our fellows—then you cannot afford to miss it.

The time is August 1941. The Vichy Government is desperate to conciliate the Nazi occupiers, even to the extent of passing a retroactive law, indefensible by any standards, which will allow them to pluck out of jail six French patriots and execute them as sacrifices to atone for the murder of a German officer.

The details of the frame-up, which demands the

willing acquiescence of a whole series of magistrates and attorneys to a perversion of justice, are taken from the German archives. (The French Government refused any access to its records.) Marxist Costa-Gavras allows a Communist editor a bravura moment of defiance, even slips into the mouth of a right-wing conservative words of praise for the Nazi-Soviet pact, but otherwise it all seems chillingly real, unhistrionic, and forensically exact . . ."

©The Sunday Times, 1977.

SPIRIT OF THE BEEHIVE, THE (EL ESPIRITU DE LA COLMENA)

Director: *Victor Erice.* Screenplay (Spanish with English subtitles): *Francisco J. Querejeta.* Based on an idea by Angel Fernandez Santos and Mr. Erice. Photography: *Luis Cuadrado.* Editor: *Pablo G. del Amo.* Music: *Luis de Pablo.* Production: *Janus Films.* Distributor: *Kino International.* Running time 98 minutes. New York opening September 23, 1976, at the D.W. Griffith Theatre. Classification: None. Origin: Spain, 1973.

Ana: *Ana Torrent.* Isabel: *Isabel Telleria.* Fernando: *Fernando Fernan Gomez.* Teresa: *Teresa Gimpera.* Monster: *Jose Villasante.* Milagros: *Lally Soldeville.* The Fugitive: *Juan Margallo.* The Doctor: *Miguel Picezo.*

New York Post, 9/24/76 (p. 13)
Archer Winsten

". . . It is a very special film dealing with the arcane world of the small child when it has been strongly affected by a viewing of James Whale's movie, *Frankenstein.* Furthermore, it is very purely that Spanish world of arid landscape, ancient, half-ruined buildings, deserted, then inhabited by a fugitive, and with blood on the ground afterwards.

What makes the film truly wonderful is the child, Ana (Ana Torrent), whose dark, intensely inquiring eyes ask every question that words do not speak. She is the one who, under the influence of her sister . . . goes to the railroad and listens to the rail telling of the approaching train, goes to the empty house, looks down the nearby well to see what mysteries it hides, waiting to see the Frankenstein monster . . .

The picture reminds me of a masterpiece from long ago, *Forbidden Games*, and there could hardly be higher praise. The feeling of children moving in an adult, alien world (Spain 1940), yet constructing their own world nevertheless, is a true work of art."

Reprinted by Permission of New York Post.
©1976, New York Post Corporation.

New York Magazine, 10/4/76 (p. 88)
John Simon

"For total incompetence . . . there is nothing like *The Spirit of the Beehive* . . . If you have admired such fine Spanish films as Bardem's *The Death of a Cyclist* or Saura's *The Hunt* and *The Garden of Delights*, don't go to see this one, which is so bad that I only wish I could blame it on the repressiveness of the Franco regime (the movie was made in 1973) rather than on the filmmakers. But, let's face it, a picture whose four principal characters all bear the Christian names of the performers who enact them immediately proclaims its lack of even the lowest kind of inventiveness . . .

Ana is played by a pretty, haunted-looking kid, and we do find out how dark it always is inside Spanish country houses, so dark that even we take a siesta during most of the film . . ."

©1976 by the NYM Corp. Reprinted with
the permission of NEW YORK Magazine.

Christian Science Monitor, 10/7/76 (p. 22)
David Sterritt

"Victor Erice's *Spirit of the Beehive*, from Spain, is a resonant, mystical voyage into the experience of youth. It is a journey into the dark dreams spawned by the meeting of innocence, puzzlement and unrest. It chooses to evoke rather than to state, to haunt rather than to explain. It is a singular experience, if not a satisfying one in the conventional movie sense . . .

The Spirit of the Beehive is a highly personal film that makes its points and tells its story in shadowy but often gentle and even beautiful visual terms. Its audience may not be wide, but those who see it are not likely to forget it in a hurry."

Reprinted by permission from The Christian
Science Monitor ©1976.
The Christian Science Publishing Society.
All rights reserved.

Films in Review, November 1976 (p. 569)
DeWitt Bodeen

". . . it is not only a major work, but it's the best film to have come out of Spain. Its director, Victor Erice, knows how to work in a clean Spartan way, evoking a mood of loneliness, of sorrow and

terror; and he understands children—one child in particular, Ana, exquisitely played by a little girl named Ana Torrent. This picture about her, like *Poil de Carotte* and *Forbidden Games*, is a study of a hungry, imaginative, lonely child lost in the maze of an embittered land.

It is 1940, and one of the few treats the villagers know comes from a film exhibitor traveling with tired, scratched prints of movies to show in the city hall. He brings *Frankenstein* to the townspeople, and Ana is transported into another world when she sees it and falls in love with the Monster. Convinced by her sister, a tease, that the Monster did not really die but is very much alive, Ana goes out alone day after day, crossing the barren countryside in search of him.

No finer foreign language film is likely to be seen in this country during the current year."

©Films in Review, 1976

Newsweek, 10/11/76 (p. 116)
Charles Michener

". . . Erice brings together all of the film's themes and images into a dramatic metaphor that seems to stand for the historical struggles of Spain itself—the struggle of generosity in a land of harsh necessities, of artistic creation in a repressive society, of life, in other words, against death. I don't want to inflate the impact of this extraordinary film. For long stretches it is quieter than a bee's hum: its loudest—and most extended—human discourse is the whispering of the little girls under the covers at night. Some of its recurring images—Ana wandering across the barren fields, an old well outlined against the vast sky—are a bit pat. But it does something that is rare in movies today: it honors the viewer's own powers of imagination. And in Ana Torrent, the little girl who plays Ana, it has a performance that will sear your soul."

©Newsweek, Inc. 1976
reprinted by permission.

Film Information, November 1976 (p. 5)
Peter P. Shillaci

". . . *The Spirit of the Beehive* is so compellingly put together that one feels let down when it leads to what seems to be a dead end. The metaphor of the beehive, for example, fills almost every scene with the promise of larger meanings, from the family house, with its hexagonal amber-colored windows, to the escaped Loyalist soldier whom Ana cares for in an abandoned farmhouse. And yet, the resolution of these leads creates a whole which is less than its parts. Everything hinges upon the 'monster' who actually appears to Ana in a midnight escapade far from home. Is the monster the political chaos of post-Civil War Spain? The dark side of the human imagination, or the large

continued on next page

continued from previous page

portion of original sin locked in the small psyches of the children?

Isabel and Ana create some remarkable moments as they improvise much of their conversation and actions—whispered revelations in bed, betrayed confidences, and unobserved cruelties . . .''

©Film Information, 1976.

SQUIRM

Director, Screenplay: *Jeff Lieberman.* Producer: *George Manasse.* Executive Producers: *Edgar Lansbury, Joseph Berule.* Photography: *Joseph Mangine.* Editor: *Brian Smedley-Aston.* Distributor: *American International Pictures.* Running time 92 minutes. New York opening July 30, 1976, at several theatres. Classification: R.

Players: *Don Scardino, Patricia Pearcy, R. A. Dow, Jean Sullivan, Peter MacLean, Fran Higgins, William Newman, Barbara Quinn, Carl Dagenhart.*

Los Angeles Times, 12/17/76 (Pt. IV, p. 21)
Kevin Thomas

"*Squirm* . . . is guaranteed to make you do just that. Made on location in Georgia, it's a nifty little horror picture that strikes a good balance between humor and terror. While not morbid, it is nevertheless graphic enough to place it out of bounds for the faint-hearted and for impressionable youngsters . . .

Squirm's special effects are terrific, and the film's writer-director Jeff Lieberman displays plenty of panache, deftly playing a folksy atmosphere against rapidly escalating peril. *Squirm* just might catch on with the midnight circuits; at any rate it's a mystery why American International didn't screen it for the press in advance when they would chance a preview of a penny dreadful like H.G. Wells' *Food of the Gods* . . ."

©Los Angeles Times, 1976.

Monthly Film Bulletin, 9/76 (p. 199)
John Pym

"This low-budget shocker adheres to a familiar plot pattern; nevertheless Jeff Lieberman's restrained use of the worms, his flourishes of black humor and, above all, his determination to trim the narrative and not to strive for overblown or fantastic effects combine to make *Squirm* a commendable and at times genuinely startling addition to a recently thriving genre. The worms are shown directly attacking only once; and when the horrors are displayed they are not allowed to interfere with the narrative thrust (Mick pulls open Willie's shirt, glimpses the heaving thorax, then hurries away to inform the sheriff; Mrs. Sanders' wormy silhouette is only momentarily glimpsed as Mick makes his way upstairs to rescue Geri). Likewise, the humor is deftly displayed: the sheriff eats a plate of spaghetti as he listens in contemptuous disbelief to Mick's story . . ."

©Monthly Film Bulletin, 1976.

New York Post, 7/31/76 (p. 37)
Archer Winsten

"If worms are your thing, vicious man-eating worms, *Squirm* . . . could make a lot of suspense for you and a bit of revulsion. What happens is a severe electrical storm in Fly Creek, Georgia, which knocks down a high-tension tower and permits electricity to permeate the ground there. This not only drives worms out of the ground, but turns them into twittering, ravening beasts which strip a man as clean of flesh as a school of piranhas . . .

. . . the picture doesn't stand up to close inspection with respect to continuity and good logic. What it does have a fair sense of character, some performers who look their parts even when they sound wrong, and horror, plenty of wormy horror . . ."

Reprinted by Permission of New York Post.
©1976, New York Post Corporation.

STAR IS BORN, A

Director: *Frank Pierson.* Screenplay: *John Gregory Dunne, Joan Didion, Mr. Pierson.* Based on a story by William Wellman and Robert Carson. Producer: *Jon Peters.* Executive Producer, Musical Concepts: *Barbra Streisand.* Photography: *Robert Surtees.* Editor: *Peter Zinner.* Music: *Phil Ramone.* Distributor: *Warner Brothers.* Running time 140 minutes. New York opening December 25, 1976, at the Ziegfeld and Baronet Theatres. Classification: R.

Esther Hoffman: *Barbra Streisand.* John Norman Howard: *Kris Kristofferson.* Bobby

Tony Orlando looks on at the climactic awards ceremony in **A Star Is Born**, starring Kris Kristofferson and Barbra Streisand. Ms. Streisand, also the film's executive producer, wrote its Oscar-winning song, "Evergreen," with Paul Williams.

Ritchie: *Gary Busey*. Gary Danziger: *Oliver Clark*. The Orsos: *Vanena Fields, Clyde King*. Quentin: *Marta Heflin*. Bebe Jesus: *M. G. Kelly*. Photographer: *Sally Kirkland*. Freddie: *Joanne Linville*. Mo: *Uncle Rudy*. Brian: *Paul Mazursky*.

Christian Science Monitor, 1/10/77 (p. 22)
David Sterritt

". . . Under the right circumstances, Streisand has more on-screen pizazz than most five performers put together. Directors too often allow her forcefulness to run roughshod over the rest of a movie, to the detriment of all concerned. But *Star* filmmaker Frank Pierson keeps her strength and talent under close control, helping her gifts to shine with more modulated grace than in any Streisand movie I can remember. It's a pleasure to watch a star serve herself, her colleagues, and her audience so well.

One Streisand, however, does not a movie make. The picture's other elements are not so fortuitous . . ."

Reprinted by permission from The Christian
Science Monitor © 1977.
The Christian Science Publishing Society.
All rights reserved.

Village Voice, 1/3/77 (p. 35)
Andrew Sarris

". . . It is no wonder that people around Warners

referred to *A Star Is Born* under their breaths as *Barbra Lyndon*.

The comparison is unfair to both Kubrick and Streisand in that they are made to seem much worse than the old movie moguls, who were presumably wise and compassionate as they went about butchering movies like Cukor's 1954 *A Star Is Born*. If the inmates seem to have taken over the asylum with brutal results, it is because they learned their lessons too well from their old keepers. Streisand could make an interesting movie sometime about how she has gained and maintained her power over people and institutions. A movie could be made about the extraordinary evils of the rock scene, which makes old Hollywood look like a holy order. Such a movie has not been made on this occasion. *A Star Is Born* is thus a compendium of lost opportunities. There is no fiction or fantasy in this Streisand vehicle, and no genuine otherness, only a monumental megalomania let loose on a once-lyrical love story . . ."

Reprinted by permission of The Village Voice.
Copyright © The Village Voice, Inc., 1977:

Los Angeles Times, 12/21/76 (Pt. IV, p. 1)
Charles Champlin

"*A Star Is Born* is not *A Star Is Born* and it is not a rock documentary or a rock epic and it is not a very successful movie unless you are one of that throng for whom Barbra Streisand, like Judy Garland, can do no wrong.

continued on next page

continued from previous page

The movie is a Streisand concert—pop, not rock, as Bob Hilburn, an expert in these matters, has pointed out—in which the star is not so much born as canonized. The songs themselves, despite the showcase treatment and the reputable hands that wrote them, sound entirely ordinary . . .

Kristofferson's performance generally is alive and interesting . . .

But movies work or they don't . . .

A Star Is Born rarely stops seeming manufactured; it can't disguise its manipulations or the process or the storytelling. You see the tangled strings, not the puppets . . .

It is at last disappointingly uninvolving for the romance it was meant to be. A half-hour in, I wrote 'A star is boring' in my notes, and was not later persuaded I'd been wrong . . ."

©Los Angeles Times, 1976.

Women's Wear Daily, 12/27/76 (p. 20)
Howard Kissel

"The original 1937 *A Star Is Born* was a witty look at the phony world of Hollywood. The 1976 remake is a witless, phony view of the even phonier world of big-time rock.

To begin with, neither Barbra Streisand nor Kris Kristofferson, the protagonists in this version, is genuinely at home in the rock world—if the film were, like its prototype, a satire, this wouldn't matter. But this *Star* is trying for realism, so it is quite implausible for a likable, but hardly charismatic figure like Kristofferson to be playing an idol screaming youngsters long to touch, or for a basically comic figure like Streisand, the Jewish Cinderella, to be playing high tragedy . . .

Beyond the basic incongruity of the casting, very little about the film seems authentic . . .

. . . This version fails utterly, because it has no real point of view. With the exception of a subtle performance by Paul Mazursky as a glib manager, the acting is as unconvincing as the material. One wonders what might have happened if writers as bright as John Gregory Dunne and Joan Didion had been allowed to develop the conception independently. But . . . this is strictly a multimillion dollar 'vanity production.' "

©Women's Wear Daily, 1976.

New York Post, 12/27/76 (p. 39)
Frank Rich

"On the posters for the new remake of *A Star Is Born* there is a sexy photo of Barbra Streisand and Kris Kristofferson locked in an ecstatic embrace—an embrace that promises a dynamic

movie romance, just like all the previous versions of *A Star Is Born*. But the poster is partially misleading. While this film is indeed a love story, the lovers are not Streisand and Kristofferson, but Streisand and Streisand. *A Star Is Born* is an $8-million exercise in unabashed narcissism—it's our number one female movie star's love sonnet to herself.

For this reason alone, the movie . . . is worth seeing; it just isn't every day of the week that a film offers us a completely uncensored glimpse into the psyche of a monomaniacal showbiz phenomenon . . .

But if *A Star Is Born* is fascinating at one level, it's disturbing at another: There's something self-destructive about Miss Streisand's self-love . . .

. . . by dominating *A Star Is Born* to the point of absurdity, she has bent the movie's dramatic line out of shape. In this film, Miss Streisand becomes her own worst enemy . . ."

Reprinted by Permission of New York Post.
©1976, New York Post Corporation.

New York Magazine, 1/10/77 (p. 56)
John Simon

". . . This is a crazy quilt of the work of countless scenarists and directors, not least (except in quality) of Barbra Streisand and her mate Jon Peters. Plot elements, like all the non-Barbra characters, including even Kristofferson, surface and vanish without making much of an impression. But, oh, is there ever Barbra! During the filming she complained that there weren't enough close-ups of her. Either she was mistaken then, or even more mistaken later, when she reedited the film to suit her enormous ego; it is full of enormous close-ups of a face that, even in medium-long shot, is an enormity . . . Streisand's notion of acting is to bulldoze her way from one end of a line to the other without regard for anyone or anything; you can literally feel her impatience for the other performer to stop talking so she can take over again. If dialogue there is, it is that between a steamroller and the asphalt beneath it . . ."

©1977 by the NYM Corp. Reprinted with the permission of NEW YORK Magazine.

Film Information, February 1977 (p. 1)
Bea Rothenbeuchner

". . . *Star* is more convincing depicting the outer manifestations of a rock star's life—the drugs, the alcohol, the demanding recording sessions, the screaming audiences, the deafening sound amplification—than it is in providing dramatic coherence and interesting character insights.

Barbra Streisand, as always, shows talent and enormous drive. When she sings, we admire her almost enough to be able to conjure up some sympathy for Esther Hoffman, the character she portrays. What causes really big problems in *Star* is what happens when she should *not* be the focus of attention . . . Streisand's awesome personality never lets us forget for one moment who really is up there on the screen, crowding out all other performers, including Kris Kristofferson . . ."

©Film Information, 1977.

Saturday Review, 2/5/77 (p. 42)
Judith Crist

". . . It is Barbra all the way, not only as star, executive producer, lyricist, and composer for several numbers (not to mention supplier of 'musical concepts,' her own clothes, and much of the interior furnishings), but also, unofficially, as editor of the film for six months. That Kristofferson survived at all is, perhaps, a tribute to her humanism (or contractual obligations) . . .

For Streisand admirers—and that we have been, with high regard for her acting as well as her singing—it is bitter to watch self-indulgence rampant. Rock 'n' roll is not her best milieu, and though a song or two (particularly a specialty bit, 'Queen Bee,' and her solo debut hit, 'The Woman in the Moon') are true Streisand numbers, most emerge as bad imitations of Mick Jagger, serving at best to interrupt the pure boredom the film generates . . ."

©Judith Crist, 1977.

New Leader, 1/17/77 (p. 26)
Robert Asahina

". . . headaches stemming from Streisand's egotistical domination of the picture. Her stridency makes Esther Hoffman unbelievable, and when she flutters her eyelashes and utters cutesy lines like, 'If you ever die, I'll kill you,' even her diehard fans must squirm. In addition, her cross-eyed, double-chinned hussy is so brazen that the whole idea of the movie is rendered ridiculous—how could *she* possibly need Kristofferson as a mentor?

Finally, Streisand is credited for her wardrobe, for 'musical concepts,' and also as 'executive producer.' Only her Shirley Temple Afro, a laughable testimony to the 'skills' of her hairdresser/boyfriend Jon Peters (who is billed as 'producer'), seems to have been out of her direct control. The movie closes with a 10-minute close-up take of Streisand singing a reprise of the film's songs—a perfectly self-indulgent finish to a tedious (two hours and 20 minutes), narcissistic epic . . ."

Reprinted with permission from The New Leader, 1977. ©The American Labor Conference on International Affairs, Inc.

Newsweek, 1/10/77 (p. 64)
Janet Maslin

". . . the movie is engrossing enough to be proof—as if any more were needed—that Streisand is exactly the kind of performer this story is about,

someone who's worth watching even in her most awkward moments. Her numbers range from terrible to so-so, but she makes a couple of them sound like hits just the same. Kristofferson has been handed a signature song that would be a disaster even if the Beatles got together and recorded it, but when Streisand performs it during a very lengthy closing medley, she manages the near-miracle of making it sound as if it had a melody. Her presence is electrifying enough to distract attention, at least temporarily, from the movie's dramatic incoherence, its gaudiness and its ragged editing. In fact, Streisand is so overwhelming a presence that she can probably get away indefinitely with making movies as slipshod as this one . . ."

©Newsweek, Inc. 1977 reprinted by permission.

Monthly Film Bulletin, March 1977 (p. 53)
Geoff Brown

". . . musically and dramatically, Streisand's *A Star Is Born* has no coherence whatever. Updating and transposing the story line from Hollywood to the rock world has proved a great mistake: the plot's hackneyed pattern of intertwined careers (one climbing upwards, one crawling down) simply does not suit the unglamorous world of monster open-air concerts, thunderous decibels, drugs and groupies . . . After the fashionably violent death of John Norman Howard, Esther sings a lengthy, maudlin version of the theme tune before a mourning audience holding aloft an array of candles. The sequence makes abundantly clear Streisand's failure to convince as a rock star, even when singing the docile brand of rock supplied here. Luckily, Kris Kristofferson makes a far better impression . . ."

©Monthly Film Bulletin, 1977.

Films in Review, February 1977 (p. 117)
Marsha McCreadie

". . . Plenty is off base . . . owing to the unrestrained egotism of one of the film's stars, Barbra Streisand, who also happens to be executive producer and final decision-maker on everything from costumes to songwriting to editing. If ever a film needed the control of outside expertise this is the one, and the shame is that Ms. Streisand did not make better use of the talent at her disposal: screenwriters Joan Didion and John Gregory Dunne, songwriters Paul Williams and Leon Russell, for just a few, plus a sure-fire, topical story line—a couple with competing careers trying to stay in love in the cutthroat entertainment business . . ."

©Films in Review, 1977.

continued on next page

continued from previous page

The Times (London), 3/25/77 (p. 9)
David Robinson

". . . The previous female stars who created the role of Esther Blodgett, the girl who achieves stardom . . . both had irresistible charm and great gifts of pathos—Janet Gaynor wistful and quiet, Judy Garland heartbreaking. When Barbra Sreisand assaults you at the end with three scenes of climactic mawkishness you are more than conscious that they are being played by the Executive Producer. The tears are all special effects.

The film will no doubt be a ball for Streisand devotees. For the rest of us, she doesn't even look very nice in it. With a hairdresser as producer they presumably knew what they were doing when they gave her a mop of yellow curls which disconcertingly recall Harpo Marx. The cameraman, at other points, has a nasty way of coming up on her from behind the left ear, catching her (cf. the bath sequence) with her singer's throat all crumpled, and giving her the look of Bernhardt in old age . . ."

©The Times, 1977.

The Sunday Times (London), 3/27/77 (p. 38)
Alan Brien

". . . *A Star Is Born* . . . is nothing if not show biz, in style and content, and the filming of it, if a tenth of the anecdotes are true, must one day make yet another What-Price-Hollywood? style musical spectacular—if they can only find someone who dare play Streisand. Whatever it says on the credits, what we see and hear on the screen is undoubtedly just what she wants us to see and hear. And, eventually, what is born is not so much a nova as a black hole—a galactic phenomenon described by its discoverer, Professor John Taylor, as 'the collapse of a heavy star to such a condensed state that nothing, not even light, can escape from its surface.'

Once this is accepted, quite an enjoyable time can be had on the way, keeping pace with Barbra Streisand as she lollops along eating up the rest of the cast, and a good deal of the props and scenery, like Bugs Bunny in a carrot field. The original unoriginal plot, now in its fourth planting, has become pretty much a dust bowl . . ."

©The Sunday Times, 1977.

STAY HUNGRY

Director: *Bob Rafelson*. Screenplay: *Charles Gaines, Mr. Rafelson*. Based on the novel by Mr. Gaines. Producers: *Harold Schneider, Mr. Rafelson*. Photography: *Victor Kemper*. Editor:

John Link 2d. Music: *Bruce Langhorne, Byron Berline*. Production: *Outov*. Distributor: *United Artists*. Running time 103 minutes. New York opening April 25, 1976, at several theatres. Classification: R.

Craig Blake: *Jeff Bridges*. Mary Tate Farnsworth: *Sally Field*. Joe Santo: *Arnold Schwarzenegger*. Thor Erickson: *R. G. Armstrong*. Franklin: *Robert Eglund*. Anita: *Helena Kallianiotes*. Newton: *Roger E. Mosley*. Craig's Uncle: *Woodrow Parfrey*. William: *Scatman Crothers*. Dorothy Stevens: *Kathleen Miller*. Amy Walterson: *Fannie Flagg*. Zoe Mason: *Joanna Cassidy*.

Women's Wear Daily, 4/23/76 (p. 11)
Howard Kissel

". . . The humor is unavoidable since much of the film centers on the bizarre, even grotesque, world of body-building. There are also excursions into country fiddling and partly comic, partly pathetic glimpses into what is left of the Old South. The film concerns the attempts of a wealthy young drifter (Jeff Bridges), who is bequeathed an old family mansion, to come to terms with himself. The basic situation is not developed into a genuine self-confrontation but used rather as a pretext for this odd journey through contemporary America. The film is at its best when its humor is good-natured and open; it is least appealing when the screenplay makes 'statements' about the American business mentality that, however true, are hardly revelations and are by now certainly more than a little stale.

This film is engaging partly because Bridges is so likable and convincing despite the material. Rafelson gets strong performances from Sally Fields, R. G. Armstrong and Scatman Crothers."

© Women's Wear Daily, 1976.

New York Magazine, 5/3/76 (p. 68)
John Simon

". . . With the current *Stay Hungry* . . . Rafelson demonstrates that a straining for eccentricity under the guise of originality, and basically trivial people and dialogue with a coating of the bizarre over them are his true hallmark. It is one thing to make a movie about body builders, the ambiguous Mister Americas or Mister Worlds who muscle in on certain beaches where, like other beached whales, they become objects of awe and ridicule; but it is quite another to make these fanatics of the superhealthy body with no room in it for a mind, healthy or otherwise, into a symbol of noble striving, a grand alternative to commercialism and greed . . .

. . . there are bad, or at least mannered, performances from R. G. Armstrong, Woodrow Parfrey, Helena Kallianiotes, Scatman Crothers, and a truly dull one from Sally Field . . . Jeff Bridges is good as always: natural and winning . . . "

© 1976 by the NYM Corp. Reprinted with the permission of NEW YORK Magazine.

New York Post, 4/26/76 (p. 20)
Frank Rich

" . . . *Stay Hungry* is an overripe, all-American mess--but it's a mess that, every so often, reverberates with the frisky beat of life . . .

. . . Various, unmanageable plot strands involving shady real-estate entrepreneurs, underworld thugs and the Mr. Universe pageant get hopelessly tangled up; the movie starts to embrace stagy and familiar dramatic crises . . .

But at its worst, *Stay Hungry* is never boring, and that is less a function of Rafelson's direction, which is as rangy as the material, than it is of his exemplary cast. The diminutive Miss Field . . . is a particular revelation . . .

Miss Field also connects superbly with Bridges, who embodies the true spirit of *Stay Hungry* . . . Here again Bridges is playing a half-innocent, half-canny country boy who's learning via picaresque adventures how to grow up . . . "

Reprinted by Permission of New York Post. © 1976, New York Post Corporation.

Newsweek, 5/17/76 (p. 111)
Jack Kroll

" . . . The screenplay, by Rafelson and Charles Gaines from the latter's novel, has all the ingredients of an American Gothic, and that's what you get. But the theme of the young dropout who opposes the system with ironic apathy until something (usually something violent) needles him to action is moldy around the edges, and by now Jeff Bridges seems to be playing that role in his sleep. The body-building angle is fresh, but Rafelson cops out in a pseudo-Nathaniel West climax that has the Mr. Universe contestants fanning out all over Birmingham, flexing their muscles in the streets.

Sally Field, the old Flying Nun herself, takes off her habit and everything else in a touching performance as a country girl who represents Possibility to Bridges, and Arnold Schwarzenegger, a former Mr. Universe, is surprisingly good as the muscle man with heart—and pectorals—of gold. A rousing fight scene, in which Bridges is wonderfully athletic as he dodges giant barbells in the gym, points to a fruitful new direction for Rafelson in which action speaks louder than words and ideas . . . "

© Newsweek, Inc. 1976
reprinted by permission.

Saturday Review, 5/29/76 (p. 48)
Judith Crist

"Bits and pieces of *Stay Hungry* would be not only more interesting but also more coherent than the whole of this new Bob Rafelson film . . .

Bridges--in a role reminiscent of his brother Beau's in *The Landlord*--does little to further his career or stretch his apparent talents as the poor little rich boy in search of something or other. But he and Sally Field do have sporadic moments of juvenile charm. Robert Eglund does a nice bit as Thor's assistant, Fannie Flagg is properly stuffy as a broadminded belle, and Helena Kallianiotes, as a karate teacher, reprises her delightful *Five Easy Pieces* spot as a zonked-out social thinker. But it's all to small purpose in a simplistic, superficial construction, based on the sort of sophomoric social approaches that even Jerry Rubin has outgrown."

© Judith Crist, 1976.

Film Information, 5/76 (p. 5)
Frederic A. Brussat

" . . . Although some of the characters fail to affect a realistic Southern accent, the cast is distinctive. Jeff Bridges is the changing Craig Blake; Sally Field is the peppy and sober Mary Tate Farnsworth (at last transcending her 'Flying Nun' image); Arnold Schwarzenegger (a former Mr. World and frequent winner in body building competitions) is Joe Santo; R. G. Armstrong is Thor. Fine supporting performances are by Joanna Cassidy, Roger E. Mosley, Scatman Crothers, Fannie Flagg, Robert Eglund, Richard Gilliand, and Helena Kallianiotes. The 'R' rating is justified for some totally gratuitous nudity scenes.

Bob Rafelson is a director who takes extreme risks with his actors/actresses and his material. *Stay Hungry* is half-successful on both counts. The genuine moments in the film where Craig Blake begins to see who he is are worth all the awkward sequences that surround it. It's almost like seeing someone reborn."

© Film Information, 1976.

Sight and Sound, Autumn 1976 (p. 255)
Tom Milne

" . . . The opening images of the film show Craig drifting moodily through a woodland glade, riding bareback with gun at his side, while a quiet, even voice—revealed to be that of his Uncle Albert reciting a letter—commiserates with his grief and urges him to 'seek the comfort of his traditions.' Yet as the romantic melancholy of the film suggests, with its echoes of Chateaubriand's noble savage and Rousseau's natural man, Craig has

continued on next page

continued from previous page

already found an alternative tradition; and when he also meets a ready-made model in Joe Santo, he is able—unlike the brothers in *The King of Marvin Gardens*— to begin living in terms of his fantasy.

The dual irony here is that fantasies tend to dissolve as soon as any reality intrudes, and that Joe Santo in fact stands for everything that Craig thinks he is rejecting: success, status, tradition . . .''

©Sight and Sound, 1976.

Christian Science Monitor, 5/10/76 (p. 23)
David Sterritt

"*Stay Hungry* is an old new romance from filmmaker Bob Rafelson, who has given us such universal diversions as *The King of Marvin Gardens* and the flawed but much admired *Five Easy Pieces*.

Rafelson does not seem to care whether his pictures are universally liked. He deals explicitly with tough, peculiar characters. *Stay Hungry* takes a well-bred Southern youth and mixes him up with a bunch of seedy capitalists. Then it adds a brilliant athlete, a training gym, and a beauty contest for men. Toss in a few complicated love affairs and you have a most unpredictable drama—sometimes charming, sometimes bitter, rarely dull . . . ''

Reprinted by permission from The Christian
Science Monitor © 1976.
The Christian Science Publishing Society.
All rights reserved.

Village Voice, 5/10/76 (p. 147)
Andrew Sarris

" . . . the one quality that is lacking in *Stay Hungry* is seductiveness. Rafelson seems to have hedged his bets on his subject by keeping it in the background as long as possible. Meanwhile, he beefed up the love story between his well-born protagonist (Jeff Bridges) and the muscle beach groupie (Sally Field), added some social and business intrigue to the plot, and tacked on a relatively happy ending in which the girl lives, and the protagonist and muscle man he admires form a business partnership. In the process, Rafelson has tended to vulgarize the class structure for easy conflicts. The main problem is that we don't see the big muscles until the end of the picture, and thus we get the impression that they have been hidden from us in teasing fashion . . . ''

Reprinted by permission of The Village Voice.
Copyright © The Village Voice, Inc., 1976

Los Angeles Times, 5/12/76 (Pt. IV, p. 1)
Charles Champlin

" . . . It is several movies not quite rolled into one, good performances and good sequences tossed together in the lap of chance, leading to a denouement that would be even cheerier if what went before had engaged belief or concern.

You sense two visions, authors' and director's, working on the same essential material, but not jointly. What could have been a deft social satire or a nice light romance or an insight into the special world of pumping iron (i.e. musclebuilding) or an impression of a changing society misses all options.

Withal, Bridges is an engaging figure, even if he never quite gets into focus here. Sally Field proves to be a fine, intense actress, displaying emotional depths hidden by the habit. Schwarzenegger is a pleasant surprise, a natural actor who gets through the plot with quiet dignity, giving evidence of a cool, clever head rising above the unbelievable musculature . . . ''

© Los Angeles Times, 1976.

Monthly Film Bulletin, 9/76 (p. 200)
Richard Combs

". . . Rafelson is probably the hardiest survivor of the fast-fading youth movies of the Sixties. What distinguishes him from other film-makers of the 'head' generation is both the poetic sureness of his fragmentary, allusive style, and the elliptical observation which prevents his social themes from being spiked too easily on the cultural antitheses of that bygone era . . . Craig Blake . . . embodies a kind of fretful, inarticulate yet still optimistic revolt that relates him to an earlier time than the locked in, isolating romances of *Marvin Gardens*, to the very beginning of the youth-movie era and *Catcher in the Rye*, with whose hero he shares a habit of evaluating things according to what is 'authentic' and what isn't . . .''

©Monthly Film Bulletin, 1976.

Cineaste, Fall 1976 (p. 37)
Tom Brom

". . . Director Bob Rafelson evidently is taking himself seriously after some positive critical response to *Five Easy Pieces* and *The King of Marvin Gardens*. He shouldn't. His efforts at presenting Jeff Bridges as an alienated Southern aristocrat looking for himself among 'low-life' real estate dealers and the crowd at a local gymnasium are simply embarrassing. Rafelson's casting of Sally Field as a sexually eager receptionist is disastrous —she was better as the Flying Nun . . .

There's nothing even mildly diverting in *Stay Hungry*. It's a decadent film directed by a moron. I can't say it any stronger. Stay away.''

Cineaste, 1976

The Sunday Times (London), 10/10/76 (p. 35)
Alan Brien

". . . There are two peaks of action, both comically horrifying. A battle in the gym, where equipment, sailing through the air as if hoisted by poltergeists, made me duck in my seat. And the Mr. Universe finals, mardi gras in the Inferno, impossible parodies of Cro-Magnon man, almost another species, materialise like inflated genii.

But it is not the sheer physicality—a society crazed on perpetual motion—with its constant undertow of rumbling menace, which makes *Stay Hungry* so gripping. It is the quirky zig-zag unpredictability of the dialogue, the twisting, tangential shifts of mood and emotion, the sudden strange surreal imagery. At the end it is all turned almost inside out into a great big bad-taste joke—but the taste lingers and should be savored."

©The Sunday Times, 1976.

The Times (London), 10/15/76 (p. 13)
Richard Combs

". . . its hero is a very regional but quite recognizable Holden Caulfield figure—though scrambled in the Rafelson manner, and pleasantly lyrical (where *Marvin Gardens* was savagely ironic) in its treatment of characters who have inadvertently slipped their moorings. The sentimental side of *Stay Hungry* is a useful reminder of Rafelson's working origins in the little revolts of the early Sixties—revolution more in the name of feelings than politics, a kind of restless, incoherent chafing at the insidious takeover of conformity and convention.

Its social comedy, taking off the Deep South cocktail party set, folksy land development sharks, and—more ambivalently—the sweat and muscle ethos of the Mr. Universe contest, also lends a useful reality to Rafelson's streak of absurdist humor. Otherwise, one can well imagine his disconnected, alienated characters floating away into . . . pained abstractions . . ."

©The Times, 1976.

STEPMOTHER, THE (MACHEKHA)

Director: *Oleg Bondaryov.* Screenplay: *Eduard Smirnow, Tatyana Doronina.* Photography: *Igor Chernykh.* Distributor: *Mosfilm Studio.* Running time 90 minutes. Los Angeles opening November 6, 1976, at several theatres. Classification: None. Origin: U.S.S.R.

Players: *Tatyana Doronina, Nadezhda Fedossova, Lena Kosterova, Leonid Nevedomsky.*

Los Angeles Times, 11/4/76 (Pt. IV, p. 14)
Linda Gross

"*The Stepmother* . . . is a sturdy and sentimental Soviet film which owns 'that children, like plants, take time and warmth to transplant.'

A happily married farm laborer (Leonid Nevedomsky) who has a preschool son and a baby daughter, receives a letter informing him that a woman he had previously loved and parted with nine years earlier has died, leaving an 8-year-old daughter (Nadezhda Fedossova), whom he had unknowingly fathered.

Begrudgingly, Nevedomsky and his wife (Tatyana Doronina) decide to bring the girl into their family . . .

The movie deals with Miss Doronina's patient struggle to render Nadezhda capable of giving and receiving love again . . .

Miss Doronina and Eduard Smirnow have written a detailed, psychologically consistent screenplay, which provides an excellent depiction of contemporary Russian working-class life, as well as a universally identifiable story of a family changing and growing in crisis . . ."

©Los Angeles Times, 1976.

STORY OF ADELE H., THE (L'HISTOIRE D'ADELE H.)

Director: *Francois Truffaut.* Screenplay: *Mr. Truffaut, Jean Gruault,* and *Suzanne Schiffman.* From **The Diary of Adele Hugo** edited by Frances V. Guille. Photography: *Nestor Almendros.* Editor: *Yann Dedet.* Music: *Maurice Jaubert.* Production: *Les Films du Carrosse/Les Productions Arvistes Associes.* Running time 97 minutes. New York opening October 12, 1975, at the New York Film Festival, Lincoln Center. Classification: None. Origin: France.

Adele H.: *Isabelle Adjani.* Lieut. Pinson: *Bruce Robinson.* Mrs. Saunders: *Sylvia Marriott.* Mr. Whistler: *Joseph Blatchley.* Colonel: *M. White.* Orderly: *Carl Hathwell.* Hypnotist: *Ivry Gillis.* Madame Baa: *Madame Louise.* Notary: *Sir Cecil de Sausmarez.* Judge Johnstone: *Sir Raymond Falla.* Dr. Murdock: *Roger Martin.*

See Volume 1 for additional reviews

continued on next page

continued from previous page

Commentary, 5/76 (p. 72)
William S. Pechter

" . . . Simple and austere though it is, there's also something faintly dull in its impeccable tastefulness.

The problem is that insofar as Adele's focus remains fixed on Lieutenant Pinson--the British officer who's loved and left her, and whom she's followed from Guernsey (where her father is in exile) to Nova Scotia--her quest obstinately fails to grow into the acting out of some soaringly romantic and magnificent obsession, but remains instead merely a clinical case of self-defeating and self-destructive behaviour by a neurotic and not entirely sympathetic young woman . . .

The Story of Adele H. isn't, I think, a great film (neither, I think, could one call Isabelle Adjani's delicately muted performance as Adele a great one), and some of it isn't even all that good, but I can think of few other films, even among better ones, that are more thematically rich, or that left me in a more profound state of emotional agitation."

© Commentary, 1976.

STORY OF SIN (DZIEJE GRZECHU)

Director: *Walerian Borowczyk*. Screenplay (Polish with English subtitles): *Mr. Borowczyk*. Based on a novel by Stefan Zeromski. Photography: *Zygmunt Samosiuk*. Production: *Polish Corporation for Film Production, "TOR" Film Unit*. Distributor: *TINC Productions*. Running time 128 minutes. New York opening October 7, 1976, at the New York Film Festival, Lincoln Center. Classification: R. Origin: Poland.

Eva: *Grazyna Dlugolecka*. Count Szczerbic: *Olgierd Lukaszewicz*. Lucas: *Jerzy Zelnik*.

Film Information, November 1976 (p. 4)
Bea Rothenbeuchner

"Polish director Walerian Borowczyk (*Immoral Tales*) lived and worked in Paris for some years and his *Story of Sin* shows French influence in its stylish decor, tasteful handling of eroticism, and, to some extent, also in its introduction of surrealist overtones. The story, one known to all cultures, is set in Victorian times: virtuous girl, seduced by a married man, goes from bad to worse.

The wages of sin is death is its familiar soap opera-like theme, one that, not surprisingly, continues to survive despite our rapidly changing sexual mores . . .

We follow the rapidly unfolding events with interest, admiring the director's flowing style, and the heroine's marvelous appearance and acting ability. However, the ultimate proof of a film's impact—did it make us feel the characters were real—is lacking. A pretty to look at but hard to believe cinematic exercise."

© Film Information, 1976.

The Times (London), 3/5/76
David Robinson

" . . . *Story of Sin* . . . seems generally to have been regarded—or ignored—as a regrettable aberration, in which Zeromski's overblown lyricism, melodramatic tendencies and muddled social notions finally took over. Borowczyk, however, draws out of the novel a mad and marvelous celebration of *l'amour fou*, in the setting of turn of the century 'decadent' literature and painting. It is the nasty tale of how a girl from a nice petit-bourgeois home falls in love with the lodger who cannot get a divorce from his estranged wife.

She pursues the loved one and the fantasy across Europe, encountering en route villainy and catastrophe that make the odysseys of Candide and Fanny Hill seem mild affairs; to die finally in an act of romantic and fulfilling sacrifice.

It is a world filled with Belle Epoque kitsch, and peopled with Zeromski's larger-than-life eccentrics . . . Grazyna Dlugolecka makes Eva, with her disaster-bent obsession with her great love and the absurd durability of a Candide, the maddest of the lot."

© The Times, 1976.

The Sunday Times (London), 3/7/76
Dilys Powell

"Walerian Borowczyk, after working for years in the West, returned to Poland to direct *Story of Sin* . . . to the phantasmagorical quality which one often finds in Polish cinema he has added his own bitter kind of romanticism—and his feeling for the look of the past . . . the piece is visually exquisite. It is based on a novel by the famous Polish writer Stefan Zeromski, from the cramped home in Warsaw through the months the girl spends in the provinces to be near her lover, to the baroque mansions and raffish bedrooms of her degradation, the narrative has the massive details of panoramic fiction. A whole society, corrupt and cruel, uncoils behind her. But the action cracks along. And the girl (Grazyna Dlugolecka) plays with a passion uncommon in novel-into-film. What is more, she has an erotic grace whether she wears a virgin's modest white, or the black corset and boots of the tart of melodrama, or, most seductively, nothing."

©The Sunday Times, 1976.

New York Post, 10/15/76 (p. 25)
Archer Winsten

". . . Walerian Borowczyk wrote the screenplay from Stefan Zeromski's novel and directed it with all the appreciation of beauty one would expect from a man who started as a painter. His sense of Polish passion must be possible only to a born Pole.

There are times when the continuity skips so violently in time, space and character change that you have trouble keeping abreast. But if you just keep your eye on Eva, she's a constant, in love, in trouble, and in her magnetism to a variety of men. Grazyna Dlugolecka handles her role with a giant swing from early modesty to the shamelessness of the professional. Jerzy Zelnik makes an appealing lover and Olgierd Lukaszewicz supplies a starch of aristocracy (Polish brand) to the role of Count Szczerbic. They all work well together in what convinces a New York observer that he is watching a True Romance of Poland, 1900."

Reprinted by Permission of New York Post.
©1976, New York Post Corporation.

STRANGE SHADOWS IN AN EMPTY ROOM

Director: *Martin Herbert.* Screenplay: *Vincent Mann, Frank Clark.* Producer: *Edmondo Amati.* Photography: *Anthony Ford.* Editor: *Vincent P. Thomas.* Music: *Armando Trovaioli.* Distributor: *American International Pictures.* Running time 99 minutes. New York opening February 11, 1977, at several theatres. Classification: R.

Tony Saitta: *Stuart Whitman.* Sergeant Matthews: *John Saxon.* The Doctor: *Martin Landau.* Julie: *Tisa Farrow.* Louise: *Carol Laure.* Margie Cohn: *Gayle Hunnicut.*

New York Post, 2/12/77 (p. 21)
Archer Winsten

". . . Murder, detection, car chases, false leads, brutal transvestites and new suspects fill the fast-moving procession as Detective Capt. Tony Saitta (Stuart Whitman) inexorably pursues the killer of his lovely, young sister Louise (Carole Laure) . . .
. . . The picture works as action melodrama. One disappointment is the early death of that prettiest girl around, Carole Laure, and when you get to

know her better, in post mortems on her wild life, that too is regrettable. However, the picture's excess of plot and fury tends to distract the would-be critic. Let's just say it's a familiar crime thriller in structure, cut from a good serviceable stencil by director Martin Herbert, following guidelines and words by Vincent Mann and Frank Clark, screenplay authors."

Reprinted by Permission of New York Post.
©1977, New York Post Corporation.

STREET PEOPLE

Director: *Maurice Lucidi.* Screenplay: *Ernest Tidyman, Randall Kleiser.* Music: *Luis Enriquez.* Art Director: *Gastogne Carsetti.* Distributor: *American International Pictures.* Running time 92 minutes. New York opening September 17, 1976, at several theatres. Classification: R.

Ulysses: *Roger Moore.* Phil: *Stacy Keach.* Salvatore Francesco: *Ivo Garrani.* Bishop Lopetri: *Entore Manni.* Continenza: *Ennio Balbo.* Nicoletta: *Fausto Tozzi.*

Films in Review, February 1977 (p. 119)
Harry Banta

"Here is another crime film centering on Mafia activities in Sicily and San Francisco. Although it never parallels the dramatic heights attained by the makers of *Godfather II*, it doesn't quite sink to the murky depths of *Lepke*, the Tony Curtis disaster film. Roger Moore, a front lawyer for 'the family' and his hit man, Stacy Keach, spend most of the footage trying to nail a traitor to the clan who has secretly imported a million dollar shipment of heroin. Approximately halfway through this Italian-American production . . . the director Maurice Lucidi, or possibly the American producers, decided to inject some broad comedy strokes, thereby giving a kind of Rover Boys relationship to the two protagonists, which doesn't meld with the grizzly earlier scenes. In fact, the film ends with a joke . . ."

©Films in Review, 1977.

New Leader, 10/11/76 (p. 24)
Robert Asahina

". . . A low-budget joint Italian-American production, it is predictably ill-made and muddled. Although the stars are Roger Moore and, somewhat

continued on next page

continued from previous page

surprisingly, Stacy Keach, the other actors mouth Italian and emit English, contributing no little to the confusion . . .

This no-nonsense manufacturing of thrills is characteristic of the current gangster movie. So is the blatant machismo of Moore and Keach: They are virile adventurers, proficient with guns, cars and women. What saves the film from being a vulgar parody of masculinity and nothing else are the straightforward script and performances that proceed in steamroller fashion, without the slightest hint of irony or condescension. *Street People*, in other words, is palatable because it neither intends nor invites any response more complex than simple-minded vicarious excitement."

Reprinted with permission from
The New Leader, 1976.
©The American Labor Conference
on international Affairs, Inc.

New York Post, 9/18/76 (p. 21)
Archer Winsten

". . . Director Maurice Lucidi has handled his people with uncommon restraint and his autos with utter abandon. No Demolition Derby could have done more to give business to the body repair shops.

The picture moves forward with such headlong momentum that one hardly has time to wonder what happened to San Francisco policemen and state cops while all this is going on. Eventually you do wonder, but by then it's too late. Nearly everyone is dead, and the heroin will never find a welcoming vein, and our heroes, Ulysses and Phil, have emerged unscathed, as heroes are wont to do in movies that have plots designed to please and extract profit from the American public."

Reprinted by Permission of New York Post.
©1976, New York Post Corporation.

STRONGEST MAN
IN THE WORLD, THE

Director: *Vincent McEveety*. Screenplay: *Joseph L. McEveety and Herman Groves*. Producer: *Bill Anderson*. Photography: *Andrew Jackson*. Editor: *Cotton Warburton*. Music: *Robert L. Brunner*. Production: *Walt Disney Productions*. Distributor: *Buena Vista*. Running time 92 minutes. New York opening July 9, 1975, at several theatres. Classification: G.

Dexter: *Kurt Russell*. Dean Higgins: *Joe Flynn*. Harriet: *Eve Arden*. A. J. Arno: *Cesar Romero*. Krinkli: *Phil Silvers*. Harry: *Dick Van Patten*. Dietz: *Harold Gould*. Schuyler: *Michael McGreevey*.

See Volume 1 for additional reviews

Monthly Film Bulletin, 8/76 (p. 176)
Sue Scott-Moncreiff

". . . here the formula reduces too many of the characters to stock responses and standard facial contortions, with the exception of Phil Silvers as Kirwood Krinkli, who provides his own idiosyncratic humor, and Joe Flynn as the harassed Dean Higgins, who generated much of the laughter . . . on the whole, the special effects are unremarkable, and the comic potential of a situation where reality becomes fantastical is rarely exploited . . . Gentle fun is poked at the world of advertising, but the establishment is never seriously challenged, and the end of the film sees the status quo firmly upheld. Fantasy finds a form but little expression when the strongest man in the world is limited to promoting breakfast cereals."

©Monthly Film Bulletin, 1976.

STUDENT BODY, THE

Director: *Gus Trikonis*. Screenplay: *Hubert Smith*. Producer: *Ed Carlin*. Photography: *Gary Graver*. Editor: *Jerry Cohen*. Music: *Don Bagley, Steve Michaels*. Production: *Brandywine*. Distributor: *Surrogate Releasing Company*. Running time 84 minutes. Los Angeles opening December 1976 at several theatres. Classification: R.

Players: *David Ankrum, Faith Bernhardt, June Fairchild, Janice Heiden, Peter Hooten, Vic Jolley, Jillian Kesner, Alan McRae, Judith Roberts, Warren Stevens*.

Los Angeles Times, 12/21/76 (Pt. IV, p. 18)
Linda Gross

"*The Student Body* . . . tries to combine exploitation and social statement. It doesn't succeed but at least it tries.

It concerns a psychology professor at a private university (Warren Stevens) who has been paid illegally to experiment with a new drug that causes increased aggression in humans. Stevens arranges for three girls from the local reformatory to be released in his custody so he can use them as guinea pigs to test the effects of the drug . . .

Hubert Smith's script lashes out against psychiatric abuses and the abuses of authority and indiscriminate drug experimentation—particularly when the patient isn't aware of what is going on. Unfortunately, the plot is not plausible and dramatic moments often deteriorate into amorphous crowd scenes. Still, Smith's anger is real and the girls are sympathetically conceived.

Jillian Kesner . . . and Janice Heiden and June Fairchild possess a softness that is unusual in exploitation films; they are also attractive and engaging performers. Director Gus Trikonis is good with actors but awkward with action scenes."

©Los Angeles Times, 1976.

SUNDAY WOMAN

Director: *Luigi Comencini*. Screenplay: *Age* and *Scarpelli*. Based on a novel by Fruttero and Lucentini. Producer: *Roberto Infascelli*. Photography: *Luciano Tovoli*. Editor: *Antonio Siciliano*. Music: *Ennio Morricone*. Distributor: *Twentieth Century-Fox*. Running time 110 minutes. New York opening September 26, 1976, at the Fine Arts Theatre. Classification: R. Origin: Italy.

Santamaria: *Marcello Mastroianni*. Ana Maria: *Jacqueline Bisset*. Massimo: *Jean-Louis Trintignant*. Lello Rivera: *Aldo Reggiani*. De Palma: *Pino Caruso*. Virginia Tabusso: *Maria Teresa Albani*. Benito: *Omero Antonutti*. Vollero: *Gigi Ballista*. Nicosia: *Renato Cecilia*. Garrone: *Claudio Gora*.

New York Post, 9/27/76 (p. 35)
Frank Rich

". . . *Sunday Woman* is somewhat better than the phone book. It's a harmless enough murder mystery set in Turin, a town so well stocked with red herrings that it seems to be the herring capital of the free world. The murder victim is a lecherous old architect (Claudio Gora)—a guy who goes to high-brow lectures about infantile masturbation for

kicks—and there are lots of people who'd like him dead. One of them bludgeons him with a stone phallus.

Marcello Mastroianni, world-weary as all get out, is the detective on the case . . .

Luigi Comencini has directed the film competently enough—though with no flair or distinctive personality—in a variety of attractive settings. Unfortunately his story is no great shakes: You don't really care who killed the disgusting architect, and there's no ingenious intellectual puzzle involved in figuring out the identity of the culprit.

Without real suspense or menace to work with, Comencini must use music and other artificial devices to create the effect. The ending is a surprise, but an arbitrary one—as if the filmmakers had drawn the murderer's name out of a hat at the last minute and then invented a motive to explain their choice . . ."

Reprinted by Permission of New York Post.
©1976, New York Post Corporation.

Film Information, October 1976 (p. 4)
David Bartholemew

"A thoroughly despicable man is bludgeoned to death, and police inspector Marcello Mastroianni is faced with a crew of suspects, all of whom with good reason hated the victim. Former critic Luigi Comencini's new film is a fluent, pungent mystery with a variety of interesting subthemes woven into the screenplay. It is on the basis of these that the film best succeeds; on the level of plotting, it falters near the end, although not illogically so, as it pounces on a fairly remote character as the culprit.

Rendered into English subtitles, the film's language, as well as its treatment of various subjects, including homosexuality—the murder weapon is a giant plaster phallus— is quite frank, although for the sake of authenticity rather than exploitation. A fine group of actors give mostly excellent, detailed performances . . ."

©Film Information, 1976.

New York Magazine, 10/11/76 (p. 80)
John Simon

". . . Alas, the film is more interested in surfaces than in cores, in effects than in causes, in cleverness than in clearsightedness. Homosexuality in particular is treated in a way that is both unconvincing and patronizing, but heterosexual relationships emerge schematic and trivial too, without much laughter as the reward of this reductionism. We do get to see quite a lot of Turin, which is good news insofar as we don't usually get to see Turin in the movies, but bad news inasmuch as Turin is not that fascinating . . .

continued on next page

continued from previous page

The acting is lively but not necessarily distinguished. Marcello Mastroianni plays Santamaria with his habitual mixture of suavity and diffidence . . .''

© 1976 by the NYM Corp. Reprinted with the permission of NEW YORK Magazine.

Christian Science Monitor, 10/7/76 (p. 22)
David Sterritt

"*Sunday Woman* has arrived on the international circuit from Italy. It is a cleverly wrought and visually precise thriller, flawed by lapses of taste and a plot with little point.

Two of Europe's most gifted male stars, Marcello Mastroianni and Jean-Louis Trintignant, join the glamorous Jacqueline Bisset to make a trio of troubled characters caught up in the aftermath of a sex-linked slaying of a disliked architect. Together, though acting from various motives, they probe the killing until the villain is unmasked at the last moment.

Director Luigi Comencini seems more interested in cinema style than in narrative suspense, forgetting that in the best movie chillers, such as Hitchcock's, these qualities go together . . .''

Reprinted by permission from The Christian Science Monitor © 1976. The Christian Science Publishing Society. All rights reserved.

SURVIVE (SUPERVIVIENTES DE LOS ANDES)

Director, Screenplay: *Rene Cardona*. Based on the book SURVIVE! by Clay Blair, Jr. English adaptation: *Martin Sherman*. Producers: *Conacine Cardona, Mr. Cardona*. Editor: *Alfredo Rosas Priego*. English Version Editor: *Marshall M. Borden*. Music: *Gerald Fried*. Postproduction, English Version: *Michael Rachmil*. Production: *Robert Stigwood-Allen Carr presentation of a Conacine-Rene Cardona Production*. Distributor: *Paramount Pictures*. Running time 87 minutes. New York opening August 4, 1976, at several theatres. Classification: R. Origin: Mexico.

Raul Cardenas: *Pablo Ferrel*. Francisco Pedraza: *Hugo Stiglitz*. Mrs. Madero: *Luiz Maria Aguilar*. Mr. Madero: *Fernando Larranaga*. Sylvia Pedraza: *Norma Lazareno*.

Los Angeles Times, 7/29/76 (p. 9)
Kevin Thomas

". . . a flat, but technically adroit English-language version of a phenomenally successful Mexican movie called *Supervivientes de los Andes* that reportedly broke box office records set by *The Exorcist* and *The Sting* in major south of the border cities.

Because we never get to know any of the victims, *Survive*, routinely though competently directed by Rene Cardona Sr. . . . is never really involving but does boast a fairly spectacular crash and rapid pace . . .

. . . In short, *Survive* is an exploitation picture with a new gimmick and best left to the undiscriminating . . .

Of far greater interest is how *Survive* was carved out of the original Mexican movie . . .

Carr and his associates . . . did not merely have a 130 minute film trimmed to 87-minute running time and dubbed into English. They went so far as to have the print bleached and have portions of the film rephotographed through various gradations of netting to make all the footage match and also to disguise that the film's fake snow looked like Ivory Flakes . . .''

© Los Angeles Times, 1976.

Women's Wear Daily, 8/5/76 (p. 8)
Howard Kissel

"If you look at *Survive* as an attempt to recreate the crude, clumsy, primitive style of Republic and Monogrom pictures, it succeeds. If you judge it on any other level it is laughable.

Survive is supposed to describe the drama of those survivors of a plane crash in the Andes who ate the frozen remains of their dead fellow passengers in order to stay alive. There is obviously incredible material here, but the film in no way deals with it. None of the characters has any real identity. Their lines are all plane-crash-pictures cliches. Even the material that must be intended to prepare us for the scenes of cannibalism is so stilted that the only way you can respond is laughter . . .

Survive, a Mexican film ineptly dubbed, is an attempt to cash in on what might be called the new voyeurism. The old voyeurism was simply concerned with sex, first conventional, then exotic. The new brand is quite literally ghoulish . . .''

© Women's Wear Daily, 1976.

New York Post, 8/5/76 (p. 19)
Archer Winsten

"*Survive* . . . tells the story of 45 people in a South American plane that crashed in the Andes.

The crew of five and several passengers died immediately. The rest of them set about in the deep snow and high altitude cold to make do without food, medicines, water or fuel . . .

The problem of cannibalism, that is, to live or die, is what the picture details in scenes that may not be for the squeamish. For any of us, I think, the picture does offer a hard, stomach-turning dilemma. It's not something that one would care to face personally, except in the direst emergency, like this true story that happened a mere four years ago.

One doesn't get to know the people very well. It's the situation that grabs you for that month of agony and suspense."

Reprinted by Permission of New York Post.
©1976, New York Post Corporation.

The Times (London), 11/12/76 (p. 9)
David Robinson

"For a while it looked as if cannibalism was going to be this year's new movie kick, with at least two different intended film versions of the 1972 Andes air disaster when the survivors stayed alive by eating the flesh of their dead companions. In the end only one of them, *Survive*, has survived; and a very odd mess it is.

Based on Clay Blair, Jr.'s, book of the same title, it seems to have originated as a Mexican production . . . 'The American version,' says the press release, 'differs greatly from the Spanish version through the wizardry and brilliance of a team of Hollywood technicians and craftsmen.'

That still leaves you guessing as to whether the original version boasted any identifiable human ·characters on this faceless package tour . . ."

©The Times, 1976.

The Sunday Times (London), 11/14/76 (p. 39)
Alan Brien

". . . rigor mortis sets in rather more quickly among the living actors than among the cold cuts from whom strips of surprisingly still moist flesh are sliced with razor blades in grisly enough detail. It is not so much that those who remain are not sufficiently individualised—I could not help wondering how even towards the end of the 72 days, some men still were unbearded and one woman kept her eye shadow—but that the decision to choose cannibalism was oddly lacking in any real debate. And when they return, we hear nothing of the accusations, explanations and justifications between the survivors and the relatives of those on whom they survived—the whole interest of the incident, which provoked world-wide speculation, lies in the mental, rather than the physical, reverberations of the ordeal. In the end, the film leaves a disappointingly flat, colourless, monotonous impression."

©The Sunday Times, 1976

SWASHBUCKLER

Director: *James Goldstone*. Screenplay: *Jeffrey Bloom*. Based on a story by Paul Wheeler. Producer: *Jennings Lang*. Photography: *Phil Lathrop*. Editor: *Edward A. Biery*. Music: *John Addison*. Distributor: *Universal Pictures*. Running time 101 minutes. New York opening July 29, 1976, at Radio City Music Hall. Classification: PG.

Ned Lynch: *Robert Shaw*. Nick Debrett: *James Earl Jones*. Lord Durant: *Peter Boyle*. Jane Barnet: *Genevieve Bujold*. Major Folly: *Beau Bridges*. Cudjo: *Geoffrey Holder*. Polonski: *Avery Schreiber*. Mr. Moonbeam: *Tom Clancy*. Woman of the Dark Visage: *Anjelica Huston*. Sir James Barnet: *Bernard Behrens*. Alice: *Dorothy Tristan*. Lute Player: *Mark Baker*. Willard Culverwell: *Kip Niven*.

Los Angeles Times, 7/30/76 (Pt. IV, p. 1)
Kevin Thomas

". . . Thankfully, *Swashbuckler* . . . is not crude burlesque. While not as sophisticated as one might wish, it manages to be lots of fun while avoiding making fun of the conventions of the traditional pirate picture (to which it actually adheres quite closely). In short, it's too good-natured to succumb to campiness.

Although Goldstone and Bloom accomplish the essential task of setting and sustaining the right tone for telling their tall tale, avoiding undue tongue-in-cheekery and overly heady old-fashioned romanticism, it's too bad they didn't try to reach beyond this to try for something of the wit, poignancy and elegance of a *Robin and Marian* . . .

Among the principal players, all of whom are pleasing, are a particularly deft Beau Bridges as a young major in Boyle's service, as pompous as he is inept, and Geoffrey Holder as an awesome knife-thrower who comes to the aid of Shaw and Jones . . ."

©Los Angeles Times, 1976.

Saturday Review, 8/21/76 (p. 45)
Judith Crist

". . . the only virtue of this ersatz romantic adventure film is that it reveals our hunger for the swash and the buckle of villainous despots, libertarian pirates, the clash of swords, and the swoons of fair ladies . . .

The script, by Jeffrey Bloom (author of *Snow Job* and *11 Harrowhouse*, mediocre caper films), is

continued on next page

continued from previous page

completely without viewpoint or wit to justify the derivative and rambling plot. Goldstone . . . has avoided any suggestion of style, let alone the panache this genre demands. As a result, an excellent cast is left to play living statues, allowed an instant of performance, and then immobilized by dumb dialogue and awkward action. Robert Shaw, as the pirate captain Ned Lynch, master of the *Blarney Cock*, is reduced to a brogue, lines like 'I'm not a gentleman—I'm an Irishman' and 'I'm no fool—I'm an Irishman,' endless fencing, and enough gymnastics to make us yearn for more; Genevieve Bujold, as the lady in distress, is given swordplay in a see-through dress and a nude-swimming scene; James Earl Jones as Shaw's lieutenant and Geoffrey Holder as a native leader are given nothing worthy of their talents . . ."

©Judith Crist, 1976.

Commonweal, 9/10/76 (p. 592)
Colin L. Westerbeck, Jr.

". . . Even more than the Western, the Swashbuckler is a genre set in a time and place so remote and peripheral none of us feels any responsibility for the history that occurs there. That makes it ideal for doing what all genres try to do: write the history of our own times under the pretense of showing us someone else's . . .

Despite the heroine's timely sauciness and other modern improvements . . . *Swashbuckler* has not tampered too much with the ancient machinery of its genre. Director Goldstone has had sense enough to realize that the fact he was making a parody did not excuse him from having as many stupendous action sequences as a straight Swashbuckler would have. On the contrary, it required that such sequences be more outlandish than ever. Shaw, Goldstone and the others so clearly enjoyed the romp they had making this movie that even if it had nothing else to recommend it, their good spirits would still be amusing . . ."

©Commonweal, 1976.

Women's Wear Daily, 7/21/76 (p. 14)
Christopher Sharp

"Hopefully Errol Flynn is so busy swordfighting in Purgatory that he will never get a chance to see *Swashbuckler*.
. . . There is a lot of swordfighting and swinging from ropes, which leaves the stunt people the real stars of the show. There is also one surprise: Beau Bridges—who plays 'Major Folly'—does an uncharacteristic bad-guy role, although he is so silly that he can't be taken seriously . . .

Goldstone makes the mistake of assuming that 'biggest, grandest, action-filled pirate movie ever' can be created with high-pitched schlock. The re-

sult is that the passion of the Flynn pirate films is replaced with a kind of loose party atmosphere in this film. It is almost as if Goldstone told his actors: 'Okay kids. Go out and pretend you're pirates the best way you know how.' The film revolves around the fighting and the gymnastics with the screenplay obsequiously serving the action scenes . . ."

©Women's Wear Daily, 1976.

Newsweek, 8/9/76 (p. 68)
Janet Maslin

". . . Much of the script sounds as if it were meant to be funny. Peter Boyle, who appears in a frightful shoulder-length black wig as the wicked British governor of Jamaica, circa 1781, says things like "I serve one master and his name is Darkness' with such gravity that you almost take him at his word. James Goldstone's direction of the action sequences is similarly confusing, mixing derring-do with slapstick, which adds to the vigor but not the excitement.

But *Swashbuckler*'s cast is unusually appealing. There's Genevieve Bujold as a feisty noblewoman, James Earl Jones as a jolly second-in-command and Beau Bridges as a bumbling British soldier—all of whom make light work of roles that are older than Long John Silver. And most of all there's Robert Shaw, who at last has found himself in a role that may elevate him, at 48, from the ranks of marvelous character actors to a full-fledged leading man . . ."

©Newsweek, Inc. 1976
reprinted by permission.

New York Magazine, 8/16/76 (p. 61)
John Simon

". . . Jeffrey Bloom's screenplay from Paul Wheeler's story is magisterially moronic, and cannot even make up its minuscule mind whether to play it straight or as a spoof of the pirate genre that might best be called *Captain Ketchup*. As a result, the incoherent whole is even worse than the scum of its parts. James Goldstone, the director, hasn't a clue about how to direct sword fights, derring-do, crowd scenes, romantic moments, orgiastic decadence, sight gags, or much of anything else . . . What he really lacks is rhythm and timing; the opening sequence, an interrupted hanging, is a model of how not to achieve either comedy or excitement . . ."

©1976 by the NYM Corp. Reprinted with
the permission of NEW YORK Magazine.

Christian Science Monitor, 8/11/76 (p. 22)
David Sterritt

"*Swashbuckler* should have been a rouser—big budget, all-star cast, wind-swept story about dashing pirates and corrupt rulers and spirited rebels . . .

. . . What a hackneyed adventure it turns out to be . . . we are struck more by the let-down than by the drama of the spectacle that lurches before our eyes . . .

Shaw has some high old moments as Ned Lynch, and James Earl Jones is feisty as his right hand. Geoffrey Holder also has fun as the pirate's colorful accomplice. In fact, the whole cast seems willing and able, except Boyle, who is desperately out of place in his flowing colonial wig. But Jeffrey Bloom's script gives nobody anything interesting to say, and James Goldstone's uneven direction only emphasizes the weariness of Paul Wheeler's story . . ."

Reprinted by permission from The Christian Science Monitor © 1976. The Christian Science Publishing Society. All rights reserved.

Village Voice, 9/13/76 (p. 111)
Marvin Deckoff

". . . Some flicks of this sort make me nervous by being too suspenseful—the hero is usually in a hell of a jam and totally humiliated before the cavalry arrives, almost too late to soothe my anxieties. No such problem here. At the very worst our friends are well in command. A carefree smile tells us that our guys still have plenty of aces left to play, and in extremis you can always dive into the water and swim back to the pirate ship. I would have liked a sea battle between the two ships, though, to break the monotony of unremitting land operations against the poor bleeding castle. Add a sea battle and some old-fashioned conviction in the characterizations and you have the makings of a classic B film here on a super-A budget."

Reprinted by permission of The Village Voice. Copyright © The Village Voice, Inc., 1976.

Film Information, 9/76 (p. 5)
Paul Coleman

". . . As piracy yarns have virtually vanished from the screens since the death of Errol Flynn, *Swashbuckler* operates under the handicap of parodying a genre with which modern audiences are not familiar. Broad comic playing—particularly from Boyle and Beau Bridges as a buffoonish major—is out of place within a complicated plot of intrigue.

Director James Goldstone seems torn between developing suspense and throwing pies . . . and neither effect carries much resonance. Even talented Broadway performers like Geoffrey Holder (of *The Wiz*), Mark Baker (of *Candide*), and Louisa Horton (of the original *One Flew Over the Cuckoo's Nest*) can do little more than suggest mysterious menace before being stirred into this Mulligan stew of a plot."

© Film Information, 1976.

Films in Review, October 1976 (p. 507)
Michael Buckley

"*Swashbuckler* buckles under too much swash! An attractive cast promises more than the screenplay by Jeffrey Bloom or direction by James Goldstone deliver.

Robert Shaw is entertaining as usual. One wonders when he has time to change makeup between film assignments. Genevieve Bujold . . . is as beautiful as ever, but her considerable acting talents are not taxed herein. James Earl Jones overplays and Peter Boyle underplays. Beau Bridges, an unappreciated actor in most circumstances, is keen when he's mean and seems slightly bored (as though he'd rather be playing something less spectacular and more meaningful, such as *The Other Side of the Mountain*). Geoffrey Holder is very tall.

All in all, it's likable but a long way from Errol Flynn."

© Films in Review, 1976.

Monthly Film Bulletin, November 1976 (p. 235)
Geoff Brown

". . . here, the swashbuckling cliches are painstakingly resurrected without the wit and energy which customarily went with them. The screen teems with activity to a tiresome degree: a typecast Shaw leads his roistering crew in a chain of noisy brawls, raids and chases, backed up by James Goldstone's nervous direction and a score by John Addison which battles for soundtrack supremacy with clashing swords, archaic oaths and full-throated yells. The only pleasures are strictly peripheral: some secondary characters are sketched with the kind of idiosyncratic detail most needed by the colourless leads . . . Addison's main theme tune, too, is characteristically buoyant, and an ironic prelude to the leaden events which follow."

© Monthly Film Bulletin, 1976.

SWEET MOVIE

Director: *Dusan Makavejev.* Dialogue: *English and French with English subtitles.* Producer: *Vincent Malle.* Photography: *Pierre L'Homme.* Editor: *Yann Dedet.* Music: *Manos Hadjidakis.* Production: *V. M. Production; Mojack Films; Maran Films.* Distributor: *Biograph Films.* Running time 95 minutes. New York opening October 8, 1975, at the D.W. Griffith Theatre. Classification: None. Origin: Canada.

continued on next page

continued from previous page

Miss Canada: *Carol Laure*. Sailor: *Pierre Clement*. Captain Ann Pianeta: *Ann Prucani*. El Macho: *Sami Frey*. Chastity Belt Lady: *Jane Mallet*. Mama Communa: *Marpessa Dawn*. Jeremiah Muscle: *Ray Callender*. Mr. Kapital: *John Vernon*. With: *Otto Muehl and members of the Therapie-Komune of Vienna*.

See Volume 1 for additional reviews

Los Angeles Times, 10/14/76 (Pt. IV, p. 20)
Kevin Thomas

"*Sweet Movie* . . . could scarcely be more misleading in its title.

Its creator, Yugoslavia's Dusan Makavejev, who also made *WR: Mysteries of the Organism*, is one of those rub-your-nose-in-it filmmakers who apparently subscribe to the very dubious theory that the more revolting they are the more liberating they are. However, the only feelings *Sweet Movie* inspires are those of profound disgust; such pretentious trash is best left to admirers of *El Topo* . . .

From time to time there are actual moments of tenderness, suggesting that Makavejev means us to believe that love, or at least a fully abandoned sensuality, is our only defense against the political tyrannies of either capitalism or communism. But Makavejev, hardly a subtle satirist, is too extravagantly trying to have it both ways, exploiting with a thudding sensationalism life's horrors while ostensibly protesting them . . ."

©Los Angeles Times, 1976.

Gennarino: *Giancarlo Giannini*. Raffaella: *Mariangela Melato*.

See Volume 1 for additional reviews

Cineaste, Spring, 1976 (p. 41)
Ruth McCormick

" . . . *Swept Away* is a fable about oppressed people--he, as a worker, she, as a woman. Both are as much victims of their own illusions and prejudices as they are of the society that predetermines their lives . . .

Wertmuller proposes the problems, not solutions, and attempts to entertain us while stripping away the romantic myths with which we have all been fed. The fact that she has become so popular with those who have no interest in or sympathy with social change, while at the same time enraging many of those who do, points less, I believe, to her lack of sincerity than to the fact that she has not yet really succeeded in coming to any conclusions herself. It's also possible that *Swept Away* is too amusing. In her efforts to enthrall and entertain us, Wertmuller, intelligent though she is, appeals more to our guts than to our brains and perhaps thereby suffers more from the emotional responses of her critics than from their rational evaluation. In this sense, a large portion of the audience is as 'swept away' as Gennario and Raffaela and, like them, develop no new perspectives but are reinforced in their old ideologies."

© Cineaste, 1976.

TAXI DRIVER

Director: *Martin Scorsese*. Screenplay: *Paul Schrader*. Producers: *Michael Phillips, Julia Phillips*. Photography: *Michael Chapman*. Editors: *Tom Rolf, Melvin Shapiro*. Music: *Bernard Herrmann*. Distributor: *Columbia Pictures*. Running time 112 minutes. New York opening February 8, 1976, at the Coronet Theatre. Classification: R.

Travis Bickle: *Robert De Niro*. Betsy: *Cybill Shepherd*. Iris: *Jodie Foster*. Sport: *Harvey Keitel*. Wizard: *Peter Boyle*. Charles Palantine: *Leonard Harris*. Tom: *Albert Brooks*. Melio: *Vic Argo*. Gun Salesman: *Steven Prince*.

SWEPT AWAY [BY AN UNUSUAL DESTINY IN THE BLUE SEA OF AUGUST]

Director: *Lina Wertmuller*. Screenplay (Italian with English subtitles): *Ms. Wertmuller*. Producer: *Romano Cardarelli*. Photography: *Giulio Battiferri, Giuseppe Fornari, and Stefano Ricciotti*. Music: *Piero Piccioni*. Production: *Medusa Films*. Distributor: *Cinema V*. Running time 116 minutes. New York opening September 17, 1975, at the Cinema II Theatre. Classification: R. Origin: Italy.

Passenger: *Martin Scorsese*. Personnel Officer: *Joe Spinell*.

See Volume 1 for additional reviews

Monthly Film Bulletin, 9/76 (p. 201)
Richard Combs

"The opening shot of *Taxi Driver* plays probably the most seductive of trumps in the recent craze for power totems that has overtaken the American screen . . . Out of a cloud of steam gushing over a New York street, a yellow cab floats majestically, mysteriously forward, its foreboding trajectory paced to the growling thunder of Bernard Herrmann's score, its surface awash with abstract patterns of neon light. The powerful physicality of the image, and the state of extreme dislocation which it conveys, are the key to a kind of muscle-flexing sense of paradox on many levels: the film is about the soul sickness of urban alienation, played out (despite the red herring and basic implausibility of Travis Bickle's Arthur Bremer-like diary) as a series of extrovert power plays involving American myths of gunmanship and Ideal Womanhood; its mood is one of determinist doom, feverishly embraced . . . and, following from this, its method is to construct a series of steel traps for its hero, all of which have firmly shut before the film is half over, though Scorsese's grandstanding and Schrader's Bressonian pretensions continue to push for moments of religious transcendence . . ."

©Monthly Film Bulletin, 1976.

The Times (London), 8/20/76 (p. 7)
David Robinson

". . . The concentration upon the solitary routines of Travis' life—the diary which is his only confidant, the endless driving through the coloured streamers of the city lights, the monotonous clicking of the meter, the succession of the fares (they include Scorsese himself as a husband murderously crazed with jealousy), the ritual nibbling of bits of bread soaked in cherry brandy, the mad method of the preparation of his mechanical armoury—gives him the obsessive private character of a Bresson hero.

It is a wonderful performance by De Niro, permitting us to see, apparently by intermittent flashes, into this ignorant, inarticulate and secret man as his personality disintegrates under stress; while he degenerates from a nondescript young citizen into some sort of grinning monster—a monster whom you uneasily suspect still survives, even after the final rehabilitation."

©The Times, 1976.

Film Quarterly, Summer 1976 (p. 37)
Michael Dempsey

. ". . . In a complete turnaround from his pinwheeling, off-the-wall Johnny Boy in *Mean Streets*, De Niro has brought Schrader's brilliant conception alive with expert minimalism: Hooded eyes, stiffly loping gait, a crinkled shadow of a grin during moments of uncertainty. Along with Scorsese's electric montages of gothic Gotham, De Niro's embodiment of this lost man is the film's most affecting element.

But once it has conjured Travis up, *Taxi Driver* does not really know what to do with him, other than baptize him in blood. Schrader uses Bressonian motifs, such as narration which describes what we already see, to make the film's climax look like the work of fate. But there is a thin line between this approach and plain old sloppy plotting . . ."

©Film Quarterly, 1976.

The Sunday Times (London), 8/22/76 (p. 28)
Philip Mackie

". . . *Taxi Driver* was all shot on location in New York, and it's one of the best arguments I've seen for all-location filming. The picture it presents of the city is an ugly one: neon signs, cheap cafeterias, garbage, junkies, teenage prostitutes. Through this sleaziness moves Robert De Niro as the taxi driver—a lonely and alienated man.

He is rejected by middle-class Cybill Shepherd, and his animosity grows: he buys a whole armoury of guns and spends his spare time in target practice. He tells himself that they're for self-defense against muggers, but the mood he's in, he might shoot anybody. The ending suggests, perhaps ironically, that he has won some kind of recognition for his final bloody shooting spree.

Robert De Niro gives a fine and truthful performance as the driver, and Jodie Foster is splendid as a teenage streetwalker."

©The Sunday Times, 1976.

Film, September 1976 (p. 10)
Peter Cargin

"The milieu of the film is similar to Scorsese's *Mean Streets* of a few years ago, the tough halflight world of New York's underbelly, but whereas that film had a driving force and power, *Taxi Driver* comes to a stop about halfway through and neither the film nor the characters progress beyond a certain point. The fault must lie with the script by Paul Schrader, who has previously written *The Yakuza*; it never convinces either in its details or its general characterisations so that one is left with an empty shell of a film. This is a pity, for Scorsese's use of

continued on next page

continued from previous page

the film medium, from the opening night-driving sequence, with De Niro looking out from his cab like some ancient gladiator onto a cruel and mean world, to the overhead reverse tracking scene down the stairway of carnage past the various killings at the finale of the film is superb. All this is backed by a superb score by Bernard Hermann . . ."

©Film 1976.

Cineaste, Fall 1976 (p. 35)
Lenny Rubinstein

". . . Sexual frustration, pervasive depravity and bloody violence—all the themes to win an audience's heart or its hatred. The problem is that neither Schrader in his script or Scorsese in his direction wanted to do more than trace that development within the confines of Travis' mentality. Themselves entranced by his kind of psychosis, their film is unable to break out of its madman's straitjacket, even at the finish, when the audience has to tell itself that Travis couldn't possibly end up a hero. In this sense, *Taxi Driver* is as much a product of America's debased human environment as it is meant to be a picture of it."

©Cineaste, 1976.

Commentary, 5/76 (p. 75)
William S. Pechter

" . . . *Taxi Driver* is Scorsese's most tautly brilliant work yet, with passages of a stylistic bravura that remain fully integrated to the work, and only one scene (a conversation between De Niro and Peter Boyle in front of the latter's cab) that has the slack feel of overextended improvisation which, for me, marred too much of *Mean Streets*. Like *Mean Streets* (which was shot by a different photographer), the film has a distinctly original look: a raw, bloody, burning look, like a neon-lit wound. And, at its center, is the image of Robert De Niro's fiery eyes: the first thing we see of him, and the last. Some have seen the movie's coda as another (weak) irony: the 'hero' snubbing the woman who's previously rejected him; but I think not. Rather, the sense I had was of his indifference (one might almost say, post-coital) to the woman he's now violently purged from his psyche. But given the last, shattered image of his eyes, it seems to me plain that she won't be the last such woman, and that it won't be long before Travis will be suicidally, murderously, purging himself of some similarly raging pain once again."

© Commentary, 1976.

Take One, 5/21/76 (p. 65)
George Morris

"From the very first image of steam rising out of a Manhattan street, *Taxi Driver* plunges into the head of its psychotic protagonist and remains there for two hours. Martin Scorsese's fifth feature-length film operates on a level of reality that verges on the surreal. The director has structured every scene so that we view New York City through the subjective viewpoint of Travis Bickle (Robert De Niro), the 26-year-old ex-Marine who drives a cab for twelve hours a day, because he has headaches and can't sleep. Looking for a direction that will give meaning to his aimless existence, he arrives at one during the course of the film: the elimination of the 'filth and scum' who people the streets of the city.

Taxi Driver is a remarkable achievement, a crazy, excessive, erratic masterpiece, but a masterpiece just the same . . .

With *Taxi Driver*, a thematic consistency becomes clear throughout Scorsese's work. The contradictions in Travis Bickle between a Puritan ethic and the need to find an outlet for his inarticulate rage and repression haunt the Harvey Keitel figure in *Mean Streets* and the headstrong Ellen Burstyn in *Alice Doesn't Live Here Any More*. The resolution of these contradictions that Travis settles upon gives this film its profoundly disturbing edge . . . The pity and terror with which we view Travis' deterioration and the pathetic irony of his redemption reflect back upon ourselves, haunting the memory long after the last image has faded from the screen."

© Take One, 1976.

TENANT, THE

Director: *Roman Polanski*. Screenplay: *Gerard Brach, Mr. Polanski*. Based on the novel by Roland Topor. Producer: *Andrew Braunsberg*. Photography: *Sven Nykvist*. Editor: *Francoise Bonnot*. Music: *Philippe Sarde*. Distributor: *Paramount Pictures*. Running time 124 minutes. New York opening June 20, 1976, at the Loews Tower East Theatre. Classification: R.

Trelkovsky: *Roman Polanski*. Stella: *Isabelle Adjani*. The Concierge: *Shelley Winters*. Mr. Zy: *Melvyn Douglas*. Mme. Diaz: *Jo Van Fleet*. Scope: *Bernard Fresson*. Mme. Gaderian: *Lila Kedrova*. Husband: *Claude Dauphin*. Neighbor: *Claude Peiplu*. Badar: *Rufus*. Simon: *Romain Bouteille*

Newsweek, 6/28/76 (p. 78)
Janet Maslin

"Roman Polanski is generous to a fault; in *The Tenant* he does his audience the dubious favor of making it privy to his apparently abundant nightmares. Here he directs himself in the role of a weaselly paranoiac, a displaced Eastern European clerk who moves into a seedy, creaky Paris apartment where the previous lodger, a woman, has jumped out the window. Gradually he becomes convinced that his oddball neighbors conspired to drive her mad and are determined to see him end the same way. Before long, he is accommodating them even to the extent of assuming his predecessor's identity by dressing up (most unbecomingly) in the clothes she left behind and wearing her make-up. When Isabelle Adjani, who is smeary-eyed and negligible as a girl who befriends him, tells Polanski he's 'strange,' she provides this debacle with its most inadvertently funny moment.

The Tenant doesn't seem to have been designed as self-parody, but it certainly comes across that way . . ."

© Newsweek, Inc. 1976
reprinted by permission.

Los Angeles Times, 6/23/76 (Pt. IV, p. 15)
Kevin Thomas

" . . . Polanski seems to be trying to stir up a little suspense, to comment on the relationship between the individual and hostile society and to pose the old 'am-I-paranoid-or-am-I-really-being-persecuted?' riddle. But *The Tenant* . . . is a flat, uninspired business from start to preposterous finish.

There's no buildup, no force of identification with Polanski and his plight. True, his neighbors are a decidedly unfriendly bunch, but we don't begin to see enough of them to consider seriously for a moment that they really might be ganging up on poor Polanski, who is seemingly coming apart for reasons of his own that are never made clear.

Sadly, all the elements and motifs that have worked so well for Polanski in the past in such pictures as *Repulsion* and *Rosemary's Baby* just don't emerge and coalesce here. As a result, *The Tenant* is a long-winded exercise in tedium and morbidity . . ."

© Los Angeles Times, 1976.

New York Post, 6/21/76 (p. 20)
Frank Rich

" . . . Essentially, *The Tenant* is a mechanical effort in which Polanski replods territory he's already covered exhaustively in his better films. At times the new movie recalls *Repulsion*, *Rosemary's Baby* and even *Two Men and a Wardrobe*--right down to some of their specific images--but *The Tenant*

doesn't elucidate Polanski's themes and passions; instead it veers into self-parody and cheapens one's memories of his other works.

This filmmaker has no one to blame, I'm afraid, but himself. Not only did he direct the movie, but he also stars in it and is the co-author of the screenplay . . .

From the outset it's clear that this film's hero is a psychotic paranoid creating his own torture--for the phenomena that scare him are all either italicized hallucinations (faces metamorphosing before his eyes, surreal images of disembodied arms and heads) or eccentric occurrences (like the bathroom shenanigans) that lend themselves to benign explanations as easily as evil ones . . .

By the time Trelkovsky starts to run around in drag, sweating furiously and talking to himself in a falsetto voice, we're less tuned into the protagonist's trauma than we are into Polanski's insistent and peculiar ambition to try his hand at female impersonation . . . "

Reprinted by Permission of New York Post.
© 1976, New York Post Corporation.

New York Magazine, 6/28/76 (p. 67)
John Simon

" . . . As always in Polanski's worst pictures, something that looks very much like stupidity takes over, though it may be nothing more than near-total lack of interest in whatever merely leads up to the kinky and maniacal sequences, the film's true *raison d'etre*. We are given here the utterly improbable story of Trelkovsky, a little Parisian office worker of Polish origin who, for no convincing reason, rents expensively a small, dismal apartment without so much as a toilet to it on the top floor of a respectable-looking house, whose owner, concierge, and tenants, however, seem to be, at the very least, unappetizing, if not downright monstrous . . .

Nothing makes sense . . . Of course, the entire film could be perceived as Trelkovsky's hallucinations, but what concern can we deploy if everything is the ravings of a madman, if we are not even accorded a normative view of reality, and if that mad protagonist is far from being a sympathetic, or merely believable, madman . . .

Script, direction, and dubbing join in making all performances insignificant, if not indeed ludicrous . . . "

© 1976 by the NYM Corp. Reprinted with
the permission of NEW YORK Magazine.

Monthly Film Bulletin, 9/76 (p. 193)
Tom Milne

"Before ultimately lapsing into deja vu with dis-

continued on next page

continued from previous page

torting lenses and clutching hands appearing from the decor which make *The Tenant* and *Repulsion* look like the His and Hers of mental derangement, Polanski stakes out an area closer to Kafka than to the earlier film's bizarre admixture of Freud and Edgar Allan Poe. Everything, really, is said in the brilliant credit sequence where the camera, roving smoothly but vertiginously up, down and around the courtyard and facade behind whose windows we momentarily see Trelkovsky merge with Simone Choule, expresses that curiosity (so easily growing through frustration into fear) evoked by the secret life going on behind the blind walls of an apartment house . . . Skillfully contriving to express subjective impressions through objective means, Polanski brilliantly merges several levels of perception as he traces the gradual ascendancy of Simone over Trelkovsky . . . Having got so far, it is a pity that Polanski then throws it all away by opting for subjective camera and Grand Guignol after a somewhat unconvincing acceleration into the gradual process of hallucination."

©Monthly Film Bulletin, 1976.

Village Voice, 7/12/76 (p. 115)
Andrew Sarris

"*The Tenant* . . . does not have to apologize for its initial premise, that is, that a tenant could conceivably be tyrannized and persecuted beyond endurance, particularly in concierge-controlled Paris. One encounters comparably Kafkaesque scenarios every so often in the Sunday Times Real Estate Section. Roman Polanski, who both acts in and directs *The Tenant*, fails to live up to the potentialities of his subject because of his lack of a consistent point of view. By juggling the occult with the satiric, the objective with the subjective, Polanski manages to dilute the suspense into very feeble outlandishness . . .

Polanski at his most ambitious tends to serve up vast portions of undigested clinical material. In this respect, *The Tenant* is his most wobbly exercise since *What?* . . ."

Reprinted by permission of The Village Voice. Copyright © The Village Voice, Inc., 1976.

Christian Science Monitor, 7/14/76 (p. 24)
David Sterritt

". . . a serious study of morbidity and madness, marked by an introspective intensity rarely encountered in more conventional melodramas . . .

It is a grim progression: feeling out of place in one's society, in one's home, in one's body, in one's life. Polanski crowds his camera closely upon his characters, peering into their faces and forms with a quarry's singlemindedness and fear. *The Tenant* stops short of explaining its own mysteries. Trelkovsky protests his victimization as sincerely as

Roman Polanski talks with Maite Nahyr (right) and Josiane Balasko in **The Tenant**, a psychological thriller he directed.

Kafka's Joseph K. in *The Trial*, yet he may be as guilty as Joseph K. on the dim levels of thought that have begun running his life. The one sure thing is the visual courage of *The Tenant*, a claustrophobic yet oddly lovely film, eerily and immaculately assembled. There is also much fine acting . . ."

Reprinted by permission from The Christian Science Monitor © 1976. The Christian Science Publishing Society. All rights reserved.

Saturday Review, 7/24/76 (p. 42)
Judith Crist

". . . the official French entry at the Cannes film festival, awkwardly dubbed into English for American consumption. With screenplay by Polanski and Gerard Brach, his collaborator on his non-Hollywood films, and with direction by Polanski and with him in the protagonist's role, this adaptation of Roland Topor's novel is a study in paranoia. On screen, however, it emerges as a near-parody of Polanski's *Repulsion*, with the filmmaker taking over Catherine Deneuve's role to demonstrate, literally in drag, how one goes bananas in style . . .

The international cast leads to a babel of dubbing. Of the leading players only Polanski, playing a naturalized Pole to compensate for his accent; Shelley Winters, wasted as an unpleásant concierge; and Melvyn Douglas, equally unexploited as the elderly owner of the house, speak for themselves. Isabelle Adjani, as the dead girl's friend, becomes as nondescript as the crisp voice allotted her. They jar with the creaky, haunting atmosphere Sven Nykvist brings to the rundown tenement and with the emphatic cello-dominated scoring by Philippe Sarde. And while Polanski initially establishes himself as the introverted little clerk with a certain glum undercurrent of macabre humor, he becomes uninteresting as he takes the obvious slide into psychosis. The tension stretches to tedium, and the mechanics of the film are exposed."

©Judith Crist, 1976.

Commonweal, 8/27/76 (p. 563)
Colin L. Westerbeck, Jr.

". . . What is the movie supposed to be, anyway, a horror film or a comedy? I don't think Polanski knows. That's what's wrong with his ending. Like a body hitting the pavement in a deadfall, it goes in all different directions at once. In neither horror films or comedies is it necessary, usually, to understand the characters' motivations. We are in a world gone crazy that we don't expect to understand in a realistic way. But Polanski's horror films try to stay close to the real world, and the causes for an action like the tenant's suicide attempt are therefore not dispensable . . .

. . . like hieroglyphs without a Rosetta stone, all these little images being sent to us by the film are ultimately indecipherable. Polanski has often taken pains to establish connections between one scene or circumstance in the film and another, but the connections do not seem in the end to have any meaning. They are just a snow job, an exercise in obscurity . . ."

©Commonweal, 1976.

The Sunday Times (London), 8/29/76 (p. 26)
Dilys Powell

". . . *The Tenant* is a film in which you can't afford to ignore details, any more than you can afford it in Hitchcock. But in a Hitchcock film the details are often there for immediate shock effect. Polanski uses them gradually . . . everything leads you further into an atmosphere of sinister suggestion. And everything is linked without emphasis.

Perhaps that is why one feels cheated when the images, at first myterious, turn savage and duplicate themselves in schizophrenic horror. Polanski, surrounded though he is by excellent players, gives a performance which still stands out: the hesitations, the summoning up of courage in the first half of the story, the terrified obstinacy of the later scenes in which he assumes the identity of his predecessor in that tomb of an apartment. Nevertheless, the transition, after the delicately uncomfortable fun at the beginning, shocks by its abruptness.

The Tenant is brilliantly made: not, perhaps, the best of Polanski but the best of his horror movies . . ."

©The Sunday Times, 1976.

The Times (London), 9/3/76 (p. 7)
Richard Combs

". . . For the most part, *The Tenant* sets its own course, an electrifying zigzagging path through the now commonplace materials of alienation. None the less, it runs into problems when it comes to tie up its ends in the second half, and succumbs to some of the horror conventions it has skirted so far . . .

At its best, *The Tenant* plays more rarified games of terror, setting its protagonist to sweat over intellectual conundrums (like the situations in *Cul de Sac* or Nabokov's *Invitation to a Beheading*) of life and death importance. Its riddling way with roles and indentities is most neatly summarized in Trelkovsky's musing, at his lowest ebb of confidence, over just who he is or might be. Without a tooth, without legs or arms, 'he' might still be said to exist; but if his head were to be separated from his body then how would he identify himself, as 'Me and my head, or me and my body'?"

©The Times, 1976.

continued on next page

357

continued from previous page

Nation, 7/17/76 (p. 60)
Robert Hatch

"I am firm in my mind that a man who will come into a cafe for a breakfast cup of coffee and accept instead the cup of chocolate that is set before him is alarmingly unsure of who he is. So I expected from the start that Trelkovsky, the hero of Roman Polanski's *The Tenant*, was about to experience that familiar contemporary disturbance, a crisis of identity . . .

. . . *The Tenant* is about the loneliness, the humiliations, the desperate social stratagems of the outsider; that is a valid theme, and the French are as adept as any people at making a foreigner aware of his deficiencies. Pathetically and foolishly, Trelkovsky keeps protesting that he is a French citizen; that is precisely what irritates the French most about him. Polanski is fine in this aspect of the character, showing us a neat man, alert, courteous, shyly dignified. Dustin Hoffman would hardly do it as well.

But I cannot relate to subjective films about madness, and from the start (that cup of chocolate) Trelkovsky is around the bend. He is clearly going to get rapidly worse, and from the moment he discovers the dresses and nail polish I knew what form his psychosis would take. So . . ."

©The Nation, 1976.

Films in Review, August/September 1976 (p. 442)
Charles Phillips Reilly

". . . The screenplay by Gerard Brach and Polanski from Roland Topor's novel is faulty. The subject of paranoia allows the writers the luxury of having a character assume a double role, but the process, whereby the character shifts identity, must have a rationale which is only sometimes evident in this film, which is often self-indulgent, particularly in its ending when Polanski as director gives Polanski the actor one of the longest death scenes since *Camille*.

Isabelle Adjani has little to do as a 'with it' secretary who was a friend of the dead girl and weaves in and out of Trelkovsky's life. Shelley Winters plays a blowsy concierge, blowsily.

Sven Nykvist's photography is not among his best work.

Despite its lacunae, *The Tenant* should be seen for Polanski's acting."

©Films in Review, 1976.

Film Information, July/August 1976 (p. 4)
David Bartholemew

". . . Polanski's world here is godless and inhospitable. His character is the most abused victim we could ever imagine and while Polanski smoothly slides his film imperceptibly in and out of fantasy, including several literally dreadful (in the horror sense) nightmare sequences, the extreme sourness of his world-view, and the lack of any possible salvation, seem just as exaggerated as the constant cheeriness of Disney movies.

Still, the film is well made and beautifully photographed by Sven Nykvist. The cast of characters confronting Polanski represent a bleak array of lost souls, lost in urban decay and isolation, headed by Shelley Winters' concierge, Melvyn Douglas' landlord, and Jo Van Fleet and Lila Kedrova as tenants. Isabelle Adjani appears as a flighty, shallow friend of both the dead girl and Polanski.

We usually forget that Polanski is as good an actor as he is, and his work—his descent into psychological and sexual confusion—is excellent, although there's an oddly distanced feel to it, which lessens the terror . . ."

©Film Information, 1976.

Women's Wear Daily, 5/26/76 (p. 30)
Howard Kissel

". . . The story of a man who rents a Paris apartment formerly occupied by a suicide and becomes paranoid to the point of committing suicide himself, *The Tenant* sounds like a '40s Hollywood psychological drama: It is, in fact, full of the unsubtle touches you would find in a '40s Hollywood psychological drama . . .

The tenant's increasing identification with his 'predecessor' ultimately reaches the point where he puts on a negligee she left behind, buys himself a wig, makes himself up grotesquely and talks to himself in a caricature of a female voice. It is in this outrageous drag that he eventually kills himself . . .

Isabelle Adjani and Shelley Winters have bit parts, but most of the time all one sees is Polanski, who performs creditably but adds no emotional depth to the trivial material . . ."

©Women's Wear Daily, 1976.

Sight and Sound, Autumn 1976 (p. 253)
Jonathan Rosenbaum

"Behind the credits, a face peering out through a window; a downward pan revealing a vertiginous drop to the courtyard below; a pan back to the window and round the court to another face, a girl's, which quickly turns into Roman Polanski's; a continuing movement past a chimney, across more windows—down one side of the building, over a railing and up another side—eventually coming to the door leading to the street, which Polanski enters . . . If the remainder of the *Tenant* were as impressive as the first shot, we conceivably might have had a masterpiece on our hands . . .

. . . when Polanski ends . . . formal interest has shrunk to the level of stylistic pirouette, and ambiguity becomes just the other side of apathy.''

©Sight and Sound, 1976.

THAT'S ENTERTAINMENT, PART 2

Director of New Sequences: *Gene Kelly.*
Screenplay: *Leonard Gershe,* Producers: *Saul Chaplin, Daniel Melnick.* Photography: *George Folsey.* Editors: *Bud Friedgan, David Blewitt.* Music: *Nelson Riddle.* Production: *Metro-Goldwyn-Mayer.* Distributor: *United Artists.* Running time 133 minutes. New York opening May 16, 1976, at the Ziegfeld Theatre. Classification: G.

Players: *An anthology of scenes from many Metro-Goldwyn-Mayer films.*

Christian Science Monitor, 5/17/76 (p. 22)
David Sterritt

''Roll out the red carpets, brass bands, and klieg lights! Fred Astaire, Gene Kelly, and the genius of old Hollywood have scored another dazzling success. *That's Entertainment, Part 2* is a sure-fire hit. And don't give all the credit to nostalgia—these rollicking sights and sounds are bound to enthrall the young in age at least as much as the young at heart . . .

. . . *Part 2* seems even more zippy, zany, and generally splendiferous than its predecessor, in sheer high spirits, if not in tunefulness. I haven't figured out just why, but it probably has to do with the sequel's easy-going good humor. For all its glory, *Part 1* seemed to snort and strain in its effort to give us every Big Moment in the M-G-M musical vaults. *Part 2* forgets about Big Moments and gives us those crazy, off-the-wall bits that we had almost forgotten about . . .

The real stuff of *Part 2* is history, however, and of this there is enough for any fan. Moreover, producers Saul Chaplin and Daniel Melnick have moved out of the musical category from time to time, allowing some choice spoken routines to enter the picture. The resulting mix is almost consistently grand . . . ''

Reprinted by permission from The Christian Science Monitor © 1976. The Christian Science Publishing Society. All rights reserved.

New York Post, 5/17/76 (p. 20)
Frank Rich

'' . . . at the risk of being run out of town at daybreak tomorrow, I must confess that I found the film . . . to be pretty much of a bore. For all its glitter, for all the memories it invokes, for all the snappy music and performers it carts out, this compilation movie never comes close to equalling the sum of its often shiny parts. *That's Entertainment 2* is not so much an entertainment as an endurance test, and only hopeless nostalgia fetishists are likely to pass its rigorous demands with flying colors . . .

That's Entertainment 2 . . . is significantly inferior to the earlier film; it has all the weaknesses and few of its glories. Here again there's a contrived format to link the numbers together, but the numbers themselves are not always worth linking, and they're rarely in the class of the best material of *That's Entertainment*. About halfway into the new film, in fact, you start to wonder if you're not watching a haphazard montage of all the footage that had been rejected the first time around . . . ''

Reprinted by Permission of New York Post. © 1976, New York Post Corporation.

The Sunday Times (London), 5/23/76 (p. 35)
Alan Brien

'' . . . 'Entertainment' is the theme, and for M-G-M that has always meant sending you out with a glow, confident that your problems are all imaginary. Above all, it is innocent fun. Yet I see now how much sex could slide by the censors, indeed by the producers, so long as it was set to a tune—Astaire singing 'I love all of you' would never have passed as dialogue.

Often it was the legs which semaphored those unmistakable messages. They would grip men round the waist, the knees, even the neck, and could be brushed by knees, hands, even lips, without a blush. The musical, Hollywood's great gift to the world, was often a choreographed orgy (see *Kiss Me Kate*) which escalated when mounted in mid-air, or underwater, by Esther Williams to an almost Roman grandiosity.

That's Entertainment could have done with some more asperity, instead of the anodyne show-biz gush Astaire and Kelly had to say, or even worse, sing. Still, this is Hollywood on its toes, with a song on its lips.''

© The Sunday Times, 1976.

Cineaste, Fall 1976 (p. 40)
Al Auster

''M-G-M has just released its latest necrophiliac concoction, *That's Entertainment, Part 2* . . .

Part 2, unfortunately, got the leftovers. The pro-

continued on next page

continued from previous page

ducers try to make do by puffing it up with mini-retrospectives of Clark Gable, Frank Sinatra, Tracy and Hepburn, and even some light teasing of film cliches . . . Overall, though, it is a sad mixture . . .

The best that can be said for *That's Entertainment, Part 2* is that it doesn't have its predecessor's pretensions. The implication of the earlier edition's advertising slogan—'Boy do we need it now'—was that it would chase away our Watergate blues. The only thing this latest version of genre-cide manages to do is to turn once-proud Leo the Lion into a mangy cur.''

©*Cineaste*, 1976.

Monthly Film Bulletin, 6/76 (p. 130)
Geoff Brown

"*That's Entertainment!* had many faults, not the least of which was the strange omission of its title song. However, the sequel (which has many more faults) rectifies this with a vengeance: after a witty title sequence by Saul Bass (aping the title designs for almost every Hollywood genre), the stars of *The Band Wagon* make their bow and 'That's Entertainment' resounds throughout the remaining two hours in so trite a fashion that one begins to wish the number had never been written. It wouldn't matter so much, perhaps, if the movie were providing solid entertainment, but the concoction of clips proves so dull and unimaginative that the song's refrain takes on overtones of hollow mockery. The number of clips is vast--counting those that appear for just a few seconds (often minus sound), the tally must be close to a hundred--but quality never keeps up with quantity: we are obviously being served left-overs from Jack Haley's foraging amongst the M-G-M vaults--the second and third choices which were left on the cutting room floor . . . "

© *Monthly Film Bulletin*, 1976.

Women's Wear Daily, 5/11/76 (p. 48)
Howard Kissel

"*That's Entertainment, Part 2* is like a 'sampler' box of chocolates--picking one's way through it, one wishes one had bought a whole box of this or that rather than the assortment. It's been so long since any full-length Betty Hutton movie has been available in a real theater--it would be more fun seeing all of *Annie Get Your Gun* than just these admittedly wonderful excerpts . . .

Much of the real interest in these seemingly harmless movies, however, is the bizarre contrast they offer to the world in which they were created. The Depression, World War II and The Bomb were the 'backdrops' for these 'numbers.' Watching them out of context would be like seeing the brilliant Flower-

land sequence from *Follies* . . . without the rest of the show--that is, the lighthearted nostalgia without the 'subtext.' Regarding the past merely as a box of bonbons may not be all that harmless."

© *Women's Wear Daily*, 1976.

The Times (London), 5/21/76 (p. 13)
Philip French

" . . . with *That's Entertainment, Part 2*, another team has been through the M-G-M archives and the result is a disappointing mess. Introduced somewhat archly in various garish surroundings by Fred Astaire and Gene Kelly, the film unrolls for two hours without apparent design and with no attempt at placing sequences in context. The superb jostles with the rotten, the camp with the sublime, and, more so than with its predecessor, *Part 2* plays dated material for easy laughs . . .

Having registered a profound dissatisfaction, one must add that this curate's egg is worth going to work on, and that there are a dozen bits of rarely seen film that no one would want to miss: among them, the teenage Garland singing 'Zing Went the Strings of My Heart' to the 14-year-old Freddie Bartholomew. Saul Bass's elegantly parodic credit titles with names written on sand, out-lined in water, engraved on burning scrolls, enclosed in a bottle, spelt out in falling dominoes, are superb . . . "

©*The Times*, 1976.

Films in Review, August/September 1976 (p. 438)
Ronald Bowers

" . . . The presence of Fred Astaire and Gene Kelly as our congenial guides makes for smoother transitions from past to present and they are greatly aided by Leonard Gershe's unsentimental narration. Best of all, however, is the use of clips from many M-G-M comedies and dramas in between the musical highlights. This gives the audience an opportunity to catch a glimpse of the likes of The Marx Brothers, Laurel and Hardy, Greta Garbo, Joan Crawford, Clark Gable, Spencer Tracy and Katherine Hepburn. There are clips from 72 M-G-M features representing the high points of those films . . .

One of the funniest sequences, and unintentionally so, shows Jeanette MacDonald singing 'Lover Come Back' to Nelson Eddy in *New Moon*. How sad it is that the lovely Jeanette rarely displayed her unique joie de vivre once she moved from Paramount to M-G-M.

The opening credits are a glorious spoof of old movie credits. *TE 2* is 133 minutes of, as the title says, 'the art that appeals to the heart.' "

©*Films in Review*, 1976.

Village Voice, 5/24/76 (p. 117)
Andrew Sarris

" . . . There is a bias . . . toward dancing over singing in this enterprise, not only because Kelly and Astaire were dancers who sang rather than singers who danced, but also because the medium itself seems more hospitable to dance than to song. Here is a space, the production design of this project seems to say, let's fill it with movement. Mere sound, however melodious, won't do . . .

But carping aside, the showstoppers far outnumber the clinkers in song as well as in dance. Judy Garland is all over the place, most excitingly, I thought with 'Have Yourself a Merry Christmas,' as sung to a lyrically tearful Margaret O'Brien from Vincente Minnelli's *Meet Me in St. Louis*, and with 'Zing Went the Strings of My Heart,' from her spectacular audition film for Metro. Ethel Waters ('Taking a Chance on Love' from *Cabin in the Sky*) and Lena Horne ('The Lady Is a Tramp' from *Words and Music*) remind us both of their electrifying styles and of the rigid segregation that kept them from mingling, even in musical numbers, with members of the white race . . .

Ah, but the dancing dominates, indeed as it should, and very much of it is done by Kelly and Astaire in no fewer than 17 of the 59 separate musical numbers, and this is apart from the new framing numbers turned out for this movie . . . "

Reprinted by permission of The Village Voice.
Copyright © The Village Voice, Inc., 1976.

Saturday Review, 5/29/76 (p. 46)
Judith Crist

" . . . *That's Entertainment, Part 2*--minus, you'll note, the exclamation point--is with us to provide a nostalgic wallow, testaments to real and fake talent, and an overdose of that self-congratulatory smugness that is encountered most often during the bleaker moments of Academy Award ceremonies. The Haley sophistication is missing this time in both the selection and grouping of numbers, with producers Saul Chaplin and Daniel Melnick taking a snickery and/or sentimental approach to the movie musical . . .

But how can one bother with reservations about a movie that offers not only the two best male dancers to have graced the screen but also their top duets with Judy Garland ('Be a Clown' with Kelly from *The Pirate* and 'A Couple of Swells' with Astaire from *Easter Parade*) and dances with Cyd Charisse (Astaire in *Silk Stockings*, Kelly in *Singin' in the Rain*)? And there's lots more . . ."

© Judith Crist, 1976.

Film Information, 5/76 (p. 3)
Paul Coleman

"Here, clearly, is a film that needs no introduc-

tion. Just as in *That's Entertainment!*, clips from old M-G-M sound films up through 1958 form a two-hour-plus agenda, complete with new musical sequences with Gene Kelly and Fred Astaire . . .

. . . M-G-M, even in presenting nostalgic entertainment for audiences presold on its quality, cannot avoid the put-down. The narration alternates between the 'Gee whizzes' of Astaire and Kelly and the sarcastic self-consciousness that holds up easy targets to ridicule. After years of insisting that Garbo was a disaster dancing in *Two-Faced Woman*, must M-G-M remind us by including two clips from her ill-fated vehicle? Jeanette MacDonald appears at her most ludicrous in scenes from *New Moon* and *Broadway Serenade* but not a shot of her at her most enchanting in *The Merry Widow*, though that film justifiably receives honored attention.

Disappointment once again is inevitable when a masterly scene appears only long enough to rivet our attention before the narration cuts to another. Kelly and Astaire's inane voice-over narration covers particularly charming dialogue and lyrics. But more offensive are their new dancing and singing sequences that provide naïve hype for moments that can stand on their own . . . "

© Film Information, 1976.

New York Magazine, 5/24/76 (p. 76)
John Simon

"*That's Entertainment, Part 2* is nowhere near its predecessor. *Part 1* had a theme, the rise and fall of the movie musical, which managed to subsume a few related and even more important themes. It also contained some spectacular footage some of us had forgotten and most of us had never seen. Here there is no theme; straight films intermingle with musicals; and excerpts known to almost everybody are torn bleeding from films to be seen, preferably and without difficulty, in toto. The whole thing is continually interrupted by scenes in which Gene Kelly and Fred Astaire dance or comment on the past. The comments, written by Leonard Gershe, are worthless; the direction of these scenes, by Gene Kelly, is flat-footed. The production design here is pretentious and routinely photographed . . . "

© 1976 by the NYM Corp. Reprinted with
the permission of NEW YORK Magazine.

Newsweek, 5/1/76 (p. 48)
Charles Michener with Martin Kasindorf

" . . . The new old quilt doesn't have the novelty or the number of first-class musical sequences the first one had, but there's good reason to believe that it will sell even better. For one thing, it includes fine scenes from old comedies and dramatic films

continued on next page

continued from previous page

as well as musicals. For another, it has Fred Astaire and Gene Kelly introducing the old footage by doing what they can still do better at ages 77 and 63 respectively, than anyone else—conjure up the old magic of song and dance. Finally, it's appearing when the appetite for old movies is keener than ever. 'Boy do we need it now'—M-G-M's tag line for *That's Entertainment!*, may have been the most smugly irritating movie pitch in a long time, but the nerve it tapped is unquestionably there.''

© Newsweek, Inc. 1976
reprinted by permission.

THIEVES

Director: *John Berry*. Screenplay: *Herb Gardner*. Based on the play by Mr. Gardner. Producer: *George Barrie*. Photography: *Arthur J. Onitz, Andrew Lazlo*. Editor: *Craig McKay*. Music: *Jule Styne*. Distributor: *Paramount Pictures*. Running time 103 minutes. New York opening February 11, 1977, at the Coronet Theatre. Classification: PG.

Sally Cramer: *Marlo Thomas*. Martin Cramer: *Charles Grodin*. Joe Kaminsky: *Irwin Corey*. Man Below: *Hector Elizondo*. Street Woman: *Mercedes McCambridge*. Gordon: *John McMartin*. Carlton: *Larry Scott*. Mr. Day: *Bob Fosse*. Mr. Night: *Norman Matlock*. Doorman: *Ian Martin*.

THEY CAME FROM WITHIN

Director, Screenplay: *David Cronenberg*. Producer: *Ivan Reitman*. Photography: *Robert Saad*. Distributor: *Trans-American Pictures*. Running time 88 minutes. New York opening July, 1976, at several theatres. Classification: R.

Roger St. Luc: *Paul Hampton*. Rollo Linsky: *Joe Silver*. Forsythe: *Lynn Lowry*. Nicholas Tudor: *Alan Magicovsky*. Janine Tudor: *Susan Petrie*. Betts: *Barbara Steele*. Merrick: *Ronald Mlodzik*.

Los Angeles Times, 5/14/76 (Pt. IV, p. 14)
Linda Gross

"*They Came From Within* . . . is a combination science fiction and horror movie about a doctor's race to stop a virulent epidemic from contaminating all of the residents of an isolated island apartment complex.

The film is a kinky and gruesome nightmare which denigrates human sexuality and assaults the audience with scene after scene of decapitations, rapes, bludgeonings, child molesting and other atrocities all committed in the guise of eroticism . . .

David Cronenberg's episodic script is obsessively full of phallic symbols, vomit and blood. Director Cronenberg maintains suspense and tension . . .

They Came From Within is an obscene personification of the victimization and violation of an audience.''

© Los Angeles Times, 1976.

Newsweek, 2/21/77 (p. 92)
Janet Maslin

"Herb Gardner's *Thieves*, based on his Broadway play, is about a New York couple called the Cramers who are in more trouble than they know. Sally Cramer (Marlo Thomas) is a perky schoolteacher who twinkles at her ghetto students as she collects their tire chains every morning and who cannot utter a sentence without making it sound like the Pledge of Allegiance. Her husband, played by Charles Grodin, speaks strangely too, lending an odd gravity to lines that are supposed to be flip . . .

Messily directed by John Berry, *Thieves* also features a lot of bleak wisecracks from the Cramers' neighbors, random aerial shots of Manhattan, Irwin Corey as a spluttering, insufferable cabdriver whose appearances are inexplicably accompanied by ukulele music, and Mercedes McCambridge as a kleptomaniac with a penchant for hats . . . Ian Martin plays the Cramers' doorman, who spends virtually all of the movie napping on the job—and finally dies in his sleep."

©Newsweek, Inc. 1977
reprinted by permission.

Films in Review, March 1977 (p. 187)
Rob Edelman

". . . Though not as cinematically blatant as in *Taxi Driver*, society's breakdown is as apparent. The metropolis' impersonality is stressed by Berry loading the film with high angle shots of the Manhattan skyline and low angle footage of the towering skyscrapers.

Gardner has written a literate screenplay and with Berry, managed to make the characters touching. Jule Styne's rag music adds to the film's flavor.

Grodin, who directed the Broadway play production, and Thomas, who starred in it with Richard Mulligan, are fine, but Irwin Corey steals the picture, as Sally's manic cabdriver father, waddling like Donald Duck and squawking about the 'tootsies' and 'bimbos' who inhabit the city. He is a frenzied caricature of the survivor of urban warfare."

©Films in Review, 1977.

New Leader, 1/14/77 (p. 23)
Robert Asahina

". . . Martin eventually makes the momentous discovery that you can never go home again, announcing to Sally that 'Loew's Delancey is closed . . . and Bogart is dead. It's all gone.' And in case we want to decipher the title, Kaminsky helpfully declares that time is 'the biggest thief in town.' Profundities like these deserve no comment except to note that Grodin and Corey are particularly ill-suited to utter them. How Grodin has managed repeatedly to be cast as a romantic lead is one of the greater mysteries of contemporary theater and films. As for Corey, his suitability for the role of wise fool seems to be grounded primarily in his undeniable ability to act foolishly. Marlo Thomas appears much prettier and less cute as she grows older, but she still looks uncomfortable on a screen larger than 19 inches across. Kaminsky is wrong. The real thieves are the pickpockets who hope to profit from this picture."

Reprinted with permission from
The New Leader, 1977.
©The American Labor Conference
on International Affairs, Inc.

New York Magazine, 2/28/77 (p. 55)
John Simon

"*Thieves* may not be the worst movie I ever saw, but it may well be the most annoyingly cloying. Herb Gardner, who wrote it and ended up pseudonymously directing much of it, is one of those horrible examples of how an extremely limited, intensely self-satisfied, repetitious, and predictable cleverness can become—within minutes—more offensive than extended witlessness . . .

Charles Grodin plays Martin as if a sufficiency of slack in the mouth absolved one from all further comedic endeavor. As Sally, Marlo Thomas is the ideal Herb Gardner interpreter. Her face is always suffused with some sort of adorable, tough wistfulness, a wisecracking yearning . . ."

©1977 by the NYM Corp. Reprinted with
the permission of NEW YORK Magazine.

Village Voice, 3/7/77 (p. 39)
Andrew Sarris

". . . this is the kind of movie that gives humanism a bad name. Marlo Thomas pokes into her part with all the charm of a mongoose, and her loudmouth poor-service cabdriver of a father (Irwin Corey) must be the most obnoxious know-it-all since the lit-

tle boy in *A Thousand Clowns*, an earlier Gardner ode to craziness as a lifestyle . . . There is no . . . balance in *Thieves*, with its sub-Saroyanesque cultivation of the uglies and the crazies for their own sakes. What is most offensive about the movie is its air of self-congratulation, as if all our problems were merely in our minds. *Thieves* provides no sense of lives being led, only of lifestyles being flaunted."

Reprinted by permission of The Village Voice.
Copyright © The Village Voice, Inc., 1977.

Los Angeles Times, 2/18/77 (Pt. IV, p. 1)
Charles Champlin

". . . it continues to feel like a stage play. The streets, the chases, the changes of pace are all natural enough and unforced, but the wonderfully calculated speech remains theatrical and so do some of the plot devices, including virtually wordless cameos by Gary Merrill and Mercedes McCambridge as light-fingered overage street urchins. Larry Scott is a superprecocious young tyrant.

No complaints from here about the theatricality; it bustles with energy and a kind of literary excitement. It is just that you need to be ready for that implicit proscenium, so to speak . . .

As you'd expect, the performances are all beautifully considered. Ms. Thomas is most ravishingly attractive but sensitive and intelligent as well, a touching comedienne who gets her first chance (*Jenny* having been a limited vehicle for her) to show her full gifts on the big screen.

Grodin has the task of being churlish at first, but not so much that you can't like him by the end. You do . . ."

©Los Angeles Times, 1977.

Christian Science Monitor, 3/7/77 (p. 21)
David Sterritt

"The new movie called *Thieves* apparently wants to be a comedy. But its pace is so uneven, its moods so morose, its subject so somber that it comes out eccentric drama instead. And not very pleasant drama, despite some bright flashes along the way . . .

Thieves has been 'opened up' from Herb Gardner's Broadway play of the same title. The best things about it are snappily edited transition scenes, unneeded but striking overhead shots of New York City, and some nifty tunes on the soundtrack. Miss Thomas shows her usual acting strength . . . but the gifted Grodin can't find an even keel between laughter and tears. Director John Berry shares the blame for this, for the film's lumpiness, and for the hammy interludes . . . In all, a picture it's hard to like more than a little."

Reprinted by permission from The Christian
Science Monitor © 1977.
The Christian Science Publishing Society.
All rights reserved.

continued on next page

continued from previous page

Saturday Review, 2/19/77 (p. 41)
Judith Crist

". . . The appeal generated by Thomas spills over
on Charles Grodin as the husband wanting to move
onward and upward and weary of his wife's cuteness. And there is an absolutely uncontrolled
scenery-chewing series of shticks by Irwin Corey as
her aged irascible cabby-father, as well as down-
played and subtle bits by . . . John McMartin and
Hector Elizondo as high-rise neighbors. But a general air of deja vu, starting with an introductory can-
tata of apartment-dweller talk taken straight from the
orchestrated opening of *Divorce American Style*,
hangs heavy over the relatively static work. A pity.
Gardner is one of the few fine social humorists at
work today—in need only of direction."

©Judith Crist, 1977.

THREE DAYS AND A CHILD

Director, Screenplay: *Uri Zohar*. Producer:
Amatziya Hiyuni. Photography: *David Bur-
finkel*. Editor: *I. Ehrlich*. Production: *S.Y.V.
Tel Aviv*. Running time 90 minutes. Los
Angeles opening October 1976 at the Royal
Theatre. Classification: None. Origin: Israel.

Players: *Misha Asherov, Stella Avni, Baruch
David, Shoshana Duer, Lily Gorlitsky, Oded
Kotler, Shuy Osherov, Judith Soleh, Germaine
Unikovski, Nissan Yafir.*

Los Angeles Times, 10/28/76 (Pt. IV, p. 15)
Linda Gross

"Contemporary Israeli writers and filmmakers
share the ability to convey extreme psychological
perceptiveness with an intangible sense of sadness.
Three Days and a Child . . . is a cold, hard and
intelligent character study, masterfully set in a root-
less and permissive atmosphere . . .
Because the viewer experiences what is happening from the point of view of a character who
is not rational, nothing is clear. Sequences of
events are interrupted by flashes of memories and
fleeting emotions and we participate in Kotler's
confusion and isolation . . .
Director Zohar is taut and skilled, moving gradually from suspense to fear to pity. As Bergman

did in *The Passion of Anna*, Zohar effectively uses
scenes of sexual intimacy to emphasize estrangement.
Kotler delivers a superb performance as a man
whose smile doesn't quite match the look in his
eyes and whose vacancy overflows with impotent
rage . . ."

©Los Angeles Times, 1976.

TO THE DEVIL . . . A DAUGHTER

Director: *Peter Sykes*. Screenplay: *Chris
Wicking, John Peacock*. Based on the novel
by Dennis Wheatley. Producer: *Roy Skeggs*.
Photography: *David Watkin*. Editor: *John
Trumper*. Music: *Paul Glass*. Production:
EMI. Distributor: *Cine Artists Picture Corp.*
Running time 90 minutes. Los Angeles open-
ing September 30, 1976, at several theatres.
Classification: R.

Players: *Anna Bentinck, Irene Bentinck, Honor
Blackman, Constantin de Goguel, Frances De
La Tour, Denholm Elliott, Derek Francis,
Michael Goodliffe, Nastassia Kinski, Chris-
topher Lee, Eva Marie Meineke, Irene Parador,
Isabella Telezynska, Anthony Valentine, Rich-
ard Widmark.*

Los Angeles Times, 10/1/76 (Pt. IV, p. 19)
Linda Gross

". . . *To the Devil . . . a Daughter* . . . the latest
offering in the burgeoning field of film demonology,
is an atmospheric, well-acted, soggily written
Gothic horror story about the struggle between
the forces of good and evil for the soul of an endangered young woman.
Demoniac forces are incarnated in the presence
of a defrocked priest-turned satanist (Christopher
Lee) who leads a convent of devil worshipers in
Bavaria . . .
To the Devil . . . a Daughter is based on a novel
by Dennis Wheatley. The screenplay by Chris
Wicking and John Peacock contains moments
of frightening bloodletting, which would be particularly traumatic to sensitive girls around the age
of puberty. Ultimately, the story is a confusing vacil-
lation between special effects, hallucinations, psychic trances and ongoing narration.
The film is distinguished by engrossing performances from Widmark, Lee, Elliott, Anthony Valen-

tine, Nastassia Kinski and Honor Blackman, superior photography by David Watkin and eerie music by Paul Glass . . ."

©Los Angeles Times, 1976.

Yang Hui-chen: *Hsu Feng.* Shih Wen-chiao: *Pai Ying.* Monk: *Roy Chiao Hung.* Ku Sheng-chai: *Shih Chun.* Ou-yang Nien: *Tien Peng.* Men Ta: *Wan Jei.*

TORA-SAN, THE INTELLECTUAL (OTOKO WA TSURAI YO TORAJIRO KATSUSHIKA RISSHI HEN)

Director, Screenplay: *Yoji Yamada.* Producer: *Kiyoshi Shimazu.* Photographer: *Tetsuo Takaba.* Editor: *Iwao Ishii.* Music: *Naozumi Yamamoto.* Distributor: *Shochiku.* Running time 97 minutes. Los Angeles opening December 1976 at the Kokusai. Classification: None. Origin: Japan.

Players: *Kiyoshi Atsumi, Chieko Baisho, Fumie Kashiyama, Keiju Kobayashi, Gin Maeda, Chieko Misaki, Hayato Nakamura, Hideji Otaki, Chishu Ryu, Gajior Sato, Masami Shimojo, Masakene Yonekura.*

Los Angeles Times, 12/31/76 (Pt. IV, p. 10)
Kevin Thomas

"*Tora-san, the Intellectual* . . . the 16th in the captivating Japanese series, arrives as a holiday treat, full of warmth and good cheer, that is far more in keeping with the spirit of the season than most of the ballyhooed year-end releases.

Once again, that very deft comedian Kiyoshi Atsumi is Tora-san, that feckless itinerant peddler who is ever the object of concern for his loving, forgiving relatives who live behind their sweet shop in a crowded working class Tokyo suburb . . .

As always, the Tora-sans' gifted writer-director Yoji Yamada celebrates the joys of family life—he has got to be one of the last commercial filmmakers in the world to do so—and the beauties of nature . . ."

©Los Angeles Times, 1976.

TOUCH OF ZEN, A (SHA-NU)

Director, Editor: *King Hu.* Screenplay (Chinese with English subtitles): *Mr. Hu.* Based on a collection of Chinese short stories. Photography: *Hua Hui-Ying.* Music: *Ng Tai-Kwong.* Distributor: *Agape Productions.* Running time 180 minutes. New York opening October 10, 1976, at the New York Film Festival, Lincoln Center. Classification: None. Origin: Taiwan.

The Sunday Times (London), 5/16/76 (p. 37)
Dilys Powell

"Trying the other day to say what I meant by a long film I came to the conclusion that physical length is irrelevant, and so is the quality of boredom; I can be bored after ten minutes. I think a long film is one which goes on after you thought it had come to an end. *A Touch of Zen* . . . is a long film.

Physically it is long all right, close on three hours, and the beginning is slow. So much action is crammed into the last two hours and three-quarters that one wishes it could have been spread out; at the start I was well on towards that ten-minute threshold of boredom. Later the mysterious encounters of the early scenes fall into place in the narrative; you understand then why the humble fifteenth-century portrait-painter is so disconcerted by the gaze of the visitor in the large hat, why the stranger so savagely assaults the blind beggar. But the enigmatic opening of this Chinese work hasn't the cohesion, the speed and the drive to which the Western cinema has accustomed us. It dawdles and with it one's attention . . ."

©The Sunday Times, 1976.

TOWN THAT DREADED SUNDOWN, THE

Director, Producer: *Charles B. Pierce.* Screenplay: *Earl E. Smith.* Photography: *Jim Roberson.* Editor: *Tom Boutross.* Music: *Jaime Mendoza-Nava.* Narrator: *Vern Stierman.* Distributor: *American International Pictures.* Running time 90 minutes. Los Angeles opening March 4, 1977, at several theatres. Classification: R.

continued on next page

continued from previous page

Players: *Robert Acquino, Cindy Butler, Jim Citty, Jimmy Clem, Bud Davis, Christine Ellsworth, Mike Hackworth, Rick Hildreth, Ben Johnson, Steve Lyons, Charles B. Pierce, Andrew Prine, Earl E. Smith, Dawn Wells, Misty West.*

Los Angeles Times, 3/5/77 (Pt. II, p. 2)
Kevin Thomas

"*The Town That Dreaded Sundown* is this week's trash picture.

In the spring and summer of 1946, the small border town of Texarkana was terrorized by a hooded homicidal maniac who murdered five citizens and severely injured three more and was never caught . . .

To describe Pierce and Smith's cinematic efforts as elementary is being overly kind. Pierce compounds the damage by supplying crass, low comedy relief by appearing as a dim-witted patrolman . . .

The Town That Dreaded Sundown likewise makes no creative use of its strongest asset, its authentic small-town setting. There's no sense of period, no suspense, no nothing, in fact. Just lots of violence."

©Los Angeles Times, 1977.

New York Post, 2/19/77 (p. 38)
Archer Winsten

". . . A real oddity of this film is that it supplies no pleasant and reassuring finale. After the last killing he simply disappears. Gradually, one assumes, Texarkana returned to normal, becoming what it doubtless is today. Despite the harsh efficiency of Capt. J. D. Morales, incarnated in Ben Johnson's weathered flesh, and the intensity of Deputy Norman Ramsey (Andrew Prine), these were crimes for which the criminal never paid. It gives you a strange feeling, movies having made such payment obligatory. Thus an ordinary picture sticks in the mind as slightly unusual."

Reprinted by Permission of New York Post.
© 1977, New York Post Corporation.

TRACKS

Director, Screenplay: *Henry Jaglom*. Producer: *Howard Zucker*. Photography: *Paul*

Glickman. Editor: *George Folsey, Jr.* Distributor: *Rainbow Films*. Running time 100 minutes. Los Angeles opening December 17, 1976, at Mann's Westwood Triplex. Classification: None.

Players: *Michael Emil, Barbara Flood, Dennis Hopper, Zack Norman, Taryn Power, Alfred Ryder, Dean Stockwell, Topo Swope.*

Los Angeles Times, 12/17/76 (Pt. IV, p. 29)
Charles Champlin

". . . It means to be a parable on the American involvement in Vietnam and, thanks to the strong, disturbing central performance by Dennis Hopper, the movie generates a certain power. But Jaglom's cleverness as a writer-director sometimes works against his intentions . . .

Hopper is an American Army sergeant back from Vietnam and escorting the body of a fallen comrade home for burial. Everything except the final sequence was shot aboard an actual Amtrak train between Los Angeles and San Diego and back again.

The sergeant is obviously at the end of his emotional tether, taunted and haunted by guilty memories of some betrayal of his pals. What he did, or didn't do, is not clear. What is clear is that he is slithering in and out of reality, hallucinating dangerously, telling improbable stories, changing clothes constantly . . .

At their best, Hopper and the film develop an alarming aura of incipient tragedy. To that extent the movie can be said to mirror the confusions and costs of the war itself. But in the end the inability to be sure what is real and what is hallucination becomes less a statement than a rather self-conscious author's mannerism . . ."

©Los Angeles Times, 1976.

TRAVELLING PLAYERS, THE (O THIASSOS)

Director: *Theodor Angelopoulos*. Screenplay (Greek with English subtitles): *Mr. Angelopoulos*. Producer: *Georges Papallos*. Photography: *George Arvanitis*. Music: *Lukianos Kilaidonis*. Running time 230 minutes. New York opening April 10, 1976, at The Museum of Modern Art. Classification: None. Origin: Greece.

Elektra: *Eva Kotamanidou.* Mother: *Aliki Georgoulis. Father: Stratos Pachis.* Orestes: *Petros Zarkadis.*

Monthly Film Bulletin, 5/76 (p. 108)
Rosalind Delmar

"Shot against the bleak and beautiful landscape of the Greek winter, a temporal metaphor which also stands for the time of fascism and foreign occupation, *The Travelling Players* is a powerful demonstration of how film can be used to explore the intermingling of private and political drama. It opens with the prologue to *Golfo the Shepherdess* in which the audience is called upon to act as witness to a drama in five acts . . . The stage has been set not for just a performance of *Golfo*, of which we see only fragments––its action being often physically interrupted by events external to it, such as the arrival by the police to arrest one of the actors, an air-raid and Oreste's revenge––but also for an enactment of the public political drama . . . Angelopoulos has created a work of amazing complexity and power which, whilst it acts as political educator, providing with great precision a history of a struggle which has met at almost every turn with obstacles and defeats, is also provocative at the emotional level. The flashback form which he has chosen is extremely difficult to handle, and the time changes which punctuate the development of the story indicate a fascinating mastery of technique and a great economy of style."

© Monthly Film Bulletin, 1976.

Sight and Sound, Winter 1975 (p. 59)
David Wilson

". . . it would be misleading to stress the formal aspects of Angelopoulos' method at the expense of the film's seductive surface, though that in itself is an element of the form. Whole sequences stay in the mind, even after one viewing. An extraordinary scene, for instance, in which the camera follows the company as they walk down a mountain road in winter and their singing is brought to a halt as a bend in the road reveals two bodies hanging from a tree—a sequence which ends with a stunning overhead shot as the actors descend on a solitary, incongruous chicken in a snow-swept field, an effectively simple metaphor for the famine which ravaged Greece during the war . . . Credit due to the camera work of George Arvantis, who also photographed Angelopoulos' previous films, *The Reconstruction* and *Days of 36*. What these films, excellent as they were, had not suggested was that Angelopoulos would go on to make a masterpiece of modern cinema, a film reverberating with metaphor and meaning."

©Sight and Sound, 1975.

Film, 6/76 (p. 8)
Lesley Robinson

"This is a film which, because of its complexity and richness, requires more than a single viewing. The action takes place on three levels, historical, cultural and personal, spans thirteen years (1939 to 1952) and keeps jumping backwards and forwards in time. The main 'personage' in the film is really Greece itself, reflected by the fortunes and misfortunes of a company of actors who tour the Greek provinces with their play *Golfo the Shepherdess*, performing in churches, halls, and other makeshift theatres. The play, a 19th century pastoral melodrama, symbolizes the country's rural past; it never gets to be finished as it is continually interrupted by bombings, shootings and other incidents . . .

Angelopoulos' camera style, his long shots and his feeling for landscape, is similar to Jancso's in *Elektreia* but unlike the Hungarian director, he has made a full-blooded film, not a series of rather sterile tableaux . . ."

©Film 1976.

The Sunday Times (London), 9/12/76 (p. 37)
Dilys Powell

". . . *The Travelling Players* is a political film and a personal film. But it operates also on a third level, the level of myth, the tragedy of adultery and retribution. Like her great predecessor, this Elektra will wait for the return of Orestes, and Orestes will execute judgment. The antique rite of vengeance is still part of the life of contemporary Greece; family honor is still sacred. And the history of the country over the years covered by the film has the mood and the stature of myth . . .

. . . about the quality of *The Travelling Players* there can be no question. It is a long film, it is overpowering. But there is no incident I would wish omitted, no extension of scene which does not contribute to the force of the message. A major work has the right to be long, and *The Travelling Players* is a major work. You might say it has a kind of grandeur."

©The Sunday Times, 1976.

The Times (London), 9/10/76 (p. 8)
David Robinson

". . . Originally deeply influenced by Jancso, Angelopoulos has developed a style altogether individual and precisely calculated to his purposes. Like Jancso he uses lengthy shots and a roaming, exploratory camera. *The Travelling Players* runs for 230 minutes yet consists of only 80 individual shots—some, like the monologue on '22, lasting for as long as nine minutes.

continued on next page

continued from previous page

Each of his shot-scenes, in the way of the film's whole overall structure, yields up its secrets and its meanings only gradually. Angelopoulos likes the effect of action off screen, or of action which his camera, prowling around, gradually or suddenly reveals. It is a style pregnant with its own kind of suspense, so that at the end of nearly four hours you are left still eager and anxious to be told more about these plain people drifted in the eddies of history."

©The Times, 1976.

TREASURE OF MATECUMBE

Director: *Vincent McEveety*. Screenplay: *Don Tait*. Based on the novel A JOURNEY TO MATECUMBE by Robert Lewis Taylor. Producers: *Bill Anderson, Ron Miller*. Distributor: *Buena Vista*. Running time 117 minutes. New York opening August 1976 at several theatres. Classification: PG.

Players: *Robert Foxworth, Joan Hackett, Peter Ustinov, Vic Morrow, Johnny Doran, Billy Attmore, Jane Wyatt, Robert DoQui, Mills Watson, Dub Taylor*.

Los Angeles Times, 8/4/76 (Pt. IV, p. 1)
Kevin Thomas

"Leave it to Disney to take us down the Mississippi via obvious and therefore distracting process shots for at least half of an otherwise exciting journey in *Treasure of Matecumbe* . . .

At a time when Disney is all but singlehandedly carrying on the family entertainment tradition it's a shame it chronically shortchanges the public with cut-rate production techniques other studios have for the most part abandoned for years. What's more, *Treasure of Matecumbe* is, frustratingly, a good yarn well-told and boasting a fine cast.

In Kentucky, just after the Civil War, two boys, one white (Johnny Doran) and one black (Billy Attmore) head for the Florida Keys with a map to treasure buried by Doran's late father that will save the family plantation. Hot on their heels, however, is nefarious carpetbagger Vic Morrow and his nasty pals . . .

Don Tait . . . has deftly adapted Robert Lewis Taylor's *A Journey to Matecumbe*, providing some exceptionally well-drawn parts for the film's principals and Joan Hackett in particular . . ."

©Los Angeles Times, 1976.

Films in Review, August/September 1976 (p. 441)
Deirdre Mack

"When a white boy (Johnny Doran) and a black (Billy Attmore) set off on a raft down the Mississippi to look for a buried treasure on a Florida key, Don Tait's screenplay based on Robt. L. Taylor's novel, *A Journey to Matecumbe*, seems to owe a large debt to Mark Twain, particularly since the boys need the gold to save Aunt Effie's (Jane Wyatt) old manse in Kentucky. But Tait and Taylor have a few tricks of their own in the person of Lauriette (Joan Hackett), a Southern belle with a mind of her own, and Dr. Snodgrass (Peter Ustinov) a quack whose heart is in the right place. Spangler (Vic Morrow) is the villain who almost foils the boys' plans but he and his gang earn a fate worse than death . . ."

©Films in Review, 1976.

New York Post, 8/28/76 (p. 15)
Archer Winsten

"*Treasure of Matecumbe* . . . is prime juvenile Disney hokum in which one finds Peter Ustinov, Joan Hackett and Jane Wyatt putting on a show for those who need it all underlined for emphasis . . .

I can't remember a single event that seemed more real than stage musical comedy, and the exaggerations that are supposed to be humorous drew no laughs and few giggles from the audience present with me. I couldn't help wondering how much that brilliant quintuple-threat actor-writer-director-producer-satirist Peter Ustinov was paid for the job and what he thought of as he was doing it. It has been proved that there is an audience for this kind of entertainment, but it is not one that reads this or any reviews . . . "

Reprinted by Permission of New York Post.
©1976, New York Post Corporation.

The Times (London), 4/1/77 (p. 21)
David Robinson

". . . *Treasure of Matecumbe* . . . a lively paraphrase of *Treasure Island*, based on a novel by Robert Lewis Taylor and set in Kentucky and the Florida Keys and Everglades just after the Civil War. The small hero receives a treasure map from his father's dying servant, and sets out in company with a black contemporary to retrieve the family fortunes . . .

With a wealth of such irresistible Americana as paddle-boats and redskins, it is kid's stuff in the best sense, exciting without being frightening (there's only one death), amusingly written, fast-moving . . . with lively children and larger-than-life adults (except, it must be said, for the romantic lead, who is about as lifelike as the Prince in *Snow White*)."

©The Times, 1977.

Monthly Film Bulletin, March 1977 (p. 54)
John Pym

". . . Vincent McEveety has a very firm grasp of the essential skills needed for the professional execution of this well-written but nonetheless routine treasure hunt: a good-humoured tone unifies a succession of brisk, vivid episodes (none set in the same spot); not a frame is wasted on unnecessary exposition; and the adult players (with the single exception of the bland Robert Foxworth) offer zestful performances stopping just short of indulgent self-parody. Peter Ustinov, in particular, all shifty-eyed rotundity, is an admirable partner for the statuesque and equally loquacious Joan Hackett . . ."

©Monthly Film Bulletin, 1977.

TUNNELVISION

Directors: *Brad Swirnoff, Neil Israel*. Screenplay: *Michael Mislove, Mr. Israel*. Executive Producer: *Mr. Israel*. Producer: *Joe Roth*. Photography: *Don Knight*. Editors: *Roger Parker, Dayle Mustain*. Music: *Dennis Lambert, Brian Potter*. Production: *International Harmony-Woodpecker Music, Inc*. Distributor: *World Wide Films*. Running time 75 minutes. New York opening July 14, 1976, at several theatres. Classification: R.

Players: *Phil Proctor, Howard Hesseman, Ernie Anderson, Edwina Anderson, Chevy Chase, Laraine Newman, William Schallert*.

New York Magazine, 7/26/76 (p. 56)
John Simon

"*Tunnelvision* purports to be a satirical look at television in 1985, when David Eisenhower is president, and a People's Network is wreaking havoc by keeping the country glued to its 'total uncensored and unorthodox' programs. This short film, which is even shorter on wit, is mostly a supposed cross section of People's Network programming, as viewed by a congressional committee investigating it. We get some 70 minutes of tiresome parodies of TV programs and commercials, which the publicity brochure describes as an only 'slightly exaggerated and mildly satirized version' of video's actual future. And that's just where the trouble lies (over and above the aforementioned shortness of wit): Slight exaggeration and mild satire are of absolutely no use here . . ."

©1976 by the NYM Corp. Reprinted with the permission of NEW YORK Magazine.

Christian Science Monitor, 6/7/76 (p. 34)
Madora McKenzie

". . . *Tunnelvision* is a perfectly dreadful movie. No, it is worse than dreadful, it is boring.
Tunnelvision is the kind of movie every 15-year-old kid in southern California dreams of making after his or her first semester of film class—something that combines biting sarcasm with socio-political overtones, and something that will shock the grown-ups (tee-hee). However, the films they make are not inflicted on a large viewing audience. And most of these young filmmakers pass through this phase rather rapidly. The makers of *Tunnelvision*, it would appear, are either all 15 or are all suffering from an extreme case of arrested development . . .
Tunnelvision is so boring the obscene humor that tries to provide most of the laughs is not even offensive. It is just dull . . ."

Reprinted by permission from The Christian Science Monitor © 1976. The Christian Science Publishing Society. All rights reserved.

Saturday Review, 8/21/76 (p. 46)
Judith Crist

". . . Neil Israel's literate, frequently funny, brash, and on occasion crass concept of what television programming will be like in 1985. More couth in content and sophisticated in execution than 1974's *The Groove Tube*, this satire—produced by Israel, a former CBS man, who wrote it with Michael Mislove and codirected with Brad Swirnoff—simply carries all the smarm and suggestiveness of today's video fare to a not illogical extreme. Envisioning a 'people's' network in an America wherein David Eisenhower has been elected President, Israel offers commercials, newscasts, serials, and specials that aren't, alas, as far out or 'sick' in their comedy as non-television-watchers might think. There are intelligence, comic sense, and only sporadic vulgarity in the material and in the performance by a large and gifted cast. Above all, it's distinguished by bright young minds at work and at play."

©Judith Crist, 1976.

New York Post, 7/15/76 (p. 40)
Frank Rich

". . . *Tunnelvision* is a collection of brief blackout sketches that spoof sitcoms, cop and game shows, eyewitness news broadcasts and commercials—but it isn't as amusing as a typically intermittent episode of *Saturday Night* and it isn't even as long . . . More annoying still, *Tunnelvision* contains only a single, one-minute appearance by Chevy Chase, *Saturday Night*'s deftest comic hand—this

continued on next page

continued from previous page

in spite of the fact that Chase receives star billing in the movie's advertising.

Since *Tunnelvision*'s principal creators, Neil Israel and Michael Mislove, are themselves network TV writers (they've collaborated on variety for the likes of Lola Falana and Mac Davis), you can correctly assume that their satirical thrusts never inflict more than superficial wounds on their targets . . .''

Reprinted by Permission of New York Post.
© 1976, New York Post Corporation.

TWILIGHT'S LAST GLEAMING

Director: *Robert Aldrich*. Screenplay: *Ronald M. Cohen, Edward Huebsch*. Based on VIPER THREE by Walter Wager. Producer: *Merv Adelson*. Photography: *Robert Hauser*. Editor: *Michael Luciano*. Music: *Jerry Goldsmith*. Production: *Lorimar-Bavaria*. Distributor: *Allied Artists*. Running time 144 minutes. New York opening February 9, 1977, at several theatres. Classification: R.

Lawrence Dell: *Burt Lancaster*. General MacKenzie: *Richard Widmark*. President Stevens: *Charles Durning*. Defense Secretary Guthrie: *Melvyn Douglas*. Powell: *Paul Winfield*. Garvas: *Burt Young*. State Secretary Renfrew: *Joseph Cotten*. James Forrest: *Roscoe Lee Browne*. General O'Rourke: *Gerald S. O'Loughlin*. Captain Towne: *Richard Jaeckel*. Attorney-General Klinger: *William Marshall*. Colonel Bernstein: *Charles Aidman*. CIA Director Whittaker: *Leif Erickson*. General Crane: *Charles McGraw*.

Women's Wear Daily, 2/7/77 (p. 16)
Howard Kissel

''. . . Everything about *Twilight* . . . is preposterous. Though the screenplay seems to understand the intricacies of gaining access to a missile site it has absolutely no understanding of things like politics or how human beings talk. As in *Cassandra* the basic impulse is to manipulate the audience . . .

. . . *Twilight* seems to be directed with full knowledge of its absurdity. At times to give the illusion that something exciting is happening and to distract the audience from thinking about what's going on, director Robert Aldrich splits the screen and has

four things happening simultaneously. If you're interested in the history of smokescreen techniques in the cinema, this must be a breakthrough.''

© Women's Wear Daily, 1977.

Newsweek, 2/21/77 (p. 90)
Janet Maslin

''. . . Despite a lot of speechifying about the sins of Vietnam, moral rearmament isn't really the movie's main concern. Action—on a puerile but crudely effective level—is, and *Twilight* works best when Aldrich cuts the chatter and cries a figurative 'Bombs away!' The suspense does become terrific, especially in a split-screen sequence that shows nine missiles emerging from their hatches, Lancaster sweating it out beside the STOP button and frantic government officials trying to settle on a counterstrategy as the seconds tick away. But it all crashes to a dead end, a violent resolution that has the caliber of a cap pistol and closing credits that feature the voice-over of Billy Preston in a soul version of 'My Country 'Tis of Thee.' It is not uplifting.''

© Newsweek, Inc. 1977
reprinted by permission.

Films in Review, March 1977 (p. 188)
Charles Phillips Reilly

''. . . Charles Durning gives an interesting performance despite many lines worthy of the Nixon tapes; Lancaster achieves a nice balance between crusader and nut, while Paul Winfield is the only one in the picture in touch with reality, particularly contrasting with the President's Security Council (Melvyn Douglas, Joseph Cotton, William Marshall, Leif Erickson, Charles McGraw . . .), here as dull a group of actors, intentionally perhaps, as we're likely to see in '77.

The ethics of this film are extraordinarily obtuse. A fitting sequel would be for scripters Ronald M. Cohen and Edward Huebsch (who worked from Walter Wager's novel) to give us a plot in which the Pope is threatened with the destruction of the Sistine Chapel if he doesn't let women become priests. (How's that for a gimmick?)

Director Robert Aldrich didn't need $2^1\!/_2$ hours to tell this story even though he does produce an effective last ten minutes of suspense and emotion.''

© Films in Review, 1977.

Film Information, March 1977 (p. 1)
James M. Wall

''. . . The story is so heavily weighted against men in power that it suffers from credibility. Burt Lancaster, as the idealistic general, and Charles Durning, as the President of the United States, give such believable performances they make the plot's weaknesses—including an overemphasis on sensationalism—less noticeable. As a Chicago politician elevated to the nomination of his party at the last moment, Durning offers a strong portrait of an average citizen who is surprised to learn that his predecessors would dare deceive the public. Richard Widmark is also effective as the commanding SAC general, a representative of the establishment determined to block Lancaster's efforts.

As a Secretary of Defense from academia, Melvyn Douglas nicely captures the uninvolved style of the 'best and brightest' who hold ideals, but can discard the ideals for the immediate pragmatic goal . . .''

©Film Information, 1977.

New York Magazine, 2/14/77 (p. 66)
John Simon

''. . . Dell and his main sidekick, the often recalcitrant Powell, are played without much subtlety by Burt Lancaster and Paul Winfield, but the director manages to make their very crassness a part of their characterizations. Worse and very nearly unbearable is Burt Young . . . But everyone else is good to excellent . . .

. . . Robert Hauser's cinematography is as routine as Jerry Goldsmith's score, but everything else about this American-German coproduction, especially the military hardware, looks convincing to these civilian eyes. If you have seen the two or three good movies playing around town, and can swallow the curious blend of over- and underwriting in this . . . screenplay, you may get some kicks out of this not good movie . . .''

©1977 by the NYM Corp. Reprinted with the permission of NEW YORK Magazine.

Saturday Review, 3/19/77 (p. 41)
Judith Crist

''Robert Aldrich's *Twilight's Last Gleaming*, based on Walter Wager's novel, *Viper Three*, is, at the very least, a conscientious and sincere statement on the Vietnam War. Beyond that, it's a feast for paranoids, what with Burt Lancaster, a general framed on a murder charge because of his opposition to the war, escaped (somehow) from prison with three other condemned men and holed up in a missile silo, threatening to release nine Titan missiles unless the President gives him $10 million 'in small denominations,' transport to a foreign country aboard Air Force One with the President along as a hostage, and a promise to 'tell the truth' to the nation about our involvement in Vietnam . . . They're all very good, right down to keeping straight faces when faced by the mind-and-denture-boggling dialogue provided by the . . . screenplay. The missile-base hardware is equally complicated. And if you're in a mood to swallow it in all its split-screen foolishness, you're welcome to it.''

©Judith Crist, 1977.

Christian Science Monitor, 3/4/77 (p. 19)
David Sterritt

''. . . *Twilight* recalls science-fiction tales . . . about well-intentioned saviors using technology to show the world the error of its ways. But Aldrich is not content to operate on this level. His movie gets historical as well, suggesting that the Vietnam War was a massive exercise in 'theater' designed to stave off nuclear conflict by showing the Soviets how 'inhuman' Americans can be.

If the film presented proof to back up this hypothesis, *Twilight* would be an important muckraking movie. But it's all presented as mere fantasy, pivoting on a fictional document and some drawn-out conversations among ersatz government officials. Thus it will convince you or not, according to your previous convictions. The rest of the long picture is sheer melodrama—sometimes cracklingly suspenseful, sometimes so limp and uneven that it's hard to believe Aldrich directed it . . .''

Reprinted by permission from The Christian Science Monitor © 1977. The Christian Science Publishing Society. All rights reserved.

Village Voice, 3/7/77 (p. 39)
Andrew Sarris

''. . . Aldrich brings it off by never flinching from the psychotic implications of the scenario. With an assortment of split-screen strategies he reinforces the impression of continual conniving. It is not that one cares about the characters, but that one comes to feel their raw anger. At any moment the anger can erupt into a cosmic explosion, and Aldrich makes us feel that *he* at least can hear the clock ticking away. He has been over this terrain many times before—*World for Ransom, Kiss Me Deadly, Attack!, Ten Seconds to Hell, The Dirty Dozen*. That is why *Twilight's Last Gleaming* is compelling without being convincing. There are plotholes big enough to drive a tank through . . . But one does not even begin asking these questions until some time after Aldrich has played his last violent trump, and it *is* a winner . . .''

Reprinted by permission of The Village Voice. Copyright © The Village Voice, Inc., 1977.

New York Post, 2/10/77 (p. 30)
Frank Rich

''If you have an afternoon that you don't mind devoting to abject silliness, you could do a lot worse than to spend it with *Twilight's Last Gleaming*, the new, long and noisy thriller . . . neither consistently exciting nor entirely coherent—sometimes it's downright ridiculous—but it's unique movie trash.

To my knowledge, this is the first American pulp movie ever to take a strong stand against the Vietnam War—and I'd even go so far as to call *Twilight's Last Gleaming* daring if only we hadn't pulled out of Vietnam two years ago . . .

continued on next page

continued from previous page

. . . this director has filled the screen with a roughneck energy that is well beyond the capabilities of the filmmakers entrusted with most of Hollywood's popcorn movies. It's that energy which keeps *Twilight's Last Gleaming* charging ahead, even when its plot, dialogue, and acting are so absurd, you can hardly believe your eyes and ears . . ."

Reprinted by Permission of New York Post.
©1977, New York Post Corporation.

Los Angeles Times, 2/10/77 (Pt. IV, p. 1)
Charles Champlin

". . . Robert Aldrich's *Twilight's Last Gleaming* structurally is a suspense melodrama in his usual muscular and meaty-fisted style. But it is thickly intercut with political attitudes.

The commentary is not discernibly from Right or Left (it is curiously indistinct in this regard). Instead, the movie is a savage and interdenominational vote of no confidence in the executive branch of the American government from Vietnam forward on grounds (here, of course, fictional) that it has deceived the people by lying or by silence in the name of dubious policies and national security . . .

Simply as movie-making, *Twilight's Last Gleaming* works less well by a good deal than Aldrich's less argumentative creations because the straight-line action stops almost dead for a great deal of solemn talk calculated not to ruffle right wing more than left wing or either more than no wing . . .

. . . The script leaves Lancaster strung between psychosis and nobility, but to the actor's credit he is not your standard fanatic and indeed is finally a rather pathetic figure, even if he would have gladly fried us all . . ."

©Los Angeles Times, 1977.

TWO KENNEDYS, THE

Documentary. Director, Screenplay: *Gianni Bislach.* Producer: *Alfredo Bini.* Editor: *M. Marco.* Distributor: *Seymour Borde & Associates.* Running time 110 minutes. Los Angeles opening September 1976 at UA Cinema Centers in Westwood and Costa Mesa. Classification: None.

Note: There is no cast in this film.

Los Angeles Times, 9/9/76 (Pt. IV, p. 18)
Linda Gross

". . . Unfortunately, Gianni Bislach's *The Two Kennedys* . . . falls short. It is a superficial, encyclopedic and exploitative film dissertation which supports a conventional European theory of conspiracy connecting the murders of John F. Kennedy and Robert Kennedy with Dr. Martin Luther King and Medgar Evers. That is not to say the movie lacks powerful and inherent dramatic appeal, but it is a moving experience which doesn't shed additional insight on the subject of American political conspiracies.

The Two Kennedys is a compilation of newsreel footage and photos tracing the Kennedys' lineage, their youth, success and sudden death. The film has been put together without discretion. Shots of the Kennedy children playing are intercut with the Ku Klux Klan, Vietnam, the assassination of Patrice Lumumba and a scene of Marilyn Monroe accepting a 1952 Photoplay fan magazine award from Lauren Bacall . . ."

©Los Angeles Times, 1976.

TWO-MINUTE WARNING

Director: *Larry Peerce.* Screenplay: *Edward Hume.* Based on the novel by George LaFountaine. Producer: *Edward S. Feldman.* Photography: *Gerald Hirschfeld.* Music: *Charles Fox.* Distributor: *Universal Pictures.* Running time 112 minutes. New York opening November 12, 1976, at several theatres. Classification: R.

Holly: *Charlton Heston.* Button: *John Cassavetes.* McKeever: *Martin Balsam.* Mike Ramsay: *Beau Bridges.* Lucy: *Marilyn Hassett.* Steve: *David Janssen.* Janet: *Gena Rowlands.* Sandman: *Jack Klugman.* Pickpocket: *Walter Pidgeon.* Gatekeeper: *Brock Peters.* Intern: *David Groh.*

Christian Science Monitor, 12/6/76 (p. 50)
David Sterritt

"*Two-Minute Warning* is the first in a mini-wave of stadium disaster movies. (*Black Sunday* will feature terrorists at the Super Bowl.) The championship game is on and a sniper is stationed behind the scoreboard. Charlton Heston is the chief cop. John

Cassavetes is head of the SWAT team called in to save the day . . .

Larry Peerce's technical skill and all these stars unfortunately don't add any sense to the script, which leads from ominous to disastrous with little intelligence along the way. There are a few weakly suspenseful twinges, but *Warning* is finally as pointless as its own violence."

Reprinted by permission from The Christian Science Monitor © 1976. The Christian Science Publishing Society. All rights reserved.

Film Information, December 1976 (p. 5)
David A. Tillyer

". . . One asks: How much farther can cinema go? We've mutilated with chain saws, annihilated with nuclear efficiency, genetically mutated and abused the human condition quite mercilessly. This normally tolerant reviewer is genuinely concerned about this trend toward mindless dehumanizing Bedlam.

Two-Minute Warning—an abrupt and disappointing turnabout for Larry Peerce, director of *A Separate Peace* and *The Other Side of the Mountain* —is technically very good, making it all the more insidious. The screenplay and direction are exacting and engaging. Perhaps we should go back to the novel, written by George LaFountaine, and ask the ultimate question of intent. Liberals have long maintained that entertainment is enough justification for most fiction, and that the question of moral purpose need not be posed. It seems our bluff has been called."

© Film Information, 1976.

Films in Review, January 1977 (p. 56)
Michael Buckley

"*Two-Minute Warning* resembles an all-star episode of the recent TV series, "SWAT," the meaning of which (Special Weapons and Tactics) is not explained herein, although the term is used frequently. The differences are the large screen, absence of commercials, inclusion of profanities, and lots of blood (stars get shot dead, featured players are only wounded). Director Larry Peerce creates a frighteningly realistic depiction of mass panic, during the final frames, as a crowd escapes a sniper who has turned a football stadium into a shooting gallery: however, everyone would have fled even faster had they been viewing this disaster . . ."

© Films in Review, 1977.

Monthly Film Bulletin, February 1977 (p. 32)
John Pym

"The wedding in *Goodbye, Columbus* demon-

strated Larry Peerce's ability to muster crowds, and the film as a whole revealed a sharp eye for the niceties of detached if sentimental characterisation. Had these modest skills (with only slight adaptation) been brought to bear on the more grandiose but less credible *Two-Minute Warning*, some of its longueurs might well have been avoided. Peerce, however, is hampered from the start by the demands of a shaky plot, chief among them being the necessity for the sustained 'mystery' of the sniper's identity . . . The most that can be said, finally, for this aimless shuffling of the disaster-movie deck is that Peerce directs the action scenes, and notably an opening sequence introducing the Special Weapons and Tactics unit (SWAT), with commendable zest."

© Monthly Film Bulletin, 1977.

The Times (London), 1/14/77 (p. 13)
David Robinson

"*Two-Minute Warning* is really the same old disaster film, though for a while you're diverted from the fact by the documentary treatment of the setting —the backstage security operation at a big ball game in Los Angeles Memorial Coliseum—and the kaleidoscopic, Altmanesque diffusion of the story.

Instead of an earthquake or a fire or a sinking ship or an exploding dirigible, you have *the crowd*— a vast and wild and many-headed beast . . .

If you like the disaster movie formula, this one is better than most, with ingenious notions like focusing much of the action on the television monitor room, where one screen has, by chance, a bead on the sniper. When it comes to juggling this sort of multiple action, however, Larry Peerce is no Altman at keeping all the balls in the air at once . . ."

© The Times, 1977.

The Sunday Times (London), 1/16/77 (p. 37)
Alan Brien

"*Two-Minute Warning* is a phrase familiar to all American football fans, the time left till the end of the game. Here it also means the moment when nice cop, Charlton Heston, who cares for everybody including the criminal, hands over the job of winkling out the barricaded sniper in the Los Angeles Coliseum to nasty cop, John Cassavetes, who cares for nobody and regards criminals as vermin to be exterminated. Between the two, one lesson is clear—if there is anything worse than obstructing the police, it is trying to help them. Either way, you'll get kneed in the groin and be held incommunicado . . .

. . . you realise that though the sniper fires at random, he will hit a minor star with every bullet. We no longer feel threatened because we know who is doomed to go . . ."

© The Sunday Times, 1977.

continued on next page

continued from previous page

Newsweek, 11/22/76 (p. 110)
Janet Maslin

"Nothing explodes, crashes, quakes, sinks or goes up in flames during *Two-Minute Warning*, but this is a disaster picture just the same. It concerns a sniper loose in the Los Angeles Memorial Coliseum at a football game and features mayhem on the grand scale. Its dramatis personae are true to form—David Janssen as The Perpetual Bachelor, Gena Rowlands as The Mistress, Jack Klugman as The Heavy Bettor, Marilyn Hassett as the Co-Ed, Beau Bridges as The Father, ad nauseam.

In fact, *Two-Minute Warning* conforms so faithfully to the conventions of the genre that it approaches parody . . ."

©Newsweek, Inc. 1976
reprinted by permission.

New York Post, 11/13/76 (p. 19)
Frank Rich

". . . What makes *Two-Minute Warning* so weird . . . and so tedious—is that there's a 90-minute gap between the time when the sniper takes his position above the scoreboard and the moment when he opens fire. Why the sniper waits 90 minutes is never explained—but this pause results in what is surely the longest intermission ever to be inserted into a two-hour film. Anyone who decides to see *Two-Minute Warning* would be well advised to bring along a good book . . .

Even by the standards of exploitation movies, this film is an unusually dehumanizing experience: Not only does it exist solely for its gore, but it reduces the victims to the dimensions of plastic ducks at a shooting gallery . . ."

Reprinted by Permission of New York Post.
©1976, New York Post Corporation.

Village Voice, 11/29/76 (p. 53)
Andrew Sarris

"*Two-Minute Warning* brings together the disaster movie and the assassination movie in the Los Angeles Coliseum on Super Bowl day. A superhuman sniper is perched above the scoreboard but he is never explained as a character. He remains a nameless, faceless evil, a sharpshooting shark derived from the *Jaws* principle of mindless entertainment through never-ending nerve jangling.

Charlton Heston and John Cassavetes lead an astonishingly impotent law-enforcement team against the mysterious assassin . . .

The cross-section of potential targets is cast for every generation and medium with Beau Bridges, Marilyn Hassett, David Janssen, Gena Rowlands, Jack Klugman, Martin Balsam, Brock Peters and

David Groh among the most prominent. There are faces and personalities there but no real characters . . ."

Reprinted by permission of The Village Voice.
Copyright ©The Village Voice, Inc., 1976.

UNDERGROUND

Documentary. By *Emile de Antonio, Mary Lampson, Haskell Wexler*. Distributor: *New Yorker Films*. Running time 88 minutes. New York opening May 9, 1976, at the Regency and Quad Cinema 1 Theatres. Classification: None.

Interviews with the following members of the Weather Underground: *Billy Ayers, Kathy Boudin, Bernardine Dohrn, Jeff Jones, Cathy Wilkerson.*

Saturday Review, 5/12/76 (p. 49)
Judith Crist

"*Underground* is a self-conscious and self-serving documentary . . . about five members of the revolutionary Weather Underground. They are Billy Ayers, Kathy Boudin, Bernardine Dohrn, Jeff Jones, and Cathy Wilkerson—all being sought by the authorities but all apparently functioning in the open . . .

Through questions and lengthy answers, the five discuss their growing up into the student and antiwar movements of the Sixties and their active revolutionary status. They give their rationale for the more than 20 bombings for which they claim credit . . . They talk, in the main, in simplistic radical cant, the jargon emphasized by its detachment from personality; faceless people make small impression—and the three expressionless filmmakers lend a static tedium to the scene. There is little here beyond what any interested person would know about the group . . . "

© Judith Crist, 1976.

Film Information, 6/76 (p. 3)
Peter P. Shillaci

" . . . what emerges is a fascinating dialogue surveying the radical politics of dissent and revolution of the Sixties from the relatively calm perspective of the Seventies. The Weather Underground speaks from experiences, personal and social, that are part of our recent history. As each person recalls his/her radicalization, we find ourselves taken back, through newsreel and video footage, to the events: draft-card burnings, the 'Days of Rage' in Chicago, the New York townhouse explosion, the whole turbulent history. From the viewpoint of the Weather people, however, this review is to a great extent a catalogue of mistakes, an elitism that alienated the oppressed from the revolution, a sexism that denied power to women in the movement, a zeal that persuaded some to take unwarranted chances with their lives and the lives of others. These fugitives make it clear they would do it differently today.

What *are* they doing today? Instead of throwing rocks, they distribute *Prairie Fire* ('A single spark can start a fire'), interview on the streets, and emphasize the fact that things *can* be different in America . . . "

© Film Information, 1976.

Village Voice, 5/17/76 (p. 140)
Mitch Tuchman

" . . . *Underground* began as a film with no images. The Weather Underground established ground rules: no faces, no recognizable locations, no prying questions whose answers might expose them unnecessarily to heat, in short, no images, and ultimately, no plot, no sympathetic characters, just a series of verbal confrontations, a discussion process that was more important than cataclysmic incidents.

Eventually three nonimages were devised to be shot in a 'safe house.' In one the Weather people sit behind a gauze scrim. In another their backs are reflected in a mirror. In a third, their out-of-focus silhouettes loom as a forbidding mass in front of de Antonio and Lampson.

None of the setups is particularly satisfactory or handsome, and yet each is redolent with powerful connotations. In the scrim shot the fugitives . . . are literally driven underground, made invisible as a result of the war in Vietnam. In the mirror shot the camera lens is reflected and appears to be pointed not at the Weather people but at the audience . . . "

Reprinted by permission of The Village Voice.
Copyright © The Village Voice, Inc., 1976.

Jump Cut, Winter 1977 (p. 13)
Thomas Waugh

" . . . In one sense, the austere visual style of the interviews provides a perfect setting for the interpolated stock material. The structural opposition of the interview passages with the archival passages can be well imagined by those familiar with the work of de Antonio and his imitators: The interviews, with their slow, deliberate, analytic rhythm and their contemplative tone, have the effect of sharply setting off the inserts, with their black and white dramatic intensity and their connotations of the turbulence and passion of the already thoroughly mythologized period.

Whatever deficiencies the three filmmakers betray as filmmakers—there might have been more dynamic interplay between the groups on either side of the camera and less feeling of intimidation on the part of the filmmakers—such deficiencies are abundantly compensated for by de Antonio's and Lampson's brilliance as editors . . ."

© Jump Cut, 1977

New York Post, 5/10/76 (p. 22)
Archer Winsten

"*Underground* . . . comes to us as a labor of love and conviction by three filmmakers who have long been associated with radical causes. They are Emile de Antonio, Haskell Wexler and Mary Lampson . . .

The three of them stand and are photographed talking with five people from the Weather Underground . . . The latter are seen through a screen so heavy that their faces are totally indistinct, or else you see the back of the head of the speaker.

What they are talking about are their careers as bombers, revolutionaries and idealists . . .

As the different members of the Underground speak there is a partly seen motto on the wall: 'The Future World is What We The People Struggle To Make It.'

It all comes back, so well remembered, and yet there is always an 'Only Yesterday' overtone. The arguments for revolution are made for now, but you still have the feeling that you are attending some extraordinarily good re-creation of the past . . . "

Reprinted by Permission of New York Post.
© 1976, New York Post Corporation.

Monthly Film Bulletin, October 1976 (p. 220)
Louise Sweet

"To judge by Emile de Antonio's most recent exercise in left-wing reportage, the members of the Weather Underground resistance movement can only provide the most rhetorical indication of which way the political winds in America are blowing. De Antonio's announced intention is to show how the five Weather people interviewed in this film came to their present 'place' in American society (a place of which he expresses his approval), and to destroy the popular media image of the group as crazed fanatics in order to prove that they are 'very rational, human, loving people.' . . . Unfortunately,

continued on next page

continued from previous page

the stilted explanations of revolution, and the tactic of presenting the five either sheltering behind a gauze curtain or with their backs to the screen, only succeed in mystifying the revolution and making the abundant jargon seem self-serving . . .''

©Monthly Film Bulletin, 1976.

Los Angeles Times, 5/19/76 (Pt. IV, p. 8)
Kevin Thomas

"At the beginning of *Underground* . . . a remarkable, deeply disturbing documentary of the Weather Underground, one has the feeling that the five Weatherpeople, fugitives all, who allowed themselves to be interviewed (but not photographed directly) are leftovers from the tumultuous '60s. At the end of the film 88 minutes later, one comes away realizing that, like it or not, they may just be the wave of the future . . .

Underground is an excellent example of documentary filmmaking. Much of it was shot in a mirror behind the group of Weatherpeople, which in effect placed the three filmmakers themselves on camera, reminding us of their constant presence and participation. This factor, plus a forthright discussion of the wide-ranging implications of the Weatherpeople being involved in a film in the first place, makes *Underground* seem an exceptionally honest endeavor in a genre whose claims to objectivity are forever suspect . . . ''

© Los Angeles Times, 1976.

Christian Science Monitor, 6/7/76 (p. 35)
David Sterritt

" . . . *Underground* is the work of three filmmakers. Emile de Antonio is the sometimes inspired documentarist who made *Point of Order*, about the army-McCarthy hearings. Haskell Wexler is the noted cinematographer who directed his own deeply committed *Medium Cool* at the end of the turbulent '60s. Mary Lampson joins them on-screen in their present effort, questioning and responding to a quintet of fugitives who belong to the radical Weather Underground.

Since the fugitives are the focus of the film, and since they won't allow their faces to be photographed, *Underground* consists largely of closeups of the backs of people's heads, interspersed with shots of the three interviewers and some newsreel-type footage (with a bit of rough language)."

Reprinted by permission from The Christian
Science Monitor © 1976.
The Christian Science Publishing Society.
All rights reserved.

Ms., 8/76 (p. 39)
Lucinda Franks

". . . One of the main complaints that has been leveled against *Underground* is that the interviews, with the backs of heads talking tag words, do not come across as real. It is true that we don't get underneath the first layer of the five fugitives, but we are somehow left with a rather strong sense of them. We see Dohrn's hands, thinner and more veined with the years, the streak of gray in her hair; we hear how Jeff Jones wakes up every morning wondering how many times he's going to be nervous that day. Above all, somehow, we understand part of what motivates them to live the harrowing life that they live. It is clear when Jones, an edge to his voice, insists they have accomplished something—'who would have thought Ho Chi Minh would win?'—and when Dohrn says they don't believe in the cynical maxim that one person can't matter. It is obvious, that to them, whatever the cost, they as individuals are going to matter."

©Ms., 1976.

UP!

Director, Producer, Photography, Editor: *Russ Meyer.* Screenplay: *B. Callum.* Based on a story by Reinhold Timme, Jim Ryan, Mr. Meyer. Music: *William Loose, Paul Ruhland.* Distributor: *American International Pictures.* Running time 80 minutes. Los Angeles opening January 1977 at several theatres. Classification: X.

Players: *Monte Bane, Elaine Collins, Raven De La Croix, Larry Dean, Mary Gavin, Harry, Wilburn Kluck, Foxy Lae, Su Ling, Robert McLane, Marianne Marks, Francesca (Kitten) Natividad, Fred Owens, Linda Sue Ragsdale, Ray Reinhardt, Edward Schaaf, Bob Schott, Janet Wood.*

New York Post, 10/30/76 (p. 37)
Archer Winsten

"Russ Meyer, the Chicago early practitioner of breast-and-buttock worship (*The Immoral Mr. Teas*) who suffered eclipse when hard-core porn made him seem naive, tries to beat his way back to the top with *Up!* . . .

The performers seem to have been chosen for size, shape, and decent looks.

The music has that beat, closely tied to sexual rhythm.

But what emerges most memorably is the sound of orgasm, very noisy. It is a picture that plunges into its representation of sex as if engaged in some cataclysmic battle made for the movies.

In brief, this is a big joke, a big bust, or just a big Russ Meyer. It has vitality, a total absence of good taste, and a well-earned X-rating that should warn off anyone who still has a decent bone in his body."

Reprinted by Permission of New York Post.
©1976. New York Post Corporation.

Los Angeles Times, 1/28/77 (Pt. IV, p. 14)
Kevin Thomas

". . . Plotting in a Meyer film is as compiicated as it is beside the point, since the whole idea is to show off as many fantastically endowed women as possible. *Up!*'s heroine Margo Winchester (Raven De La Croix) has dimensions as incredible as her adventures in a small Northern California mountain community where a very kinky old German (who just might be Hitler) resides—until somebody puts a killer fish in his Jacuzzi. This makes *Up!* a mystery only nominally, for the real guessing has to do with the measurements of Miss De La Croix and various other lovelies.

As always, Meyer is a terrific cameraman and razzle-dazzle editor, but *Up!* is so blood-drenched it's more of a turnoff than a turn-on. The irony is that more explicit sex would be far more preferable than so much explicit violence."

©Los Angeles Times, 1977.

VERONIQUE, OR THE SUMMER OF MY 13TH YEAR (VERONIQUE, OU L'ETE DE MES 13 ANS)

Director: *Claudine Guilmain.* Screenplay (French with English subtitles): *Ms. Guilemain.* Dialogue: *Pierre Lartha.* Executive Producer: *George Dybman.* Photography: *Jean-Jacques Rochut.* Editors: *Alfredo Muschietti, Caroline Roulet.* Production: *Film du Losange/Felix Films.* Running time 88 minutes. New York opening April 6, 1976, at The Museum of Modern Art. Classification: None. Origin: France.

Véronique: *Anne Teyssedre.* Anne: *Anouk Ferjak.* Jean: *Michel Peyrelon.* Father:

Jean-Pierre Mouiln. Mother: *Edith Loria.* Michele: *Anne Karylen.* Sylvain: *Christophe Perring.*

Women's Wear Daily, 6/18/76 (p. 32)
Howard Kissel

"The sexual tensions and discoveries of adolescence have rarely been treated with as much subtlety and depth as they are in *Véronique*, a gem of a film by a young Frenchwoman, Claudine Guilemain.

Instead of concentrating, as most such films do, on the relations of a young girl and her boyfriend or a young girl and her parents, Guilemain shows us a 13-year-old girl who goes on vacation with her godparents, an attractive couple, seemingly warmer and more open than her parents. The unspoken anxieties that characterize the relations between generations can here be articulated. Véronique can confide in both her godparents more than she can with her parents; she can also observe their relationship more dispassionately. Her gradual awareness of their frustrations and difficulties with one another is a sort of initiation for her, a rite of passage into maturity.

Guilemain has written the screenplay with extraordinary delicacy, leaving many points in the story muted or open to question, rather than hammering things home. She has directed the film with similar subtlety, drawing beautiful, extremely intelligent, sensitive performances from Anne Teyssedre as the young girl and Michel Peyrelon and Anouk Ferjak as her godparents . . . "

© Women's Wear Daily, 1976.

Los Angeles Times, 10/27/76 (Pt. IV, p. 1)
Charles Champlin

". . . Emotional events and changes are the events of *Veronique* and, as in life, are the more fascinating because they prove so universal. Coming of age does not sound drastically different with a French accent, and the laughter, of which *Veronique* produces a lot, sounds exactly the same.

The godparents are played by Anouk Ferjak and Michel Peyrelon and they are said to be, like everyone else in the cast, nonactors recruited from the ranks of the director's friends and acquaintances. It is astonishing if true, because they achieve that unfeigned and attractive naturalness that eludes most amateurs and all but the best professionals . . .

. . . it is wise, involving, insightful and enjoyable. There is reassurance in it for anyone who still chooses to believe that substance is what counts most, more than stars or budgets . . ."

©Los Angeles Times. 1976.

continued on next page

continued from previous page

New York Magazine, 6/28/76 (p. 69)
John Simon

" . . . a slight but honorable film . . . This is one of those extended young-girl-coming-of-age vignettes that, paradoxically, can clobber us with excess of sensitivity; but the girl who here begins —only begins—to grow up is inspiritingly tomboyish, commonsensical and unextraordinary. If the film suffers from anything, it is from an intermittent tendency to pseudoprofound speechifying (which Mlle. Guilemain could have picked up while acting as an assistant director to Eric Rohmer), but this is more than made up for by wonderful composition, a delightful sense of how to make characters enter and exit from the frame, and a splendid ability to choreograph certain wordless scenes in long shot. The outstanding performance is by Anouk Ferjak as the heroine's godmother . . . "

© 1976 by the NYM Corp. Reprinted with the permission of NEW YORK Magazine.

Village Voice, 8/12/76 (p. 117)
Molly Haskell

". . . Sensuality and reflection go hand in hand. The film has been called the female counterpart to *Claire's Knee*, and one feels the influence of Eric Rohmer, with whom Guilmain worked as assistant. But whereas Rohmer's films work from a metaphysical premise, a cerebral puzzle that is the tantalizing parlor to the film's flies, Guilmain's film takes a looser, more episodic course. Her position is one of creative passivity, and even when the film seems to meander, there are acute social observations on French middle-class family life . . .

Claudine Guilmain still has something to learn technically . . . But she has a great gift for understated drama—for conveying the meaning to be found in the look, the offhand comment, and the uncompleted act . . . "

Reprinted by permission of The Village Voice. Copyright © The Village Voice, Inc., 1976.

New York Post, 6/21/76 (p. 21)
Frank Rich

" . . . *Véronique* has beautiful French countryside settings, smart and likable characters, fine acting and off-hand wit; it also builds steadily toward an erotic climax that never happens.

The story is about a pubescent 13-year-old girl (a highly appealing Anne Teyssedre) who goes on vacation with her godparents (Michel Peyrelon and Anouk Ferjak) and learns a little more about growing up than she bargained for. It's a perfectly competent little pastiche by a director who seems to have talent but who has not yet begun her career in earnest."

Reprinted by Permission of New York Post. © 1976, New York Post Corporation.

VIGILANTE FORCE

Director, Screenplay: *George Armitage.* Producer: *Gene Corman.* Photography: *William Cronjager.* Editor: *Morton Tubor.* Music: *Gerald Fried.* Production: *Gene Corman.* Distributor: *United Artists.* Running time 91 minutes. Los Angeles opening April, 1976, at several theatres. Classification: PG.

Players: *Kris Kristofferson, Jan-Michael Vincent, Victoria Principal, Bernadette Peters, Brad Dexter, Judson Pratt, David Doyle, Antony Carbone, Andrew Stevens, Shelly Novack, Paul X. Gleason, John Steadman, Lilyan McBride, James Lydon, Peter Coe, Charles Cyphers, Debbie Lytton, Cerman Argenziano, Don Pulford, Suzanne Horton.*

Los Angeles Times, 4/29/76 (Pt. IV, p. 12)
Kevin Thomas

"*Vigilante Force* . . . is yet another numbing, ultra violent variation on *Walking Tall* that wastes its capable stars and buries a viable premise deep beneath unspeakable carnage.

This blood-soaked United Artists release envisions what could happen after the government at long last opens up the oil reserves at Elk Hills, turning the pleasant little community into a boom town seething with avarice and mayhem.

Things get so out of hand that mayor Brad Dexter and police chief Judson Pratt get upstanding Jan-Michael Vincent to persuade his Vietnam vet brother Kris Kristofferson to head up a special force to restore law and order.

Kristofferson, however, proves to be a raging psychopath . . .

Sixty-five minutes into this 90-minute movie Vincent finally sees through Kristofferson and now promptly leads his fellow citizens in battle against his brother and his minions . . .

In such circumstances it's scarcely surprising that characterizations are strictly one-dimensional, with the cast having little opportunity but to give one-note performances. Vincent's portrayal is dumb but good, Kristofferson's pure evil and Vincent's lovely schoolteacher girlfriend Victoria Principal is asked only to be understandably distraught.

Somehow managing to make a little something from next to nothing is multitalented Bernadette Peters . . ."

© Los Angeles Times, 1976.

Monthly Film Bulletin, 7/76 (p. 154)
Tom Milne

"As one might expect from George Armitage's previous credits (script for Corman's *Gas*, writer-director on *Private Duty Nurses* and a Pam Grier vehicle, *Hit Man*), *Vigilante Force* is sharp, bright, and not averse to exploitation bandwagons. Buried somewhere in the script and kept more or less in sight by Kris Kristofferson's broodingly ambivalent performance is the thesis that, after Vietnam, America deserves what it gets from the calloused veterans it created . . . So far, so good, with the small town atmosphere (a tidy civic facade revealing some nasty back street cracks) admirably enhanced by the locations in and around Los Angeles which take in what is obviously a real Fourth of July parade, and with Armitage's laconically witty dialogue giving a vivid edge to most of the minor characters . . . But the sense of personal disillusionment and despair carefully built up through allusions to Aaron's past and brilliantly encapsulated by the curious mixture of callousness and regret with which he sentences his brother's girlfriend to death . . . unfortunately doesn't match with the other side of his character: the ruthless demagogue who marshals his blackshirt forces and stockpiles armaments in cool expectation of a revolutionary coup. This neo-Fascist motif, in fact, is little more than a red herring . . ."

©Monthly Film Bulletin, 1976.

VINCENT, FRANCOIS, PAUL AND THE OTHERS

Director: *Claude Sautet*. Screenplay (French with English subtitles): *Jean-Loup Dabadie, Claude Neron, Mr. Sautet*. Based on the novel LA GRANDE MARRADE by *Mr. Neron*. Producer: *Raymond Danon*. Photography: *Jean Boffety*. Music: *Philippe Sarde*. Production: *Lira Films/President Films*. Distributor: *Joseph Green Pictures*. Running time 113 minutes.

New York opening March 7, 1976, at the Regency and D.W. Griffith Theatres. Classification: None. Origin: France.

Vincent: *Yves Montand*. Francois: *Michel Piccoli*. Paul: *Serge Reggiani*. Jean: *Gerard Depardieu*. Catherine: *Stéphane Audran*. Marie: *Ludmilla Mikael*. Lucie: *Marie Dubois*. Julia: *Antonella Lualdi*. Colette: *Catherine Allegret*. Jacques: *Umberto Orsini*.

See Volume 1 for additional reviews

Film Information, 5/76 (p. 4)
Barbara Bauer

"*Vincent, Francois, Paul and the Others* is a poignant study of three old friends, who at fifty, face up to the unsettling realization that--at some point in their lives--they have pulled over to the side of the road. Their wives and mistresses, their troubled businesses and shattered ambitions reveal the compromises they have accepted. Slowly, their frustration creeps from malaise to despair . . .
. . . The problem is that director Claude Sautet could not settle for telling his story with subtlety. His cast--including Yves Montand and a host of equally attractive French stars--is too elegant to make the characters' crises believable. Photography, music, and sets are too sophisticated. It is thus impossible to feel the cathartic angst that we are meant to feel. *Vincent*, a film about the repressed and unexplored gray areas in our lives, should have been made with balding and paunchy actors, with real-life settings and with black-and-white photography. Its Hollywood glitter, unfortunately, only diminishes the power of its depressing but all too fundamental statement."

© Film Information, 1976.

Films in Review, June/July 1976 (p. 379)
Marsha McCreadie

"Sautet is very good at showing clashes among life styles, particularly at dinner table scenes where such tensions frequently emerge. And if the film leaves us slightly depressed it's because no solutions are offered—just a meditation on the failures, compromises, and lost opportunities that the characters are still mulling over. For Vincent, his happy past is epitomized in an old photograph of all the friends dancing with their wives; he with the elegant Stephane Audran, now lost to him forever.

That these portraits stick with us, no matter however melancholically, is a tribute to the director, the actors, and the rhythmic editing which makes us interested in the bits and pieces of the lives we see."

©Films in Review, 1976.

VOYAGE OF THE DAMNED

Director: *Stuart Rosenberg.* Screenplay: *Steve Shagan, David Butler.* Based on the novel by Gordon Thomas and Max Morgan-Witts. Producer: *Robert Fryer.* Photography: *Billy Williams.* Editor: *Tom Priestly.* Music: *Lalo Schifrin.* Presented by Sir Lew Grade. Production: *ITC Entertainment Film.* Distributor: *Avco Embassy Pictures.* Running time 158 minutes. New York opening December 22, 1976, at several theatres. Classification: PG.

Denise Kreisler: *Faye Dunaway.* Capt. Schroeder: *Max Von Sydow.* Dr. Kreisler: *Oskar Werner.* Max Gunter: *Malcolm McDowell.* Estedes: *Orson Welles.* Remos: *James Mason.* Lillian Rosen: *Lee Grant.* Morris Troper: *Ben Gazzara.* Mira Hauser: *Katharine Ross.* Prof. Weiler: *Luther Adler.* Clasing: *Michael Constantine.* Adm. Canaris: *Denholm Elliott.* Benitez: *Jose Ferrer.* Anna Rosen: *Lynne Frederick.* Schiendick: *Helmut Griem.* Alice Feinchild: *Julie Harris.* Rebecca Weiler: *Wendy Hiller.* Dr. Glauner: *Donald Houston.* Aaron Pozner: *Paul Koslo.* Mr. Hauser: *Nehemiah Persoff.* President Bru: *Fernando Rey.* Commander von Bonin: *Leonard Rossiter.* Mrs. Hauser: *Maria Schell.* Dr. Max Strauss: *Victor Spinetti.* Leni Strauss: *Janet Suzman.* Carl Rosen: *Sam Wanamaker.* Joseph Manasse: *Jonathan Pryce.*

Women's Wear Daily, 12/20/76 (p. 5)
Howard Kissel

". . . you can't really judge *Voyage* as a film because it's more like vaudeville, where each performer has his moment in the spotlight and then moves along to make room for the next act. With so many stars you find yourself wondering, 'Now how big a part will Orson Welles have?' or, 'Is that woman in the funny wig really Maria Schell?' Concerned with such matters, it is a little hard to maintain equal interest in the plot, which happens to be about the ship of Jews that left Germany in the spring of 1939 bound for Cuba. Cuba would not admit them, nor would the U.S.—ultimately the ship went back to Europe, where a consortium of nations divided up the passengers and granted them a temporary reprieve from the Holocaust. The subject is obviously a crucial one, but it is handled as a series of cliches—*Ship of Fools* A La Juive . . ."

©Women's Wear Daily, 1976.

Newsweek, 12/27/76 (p. 57)
Janet Maslin

". . . Ultimately, the script becomes so manipulatively weepy that it's a wonder nobody drowns. Director Stuart Rosenberg compounds the problem by getting the characters' individual stories hopelessly tangled and making cuts so arbitrary that they are sometimes unintentionally appalling. After Sam Wanamaker, as an embittered, disbarred lawyer, has slashed his wrists in front of his family and then leaped overboard, Rosenberg cuts abruptly to a Cuban nightclub in full swing.

Voyage's most disturbing quality is that it seems to have been put together as an international business venture. The enormous cast . . . is of the sort that prompts you to whisper, 'Isn't that Jose Ferrer?' (It is—as Cuba's director of immigration.) Some of the players, like Julie Harris, have virtually nothing to do and seem to have been recruited only to fill out crowd scenes . . ."

©Newsweek, Inc. 1976
reprinted by permission.

Los Angeles Times, 12/24/76 (Pt. IV, p. 1)
Charles Champlin

". . . The movie . . . has to be counted a kind of homage to past sufferings, because there can have been only the thinnest hope that so grim and foreboding a story would return the unstinting millions that have been spent on it.

Whether correct or not, the aesthetic decision has been to go all-out, all-star, first-cabin and the result is an old-fashioned and expansive work of high film craftsmanship within which virtually every face is familiar . . .

On and on it goes, with moments of quite affecting poignance . . . Over it all, unless one is blind to history, hangs the remembered pall of the unthinkable taking place.

But in the end it is too much, the impact weakened by the picture's scale, which defeats the sustained intimacy that would have brought home the full horror . . .

Stuart Rosenberg has directed with an admirable and indeed very impressive command of the logistics (which must have been boggling) and with performances that one by one are generally efficient and accurate.

But the movie stays surprisingly distanced and impersonal, like a panning shot that moves too quickly for the details to register . . ."

©Los Angeles Times, 1976

Film Information, December 1976 (p. 3)
John Evenson

"*Voyage of the Damned* is another 'disaster' movie with a cast of more than 20 well-known actors and a tragic plot. But in this film, the disaster is based on historical fact. The year is 1939 and 937 passengers embark in Hamburg bound for Havana, Cuba. The passengers are all Jews, allowed to leave Nazi Germany in a public relations gesture . . .

Voyage of the Damned attempts to capture the despair and hope of the outcast, in this case the Jew who has been so often despised by the Christian world. Unfortunately, the episodic story does not give us a chance to empathize in depth with any of its large cast of characters who, despite their presumed intelligence, speak mostly shallow dialogue. The tension, however, does mount, and the violence of the Nazi element in the crew is believable, as is the dilemma of the well-meaning captain, believably protrayed by Von Sydow . . ."

©Film Information, 1976.

Christian Science Monitor, 12/31/76 (p. 19)
David Sterritt

". . . Sir Lew Grade, the British impresario, must have thought this would make a dandy *Ship of Fools* type of movie, and he set about filming it in the grand manner. As they used to say in Hollywood, whatta cast! Max Von Sydow as the well-meaning captain, Malcolm McDowell as his feisty steward, Oskar Werner as a compassionate doctor who tries to be above it all, Faye Dunaway as his lovely wife.

And more . . .

All these famous stars do just what we want and expect them to, yet *Voyage* soon becomes a rather dull cruise. Director Stuart Rosenberg fails to lend visual flair or narrative tension to the story, which floats lazily from one character sketch to another . . . In all, it's another of those projects that probably looked better on the drawing board than it looks on the screen."

Reprinted by permission from The Christian Science Monitor ©1976. The Christian Science Publishing Society. All rights reserved.

New York Magazine, 12/27/76 (p. 79)
John Simon

"*Voyage of the Damned* is numbingly earnest in its intentions and crushingly dull in its execution. A pity that, for several reasons. It is based on a shattering historical event with serious present-day implications; a good deal of effort by famous and capable people has gone into it; and the financing was lavish to the point of recklessness. There are fleeting instants when the power of the facts depicted, however flat-footedly, inundates the screen; for the rest of its 158 minutes, this unhappy vessel might as well be sailing under the pious but inept helmsmanship of Stanley Kramer and called *The Return Voyage of the Ship of Fools* . . .''

©1976 by the NYM Corp. Reprinted with the permission of NEW YORK Magazine.

Saturday Review, 1/22/77 (p. 50)
Judith Crist

". . . thanks to a number of performers, if not to Stuart Rosenberg's pedestrian direction and the unsubtle Steve Shagan-David Butler screenplay, it carries a strong emotional impact most of the way and in its documented conclusion.

The memorable moments are contributed by Max von Sydow, as the non-Nazi German captain of the ship; Faye Dunaway, as a professor's wife (although Oskar Werner, as the professor, is strangely without character); Katharine Ross, as a prostitute; Maria Schell and Nehemiah Persoff, as her parents; Jose Ferrer, as a corrupt Cuban official; and as passengers, Lee Grant, Julie Harris and Wendy Hiller. Their performances—and the shocking reminder of pre-World War II attitudes toward refugees—make the film worthwhile."

©Judith Crist, 1977.

Films in Review, January 1977 (p. 58)
Jane Morgan

". . . When producer Robert Fryer bought film rights, he intended a TV movie, but the project was too expensive. Sir Lew Grade agreed to do it as the first big-budget movie of the Grade-General Cinema merger, Associated General Films, with the proviso that it have a star-studded cast for the international market. The movie was thus almost damned from the outset . . .

Max von Sydow does an admirable job as the captain torn between conscience and fascism. Helmut Griem is a stereotype Nazi crewman. Ben Gazzara is static as the main negotiator. Oskar Werner is not believable. Faye Dunaway and Lee Grant hold attention but must make room for cameos by Julie Harris, Maria Schell, Katharine Ross, Orson Welles, James Mason, Jose Ferrer, Fernando Rey, Victor Spinetti et al. . . ."

©Films in Review, 1977.

W. C. FIELDS AND ME

Director: *Arthur Hiller*. Screenplay: *Bob Merrill*. Based on the book by *Carlotta Monti* with *Cy Rice*. Producer: *Jay Weston*. Photography: *David M. Walsh*. Editor: *John C. Howard*. Music: *Henry Mancini*. Production Designer: *Robert Bovie*. Costumes: *Edith Head*.

continued on next page

continued from previous page

Distributor: *Universal **Pictures**.* Running time 111 minutes. New York opening March 31, 1976, at the Criterion, Baronet and 34th Street East Theatres. Classification: PG.

Players: *Rod Steiger, Valerie Perrine, John Marley, Jack Cassidy, Bernadette Peters, Dana Elcar, Paul Stewart, Billy Barty, Allan Arbus, Milt Kamen, Louis Zorich, Andrew Parks, Hank Rolike, Kenneth Tobey, Paul Mantee, Elizabeth Thompson, Eddie Firestone, Linda Purl, Clay Tanner, George Loros.*

See Volume 1 for additional reviews

Saturday Review, 4/17/76 (p. 47)
Judith Crist

" . . . Hollywood, of course, can't miss a main chance at exploitation, let alone at diminution--as *W. C. Fields and Me*, produced by Jay Weston, demonstrates . . .

. . . Rod Steiger . . . presumably has kept many a cocktail-party backwash in stitches with his Fields impersonation. On screen it comes out as wearying second-hand Rich Little or potato-chip commercial--particularly since Steiger's make-up, of the death-mask-and-Pancake variety, makes him look like Van Johnson decked out with a clown nose . . . It's a dismal concoction, moving at snail's pace under Arthur Hiller's direction, with small regard for the facts of Fields' career (typically there is no mention whatsoever of radio) and less for his true accomplishments. The point of the fiction is impossible to guess. The real article is available --and unbeatable."

© Judith Crist, 1976.

Film Information, 4/76 (p. 5)
Charles M. Austin

"*W. C. Fields and Me* has Rod Steiger, which is better than it deserves. Based on the book by Fields' secretary-mistress, the movie is like one of those fan club biographies. vacillating between adulation of the stars and feigning shock at the nasty lives they lead.

There are some fine moments, thanks to the superb characterization by Steiger. He brings sensitivity and depth to a role that might have been little more than an impersonation.

The rest of the cast does not fare so well. Valerie Perrine tries hard as the mistress and Jack Cassidy is amusing as the wild-living John Barrymore. But there is no sparkle or insight into their characters.

And everyone else is around merely as decoration.

Most tragically, Fields himself is somewhat degraded by the movie, although the film obviously intends to uplift him. Most of his comic genius is missing--the bits of stage business, the double takes, the light-weight larceny which marked his best films. Instead, the Fields in this movie is reduced to some choleric one-liners, making him a vintage Don Rickles . . . "

© Film Information, 1976.

Village Voice, 4/26/76 (p. 145)
Andrew Sarris

"Rod Steiger's incarnation of W. C. Fields in *W. C. Fields and Me* is about as good as one can expect in waxworks enterprises of this kind, which is not bad, not bad at all. Unlike the poor wretches impersonating Gable and Lombard, the substantially talented Mr. Steiger establishes a screen presence to which we can respond with some intelligent speculation. At the very least, he makes us wonder what the real W. C. Fields was like, what made him tick . . .

. . . the Steiger movie . . . seems to go out of its way to invent outright falsehoods as a way of goosing up the plot. The career chronology is all wrong. Fields is shown trying to get into movies around 1932 (via a still of *Shanghai Express* on the Paramount lot). Actually, he had made his first screen appearance back in 1915, and had appeared in several prominent pictures in the '20s. Nor did he arrive in Hollywood penniless but for the generosity of a midget friend. Actually, he had upward of $300,000 in his pockets . . . "

Reprinted by permission of The Village Voice.
Copyright © The Village Voice, Inc., 1976.

Christian Science Monitor, 4/12/76 (p. 22)
David Sterritt

"Rod Steiger is one of the few screen actors who has the gift of submerging his entire personality into the character he is playing. When the character is complex and fascinating in its own right, the result can be scintillating.

That is what almost happens in *W. C. Fields and Me*, the latest in Hollywood's new wave of 'biopics' on legendary movie subjects . . .

Based on a book co-written by Field's long-time companion, Carlotta Monti, *W. C. Fields and Me* capitalizes on the comic's appeal in a direct and imitative way. Much of Steiger's portrayal is sheer impersonation, but it must have been a major challenge to capture Field's on-screen persona--and then carry the image through to his turbulently emotional off-screen life.

Taken as a whole, the film is sometimes provocative, as when it depicts Fields' jealousy of Charlie Chaplin. But there is a rankling indelicacy that

W. C. Fields (Rod Steiger) and his chauffeur (Hank Rolike) grieve over John Barrymore's death in **W. C. Fields and Me.**

spoils much of the movie's atmosphere. Unflinching biography is one thing. Sniggering vulgarity is quite another . . .

None of this detracts, however, from the inspiration of Steiger's performance, which comes as an especially welcome relief after the stiff mimicry of James Brolin in *Gable and Lombard* from the same studio, Universal . . . "

Reprinted by permission from The Christian Science Monitor © 1976. The Christian Science Publishing Society. All rights reserved.

Monthly Film Bulletin, 6/76 (p. 132)
John Pym

" . . . In her effusively anecdotal, ghost-written memoir of W. C. Fields, on which this film loosely draws, his last mistress Carlotta Monti provides no new insights into the nature of Fields' genius or any indication--which is surely strange from one who repeatedly states her love for him--that the comedian was anything but the cruel, mean, paranoid misogynist of the popular imagination. The tone of *W. C. Fields and Me* varies from Miss Monti's partial recollections only in that it frequently succumbs to sentiment--the emotion which most disgusted the comedian . . . Even Steiger's uncanny imitation of the voice and mannerisms of the performing Fields

cannot disguise the emptiness of a script which never attempts to answer the one interesting question: what manner of man lay behind the self-protective greasepaint?"

© Monthly Film Bulletin, 1976.

Films in Review, 5/76 (p. 312)
Michael Deskey

"The 'Me' of the title is Carlotta Monti who was mistress, nurse and secretary to the great comedian for the last fourteen years of his life . . . This sums up the basic fault of this movie: it is neither faithful to her book nor to the facts (which were sometimes at variance to her recollections) as reported in Fields' various biographies, including the definitive one by Robert Lewis Taylor.

Fields (Rod Steiger) is shown quitting Broadway after Ziegfeld criticizes the coarseness of his dentist office sketch, and travelling to Hollywood, broke and unknown, with a midget pal (Billy Barty). All this is fictitious . . .

Steiger is good at times at what is really an impossible job; however his stance looks more like a boxer's than Field's pompous padding, and his nasal, side-of-mouth talking often comes dangerously close to emulating Van Johnson . . . "

© Films in Review, 1976.

WALKING TALL-PART II

Director: *Earl Bellamy.* Screenplay: *Howard B. Kreitsek.* Producer: *Charles A. Pratt.* Photography: *Keith Smith.* Editor: *Art Seid.* Music. *Walter Scharf.* Distributor: *Cinerama/ American International.* Running time 109 minutes. Los Angeles opening August, 1975, at several theatres. Classification: PG.

Buford Pusser: *Bo Svenson.* Pinky Dobson: *Luke Askew.* Carl Pusser: *Noah Beery.* Ray Henry: *John Chandler.* Obra Eaker: *Robert Doqui.* Grady Coker: *Bruce Glover.* Stud Pardee: *Richard Jaeckel.* Ruby Ann: *Brooke Mills.* John Witter: *Logan Ramsey.* Marganne Stilson: *Angel Tompkins.*

See Volume 1 for additional reviews

Monthly Film Bulletin, October 1976 (p. 215)
Jonathan Rosenbaum

". . . leads off with a written *and* spoken statement, signed by scriptwriter Howard B. Kreitsek and stamped by a Notary Public, asserting that the details of this film are true, even if some names have been changed . . . It seems worth reporting, in any case, that the Pusser portrayed by Bo Svenson in *Legend of the Lawman* is still provided with the fictional son he had in *Walking Tall.* It also seems rather unlikely that any of his friends (or anyone else) ever said, 'There's more ideas flyin' around here than a possum has tricks,' that so many of his adversaries and friends bore striking resemblances to unconvincing actors, or that any aspect of his life could have been quite as sluggish as Earl Bellamy's direction makes it seem . . ."

©Monthly Film Bulletin, 1976.

WELCOME TO L.A.

Director, Screenplay: *Alan Rudolph.* Producer: *Robert Altman.* Photography: *Dave Myers.* Editors: *William A. Sawyer, Tom Walls.* Music and Songs: *Richard Baskin.* Distributor: *United Artists.* Running time 106 minutes. New York opening March 10, 1977, at the Baronet Theatre. Classification: R.

Carroll Barber: *Keith Carradine.* Ann Goode: *Sally Kellerman.* Karen Hood: *Geraldine Chaplin.* Ken Hood: *Harvey Keitel.* Nona Bruce: *Lauren Hutton.* Susan Moore: *Viveca Lindfors.* Linda Murray: *Sissy Spacek.* Carl Barber: *Denver Pyle.* Jack Goode: *John Considine.* Eric Wood: *Richard Baskin.*

Newsweek, 2/21/77 (p. 88)
Jack Kroll

". . . Rudolph does a remarkable job of weaving this gallery of neurotics into a vivid pattern of sharp, distilled performances. Pattern is the key word for this film. Rudolph has worked with Robert Altman . . . and technically he's gone beyond even Altman's example in shaping a film from a total design concept. Rudolph creates a Los Angeles that's a shimmering Xanadu of psychic uncertainty. Mirrors reassemble people into soulless human collages. The swoosh of Hutton's ever-present Nikon sounds like a little guillotine beheading reality. The quavering cadences of Baskin's music evoke both the sweetness and self-indulgence of Carroll Barber. Cinematographer Dave Myers works like the new realist painters, capturing a metropolis of burnished surfaces that seem to dissolve the will in an amber nullity of light. Even Rudolph's occasional fin de siecle overripenesses (a nude Chaplin presents herself to Carradine in front of a Matisse odalisque) are the excesses of a young talent making an extraordinary debut . . ."

©Newsweek, Inc. 1977
reprinted by permission.

Commonweal, 4/1/77 (p. 214)
Colin L. Westerbeck, Jr.

". . . *Welcome to L.A.* is really very close— uncomfortably close—to Altman's *Nashville* . . . In effect his film is the road show of *Nashville,* moving to L.A. that same pop music scene which *Nashville* exploited so successfully. Here the music is rock instead of country and western, but the setting of recording studios and overly impressive offices is the same. The personnel is pretty much the same too, with Keith Carradine, Geraldine Chaplin . . . and Richard Baskin all reappearing from the earlier film (Baskin again in the dual role of on-screen performer and off-screen musical director). Even the characters are the same in Rudolph's film. The one that Ned Beatty played in *Nashville*—the executive who's cheating on his wife—is played here by Harvey Keitel. The wife, played by Lily Tomlin before and by Ms. Chaplin now, is again cheating on her husband as well. And the man with whom the wife does this cheating in both films is a pop singer played by Keith Carradine.

Yet it is not ultimately in some particular character of situation that Rudolph's film is most like Altman's, but rather in its manner of execution, its style . . ."

©Commonweal, 1977.

Saturday Review, 3/19/77 (p. 41)
Judith Crist

"There is indulgence in Welcome to L.A., and it . . . can be forgiven, because this first film by Alan Rudolph is so filled with promise so largely fulfilled. Its major fascination is that Rudolph, as writer-director, and Richard Baskin, who provided the music and songs, have come up with so perceptive a probe of the female psyche in the course of their exploration of encounters between ten people during the ersatz Christmas season typical of Los Angeles. The interlocking relationships are, of course, a mini-Nashville, and not surprisingly, since Robert Altman produced the film and both young men have been his associates . . .

But the work itself is very much their own, an exploration of the search for love, the futility of seeking more than physical contacts, the abiding loneliness of the seekers . . ."

©Judith Crist, 1977.

New York Magazine, 3/21/77 (p. 65)
John Simon

". . . Well, you can't have it both ways, as this stupid and corrupt film would have it; what gets stretched here is our endurance—cinema merely gets shriveled. Special mention must be made of Dave Myers' grandiloquent cinematography, in which some of Sven Nykvist's most wonderful effects (e.g. dark silhouettes outlined by an edge of light) are reduced to visual vulgarisms. The direction is, at best, nonexistent, shrinking good actors into nonentities, and bad ones, like Chaplin and Viveca Lindfors, into thoroughgoing zombies. With typical uninventiveness trying to pass for cleverness, most of the characters have names like Hood, Wood, or Goode. It would have made more sense to call them Sad, Mad, or just Bad. Only one actor survives the mess with a genuinely human performance: I doff my hat to Harvey Keitel . . ."

© 1977 by the NYM Corp. Reprinted with the permission of NEW YORK Magazine.

New Leader, 1/14/77 (p. 24)
Robert Asahina

". . . By the fourth or fifth bedhopping it is obvious that Rudolph has nothing illuminating to say about alienation, West Coast style, besides repeating over and over again the rather insignificant observation that impersonal sex reflects the emptiness of L.A. existence. The brief encounters that he attempts to

flavor with existential angst turn out to be less meaningful than mechanical and predictable. After Ken Hood (Harvey Keitel) is shown being unfaithful to his wife, for instance, we know it is only a matter of time before she runs into Carroll Barber, whose primary dramatic function is apparently to service women searching for the meaning of life in bed.

All these lame activities soon sink to the level of middlebrow melodrama . . ."

Reprinted with permission from
The New Leader, 1977.
©The American Labor Conference
on International Affairs. Inc.

Nation, 3/26/77 (p. 380)
Robert Hatch

". . . it sprawls and lacks character.

But it has a lot of 'style.' Welcome to L.A. is a decor film. It occurs for the most part in an environment of dark, rich-grained plastic, synthetic leather and amber light, suggesting what not quite first-rate department stores use in their men's boutiques to create the illusion that price should be no impediment to vulgarity. And the story is transmitted in fragmented time frames, a device that only partially conceals the fact that it is not of sufficient interest to survive coherent narration . . .

The dialogue, expressing various states of desperation in elliptical cliches, competes on the soundtrack with Barber's songs . . .

The moral of the picture is that everything and everybody these days is being merchandised. It is a cheaply cynical message, designed to impress the gullible. Maybe it will work—they're merchandising the hell out of Welcome to L.A."

©The Nation, 1977.

Women's Wear Daily, 3/7/77 (p. 16)
Howard Kissel

"Welcome to L.A. is a look at the malaise of American life as represented by ten boring phonies. If the picture had been called Welcome to N.Y. at least we could see the malaise represented in 10 witty and interesting phonies, but that would have been beyond the powers of screenwriter-director Alan Rudolph and most of his actors, whose emotional range rarely goes beyond solemn and ponderous . . .

Rudolph's strengths as a director seem mainly visual—he has a good sense of how to use the space of the screen to create mood, especially to create feelings of isolation. With a meatier script, his strong feeling for how to make a face seem like rounded sculpture might make exciting film. But here there's nothing to back up the visual sense. All the characters are prejudged . . ."

©Women's Wear Daily, 1977.

continued on next page

continued from previous page

New York Post, 3/11/77 (p. 20)
Frank Rich

". . . it takes patience to ferret out *Welcome to L.A.*'s gold from the muck that surrounds it . . .

During the movie's first half, Rudolph mixes . . . characters up in a mechanical manner that is a poor equivalent to Altman's improvisational style.

It's only when night falls and the couples come together for their one-night stands that *Welcome to L.A.* finds its own rhythm: As the film's sad women and angry men set out on their nocturnal search for human contact, the movie becomes a celebration of the courage that fuels their doomed quest for love.

At that point, the film's style coalesces along with its content—and *Welcome to L.A.* ceases to be a paint-by-numbers Altman film and becomes a touching Rudolph film instead . . ."

Reprinted by Permission of New York Post.
© 1977, New York Post Corporation.

Village Voice, 3/21/77 (p. 45)
Molly Haskell

". . . Rudolph's sensibility is California Modern and his talent is rhythmically visual—though, happily, he is neither film-school showy nor politically preachy. I suspect that like others of the 'visual' generation, the nonverbal half of his brain is overdeveloped while the other half withers with disuse. It is this hemisphere—where dialogue is hatched, and, more importantly, duties of the conceptual imagination are fulfilled—that has been neglected, and seems often at war, in *Welcome to L.A.*, with the other half. What I mean is that the characters . . . have been conceived as stereotypes but arranged on the screen and viewed with vivid individuality . . .

Welcome to L.A. is a strange film, in many ways hard to defend. I suppose I like it as much for what it refrained from doing as for what it did, the fact that, for all its emphasis on composition and color and planes, it never completely subordinated the characters to the visual scheme . . ."

Reprinted by permission of The Village Voice.
Copyright © The Village Voice, Inc., 1977.

WELCOME TO MY NIGHTMARE

Director, Producer: *David Winters*. Show Conception: *Alice Cooper, Shep Gordon, Joe Gannon, Mr. Winters*. Photography: *Larry Pizer*. Editor: *Stuart Baird*. Music: *Bob Ezrin,*

Mr. Cooper, Mr. Winters. Production: *P.R.O. International*. Distributor: *Key Pictures*. Running time 80 minutes. Los Angeles opening October 2, 1976, at several theatres. Classification: PG.

Players: *Robyn Blythe, Josef Chirowski, Alice Cooper, Pentti Glan, Sheryl Goddard, Steve Hunter, Eugene Montoya, John Prakash, Uchi Sugiyama, Dick Wagner.*

Los Angeles Times, 10/2/76 (Pt. IV, p. 10)
Kevin Thomas

"The Alice Cooper revue *Welcome to My Nightmare* . . . has been seen on many stages—including the Sahara Tahoe's—on television and has now been filmed. Produced and directed by David Winters, it's strictly a concert film (with a few hokey inserts) made during a London stand—and strictly for Alice Cooper fans.

Welcome to My Nightmare is a slick, Vegas-type show, fairly cleverly assembled to string together a large slice of Cooper's ghoulish-accented schlock-rock. Stringy-haired and skinny as ever, Cooper, seen mainly in tattered red tights, performs between a pair of immense, vaguely Frankensteinian riveted obelisks. In the middle, there's a huge toy box and a sort of junk sculpture bed behind which Cooper's first-rate musicians play . . ."

© Los Angeles Times, 1976.

WHERE THE RED FERN GROWS

Director: *Norman Tokar*. Screenplay: *Douglas Stewart, Eleanor Lamb*. Based on the novel by Wilson Rawls. Producer: *Lyman D. Dayton*. Photography: *Dean Cundey*. Editor: *Marsh Hendry*. Distributor: *Cinema Shares International Distribution Corporation*. Running time 97 minutes. New York opening September 1976 at the Guild 50th Theatre. Classification: G.

Players: *James Whitmore, Beverly Garland, Jack Ging, Lonny Chapman, Stewart Petersen, Jill Clark, Rex Clark, Jeanna Wilson, John Lindsey.*

Monthly Film Bulletin, 11/75 (p. 245)
John Pym

". . . The makers of *Where the Red Fern Grows* seem to have set about reaffirming the old settler virtues of hard work, thrift and godliness . . . The unashamedly romantic formula plot is set in the depressed Thirties, and we victims of the recessive Seventies are clearly meant to take heart at the optimistic outcome. Opening with an evocative tracking shot of a placid Oklahoma river, the film is inextricably linked to its location; nevertheless, Billy's supporting morality has as much to do with the reality of life in the Thirties as did that of Tarzan, another Thirties innocent . . . The plot's binding sentimentality is so complete that it almost surpasses itself; the characters' certainties are so unshakeable as to be almost believable."

©Monthly Film Bulletin, 1975.

New York Post, 9/30/76 (p. 30)
Archer Winsten

"*Where the Red Fern Grows* . . . is a dog and boy story set in the Ozarks of the '30s and well known since publication in 1961. As a movie written by Douglas Stewart and Eleanor Lamb and directed by Norman Tokar, it is remarkably true to its source, the Wilson Rawls novel.

The boy, Billy Coleman, is well played by Stewart Petersen, and the two redbone coon hounds are full of voice and hunting energy.

The plot turns on the desire of this small boy for two hunting dogs, and the sacrifices he makes in saving $40 in two years to buy them . . .

It's the kind of picture, strongly sentimental and awash in family virtues of the backwoods, that can be unhesitatingly recommended as entertainment for children and their parents . . ."

Reprinted by Permission of New York Post.
©1976, New York Post Corporation.

WHERE THERE'S SMOKE (IL-N'Y-A PAS DE FUMEE SANS FEU)

Director: *Andre Cayatte.* Screenplay (French with English subtitles): *Mr. Cayatte.* Producer: *Lucien Masse.* Photography: *Maurice Fellous.* Distributor: *Libra Films Corporation.* Running time 112 minutes. New York opening December 10, 1975, at the Cinema Studio Theatre. Classification: None. Origin: France.

Sylvie: *Annie Girardot.* Olga: *Mireille Darc.*

Michel Peyrac: *Bernard Fresson.* Morlaix: *Michel Bouquet.* Ulrich: *Mathieu Carriere.* Boussard: *Andre Falcon.*

See Volume 1 for additional reviews

Los Angeles Times, 10/28/76 (Pt. IV, p. 17)
Kevin Thomas

". . . while *Where There's Smoke* is earnest to the point of becoming plodding, its timeliness and Cayatte's sheer doggedness command respect and pay off in a strong, uncompromising finish.

Actually, the getting there is reasonably absorbing, if somewhat obvious and talky, thanks largely to the solid impressions by the film's well-established stars, Bernard Fresson, Annie Girardot and Mireille Darc . . .

. . . *Where There's Smoke* shows us with complete conviction just how dirty contemporary politics can get.

Where There's Smoke is hard-hitting and harrowing but could have been stronger if Cayatte had made specific the nature of Falcon's corrupt activities and made Fresson's doctor somewhat less naive . . ."

©Los Angeles Times, 1976.

WHITE LINE FEVER

Director: *Jonathan Kaplan.* Screenplay: *Ken Friedman and Mr. Kaplan.* Producer: *John Kemeny.* Photography: *Fred Koenekamp.* Editor: *O. Nicholas Brown.* Distributor: *Columbia Pictures.* Running time 92 minutes. New York opening August 26, 1975, at several theatres. Classification: PG.

Carrol Jo Hummer: *Jan-Michael Vincent.* Jerri Hummer: *Kay Lenz.* Duane Haller: *Slim Pickens.* Buck Wessle: *L. Q. Jones.* Lucy: *Leigh French.* Josh Cutler: *Don Porter.* Pops Dinwiddie: *Sam Laws.*

See Volume 1 for additional reviews

continued on next page

continued from previous page

Cineaste, Spring 1976 (p. 40)
Gerald Peary

"This is what the movie is finally about: bodies leaping upon each other, kicking and kneeing, trucks pushing other vehicles off the road, and nothing motivated. Here are some of the most lame and soporific action sequences this side of Made-for-Television. (Kaplan is clearly emulating Bruce Lee movies, yet he never captures their gymnastic inventiveness.)

However clumsy and juvenile, the violence in *White Line Fever* becomes, for some, vindicated in progressive political terms. Hummer takes after not only the nefarious middlemen (Slim Pickens and L. Q. Jones) but the fat cats at the top, a contingent of sauna bath slobs who plot evil on the golf course of their San Clemente-like estate, the Glass House. Our hero sends his truck plummeting through their impenetrable, guarded gate in near-suicidal defiance.

True, Kaplan takes a solid and consistent stand for his workers in the great ideological war. Nevertheless, Carrol Jo's actions (developed from the script by Kaplan and Ken Friedman) smack much more of kamikaze adventurism and brute revenge than the militant extensions of a political philosophy . . . "

© Cineaste, 1976.

WHITE WALL, THE

Director, Screenplay: *Stig Bjorkman*. Producer: *Bengt Forslund*. Photography: *Peter Davidsson*. Editors: *Margit Nordqvist, Mr. Bjorkman*. Running time 80 minutes. New York opening September 22, 1976, at the second International Festival of Women's Films, at the Cinema Studio. Classification: None. Origin: Sweden.

Monika: *Harriet Andersson*. Berit: *Lena Nyman*. Kjell: *Sven Wolter*. Arne: *Tomas Ponten*.

Village Voice, 9/20/76 (p. 91)
Molly Haskell

"*The White Wall* . . . stars Harriet Andersson as (yet another) 35-year-old lower-middle-class divorcee trying to thread her way between abject humiliation (having to beg her 'ex' for money, being used by a one night lover, and made to feel expendable in a job interview) and the authority her inborn dignity, constantly under assault, gives her. The socially conscious naturalism of the film is balanced by an elegant visual style and verbal wit that, along with Andersson's fine performance, raises the housewife's dilemma to something beyond the sociological platitudinous. It was directed—here's the kicker—by a man, ex-Bergman actor Stig Bjorkman."

Reprinted by permission of The Village Voice.
Copyright © The Village Voice, Inc., 1976.

WILD GOOSE CHASE, THE

Director: *Claude Zidi*. Screenplay: *Michel Fabre, Jean-Luc Voulfow, Mr. Zidi*. Producer: *Pierre Grunstein*. Distributor: *EDP Films*. Running time 87 minutes. New York opening July 21, 1976, at the Cinema 2 Theatre. Classification: PG. Origin: France.

Pierre Vidal: *Pierre Richard*. Janet: *Jane Birkin*. Bertrand de Rovere: *Claude Dauphin*.

New York Post, 7/22/76 (p. 16)
Archer Winsten

". . . offers that amiable French redhead, Pierre Richard, as Pierre Vidal, a young bank executive whose other life is occupied with Janet (Jane Birkin), a nearby beautician who considers ousting him because he bores her.

That is before they, and we, become enmeshed in a plot so wildly slapsticky international and transvestite that all boundaries of the probable and possible are exceeded. It has to do with bank vault papers, a heist, and a chase that crosses the English Channel, goes underwater, endures fire and ends up on a stage in Britain's Brighton.

One must admit that the picture has everything. And nothing . . . "

Reprinted by Permission of New York Post.
©1976, New York Post Corporation.

WINTERHAWK

Director, Screenplay, Producer: *Charles B. Pierce*. Narration: *Earl E. Smith*. Photography: *Jim Roberson*. Editor: *Tom Boutrouss*. Music: *Lee Holdridge*. Distributor: *Howco International Pictures*. Running time 98 minutes. Los Angeles opening January, 1976, at several theatres. Classification: PG.

Players: *Michael Dante, Leif Erickson, Woody Strode, Denver Pyle, Elisha Cook Jr., L. Q. Jones, Arthur Hunnicutt, Dawn Wells, Chuck Pierce Jr., Sacheen Littlefeather, Dennis Fimple, Seaman Glass, Jimmy Clem, Ace Powell*.

See Volume 1 for additional reviews

New York Post, 6/10/76 (p. 23)
Archer Winsten

" . . . It introduces Michael Dante as Winterhawk, a Blackfoot Indian chief who travels to the whites to get a cure for their disease, smallpox. Instead he gets two of his braves killed, which inspires him to kidnap a pretty white miss (Dawn Wells) and her young brother (Chuck Pierce, Jr.).

For a long time thereafter, through Montana and on into wintery and snowy Canada the Indians and their victims are pursued. As it turns out, the whites include some pretty mangy characters, who get their just desserts in the end, and the noble Winterhawk is eventually rewarded for his forbearance. He himself has scalped no one.

As a picture of the time and place--the romantic view--the picture is not lacking in merit. Director-writer-producer Charles B. Pierce has poured in a lot of emotion, and some of it gets into your eyes as moisture."

Reprinted by Permission of New York Post.
© 1976, New York Post Corporation.

WON TON TON, THE DOG WHO SAVED HOLLYWOOD

Director: *Michael Winner*. Screenplay: *Arnold Schulman, Cy Howard*. Producers: *David V. Picker, Mr. Schulman, Mr. Winner*. Photography: *Richard H. Kline*. Music: *Neal Hefti*. Distributor: *Paramount Pictures*.

Running time 92 minutes. New York opening May 26, 1976, at the Sutton and Paramount Theatres. Classification: PG.

Estie Del Ruth: *Madeline Kahn*. Grayson Potchuck: *Bruce Dern*. J. J. Fromberg: *Art Carney*. Murray Fomberf: *Phil Silvers*. Dancing Butler: *Stepin Fetchit*. Rudy Montague: *Ron Leibman*.

Los Angeles Times, 5/26/76 (Pt. IV, p. 1)
Kevin Thomas

"Sixty guest stars can't save *Won Ton Ton, the Dog Who Saved Hollywood* . . . from its unrelentingly crass tone and steady stream of unfunny jokes. Unquestionably, the best performance is given by an appealing German Shepherd named Augustus von Schumacher, who plays Won Ton Ton . . .

. . . *Won Ton Ton* is loaded with anachronisms both deliberate and otherwise. In hands with a lighter touch than Winner's they might have been amusing in themselves; as it is, however, they are simply distracting.

Miss Kahn and Dern, gifted, proven performers both, try hard and at least make favorable individual impressions, although Miss Kahn really gets not much opportunity to do anything but register dumbfoundedness over and over. Ron Leibman's travesty of Rudolph Valentino is offensive not so much because he makes him a drag queen but because Leibman here is not nearly as funny as Valentino was charismatic. Indeed, Leibman typifies the film's tendency to diminish--in fact, to demolish--what it could have at once celebrated and good-naturedly satirized . . . "

© Los Angeles Times, 1976.

The Times (London), 7/16/76 (p. 13)
David Robinson

" . . . It is just a mean film (which is small recommendation for a comedy, you might think). It has a mean view of what Hollywood and its artists were and represented; it has a mean view of the achievement of the silent cinema. The audience does not have such a great time either: the film tries to conceal its deficiencies in comic ideas and comic skill by doing everything at the pace of a clockwork toy with a too-tight spring.

Vaguely pretending to be based on the real-life dog star Rin Tin Tin, it is particularly mean about him. He was certainly a lot more fun than this (admittably not unlovable) counterfeit . . . "

© The Times, 1976.

continued on next page

continued from previous page

Newsweek, 6/14/76 (p. 90)
Katrine Ames

" . . . In Michael Winner's *Won Ton Ton, the Dog Who Saved Hollywood*, a would-be actress (Madeline Kahn), a would-be director (Bruce Dern) and a studio mogul *manqué* (Art Carney) make good by riding in on the tail of a talented German shepherd as he becomes a star of the silent screen.

It's hard to hate a movie about a dog . . . But in this case it's equally hard not to make cracks about the movie being dog-eared or dog-tired or just that it shouldn't happen to a dog. Winner apparently believes that if a joke, like a pie in the face, is funny once, it gets more hilarious every time it's used. He trots out some of his gags until they roll over and play dead . . .

Kahn, Dern, Carney and Ron Leibman (who plays a wonderfully narcissistic matinee idol) would probably have fared better without a director. They are backed up by dozens of 'guest stars' in cameo roles, some of whom––like Andy Devine as a priest who intones prayers while Won Ton Ton walks to a death chamber (from which he is, of course, reprieved)––almost make this uninspired lunacy worth seeing."

© Newsweek, Inc. 1976
reprinted by permission.

New York Post, 5/27/76 (p. 42)
Frank Rich

"*Won Ton Ton, the Dog Who Saved Hollywood*, a dog of a movie . . . is a ragtag collection of crudely shot slapstick footage that attempts, as far as I could make out, to retell the *Star is Born* story with a German shepherd in the Judy Garland role. It's either the worst idea for a movie in recent years or a sick inside joke of psychotic dimensions. In either case, it's a bone-crunching bore.

The movie has been assembled by a crew of Hollywood hacks led by Michael Winner, a pedestrian director (*Death Wish*) whose qualifications for staging a huge Hollywood farce aren't readily apparent. I don't have any sympathy for him or writers Arnold Schulman and Cy Howard, but it's hard not to feel a little sorry for *Won Ton Ton*'s cast, which must play second fiddle to an oppressively cute trained dog . . . "

Reprinted by Permission of New York Post.
© 1976, New York Post Corporation.

Christian Science Monitor, 6/24/76 (p. 30)
David Sterritt

"The supporting cast is absolutely mammoth in *Won Ton Ton, the Dog Who Saved Hollywood*, which tries to boost its appeal by filling bit parts with famous faces. If you've been missing Andy

Devine or Dean Stockwell or Henny Youngman or the Ritz Brothers, or almost anyone else, now's your chance.

Most of the picture centers on Madeline Kahn and Bruce Dern, though, and a dog named Augustus von Schumacher. He plays Won Ton Ton, who becomes the movies' biggest star back in the silent era, and causes sundry misadventures for the would-be mogul who owns him and the would-be starlet who loves him.

That much said, be it known that Won Ton Ton is a dog of a picture. Director Michael Winner works in every gag he can come up with, appropriate or not, and dumps the ensuing stew over our heads with nary a thought to scripting sense or editing grace. Mr. Dern and Miss Kahn have flashes of easy charm, but such gifted actors as Art Carney and Ron Leibman are wasted on crass caricatures . . . "

Reprinted by permission from The Christian
Science Monitor © 1976.
The Christian Science Publishing Society.
All rights reserved

Monthly Film Bulletin, 8/76 (p. 177)
John Pym

". . . Michael Winner does not have Mel Brooks' frenzied gift for marshalling this sort of material; and to make matters worse, the script attains a level of parody no higher than Ron Leibman's mincing caricature of Valentino, embellished with little more than the standard mannerisms of the familiar theatrical queen . . . Any unified sense of direction that the film may once have had (and there is a final indication of a moral on the price of stardom) is subordinated to a below-par series of one-liners and sight gags . . . The brassy vulgarity which Madeline Kahn has up to now made particularly her own is here subordinated to the antics of the indolent, overweight Won (no descendant of the sleek Rin Tin Tin) whose most characteristic show of animation is to sluice his tongue over the versatile face of the admirably forbearing Ms. Kahn. In its way, an image that sums up the whole film."

©Monthly Film Bulletin, 1976.

Film Information, July/August 1976 (p. 5)
Dave Pomeroy

"*Won Ton Ton, the Dog Who Saved Hollywood* is a film trying to be all things to all people—and as a result falls flat on its face. It is a satire on Hollywood lifestyles and conventions; yet it is a picture-postcard to Silent Hollywood of the '20s. It is a parody of film-star biographies; yet Paramount is ballyhooing Augustus von Schumacher (the German Shepherd who plays Won Ton) as the 'hottest discovery since Valentino.' It is a comedy that reaches for a semi-serious sentimental ending.

And *Won Ton Ton* may have set the world's record for stars in cameo roles—67 of them . . .

Typical Hollywood cliches come about one-a-frame—from custard pies to the producer seducing the starlet. And the level of parody finds hopeful-director Dern bringing sure-fire script ideas (a large shark, a huge burning building, a little girl possessed by the devil) to producer Carney, who keeps insisting they won't sell.

To those who have some reverence for the real artistic talent that existed in Hollywood in the '20s *Won Ton Ton* amounts to a travesty. To those who would find much to satirize in the star-system Hollywood produced, this film misses by a wide mark."

©Film Information, 1976.

WONDERFUL CROOK, THE
(PAS SI MECHANT QUE CA)

Director: *Claude Goretta*. Screenplay (French with English subtitles): *Mr. Goretta*. Executive Producers: *Yves Gasser and Yves Peyrot*. Photography: *Renato Berto*. Editor: *Joel van Effenterre*. Music: *Arle Dzieriatka*. Production: *Citel Films/Artco Films/Action Films; M. J. Productions*. Running time 112 minutes. New York opening October 1, 1975, at the New York Film Festival, Lincoln Center. Classification: None. Origin: Switzerland.

Nelly: *Marlene Jobert*. Pierre: *Gerard Depardieu*. Marthe: *Dominique Labourier*. Julien: *Philippe Leotard*. Pierre's father: *Jacques Debary*. Francois: *Michel Robin*. Drunkard: *Paul Crauchet*.

See Volume 1 for additional reviews

Nation, 3/26/77 (p. 380)
Robert Hatch

". . . As to Mr. Goretta's motive, I can only guess. He is an able director, one who gets eloquent performances from his cast and who tells his story with elegant economy. His is a good-looking film, full of life and air. I think he achieved what he set out to do—to give weight to a crime comedy by painting a wash of somber implications behind the bright morality. But it seems to me an unsatisfactory accomplishment because the viewer cannot find a way to relate to the picture . . .

Perhaps this is to take the film much too seriously; it is not, obviously, intended to be a great drama of souls in torment. Nevertheless, I felt that Goretta was asking us to care more than casually about his people, but then was unable to break enough out of the caper formula to let us do so."

©The Nation, 1977.

New York Magazine, 2/7/77 (p. 78)
John Simon

". . . A true, if seemingly farfetched, tale is told here with unaffected brilliance, with stunning control of both the cinematic medium and a verite far beyond mere cinema . . .*The Wonderful Crook* . . . is a film to which laughter and tears come in the most natural way: unpredictably, pell-mell, and irresistibly.

What makes this picture so extraordinary is the amount of truth and poetry it carries with such unostentatious ease that casual moviegoers will miss a great deal of it, though even for them there is enough inventive clowning to make the experience worthwhile. For underneath the clever yet apparently simple plot is the most acute analysis of human differences and similarities within differences, of the clash between legality and morality, of the contradictions in various lovers' attitudes toward one another and toward love itself—the very thing that gives love its bittersweet, tragi-comic, and wholly irreplaceable savor . . ."

©1977 by the NYM Corp. Reprinted with the permission of NEW YORK Magazine.

XALA

Director: *Ousmane Sembene*. Screenplay: *Mr. Sembene*. Photography: *Georges Caristan*. Editor: *Florence Evmon*. Distributor: *New Yorker Films*. Running time 123 minutes. New York opening October 1, 1975, at the New York Film Festival, Lincoln Center. Classification: None. Origin: Senegal.

Players: *Thierno Leye, Seum Samb, Younouss Seye, Myriam Niang, Douta Seck, Fatim Diagne, Diaynaba Niang, Moustapha Toure, Llimane Sagnan, and Makouredia Gueye*.

See Volume 1 for additional reviews

Monthly Film Bulletin, December 1976 (p. 260)
Jill Forbes

". . . Clearly, the film's lesson is that the forms of exploitation which characterised the colonial period

continued on next page

continued from previous page

The Times (London), 11/25/76 (p. 9)
David Robinson

are more than reinforced by liberation and now take the form of distinctions between the city and the country, the healthy and the sick, the skilled and the uneducated. But what makes it enjoyable is a verisimilitude which takes no account of the voyeuristic impulses of Western audiences, a sense of humour which rejects a sentimental view either of the exploiters or the exploited, and a sophisticated narrative style which makes no concession to the novelty of the subject, but allows Ousmane Sembene to put African cinema 'on the map' by exploiting the best traditions of the French cinema. In this sense *Xala* is, in a quiet way, a revolutionary film."

© Monthly Film Bulletin. 1976.

". . . The freshness and vitality of a film like *Xala* (for which, because of its theme, Sembene returns to the French language) have nothing of the primitive about them; and the satire at the expense of the Europeanized and colonial attitudes that linger in the new Africans is unsparing. The precredit sequence of *Xala* shows the board of the fictitious Senegalese Chamber of Commerce and Industry on the proud day when the Africans take over. Representatives of the former French masters—who now adopt their new position as 'advisers' with all the mocking deference of old retainers—hand over the symbols of status: a briefcase apiece helpfully stuffed with banknotes. The Africans, in their European suits and Mercedes limousines, keep reassuring one another how truly African they are . . ."

© The Times. 1976.

49th ANNUAL ACADEMY AWARDS
March 28, 1977

Best Picture - **Rocky.**

Best Actor - Peter Finch in **Network.**

Best Actress - Faye Dunaway in **Network.**

Best Supporting Actor - Jason Robards in **All the President's Men.**

Best Supporting Actress - Beatrice Straight in **Network.**

Best Director - John G. Avildsen for **Rocky.**

Foreign Language Film - **Black and White in Color** (Ivory Coast).

Short Subject, animated - **Leisure** (Australia).

Short Subject, live - **In the Region of Ice.**

Sound - Arthur Piantadosi, Les Fresholtz, Dick Alexander and Jim Webb for **All the President's Men.**

Documentary Feature - **Harlan County, U.S.A.**

Documentary Short Subject - **Number Our Days.**

Costume Design - Danilo Donati for **Fellini's Casanova.**

Art Direction - George Jenkins for **All the President's Men**; set decoration, George Gaines.

Original Music Score - Jerry Goldsmith for **The Omen.**

Originl Song Score and Adaptation - Leonard Rosenman for **Bound for Glory.**

Cinematography - Haskell Wexler for **Bound for Glory.**

Film Editing - Richard Halsey, Scott Conrad for **Rocky.**

Original Song - "Evergreen" from **A Star is Born**; music by Barbra Streisand; lyrics by Paul Williams.

Original Screenplay - Paddy Chayefsky for **Network.**

Screenplay Adaptation - William Goldman for **All the President's Men.**

NATIONAL SOCIETY OF FILM CRITICS AWARDS
January 4, 1977

Best Picture - **All the President's Men.**

Best Director - Martin Scorsese for **Taxi Driver.**

Best Actress - Sissy Spacek in **Carrie.**

Best Actor - Robert De Niro in **Taxi Driver.**

Best Supporting Actress - Jodie Foster in **Taxi Driver.**

Best Supporting Actor - Jason Robards in **All the President's Men.**

Best Screenplay - Alain Tanner and John Berger for **Jonah Who Will Be 25 in the Year 2000.**

Best Cinematography - Haskell Wexler for **Bound for Glory.**

NEW YORK FILM CRITICS CIRCLE AWARDS
January 3, 1977

Best Picture - **All The President's Men.**

Best Director - Alan Pakula for **All the President's Men.**

Best Actress - Liv Ullmann in **Face to Face.**

Best Actor - Robert De Niro in **Taxi Driver.**

Best Supporting Actress - Talia Shire in **Rocky.**

Best Supporting Actor - Jason Robards in **All the President's Men.**

Best Screenplay - Paddy Chayefsky for **Network.**

NATIONAL BOARD OF REVIEW OF MOTION PICTURES AWARDS
December 1976

Ten best English-language films of 1976:

All the President's Men
Network
Rocky
The Last Tycoon
The Seven-Per-Cent Solution
The Front
The Shootist
Family Plot
Silent Movie
Obsession

Five best foreign-language films of 1976:

The Marquise of O . . .
Face to Face
Small Change
Cousin, Cousine
The Clockmaker

Best Director—Alan Pakula for **All the President's Men.**

Best Actress—Liv Ullmann in **Face to Face.**

Best Actor—David Carradine in **Bound for Glory.**

Best Supporting Actress—Talia Shire in **Rocky.**

Best Supporting Actor—Jason Robards in **All the President's Men.**

WRiTERS GUILD OF AMERICA AWARDS
March 24, 1977

Best American Drama Adapted From Another Medium - William Goldman for **All the President's Men.**

Best American Comedy Written Directly for the Screen - Bill Lancaster for **The Bad News Bears.**

Best American Comedy Adapted From Another Medium - Frank Waldman and Blake Edwards for **The Pink Panther Strikes Again.**

Best American Drama Written Directly For the Screen - Paddy Chayefsky for **Network.**

Writers Guild Laurel For Screen Writing Achievement - Samson Raphaelson.

Valentine Davies Award for "contributions to the motion picture community" - Carl Foreman.

Writers Guild Medallion - Cesare Zavattini.

CANNES FILM FESTIVAL AWARDS
May 28, 1976

Golden Palm for Best Film - **Taxi Driver** (U.S.A.)

Best Director - Ettore Scola for **Disgusting, Dirty and Mean** (Italy).

Best Actress - shared by Dominique Sanda in **The Ferramount Heritage** (France) and Marie Torocsik in **Where Are You, Madame Dery?** (Hungary).

Best Actor - Jose Luis Gomez in **The Family of Pascal Duarte** (Spain).

Special Grand Prize - shared by **Feed the Crows** (Carlos Saura - Spain) and **The Marquise of O** (Eric Rohmer - West Germany).

International Federation of Film Critics Prize - shared by **The Course of Time** (Win Wenders - West Germany) and **Ferdinand the Radical** (Alexander Klug - West Germany).

Award Given by Commission of Technique in France - Soundman Michael Fano for the documentary, **Fang & Claw**, by Gerard Vienne and Francois Bel.

Golden Palm for Best Short Film - **Metamorphosis** (Barry Greenwald - Canada).

BERLIN FILM FESTIVAL AWARDS
July 6, 1976

Golden Bear for Best Film - **Buffalo Bill and the Indians or Sitting Bull's History Lesson** (U.S.A.), directed by Robert Altman.

Silver Bear for Best Director - Mario Monicelli for **Dear Michael** (Italy).

Silver Bear for Best Actress - Jadwiga Baranski in **Nights and Days** (Poland).

Silver Bear for Best Actor - Gerhard Olschewski in **Lost Life** (West Germany).

Silver Bear - **Garden of Stones** (Iran), directed by Parviz Kimiavi.

Silver Bear for Best Jury Prize - **Canoa** (Mexico), directed by Felipe Cazals.

Silver Bear for Best First Film - Laszlo Lugossy, director, for **Azonositas** (Hungary).

Golden Bear for Best Short Subject - **Munakata, The Woodcarver** (Japan).

Silver Bear for Best Short Subject - **Trains** (U.S.A.).

International Critics Prize - **Long Vacations of '36** (Spain).

Catholic and Protestant Awards - **Loneliness of Konrad Steiner** (Switzerland).

index

411

index of reviewers